Rick Steves

FRANCE

2005

Rick Steves & Steve Smith

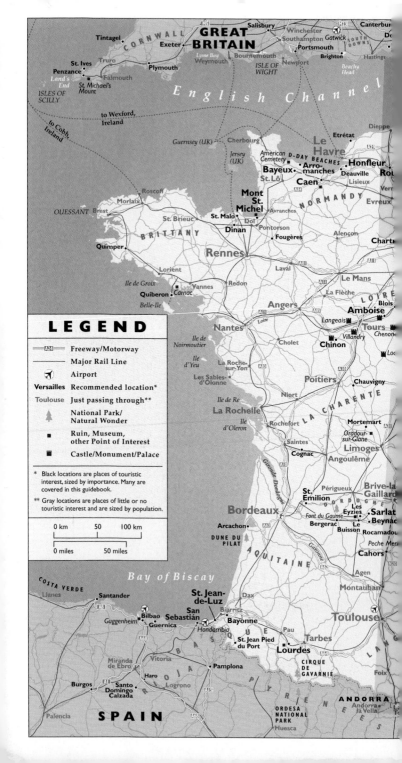

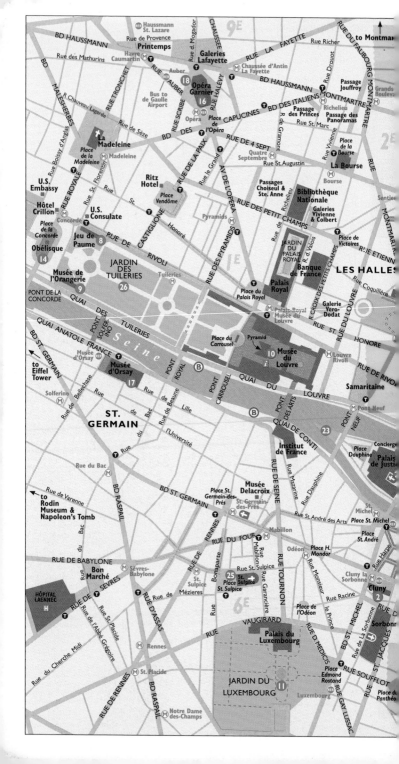

KEY

- ═■ Pedestrian-friendly Area
- ═■ Popular Shopping Area
- ═ ═ ═ Tunnel
- Ⓜ Ⓡ Metro Station, RER Station
- ⓣ Taxi Stand
- Ⓑ Bâtobus Boat Stops (April-Oct)
- ■ Landmark or Point of Interest
- 🄸 Tourist Information

```
0 km                    .5 km
├──────────┬──────────┤

0 mi                    .25 mi
├──────────┬──────────┤
```

CENTRAL PARIS SIGHTS

1. Carnavalet Museum
2. Cluny Museum
3. Conciergerie
4. Deportation Memorial
5. Flower Market
6. Ile St. Louis
7. Jardin des Plantes
8. Jeu de Paume Museum
9. L'Orangerie Museum
10. Louvre Museum
11. Luxembourg Garden
12. Museum of Jewish Art & History
13. Notre-Dame Cathedral
14. Obelisk, Place de la Concorde
15. Opéra Bastille
16. Opéra Garnier (Old Opera)
17. Orsay Museum
18. Paris Story Film
19. Picasso Museum
20. Pompidou Center
21. Promenade Plantée Park Entry
22. Sainte-Chapelle
23. Seine River Boat Rides
24. St. Severin Church
25. St. Sulpice Church
26. Tuileries Garden

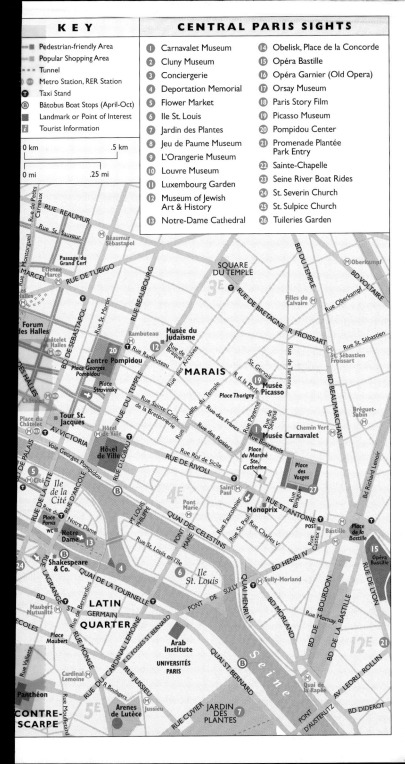

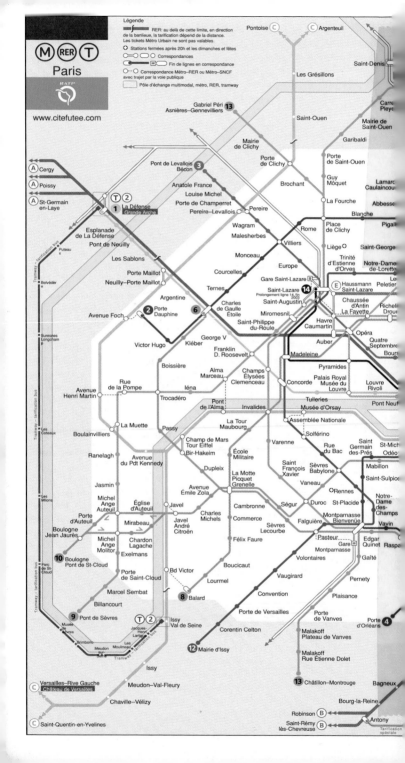

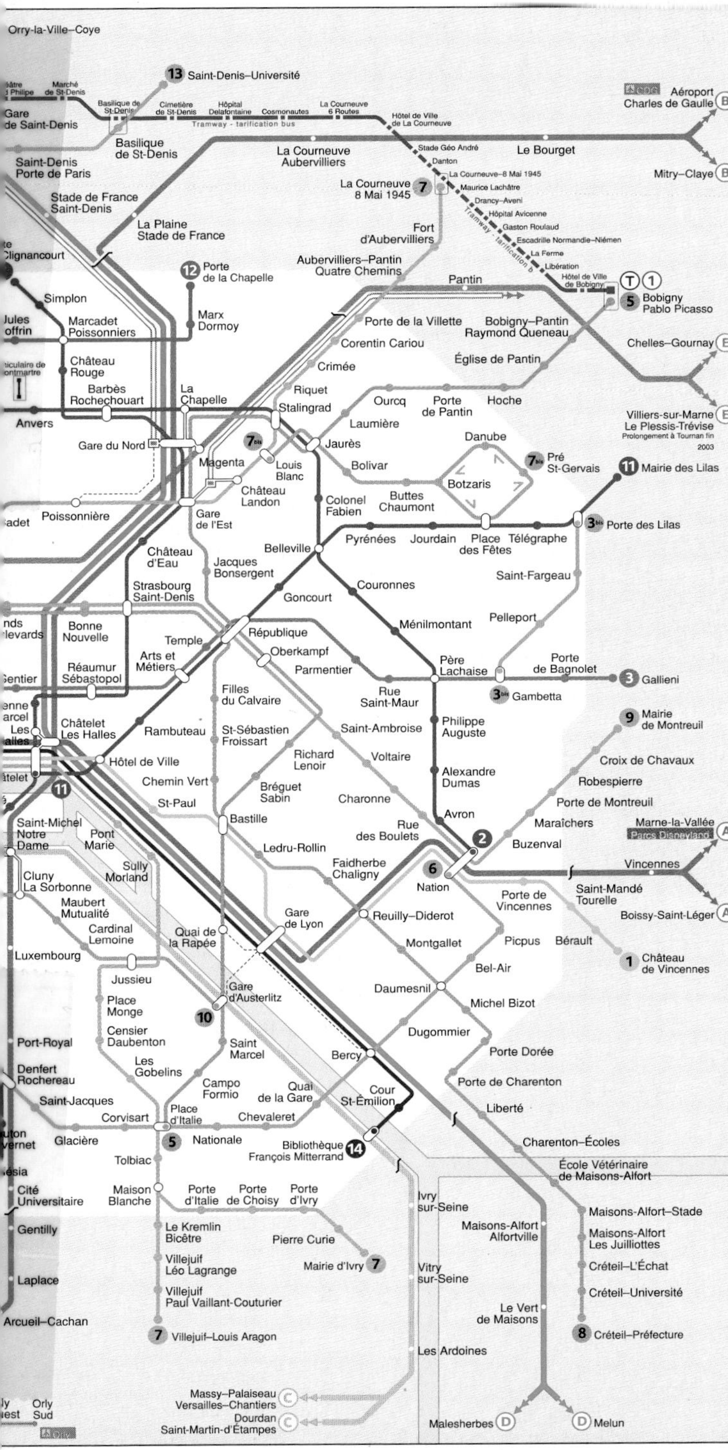
Orry-la-Ville–Coye
13 Saint-Denis–Université
Marché de St-Denis
Gare de Saint-Denis
Basilique de St-Denis
Cimetière de St-Denis
Hôpital Delafontaine
Cosmonautes
La Courneuve 6 Routes
Hôtel de Ville de La Courneuve
Tramway - tarification bus
Aéroport Charles de Gaulle B
Basilique de St-Denis
La Courneuve Aubervilliers
Le Bourget
Stade Géo André
Danton
La Courneuve–8 Mai 1945
Maurice Lachâtre
Drancy–Avenir
Hôpital Avicenne
Gaston Roulaud
Escadrille Normandie–Niémen
La Ferme
Libération
Hôtel de Ville de Bobigny
Tramway - tarification bus
Mitry–Claye B
Saint-Denis Porte de Paris
Stade de France Saint-Denis
La Plaine Stade de France
La Courneuve 8 Mai 1945 7
Fort d'Aubervilliers
Aubervilliers–Pantin Quatre Chemins
Clignancourt
12 Porte de la Chapelle
Pantin
T 1
5 Bobigny Pablo Picasso
Simplon
Jules Joffrin
Marcadet Poissonniers
Marx Dormoy
Porte de la Villette
Bobigny–Pantin Raymond Queneau
Corentin Cariou
Chelles–Gournay E
Funiculaire de Montmartre
Château Rouge
Crimée
Église de Pantin
Barbès Rochechouart
La Chapelle
Riquet
Ourcq
Porte de Pantin
Hoche
Anvers
Stalingrad
Laumière
Villiers-sur-Marne Le Plessis-Trévise E
Prolongement à Tournan fin 2003
Gare du Nord
Jaurès
Danube
Magenta
7bis
Louis Blanc
Bolivar
7bis Pré St-Gervais
11 Mairie des Lilas
Château Landon
Botzaris
Colonel Fabien
Buttes Chaumont
Poissonnière
Gare de l'Est
Cadet
3bis Porte des Lilas
Pyrénées
Jourdain
Place des Fêtes
Télégraphe
Château d'Eau
Belleville
Jacques Bonsergent
Saint-Fargeau
Strasbourg Saint-Denis
Goncourt
Couronnes
Pelleport
Grands Boulevards
Bonne Nouvelle
République
Ménilmontant
Temple
Oberkampf
Arts et Métiers
Parmentier
Père Lachaise
Porte de Bagnolet
Réaumur Sébastopol
3 Gallieni
Sentier
3bis Gambetta
Étienne Marcel
Filles du Calvaire
Rue Saint-Maur
Les Halles
Châtelet Les Halles
Rambuteau
Philippe Auguste
9 Mairie de Montreuil
St-Sébastien Froissart
Saint-Ambroise
Châtelet
Hôtel de Ville
Richard Lenoir
Voltaire
Croix de Chavaux
Chemin Vert
Alexandre Dumas
Robespierre
11
St-Paul
Bréguet Sabin
Charonne
Porte de Montreuil
Saint-Michel Notre Dame
Pont Marie
Bastille
Avron
Maraîchers
Marne-la-Vallée Parcs Disneyland A
Rue des Boulets
2
Buzenval
Sully Morland
Ledru-Rollin
Faidherbe Chaligny
6 Nation
Vincennes
Cluny La Sorbonne
Saint-Mandé Tourelle
Porte de Vincennes
Maubert Mutualité
Gare de Lyon
Reuilly–Diderot
Boissy-Saint-Léger A
Cardinal Lemoine
Quai de la Rapée
Picpus
Bérault
Montgallet
Luxembourg
1 Château de Vincennes
Jussieu
Bel-Air
Gare d'Austerlitz
Daumesnil
Place Monge
Michel Bizot
10
Censier Daubenton
Port-Royal
Dugommier
Saint Marcel
Bercy
Porte Dorée
Les Gobelins
Denfert Rochereau
Campo Formio
Quai de la Gare
Cour St-Émilion
Porte de Charenton
Saint-Jacques
Place d'Italie
Liberté
Corvisart
Chevaleret
Mouton Duvernet
Glacière
5
Nationale
Bibliothèque François Mitterrand 14
Charenton–Écoles
Tolbiac
Alésia
École Vétérinaire de Maisons-Alfort
Cité Universitaire
Maison Blanche
Porte d'Italie
Porte de Choisy
Porte d'Ivry
Ivry sur-Seine
Maisons-Alfort–Stade
Gentilly
Maisons-Alfort Alfortville
Maisons-Alfort Les Juilliottes
Le Kremlin Bicêtre
Pierre Curie
Villejuif Léo Lagrange
Mairie d'Ivry 7
Vitry sur-Seine
Créteil–L'Échat
Laplace
Villejuif Paul Vaillant-Couturier
Créteil–Université
Le Vert de Maisons
Arcueil–Cachan
7 Villejuif–Louis Aragon
8 Créteil–Préfecture
Les Ardoines
Massy–Palaiseau Versailles–Chantiers C
Orly Sud
Dourdan Saint-Martin-d'Étampes C
Malesherbes D
D Melun

Rick Steves'

FRANCE

2005

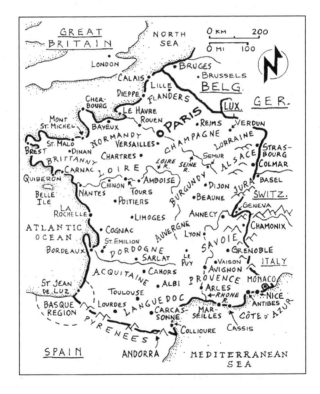

AVALON
TRAVEL

CONTENTS

Top Destinations in France

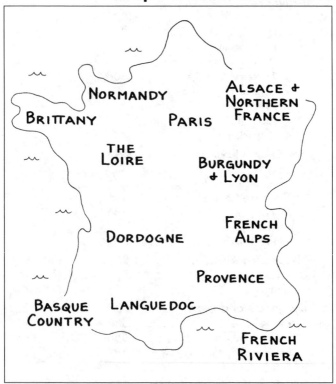

INTRODUCTION

Bienvenue! You've made a great choice. France is Europe's most diverse, tasty, and, in many ways, exciting country to explore. It's a multifaceted cultural fondue.   USA – 297 million

France is nearly as big as Texas, with 60 million people and more than 400 different cheeses. *Diversité* is a French forte. This country features three distinct mountain ranges (the Alps, the Pyrénées, and the Massif Central), two coastlines that are as different as night and day (Atlantic and Mediterranean), cosmopolitan cities (such as Paris, Lyon, Strasbourg, and Nice—all featured in this book), and sleepy villages. From the Swiss-like Alps to the *molto* Italian Riviera, and from the Spanish Pyrénées to *das* German Alsace, you can stay in France and feel like you've sampled much of Europe—and never be more than a short stroll from a good *vin rouge*.

Throughout 17 years of guiding tours and working on this book together, Rick Steves and francophile Steve Smith have worked hard to discover and describe France's most interesting destinations, giving you tips on how to use your time and money most efficiently. Each of our recommended destinations is a dripping forkful (complete with instructions on how to enjoy the full flavor without burning your tongue).

This book covers the predictable biggies and mixes in a healthy dose of "Back Door" intimacy. Along with seeing the Eiffel Tower, Mont St. Michel, and the French Riviera, you'll take a minivan tour of the D-Day beaches with our favorite guides, pedal your way from villages to vineyards in the Alsace, marvel at 15,000-year-old cave paintings, and paddle a canoe down the lazy Dordogne River. You'll find a *magnifique* hill-town perch to catch a Provençal sunset, ride Europe's highest mountain lift over the Alps, and touch the quiet Romanesque soul of Burgundian abbeys and villages. You'll learn about each region's key monuments and cities with our walking tours and thoughtfully presented background information. Just as important, you'll meet the intriguing people who run your hotel, bed-and-breakfast, or restaurant. We've also listed the best local guides, all well worth the time and money, to help you gain a better understanding of this marvelous country's past and present.

Rick Steves' France is a tour guide in your pocket—actually, two tour guides in your pocket. Destinations covered in this book are balanced to include the most famous cities and intimate villages, from jet-setting beach resorts to the traditional heartland. We've been selective, including only the most exciting sights and romantic villages. For example, there are *beaucoup de* beautiful châteaux in the Loire region. We cover just the best. And while there are dozens of Loire towns where you could base yourself, we recommend only the top two.

The best is, of course, only our opinion. But after more than 35 busy years between us spent travel writing, lecturing, guiding tours, and satisfying our Francophilia, we've developed a sixth sense for what touches the traveler's imagination.

This Information is Accurate and Up-to-Date

This book is completely updated every year. Most publishers of guidebooks that cover a region from top to bottom can afford an update only every two or three years (and even then, it's often by letter or phone). Since this book is selective, covering only the places we think make the top month of sightseeing, we can update it in person each spring and summer. Of course, even with an annual update, things change. But if you're traveling with the current edition of this book, we guarantee you're using the most up-to-date information available in print. For the latest, see www.ricksteves .com/update. Also at our Web site, check our Graffiti Wall (select "Rick Steves' Guidebooks," then "France") for a huge, worthwhile list of reports and experiences—good and bad—from fellow travelers.

This book will help you have an inexpensive, hassle-free trip. Use this year's edition. Saving a few bucks by traveling on old information is not smart. If you're packing an old book, you'll learn the seriousness of your mistake...in France. Your trip costs at least $10 per waking hour. Your time is valuable. This guidebook saves lots of time.

About This Book

This book is organized by destination. Each of these destinations is a mini-vacation on its own, filled with exciting sights, strollable towns, homey, affordable places to stay, and memorable places to eat. For each chapter, you'll find the following:

Orientation includes tourist information, public transportation basics, and easy-to-read maps. The "Planning Your Time" section offers a suggested schedule with thoughts on how best to use your limited time.

Sights provides a succinct overview of France's most important sights. They're arranged by neighborhood and include ratings: ▲▲▲—Don't miss; ▲▲—Try hard to see; ▲—Worthwhile if you can make it; No rating—Worth knowing about.

Sleeping is a guide to our favorite hotels, from unbeatable deals to cushy splurges.

Eating offers good-value restaurants ranging from inexpensive eateries to romantic bistros.

Transportation Connections lays the groundwork for your smooth arrival and departure, covering connections by train and plane. Drivers will find route tips.

The handy **appendix** includes telephone tips, a festival calendar, a climate chart, and French survival phrases.

Browse through this book, choose your favorite destinations, and create your own recipe. Then have a *fantastique* trip! You'll travel like a temporary local, getting the absolute most out of every mile, minute, and euro. You won't waste time on mediocre sights because, unlike other guidebooks, we cover only the best. This selective coverage also allows us to spend more time describing a sight, giving you a better appreciation of what you came to see and learn about. And since your major financial pitfall can be lousy, expensive hotels, we've worked hard to assemble the best accommodation values for each stop. As you travel the route we know and love, we're happy you'll be meeting some of our favorite French friends.

PLANNING

Trip Costs

Five components make up your total trip cost: airfare, surface transportation, room and board, sightseeing/entertainment, and shopping/miscellany.

Airfare: Don't try to sort through the mess. Find and use a good travel agent. A basic round-trip United States-to-Paris flight costs $700 to $1,200 (even cheaper in winter), depending on where you fly from and when. Always consider saving time and money in Europe by flying "open jaw" (into one city and out of another). Flying into Nice and out of Paris costs roughly the same as flying round-trip to Paris. (Many find relaxed, Mediterranean Nice far easier than Paris as a starting point for their trip.) You can find cheaper round-trip flights from the United States to London or Amsterdam, but the cost of train tickets (to get you back to London or Amsterdam for your flight home) eliminate most of your savings. Smaller airlines provide bargain service from several European capitals to many French cities (consider www.easyjet.com, www.ryanair.com, and www.virgin-express.com, among many others). Within France, inexpensive flights can get you from Paris or Nice to all major cities, such as Strasbourg, Toulouse, Lyon, and Bordeaux, sometimes at less cost than by train.

Surface Transportation: For a three-week whirlwind trip of our recommended destinations, allow $600 per person for public transportation (trains and buses) or $700 per person (based on 2 people sharing) for a three-week car rental, tolls, gas, and insurance. Car rental is cheapest if arranged from the United States (see page 24 for money-saving ideas). Train passes are normally available only outside of Europe. You may save money by simply buying tickets as you go (see map in sidebar on page 22).

Room and Board: You can thrive in France on $80 a day per person for room and board (allow $100 a day for Paris). An $80-a-day budget allows $10 for a simple lunch, $20 for dinner, and $50 for lodging (based on two people splitting the cost of a $100 double room that includes breakfast). That's definitely doable. Students and tightwads do it on $45 a day ($25 per bed, $20 for meals and snacks). But budget sleeping and eating require the skills and information covered later in this chapter (and in much greater depth in *Rick Steves' Europe Through the Back Door*).

Sightseeing and Entertainment: In cities, figure $6 to $9 per major sight (Rodin Museum-$6, Louvre-$9), $3 for minor ones (climbing church towers), $12 for guided walks, and $30 for bus tours and splurge experiences (concerts in Paris' Sainte-Chapelle or a ride on the Chamonix gondola). An overall average of $15 a day works for most. Don't skimp here. After all, this category directly powers most of the experiences all the other expenses are designed to make possible.

Shopping and Miscellany: Figure $3–4 per ice-cream cone, coffee, or soft drink. Shopping can vary in cost from nearly nothing to a small fortune. Good budget travelers find that this category has little to do with assembling a trip full of lifelong and wonderful memories.

When to Go

Late spring and fall are best, with generally good weather and lighter crowds, though summer brings festivals, reliable weather, and long opening hours at sights. Book ahead for the holidays that occur throughout the year (see list on page 13).

Europeans vacation in July and August, jamming the Riviera and the Alps (worst July 15–Aug 20), but leaving the rest of the country reasonably tranquil. And while many French businesses close in August, the traveler hardly notices. Winter travel is fine for Paris, Nice, and Lyon, but you'll find smaller cities and villages buttoned up tight. Winter weather is gray, noticeably milder in the south (unless the wind is blowing), and colder and wetter in the north. Sights and tourist information offices keep shorter hours, and some tourist activities (like English-language castle tours) vanish altogether.

Thanks to France's relatively mild climate, fields of flowers greet the traveler much of the year:

April–May: Crops of brilliant yellow colza bloom, mostly in the north (best in Burgundy). Wild red poppies *(coquelicots)* begin sprouting in the south.

June: Red poppies pop up throughout the country. Lavender begins to bloom in the hills of Provence, generally during the last week of the month.

July: Lavender is in full swing in Provence, and sunflowers are awakening. Cities, towns, and villages everywhere overflow with carefully tended flowers.

August–September: Sunflowers flourish north and south.

October: In the latter half of the month, the countryside glistens with fall colors, as most trees are deciduous. Vineyards go for the gold.

Sightseeing Priorities

Depending on the length of your trip, here are our recommended priorities:

3 days:	Paris and maybe Versailles
5 days, add:	Normandy
7 days, add:	The Loire
10 days, add:	Dordogne, Carcassonne
15 days, add:	Provence, the Riviera
18 days, add:	Burgundy, Chamonix
21 days, add:	Alsace, Champagne
23 days, add:	Basque Country

For a day-by-day itinerary of this three-week trip—geared for drivers and train travelers—see "Whirlwind Three-Week Trip," page 14. For a more focused two-week trip that highlights Paris, Provence, and the Riviera, fly into Paris and out of Nice (or vice versa), and connect these areas in 5 hours by TGV train or in one hour by plane. For travelers with a little more time, Burgundy and the Alps are about halfway between Paris and Provence and are easy to reach by car or train. If all you have is a week and it's your first trip to France, do Paris, Normandy, and the Loire.

RESOURCES

French Tourist Offices in the United States

France's national tourist offices are a wealth of information. Before your trip, request any specific information you may want (such as city maps and schedules of upcoming festivals).

French Government Tourist Offices: For questions and brochures, call 410/286-8310. Ask for the France Guide. Materials delivered in four to six weeks are free; there's a $4 shipping fee for information delivered in 5 to 10 days. Their Web site is www .franceguide.com, their e-mail is info@franceguide.com, and their offices are in:

New York: 444 Madison Ave., 16th floor, New York, NY 10022, tel. 212/838-7800, fax 212/838-7855, Mon–Fri 10:00–16:00, closed Sat–Sun.

California: 9454 Wilshire Blvd. #310, Beverly Hills, CA 90212, tel. 310/271-6665, fax 310/276-2835, Mon–Fri 9:00–13:00 & 14:00–17:00, closed Sat–Sun.

Rick Steves' Books and Public Television Shows

Rick Steves' Europe Through the Back Door 2005 gives you budget travel tips on minimizing jet lag, packing light, planning your itinerary, traveling by car or train, finding budget beds, avoiding rip-offs, using mobile phones, hurdling the language barrier, staying healthy, using your bidet, and lots more. The book also has chapters on 38 of Rick's favorite "Back Doors," including three in France.

Rick Steves' Country Guides are a series of 11 annually updated guidebooks—including this one—that cover Europe, offering you the latest on the top sights and destinations, with tips on how to make your trip efficient and fun.

Rick Steves' City and Regional Guides include our *Provence & the French Riviera* guidebook, along with Paris, Venice, Florence, London, and Amsterdam/Bruges/Brussels. These practical, annually updated guides offer in-depth coverage of the sights, hotels, restaurants, and nightlife in these grand cities and regions, along with illustrated tours of their great museums.

Rick Steves' Easy Access Europe, written for travelers with limited mobility, covers London, Paris, Bruges, Amsterdam, and the Rhine River.

Rick Steves' Europe 101: History and Art for the Traveler (with Gene Openshaw) gives you the story of Europe's people, history, and art. Written for smart people who were sleeping in their history and art classes before they knew they were going to Europe, *101* really helps Europe's sights come alive.

Rick Steves' Best European City Walks & Museums (with Gene Openshaw) gives you self-guided tours of the major museums and historic neighborhoods in Paris, London, Amsterdam, Rome, Florence, Venice, and Madrid.

Rick Steves' French Phrase Book helps you meet the people and stretch your budget. It's written by a monoglot who, for 25 years, has fumbled through France struggling with all the other phrase books. This handy book has everything you'll need, including a menu decoder, conversation starters for connecting with locals, and an easy-to-follow telephone template for making hotel reservations.

Rick Steves' Guidebooks

Rick Steves' Europe Through the Back Door
Rick Steves' Best European City Walks & Museums
Rick Steves' Easy Access Europe

Country Guides
Rick Steves' Best of Europe
Rick Steves' Best of Eastern Europe
Rick Steves' France
Rick Steves' Germany & Austria
Rick Steves' Great Britain
Rick Steves' Ireland
Rick Steves' Italy
Rick Steves' Portugal
Rick Steves' Scandinavia
Rick Steves' Spain
Rick Steves' Switzerland

City and Regional Guides
Rick Steves' Amsterdam, Bruges & Brussels
Rick Steves' Florence & Tuscany
Rick Steves' London
Rick Steves' Paris
Rick Steves' Prague & the Czech Republic*
Rick Steves' Provence & the French Riviera
Rick Steves' Rome
Rick Steves' Venice

*New in 2005

(Avalon Travel Publishing)

Our public television series, *Rick Steves' Europe*, keeps churning out shows. Several of the 95 episodes (from the new series and from *Travels in Europe with Rick Steves*) feature sights covered in this book, including three shows on Paris and seven on other parts of France.

Rick Steves' Postcards from Europe, Rick's autobiographical book, packs 25 years of travel anecdotes and insights into the ultimate 2,000-mile European adventure.

Other Guidebooks
For most travelers, this book is all you need. But if you'd like more information, you may want to get supplemental materials, especially if you're traveling beyond our recommended destinations. Considering the improvements they'll make in your $3,000 vacation, $25 or $35 for extra maps and books is money well spent. One

simple budget tip can easily save the price of an extra guidebook.

I like Cadogan's *France* guide for its well-presented background information and its coverage of cultural issues. The recommendations suit upscale travelers and can get stale, as they are not updated annually. Lonely Planet's *France* is well-researched, with good maps and hotel recommendations for low- to moderate-budget travelers (but it's also not updated annually). The highly opinionated, annually updated *Let's Go: France* (St. Martin's Press) is ideal for students and vagabonds. The popular, skinny, green Michelin guides are dry but informative, especially for drivers. They're known for their city and sightseeing maps and concise, helpful information on all major sights. English editions, covering most of the regions you'll want to visit, are sold in France for about €14 (or in the U.S. for $20). Of the multitude of other guidebooks on France and Paris, many are high on facts and low on opinion, guts, or personality.

Recommended Books and Movies

For information on France past and present, consider reading some of these books or seeing these films:

Non-Fiction: To better understand the French, check out *French or Foe* or *Savoir-Flair!* (both by Polly Platt). To better appreciate village life, read *A Year in Provence* and *Toujours Provence* (Peter Mayle). *The Course of French History* (Pierre Goubert) provides a good, succinct summary of French history. Ina Caro's *The Road from the Past* is filled with enjoyable essays on her travels through France, with an accent on history.

Here are more: *Travelers' Tales: France* (edited by James O'Reilly), *Portraits of France* (Robert Daley), *Holy Blood, Holy Grail* (Michael Baigent, Richard Leigh, and Henry Lincoln), *The Longest Day* (Cornelius Ryan), *Wine & War: The French, the Nazis, and the Battle for France's Greatest Treasure* (Don and Petie Kladstrup), *Is Paris Burning?* (Larry Collins), *At Home in France* (Ann Barry), *Postcards from France* (Megan McNeill Libby), *Adapter Kit France: A Traveler's Tools for Living Like a Local* (Terry Link), *Culture Shock: France* (Sally A. Taylor), and *Marling Menu-Master for France*.

Fiction: *City of Darkness, City of Light* (Marge Piercy), *Le Divorce* and *Le Mariage* (both by Diane Johnson), *Versailles* (Kathryn Davis), *Chocolat* (Joanne Harris), *Inspector Maigret* series (Georges Simenon), *A Very Long Engagement* (Sébastien Japrisot), *Birdsong* (Sebastian Faulks), and *Les Misérables* and *The Hunchback of Notre-Dame* (both by Victor Hugo).

Flicks: *Queen Margot, Jean de Florette, My Mother's Castle, My Father's Glory, Manon of the Spring, To Catch A Thief, The Return of Martin Guerre, Mr. Hulot's Holiday, The Horseman on the Roof, Jules et Jim, The 400 Blows, The Red Balloon, Ridicule, Les Misérables, Lust for Life, Cyrano de Bergerac, Danton, Is Paris Burning?, Moulin Rouge*

Begin Your Trip at www.ricksteves.com

At ricksteves.com, you'll find a wealth of **free information** on destinations covered in this book, including fresh European travel and tour news every month, and helpful "Graffiti Wall" tips from thousands of fellow travelers.

While you're there, Rick Steves' **online Travel Store** is a great place to save money on travel bags and accessories specially designed by Rick Steves to help you travel smarter and lighter. These include Rick's popular carry-on bags (wheeled and rucksack versions), money belts, day bags, totes, toiletries kits, packing cubes, clotheslines, locks, clocks, sleep sacks, adapters, and a wide selection of guidebooks, planning maps, and *Rick Steves' Europe* DVDs.

Traveling through Europe by rail is a breeze, but choosing the right railpass for your trip (amidst hundreds of options) can drive you nutty. At ricksteves.com, you'll find **Rick Steves' Annual Guide to European Railpasses**—your best way to convert chaos into pure travel energy. Buy your railpass from Rick, and you'll get a bunch of free extras to boot.

Travel agents will tell you about mainstream tours of Europe, but they won't tell you about **Rick Steves' tours**. Rick Steves' Europe Through the Back Door travel company offers more than two dozen itineraries and 250+ departures reaching the best destinations in this book...and beyond. You'll enjoy the services of a great guide, a fun bunch of travel partners (with group sizes in the mid-20s), and plenty of room to spread out in a big, comfy bus. You'll find tours to fit every vacation size, from week-long city getaways (Paris, London, Venice, Florence, Rome), to 12–18-day country tours, to three-week "Best of Europe" adventures. For details, visit www.ricksteves.com or call 425/771-8303 ext 217.

(1952), *French Kiss, Amélie, An American in Paris, Can-Can, Funny Face, Charade, The Last Time I Saw Paris, Gigi, The Phantom of the Opera* (1943), *Saving Private Ryan,* and *Chocolat.*

Maps

The black-and-white maps in this book, drawn by Dave Hoerlein, are concise and simple. Dave, who is well-traveled in France, designed the maps to help you locate recommended places and reach tourist information offices, where you'll find more in-depth (and often free) maps of cities or regions. Better maps are sold at newsstands—take a look before you buy to be sure the map has the level of detail you want. Also, see the handy color city and Métro maps in the beginning of this book.

Don't skimp on maps. Michelin maps are available throughout France at bookstores, newsstands, and gas stations (about €5–6, half the U.S. price). Train travelers can do fine with Michelin's #989

France map (1:1,000,000). For better detail, pick up the yellow Michelin Local series maps as you travel. Drivers should consider the soft-cover Michelin France atlas (the entire country at 1:200,000, well-organized in a €20 book with an index and 75 maps of major cities). Learn the Michelin key to get the most sightseeing value out of their maps.

PRACTICALITIES

Red Tape: You need a passport, but no visa or shots, to travel in France. It's a good idea to bring photocopies of your identity papers in case the originals are lost or stolen. You are required to have proof of identity on you at all times in France.

Time: In Europe, you'll be using the 24-hour clock. It's the same through 12:00 noon, then keep going: 13:00, 14:00, and so on. For anything over 12, subtract 12 and add p.m. (14:00 is 2:00 p.m.).

Business Hours: You'll find much of rural France closed on weekdays from noon to 14:00 (lunch is sacred). On Sunday and during the numerous holidays (see below), most businesses are closed (family is sacred), though small shops, such as *boulangeries* (bakeries), are open until noon, and museums are open all day. On Monday, many businesses are closed until 14:00, and possibly all day. Smaller towns are usually quiet on Sundays and Mondays. Saturdays are like weekdays. Note that on any day, sights stop admitting people 30 to 60 minutes before they close.

Shopping: Shoppers interested in customs regulations and VAT refunds (the tax refunded on large purchases made by non-EU residents) can refer to page 11.

Discounts: While discounts for sights and transportation generally are not listed in this book, seniors (60 and over) and students (with International Student Identification Cards; contact STA Travel, below) may get discounts—but only by asking. Those under 18 or even 26 can get discounts—but you'll need to ask. Teachers with an International Teacher ID Card might be given discounts or free admission to some sights. To get a Teacher or Student ID Card, contact STA Travel (U.S. tel. 800/777-0112, www.statravel.com) or the International Student Travel Confederation (www.isic.org).

Metric: Get used to metric. A liter is about a quart (four quarts to a gallon). A kilometer is six-tenths of a mile. We figure kilometers to miles by cutting them in half and adding back 10 percent of the original (120 km: 60 + 12 = 72 miles, 300 km: 150 + 30 = 180 miles).

Watt's Up? If you're bringing electrical gear, you'll need a two-prong adapter plug and a converter. Travel appliances often have convenient, built-in converters; look for a voltage switch marked 120V (U.S.) and 240V (Europe).

MONEY

Exchange Rate
We've priced things throughout this book in the local currency: the euro.

> 1 euro (€) = about $1.20

To convert prices in euros to dollars, add 20 percent: €20 = about $24, €50 = about $60. Just like the dollar, the euro is broken down into 100 cents *(centimes)*. You'll find coins ranging from one cent to two euros, and bills from five euros to 500 euros.

Banking
Bring a debit card (or ATM card) and a credit card, along with a couple hundred dollars in cash as a backup. Travelers checks are a waste of your time and money.

The best and easiest way to get cash in euros is to use the omnipresent French bank machines (always open, low fees, and quick processing). You'll need a PIN code—numbers only, no letters—to use with your Visa or Mastercard. "Cash machines" in French are signed *point d'argent* or *distributeur des billets;* the French call these *D.A.B.* (day ah bay).

Before you go, verify with your bank that your card will work and alert them that you'll be making withdrawals in Europe; otherwise, the bank may not approve transactions if it perceives unusual spending patterns. Bring two cards in case one gets damaged.

Just like at home, credit or debit cards work easily at larger hotels, restaurants, and shops. Visa and MasterCard are more commonly accepted than American Express. Smaller businesses prefer payment in local currency. Smart travelers function with hard cash and plastic.

Keep your credit and debit cards and most of your money hidden away in a money belt (a cloth pouch worn around your waist and tucked under your clothes). Thieves target tourists. A money belt provides peace of mind and allows you to carry lots of cash safely. Don't be petty about changing money. Change a week's worth of money, stuff it in your money belt, and travel!

VAT Refunds and Customs Regulations
VAT Refunds for Shoppers: Wrapped into the purchase price of your French souvenirs is a Value Added Tax (VAT) of 19.6 percent. If you make a purchase of more than €175 in France at a store that participates in the VAT refund scheme, you're entitled to get most of that tax back. Personally, we've never felt that VAT refunds are worth the hassle, but if you do, here's the scoop.

You must be over 15, and, if you're lucky, the merchant will

Visa 701-461-1552
Debit 1-800-673-3555
US Bank - Busi Check card

Damage Control for Lost or Stolen Cards

You can stop thieves from using your ATM, debit, or credit card by reporting the loss immediately to the proper company. Call these 24-hour U.S. numbers collect: Visa (tel. 410/581-9994), MasterCard (tel. 636/722-7111), and American Express (tel. 336/393-1111).

Providing the following information will help expedite the process: the name of the financial institution that issued you the card, full card number, the cardholder's name as printed on the card, billing address, home phone number, circumstances of the loss or theft, and identification verification, including a Social Security Number or birth date and your mother's maiden name. (Packing along a photocopy of the front and back of your cards helps you answer the harder questions.) If you are the secondary cardholder, you'll also need to provide the primary cardholder's identification verification details. You can generally receive a temporary card within two or three business days in Europe.

If you promptly report your card lost or stolen, you typically won't be responsible for any unauthorized transactions on your account, although many banks charge a liability fee of $50.

subtract the tax when you make your purchase; this is more likely if the store ships the goods to your home. Otherwise, you'll need to:

- Get the paperwork. Have the merchant completely fill out the necessary refund document (Bordereau de Vente à l'Exportation—also called a "cheque"). You'll have to present your passport at the store.
- Get your stamp at the border. Process your cheque(s) at your last stop in the EU with the customs agent who deals with VAT refunds. It's best to keep your purchases in your carry-on for viewing, but if they're too large or considered too dangerous (such as knives) to carry on, then track down the proper customs agent to inspect them before you check your bag. You're not supposed to use your purchased goods before you leave. If you show up at customs wearing your chic new French ensemble, officials might look the other way—or deny you a refund.
- Collect your refund. You'll need to return your stamped document to the retailer or its representative. Many merchants work with a service, such as Global Refund or Premier Tax Free, which have offices at major airports, ports, or border crossings. These services, which extract a 4 percent fee, can refund your money immediately in your currency of choice or credit your card (within two billing cycles). If you have to deal directly with the retailer, mail the store your stamped documents and wait. It could take months.

Customs Regulations: You can take home $800 in souvenirs per person duty-free. The next $1,000 is taxed at a flat 3 percent. After that, you pay the individual item's duty rate. You can also bring in duty-free a liter of alcohol (slightly more than a standard-sized bottle of wine, but don't bring home absinthe—illegal in the United States), a carton of cigarettes, and up to 100 cigars. As for food, anything in sealed jars or cans (such as foie gras or most meat products) is acceptable. Skip cheeses, dried meats, fruits, and vegetables. To check customs rules and duty rates, visit www.customs.gov.

TRAVEL SMART

Your trip to France is like a complex play—easier to follow and really appreciate on a second viewing. While no one does the same trip twice to gain that advantage, reading this book in its entirety before your trip accomplishes much the same thing.

Reread this book as you travel, and visit local tourist information offices (abbreviated as "TI" in this book). If you're using public transportation, read up on the tips for trains and buses, both listed later in this chapter. Upon arrival in a new town, lay the groundwork for a smooth departure; write down the schedule for the train or bus you'll take when you depart. If you're driving, be sure to peruse our driving tips and study the examples of road signs (see page 26).

Slow down and ask questions. Most locals are eager to tell you about their town's history and point you in their idea of the right direction. Buy a phone card or mobile phone and use it for reservations and confirmations. Those who expect to travel smart, do.

Maximize rootedness by minimizing one-night stands. Plan ahead for banking, laundry, post-office chores, and picnics. Mix intense and relaxed periods. Every trip (and every traveler) needs at least a few slack days. Pace yourself. Assume you will return.

As you read through this book, plan your itinerary. Note the days when sights are closed. Sundays have pros and cons, as they do for traveling in the United States (special events and weekly markets, limited hours, shops and banks closed, limited public transportation, no rush hours). Saturdays are virtually weekdays.

Holidays: Popular places are even busier on weekends and inundated on three-day weekends. Holiday weekends can make towns, trains, roads, and hotels more crowded than summer.

In 2005, be ready for unusually big crowds during these holiday periods, and book your accommodations well in advance: Easter week (March 21–29), Labor Day weekend (April 29–May 1), Ascension weekend (May 5–8), Bastille Day (July 14), Assumption (Aug 15), All Saints' Day weekend (Oct 29–Nov 1), Armistice Day weekend (Nov 11–13), and the winter holidays (Dec 17–Jan 3). Many sights close on the actual holiday (confirm closures at local tourist information offices).

Whirlwind (Kamikaze) Three-Week Trip of France by Car

Day	Plan
1	Fly into Paris, pick up car, visit Giverny or Rouen, and spend the afternoon and night in Honfleur (save Paris sightseeing for end of trip). If arriving late in Paris, you can sleep in Giverny or Rouen.
2	9:00–Depart Honfleur, 10:00–Caen WWII Museum, 12:30–Drive to Arromanches for lunch and museum, 15:30–American cemetery, 17:00–Pointe du Hoc, with dinner and overnight in Bayeux.
3	9:00–Bayeux tapestry and church, 12:00–Drive to Dinan, 13:00–Arrive in Dinan for a quick look at Brittany, 17:00–Scenic drive to Mont St. Michel. Sleep on Mont St. Michel.
4	Visit abbey of Mont St. Michel this morning. 11:00–Drive to Loire, 15:30–Tour Chambord, 18:00–Arrive in Amboise, sleep in Amboise.
5	8:45–Depart Amboise, 9:00–Chenonceaux, 11:30–Cheverny château and lunch, 14:00–Possible stop in Chaumont, back in Amboise for Leonardo's house and free time in town, sleep in Amboise.
6	8:30–Depart Amboise, with café stop in Chauvigny and lunch at Mortemart, 13:30–Oradour-sur-Glane, 14:30–Drive to Sarlat or Beynac, 17:30–Wander Beynac or Sarlat. Have dinner and overnight in Beynac or Sarlat.
7	9:00–Browse the town and market of Sarlat, 12:00–Font-de-Gaume tour, 14:00–More caves, castles, or canoe extravaganza. Dinner and sleep in Beynac or Sarlat.
8	9:00–Depart, 10:00–Short stop at Cahors bridge, 12:30–Arrive in Albi and have lunch, 14:00–Tour church and Toulouse-Lautrec Museum, 16:00–Depart for Carcassonne, 18:00–Explore, have dinner, and sleep in Carcassonne.
9	10:30–Depart Carcassonne, 11:15–Café stop in Minerve, 14:00–Pont du Gard, 16:30–Drive to Arles, 17:30–Set up for evening in Arles.
10	All day for Arles and Avignon, evening back in Arles.
11	8:30–Depart Arles, 9:00–Les Baux, 11:00–Depart Les Baux, 12:00–Lunch and wander in Roussillon, 14:00–Luberon hill-town drive, 15:30–Depart for the Riviera, 18:30–Arrive in Nice or Antibes.
12	Sightsee in Nice and Monaco, then sleep in Nice or Antibes.
13	Morning free (Chagall and/or Matisse museums), 12:00–Drive north, sleep in Annecy.

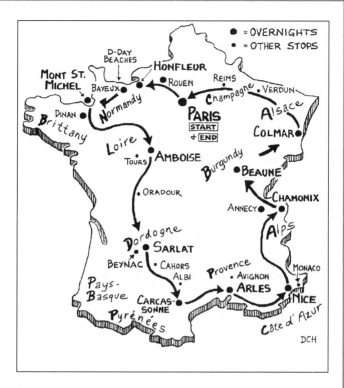

14	Most of day in Annecy, afternoon drive to Chamonix. With clear weather, do Aiguille du Midi. Sleep in Chamonix.
15	All day for the Alps. Sleep in Chamonix.
16	9:00–Depart Chamonix, 12:00–Lunch in Brancion, 14:00–Depart Brancion, 15:00–Arrive in Beaune for Hôtel Dieu and wine-tasting, sleep in Beaune.
17	9:00–Depart for Burgundy village treats or get to Alsace early. Arrive in Colmar after 3.5-hour drive.
18	9:00–Unterlinden Museum, 10:00–Free time in town, 14:00–Wine Road villages, evening back in Colmar.
19	8:00–Depart Colmar, 12:00–Lunch and tour Verdun battle-field, 15:00–Depart, 16:00–Arrive Reims, church and a champagne cave, 18:00–Turn in car at Reims, picnic dinner celebration on train to Paris, 21:00–Collapse in Paris hotel.
20 & 21	Sightsee Paris.
22	Sightsee Paris, trip over.

Three-Week Trip of France by Train and Bus

Day **Plan**

All times are approximate. Fewer buses and trains run on Sunday.

1   Fly into Paris, find your hotel, go for an afternoon walk.

2   Sightsee all day in Paris.

3   Head to Rouen (check bags at station), sightsee there, and then head to Honfleur (from Rouen, take afternoon train to Le Havre, and catch bus to Honfleur). Sleep in Honfleur.

4   Morning in Honfleur, then take midday bus to Caen (or go in morning to Caen for more time at WWII museum), then train to Bayeux to see tapestries in the afternoon. Sleep in Bayeux.

5   All day for D-Day beaches by minivan excursion or one-day car rental, late afternoon train (about 17:00) to Pontorson. Taxi to Mont St. Michel, sleep on Mont St. Michel.

6   Early-morning walk on the island, then catch a bus or taxi to Pontorson, 10:00–Train to Rennes, transfer to Le Mans, train to Tours, and then train to Amboise. Sleep in Amboise.

7   Minivan tour of the Loire or one-day car rental. Sleep in Amboise.

8   Early-morning train to Sarlat (probable transfers at Tours and Bordeaux St. Jean), afternoon in Sarlat, sleep in Sarlat. (Note: It's possible to visit Oradour-sur-Glane on this day; see Amboise's and Sarlat's Transportation Connections on pages 254 and 283, respectively.)

9   All day in the Dordogne, take a taxi-van tour (see page 272, and ask driver to drop you in Cenac for canoe trip to Beynac), then taxi from Beynac to Sarlat, or take morning train to Les Eyzies (rent a bike and visit Grotte de Font-de-Gaume and Abri du Cap Blanc). At the end of the day, train back to Sarlat, sleep in Sarlat.

Tourist Information

Except in Paris, where they aren't very helpful, the tourist information office (abbreviated in this book as **TI**) is your best first stop in any new city, offering useful maps, special events information, English-language tour information, and much more. If you're arriving in town after the office closes, consider calling ahead or picking up a map in a neighboring town. Throughout France, you'll find TIs are usually well-organized and have English-speaking staff. Most will help you find a room by calling hotels (for a small fee) or by giving you a complete listing of available bed-and-breakfasts. Towns with a lot of tourism generally have English-speaking guides available for private hire (about $100 for a 2-hr guided town walk).

    The French call TIs by different names. *Office de Tourisme* and

10	Morning train to Carcassonne (transfer in Souillac or Bordeaux and in Toulouse), afternoon wall walk, sleep in Carcassonne.
11	Morning train to Arles, sightsee and sleep in Arles.
12	Morning train to Nîmes, late-morning bus to Pont du Gard (about 11:00), early-afternoon bus from Pont du Gard to Avignon (about 13:30). Afternoon in Avignon, evening train back to Arles, sleep in Arles.
13	Taxi to Les Baux (about 8:30), return midday to Arles, afternoon train to Nice, stroll the promenade, sleep on the Riviera.
14	Morning in Nice's old city, bus to Monaco, see casino and Changing of the Guard, return to Nice for beach time or Chagall Museum, sleep in Nice.
15	Take a vacation from your vacation and spend a day on the beach. Spend part of the day in Antibes or Villefranche-sur-Mer.
16	Train to Annecy, afternoon bike ride and boat trip, sleep in Annecy.
17	Morning in Annecy's old town, midday train to Chamonix, afternoon and night in Chamonix.
18	Hike all day in the Alps, sleep in Chamonix.
19	Train to Colmar (via Martigny, Lausanne, and Basel*), sleep in Colmar, or TGV to Paris (via Aix-les-Bains).
20	All day in Alsace, sleep in Colmar (or evening train to Paris if you must leave the next day).
21	Train to Paris (consider a stop in Reims en route).

*If you have a French railpass, you'll need a ticket for the Swiss segment of your journey.

Bureau de Tourisme are used in cities, while *Syndicat d'Initiative* or *Information Touristique* are used in small towns. Also look for *Accueil* signs in airports and at popular sights. These are information booths staffed with seasonal helpers who provide tourists with limited, though generally sufficient, information. TIs are often closed from noon to 14:00.

TRANSPORTATION

By Car or Train?

Cars are best for three or more traveling together (especially families with small kids), those packing heavy, and those scouring the countryside. Trains and buses are best for solo travelers, blitz tourists, and city-to-city travelers. Train stations are usually centrally located in cities, which makes hotel-hunting and sightseeing easy. But because so many of your destinations are likely to be small places, such as Honfleur, Mont St. Michel, D-Day beaches, Loire châteaux, Dordogne caves, and villages in Provence and Burgundy, trains and buses require great patience, planning, and time. If relying on public transportation, seriously consider the value of a train or bus detour and focus on fewer key destinations.

Trains

France's rail system (SNCF) sets the pace in Europe. Its super TGV (tay zhay vay; *train à grande vitesse*) system has inspired bullet trains throughout the world. The TGV runs at 170 to 220 mph. Its rails are fused into one long, continuous track for a faster and smoother ride. The TGV has changed commuting patterns in much of France and put most of the country within day-trip distance of Paris. The Eurostar English Channel tunnel train to Britain and the Thalys bullet train to Brussels are two more links in the grand European train system of the 21st century. The fastest TGV Mediterranean line opened in 2001, with trains screaming from Paris' city center and Charles de Gaulle airport to Avignon (in Provence) in 2.5 hours.

Schedules change by season, weekday, and weekend. Verify TGV train times shown in this book (to study ahead on the Web, check http://bahn.hafas.de/bin/query.exe/en), and make your reservations. The nationwide information line for train schedules and reservations is tel. 3635. Dial this four-digit number, then press "3" (for reservations or to purchase a ticket) when you get the message. This incredibly helpful, time-saving service costs €0.34 per minute from anywhere in France. Ask for an English-speaking agent and hope for the best (allow 5 min per call). The time and energy you save easily justifies the telephone torture, particularly when making seat reservations. Phoned-in reservations must be picked up at the station at least 30 minutes prior to departure.

Bigger stations have helpful information agents (often in red vests) roaming the station and/or at *Accueil* offices or booths. They're capable of answering rail questions more quickly than the information or ticket windows. Make use of these people; don't stand in a ticket line if all you need is a train schedule. Many cities have neighborhood SNCF Boutiques, small offices where you can confirm schedules, buy tickets, and make reservations. I've listed some offices in this book, but ask your hotelier for the location nearest your hotel.

Long-distance travelers can save big money with a France Railpass, sold only outside France (through travel agents or Europe Through the Back Door; see Railpass sidebar on page 22). For roughly the cost of a Paris–Avignon–Paris ticket, the France Railpass offers four days of travel (within a month) anywhere in

The French Rail System

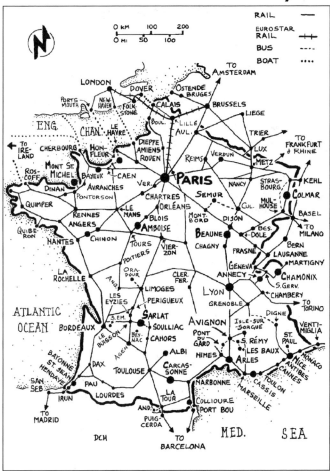

France. You can add up to six additional days for the cost of a two-hour ride each. Save money by getting the second-class instead of the first-class version and/or travel with a companion (the flexi-saver gives two people traveling together a 20 percent discount). Each day of use allows you to take as many trips as you want until midnight (you could go from Paris to Chartres, see the cathedral, then continue to Avignon, stay a few hours, and end in Nice—though we don't recommend it). Buy second-class tickets in France for shorter trips, and spend your valuable railpass days wisely. If you're connecting the French Alps with Alsace, you might travel through Switzerland, requiring France railpass holders to buy a ticket for that segment (about €50).

Train and Bus Tips

Trains

- Arrive at the station with plenty of time before your departure to find the right platform, confirm connections, and so on. In small towns, your train may depart before the station opens; go directly to the tracks and find the overhead sign that confirms your train stops at that track.
- Check schedules in advance. Upon arrival at a station, find out your departure possibilities. Large stations have a separate information window or office; at small stations, the ticket office gives information.
- Write the date on your flexi-pass each day you travel.
- Validate tickets (not passes) and reservations in orange machines before boarding. If you're traveling with a pass and have a reservation for a certain trip, you must validate the reservation.
- Before getting on a train, confirm that it's going where you think it is. For example, ask the conductor or any local passenger, *"A Bayeux?"* (ah Bayeux; meaning, "To Bayeux?").
- Some trains split cars en route. Make sure your train car is continuing to your destination by asking, *"Cette voiture va à Bayeux?"* (set vwa-ture vah ah Bayeux; meaning, "This car goes to Bayeux?").
- If a seat is reserved, it will be labeled *réservé*, with the cities to and from which it is reserved.
- Verify with the conductor all transfers you must make (*"Correspondance à?"*; meaning, "Transfer to where?").
- To guard against theft, keep your bags right overhead; don't store them on the racks at the end of the car.
- Note your arrival time, so you'll be ready to get off.
- Use the trains' free WCs before you get off.

If traveling *sans* railpass, inquire about the many point-to-point discount fares possible (for youths, those over 60, married couples, families, travel during off-peak hours, and more).

Second-class tickets, available to people of any age, provide the same transportation for 33 percent less (and many regional trains to less trafficked places often have only second-class cars). Travelers of any age can also choose first or second class with the France Railpass. (But travelers who want a Eurailpass—and are 26 or older—must buy a first-class pass.) You can buy tickets on the train for a €4 surcharge, but you must find the conductor

Automatic Train Ticket Machines
Ticket machines available at most stations are great time-savers when ticket-window lines are long. Some have English instructions, but for those that don't, here is what you are prompted to do. (The default is usually what you want; turn the dial or move the cursor to your choice, and press "Validez" to agree to each step.)
1. *Quelle est votre destination?* (What's your destination?)
2. *Billet Plein Tarif* (Full fare ticket—yes for most.)
3. *1ère ou 2ème* (First or second class; normally second is fine.)
4. *Aller simple ou aller-retour?* (One-way or round-trip?)
5. *Prix en Euro* (The price should be shown if you get this far.) Pay with Visa, MasterCard, or coins.

Buses
- Read the train tips above, and use those that apply.
- TIs often have regional bus schedules and can help plan your trip.
- Service is sparse on Sunday. Wednesday bus schedules are often different during the school year.
- Be at stops at least five minutes early.
- On schedules, *en semaine* means Monday through Saturday, and *jours fériés* are holidays.

Key Phrases for Train or Bus
- *Bonjour, monsieur/madame, parlez-vous anglais?*
  Pron: bohn-zhoor, muhs-yur/mah-dahm, par-lay-voo ahn-glay?
  Meaning: Hello, sir/madam, do you speak English?
- *Je voudrais un départ pour* ___ (destination), *pour le* ___ (date), *vers* ___ (general time of day), *la plus direct possible*.
  Pron: zhuh voo-dray day-par poor ___ (destination), poor luh ___ (date), vehr ___ (time), lah ploo dee-rehk poh-see-bluh.
  Meaning/Example: I would like a departure for Avignon, on 23 May, about 9:00, the most direct way possible.

immediately on boarding, otherwise it's a €35 minimum charge.
Reservations, while generally unnecessary for non-TGV trains, are advisable during busy times (e.g., Fri and Sun afternoons, weekday rush hours, and particularly holiday weekends; see "Holidays," page 13). Reservations are required for any TGV train (usually about €3, more during peak periods) and for *couchettes* (berths, €15) on night trains. Even railpass-holders need reservations for the TGV trains, and only a limited number of reservations are available for passholders. To avoid the more expensive fares, don't travel at peak times; ask at the station. Validate (*composter,* kohm-poh-stay) all

Cost of Railpasses

Prices listed are for 2004. My free *Rick Steves' Guide to European Railpasses* has the latest prices and details (and easy online ordering) at www.ricksteves.com/rail. Note that France-only passes are not valid on Paris-Berlin night train.

FRANCE FLEXIPASS

	Adult 1st class	Adult 2nd class	Senior 1st class	Youth 1st class	Youth 2nd class
Any 4 days in 1 month	$252	$218	$228	$189	$164
Extra rail days (max 6)	32	28	29	24	21

Seniors 60+, youth under 26, kids 4-11 half adult fare.

FRANCE FLEXI SAVERPASS

	Adult 1st class	Adult 2nd class
Any 4 days in 1 month	$215	$186
Extra rail days (max 6)	28	24

Prices are per person for two or more traveling together. OK to mix kids and adults (kids 4–11 half adult fare).

FRANCE RAIL & DRIVE PASS

Any 2 days of rail and 2 days of Avis rental car in 1 month.

France: The map shows approximate point-to-point one-way 2nd class rail fares in $US. 1st class costs 50% more. Add up fares for your itinerary to see if a railpass will save you money.

Car category	1st class	Extra car day
Economy	$205	$39
Compact	219	49
Intermediate	235	55
Full-size car	255	79
Minivan	299	129

Rail and Drive prices are approximate per person, two traveling together. Solo travelers pay about $100 extra, third and fourth members of a group need only buy the equivalent flexi railpass. Extra rail days (6 max) cost $29 per day for first or second class. To order a France Rail & Drive pass, call your travel agent or Rail Europe at 800/438-7245.

EURAIL SELECTPASSES

These prices cover travel in three adjacent countries. For four- and five-country options, please see the railpass guide at www.ricksteves.com/rail.

	1st class Selectpass	1st class Saverpass	2nd class Youthpass
5 days in 2 months	$356	$304	$249
6 days in 2 months	394	336	276
8 days in 2 months	470	400	329
10 days in 2 months	542	460	379

Saverpass: Price is per person for 2 or more adults traveling together at all times.
Youthpasses: Under age 26 only. Kids 4-11 pay half adult fare; under 4: free.

FRANCE 'N SWITZERLAND PASS

	1st class Individ.	1st class Saver	2nd class Youthpass
4 days in 2 months	$299	$259	$209
Extra rail days (max 6)	36	30	27

Youthpasses are for travelers under age 26 only. Saverpass prices are per person for two or more people traveling together. Children 4-11: half adult or saver price, under 4: free.

FRANCE 'N ITALY PASS

	1st class Individual	1st class Saver	2nd class Individual	2nd class Saver	2nd class Youth
Any 4 days in 2 months	$299	$259	$259	$229	$199
Extra rail days (max 6)	30	27	27	24	21

Youthpasses are for travelers under 26 only. Saver prices are per person for 2 or more traveling together. Children 4-11: half adult or saver price, under 4: free.

Be aware of your route. Many daytime connections from Paris to Italy pass through Switzerland (an additional $50 2nd class or $75 1st class if not covered by your pass). Routes via Nice, Torino, or Modane, will bypass Switzerland. Paris-Italy night trains are covered by the pass, regardless of their route.

FRANCE 'N SPAIN PASS

	1st class Individual	1st class Saver	2nd class Individual	2nd class Saver	2nd class Youth
Any 4 days in 2 months	$299	$259	$259	$229	$199
Extra rail days (max 6)	33	29	29	25	22

Saverpass prices are per person for two or more people traveling together. Youthpasses are for travelers under age 26 only. Children 4-11: half adult or saver price, under 4: free.

If you're only dipping into a bit of Spain, you may not need the France 'n Spain pass. For instance, a ticket from the French border at Cerbere to Barcelona costs only $25. From the French border at Hendaye to Madrid costs $40, but if you cover this ground via the fancy Paris-Madrid "Elipsos" night train, the same passholder fares ($85 and up) apply whether your pass covers one or both countries.

train tickets and reservations in the orange machines located before the platforms. (Do not *composte* your railpass, but do validate it at a ticket window before the first time you use it.) Watch others and imitate.

Baggage check is available only at large train stations (about €4.50 per bag), and is listed by station throughout this book. The availability of baggage check changes frequently depending on security concerns, so be prepared to keep your bag.

For mixing train and bike travel, ask at stations for information booklets *(Train + Vélo)*.

Buses

Regional bus service takes over where the trains stop. You can get most places by rail and bus if you're well-organized, patient, and allow enough time. Review our bus-schedule information, and always verify times at the local TI or bus station; call ahead when possible. A few bus lines are run by SNCF (France's rail system) and are included with your railpass (show railpass at station to get free bus ticket), but most bus lines are independent of the rail system and are not covered by railpasses. Train stations often have bus information where train-to-bus connections are important—and vice versa for bus companies. On Sunday, regional bus service virtually disappears.

Regional Minivan Excursions

Some French companies offer organized day tours of regions where bus and train service is sparse. For the D-Day beaches, châteaux of the Loire Valley, Dordogne Valley villages and caves, Languedoc, the Route du Vin in the Alsace, and wine-tasting in Burgundy, we list companies within each chapter that provide this helpful service at reasonable rates. Some of these minivan excursions offer just trans-portation between the sights; others add a running commentary and information on regional history.

Rental Cars and Rail 'n' Drive Passes

Car rental is cheapest if arranged in advance from home. Call various companies, look online, or arrange a rental through your hometown travel agent, who can also help you out if anything goes wrong during your trip. The best rates are weekly, with unlimited mileage or leasing (see "Leasing," below). You can pick up and drop off in moderate-sized to larger cities anytime. Big companies have offices in more cities and towns. Small rental companies can be cheaper, but aren't as flexible.

You can rent a car on the spot just about anywhere. In many cases, this is a worthwhile splurge. All you need is your American driver's license and money (roughly €65/day with 100–200 kilometers/60–120 miles included). If you only want a car only for a day (e.g., for D-Day beaches or Loire châteaux-hopping), you'll find it cheaper to rent it in France, as most U.S.-arranged rentals have a three-day minimum (which is still cheaper than 2 days of a car rental arranged in Europe).

When you drive a rental car, you are liable for its replacement value. CDW (Collision-Damage Waiver) insurance gives you the peace of mind that comes with low-deductible coverage for about $15 a day; a few "gold" credit cards provide this coverage for free if you use their card for the rental. Quiz your credit-card company on the worst-case scenario, or consider the $7-a-day policy offered by Travel Guard (U.S. tel. 800/826-1300, www.travelguard.com).

Leasing: For a trip of three weeks or more, leasing is a bargain. By technically buying and then selling back the car, you save lots of money on tax and insurance (CDW is included). Leasing, which you should arrange from the United States, usually requires a 22-day minimum contract, but Europe by Car leases cars in France for as few as 17 days for $700 (U.S. tel. 800/223-1516, www.europebycar .com). Auto France has good deals on leasing Peugeot cars (U.S. tel. 800/572-9655, fax 201/934-7501, www.autofrance.net).

Rail 'n' drive passes allow you to mix car and train travel economically (available only outside of France, from your travel agent). Generally, big-city connections are best done by train, and rural regions are best done by car. With a rail 'n' drive pass, you get an economic flexi-railpass with flexi car days. This allows you to combine rail and drive into one pass. For a very reasonable package price, you can take advantage of the high speed and comfort of the TGV trains for longer trips, and rent a car for as little as one day at a time for the day trips that can't be done without one (such as the Loire, the Dordogne, and Provence). Within the same country, you can pick up a car in one city and drop it off in another city without problems. While you're only required to reserve the first car day, it's safer to reserve all days, as cars are not always available on short notice.

Driving

An international driver's license is not necessary in France. Seat belts are mandatory for all, and children under age 10 must be in the back seat. Gas (*essence* in French) is expensive—about $5 per gallon. Diesel *(gazole)* is less—about $3.80 per gallon—so rent a diesel car if you can. Gas is most expensive on autoroutes and cheapest at big supermarkets (closed at night and on Sunday). Many gas stations close on Sunday.

Four hours of autoroute tolls cost about €20, but the alternative to these super "feeways" is often being marooned in rural traffic. Autoroutes usually save enough time, gas, and nausea to justify the splurge. Mix high-speed "autorouting" with scenic country-road rambling (be careful of sluggish tractors on country roads). You'll usually take a ticket when entering an autoroute and pay when you leave, though shorter sections have periodic unmanned toll booths, where you can pay by dropping coins into a basket (change given, but keep a good supply of coins handy to avoid waiting) or by inserting a credit card. Autoroute gas stations usually come with well-stocked mini-marts, clean rest rooms, sandwiches, maps, local products, and cheap vending-machine coffee (€1). Many have small cafés or more elaborate cafeterias with reasonable prices.

Roads are classified into departmental (D), national (N), and autoroutes (A). D routes (usually yellow lines on maps) are slow and often the most scenic. N routes (usually red lines) are the fastest after autoroutes (orange lines). Green road signs are for national routes; blue are for autoroutes. There are plenty of good facilities, gas stations, and rest stops along most French roads.

Speed limits are by road type and typically not posted, so it's best to remember these limits: 90k/hour on two-lane N and D roads outside cities and towns; 110k/hour on divided highways outside cites and towns; 130k/hour on toll autoroutes (10k/hour less if it's raining on N and D roads, 20k/hour less on autoroutes). When you

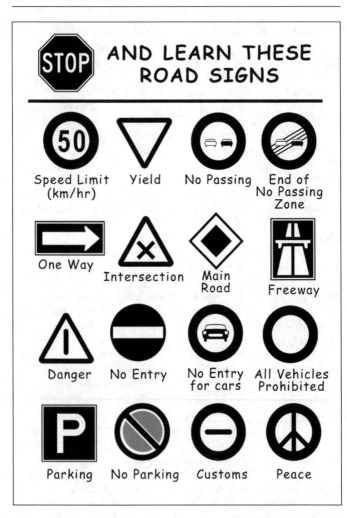

STOP AND LEARN THESE ROAD SIGNS

Speed Limit (km/hr) — Yield — No Passing — End of No Passing Zone

One Way — Intersection — Main Road — Freeway

Danger — No Entry — No Entry for cars — All Vehicles Prohibited

Parking — No Parking — Customs — Peace

do see a speed limit sign, it's a red circle around the number; when you see that same number again in grey with a broken line diagonally across it, this means that limit no longer applies.

Here are a few French road tips: In city centers, traffic merging from the right normally has the right-of-way *(priorité à droite)*, though cars entering the many suburban roundabouts must yield *(cédez le passage)*. It's an art to navigate roundabouts. The key is to know your direction and stay in the outer lane of the circle. When navigating through cities, approach intersections cautiously, stow the map, and follow the signs to *Centre-Ville* (downtown). From there, head to the TI *(Office de Tourisme)*. When leaving or just passing through, follow the signs for *Toutes Directions* or *Autres Directions*

Quick-and-Dirty Road Sign Translation

Instructional Signs that You Must Obey

Cédez le Passage	Yield
Priorité à Droite	Right-of-way is for cars coming from the right
Vous n'avez pas la priorité	You don't have the right of way (when merging)
Rappel	Remember to obey the sign
Allumez vos feux	Turn on your lights
Doublage Interdit	No passing
Parking Interdit/ Stationnement Interdit	No parking

Signs for Your Information

Centre Commercial	Grouping of large, suburban stores (not city center)
Centre-Ville	City center
Feux	Traffic signal
Horadateur	Remote parking meter, usually at the end of the block
Parc de Stationnement	Parking lot
Rue Piétonne	Pedestrian-only street
Sauf Riverains	Local access only

Signs Unique to Autoroutes

Aire	Rest stop with WCs, telephones, and sometimes gas stations
Bouchon	Traffic jam ahead
Fluide	No slowing ahead ("fluid conditions")
Péage	Toll
Télépéage	Toll booths—automatic toll payment only
Toutes Directions	All directions (leaving city)
Autres Directions	Other directions (leaving city)

(meaning anywhere else) until you see a sign for your specific destination. While locals are eating lunch (12:00–14:00), many sights (and gas stations) are closed, so you can make great time driving. The French drive fast and live to tailgate. U-turns are illegal throughout France, and you can not turn right on red lights. Be very careful when driving on smaller roads—most are narrow, with little ditches on either side that are easy to slide into. We've met several readers who "ditched" their cars (and were successfully pulled out by local farmers).

Parking is a headache in the larger cities, and theft is a problem throughout France. Ask your hotelier for ideas, and pay to park

Driving in France: Distance and Time

at well-patrolled lots (blue *P* signs direct you to parking lots in French cities). Parking structures often require that you take a ticket with you and prepay at a machine (called a *caisse*, credit cards usually accepted) on your way back to the car. Overnight parking (usually 19:00–8:00) is generally very reasonable. Curbside metered parking also works (usually free 12:00–14:00 & 19:00–9:00, and in August). Look for a small machine selling time (called *horadateur*, usually one per block), plug in a few coins (about €1 gets about an hour), push the green button, get a receipt showing the amount of time you have, and display it inside your windshield. Keep a pile of coins in your ashtray for parking meters, public restrooms, launderettes, and short stints on autoroutes.

Biking

Throughout France, you'll find areas where public transportation is limited, and bicycle touring is a good idea for some. For many, biking is a romantic notion that is less so after the first hill—realistically evaluate your physical condition, and understand the limitations bikes present. Start with an easy pedal to a nearby village or through the vineyards, then decide how ambitious you want to be. Most find that two hours on a narrow, hard seat is enough. We've listed bike rental shops where appropriate. The TI will always have addresses for bike rental places. For a good touring bike, allow about €10 for a half day and €16 for a full day. You'll pay more for better equipment; generally the best is available through bike shops, not at train stations or other outlets. French cyclists usually don't use bike helmets, though most bike rental outfits have them.

COMMUNICATING

The Language Barrier and That French Attitude

You've no doubt heard that the French are "mean and cold and refuse to speak English." This out-of-date preconception is left over from the days of Charles de Gaulle. The French are as sincere as any other people. Parisians are no more disagreeable than New Yorkers. And, without any doubt, the French speak more English than Americans speak French. Be reasonable in your expectations: Waiters are paid to be efficient, not chatty. And small-town French postal clerks are every bit as speedy, cheery, and multilingual as ours are back home.

The biggest mistake most Americans make when traveling in France is trying to do too much with limited time. Hurried, impatient travelers who miss the subtle pleasures of people-watching from a sun-dappled café and taking walks in the countryside often misinterpret French attitudes. By slowing your pace and making an effort to understand French culture, you're more likely to have a richer experience. With five weeks' paid time off, your hosts can't comprehend why anyone would rush through a vacation, let alone a meal.

The French take great pride in their customs, clinging to their belief in cultural superiority despite the fact that they're no longer a world superpower. Let's face it—it's tough to keep on smiling when you've been crushed by a Big Mac, Mickey-Moused by Disney, and drowned in instant coffee. Your hosts are cold only if you decide to see them that way. Polite and formal, they respect the fine points of culture and tradition. In France, strolling down the street with a big grin on your face (and saying hello to people you don't know) is a sign of senility, not friendliness (seriously). They think that Americans, while friendly, are hesitant to pursue more serious friendships. Recognize sincerity and look for kindness. Give them the benefit of the doubt.

French communication difficulties are exaggerated. To hurdle the language barrier, bring a small English/French dictionary, a phrase book (look for ours), a menu reader, and a good supply of patience. If you learn only five phrases, choose these: *bonjour* (good day), *pardon* (pardon me), *s'il vous plaît* (please), *merci* (thank you), and *au revoir* (good-bye). The French place great importance on politeness. Begin every encounter with "*Bonjour, madame/monsieur,*" and end every encounter with "*Au revoir, madame/monsieur.*"

The French are language perfectionists—they take their language (and other languages) seriously. They often speak more English than they let on. This isn't a tourist-baiting tactic, but timidity on their part with speaking another language less than fluently. Start any conversation with "*Bonjour, madame/monsieur. Parlez-vous anglais?*" and hope they speak more English than you speak French.

Telephones

You'll want a locally purchased phone card for making hotel/restaurant reservations, verifying hours at sights, phoning home, and checking e-mail (at some places, see below).

Phone Cards: Instead of putting coins in pay phones, you can buy cards with prepaid time. Look for them at any post office and from most newsstands and tobacco shops *(tabacs)*, including at train stations and airports. There are two kinds of cards available.

1. A ***télécarte*** (tay-lay-kart) can be used only in a public phone booth. The *télécarte* represents the efficient card-operated system that has replaced coin-operated public phones throughout Europe. Insert the card in the phone and dial away. There are two denominations: *une petite* costs about €7; *une grande* about €15. To use the *télécarte*, simply take the phone off the hook, insert the card, and wait for a dial tone; the price of the call (local or international) is automatically deducted.

2. A ***carte à code*** (cart ah code) comes with a dial-up code that can be used from any phone, including the one in your hotel room (if it's set on "pulse," switch it to "tone"). Cards are marked as national (France only), international, or for both, but all work for calls inside and outside the country. (You get a better rate if your card corresponds to the type of call you're making.) If you're not sure what kind of calls you'll make, buy one that does both. *Le Ticket de Téléphone, 365-Universel,* and *Kosmos* seem like the most common calling-card brands, with denominations in €7, €10 (sometimes), and €15 amounts. They're all good values—my €15 international card lasted for four weeks of regular calls home (about 15 cents a minute).

These cards all work the same way and are simple to use, once you learn the rules (English instructions provided). Scratch to get your code. After you dial the access code, the message tells you to enter your code and then press (*touche*, pronounced toosh) the pound key (#, *dièse*, dee-ehz) or the star key (*, *étoile*, eh-twahl); once the next message arrives, dial your number, again followed by pound or star (you don't have to listen through the entire sales pitch). While per-minute rates are much cheaper with a *carte à code* than with a *télécarte*, it's slower to use (more numbers to dial)—so local calls are quicker with a *télécarte* from a phone booth.

When spelling out your name on the phone, you'll find that some letters are pronounced differently in French: *a* is pronounced "ah," *e* is pronounced "eh," and *i* is pronounced "ee." To avoid confusion, say "*a*, Anne," "*e*, euro," and "*i*, Isabelle," etc.

U.S. Calling Card Services: Since direct-dialing rates have dropped, calling cards (offered by AT&T, MCI, and Sprint) are no longer the good value they used to be. In fact, they are a rip-off. You're likely to pay a $4 connection fee and $3 for the first minute; if you get an answering machine, it'll cost you $7 to say, "Sorry I missed you." Now it's much cheaper to make your international calls with a phone card purchased in Europe.

Dialing Direct: France has a direct-dial 10-digit telephone system. There are no area codes. To call to or from anywhere in France, you dial the 10 numbers directly. (All Paris numbers start with 01.)

To call France from another country, start with the international access code (00 if you're calling from a European country; 011 from the United States and Canada), dial France's country code (33), and then drop the initial 0 of the 10-digit local number and dial the remaining nine digits. For example, the phone number of a good hotel in Paris is 01 47 05 49 15. To call it from home, dial 011 33 1 47 05 49 15.

To dial out of France, start your call with its international code (00), then dial the country code of the country you're calling, then the number you're calling. For example, to call our office in the United States, dial 00 (France's international access code), 1 (U.S. country code), then 425/771-8303 (our area code plus local number).

For a list of international access codes and country codes, see the appendix. European time is six/nine hours ahead of the East/West Coast of the United States.

Mobile Phones: You can buy relatively cheap mobile phones in Europe to make both local and international calls (parents with independent-minded traveling teens find these phones invaluable). Typical American mobile phones don't work in Europe, and those that do have horrendous per-minute costs. For about $120, you can get a phone with $20 worth of calls that will work in the country where you purchased it. (You can buy more time at newsstands or mobile phone shops.) Pricier phones (about $150–200) work in most countries once you pick up the necessary chip per country (about $25). If you're interested, stop by any European shop that sells mobile phones; you'll see prominent store window displays.

Depending on your trip, ask for a phone that works only in that country or one that can be used throughout Europe. If you're on a budget, skip mobile phones and buy phone cards instead.

E-mail and Mail

E-mail: E-mail has caught on among hoteliers; today, very few lack an e-mail address. Many hotels have computers in their lobby—usually with slow Internet connections—for guests to use. The terminals might be free, or operated with coins or a telephone card.

For high-speed Web access, ask at your hotel if there is a nearby Internet (an-ter-net) café. Post offices that offer Internet access *(cyberposte)* charge less than the cafés; buy a chip-card (for about same prices as phone cards) and you're in business.

The current rage is wireless access, called *Wi-Fi* (wee fee), available to laptop users for a minimal fee at Internet cafés and some post offices and hotels.

Mail: French post offices are called PTT for "Post, Telegraph, and Telephone"—look for signs for *La Poste.* Hours vary, though most are open weekdays 8:00–19:00 and Saturday morning 8:00–12:00. Stamps and phone cards are also sold at *tabac* (tobacco) shops. It costs about €0.90 to mail a postcard to the United States.

To arrange for mail delivery, reserve a few hotels along your route in advance, and give their addresses to friends. If you have an American Express card, most AmEx offices will hold your mail for you for free. Allow 10 days for a letter to arrive. Federal Express makes pricey two-day deliveries. E-mailing and phoning are so easy that we've dispensed with mail stops altogether.

SLEEPING

Accommodations in France are a good value and easy to find. Choose from hotels, bed-and-breakfasts *(chambres d'hôte)*, rental homes *(gîtes)*, hostels, and campgrounds. We like places that are clean, small, central, traditional, inexpensive, friendly, and not listed in other guidebooks. Most places we list have at least five of these seven virtues.

Hotels

In this book, the price for a double room will range from €30 (very simple, toilet and shower down the hall) to €200 (maximum plumbing and more), with most clustering around €70.

The French have a simple hotel rating system based on amenities (0–4 stars, indicated in this book by * through ****). One star is simple, two has most of the comforts, and three is generally a two-star with a minibar and fancier lobby. Four stars offer more luxury than you have time to appreciate. One- and two-star hotels are the best budget values, though some three-star hotels (and even a few four-star hotels) can justify the extra cost. In recent years, the star system has become less reliable. Unclassified hotels (no stars) can be bargains or depressing dumps. Look before you leap, and lay before you pay (upon departure).

Most hotels have lots of doubles and a few singles, triples, and quads. Traveling alone can be expensive, as single rooms (except for the rare closet-type rooms that fit only one twin bed) are simply doubles used by one person—so they cost about the same as a double. Room prices vary within each hotel, depending on size and whether the room has a bath or shower and twin beds or a double bed (tubs and twins cost more than showers and double beds). A triple is often a double room with a small double bed plus a sliver-sized single, and quad rooms usually have two double beds. Hotels cannot legally allow more in the room than what's shown on their price list.

Receptionists often don't mention the cheaper rooms—they assume you want a private bathroom or a bigger room. Study the price list on the Web site or posted at the desk. These are the types of rooms and beds:

- *Une chambre sans douche* or *sans WC:* Room without a private shower or toilet (uncommon these days).
- *Une chambre avec cabinet de toilette:* Room with a toilet but no shower (some hotels charge for down-the-hall showers).
- *Une chambre avec salle de bain et WC:* Room with private bathtub and toilet.
- *Une chambre avec douche et WC:* Room with private shower and toilet.
- *Chambres communiquantes:* Connecting rooms (ideal for families), available only at more modern hotels.
- *Un grand lit:* Double bed (55 inches wide).
- *Deux petits lits:* Twin beds (30–36 inches wide).
- *Deux lits séparés:* Two beds separated.
- *Un lit de cent-soixante:* Queen-size bed (literally 160 centimeters, or 63 inches, wide).
- *Un lit dépliant:* Folding bed.
- *Un berceau:* Baby crib.
- *Un lit d'enfant:* Children's bed.

You can save as much as €20–25 by finding the rare room without a private shower or toilet. A room with a bathtub costs €5–10 more than a room with a shower and is generally larger. Hotels often have more rooms with tubs than showers and are inclined to give you a room with a tub (which the French prefer).

A double bed is €5–10 cheaper than twins, though rooms with twin beds tend to be larger, and French double beds are smaller than American double beds. Hotels occasionally offer queen-size beds, which are 160 centimeters wide (over 5 feet wide); most doubles are

140 centimeters (about 4.5 feet). To see if a hotel has queen-size beds, ask, *"Avez-vous un lit de cent-soixante?"* (ah-vay-voo uh lee duh sahn-swah-sahnt). Some hotels push two twins together under king-size sheets and blankets.

If you prefer a double bed (instead of twins) and a shower (instead of a tub), you need to ask for it—and you'll save up to €20. If you're willing to take either twins or a double, ask generically for *une chambre pour deux* (room for two) to avoid being needlessly turned away.

Hotels in France must charge a daily tax *(taxe du séjour)* that is normally added to the bill. It varies from €0.55 to €1.10 per day per person depending on the hotel's number of stars. While some hotels include it in the price list, most add it to your bill.

You'll almost always have the option of breakfast at your hotel, which is pleasant and convenient, but it's more than the price of breakfast at the corner café, and with less ambience (though you get more coffee at your hotel). Some hotels offer only the classic continental breakfast for about €6–8, but others offer buffet breakfasts for about €8–15 (cereal, yogurt, fruit, cheese, croissants, juice, and hard-boiled eggs)—which we usually spring for. While hotels hope you'll buy their breakfast, it's optional unless otherwise noted.

Some hotels strongly encourage their peak-season guests to take "half pension"—that is, breakfast and either lunch or dinner. By law, they can't require you to take half pension unless you are staying three or more nights, but, in effect, many do during summer. While the food is usually good, it limits your ability to shop around. We've indicated where we think *demi-pension* is a good value.

Rooms are safe. Still, keep cameras and money out of sight. Towels aren't routinely replaced every day; drip-dry and conserve. If that Lincoln-log pillow isn't your idea of comfort, American-style pillows (and extra blankets) may be in the closet or available on request. For a pillow, ask for *"Un oreiller, s'il vous plaît"* (uhn oar-ray-yay, see voo play).

Some hoteliers will ask you to sign their *Livre d'Or* (literally, "Golden Book," for client comments). They take this seriously and enjoy reading your remarks.

France is littered with sterile, ultramodern hotels, usually located on cheap land just outside of town, providing drivers with low-stress accommodations. The antiseptically clean and cheap Formule 1 and ETAP chains (about €30–40/room for up to 3 people), the more attractive Ibis hotels (€50–70 for a double), and the cushier Mercure and Novotels hotels (€70–110 for a double) are all run by the same company, Accor. While far from quaint, these can be a good value; check their Web site at www.accorhotels.com. A smaller, up-and-coming chain, Kyriad, has its act together, offering good prices and quality (toll-free in France tel. 08 25 00 30 03, from overseas tel. 01 64 62 46 46, www.kyriad.com; these telephone numbers also work for 8 other affiliated chains, including Clarine, Climat de France, and Campanile).

Making Reservations

It's possible to travel at any time of year without reservations, but given the high stakes and the quality of the places I've found for this book, I'd recommend making reservations. You can call long in advance from home, or, for more flexibility, book rooms a few days to a week in advance as you travel. (If you have difficulty, ask the fluent receptionist at your current hotel to call for you.) If you like spontaneity (or if you're traveling off-season), you might make a habit of calling between 9:00 and 10:00 on the day you plan to arrive, when the hotel clerk knows who'll be checking out and just which rooms will be available. We've taken great pains to list telephone numbers with long-distance instructions (see "Telephones," page 30; also see the appendix). Use a public phone, the convenient prepaid telephone cards, or your mobile phone. Most hotels listed here are accustomed to English-only speakers. A hotel receptionist will trust you and hold a room until 16:00 without a deposit, though some will ask for a credit-card number.

If you know where you want to stay each day (and you don't need or want flexibility), reserve your rooms a month or two in advance from home. This is particularly smart for Paris and during holiday periods (see "Holidays," page 13). To reserve from home, e-mail, fax, or call the hotel. E-mail is preferred. To fax, use the handy form in the appendix (or find it online at www.ricksteves .com/reservation). If you don't get an answer to your faxed or emailed request within a week, consider that a "no." (Many little places get many emails and faxes after they're full, and they can't afford to respond.)

A two-night stay in August would be "2 nights, 16/8/05 to 18/8/05." (Europeans write the date in this order—day/month/year—and hotel jargon uses your day of departure.)

If you receive a response from the hotel stating its rates and room availability, it's not a confirmation. You must confirm that you indeed want a room at the given rate. One night's deposit is generally required. A credit-card number is often accepted as a deposit (though you may need to send a signed traveler's check or, rarely, a bank draft in the local currency). To make things easier on yourself and the hotel, be sure you really intend to stay at the hotel on the dates you requested. These small, family-run businesses lose money if they turn away customers while holding a room for someone who doesn't show up. Understandably, some hotels bill no-shows for one night. *If you must cancel, give at least two days' notice.* Long-distance calls are cheap and easy from public phone booths; don't let these people down.

Reconfirm your reservations a few days in advance for safety. Don't needlessly confirm rooms through the tourist office; they'll take a commission.

Bed-and-Breakfasts (Chambres d'Hôte)

B&Bs offer double the cultural intimacy for a good deal less than most hotel rooms. This book and local tourist offices list B&Bs. *Chambres d'hôte* (abbreviated CH in this book) are found mostly in smaller towns and rural areas. They are listed by the owner's family name. While some post small *Chambres* or *Chambres d'hôte* signs in their front windows, many are found only through the local tourist office. We list reliable CHs that offer a good value and/or unique experience (such as CHs in renovated mills, châteaux, and wine *domaines*). Most have private bathrooms in all rooms, but don't change sheets on a daily basis or have reception areas or lounges to stretch out in. Doubles with breakfast generally cost €35–50, fancier ones €60–70 (breakfast may or may not be included—ask). While your hosts may not speak English, they will almost always be enthusiastic and pleasant.

Hostels (Auberges de Jeunesse)

Hostels charge about €14 per bed. Get a hostel card before you go (contact Hostelling International, 202/783-6161, www.hiayh.org). Travelers of any age are welcome if they don't mind dorm-style accommodations (usually in rooms of 4 to 8 beds) or meeting other travelers. Travelers without a hostel card can generally spend the night for a small extra "one-night membership" fee. Cheap meals are sometimes available, and kitchen facilities are usually provided for do-it-yourselfers. Expect youth groups in spring, crowds in the summer, snoring, and incredible variability in quality from one hostel to the next. Family rooms are sometimes available on request, but it's basically boys' dorms and girls' dorms. You usually can't check in before 17:00 and must be out by 10:00. There is often a 23:00 curfew. Official hostels are marked with a triangular sign that shows a house and a tree. Some hostels only accept reservations by e-mail (www.hihostels.com).

Gîtes and Apartments

Throughout France, you can find reasonably priced rental homes. A good idea when you're exploring an area with plenty of sights within easy driving distance, it can make a lot of sense to spend your vacation at one home base.

Gîtes (zheet) are country homes (usually urbanites' second homes) that the government rents out to visitors who want a week in the countryside. The original objective of the *gîte* program was to save characteristic rural homes from abandonment and to make it easy and affordable for families to reacquaint themselves with the

Sleep Code

To help you sort easily through these listings, I've divided the rooms into three categories based on the price for a standard double room with bath:

$$$ **Higher Priced**
$$ **Moderately Priced**
$ **Lower Priced**

To give maximum information in a minimum of space, I use the following code to describe the accommodations. Prices listed are per room, not per person. Unless otherwise noted, breakfast is included (but usually optional). English is generally spoken.

S = Single room (or price for one person in a double).
D = Double or Twin. French double beds can be very small.
T = Triple (generally a double bed with a single).
Q = Quad (usually two double beds).
b = Private bathroom with toilet and shower or tub.
s = Private shower or tub only (the toilet is down the hall).
no CC = Doesn't accept credit cards; pay in local cash.
SE = Speaks English. This code is used only when it seems predictable that you'll encounter English-speaking staff.
NSE = Does not speak English. Used only when it's unlikely you'll encounter English-speaking staff.
* = French hotel rating system, ranging from zero to four stars.

According to this code, a couple staying at a "Db-€90, SE" hotel would pay a total of 90 euros (about $110) for a double room with a private bathroom. The staff speaks English. The hotel accepts credit cards or cash in payment; you can assume a hotel takes credit cards unless you see "no CC" in the listing.

French countryside. The government offers subsidies to renovate such homes, then coordinates rentals to make it financially feasible for the owner. Today, France has more than 8,000 *gîtes*. One of your authors restored a farmhouse a few hours north of Provence, and even though he and his wife are 100 percent American, they received the same assistance French owners do.

Gîtes are best for drivers (usually rural, with little public-transport access) and ideal for families and small groups (since they can sleep many for the same price). Homes range in comfort from simple cottages and farmhouses to restored châteaux. Most have at least two bedrooms, a kitchen, a living room, a bathroom or two, and no sheets or linens (though you can usually rent them for extra). Like hotels, all *gîtes* are rated for comfort from one to four (using ears of corn—*épis*—rather than stars). Two or three *épis* are generally sufficient quality, but I'd lean towards three for more comfort. Prices generally range €300–1,200 per week, depending on house size and amenities, such as pools. For more information on *gîtes*, visit www.gites-de-france.fr/eng or www.gite.com. Our readers also report finding long lists of non-*gîte* homes for rent through TIs and on the Internet, though these are usually more expensive than staying in a *gîte*.

While less common than *gîtes*, **apartments** can be rented in cities and towns along the Riviera (one-week minimum). Tourist offices have lists.

Camping

In Europe, camping is more of a social than an environmental experience. It's a great way for American travelers to make European friends. Camping costs about €14 per campsite per night, and almost every destination recommended in this book has a campground within a reasonable walk or bus ride from the town center and train station. A tent and sleeping bag are all you need. Many campgrounds have small grocery stores and washing machines, and some even come with discos and miniature golf. Hot showers are better at campgrounds than at many hotels. Local TIs have camping information. You'll find more detailed information in the annually updated *Michelin Camping/Caravanning Guide*, available in the United States and at most French bookstores.

EATING

The French eat long and well. Relaxed lunches, three-hour dinners, and endless hours sitting in outdoor cafés are the norm. The French have a legislated 35-hour workweek and a self-imposed 36-hour eatweek. Here, chefs are as famous as great athletes. Local cafés, cuisine, and wines should become a highlight of any French adventure—sightseeing for your palate. Even if the rest of you is sleeping in cheap hotels, let your taste buds travel first class in France. (They can go coach in England.) You can eat well without going broke—but choose carefully: You're just as likely to blow a small fortune on a mediocre meal as you are to dine wonderfully for €20. Carefully read the information below, consider my restaurant suggestions in this book, and you'll do fine.

Breakfast

Petit déjeuner (puh-tee day-zhu-nay) is typically *café au lait*, hot chocolate, or tea; a roll with butter and marmalade; and a croissant, though more hotels are starting to provide breakfast buffets with fruit, cereal, yogurt, and cheese (usually for a few extra euros and well worth it). While breakfasts are available at your hotel (about €6–15), they're cheaper at corner cafés (but don't come with coffee refills; see "Café Culture," below). It's okay to buy a croissant or roll at a bakery and eat it with your cup of coffee at a café. Better still, some bakeries offer worthwhile breakfast deals with juice, croissant, and coffee or tea for about €4 (look for the bakery chain La Brioche Dorée). If you crave eggs for breakfast, drop into a café and order *une omelette* or *œufs sur le plat* (fried eggs). You could also buy (or bring from home) plastic bowls and spoons, buy a box of cereal and a small box of milk, and eat in your room before heading out for coffee.

Picnics

For many lunches—*déjeuner* (day-zhuh-nay)—we picnic or munch a take-away sandwich from a *boulangerie* (bakery) or a crêpe from a *crêperie*.

Picnics can be first-class affairs and adventures in high cuisine. Be daring. Try the smelly cheeses, ugly pâtés, sissy quiches, and baby yogurts. Local shopkeepers are accustomed to selling small quantities of produce. Try the tasty salads-to-go and ask for a plastic fork (*une fourchette en plastique;* oon foor-sheht en plah-steek). A small container is *une barquette* (oon bar-keht).

Gather supplies early; you'll want to visit several small stores to assemble a complete meal, and many close at noon. Look for a *boulangerie*, a *crémerie* or *fromagerie* (cheeses), a *charcuterie* (deli items, meats, and pâtés), an *épicerie* or *magasin d'alimentation* (small grocery with veggies, drinks, and so on), and a *pâtisserie* (delicious pastries). Open-air markets *(marchés)* are fun and photogenic and close at about 13:00 (many are listed in this book, see page 43; local TIs have complete lists). Local *supermarchés* offer less color and cost, more efficiency, and adequate quality. On the outskirts of cities, you'll find the monster *hypermarchés*. Drop in for a glimpse of hyper-France in action.

In stores, unrefrigerated soft drinks, bottled water, and beer are one-third the price of cold drinks. Milk, bottled water, and boxed fruit juice are the cheapest drinks. Avoid buying drinks to go at streetside stands; you'll find them far cheaper in a shop. Try to keep a water bottle with you. Water quenches your thirst better and cheaper than anything you'll find in a store or café. We drink tap water throughout France, filling our bottles in hotel rooms as we go.

Sandwiches, Quiche, and Pizza

Throughout France, you'll find bakeries and small stands selling baguette sandwiches, quiche, and pizza-like items to go for €3–5. Usually filling and tasty, they also streamline the picnic process. (If

Tipping

Tipping *(donner un pourboire)* in France isn't as automatic and generous as it is in the United States, but for special service, tips are appreciated, if not expected. As in the United States, the proper amount depends on your resources, tipping philosophy, and the circumstance, but some general guidelines apply.

Restaurants: Almost all restaurants include tax and a 15 percent service charge *(service compris)* in their prices, but it's polite to round up for a drink or meal well-served. This bonus tip is usually about 5 percent of the bill (for example, if your bill is €19, leave €20). For exceptional service, tip up to 10 percent. In the rare case where service is not included (the menu would state *service non compris* or *s.n.c.*), a 15 percent tip is appropriate. When you hand your payment plus a tip to your waiter, you can say, *"C'est bon"* (say bohn), meaning, "It's good." It's best to tip in cash even if you pay with your credit card. Otherwise, the tip may never reach your server. If you order your food at a counter, don't tip.

Taxis: To tip the cabbie, round up. For a typical ride, round up to the next euro on the fare (to pay a €13 fare, give €14); for a long ride, round up to the nearest €5 (for a €51 fare, give €55). If the cabbie hauls your bags and zips you to the airport to help you catch your flight, you might want to toss in a little more—but not more than €5. But if you feel like you're being driven in circles or otherwise ripped off, skip the tip.

Special services: Tour guides at public sites and tour bus drivers often hold out their hands for tips after the tour; since we've already paid for the tour, we don't tip extra—but some tourists do give a euro or two, particularly for a job well done. If the tour was free, then we tip the guide €1 to €2 per person in our group or family. We don't tip at hotels, but if you do, give the porter a euro for carrying bags and leave a couple of euros in your room at the end of your stay for the maid if the room was kept clean. In general, if someone in the service industry does a super job for you, a tip of a couple euros is appropriate...but not required.

When in doubt, ask: If you're not sure whether (or how much) to tip for a service, ask your hotelier or the tourist information office; they'll fill you in on how it's done on their turf.

you don't want your sandwich drenched in mayonnaise, ask for it *sans mayonnaise;* sahn my-oh-nehz). Here are some sandwiches you'll see:

- *Jambon beurre* (zhahn-bohn bur): Ham and butter (boring).
- *Fromage beurre* (froh-mahzh bur): Cheese and butter (also dull).
- *Poulet crudités* (poo-lay krew-dee-tay): Chicken with tomatoes, lettuce, carrots, and cucumbers.
- *Thon crudités* (tohn krew-dee-tay): Tuna with veggies.
- *Jambon crudités* (zhahn-bohn krew-dee-tay): Ham with veggies.

Café Culture

French cafés (or *brasseries*) provide light meals and a refuge from museum and church overload. They are carefully positioned places from which to watch the river of local life flow by. Feel free to order only a bowl of soup or a salad at a café.

Cafés generally open by 7:00, but closing varies wildly. Food is served throughout the day—so, if you want a late lunch or an early dinner, find a café instead of a restaurant (which opens only for regular lunch and dinner hours).

It's easier for the novice to sit and feel comfortable when you know the system. Check the price list first. Prices, which must be posted prominently, can vary a great deal between cafés. Cafés charge different prices for the same drink, depending on where you want to be seated. Prices are posted: *comptoir* (counter/bar) or the more expensive *salle* (seated). Don't pay for your drink at the bar if you want to sit at a table (as you might do at home).

Your waiter probably won't overwhelm you with friendliness. Notice how hard they work. They almost never stop. Cozying up to clients (French or foreign) is probably the last thing on their minds. To get a waiter's attention, say, "*S'il vous plaît.*"

The **standard menu items** (generally served day and night) are the *croque monsieur* (grilled ham and cheese sandwich) and *croque madame* (*monsieur* with a fried egg on top). The *salade composée* (sah-lahd cohm-poh-zay) is a hearty chef's salad. To get salad dressing on the side, order *la sauce à part* (lah sohs ah par). Sandwiches are least expensive but plain—and much better—at the *boulangerie* (bakery). To get more than a piece of ham *(jambon)* on a baguette, order a sandwich *jambon crudité*, which means garnished with veggies. Omelettes come lonely on a plate with a basket of bread. The **daily special**—*plat du jour* (plah dew zhoor)—is your fast, hearty hot plate for €10–14. Regardless of what you order, bread is free; to get more, just hold up your bread basket and ask, "*Encore, s'il vous plaît.*"

For tips on beverages, see below.

Beverages at Cafés and Restaurants

House **wine** at the bar is generally cheap and good (about €3 per glass, especially in Provence). At a restaurant, a bottle or carafe of house wine—invariably good enough for Rick Steves, if not always Steve Smith—costs €6–11. To get inexpensive wine, order regional table wine (*un vin du pays;* uhn van duh pay) in a pitcher (*un pichet;* uhn pee-shay), rather than a bottle (though finer restaurants usually offer only bottles of wine). If all you want is a glass of wine, ask for *un verre de vin rouge* for red wine or *blanc* for white wine (uhn vehr duh van roozh/blahn). A half carafe of wine is *un demi-pichet* (uhn duh-mee pee-shay); a quarter carafe (ideal for one) is *un quart* (uhn kar).

The local **beer**, which costs about €3 at a restaurant, is cheaper on tap (*une pression;* oon pres-yohn) than in the bottle (*bouteille;* boo-teh-ee). France's best beer is Alsatian; try Kronenbourg or the heavier Pelfort. *Une panaché* (oon pah-nah-shay) is a refreshing French shandy (beer and 7-Up).

Try some regional specialty **drinks**. For a refreshing before-dinner drink, order a *kir* (keer): a thumb's level of *crème de cassis* (black currant liqueur) topped with white wine. If you like brandy, try a *marc* (regional brandy, e.g., *marc de Bourgogne)* or an Armagnac, cognac's cheaper twin brother. *Pastis,* the standard southern France aperitif, is a sweet anise (licorice) drink that comes on the rocks with a glass of water. Cut it to taste with lots of water.

The French are willing to pay for **bottled water** with their meal (*eau minérale;* oh mee-nay-rahl) because they prefer the taste over tap water. If you prefer a free pitcher of tap water, ask for *une carafe d'eau* (oon kah-rahf doh). Otherwise, you may unwittingly buy bottled water.

Soft drinks cost about €3 in restaurants. Kids love the local lemonade (*citron pressé;* see-trohn preh-say) and the flavored syrups mixed with bottled water (*sirops à l'eau;* see-roh ah loh), try *un diablo menthe* (7-Up with mint syrup; uh dee-ah-bloh mahnt). The ice cubes melted after the last Yankee tour group left.

If you order **coffee or tea,** here's the lingo:

Coffee

- *Un express* (uh nex-prehs): A shot of espresso.
- *Une noisette* (oon nwah-zeht): An espresso with a shot of milk.
- *Un café au lait* (uh kah-fay oh lay): Coffee with lots of milk, also called *un grand crème* (large size; uhn grahn krehm) or *un petit crème* (average size; uh puh-tee krehm) in big cities.
- *Un grand café noir* (uh grahn kah-fay nwahr): A cup of black coffee, closest to American style.
- *Un décaffiné* (uh day-kah-fee-nay): A decaf coffee; can modify any of the above drinks.

By law, the waiter must give you a glass of tap water with your coffee if you request it; ask for *un verre d'eau, s'il vous plaît* (uh vehr doh, see voo play).

Tea

- *Un thé nature* (uh tay nah-toor): A cup of plain tea.
- *Un thé au lait* (uh tay oh lay): Tea with milk.
- *Un thé citron* (uh tay see-trohn): Tea with lemon.
- *Un infusion* (uh an-few-see-yohn): Herbal tea. Provence is known for its herbal and fruit teas. Look for *tilleul* (linden), *verveine* (verbena), or interesting blends such as *poire-vanille* (pear-vanilla).

Restaurants

Choose restaurants filled with locals, not places with signs boasting, "We Speak English." Consider our suggestions and your hotelier's

Market Day *(Jour du Marché)*

Try to buy at least one of your picnics at an open-air market. Market days are a big deal throughout France. They have been a central feature of life in rural areas since the Middle Ages. No single event better symbolizes the French preoccupation with fresh products and their strong ties to the small farmer than the weekly market. It's said that locals mark their calendars with the arrival of fresh produce. Notice the signs as you enter towns indicating the *jours du marché* (essential information to any civilized soul, and a reminder to non-locals not to park on the streets the night before).

Most *marchés* take place once a week in the town's main square and, if large enough, spill into nearby streets. Markets combine fresh produce; tastings of wine and other locally produced beverages (such as brandies and ciders); and a smattering of nonperishable items, such as knives, berets, kitchen goods, and cheap clothing. The bigger the market, the greater the overall selection—particularly for nonperishable goods. Bigger towns (such as Beaune and Arles) may have two weekly markets, one for produce and another for nonperishable goods. In other towns, the second weekly market may simply be a smaller version of the main market day. Biggest market days are usually on weekends, so that everyone can go.

Providing far more than fresh produce, market day is a weekly chance to resume friendships and get current on gossip. Here, locals can catch up on Henri's barn renovation, see photos of Jacqueline's new grandchild, and relax over *un café* with an old friend. Dogs are tethered to café tables while friends exchange kisses. Tether yourself to a café table, and observe: three cheek-kisses for good friends (left-right-left), a fourth for friends you haven't seen in a while. You should never be in a hurry on market day. Allow the crowd to set your pace. Watch the interaction between vendor and client, then think of your home supermarket routine.

All perishable items are sold directly from the producers— no middlemen, no Visa cards, just really fresh produce. Most vendors follow a weekly circuit of markets they feel work best for them, and most show up every market day, year in and year out. Notice how much fun they have chatting up their customers and each other. Many speak enough English to allow you to learn about their product. Space rental is cheap (about €5–10, depending on the size). Markets end by 13:00—in time for lunch, allowing the town to reclaim its streets and squares.

opinion, but trust your instinct. If the menu *(la carte)* isn't posted outside, move along. Refer to our restaurant recommendations to get a sense of what a reasonable meal should cost.

French restaurants open for dinner at 19:00 and are typically most crowded about 20:30 (the early bird gets the table). Last seating is usually about 21:00 or 22:00 in cities (even later in Paris), and earlier in small villages during the off-season. When lunch is served at restaurants, it generally begins at 11:30 and goes until 14:00, with last orders taken around 13:30.

La carte is the menu; if you ask for *le menu*, you'll get a fixed-price meal. This fixed-price *menu* gives you a choice of soup, appetizer, or salad *(entrée);* a choice of three or four main courses (called *plat principal*) with vegetables; plus a cheese course and/or a choice of desserts. (The same *menu* can cost €6 or so more at dinner.) Cheaper versions of *menus* are sometimes called *formules*, allowing a choice of two courses *(entrée* and *plat*, or *plat* and *dessert)*, but these are less common and usually available at lunch only. Most restaurants offer a reasonable *menu-enfant* (kids' menu). Service is included, but wine or drinks are generally extra. Wines are often listed in a separate *carte des vins.*

To order à la carte, ask the waiter for help in deciphering *la carte.* Go with the waiter's recommendations and anything *de la maison* (of the house), unless it's an organ meat *(tripes, rognons,* or *andouillette).* Galloping gourmets should bring a menu translator; the *Marling Menu-Master* is excellent. The *entrée* is the first course, and *le plat principal* is the main course. The *plat du jour* (€9–14 plate of the day) is served all day at bistros and cafés, but usually only at lunch (when available) at restaurants. Because small-sized dinner salads are usually not available on *la carte,* we often split a big salad (of which several are usually available) and each get a *plat principal.* At finer restaurants, it's not considered appropriate for two diners to share one main course; if all you want for dinner is a salad, find a café instead of a restaurant.

At the end of your meal, your server is likely to ask, *"Ca y était?"* (sah ee ay-tay, "Was it good?"), then, *"Desirez-vous autre choses?"* (day-zee-ray voo oh-truh shohz, "Would you like anything else?")

Restaurants are almost always a better value in the countryside than in Paris. If you're driving, look for red-and-blue Relais Routier decals on main roads outside cities, indicating that the place is recommended by the truckers' union. These truck stop cafés offer inexpensive and hearty fare.

French Cuisine

The following listing of items found commonly throughout France should help you navigate a typical French menu. For dishes specific to each region, see the "Cuisine Scene" section in the introduction for that region.

First Course *(Entrée)*

Salades: With the exception of a *salade mixte* (simple green salad, often difficult to find), the French get creative with their *salades.* They're typically large—one is perfect for lunch or a light dinner, or split between two people as a first course. Among the classics are *salade niçoise* (nee-swaz), a specialty from Nice that typically includes green salad topped with green beans, boiled potatoes (sometimes rice), tomatoes (sometimes corn), anchovies, olives, hard-boiled eggs, and lots of tuna; *salade au chèvre chaud,* a mixed green salad topped with warm goat cheese and toasted bread croutons; and *salade composée,* "composed" of any number of ingredients, such as *lardons* (bacon), *comte* (a Swiss-style cheese), *roquefort* (blue cheese), *œuf* (egg), *noix* (walnuts), *jambon* (ham, generally thinly sliced), *saumon fumé* (smoked salmon), and the highly suspect *gesiers* (chicken livers).

Crudités: Made of raw and lightly cooked fresh vegetables, this mix usually includes grated carrots, celery root, tomatoes, and beets, often with a hefty dose of vinaigrette dressing. If you want the dressing on the side, say, *"La sauce à part, s'il vous plaît"* (lah sohs ah par, see voo play).

Escargots: The snails of this famous French dish are usually cooked in parsley-garlic butter. You don't even have to like the snail itself. Just dipping your bread in garlic butter is more than satisfying. Prepared a variety of ways, the classic is *à la bourguignonne* (served in their shells).

Huitres: Oysters, served raw any month, are particularly popular at Christmas and New Year's, when every café seems to have overflowing baskets lining the storefront.

Pâtés and ***Terrines:*** Slowly cooked, ground meat (usually pork, though chicken and rabbit are also common) is highly seasoned and served in slices with mustard and *cornichons* (little pickles). Pâtés are smoother than the similarly prepared but chunkier *terrines.*

Foie gras: Rich, buttery in consistency, and pricey, foie gras is made from the swollen livers of force-fed geese *(foie d'oie)* or ducks *(foie de canard).* Spread it on toast with your knife, and never add mustard. For a real French experience, try this dish with a some sweet white wine (often offered by the glass for an additional cost).

Main Course *(Plat Principal)*

Duck, lamb, and rabbit are popular in France, and each is prepared in a variety of ways. You'll also encounter various stew-like dishes that vary by region. The most common regional specialties are available almost everywhere and are described below.

Coq au vin: Native to Burgundy, this dish consists of chicken marinated ever so slowly in red wine, then cooked until it melts in your mouth. It's served (often family-style) with vegetables.

French Wine-Tasting 101

France is peppered with opportunities to taste wines. Look for vineyards posted with *Dégustation Gratuite* signs, which mean you're welcome to stop in for a free tasting. Some towns have *cave coopératives*, providing an excellent opportunity to taste wines from a number of local vintners in a single less intimidating setting.

The American wine-tasting experience (we're thinking Napa Valley) is generally informal, chatty, and entrepreneurial (baseball caps and golf shirts festooned with logos). Throughout France, wine-tasting is a more serious, wine-focused experience.

Vintners are happy to work with you—if they can figure out what you want. When you enter a winery, it helps to know what you like (drier or sweeter, lighter or full-bodied, fruity or more tannic, and so on). The people serving you may know those words in English, but you're better off knowing and using the key words in French (see next page).

For reds, you'll be asked if you want to taste a younger wine (that still needs maturing), or older wines, ready to drink now. (Whites and rosés are always ready to drink.) The French like to sample younger wines and determine how they will taste in a few years, which allows them to buy at cheaper prices and stash the bottles in their cellars. Americans want it now—for today's picnic. While many Americans like a big, full-bodied wine, the French tend to prefer more subtle flavors. They judge a wine by virtue of what food it would go well with—and a big, oaky wine would overwhelm most French cuisine (yes, even cheese courses).

Remember that the vintner is hoping that you'll buy at least a bottle or two. If you don't buy, you may be asked to pay a minimal fee for the tasting. They all know that Americans can't export much wine, and don't expect to make a big sale—but they do hope you'll look for their wines in the United States.

Bœuf Bourguignon: Another Burgundian specialty, the classy beef stew is cooked slowly in red wine, with onions, potatoes, and mushrooms.

Gigot d'agneau: A specialty of Provence, a leg of lamb often grilled and served with white beans.

Confit de canard: A Southwest favorite (think Dordogne region) is duck that has been preserved and cooked, and is often served, in the same fat with potatoes (which have also been cooked in the fat). Not for dieters.

Steak: Referred to as *pavé, bavette,* or *entrecôte,* French steak is usually thinner than American steak and is always served with sauces (*au poivre* is a pepper sauce, *une sauce roquefort* is a blue-cheese sauce).

By American standards, the French undercook meats: rare, or *saignant* (seh-nyahn), is close to raw; medium, or *à point* (ah pwahn),

French Wine Lingo

Here are the steps you should follow when entering any wine-tasting:

1. Greetings, Sir/Madam: *Bonjour, Monsieur/Madame.*

2. We would like to taste a few wines.
    Nous voudrions déguster quelques vins.
    (noo voo-dree-ohn day-goo-stay kehl-kuh van)

3. We want a wine that is ___ and ___.
    Nous voudrions un vin ___ et ____.
    (noo voo-dree-ohn uhn van ___ ay ___)

Fill in the blanks with your favorites from this list:

English	French	Pronounciation
wine	*vin*	van
red	*rouge*	roozh
white	*blanc*	blahn
rosé	*rosé*	roh-zay
light	*léger*	lay-zhay
full-bodied, heavy	*robuste*	roh-boost
fruity	*fruité*	frwee-tay
sweet	*doux*	doo
tannic	*tannique*	tah-neek
fine	*fin, avec finesse*	fahn, ah-vehk fee-nehs
ready to drink (mature)	*prêt à boire*	preh ah bwar
not ready to drink	*fermé*	fair-may
oaky	*goût de la chêne*	goo duh lah sheh-nuh
from old vines	*de vieille vignes*	duh vee-yay-ee veen-yah
sparkling	*pétillant*	pay-tee-yahn

is rare; and well-done, or *bien cuit* (bee-yehn kwee), is medium.

Steak tartare: This wonderfully French dish is for adventurous types only. It's very lean, raw hamburger served with spices (usually Tabasco, onions, salt, and pepper on the side) and topped with a raw egg.

Saumon and **truite:** You'll see salmon dishes served in various styles. Like steak, salmon always comes with sauce, most commonly a sorrel *(oiseau)* sauce. Trout *(truite)* is also fairly routine on menus.

Daube: Generally made with beef but sometimes lamb, this is a long and slowly simmered dish, typically paired with noodles or other pasta.

Cheese Course *(Le Fromage)*

In France, the cheese course is served just before (or instead of) dessert. This not only helps with digestion, but also gives you a great opportunity to sample the tasty regional cheeses—there are more than 400 to choose from. Most restaurants will offer a platter from which you select a few different cheeses (3 is average). If you'd like a little of each, say, *"Un peu de chaque, s'il vous plaît"* (uh puh duh shahk, see voo play). If you serve yourself from the cheese plate, observe French etiquette and keep the shape of the cheese, carefully shaving off a slice from the side or cutting a small wedge.

A typical plate contains a mixture of cheeses varying in strength and age (older cheeses can smell quite toxic, but they're milder in taste, and covered with edible mold). Cheeses are made from the milk of three animals: cow *(vache)*, goat *(chevre)*, and sheep *(brebi)*. Look for Brie (mild and creamy, from just outside Paris), Camembert, (semi-creamy and pungent, from Normandy), different *bleu* cheeses, such as Roquefort (strong and deeply blue-veined, from south-central France), and artery-clogging triple creams such as *boursault* and *explorateur*. Harder cheeses might include a *comté* (nutty and rich, from the Alps region) or *tomme* (produced in most regions, but *tomme de Savoie* is perhaps the most widely available). For a truly stinky experience, try *Munster* or *Livarot*. When it comes to goat cheese *(chèvre)*, ask for *frais* if you want it fresh and soft, *demi-sec* for medium hardness, and *sec* for dry and crumbly. The cheese plate is always served with bread.

Dessert *(Le Dessert)*

Here are typical desserts you'll find on many menus:

Crème brûlée: A rich, creamy, dense, and caramelized custard.

Tarte tatin: This is apple pie like grandma never made, with caramelized apples cooked upside down, but served upright.

Mousse au chocolat: Chocolate mousse.

Ile flottante: This lighter dessert consists of islands of meringue floating on a pond of custard sauce.

Profiteroles: Cream puffs filled with vanilla ice cream, smothered in warm chocolate sauce.

Tartes: Narrow strips of fresh fruit, baked in a crust and served in thin slices (without ice cream).

Sorbets: Known to us as sherbets, these light, flavorful, and fruity ices are sometimes laced with brandy. *Citron* (lemon) and *citron-vert* (lime) are particularly popular and refreshing.

Glaces: Ice cream, typically vanilla, chocolate, or strawberry *(fraise)*.

Traveling with Kids

France is young-kid-friendly, partly because so much of it is rural. (Our teenagers, on the other hand, tend to prefer cities.) Our kids' favorite places have been Mont St. Michel, the Alps, the Loire châteaux, Carcassonne, and Paris (especially the Eiffel Tower and Seine River boat ride)—and any hotel with a pool. To make your trip fun for everyone in the family, mix heavy-duty sights with kids' activities (playing miniature golf, renting bikes, and riding the little tourist trains popular in many towns). While Disneyland Paris is the predictable draw, our kids had more fun for half the expense simply by enjoying the rides in the Tuileries Garden in downtown Paris. If you're in France near Bastille Day, remember that firecracker stands pop up everywhere on the days leading up to July 14. Putting on their own fireworks show can be a highlight for teenagers.

Minimize hotel changes by planning three-day stops. Aim for hotels with restaurants, so the kids can go back to the room and play while you finish a pleasant dinner. We've listed public pools in many places (especially the south), but be warned: Public pools in France commonly require a small, Speedo-like bathing suit for boys and men (American-style swim trunks won't do)—though they usually have these little suits to loan.

For breakfast, croissants are a hit. For lunch and dinner, we developed a knack for finding *crêperies* with plenty of kid-friendly stuffings for both savory and dessert crêpes. It's easy to find fast-food places and restaurants with kids' menus, but for food emergencies, we travel with a plastic container of peanut butter brought from home and smuggle small jars of jam from breakfast.

Swap baby-sitting duties with your partner if one of you wants to take in an extra sight. Kids homesick for friends can keep in easy touch with cheap international phone cards (a dollar buys 10 minutes of time for catching up) and through Internet cafés.

For memories that will last long after the trip, keep a family journal. Pack a small diary and a glue stick. While relaxing at a café over a *citron pressé* (lemonade), take turns writing down the day's events, and include mementos such as ticket stubs from museums, postcards, or stalks of lavender.

Coffee (Café)

If you order espresso at a restaurant, it will always come after dessert. To have coffee with dessert, ask for *"café avec le dessert"* (kah-fay ah-vehk luh day-sayr). For more on tea and coffee, see page 42.

TRAVELING AS A TEMPORARY LOCAL

We travel all the way to Europe to enjoy differences—to become temporary locals. You'll experience frustrations. Certain truths that we find "God-given" or "self-evident," like friendly waiters, ice in drinks, bottomless cups of coffee, hot showers, and bigger being better, are suddenly not so true. One of the benefits of travel is the eye-opening realization that there are logical, civil, and even better alternatives.

France is an understandably proud country. To enjoy its people, you need to celebrate the differences. A willingness to go local ensures that you'll enjoy a full dose of French hospitality.

While updating our guidebooks, we hear over and over again that our readers are considerate and fun to have as guests. Thank you for traveling as temporary locals who are sensitive to the culture. It's fun to follow you in our travels.

Send Us a Postcard, Drop Us a Line

If you enjoy a successful trip with the help of this book and would like to share your discoveries, please fill out the survey at www .ricksteves.com/feedback or contact us at rick@ricksteves.com. We personally read and value all feedback.

For our latest travel information on France, visit www .ricksteves.com. To check on any updates for this book, visit www.ricksteves.com/update. Anyone is welcome to sign up for our monthly e-mail newsletters.

Judging from all the happy postcards we receive from travelers who have used this book, it's safe to assume you'll enjoy a great, affordable vacation—with the finesse of an independent, experienced traveler.

From this point, "we" (your co-authors) will drop our respective egos and become "I."

Thanks, and *bon voyage!*

BACK DOOR TRAVEL PHILOSOPHY
From *Rick Steves' Europe Through the Back Door*

Travel is intensified living—maximum thrills per minute and one of the last great sources of legal adventure. Travel is freedom. It's recess, and we need it.

Experiencing the real Europe requires catching it by surprise, going casual..."Through the Back Door."

Affording travel is a matter of priorities. (Make do with the old car.) You can travel—simply, safely, and comfortably—anywhere in Europe for $100 a day (less in the countryside) plus transportation costs. In many ways, spending more money only builds a thicker wall between you and what you came to see. Europe is a cultural carnival, and, time after time, you'll find that its best acts are free and the best seats are the cheap ones.

A tight budget forces you to travel close to the ground, meeting and communicating with the people, not relying on service with a purchased smile. Never sacrifice sleep, nutrition, safety, or cleanliness in the name of budget. Simply enjoy the local-style alternatives to expensive hotels and restaurants.

Extroverts have more fun. If your trip is low on magic moments, kick yourself and make things happen. If you don't enjoy a place, maybe you don't know enough about it. Seek the truth. Recognize tourist traps. Give a culture the benefit of your open mind. See things as different, but not better or worse. Any culture has much to share.

Of course, travel, like the world, is a series of hills and valleys. Be fanatically positive and militantly optimistic. If something's not to your liking, change your liking. Travel is addictive. It can make you a happier American, as well as a citizen of the world. Our Earth is home to six billion equally important people. It's humbling to travel and find that people don't envy Americans. They like us, but, with all due respect, they wouldn't trade passports.

Globe-trotting destroys ethnocentricity. It helps you understand and appreciate different cultures. Travel changes people. It broadens perspectives and teaches new ways to measure quality of life. Many travelers toss aside their hometown blinders. Their prized souvenirs are the strands of different cultures they decide to knit into their own character. The world is a cultural yarn shop. And Back Door travelers are weaving the ultimate tapestry.

Come on, join in!

PARIS

The City of Light has been a beacon of culture for centuries. As a world capital of art, fashion, food, literature, and ideas, it stands as a symbol of all the fine things that human civilization can offer.

Paris offers sweeping boulevards, chatty crêpe stands, chic boutiques, and world-class art galleries. Sip decaf with deconstructionists in a sidewalk café, then step into an Impressionist painting in a tree-lined park. Climb Notre-Dame and rub shoulders with the gargoyles. Cruise the Seine, zip up the Eiffel Tower, and saunter down the avenue des Champs-Elysées. Master the Louvre and Orsay museums. Save some after-dark energy for one of the world's most romantic cities.

Some see the essentials and flee, overwhelmed. But with the proper approach and a good orientation, you'll fall head over heels for Europe's capital.

Planning Your Time:
Paris in One, Two, or Three Days

Day 1

Morning: Follow my self-guided "Historic Core of Paris Walk" (see page 68), featuring Ile de la Cité, Notre-Dame, the Latin Quarter, and Sainte-Chapelle.

Afternoon: Visit the Pompidou Center (at least from the outside), then walk to the Marais neighborhood, visit place des Vosges, and consider touring any of three museums nearby: Carnavalet Museum (city history), Jewish Art and History Museum, or Picasso Museum.

Evening: Cruise the Seine River or take the "Paris Illumination" nighttime bus tour.

Day 2

Morning: Visit Arc de Triomphe, then take my self-guided "Champs-Elysées Walk" (page 101).

Afternoon: Have lunch in the Tuileries (several lunch cafés in the park), then tour the Louvre.

Evening: Enjoy the Trocadéro scene and a twilight ride up the Eiffel Tower.

Day 3

Morning: Tour the Orsay Museum.

Afternoon: Either tour the nearby Rodin Museum and Napoleon's Tomb or visit Versailles (take RER-C train direct from Orsay).

Evening: Visit Montmartre and the Sacré-Cœur basilica.

ORIENTATION

Paris (city center pop. 2,150,000) is split in half by the Seine River, divided into 20 *arrondissements* (proud and independent governmental jurisdictions), circled by a ring-road freeway (the *périphérique*), and speckled with Métro stations. You'll find Paris easier to navigate if you know which side of the river you're on, which *arrondissement* you're in, and which subway (Métro) stop you're closest to. If you're north of the river (the top half of any city map), you're on the Right Bank *(rive droite)*. If you're south of it, you're on the Left Bank *(rive gauche)*. The bull's-eye of your Paris map is Notre-Dame, which sits on an island in the middle of the Seine. Most of your sightseeing will take place within five blocks of the river.

Arrondissements are

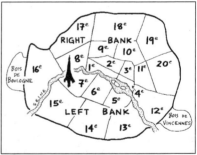

Paris Arrondissements

numbered, starting at the Louvre and moving in a clockwise spiral out to the ring road. The last two digits in a Parisian zip code are the *arrondissement* number. The abbreviation for the Métro stop is "Mo." In Parisian jargon, Napoleon's tomb is on *la rive gauche* (the Left Bank) in the *7ème* (7th *arrondissement*), zip code 75007, Mo: Invalides. Paris Métro stops are used as a standard aid in giving directions, even for those not using the Métro. As you're tracking down addresses, these words and pronunciations will help: *place* (plahs; square), *rue* (roo; road), *avenue* (ah-vuh-noo), *boulevard* (boo-luh-var), *pont* (pohn; bridge), and Métro (may-troh).

Daily Reminder

Monday: These sights are closed today—Orsay, Rodin, Marmottan, Montmartre Museum, Carnavalet, Catacombs, Giverny, and Versailles; the Louvre and Eiffel Tower are more crowded because of this. Napoleon's Tomb is closed the first Monday of each month (except July–Sept). Some small stores don't open until 14:00. Street markets such as rue Cler and rue Mouffetard are dead today. Some banks are closed. It's discount night at most cinemas.

Tuesday: Many museums are closed today, including the Louvre, Picasso, Cluny, and Pompidou Center, as well as the châteaux of Chantilly (except July–Aug) and Fontainebleau. The Eiffel Tower, Orsay, Versailles, and Giverny are particularly busy today.

Wednesday: All sights are open (Louvre until 21:45). The weekly *Pariscope* magazine comes out today. Most schools are closed, so many kids' sights are busy. Some cinemas offer discounts.

Thursday: All sights are open except the Sewer Tour. The Orsay is open until 21:45. Department stores are open late.

Friday: All sights are open except the Sewer Tour (Louvre until 21:45). Afternoon trains and roads leaving Paris are crowded; TGV train reservation fees are higher.

Saturday: All sights are open (except the Jewish Art and History Museum). The fountains run at Versailles (July–Sept), and Vaux-le-Vicomte hosts candlelight visits (May–Oct); otherwise, avoid weekend crowds at area châteaux and Impressionist sights. Department stores are jammed. The Jewish Quarter is quiet.

Sunday: Some museums are free the first Sunday of the month—and therefore more crowded (e.g., Louvre, Rodin, Pompidou, Cluny, and Picasso). Several museums offer reduced prices every Sunday (Orsay plus Cluny and Rodin—other than first Sun, when they're free). Napoleon's Tomb is open until 19:00 in summer, and the fountains run at Versailles (early April–early Oct). Most of Paris' stores are closed on Sunday, but shoppers will find relief in the Marais neighborhood's lively Jewish Quarter and in Bercy Village, where many stores are open. Look for organ concerts at St. Sulpice and possibly other churches. The American Church often hosts a free evening concert at 18:00 (Sept–May only). Many recommended restaurants in the rue Cler neighborhood are closed for dinner.

Tourist Information

Avoid the Paris TIs because of their long lines, short information, and charge for maps. This chapter, the *Pariscope* magazine (described below), and one of the freebie maps available at any hotel (or in the front of this book) are all you need. Paris' TIs share a single phone number: 08 92 68 30 00 (from the United States, dial 011 33 8 92 68 30 00).

If you must visit a TI, there are several locations: **Grands Magasins** (Mon–Sat 9:00–18:30, closed Sun, near Opéra Garnier at 11 rue Scribe), **Gare de Lyon** (Mon–Sat 8:00–20:00, closed Sun), **Montmartre** (daily 10:00–19:00, place du Tertre), at the **Eiffel Tower** (May–Sept daily 11:00–18:42, closed Oct–April), and at the **Louvre** (Wed–Mon 10:00–19:00, closed Tue). Both **airports** have handy information offices (called ADP) with long hours and short lines (see "Transportation Connections," page 162).

For a complete schedule of museum hours and English-language museum tours, pick up the free *Musées, Monuments Historiques, et Expositions* booklet from any museum.

Web sites: Paris' TIs have an official Web site (www.paris -touristoffice.com) offering practical information on hotels, special events, museums, children's activities, fashion, nightlife, and more. Two other Web sites that are entertaining and at times useful are www.bonjourparis.com (which claims to offer a virtual trip to Paris, featuring interactive French lessons, tips on wine and food, and news on the latest Parisian trends) and the similar www.paris-anglo.com (with informative stories on visiting Paris, plus a directory of over 2,500 English-speaking businesses).

Pariscope: The *Pariscope* weekly magazine (or one of its clones, €0.40 at any newsstand) lists museum hours, art exhibits, concerts, festivals, plays, movies, and nightclubs. Smart tour guides and sight-seers rely on this for the latest listings.

Maps: While Paris is littered with free maps, they don't show all the streets. You may want the huge Michelin #10 map of Paris. For an extended stay, I prefer the pocket-size, street-indexed *Paris Pratique* or Michelin's *Paris par Arrondissement* (both about €6, sold at newsstands and bookstores in Paris). Before you buy a map, look at it to make sure it has the level of detail you want.

Bookstores: There are many English-language bookstores in Paris where you can pick up guidebooks (for nearly double their American prices). Most carry this book. My favorite is the friendly Red Wheelbarrow Bookstore in the Marais neighborhood, run by charming Penelope and Abigail (main store at 22 rue St. Paul, Mon–Sat 10:00–19:00, Sun 14:00–19:00; children's bookstore nearby at 13 rue Charles V, Wed–Sun 10:00–19:00, closed Mon–Tue; Mo: St. Paul for both, tel. 01 42 77 42 17). Others include Shakespeare and Company (daily 12:00–24:00, some used

Paris Overview

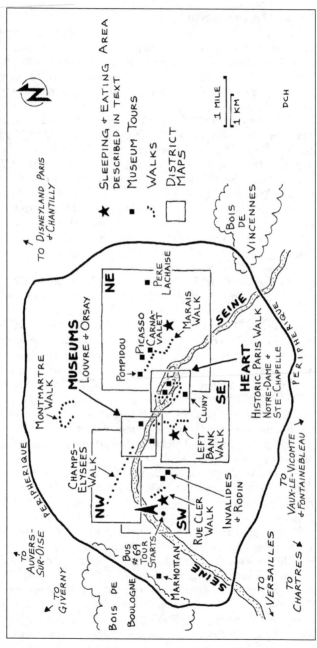

travel books, 37 rue de la Bûcherie, across the river from Notre-Dame, Mo: St. Michel, tel. 01 43 26 96 50), W.H. Smith (Mon–Sat 10:00–19:00, 248 rue de Rivoli, Mo: Concorde, tel. 01 44 77 88 99), and Brentanos (closed Sun, 37 avenue de l'Opéra, Mo: Opéra, tel. 01 42 61 52 50).

American Church: The American Church is a nerve center for the American émigré community. It distributes a free, handy, and insightful monthly English-language newspaper called the *Paris Voice*, which has useful reviews of concerts, plays, and current events; find it at about 200 locations in Paris (www.parisvoice.com). Also available is an advertisement paper called *France–U.S.A. Contacts* (www.fusac.fr), full of useful information for those seeking work or long-term housing. The church faces the river between the Eiffel Tower and Orsay Museum (reception open Mon–Sat 9:30–22:30, Sun 9:00–19:30, 65 quai d'Orsay, Mo: Invalides, tel. 01 40 62 05 00).

Arrival in Paris

By Train: Paris has six train stations, all connected by Métro, bus, and taxi (see map on page 164). All have ATMs, banks or change offices, information desks, telephones, cafés, newsstands, and clever pickpockets. Most have lockers *(consigne automatique)*, listed per station; see page 165. Hop the Métro to your hotel (see "Getting Around Paris," below).

By Plane: For detailed information on getting from Paris' airports to downtown Paris (and vice versa), see "Transportation Connections" on page 162.

Helpful Hints

Heightened Security *(Plan Vigipirate)*: You may notice an abundance of police at monuments, on streets, and on the Métro, as well as security checks to enter many public buildings. This is part of Paris' anti-terror plan. The police are helpful, the security lines move quickly, and there are fewer pickpocket problems on the Métro.

Theft Alert: Métro and RER lines that serve high-profile tourist sights are popular with thieves. Wear a money belt, put your wallet in your front pocket, loop your day bag over your shoulders (consider wearing it in front), and keep a tight grip on your purse or shopping bag. Muggings are rare but do occur. If you're out late, avoid the dark riverfront embankments and any place where the lighting is dim and pedestrian activity is minimal.

Paris Museum Pass: This worthwhile pass, covering most sights in Paris, is available at major Métro stations, TIs, and museums. For information, see page 76.

Museum Strategy: When possible, visit key museums first thing (when your energy is best) and save other activities for the afternoon. Arriving 20 minutes before major museums open is line-time well spent. Remember, most museums require you to check daypacks and coats, and important museums have metal detectors that will slow your entry. If you're still ahead of the pack when you get inside, consider hustling to the most popular works first. The Louvre, Orsay, and Pompidou are open on selected nights (see "Paris at a Glance," page 64), making for peaceful visits with fewer crowds.

Useful Telephone Numbers: American Hospital—01 46 41 25 25; English-speaking pharmacy—01 45 62 02 41 (Pharmacie les Champs, 24 hrs, 84 avenue des Champs-Elysées, Mo: Georges V); Police—17; U.S. Embassy—01 43 12 22 22; Paris and France directory assistance—12 (see appendix for additional numbers).

Street Safety: Parisian drivers are notorious for ignoring pedestrians. Look both ways (many streets are one-way) and be careful of seemingly quiet bus/taxi lanes. Don't assume you have the right of way, even in a crosswalk. When crossing a street, keep your pace constant and don't stop suddenly. By law, drivers must miss pedestrians by one meter—a little more than a yard (1.5 meters in the countryside). Drivers carefully calculate your speed and won't hit you, provided you don't alter your route or pace.

Watch out for a lesser hazard: *merde.* Parisian dogs decorate the city's sidewalks with 16 tons of droppings per day. People get injured by slipping in it.

Toilets: Carry small change for pay toilets, or walk into any sidewalk café like you own the place and find the toilet in the back. The restrooms in museums are free and the best you'll find, and if you have a Museum Pass, you can drop into almost any museum for the toilets. Modern, sanitary, street-booth toilets provide both relief and a memory (coins required, don't leave small children inside unattended). Keep toilet paper or tissues with you, as some toilets are poorly supplied.

Parking: Drivers pay to park curbside (except Sunday year-round, or any day in Aug). There are good parking garages under Ecole Militaire, St. Sulpice Church, Les Invalides, the Bastille, and the Panthéon for about €20–25 per day. Some hotels offer parking for less—ask.

Getting Around Paris

By Métro: In Paris, you're never more than a 10-minute walk from a Métro station. Europe's best subway allows you to hop from sight to sight quickly and cheaply (runs daily 5:30–24:30). Learn to use it.

Pickpockets and Panhandlers: Thieves spend their days in the Métro. Be on guard. For example, if your pocket is picked as you pass through a turnstile, you end up stuck on the wrong side while the thief strolls away. Stand away from Métro doors to avoid being a

Paris

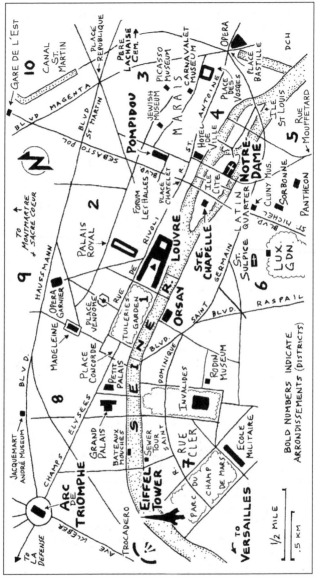

target for a theft-and-run just before the doors close. Any jostling or commotion, especially when boarding or leaving trains, is likely the sign of a thief or a team of thieves in action. Make any fare inspector show proof of identity (ask locals for help if you're not certain).

Paris has a huge homeless population and higher than 11 percent unemployment; expect a warm Métro welcome from panhandlers, musicians, and those selling magazines produced by the homeless community.

Tickets and Passes: One ticket (€1.40) takes you anywhere in the system, with unlimited transfers. Tickets are also good on the RER suburban trains (see below) and on city buses, although one ticket cannot be used to transfer between subway and bus. Save 30 percent by buying a ***carnet*** (car-nay) of 10 tickets for €10.50 (a single ticket is €1.40, kids 4–10 pay €5 for a *carnet*). Buy tickets at any Métro station from a human or a machine (some machines also accept credit cards).

If you're staying in Paris for a week or more, consider the **Carte Orange** (kart oh-rahnzh) for about €15, which gives you free run of the bus and Métro system for one week, starting Monday and ending Sunday; ask for the Carte Orange *hebdomadaire* and supply a passport-size photo. The month-long version costs about €50; request a Carte Orange *mensuel* (good from the first day of the month to the last). These passes cover only central Paris. You can pay more for passes covering regional destinations (like Versailles), but for most visitors, this is a bad value (buy individual tickets for longer-distance destinations). All passes can be purchased at any Métro station, most of which have photo booths where you can get the photo required for the pass. Despite what some Métro agents say, Carte Orange passes are definitely not limited to residents; if you're refused, simply go to another station to buy your pass.

The overpriced **Paris Visite** passes were designed for tourists and offer minor reductions at minor sights (1 day-€9, 2 days-€14, 3 days-€19, 5 days-€28), but you'll get a better value with a cheaper *carnet* of 10 tickets or a Carte Orange.

How the Métro works: To get to your destination, determine the closest "Mo" stop and which line or lines will get you there. The lines have numbers, but they're best known by their end-of-the-line stops. (For example, the La Défense/Château de Vincennes line, also known as line 1, runs between La Défense in the west and Vincennes in the east.) Once in the Métro station, you'll see blue-and-white signs directing you to the train going in your direction (e.g., "*direction:* La Défense"). Insert your ticket in the automatic turnstile, pass through, reclaim your ticket, and *keep it until you exit the system.* Fare inspectors regularly check for cheaters and accept absolutely no excuses.

Transfers are free and can be made wherever lines cross. When

you transfer, look for the *corre-spondance* (connections) signs when you exit your first train, then follow the proper direction sign.

While the Métro whisks you quickly from one point to another, be prepared to walk significant distances within stations to reach your platform (most noticeable when you transfer). Escalators are usually available for vertical movement, but they're not always in working order. To limit excessive walking, avoid transferring at these sprawling stations: Montparnasse-Bienvenüe, Chatelet-Les Halles, Charles de Gaulle-Etoile, Gare du Nord, and Bastille.

Before taking the *sortie* (exit) to leave the Métro, check the helpful *plan du quartier* (map of the neighborhood) to get your bearings, locate your destination, and decide which *sortie* you want. At stops with several *sorties*, you can save lots of walking by choosing the best exit.

After you exit the system, toss or tear your used ticket so you don't confuse it with your unused ticket—they look virtually identical.

By RER: The RER (Réseau Express Régionale; air-ay-air) is the suburban arm of the Métro, serving destinations further out of the center (such as Versailles, Disneyland Paris, and the airports). These routes are indicated by thick lines on your subway map and identified by letters A, B, C, and so on. Some suburban routes are operated by France's railroad (SNCF), and are called **Transilien**; they function the same way and use the same tickets as the RER. On Transilien trains (but not RER trains), railpasses are accepted (show your pass at a ticket window to get a free ticket to get through the turnstiles).

Within the city center, the RER works like the Métro but can be speedier (if it serves your destination directly) because it makes fewer stops. Métro tickets are good on the RER when traveling in the city center. (You can transfer between the Métro and RER systems with the same ticket.) But to travel outside the city (to Versailles or the airport, for example), you'll need to buy a separate, more expensive ticket at the station window before boarding. Unlike in the Métro, you need to insert your ticket in a turnstile to exit the RER lines. Also unlike the Métro, not every train stops at every station along the way; check the sign over the platform to see if your destination is listed as a stop (*toutes les gares* means it makes all stops along the way), or confirm with a local before you board.

By City Bus: The trickier bus system is worth figuring out. Métro tickets are good on buses and the Métro, though you can't

Key Words for the Métro and RER

- *direction* (dee-rek-see-ohn): direction
- *ligne* (leen-yuh): line
- *correspondance* (kor-res-pohn-dahns): transfer
- *sortie* (sor-tee): exit
- *carnet* (kar-nay): cheap set of 10 tickets
- *Pardon, madame/monsieur* (par-dohn, mah-dahm/mes-yur): Excuse me, lady/bud.
- *Je descend* (juh day-sahn): I'm getting off.
- *Donnez-moi mon porte-monnaie!* (duh-nay-mwah mohn port-moh-nay): Give me back my wallet!

Etiquette
- When waiting at the platform, get out of the way of those exiting their train. Board only once everyone is off.
- Avoid using the hinged seats near the doors when the car is jammed; they take up valuable standing space.
- In a crowded train, try not to block the exit. If you're blocking the door when the train stops, step out of the car and to the side, let others off, then get back on.
- Talk softly in the cars. Listen to how quietly Parisians can communicate and follow their lead.
- On escalators, stand on the right, pass on the left.

use the same ticket to transfer between the two systems. One ticket gets you anywhere in central Paris, but if you leave the city center (shown as zone 1 on the diagram onboard the bus), you must validate a second ticket. While the Métro shuts down about 24:30, some buses continue much later.

Enter buses through the front door. Punch your Métro ticket in the machine behind the driver, or pay the higher cash fare. Get off buses using the rear door. Even if you're not certain you've figured it out, do some joyriding (outside of rush hour: Mon–Fri 8:00–9:30 & 17:30–19:30). Lines #24, #63, #87, and #69 are a few of Paris' most scenic routes, and make a great introduction to the city. Buses #69 and #87 are particularly handy. The #69 runs east–west between the Eiffel Tower and Père Lachaise Cemetery by way of rue Cler (recommended hotels), quai d'Orsay, the Louvre, and the Marais (more recommended hotels). Bus #87 also links the Marais and rue Cler areas, as well as the Luxembourg Garden neighborhood (with more recommended hotels). The #87 stays mostly on the Left Bank, connecting the Eiffel Tower, St. Sulpice, Luxembourg Garden, St. Germain-des-Prés, the Latin Quarter, and the Bastille.

Schedules are posted at bus stops. Handy bus-system maps *(plan des autobus)* are available in any Métro station (and in the €6

Paris Pratique map book—see "Tourist Information," above). Big system maps, posted at each bus and Métro stop, display the routes. Individual route diagrams show the exact routes of the lines serving that stop. Major stops are displayed on the side of each bus. The handiest bus routes are listed for each recommended hotel neighborhood (see "Sleeping," page 123).

By Taxi: Parisian taxis are reasonable—especially for couples and families. The meters are tamper-proof. Fares and supplements (described in English on the back windows) are straightforward. There's a €5.20 minimum. A 10-minute ride (e.g., Bastille to Eiffel Tower) costs about €10 (versus about €1 to get anywhere in town using a *carnet* ticket on the Métro). You can try waving down a taxi, but it's easier to ask for the nearest taxi stand (*"Où est une station de taxi?"*; oo ay oon stah-see-ohn duh taxi). Taxi stands are indicated by a circled T on many city maps, including Michelin's #10 Paris. A typical taxi takes three people (maybe 4, if you're polite and pay about €3 extra); groups of up to five can use a *grand taxi,* which must be booked in advance—ask your hotel to call. If a taxi is summoned by phone, the meter starts as soon as the call is received, adding €3–4 to the bill. Higher rates are charged at night from 19:00 to 7:00, all day Sunday, and to either airport. There's a €1 charge for each piece of baggage and for train station pick-ups. To tip, round up to the next euro (minimum €0.50). Taxis are tough to find on Friday and Saturday nights, especially after the Métro closes (around 24:30). If you need to catch a train or flight early in the morning, book a taxi the day before.

TOURS

Bus Tours—Paris Vision offers bus tours of Paris, day and night (advertised in hotel lobbies); their "Paris Illumination" night tour is much more interesting (see "Nightlife," page 122).

Far better daytime bus tours are the hop-on, hop-off double-decker buses that connect Paris' main sights while providing running commentary. You can hop off at any stop, tour a sight, then catch a later bus. These are ideal in good weather, when you can sit on top. (See also "Batobus" under "Boat Tours," below.)

Two companies provide hop-on, hop-off bus service: **L'Open Tours** and **Les Cars Rouges;** pick up their brochures showing routes and stops from any TI or on their buses. You can start either tour at nearly any of the major sights, such as the Eiffel Tower (both companies stop on avenue Joseph Bouvard).

L'Open Tours uses yellow buses and provides more extensive coverage on four different routes, rolling by most of the important sights in Paris. Their Paris Grand Tour offers the best introduction. Tickets are good for any route. Buy your tickets from the driver

Paris at a Glance

▲▲▲**Louvre** Europe's oldest and greatest museum, starring Mona Lisa and Venus di Milo. **Hours:** Wed–Mon 9:00–18:00, closed Tue. Most wings open Wed and Fri until 21:45.

▲▲▲**Orsay Museum** 19th-century art, including Europe's greatest Impressionist collection. **Hours:** June 20–Sept 20 Tue–Sun 9:00–18:00; Sept 21–June 19 Tue–Sat 10:00–18:00, Sun 9:00–18:00; Thu until 21:45 year-round, closed Mon.

▲▲▲**Eiffel Tower** Paris' soaring exclamation point. **Hours:** Daily March–Sept 9:00–24:00, Oct–Feb 9:30–23:00.

▲▲▲**Arc de Triomphe** Triumphal arch with viewpoint, marking start of Champs-Elysées. **Hours:** Outside always open; inside open daily April–Sept 10:00–23:00, Oct–March 10:00–22:30.

▲▲▲**Sainte-Chapelle** Gothic cathedral with peerless stained glass. **Hours:** Daily March–Oct 9:30–18:00, Nov–Feb 9:00–17:00.

▲▲▲**Versailles** The ultimate royal palace, with Hall of Mirrors, vast gardens, a grand canal, and smaller palaces. **Hours:** May–Sept Tue–Sun 9:00–18:30, Oct–April Tue–Sun 9:00–17:30, closed Mon. Gardens open early (7:00) and smaller palaces open late (12:00).

▲▲**Notre-Dame Cathedral** Paris' most beloved church, with towers and gargoyles. **Hours:** Church daily 8:00–18:45; tower daily April–Sept 9:30–19:30, Oct–March 10:00–17:30; treasury daily 9:30–17:30.

▲▲**Sacré-Cœur** White basilica atop Montmartre with spectacular views. **Hours:** Daily 7:00–23:00.

▲▲**Napoleon's Tomb** The emperor's imposing tomb, flanked by army museums. **Hours:** April–Sept daily 10:00–18:00, summer Sun until 19:00, Oct–March daily 10:00–17:00, closed first Mon of month except July–Sept.

▲▲**Rodin Museum** Works by the greatest sculptor since Michelangelo. **Hours:** April–Sept Tue–Sun 9:30–17:45; Oct–March Tue–Sun 9:30–16:45, closed Mon.

▲▲**Marmottan Museum** Untouristy art museum focusing on Monet. **Hours:** Tue–Sun 10:00–18:00, closed Mon.

▲▲**Pompidou Center** Modern art in colorful building with city views. **Hours:** Wed–Mon 11:00–21:00, closed Tue.

▲▲**Jacquemart-André Museum** Art-strewn mansion. **Hours:** Daily 10:00–18:00.

▲▲**Cluny Museum** Medieval art with unicorn tapestries. **Hours:** Wed–Mon 9:15–17:45, closed Tue.

▲▲**Carnavalet Museum** Paris' history wrapped up in a 16th-century mansion. **Hours:** Tue–Sun 10:00–18:00, closed Mon.

▲▲**Jewish Art and History Museum** Displays history of Judaism in Europe. **Hours:** Mon–Fri 11:00–18:00, Sun 10:00–18:00, closed Sat.

▲▲**Deportation Memorial** Monument to Holocaust victims, near Notre-Dame. **Hours:** Daily April–Sept 10:00–12:00 & 14:00–19:00, Oct–March 10:00–12:00 & 14:00–17:00.

▲▲**Champs-Elysées** Paris' grand boulevard. **Hours:** Always open.

▲▲**Picasso Museum** World's largest collection of Picasso's works. **Hours:** April–Sept Wed–Mon 9:30–18:00; Oct–March Wed–Mon 9:30–17:30, closed Tue.

▲**Opéra Garnier** 19th-century opera house open for tours. **Hours:** Daily 10:00–17:00 except during performances.

▲**La Défense and La Grande Arche** Paris' modern arch on outskirts of city. **Hours:** Elevator daily 10:00–19:00.

▲**Catacombs** Underground tunnels lined with bones. **Hours:** Tue–Sun 10:00–17:00, closed Mon.

▲**Paris Sewer Tour** The lowdown on Paris plumbing. **Hours:** May–Sept Sat–Wed 11:00–17:00, Oct–April Sat–Wed 11:00–16:00, closed Thu–Fri.

(1-day ticket-€25, 2-day ticket-€28, kids 4–11 pay €13 for 1 or 2 days, allow 2 hours per tour). Two or three buses depart hourly from about 10:00 to 18:00; expect to wait 10–20 minutes at each stop (stops can be tricky to find—look for yellow signs). You'll see these bright-yellow, topless, double-decker buses all over town (tel. 01 42 66 56 56, www.paris-opentour.com).

Les Cars Rouges' bright red buses offer largely the same service with fewer stops on a single Grand Tour Route, for a bit less money (2-day ticket: adult-€23, kids 4–12 pay €12; tel. 01 53 95 39 53, www.carsrouges.com).

Boat Tours—Several companies offer one-hour boat cruises on the Seine (by far best at night). The huge, mass-production **Bateaux-Mouches** or **Bateaux Parisien** boats are convenient to rue Cler hotels (depart every 20–30 min from the pont de l'Alma's right bank, or from just in front of the Eiffel Tower, respectively; €7, kids 4–12 pay €4, daily 10:00–22:30, useless recorded explanations in 6 languages and tour groups by the dozens, tel. 01 40 76 99 99). The smaller and more intimate **Vedettes du Pont-Neuf** depart only once an hour from the center of Pont-Neuf (2/hr after dark), but they come with a live guide giving explanations in French and English and are convenient to Marais and Luxembourg area hotels (€10, kids 4–12 pay €5, tel. 01 46 33 98 38).

From April through October, the **Batobus** hop-on, hop-off boats on the Seine connect eight popular stops every 15–25 minutes: Eiffel Tower, Champs-Elysées, Orsay/place de la Concorde, Louvre, Notre-Dame, St. Germain-des-Prés, Hôtel de Ville, and Jardin des Plantes. Pick up a schedule at any stop (or TI) and use the boats as a scenic alternative to the Métro (€7.50 for a one-way trip of up to 4 stops, €11 for unlimited use for 1 day, €13 for 2 days, under 12 about 50 percent less, www.batobus.com). Boats run from 10:00 to 19:00 (and until 21:00 June–Sept).

Canauxrama runs a 2.5-hour cruise on a peaceful canal without the Seine in sight, starting from place de la Bastille and ending at Bassin de la Villette (near Mo: Stalingrad). The first segment of your trip is through a tunnel, as the canal runs under boulevard Richard Lenoir for about 20 blocks (€14, kids-€9, seniors and students-€11, departs at 9:45 and 14:30 across from Opéra Bastille, just below boulevard de la Bastille, opposite #50, where the canal meets place de la Bastille, tel. 01 42 39 15 00).

Walking Tours—The company **Paris Walks** offers a variety of excellent two-hour walks, led by British or American guides, nearly daily for €10 (Peter and Oriel Caine, tel. 01 48 09 21 40 for recorded schedule in English, fax 01 42 43 75 51, see www.paris-walks.com for their complete schedule and private tour options, paris@paris-walks.com). Tours focus on the Marais, Montmartre, Ile de la Cité and Ile St. Louis, and Hemingway's Paris. Ask about their family-friendly tours. Call a day or two ahead to learn their schedule and starting point. No reservations are required. These are thoughtfully prepared, relaxing, and humorous. Don't hesitate to stand close to the guide to hear.

Private Guides—For many, Paris merits hiring a Parisian as your personal guide. **Arnaud Servignat**, who runs Global Travel Partners, is an excellent licensed local guide (€215/half-day, €335/day; also does car tours of the countryside around Paris for €300/half-day, €505/day; tel. 06 68 80 29 05, fax 01 42 57 00 38, arnaud.servignat@noos.fr). Elizabeth Van Hest is another likeable and capable guide (€170/half-day, €250/day, tel. 01 43 41 47 31, e.van.hest@noos.fr). Paris Walks can also set you up with one of their guides; some are trained to work with families and children (see "Walking Tours," above).

Bike Tours—**Fat Tire Bike Tours** attract a younger crowd for fun and frolicking three- to four-hour guided rides through Paris. These are well done and surprisingly informative, whether by day (€24, March–Nov daily at 11:00, also at 15:00 June–July) or by night (€28, April–Oct daily at 19:00, cash only, in English, no bikes or reservations needed, meet at south pillar of Eiffel Tower, tel. 01 56 58 10 54, www.fattirebiketours.com). They also offer bike tours of Giverny (€65) and of Versailles (€50, mid-April–mid-Oct, depart at 9:30, mid-May–July Tue–Sun, otherwise Sun, Tue, and Thu, meet at office near Eiffel Tower, 24 rue Edgar Faure, Mo: Dupleix). Fat Tire's pricey new **Segway Tours** are making a splash with an older clientele (€70, April–Oct daily at 10:30 and 18:00, www.parissegwaytours.com).

Excursion Tours—Many companies offer minivan and big bus tours to regional sights, including all of the day trips described in this book. **Paris Walks** (mentioned above) is the best, with educational though infrequent tours of the Impressionist artist retreats of Giverny and Auvers-sur-Oise (€47–56, includes admissions, tel. 01 48 09 21 40 for recording in English, www.paris-walks.com).

Paris Vision and **Touringscope** both offer mass-produced, full-size bus and minivan tours to several popular regional destinations, including the Loire Valley, Champagne region, D-Day beaches, and Mont St. Michel. Minivan tours are more expensive but more personal, given in English, and offer convenient pick-up at your hotel (€130–200/person). Their full-size bus tours are multilingual and cost about half the price of a minivan tour—worth it for some simply for the ease of transportation to the sights (about €60, destinations include Versailles, Chartres, and Giverny). Paris Vision's full-size buses depart from 214 rue de Rivoli (Mo: Tuileries, tel. 01 42 60 30 01, fax 01 42 86 95 36, www.parisvision.com); Touringscope's leave from 11 boulevard Haussmann (Mo: Opéra or Chausée d'Antin, tel. 01 53 34 11 94, www.touringscope.com).

Historic Core of Paris Walk

(This information is distilled from the Historic Paris Walk chapter in *Rick Steves' Paris*, by Gene Openshaw, Steve Smith, and Rick Steves.)

Allow four hours for this self-guided tour, including sightseeing. Start where the city did—on the Ile de la Cité. Face Notre-Dame and follow the dotted line on the "Core of Paris" map (see page 69). To get to Notre-Dame, ride the Métro to Cité, Hôtel de Ville, or St. Michel and walk to the big square facing the...

▲▲Notre-Dame Cathedral—This 700-year-old cathedral is packed with history and tourists. Study its sculpture and windows, take in a Mass, eavesdrop on guides, and walk all around the outside (free, daily 8:00–18:45; treasury-€2.50, not covered by Museum Pass, daily 9:30–17:30; ask about free English tours, normally Wed and Thu at 12:00 and Sat at 14:30; Mo: Cité, Hôtel de Ville, or St. Michel). Climb to the top for a great view of the city; you get 400 steps for only €6.10 (daily April–Sept 9:30–19:30, Oct–March 10:00–18:00, last entry 45 min before closing, covered by Museum Pass though you can't bypass line, arrive early to avoid long lines). There are clean toilets in front of the church near Charlemagne's statue.

The **cathedral facade** is worth a close look. The church is dedicated to "Our Lady" (Notre-Dame). Mary is center stage—cradling Jesus, surrounded by the halo of the rose window. Adam is on the left and Eve is on the right.

Below Mary and above the arches is a row of 28 statues known as the Kings of Judah. During the French Revolution, these biblical kings were mistaken for the hated French kings. The citizens stormed the church, crying, "Off with their heads!" All were decapitated, but have since been recapitated.

Speaking of decapitation, look at the carving above the doorway on the left. The man with his head in his hands is St. Denis. Back when there was a Roman temple on this spot, Christianity began making converts. The 4th-century bishop of Roman Paris, Denis, was beheaded. But these early Christians were hard to keep down. The man who would become St. Denis got up, tucked his head under his arm, and headed north until he found just the right place to meet his maker: Montmartre. (Although the name "Montmartre" comes from the Roman "Mount of Mars," later generations—thinking of their beheaded patron St. Denis—preferred a less pagan version, "Mount of Martyrs.") The Parisians were

Core of Paris

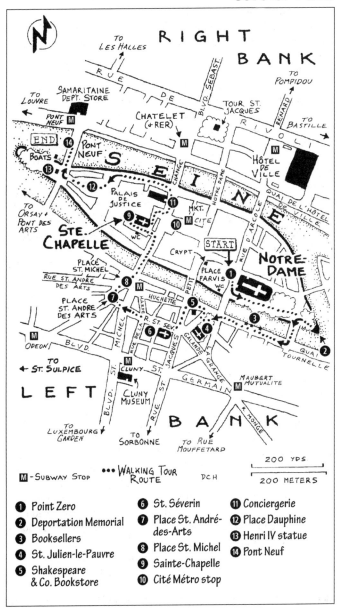

M – SUBWAY STOP   •••WALKING TOUR ROUTE   DCH

200 YDS

200 METERS

① Point Zero

② Deportation Memorial

③ Booksellers

④ St. Julien-le-Pauvre

⑤ Shakespeare & Co. Bookstore

⑥ St. Séverin

⑦ Place St. André-des-Arts

⑧ Place St. Michel

⑨ Sainte-Chapelle

⑩ Cité Métro stop

⑪ Conciergerie

⑫ Place Dauphine

⑬ Henri IV statue

⑭ Pont Neuf

convinced of this miracle, Christianity gained ground, and a church soon replaced the pagan temple.

Medieval art was OK if it embellished the house of God and told Bible stories. For a fine example, move to the base of the central column (at the foot of Mary, about where the head of St. Denis could spit if he were really good). Working around from the left, find God telling a barely created Eve, "Have fun, but no apples." Next, the sexiest serpent I've ever seen makes apples à la mode. Finally, Adam and Eve, now ashamed of their nakedness, are expelled by an angel. This is a tiny example in a church covered with meaning.

Now move to the right and study the carving above the **central portal**. It's the end of the world, and Christ sits on the throne of Judgment (just under the arches, holding his hands up). Below him an angel and a demon weigh souls in the balance. The "good" stand to the left, looking up to heaven. The "bad" ones to the right are chained up and led off to a six-hour tour of the Louvre on a hot day. The "ugly" ones must be the crazy, sculpted demons to the right, at the base of the arch.

Wander through the interior. You'll be routed around the ambulatory, much as medieval pilgrims would have been. Don't miss the rose windows filling each of the transepts. Back outside, walk around the church through the park on the riverside for a close look at the flying buttresses.

The neo-Gothic, 300-foot **spire** is a product of the 1860 reconstruction. Around its base are apostles and evangelists (the green men) as well as Eugène-Emmanuel Viollet-le-Duc, the architect in charge of the work. Notice how the apostles look outward, blessing the city, while the architect (at top, seen from behind the church) looks up, admiring his spire.

The **archaeological crypt** is a worthwhile 15-minute stop with your Museum Pass (€3.50, Tue–Sun 10:00–18:00, closed Mon, enter 100 yards in front of cathedral). You'll see Roman ruins, trace the street plan of the medieval village, and see diagrams of how the earliest Paris grew and grew, all thoughtfully explained in English.

If you're hungry near Notre-Dame, the nearby Ile St. Louis has inexpensive *crêperies* and grocery stores open daily on its main drag. Plan a picnic for the quiet, bench-filled park immediately behind the church (public WC available).

Behind Notre-Dame, squeeze through the tourist buses, cross the street, and enter the iron gate into the park at the tip of the island. Look for the stairs and head down to reach the...

▲▲**Deportation Memorial (Mémorial de la Déportation)**—This memorial to the 200,000 French victims of the Nazi concentration camps draws you into their experience. As you descend the steps, the city around you disappears. Surrounded by walls, you have become a prisoner. Your only freedom is your view of

Ile St. Louis

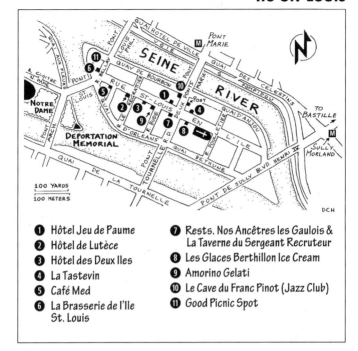

1 Hôtel Jeu de Paume

2 Hôtel de Lutèce

3 Hôtel des Deux Iles

4 La Tastevin

5 Café Med

6 La Brasserie de l'Ile St. Louis

7 Rests. Nos Ancêtres les Gaulois & La Taverne du Sergeant Recruteur

8 Les Glaces Berthillon Ice Cream

9 Amorino Gelati

10 Le Cave du Franc Pinot (Jazz Club)

11 Good Picnic Spot

the sky and the tantalizing glimpse of the river below.

Enter the single-file chamber ahead. Inside, the circular plaque in the floor reads, "They went to the end of the earth and did not return." A hallway stretches in front of you, lined with 200,000 lighted crystals, one for each French citizen that died. Flickering at the far end is the eternal flame of hope. The tomb of the unknown deportee lies at your feet. Above, the inscription reads, "Dedicated to the living memory of the 200,000 French deportees sleeping in the night and the fog, exterminated in the Nazi concentration camps."

Above the exit as you leave is the message you'll find at all Nazi sights: "Forgive, but never forget." (Free, daily April–Sept 10:00–12:00 & 14:00–19:00, Oct–March 10:00–12:00 & 14:00–17:00, east tip of the island Ile de la Cité, behind Notre-Dame and near Ile St. Louis, Mo: Cité.)

Ile St. Louis—Look across the river to the Ile St. Louis. If the Ile de la Cité is a tug laden with the history of Paris, it's towing this classy little residential dinghy laden only with boutiques, famous sorbet shops, and restaurants (see "Eating," page 158). This island wasn't developed until much later (18th century). What was a swampy mess is now harmonious Parisian architecture. The pedestrian bridge, pont St. Louis, connects the two islands, leading right to rue St. Louis-en-l'Ile. This spine of the island is lined with interesting shops. A short stroll takes you to the famous Berthillon ice-cream parlor (#31). Loop back to the pedestrian bridge along the parklike quays (walk north to the river and turn left). This walk is about as peaceful and romantic as Paris gets.

Before walking to the opposite end of the Ile de la Cité, loop through the Latin Quarter (as indicated on the map on page 69). From the Deportation Memorial, cross the bridge onto the Left Bank and enjoy the riverside view of Notre-Dame, window-shopping among the green book stalls and browsing through used books, vintage posters, and souvenirs. At the little park and church (over the bridge from the front of Notre-Dame), venture inland a few blocks, basically arcing through the Latin Quarter and returning to the island two bridges down at place St. Michel.

▲**Latin Quarter**—This neighborhood's touristic fame relates to its intriguing artsy, bohemian character. This was perhaps Europe's leading university district in the Middle Ages—home, since the 13th century, to the prestigious Sorbonne University. Back then, Latin was the language of higher education. And, since students here came from all over Europe, Latin served as their linguistic common denominator. Locals referred to the quarter by its language: Latin.

The neighborhood's main boulevards (St. Michel and St. Germain) are lined with far-out bookshops, street singers, and jazz clubs. While still youthful and artsy, the area has become a tourist ghetto filled with cheap North African eateries. The cafés that were once the haunts of great poets and philosophers are now the hangout of tired tourists. For colorful wandering or café sitting, afternoons and evenings are best (Mo: St. Michel).

Walking along rue St. Séverin, you can still see the shadow of the medieval sewer system (the street slopes into a central channel of bricks). In the days before plumbing and toilets, when people still went to the river or neighborhood wells for their water, "flushing" meant throwing it out the window. Certain times of day were flushing times. Maids on the fourth floor would holler, *"Garde de l'eau!"* ("Watch out for the water!") and heave it into the streets, where it would eventually be washed down into the Seine.

Consider a visit to the Cluny Museum for its medieval art and unicorn tapestries (see page 89).

Place St. Michel (facing the St. Michel bridge) is the traditional core of the Left Bank's artsy, liberal, hippie district of poets, philosophers, winos, and tourists. In less commercial times, place St. Michel was a gathering point for the city's malcontents and misfits. Here, in 1871, the citizens took the streets from government troops, set up barricades *Les Miz*–style, and established the Paris Commune. During World War II, the locals rose up against their Nazi oppressors (read

Sainte-Chapelle

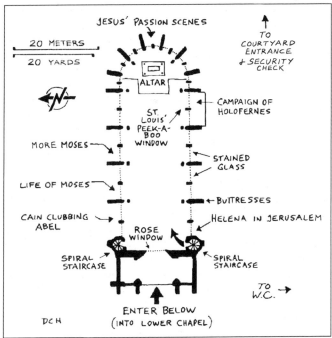

JESUS' PASSION SCENES

20 METERS

20 YARDS

TO
COURTYARD
ENTRANCE
& SECURITY
CHECK

ALTAR

N

CAMPAIGN OF
HOLOFERNES

ST.
LOUIS'
PEEK-A-
BOO
WINDOW

MORE MOSES

STAINED
GLASS

LIFE OF MOSES

BUTTRESSES

CAIN CLUBBING
ABEL

HELENA IN JERUSALEM

ROSE
WINDOW

SPIRAL
STAIRCASE

SPIRAL
STAIRCASE

TO
W.C.

DCH

ENTER BELOW
(INTO LOWER CHAPEL)

the plaques by St. Michel fountain). And in the spring of 1968, a time of social upheaval all over the world, young students—battling riot batons and tear gas—took over the square and demanded change.

From place St. Michel, look across the river and find the spire of Sainte-Chapelle church and its weathervane angel (below). Cross the river on pont St. Michel and continue along boulevard du Palais. On your left, you'll see the high-security doorway to the Sainte-Chapelle. You'll need to pass through a metal detector to get into the Sainte-Chapelle complex. Once past security, restrooms are ahead on the left. The line into the church may be long. (Museum Pass–holders can bypass this line; pick up an English info flier.) Enter the humble ground floor of...

▲▲▲**Sainte-Chapelle**—This triumph of Gothic church architecture is a cathedral of glass like no other. It was speedily built from 1242 to 1248 for Louis IX (the only French king who is now a saint) to house the supposed Crown of Thorns. Its architectural harmony is due to the fact that it was completed under the direction of one architect in only six years—unheard of in Gothic times. (Notre-Dame took more than 200 years to build.)

The design clearly shows an Old Regime approach to worship. The basement was for staff and other common folk. Royal

Christians worshipped upstairs. The ground-floor paint job, a 19th-century restoration, is a reasonably accurate copy of the original.

Climb the spiral staircase to the **Chapelle Haute**. Fill the place with choral music, crank up the sunshine, face the top of the altar, and really believe that the Crown of Thorns is there, and this becomes one awesome space.

"Let there be light." In the Bible, it's clear: Light is divine. Light shining through stained glass was a symbol of God's grace shining down to earth. Gothic architects used their new technology to turn dark stone buildings into lanterns of light. The glory of Gothic shines brighter here than in any other church.

There are 15 separate panels of stained glass (6,500 square feet—two-thirds of it 13th-century original), with more than 1,100 different scenes, mostly from the Bible.

The altar was raised up high to better display the relic—the Crown of Thorns—around which this chapel was built. The supposed crown cost King Louis three times as much as this church. Today, it is kept in the Notre-Dame treasury and shown only on Fridays during Lent.

Louis IX's little private viewing window is in the wall to the right of the altar. Louis IX, both saintly and shy, liked to go to church without dealing with the rigors of public royal life. Here, he could worship while still dressed in his jammies.

Lay your camera on the ground and shoot the ceiling. Those ribs growing out of the slender columns are the essence of Gothic.

Books in the gift shop explain the stained glass in English. (€6.10 entry fee, €9 combo-ticket covers Conciergerie, both covered by Museum Pass, daily March–Oct 9:30–18:00, Nov–Feb 9:00–17:00, Mo: Cité). There are concerts almost every summer evening (€15–23, tel. 01 44 07 12 38 for concert information).

Palais de Justice—Back outside, as you walk around the church exterior, look down and notice how much Paris has risen in the 800 years since Sainte-Chapelle was built. You're in a huge complex of buildings that has housed the local government since ancient Roman times. It was the site of the original Gothic palace of the early kings of France. The only surviving medieval parts are the Sainte-Chapelle church and the Conciergerie prison.

Most of the site is now covered by the giant Palais de Justice, home of France's supreme court (built in 1776). "*Liberté, Egalité, Fraternité,*" emblazoned over the doors, is a reminder that this was also the headquarters of the Revolutionary government.

Now pass through the big iron gate to the noisy boulevard du Palais. Cross the street to the wide pedestrian-only rue de Lutèce and walk about halfway down.

Cité "Métropolitain" Stop—Of the 141 original early-20th-century subway entrances, this is one of only a few survivors—now preserved as a national art treasure. The curvy, plantlike ironwork is a textbook example of Art Nouveau, the style that rebelled against the erector-set squareness of the Industrial Age (e.g., Mr. Eiffel's tower).

The flower and plant market on place Louis Lépine is a pleasant detour. On Sundays, this square is all aflutter with a busy bird market. And across the way is the Prefecture de Police, where Inspector Clouseau of *Pink Panther* fame used to work, and where the local resistance fighters took the first building from the Nazis in August of 1944, leading to the Allied liberation of Paris a week later.

Pause here to admire the view. Sainte-Chapelle is a pearl in an ugly architectural oyster. We'll double back to the Palais de Justice, turn right and enter the...

Conciergerie—Though barren inside, this former prison echoes with history. It's a gloomy place. Kings used it to torture and execute failed assassins. The leaders of the Revolution put it to similar good use. A tower along the river, called "the babbler," was named for the painful sounds that leaked from it.

Marie-Antoinette was imprisoned here. During a busy eight-month period in the Revolution, she was one of 2,600 prisoners kept here on the way to the guillotine. You can see Marie-Antoinette's cell, which houses a collection of her mementos. In another room, a list of those made "a foot shorter at the top" by the "national razor" includes ex-King Louis XVI, Charlotte Corday (who murdered Jean-Paul Marat in his bathtub), and the chief revolutionary who got a taste of his own medicine, Maximilien de Robespierre (€6.10, €9 combo-ticket covers Sainte-Chapelle, both covered by Museum Pass, daily April–Sept 9:30–18:30, Oct–March 10:00–17:00, good English descriptions).

Back outside, turn left on boulevard du Palais and head toward the river (north). On the corner is the city's oldest public clock. The mechanism of the present clock is from 1334, and even though the case is Baroque, it keeps on ticking.

Turn left onto quai de l'Horloge and walk west along the river, past the round medieval tower called "the babbler." The bridge up ahead is the pont Neuf, where we'll end this walk. At the first corner, veer left into a sleepy triangular square called place Dauphine. Marvel at how such quaintness could be lodged in the midst of such greatness as you walk through the park to the end of the island (the departure point for Seine river cruises offered by Vedettes du Pont-Neuf; see page 66). At the equestrian statue of Henry IV, turn right onto the bridge and take refuge in one of the nooks on the Eiffel Tower side.

Pont Neuf—This "new bridge" is now Paris' oldest. Built during Henry IV's reign (around 1600), its 12 arches span the widest part of the river. The fine view includes the park on the tip of the island

The Paris Museum Pass

In Paris, there are two classes of sightseers—those with a Paris Museum Pass, and those who stand in line. Serious sightseers save time and money by getting this pass.

Most of the sights listed in this chapter are covered by the pass (see list below), except for the Eiffel Tower, Montparnasse Tower, Marmottan Museum, Opéra Garnier, Notre-Dame treasury, Jacquemart-André Museum, Jewish Art and History Museum, Grande Arche de La Défense, Jeu de Paume and Grand Palais exhibition halls, Catacombs, *Paris Story* film, Montmartre Museum, Dalí Museum, and the ladies of Pigalle.

The pass pays for itself with three admissions and gets you into most sights with no lining up to buy tickets (1 day-€18, 3 consecutive days-€36, 5 consecutive days-€54, no youth or senior discount). It's sold at museums, main Métro stations (including Ecole Militaire and Bastille), and TIs (even at airports). Try to avoid buying the pass at a major museum (such as the Louvre), where supply can be spotty and lines long.

The pass isn't activated until the first time you use it (you write the starting date on the pass). Think and read ahead to make the most of your pass, since some museums are free (e.g., Carnavalet and Victor Hugo's House), many sights are discounted on Sundays, and your pass must be used on consecutive days. The free directory that comes with your pass lists the current hours of sights, phone numbers, and the price kids pay (where applicable—see below).

The pass isn't worth buying for children and teens, as most museums are free for those under 18 (teenagers may need to show proof of age). Of the museums that charge for children, some allow kids in free if their parent has a Museum Pass, while others charge admission, depending on age (the cutoff age varies from 5 to 18). If a sight is free for kids, they can skip the line with their passholder parents.

Included sights you're likely to visit (and admission prices without the pass): Louvre (€8.50), Orsay Museum (€7), Sainte-Chapelle (€6.10), Arc de Triomphe (€7), Les Invalides/Napoleon's

(note Seine tour boats), the Orsay Museum, and the Louvre. These turrets were originally for vendors and street entertainers. In the days of Henry IV, who originated the promise of "a chicken in every pot," this would have been a lively scene.

As for now, you can tour the Seine by boat, shop at the Samaritaine (across the bridge), continue to the Louvre, or head to the beach *(plage)*.

Paris *Plage* and In-Line Skaters—The year 2005 will be the fourth consecutive summer that Paris officials remove cars from a key section of busy Right Bank express lanes to make room for an

Tomb (€7), Conciergerie (€6.10), Panthéon (€7), Sewer Tour (€4), Cluny Museum (€5.50), Pompidou Center (€7), Notre-Dame towers (€6.10), Archaeological Crypt (€3.50), Picasso Museum (€5.50), Rodin Museum (€5), L'Orangerie Museum (when it re-opens, about €6), Maritime Museum (€7). Outside Paris, the pass covers the Palace of Versailles (€7.50, plus its Trianon châteaux-€5), Château of Fontainebleau (€5.50), and Château of Chantilly (€7).

Tally up what you want to see—and remember, an advantage of the pass is that you skip to the front of some lines, which saves hours of waiting, especially in summer. (Nevertheless, everyone must pass through the slow-moving, metal-detector lines at some sights, and a few places, such as Notre-Dame's tower, can't accommodate a bypass lane.) With the pass, you'll pop freely into sights that you're walking by (even for a few minutes) that otherwise might not be worth the expense (e.g., Archaeological Crypt, Conciergerie, and the Panthéon).

Museum Tips: The Louvre and many other museums are closed on Tuesday. The Orsay, Rodin, Marmottan, Carnavalet, Catacombs, Victor Hugo's House, Versailles, and Giverny are closed Monday. Some museums offer reduced prices on Sunday. Most sights stop admitting people 30–60 minutes before closing time, and many begin shutting down rooms 45 minutes before.

For the fewest crowds, visit very early, at lunch, or very late. Most museums have slightly shorter hours October through March. French holidays can really mess up your sightseeing plans on Jan 1, May 1, July 14, Nov 1, Nov 11, and Dec 25.

The best Impressionist art museums are the Orsay (page 83), Marmottan (page 88), and L'Orangerie (closed until late 2005 or 2006).

Many museums also host optional temporary exhibitions, which are not covered by the Paris Museum Pass (generally €3–5 extra). You can find good information on many of Paris' sights on the French TI's official Web site: www.paris.fr/EN/Visiting/musees.asp.

artificial beach (mid-July–mid-Aug). Tons of sand are poured over black asphalt, then sprinkled lightly with beach chairs and changing rooms, and *voilà!*—a summer scene that the Beach Boys would appreciate (though you can't swim in the river). The faux beach extends two miles along the Seine on voie Georges Pompidou (just north of the Ile de la Cité), from pont des Arts to pont de Sully, with three main sub-areas: one sandy, one grassy, and one with wood decking. You'll also find climbing walls, a swimming pool, trampolines, a library, beach volleyball, badminton, and Frisbee areas.

The same riverside highway also provides a long fun-filled traffic-free zone for joggers, bicyclists, and in-line skaters (mid-July–mid-Aug Sun–Fri 9:00–16:00). For even more high-rolling fun, thousands of rollerbladers take to the streets Fridays at 22:30 and summer Sunday afternoons as police close off various routes in different parts of downtown (ask at your hotel or a TI).

SIGHTS

Paris Museums near the Tuileries Garden

Paris' grandest park, the Tuileries Garden, was once the private property of kings and queens. Today it links the museums of the Louvre, L'Orangerie, Jeu de Paume, and the Orsay.

▲▲▲**Louvre**—This is Europe's oldest, biggest, greatest, and second-most-crowded museum (after the Vatican). Housed in a U-shaped, 16th-century palace (accentuated by a 20th-century glass pyramid), the Louvre is Paris' top museum and one of its key landmarks. It's home to *Mona Lisa*, *Venus de Milo*, and hall after hall of Greek and Roman masterpieces, medieval jewels, Michelangelo statues, and paintings by the greatest artists from the Renaissance to the Romantics (mid-1800s).

Touring the Louvre can be overwhelming, so be selective. Consider taking a tour (see "Tours," below), or follow my self-guided tour at the end of this listing. Focus on the **Denon Wing** (south, along the river): Greek sculptures, Italian paintings (by the likes of Raphael and da Vinci), and—of course—French paintings (neoclassical and Romantic). For extra credit, tackle the **Richelieu Wing** (north, away from the river), with works from ancient Mesopotamia (today's Iraq), as well as French, Dutch, and Northern art; or the **Sully Wing** (connecting the other two wings), with Egyptian artifacts and more French paintings.

Cost: €8.50, €6 after 16:00 on Wed and Fri, free on first Sun of month, covered by Museum Pass. Tickets good all day; reentry allowed. The new self-serve ticket machines are faster than the ticket windows (accepts euro notes, coins, and Visa cards, not MasterCard).

Hours: Wed–Mon 9:00–18:00, closed Tue. Most wings open Wed and Fri until 21:45. Galleries start closing 30 minutes early. Evening visits are peaceful and the pyramid glows after dark. Galleries start shutting down 30 minutes early. The last entry is 45 minutes before closing. Crowds are worst on Sun, Mon, Wed, and mornings.

Information: Tel. 01 40 20 53 17, recorded info tel. 01 40 20 51 51, www.louvre.fr. Pick up the free *Louvre Plan Information* in English at the information desk under the pyramid as you enter.

Crowd-Beating Tips: There is no grander entry than through the pyramid, but metal detectors (not ticket-buying lines) create a

Paris Museums near the Tuileries Garden

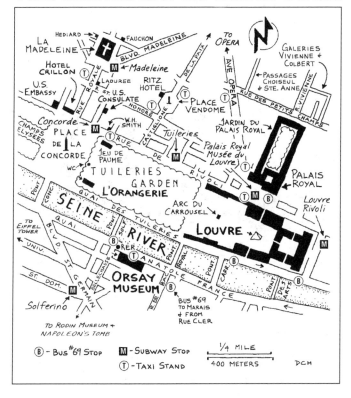

long line at times. There are several ways to avoid the line. Museum Pass–holders can use the group entrance in the pedestrian passageway between the pyramid and rue de Rivoli (under the arches, a few steps north of the pyramid, find the uniformed guard at the entrance, with the escalator down). Otherwise, you can enter the Louvre from its (usually less-crowded) underground entrance, accessed through the "Carrousel du Louvre" shopping mall. Enter the mall at 99 rue de Rivoli (the door with the red awning, daily 8:30–23:00) or directly from the Métro stop Palais Royal-Musée du Louvre (stepping off the train, exit to the left, following signs to Carrousel du Louvre-Musée du Louvre). The taxi stand is across rue de Rivoli next to the Métro station.

Tours: The 90-minute English-language tours leave three times daily except Sun (normally at 11:00, 14:00, and 15:45, €6 plus your entry ticket, tour tel. 01 40 20 52 63). Digital audioguides (available for €5 at entries to the three wings, at top of escalators) give you a directory of about 130 masterpieces, allowing you to dial a rather dull commentary on included works as you stumble upon them.

The Louvre

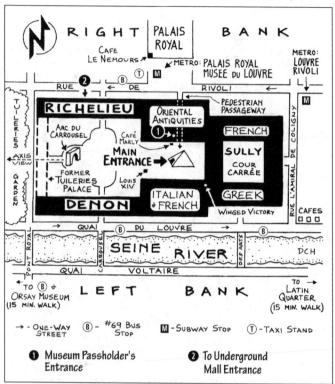

Underground Louvre: To explore the subterranean shopping mall, enter through the pyramid, walk toward the inverted pyramid, and uncover a post office, a handy TI and SNCF (train tickets) office, glittering boutiques and a dizzying assortment of good-value eateries (up the escalator), and the Palais Royal-Musée du Louvre Métro entrance. Stairs at the far end take you right into the Tuileries Garden, a perfect antidote to the stuffy, crowded rooms of the Louvre.

Self-Guided Tour: Start in the Denon wing and visit the high-lights, in the following order (thanks to Gene Openshaw for his help with this).

Wander through the **ancient Greek and Roman works** to see the Parthenon frieze, Pompeii mosaics, Etruscan sarcophagi, and Roman portrait busts. You can't miss lovely *Venus de Milo (Aphrodite)*. This goddess of love (c. 100 B.C., from the Greek island of Melos) created a sensation when she was discovered in 1820. Most "Greek" statues are actually later Roman copies, but Venus is a rare Greek original. She, like Golden Age Greeks, epitomizes stability, beauty, and balance. Later Greek art was Hellenistic, adding motion and drama. For a good example, see the exciting *Winged Victory of Samothrace* (*Victoire de Samothrace,* on the landing). This statue of a woman with wings, poised on the prow of a ship, once stood on a hilltop to commemorate a great naval victory. This is the *Venus de Milo* gone Hellenistic.

The **Italian collection** is on the other side of the Winged Victory. The key to Renaissance painting was realism, and for the Italians "realism" was spelled "3-D." Painters were inspired by the realism and balanced beauty of Greek sculpture. Painting a 3-D world on a 2-D surface is tough, and after a millennium of Dark Ages, artists were rusty. Living in a religious age, they painted mostly altarpieces full of saints, angels, Madonnas-and-bambinos, and crucifixes floating in an ethereal gold-leaf heaven. Gradually, though, they brought these otherworldly scenes down to earth. The Italian collection—including the *Mona Lisa*—is scattered through-out rooms *(salles)* 3 and 4, in the long Grand Gallery, and in adjoin-ing rooms. These paintings are likely to be moving targets in 2005, when the room they usually occupy (Salle des Etats) is renovated. *Mona Lisa* and other Italian Renaissance works described here will be close by. Just ask.

Two masters of the Italian High Renaissance (1500–1600) were Raphael (see his *La Belle Jardinière,* showing the Madonna, Child, and John the Baptist) and Leonardo da Vinci. The Louvre has the greatest collection of Leonardos in the world—five of them, includ-ing the exquisite *Virgin, Child, and St. Anne,* the neighboring *Madonna of the Rocks,* and the androgynous *John the Baptist.* His most famous, of course, is the *Mona Lisa.*

Leonardo was already an old man when François I invited him to France. Determined to pack light, he took only a few paintings. One was a portrait of Lisa del Giocondo, the wife of a wealthy Florentine merchant. When Leonardo arrived, François I immedi-ately fell in love with the painting and made it the centerpiece of the small collection of Italian masterpieces that would, in three cen-turies, become the Louvre museum. He called it *La Gioconda.* We know it as a contraction of the Italian for "my lady Lisa"—*Mona Lisa.* Warning: François I was impressed, but *Mona* may disappoint you. She's smaller and darker than you'd expect, engulfed in a huge room, and hidden behind a glaring pane of glass.

Mona's overall mood is one of balance and serenity, but there's also an element of mystery. Her smile and long-distance beauty are subtle and elusive, tempting but always just out of reach, like strands of a street singer's melody drifting through the Métro tunnel. *Mona* doesn't knock your socks off, but she winks at the patient viewer.

Now for something **neoclassical**. Notice the fine work, such as *The Coronation of Napoleon* by Jacques-Louis David, near *Mona* in the Salle Daru. Neoclassicism, once the rage in France (1780–1850), usually features Greek subjects, patriotic sentiment, and a clean, simple style. After Napoleon quickly conquered most of Europe, he insisted on being made emperor (not merely king) of this "New Rome." He staged an elaborate coronation ceremony in Paris, and rather than let the pope crown him, he crowned himself. The setting is the Notre-Dame Cathedral, with Greek columns and Roman arches thrown in for effect. Napoleon's mom was also added, since she couldn't make it to the ceremony. A key on the frame describes who's who in the picture.

The **Romantic** collection, in an adjacent room (Salle Mollien), has works by Théodore Géricault *(The Raft of the Medusa)* and Eugène Delacroix *(Liberty Leading the People)*. Romanticism, with an emphasis on motion and emotion, is the complete flip side of neoclassicism, though they both flourished in the early 1800s. Delacroix's *Liberty*, commemorating the stirrings of democracy in France, is also a fitting tribute to the Louvre, the first museum opened to the common rabble of humanity. The good things in life don't belong only to a small wealthy part of society, but to all. The motto of France is *"Liberté, Egalité, Fraternité"*—liberty, equality, and brotherhood.

Exit the room at the far end (past the café) and go downstairs, where you'll bump into the bum of a large, twisting male nude who looks like he's just waking up after a thousand-year nap. The two *Slaves* (1513–1515) by Michelangelo are a fitting end to this museum—works that bridge the ancient and modern worlds. Michelangelo, like his fellow Renaissance artists, learned from the Greeks. The perfect anatomy, twisting poses, and idealized faces look like they could have been done 2,000 years earlier. Michelangelo said that his purpose was to carve away the marble to reveal the figures God put inside. The *Rebellious Slave,* fighting against his bondage, shows the agony of that process and the ecstasy of the result.

Jeu de Paume (Galerie Nationale du Jeu de Paume)—This museum hosts rotating exhibits of top contemporary artists (€6, not covered by Museum Pass, Tue 12:00–21:30, Wed–Fri 12:00–19:00, Sat–Sun 10:00–19:00, closed Mon, on place de la Concorde, just inside Tuileries Garden on rue de Rivoli side, Mo: Concorde).

▲Musée de l'Orangerie—This Impressionist museum, lovely as a water lily, is due to reopen sometime in late 2005 or 2006. (For the latest, ask at any Paris TI.) When it opens, you can step out of the tree-lined, sun-dappled Impressionist painting that is the Tuileries Garden, and into L'Orangerie (loh-rahn-zheh-ree), a little *bijou* of select works by Utrillo, Cézanne, Renoir, Matisse, and Picasso. On the ground floor, you'll find a line of eight rooms dedicated to these artists. Downstairs is the finale: Monet's water lilies. The museum's collection is small enough to enjoy in a short visit, but complete enough to see the bridge from Impressionism to the Moderns. And it's all beautiful (located in Tuileries Garden near place de la Concorde, Mo: Concorde). If you need a Monet fix before L'Orangerie reopens, visit the Marmottan Museum (see page 88).

▲▲▲**Orsay Museum**—The Musée d'Orsay (mew-zay dor-say) houses French art of the 1800s (specifically, art from 1848 to 1914),

picking up where the Louvre leaves off. For us, that means Impressionism. The Orsay houses the best general collection anywhere of Edouard Manet, Claude Monet, Pierre-Auguste Renoir, Edgar Degas, Vincent van Gogh, Paul Cézanne, and Paul Gauguin.

The museum shows art that is also both old and new, conservative and revolutionary. You'll start on the ground floor with the Conservatives and the early rebels who paved the way for the Impressionists, then head upstairs to see how a few visionary young artists bucked the system, revolutionized the art world, and paved the way for the 20th century.

For most visitors, the most important part of the museum is the Impressionist collection upstairs. Here, you can study many pictures you've probably seen in books, such as Manet's *Luncheon on the Grass*, Renoir's *Dance at the Moulin de la Galette*, Monet's *Gare St. Lazare*, James Abbott McNeill Whistler's *Portrait of the Artist's Mother*, van Gogh's *The Church at Auvers-sur-Oise*, and Cézanne's *The Card Players*. As you approach these beautiful, easy-to-enjoy paintings, remember that there is more to this art than meets the eye.

Impressionism 101: The camera threatened to make artists obsolete. A painter's original function was to record reality faithfully, like a journalist. Now a machine could capture a better likeness faster than you could say Etch-A-Sketch.

But true art is more than just painted reality. It gives us reality from the artist's point of view, putting a personal stamp on the work. It records not only a scene—a camera can do that—but the artist's impressions of that scene. Impressions are often fleeting, so the artist has to work quickly.

The Impressionist painters rejected camera-like detail for a quick style more suited to capturing the passing moment. Feeling stifled by the rigid rules and stuffy atmosphere of the Academy, the Impressionists took as their motto, "Out of the studio, into the open air." They grabbed their berets and scarves and took excursions to the country, where they set up their easels on riverbanks and hillsides, or sketched in cafés and dance halls. Gods, goddesses, nymphs, and fantasy scenes were out; common people and rural landscapes were in.

The quick style and simple subjects were ridiculed and called

Orsay Museum—Ground Floor

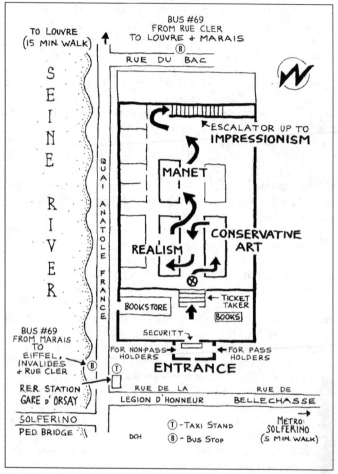

childish by the "experts." Rejected by the Salon, the Impressionists staged their own exhibition in 1874. They brashly took their name from an insult thrown at them by a critic, who laughed at one of Monet's impressions of a sunrise. During the next decade, they exhibited their own work independently. The public, opposed at first, was slowly drawn in by the simplicity, color, and vibrancy of Impressionist art.

Cost: €7; €5 after 16:15 and on Sun, free first Sun of month, covered by Museum Pass. Tickets are good all day. Museum Pass–holders can enter quickly on the right side of the building, ticket-buyers enter along the left (river) side.

Hours: June 20–Sept 20 Tue–Sun 9:00–18:00, Sept 21–June 19

Tue–Sat 10:00–18:00, Sun 9:00–18:00, Thu until 21:45 year-round, always closed Mon. Last entry is 45 min before closing. The Impressionist galleries start closing at 17:15, frustrating unwary visitors. Note that the Orsay is crowded on Tuesday, when the Louvre is closed.

Location: The Orsay sits above the RER-C stop called Musée d'Orsay. The nearest Métro stop is Solférino, three blocks south of the Orsay. Bus #69 from the Marais neighborhoods stops at the museum on the river side (quai Anatole France); from the rue Cler area, it stops behind the museum on the rue du Bac. A taxi stand is in front of the museum on quai Anatole France.

Information: The booth inside the entrance gives free floor plans in English. Tel. 01 40 49 48 41, www.musee-orsay.fr.

Tours: Audioguides are €5. English-language guided tours usually run daily (except Sun) at 11:30 (90-min tours–€6). Tours in English focusing on the Impressionists are offered Tuesdays at 14:30 (€6, sometimes also on other days).

Cafés: The elegant second-floor restaurant has a pricey but *très* elegant restaurant, serving tea and coffee from 15:00–17:30. A simple fifth-floor café is sandwiched between the Impressionists; above it is an easy self-service place.

Southwest Paris: The Eiffel Tower Neighborhood

▲▲▲**Eiffel Tower (La Tour Eiffel)**—It's crowded and expensive, but this 1,000-foot-tall ornament is worth the trouble. In hot weather, it's six inches taller. It covers 2.5 acres and requires 50 tons

of paint. Its 7,000 tons of metal are spread out so well at the base that it's no heavier per square inch than a linebacker on tiptoes. Visitors to Paris may find *Mona Lisa* to be less than expected, but the Eiffel Tower rarely disappoints, even in an era of skyscrapers.

Built a hundred years after the French Revolution (and in the midst of an Industrial one), the tower served no function but to impress. Bridge-builder Gustave Eiffel won the contest for the 1889 Centennial World's Fair by beating out such rival proposals as a giant guillotine. To a generation hooked on technology, the tower was the marvel of the age, a symbol of progress and man's ingenuity. To others it was a cloned-sheep monstrosity. The writer Guy de Maupassant routinely ate lunch in the tower just so he wouldn't have to look at it.

Delicate and graceful when seen from afar, the Eiffel is massive—even a bit scary—from close up. You don't appreciate the size

Eiffel Tower to Les Invalides

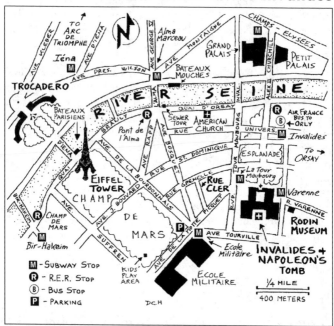

until you walk toward it; like a mountain, it seems so close but takes forever to reach.

There are three observation platforms, at 200, 400, and 900 feet; the higher you go, the more you pay. Each requires a separate elevator (and line), so plan on at least 90 minutes if you want to go to the top and back. For most, the view from the second level is plenty.

A TI/ticket booth is between the Pilier Nord (north pillar) and Pilier Est (east pillar). The stairs (yes, you can walk up partway) are next to the Jules Verne restaurant entrance (allow $300 per person for the restaurant, reserve 3 months in advance). A sign in the cheek-to-jowl elevator tells you to beware of pickpockets.

As you ascend through the metal beams, imagine being a worker, perched high above nothing, riveting this giant erector set together. On top, all of Paris lies before you, with a panorama guide. On a good day, you can see for 40 miles.

The **first level** has exhibits, a post office (daily 10:00–19:00, cancellation stamp will read Eiffel Tower), a snack bar, WCs, and souvenirs. Read the informative signs (in English) describing the major monuments, see the entertaining free movie on the history of the tower, and don't miss a century of fireworks—including the entire millennium blast—on video. Then consider a drink or a sandwich overlooking all of Paris at the snack café (outdoor tables in summer) or at the city's best view bar/restaurant, Altitude 95 (see page 151).

The **second level** has the best views (walk up stairway to get above netting), a cafeteria, and WCs.

While you'll save no money, consider taking the elevator up and the stairs down (from second level) for good exercise and views.

Cost and Hours: It costs €4 to go to the first level, €7.50 to the second, and €11 to go all the way (not covered by Museum Pass). On a budget? You can climb the stairs to the second level for only €3.50 (daily March–Sept 9:00–24:00, Oct–Feb 9:30–23:00, last entry 1 hour before closing, shorter lines at night, can catch Bateaux-Parisiens boat for Seine cruise at base of tower, Mo: Trocadéro, RER: Champ de Mars-Tour Eiffel, tel. 01 44 11 23 23, www.tour-eiffel.fr).

Crowd-Beating Tips: To avoid most crowds, go early (by 8:45) or late in the day (after 18:00, after 20:00 May–Aug, last entry 1 hr before closing); weekends are worst. Ideally you'd arrive with some light and stay as it gets dark.

Best Views: The best place to view the tower is from **Trocadéro Square** to the north; it's a 10-min walk across the river, a happening scene at night, and especially fun for kids. Consider arriving at the Trocadéro Métro stop for the view, then walking toward the tower. Another great viewpoint is the long, grassy field, **Parc du Champ de Mars**, to the south (great for dinner picnics). However impressive it may be by day, the tower is an awesome thing to see at twilight, when it becomes engorged with light, and virile Paris lies back and lets night be on top.

National Maritime Museum (Musée National de la Marine)—This extensive museum houses an amazing collection of ship models, submarines, torpedoes, cannonballs, *beaucoup de* bowsprits, and naval you-name-it—including a small boat made for Napoleon. You'll find some English information on the walls. The €3 audio-guide is an essential investment for *Master and Commander* types; kids like the museum either way (adults-€7, kids-€4, covered by Museum Pass, Wed–Mon 10:00–18:00, closed Tue, on left side of Trocadéro Square with your back to Eiffel Tower, www.musee-marine.fr).

▲Paris Sewer Tour (Les Egouts de Paris)—This quick and easy visit takes you along a few hundred yards of underground water tunnel lined with interesting displays, well-described in English, that explain the evolution of the world's longest sewer system. (If you straightened out Paris' sewers, they would reach beyond Istanbul.) Don't miss the slideshow, the fine WCs just beyond the gift shop, and the occasional tour in English (€4, covered by Museum Pass, May–Sept Sat–Wed 11:00–17:00, Oct–April Sat–Wed 11:00–16:00, closed Thu–Fri, located where pont de l'Alma greets the Left Bank, Mo: Alma-Marceau, RER: Pont de l'Alma, tel. 01 53 68 27 81).

▲▲**Napoleon's Tomb and Army Museum (Les Invalides)**—The emperor lies majestically dead inside several coffins under a grand dome—a goose-bumping pilgrimage for historians. Napoleon is surrounded by the tombs of other French war heroes and a fine military museum in Hôtel des Invalides. Check out the interesting World War II wing. Follow signs to the "crypt" to find Roman Empire-style reliefs that list the accomplishments of Napoleon's administration. The restored dome glitters with 26 pounds of gold (€7, covered by Museum Pass, April–Sept daily 10:00–18:00, summer Sun until 19:00, Oct–March daily 10:00–17:00, closed the first Mon of every month except July–Sept; Mo: La Tour Maubourg or Varenne, tel. 01 44 42 37 72, www.invalides.org).

▲▲**Rodin Museum (Musée Rodin)**—This user-friendly museum is filled with passionate works by the greatest sculptor since Michelangelo. You'll see *The Kiss, The Thinker, The Gates of Hell*, and many more.

Well-displayed in the mansion where the sculptor lived and worked, exhibits trace Rodin's artistic development, explain how his bronze statues were cast, and show some of the studies he created to work up to his masterpiece (the unfinished *Gates of Hell*). Learn about Rodin's tumultuous relationship with his apprentice and lover, Camille Claudel. Mull over what makes his sculptures some of the most evocative since the Renaissance. And stroll the gardens, packed with many of his greatest works (including *The Thinker*). The beautiful gardens are ideal for artistic reflection...or a picnic.

Cost, Hours, Location: €5, €3 on Sun, free first Sun of month, covered by Museum Pass. You'll pay €1 to get into the gardens only—which may be Paris' best deal, as many works are on display there. April–Sept Tue–Sun 9:30–17:45, closed Mon, gardens close 18:45, Oct–March Tue–Sun 9:30–16:45, closed Mon, gardens close 17:00. It's at 77 rue de Varenne, near Napoleon's Tomb (Mo: Varenne, tel. 01 44 18 61 10, www.musee-rodin.fr).

▲▲**Marmottan Museum (Musée Marmottan Monet)**—In this private, intimate, untouristy museum, you'll find the best collection anywhere of works by Impressionist headliner Claude Monet. Follow Monet's life through over a hundred works, from simple sketches to the *Impression: Sunrise* painting that gave his artistic movement its start—and a name. You'll also enjoy classic Monet canvases featuring the water lilies from his garden at Giverny.

Cost, Hours, Location: €7, not covered by Museum Pass, Tue–Sun 10:00–18:00, last entry is 17:30, closed Mon, 2 rue Louis Boilly, Mo: La Muette, follow brown museum signs 6 blocks down chaussée de la Muette through park to museum, tel. 01 44 96 50 33, www.marmottan.com.

Post-Museum Stroll: Wander down one of Paris' most pleasant (and upscale) shopping streets, the rue de Passy (2 blocks up chaussée

Latin Quarter

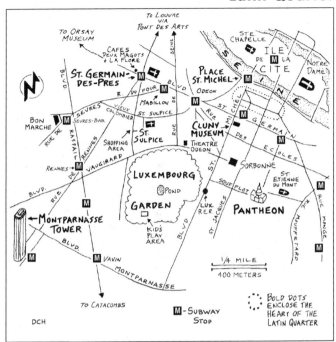

de la Muette in opposite direction from La Muette Métro stop).

Southeast Paris: The Latin Quarter

This Left Bank neighborhood, just opposite Notre-Dame, is the Latin Quarter. (For more information and a walking tour, see the "Historic Core of Paris Walk," page 68.)

▲▲**Cluny Museum (Musée National du Moyen Age)**—This treasure-trove of Middle Age ("Moyen Age") art fills the old Roman baths, offering close-up looks at stained glass, Notre-Dame carvings, fine goldsmithing and jewelry, and rooms of tapestries. The star here is the exquisite "Lady and the Unicorn" tapestry: In five panels, a delicate-as-medieval-can-be noble lady introduces a delighted unicorn to the senses of taste, hearing, sight, smell, and touch.

Cost, Hours, Location: €5.50, €4 on Sun, free first Sun of month, covered by Museum Pass, Wed–Mon 9:15–17:45, closed Tue, near corner of boulevards St. Michel and St. Germain; Mo: Cluny-La Sorbonne, St. Michel, or Odéon; tel. 01 53 73 78 16, www.musee-moyenage.fr.

St. Germain-des-Prés—A church was first built on this site in A.D. 452. The church you see today was constructed in 1163 and is all that's left of a once sprawling and influential monastery. The colorful interior reminds us that medieval churches were originally painted in bright colors. The surrounding area hops at night with venerable cafés, fire-eaters, mimes, and scads of artists (free, daily 8:00–20:00, Mo: St. Germain-des-Prés).

▲**St. Sulpice Organ Concert**—For pipe-organ enthusiasts, this is a delight. The Grand Orgue at St. Sulpice Church has a rich history, with a succession of 12 world-class organists (including Charles-Marie Widor and Marcel Dupré) going back 300 years. Widor started the tradition of opening the loft to visitors after the 10:30 service on Sundays. Daniel Roth continues to welcome guests in three languages while playing five keyboards at once. (See www.danielrothsaintsulpice.org for his exact dates and concert plans.) The 10:30 Sunday Mass is followed by a high-powered 25-minute recital at about

11:35. Then, just after noon, the small, unmarked door is opened (left of entry as you face the rear). Visitors scamper like sixteenth notes up spiral stairs, past the 19th-century Stairmasters that five men once pumped to fill the bellows, into a world of 7,000 pipes. Here, they watch the master play during the next Mass. You'll generally have 30 minutes to kill (there's a plush lounge) before the organ plays; visitors can leave at any time. If late or rushed, show up around 12:30 and wait at the little door. As someone leaves, you can slip in (church open daily 7:30–19:30, Mo: St. Sulpice or Mabillon).

The Luxembourg Garden and St. Germain street market are both nearby and open daily (the St. Germain market is between St. Sulpice and Métro stop Mabillon on rue Clément).

▲▲**Luxembourg Garden (Jardin du Luxembourg)**—Paris' most beautiful, interesting, and enjoyable garden/park/recreational area is a great place to watch Parisians at rest and play (open daily until dusk, Mo: Odéon, RER: Luxembourg). It's ideal for families. These private gardens are property of the French Senate (housed in the château) and have special rules governing their use (e.g., where cards can be played, where dogs can be walked, where joggers can run, when and where music can be played). The brilliant flower beds are completely changed three times a year, and the boxed trees are brought out of the orangery in May. Challenge the card and chess players to a game (near the tennis courts), rent a toy sailboat, or find a free chair near the main pond and take a breather. Notice any pigeons? The story goes that a poor Ernest Hemingway used to hand-hunt (read: strangle) them here. Paris Walking Tours offers a good tour of the park (see "Tours," page 63).

The grand, neoclassical-domed Panthéon, now a mausoleum

housing the tombs of several great Frenchmen, is a block away and only worth entering if you have a Museum Pass.

If you enjoy the Luxembourg Garden and want to see more, visit the nearby, colorful Jardin des Plantes (Mo: Jussieu or Gare d'Austerlitz, RER: Gare d'Austerlitz) and the more elegant Parc Monceau (Mo: Monceau).

Montparnasse Tower (La Tour Montparnasse)—The 59-story superscraper is cheaper and easier to get to the top of than the Eiffel Tower, with the added bonus of offering one of Paris' best views—the Eiffel Tower is in sight and the Montparnasse Tower isn't. Buy the €3 photo guide to the city, then go to the rooftop and orient yourself. As you zip 56 floors in 38 seconds, watch the altitude meter above the door. Up top, enjoy the surreal scene with a man in a box and a helipad surrounded by the window-cleaner track. Then scan

the city, noticing the lush courtyards hiding behind grand street fronts. Downstairs you'll find fascinating historic black-and-white photos and a plush little theater playing *Paris Like Never Seen* (free, 12 min, shows continuously). You'll float past unseen visual delights, spiraling down the Eiffel Tower as the French narration explains, "Paris is radiant and confident, like a lover who finally took her blouse off."

Cost, Hours, Location: €8.50, not covered by Museum Pass, daily April–Sept 9:30–23:30, Oct–March 9:30–22:30, disappointing after dark, entrance on rue de l'Arrivée, Mo: Montparnasse-Bienvenüe. The tower is an efficient stop when combined with a day trip to Chartres (see page 113), which begins at the Montparnasse train station.

▲**Catacombs**—These underground tunnels contain the anonymous bones of six million permanent Parisians. In 1785, the Revolutionary Government of Paris decided to relieve congestion and improve sanitary conditions by emptying the city cemeteries (which traditionally surrounded churches) into an official ossuary. The perfect locale was the many miles of underground tunnels from limestone quarries, which were, at that time, just outside the city. For decades, priests led ceremonial processions of black-veiled, bone-laden carts into the quarries, where the bones were stacked into piles five feet high and as much as 80 feet deep behind neat walls of skull-studded tibiae. Each transfer was completed with the placement of a plaque indicating the church and district from which that stack of bones came and the date they arrived.

From the entry, a spiral staircase leads 60 feet down. Then you begin a one-mile subterranean walk. After several blocks of empty passageways, you ignore a sign announcing: "Halt, this is the empire of the dead." Along the way, plaques encourage visitors to reflect upon their destiny: "Happy is he who is forever faced with the hour of his death and prepares himself for the end every day." You emerge far from where you entered, with white-limestone-covered toes, telling anyone in the know you've been underground gawking at bones. Note to wannabe Hamlets: An attendant checks your bag at the exit for stolen souvenirs. A flashlight is handy. Being under 6'2" is helpful.

Cost, Hours, Location: €5, not covered by Museum Pass, Tue–Sun 10:00–17:00, ticket booth closes at 16:00, closed Mon, 1 place Denfert-Rochereau, tel. 01 43 22 47 63. Take the Métro to Denfert-Rochereau, then find the lion in the big traffic circle; if he looked left rather than right, he'd stare right at the green entrance to the Catacombs.

Northwest Paris:
Champs-Elysées, Arc de Triomphe, and Beyond

▲▲**Place de la Concorde and the Champs-Elysées**—This famous boulevard is Paris' backbone, and has the greatest concentration of traffic. All of France seems to converge on the place de la Concorde, the city's largest square. It was here that the guillotine took the lives of thousands—including King Louis XVI and Marie-Antoinette. Back then it was called the place de la Revolution.

Catherine de Médicis wanted a place to drive her carriage, so she started draining the swamp that would become the avenue des Champs-Elysées. Napoleon put on the final touches, and it's been the place to be seen ever since. The Tour de France bicycle race ends here, as do all parades (French or foe) of any significance. While the boulevard has become a bit hamburgerized, a walk here is a must. Follow my self-guided "Champs-Elysées Walk" on page 101. Take the Métro to the Arc de Triomphe (Mo: Charles de Gaulle-Etoile) and saunter down the Champs-Elysées (Métro stops every few blocks: Franklin D. Roosevelt, George V, and Charles de Gaulle-Etoile).

▲▲▲**Arc de Triomphe**—Napoleon had the magnificent Arc de Triomphe commissioned to commemorate his victory at the battle of Austerlitz. There's no triumphal arch bigger (165 feet high, 130 feet wide). And, with 12 converging boulevards, there's no traffic circle more thrilling to experience—either from behind the wheel or on foot (take the underpass).

The foot of the arch is a stage on which the last two centuries of Parisian history have played out—from the funeral of Napoleon, to the goose-stepping arrival of the Nazis, to the triumphant return of Charles de Gaulle after the Allied liberation. Ponder the Tomb of the Unknown Soldier (from World War I, at base of arch), where the flame is rekindled daily at 18:30. Find François Rude's famous

Northwest Paris: Champs-Elysées, Arc de Triomphe, and Beyond

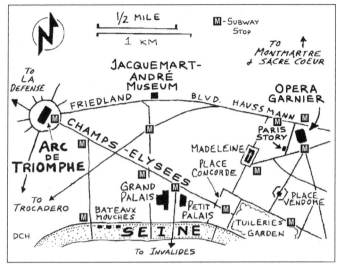

relief, "La Marseillaise" (on the right pillar), showing a shouting Lady Liberty rallying weary troops.

The 284 steps lead to a cute museum about the arch, sweeping skyline panoramas, and a mesmerizing view down onto the traffic that swirls around the arch.

Cost, Hours, Location: €7, covered by Museum Pass, daily April–Sept 10:00–23:00, Oct–March 10:00–22:30, Mo: Charles de Gaulle-Etoile, use underpass to reach arch. At the arch, the elevator—which is only for people with disabilities—goes to the museum but not to the top.

▲**Opéra Garnier**—This grand palace of the belle époque was built for Napoleon III and finished in 1875. From the grand avenue de l'Opéra, once lined with Paris' most fashionable haunts, the newly restored facade seems to say "all power to the wealthy." And Apollo, holding his lyre high above the buidling, seems to declare "this is a temple of the highest arts." While huge, the actual theater seats only 2,000. The real show was before and after, when the elite of Paris—out to see and be seen—strutted their elegant stuff in the extravagant lobbies. Think of the grand marble stairway as a theater itself. As you wander the halls and gawk at the decor, imagine the place filled with the beautiful people of the day. The massive foundations straddle an underground lake (creating the mysterious world of the *Phantom of the Opera*). Tourists can peek from two boxes into the actual red-velvet theater, where they see Marc Chagall's colorful ceiling (1964) playfully dancing around the eight-ton chandelier. Note the box seats next to the stage—the most expensive in the house, with an obstructed view of the stage...but just right if you're there only to be seen. The elitism of this place prompted President François Mitterand to have a people's opera house built in the 1980s (symbolically on place de la Bastille, where the French Revolution started in 1789). This left the Opéra Garnier home only to ballet and occasional concerts (usually no performances from mid-July to mid-Sept). While the library/museum is of interest to opera buffs, anyone will enjoy the second-floor grand foyer and Salon du Glacier, iced with decor typical of 1900.

Cost, Hours, Location: €6, not covered by Museum Pass, daily 10:00–17:00, July–Aug until 18:00, closed during performances, 8 rue Scribe, Mo: Opéra, tel. 01 40 01 22 53, www.opera-de-paris.fr.

Tours: There are English tours of the building on most afternoons (€10, includes entry, 90 min, call to confirm, tour ticket window at opposite end of entry from regular ticket booth).

Nearby: American Express, a TI, and the *Paris Story* film (see below) are on the left side of the Opéra, and the venerable Galeries Lafayette department store is just behind. Across the street, the illustrious Café de la Paix has been a meeting spot for the local glitterati for generations. If you can afford the coffee, this offers a delightful break.

Paris Story Film—This entertaining film offers a good and painless overview of the city's turbulent and brilliant past, covering 2,000 years in 45 fast-moving minutes. The theater's widescreen projection and cushy chairs provide an ideal break from bad weather and sore feet, and the movie's a fun activity with kids.

Cost, Hours, Location: Adults-€8, kids-€5, family of 4-€21, not covered by Museum Pass. Individuals get a 20 percent discount with this book in 2005 (no discount on family rate). The film shows on the hour daily 9:00–19:00. Next to Opéra Garnier at 11 rue Scribe, Mo: Opéra, tel. 01 42 66 62 06.

▲▲Jacquemart-André Museum (Musée Jacquemart-André)— This thoroughly enjoyable museum showcases the lavish home of a wealthy, art-loving, 19th-century Parisian couple. After wandering the grand boulevards, you now get inside for an intimate look at the lifestyles of the Parisian rich and fabulous. Edouard André and his wife Nélie Jacquemart—who had no children—spent their lives and fortunes designing, building, and then decorating a sumptuous mansion. What makes this visit so rewarding is the fine audioguide tour (in English, free with admission). The place is strewn with paintings by Rembrandt, Botticelli, Uccello, Mantegna, Bellini, Boucher, and Fragonard—enough to make a painting gallery famous. Plan on spending an hour with the audioguide.

Cost, Hours, Location: €8.50, not covered by Museum Pass, daily 10:00–18:00, elegant café, boulevard Haussmann, Mo:

Miromesnil or St Philippe de Roule, tel. 01 45 62 11 59, www
.musee-jacquemart-andre.com/jandre.

Petit Palais (and its Musée des Beaux-Arts)—The free museum
is due to reopen after renovation in the spring of 2005. When it
does, you'll find a broad collection of paintings and sculpture from
the 1600s to the 1900s. To some it feels like a museum of second-
choice art, as the more famous museums in Paris have better
collections from the same periods. Others find a few diamonds in
the rough from Monet, Renoir, Boudin, and more; some interesting
Art Nouveau pieces; and a smattering of works by Dutch, Italian,
and Flemish Renaissance artists (across from Grand Palais, avenue
Winston Churchill, just west of place de la Concorde, tel.
01 40 05 56 78).

Grand Palais—This grand exhibition hall, built for the 1900
World's Fair, is busy with generally worthwhile temporary exhibits.
Get details on the current schedule from TIs or in *Pariscope* maga-
zine (€9, not covered by Museum Pass, avenue Churchill, Mo: Rond
Point or Champs-Elysées).

▲**View from Hôtel Concorde-Lafayette**—For a remarkable Parisian
panorama, take the Métro to the pedestrian-unfriendly Porte Maillot
stop, then follow *Palais de Congrés* signs to the glass-and-steel tower
that houses this luxury hotel. Take an elevator in the rear of the lobby
to floor 33, walk one flight up, and enter a sky-high world of semicircular booths (rooftop bar open 17:30–02:00, €8 beers, €6 espressos,
and jaw-dropping views, best before dark). If it's clear and the sun's
about to set, spring for a drink—the ride was free (rooms start at €400,
3 place du General Koening, tel. 01 40 68 50 68, www.concorde
-lafayette.com).

▲**La Défense and La Grande Arche**—On the outskirts of Paris,
the centerpiece of Paris' ambitious skyscraper complex (La Défense)
is the Grande Arche. Inaugurated in 1989 on the 200th anniversary
of the French Revolution, it was dedicated to human rights and
brotherhood. The place is big—38 floors holding offices for 30,000

people on more than 200 acres. Notre-
Dame Cathedral could fit under its arch.
The complex at La Défense is an interesting study in 1960s land-use planning.
More than 100,000 workers commute
here daily, directing lots of business and
development away from downtown and
allowing central Paris to retain its more
elegant feel. This makes sense to most Parisians, regardless of whatever else they feel about this controversial complex. You will enjoy
city views from the Grande Arche elevator.

Cost, Hours, Location: Grande Arche elevator-€7.50, kids-
€6, family deals, not covered by Museum Pass, daily 10:00–19:00,

RER or Mo: La Défense, follow signs to Grande Arche, tel. 01 49 07 27 57. The entry price includes art exhibits and a film on the Arche's construction.

Northeast Paris:
Marais Neighborhood and More

The Marais neighborhood extends along the Right Bank of the Seine from the Pompidou Center to the Bastille. It contains more pre-revolutionary lanes and buildings than anywhere else in town and is more atmospheric than touristy. It's medieval Paris. This is how much of the city looked until, in the mid-1800s, Napoleon III had Baron Haussmann blast out the narrow streets to construct broad boulevards (wide enough for the guns and ranks of the army, too wide for revolutionary barricades), thus creating modern Paris. Originally a swamp *(marais)* during the reign of Henry IV, this area became the hometown of the French aristocracy. In the 17th century, big shots built their private mansions *(hôtels)*, close to Henry IV's place des Vosges. When strolling the Marais, stick to the west–east axis formed by rue Sainte-Croix de la Bretonnerie, rue des Rosiers (heart of Paris' Jewish community), and rue St. Antoine. On Sunday afternoons, this trendy area pulses with shoppers and café crowds.

▲**Place des Vosges**—Study the architecture in this grand square: nine pavilions per side. Some of the brickwork is real, some is fake. Walk to the center, where Louis XIII sits on a horse surrounded by locals enjoying their community park. Children frolic in the sandbox, lovers warm benches, and pigeons guard their fountains while trees shade this retreat from the glare of the big city. Henry IV built this centerpiece of the Marais in 1605. As hoped, this turned the Marais into Paris' most exclusive neighborhood. As the nobility flocked to Versailles in a later age, this too was a magnet for the rich and powerful of France. With the Revolution, the aristocratic elegance of this quarter became working-class, filled with gritty shops, artisans, immigrants, and Jews. **Victor Hugo** lived at #6, and you can visit his house (free, Tue–Sun 10:00–18:00, closed Mon, 6 place des Vosges, tel. 01 42 72 10 16). Leave the place des Vosges through the doorway at southwest corner of the square (near the three-star Michelin restaurant, l'Ambroisie) and pass through the elegant **Hôtel de Sully** (great example of a Marais mansion) to rue St. Antoine.

▲▲**Pompidou Center (Centre Pompidou)**—One of Europe's greatest collections of far-out modern art is housed in the Musée National d'Art Moderne, on the fourth and fifth floors of this colorful, exoskeletal building. Once ahead of its time, this 20th-century (remember that century?) art has been waiting for the world to catch up with it. After so many Madonnas-and-Children, a piano smashed to bits and glued to the wall is refreshing.

Northeast Paris:
Marais Neighborhood and More

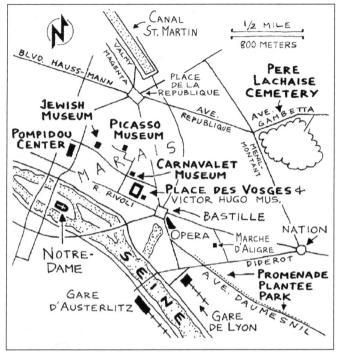

The Pompidou Center and its square are lively, with lots of people, street theater, and activity inside and out—a perpetual street fair. Kids of any age enjoy the fun, colorful fountain called *Homage to Stravinsky*, next to the Pompidou Center. Don't miss the free exhibits on the ground floor of the Center. Ride the escalator for a great city view from the top (ticket or Museum Pass required), and consider the good mezzanine-level café.

Cost, Hours, Location: €7, free first Sun of month, covered by Museum Pass, Wed–Mon 11:00–21:00, closed Tue, Mo: Rambuteau, tel. 01 44 78 12 33, www.centrepompidou.fr.

Lunch: You'll find the cool Café La Mezzanine on Level 1 of the Pompidou and the snobby Chez Georges view restaurant on Level 6. Across from the entrance/exit, on rue Rambuteau, is the cheap, efficient Flunch self-service cafeteria. My favorite places line the Stravinsky fountain: Dame Tartine and Crêperie Beaubourg (to the right as you face the museum entrance).

▲▲**Jewish Art and History Museum (Musée d'Art et Histoire du Judaïsme)**—This fascinating museum is located in a beautifully restored Marais mansion and tells the story of Judaism throughout

Marais Sights

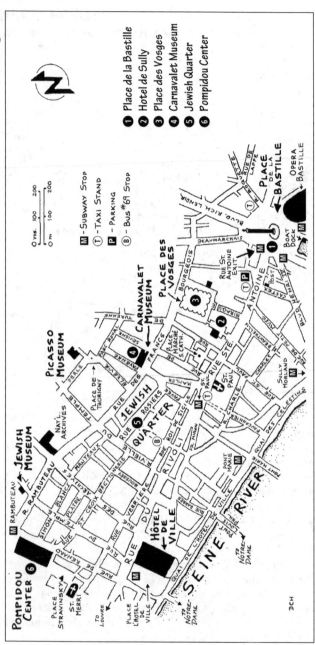

1. Place de la Bastille
2. Hotel de Sully
3. Place des Vosges
4. Carnavalet Museum
5. Jewish Quarter
6. Pompidou Center

M - Subway Stop
T - Taxi Stand
P - Parking
B - Bus #69 Stop

Europe, from the Roman destruction of Jerusalem to the theft of famous artworks during World War II.

The museum illustrates the cultural unity maintained by this continually dispersed population. You'll learn about the history of Jewish traditions from bar mitzvahs to menorahs, and see the exquisite traditional costumes and objects around which daily life revolved. Don't miss the explanation of "the Dreyfus affair," a major event in early 1900s French politics. You'll also see photographs of and paintings by famous Jewish artists, including Chagall, Modigliani, and Soutine. A small but moving section is devoted to the deportation of Jews from Paris.

Helpful, free audioguides and many English explanations make this an enjoyable history lesson (red numbers on small signs indicate the number you should press on your audioguide). Move along at your own speed.

Cost, Hours, Location: €7, includes audioguide, not covered by Museum Pass, Mon–Fri 11:00–18:00, Sun 10:00–18:00, closed Sat, 71 rue du Temple, Mo: Rambuteau or Hôtel de Ville a few blocks farther away, tel. 01 53 01 86 60, www.mahj.org.

▲▲**Picasso Museum (Musée Picasso)**—Tucked into a corner of the Marais and worth ▲▲▲ if you're a Picasso fan, this museum contains the world's largest collection of Picasso's paintings, sculptures, sketches, and ceramics, and includes his small collection of Impressionist art. The art is well-displayed in a fine old mansion with a peaceful garden café. The room-by-room English introductions help make sense of Picasso's work—from the Toulouse-Lautrec-like portraits at the beginning of his career to his gray-brown Cubist period to his return-to-childhood, Salvador Dalí-like finish. The well-done €3 English guidebook helps Picassophiles appreciate the context of his art and learn more about his interesting life. Most will be happy reading the posted English explanations while moving at a steady pace through the museum—the ground and first floors satisfied my curiosity.

Cost, Hours, Location: €5.50, free first Sun of month, covered by Museum Pass, April–Sept Wed–Mon 9:30–18:00, Oct–March Wed–Mon 9:30–17:30, closed Tue, 5 rue de Thorigny, Mo: St. Paul or Chemin Vert, tel. 01 42 71 25 21, www.musee-picasso.fr.

▲▲**Carnavalet Museum (Musée Carnavalet)**—The tumultuous history of Paris is well portrayed in this converted Marais mansion. Explanations are in French only, but many displays are fairly self-explanatory. You'll see paintings of Parisian scenes, French Revolution paraphernalia, old Parisian store signs, a small guillotine, a model of 16th-century Ile de la Cité (notice the bridge houses), and rooms full of 17th-century Parisian furniture.

Cost, Hours, Location: Free, Tue–Sun 10:00–18:00, closed Mon; avoid lunchtime (12:00–14:00), when many rooms close; 23 rue de Sévigné, Mo: St. Paul, tel. 01 44 59 58 58.

▲**Promenade Plantée Park**—This two-mile-long, narrow garden walk on a viaduct was once used for train tracks and is now a joy. Part of the park is elevated. At times, you'll walk along the street until you pick up the next segment. The shops below the viaduct's arches make for entertaining window-shopping.

Cost, Hours, Location: Free, opens Mon–Fri at 8:00, Sat–Sun at 9:00, closes at sunset. It runs from place de la Bastille (Mo: Bastille) along avenue Daumesnil to Saint-Mandé (Mo: Michel Bizot). From place de la Bastille (follow "Sortie Opéra" or "Sortie rue de Lyon" from Bastille Métro station), walk down rue de Lyon with the Opéra immediately on your left. Find the steps up the red brick wall a block after the Opéra.

▲**Père Lachaise Cemetery (Cimetière du Père Lachaise)**— Littered with the tombstones of many of the city's most illustrious dead, this is your best one-stop look at the fascinating, romantic world of "permanent Parisians." More like a small city, the cemetery is confusing, but maps will direct you to the graves of Frédéric Chopin, Molière, Edith Piaf, Oscar Wilde, Gertrude Stein, Jim Morrison, Héloïse and Abélard, and more (helpful €2 maps sold at flower stores near either entry).

Cost, Hours, Location: Free, Mon–Sat from 8:00, Sun from 9:00, closes at dusk. It's down rue Père Lachaise from Mo: Gambetta, or across the street from the Père Lachaise Métro stop (also reachable via bus #69).

North Paris: Montmartre

▲▲**Sacré-Cœur and Montmartre**—The five-domed, Roman-Byzantine basilica of Sacré-Cœur took 44 years to build (1875–1919). It stands on a foundation of 83 pillars sunk 130 feet deep, necessary because the ground beneath was honeycombed with gypsum mines. The exterior is laced with gypsum, which whitens with age.

For an unobstructed panoramic view of Paris, climb 260 feet up the tight and claustrophobic spiral stairs to the top of the **dome** (church free, open daily 7:00–23:00; €5 to climb dome, daily June–Sept 9:00–19:00, Oct–May 10:00–18:00).

One block from the church, the **place du Tertre** was the haunt of Henri de Toulouse-Lautrec and the original bohemians. Today, it's mobbed with tourists and unoriginal bohemians, but it's still fun (go early in the morning to beat the crowds).

To get to Montmartre, take the Métro to the Anvers stop (one more Métro ticket buys your way up the funicular and avoids the stairs) or the closer but less scenic Abbesses stop. A taxi to the top of the hill saves time and avoids sweat. For restaurant recommendations, see "Eating," page 147.

Pigalle—Paris' red-light district, the infamous "Pig Alley," is at the foot of butte Montmartre. *Oo la la*. It's more shocking than dangerous. Walk from place Pigalle to place Blanche, teasing desperate barkers and fast-talking temptresses. In bars, a €150 bottle of cheap champagne comes with a friend. Stick to the bigger streets, hang on to your wallet, and exercise good judgment. Cancan can cost a fortune, as can con artists in topless bars. After dark, countless tour buses line the streets, reminding us that tour guides make big bucks by bringing their groups to touristy nightclubs like the famous Moulin Rouge (Mo: Pigalle or Abbesses).

Disappointments de Paris

Here are a few negatives to help you manage your limited time:

La Madeleine is a big, neoclassical church with a postcard facade and a postbox interior.

Paris' **Panthéon** (nothing like Rome's) is another neoclassical edifice filled with the mortal remains of great Frenchmen.

The **Bastille** is Paris' most famous non-sight. The square is there, but confused tourists look everywhere and can't find the famous prison of Revolution fame. The building's gone, and the square is good only as a jumping-off point for Promenade Plantée Park (see previous page).

Finally, much of the **Latin Quarter** is a frail shadow of its once-bohemian self. The blocks nearest the river (across from Notre-Dame) are more Tunisian, Greek, and Woolworth's than old-time Paris. The neighborhood merits a wander, but you're better off focusing on the area around boulevard St. Germain and rue de Buci, and on the streets around the Maubert-Mutualité Métro stop.

SELF-GUIDED WALKS

Champs-Elysées Walk

Don't leave Paris without strolling the avenue des Champs-Elysées. This is Paris at its most Parisian: monumental sidewalks, stylish shops, grand cafés, and glimmering showrooms. This walk covers about two miles—from the Arc de Triomphe to the Rond-Point,

the bottom of the commercial half of the Champs-Elysées—and takes two hours if done completely. It's a great stroll day or night. Métro stops are located about every three blocks on the Champs-Elysées (shahn-zay-lee-zay).

Start at the **Arc de Triomphe** by taking the Métro to Charles de Gaulle-Etoile (then follow *sortie Champs-Elysées/Avenue Friedland* signs to *access Arc de Triomphe*

Champs-Elysées Walk

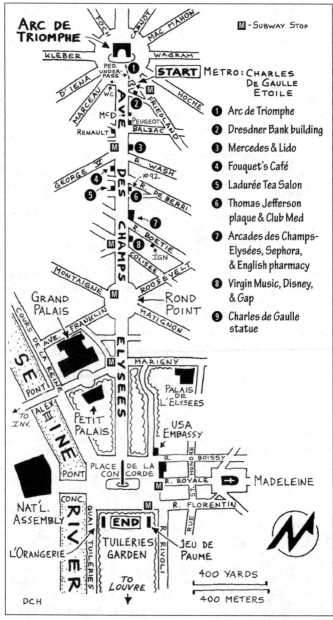

☐ – Subway Stop

START   METRO: Charles
           De Gaulle
           Etoile

❶ Arc de Triomphe

❷ Dresdner Bank building

❸ Mercedes & Lido

❹ Fouquet's Café

❺ Ladurée Tea Salon

❻ Thomas Jefferson
   plaque & Club Med

❼ Arcades des Champs-
   Elysées, Sephora,
   & English pharmacy

❽ Virgin Music, Disney,
   & Gap

❾ Charles de Gaulle
   statue

signs). At the top of the Champs-Elysées, face the arch. The underground WCs are on the other (south) side of Champs-Elysées, and an underground walkway leading to the arch is in front of you. Get to that arch. It's worthwhile even if you don't climb it; there's no charge to wander around the base (€7, skip ticket line and fee if you have Museum Pass, daily April–Sept 10:00–23:00, Oct–March 10:00–22:30, Mo: Charles de Gaulle-Etoile, tel. 01 43 80 31 31). For more information on the arch, see page 92.

Starting at the top, stroll the Champs-Elysées, one of the world's grandest, most elegant, and celebrated streets, home to big business, celebrity cafés, glitzy nightclubs, high-fashion shopping, and international people-watching.

In 1667, Louis XIV opened the first section of the street as a short extension of the Tuileries Garden. This date is considered the birth of Paris as a grand city. The Champs-Elysées soon became *the* place to cruise in your carriage. (It still is today—traffic can be jammed up even at midnight.) One hundred years later, the café scene arrived.

From the 1920s until the 1960s, this boulevard was pure elegance. Locals actually dressed up to come here. It was mainly residences, rich hotels, and cafés. Then, in 1963, the government pumped up the neighborhood's commercial metabolism by bringing in the RER (commuter underground). Suburbanites had easy access, and bam—there went the neighborhood.

Start your descent and pause at the first tiny street you cross, rue de Tilsitt. This street is part of a shadow ring road—an option for drivers who'd like to avoid the chaos of the arch, complete with stoplights. A half-block down rue de Tilsitt is the **Dresdner Bank building**. It's one of the few survivors of a dozen uniformly U-shaped buildings in Baron Haussman's original 1853 grand design. Peek into the foyer for a glimpse of 19th-century Champs-Elysées classiness.

Back on the main drag, look across to the other side of the Champs-Elysées at the big, gray concrete-and-glass **"Publicis" building**. Ugh. In the 1960s, venerable old buildings (similar to the Dresdner Bank building) were leveled to make way for new commercial operations, like Publicis. Then in 1985, a law prohibited the demolition of the old building fronts that gave the boulevard a uniform grace. Today, many modern businesses hide behind preserved facades.

The coming of **McDonald's** was a shock to the boulevard. At first, it was allowed only white arches painted on the window. Today, it spills out legally onto the sidewalk—provided it offers café-quality chairs and flower boxes—and dining "chez McDo" has become typically Parisian. A €3 Big Mac here buys an hour of people-watching. (There's a WC nearby.)

The *nouveau* Champs-Elysées, revitalized in 1994, has new

benches and lamps, broader sidewalks, and an army of green-suited workers armed with high-tech pooper-scoopers. Blink away the modern elements, and it's not hard to imagine the boulevard pre-1963, with only the finest structures lining both sides all the way to the palace gardens.

Then come the fancy car dealerships—**Peugeot** at #136 (showing off its futuristic concept cars next to the classic models) and **Mercedes** at #118 (like an English-language car show). In the 19th century, this was an area for horse stables; today, it's the district of garages, limo companies, and car dealerships.

Next to Mercedes is the famous **Lido**, Paris' largest cabaret (and a multiplex cinema). Check out the perky photos, R-rated videos, and shocking prices. Paris still offers the kind of burlesque-type spectacles combining music, comedy, and scantily-clad women performed here since the 19th century. Movie-going on the Champs-Elysées is also popular, with theaters showing the very latest releases. Check to see if there are films you recognize, then look for the showings *(séances)*. A "v.o." *(version originale)* next to the time indicates the film will be in its original language.

Now cross the boulevard. Spend one traffic light cycle at the island mid-stream and enjoy the view. Look up at the Arc de Triomphe, with its rooftop bristling with tourists. Notice the architecture—old and elegant, new, and new-behind-old facades. Then take some time to soak up a bit of the city's fabled **café culture.**

Fouquet's café-restaurant (#99), under the red awning, is a popular spot among French celebrities and charges accordingly (€4.60 for espresso). Opened in 1899 as a coachman's bistro, Fouquet's gained fame as the hangout of France's WWI biplane fighter pilots—those who weren't shot down by Germany's infamous "Red Baron." It also served as James Joyce's dining room. Since the early 1900s, Fouquet's has been a favorite of French actors and actresses. The golden plaques by the entrance honor winners of France's Oscar-like film awards, the Césars—see plaques to Gérard Depardieu, Catherine Deneuve, Roman Polanski, Juliette Binoche, and many famous Americans (but not Jerry Lewis). While the impressive interior is intimidating, the outdoor setting is great. Fouquet's was recently saved from foreign purchase and eventual destruction when the government declared it a historic monument.

Ladurée (a block downhill at #75, with green and purple awning) is a classic 19th-century tea salon/restaurant/*pâtisserie*. Its interior is right out of the 1860s. Wander around...even peeking into the cozy rooms upstairs. A coffee here is *très élégant*. The bakery makes traditional macaroons, cute little cakes, and gift-wrapped finger sandwiches.

Cross back to the lively (north) side of the street. At #92 (a bit uphill), a wall plaque marks the place **Thomas Jefferson** lived (with his 14-year-old slave, Sally Hemings) while minister to France (1785–1789). He'd replaced the popular Benjamin Franklin, but quickly made his own mark, extolling the virtues of America's Revolution to a country approaching its own. A plaque just below marks the spot where a soldier (Robert Birlinger) died fighting the Germans during the liberation of Paris in August 1944.

The nearby **Club Med** (#88), with its travel ads to sunny destinations, is a reminder of the French commitment to the vacation. Since 1936 the French, by law, have enjoyed one month of paid vacation. In the swinging '60s, Club Med made hedonism accessible to the middle-class French masses.

Stroll into the **Arcades des Champs-Elysées** mall at #76. With its fancy lamps, mosaic floors, glass skylight, and classical columns, it captures faint echoes of the *années folles*—the "crazy years," as the roaring '20s were called in France. Architecture buffs can observe how flowery Art Nouveau became simpler, more geometrical Art Deco. Down the street, the **Galerie du Claridge** (at #74) is a fine example of an old facade—with an ironwork awning, balconies, *putti*, and sculpted fantasy faces—fronting a new building.

At #72, glide down **Sephora**'s ramp into a vast hall of cosmetics and perfumes (Mon–Sat 10:00–24:00, Sun 11:00–24:00). Grab a disposable white strip, spritz it with a sample, and sniff. The huge chain's flagship store is thoughtfully laid out: The entry hall is lined with the new products—all open and ready (with sniff strips) to sample. In the main showroom of this scent seller's flagship store, women's fragrances line the left wall and men's line the (shorter) right wall—organized alphabetically by company from Armani to Versace. The store has over 400 samples to help you find the scent of your dreams and assemble a list of products to match. There's a logical progression when sampling perfume scents, starting with fresh, sea, flower, fruit, herb, wood, spicy, amber, and leather. Lemon is freshest. *Civette*—eau de cow pie—is strongest. (I'm not kidding…give it a whiff. Now you can mark your territory.) The bestseller: chocolate. Worst seller? Guess. Grab a basket and follow your nose. The mesmerizing music, chosen just for Sephora, actually made me crave cosmetics. Halfway down on your left in red, flashing numbers show the current prices of perfumes *(cours des parfums)* in cities throughout the world—allowing jet-setters to comparison shop.

Car buffs and Star Trek fans should detour across the Champs and park themselves at the space-age bar in the Renault store (open until midnight with €2.50 espresso). The car exhibits change regularly, but the high-backed leather chairs looking down onto the Champs-Elysées are permanent.

The English **pharmacy** is open until midnight at the corner of rue la Boétie, and map-lovers can detour one block down this street to shop at Espace IGN (Institut Géographique National), France's version of the National Geographic Society (Mon–Fri 9:30–19:00, Sat 11:00–12:30 & 14:00–18:30, closed Sun, tel. 03 80 30 33 67).

A block farther down, the **Virgin Megastore** (#54) sells a world of music. The **Disney**, **Gap**, and **Quicksilver** stores are reminders of global economics—the French seem to love these places as much as Americans do.

At the **Rond-Point** des Champs-Elysées, the shopping ends and the park begins. This round, leafy traffic circle is always colorful, lined with flowers or seasonal decorations (thousands of pumpkins at Halloween, hundreds of decorated trees at Christmas). Your guided walk is over. From here you can go to the closest Métro stop (Franklin D. Roosevelt), or continue for 20 minutes straight down the Champs-Elysées to the place de la Concorde and Tuileries Garden, leading to the Louvre Museum.

DAY TRIPS

Palace of Versailles

Every king's dream, Versailles was the residence of the French king and the cultural heartbeat of Europe for about 100 years—until the Revolution of 1789 ended the notion that God deputized some people to rule for Him on Earth. Louis XIV spent half a year's income of Europe's richest country turning  his dad's hunting lodge into a palace fit for a divine monarch. Louis XV and Louis XVI spent much of the 18th century gilding Louis XIV's lily. In 1837, about 50 years after the royal family was evicted, King Louis Philippe opened the palace as a museum. Europe's next-best palaces are Versailles wannabes.

Cost: There are several different parts of the palace, each with a separate admission. The **State Apartments,** which are the most essential component, costs €7.50 (€5.50 after 15:30, covered by Museum Pass). Guided tours cost extra; see the "Touring Versailles from A to D" sidebar, page 108.

The **gardens** are normally €3 (not covered by Museum Pass), except on summer weekends, when the fountains blast and the price shoots up to €6 (see "Fountain Spectacles," page 112).

Entering the **Grand and Petit Trianon Palaces** costs €5 together (both covered by Museum Pass).

Two types of **all-day Versailles passes** are available for those without a Paris Museum Pass. Unless you plan to visit most of the

Versailles

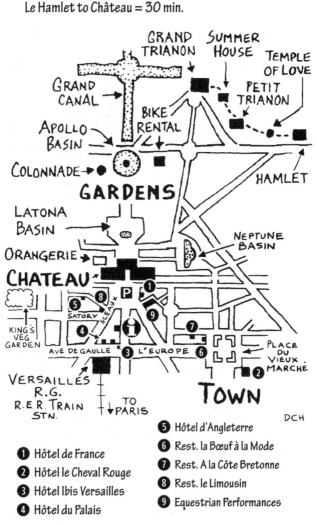

WALKING TIMES
Train Station to Château = 10 min.
Château to Grand Trianon = 30 min.
Grand Trianon to Hamlet = 20 min.
Le Hamlet to Château = 30 min.

GRAND TRIANON
SUMMER HOUSE
TEMPLE OF LOVE
GRAND CANAL
PETIT TRIANON
BIKE RENTAL
APOLLO BASIN
COLONNADE
HAMLET

GARDENS

LATONA BASIN
ORANGERIE
NEPTUNE BASIN
CHATEAU

KING'S VEG. GARDEN
SATORY
AVE DE GAULLE
L'EUROPE
PLACE DU VIEUX MARCHÉ

VERSAILLES R.G. R.E.R. TRAIN STN.
TO PARIS
TOWN

DCH

❶ Hôtel de France
❷ Hôtel le Cheval Rouge
❸ Hôtel Ibis Versailles
❹ Hôtel du Palais
❺ Hôtel d'Angleterre
❻ Rest. la Bœuf à la Mode
❼ Rest. A la Côte Bretonne
❽ Rest. le Limousin
❾ Equestrian Performances

Touring Versailles from A to D

Versailles' highlights are the State Apartments (including the magnificent Hall of Mirrors) and the gardens, dotted with the Trianon Palaces—both covered on our self-guided tour. Versailles aficionados should spend extra time and money to see the lavish King's Private Apartments, the Opera House, and more, which can be visited only with an audioguide or live guide.

Whether you have a Paris Museum Pass or one of the Versailles passes or you've paid admission (€7.50) to enter the palace, you have to pay extra to take a tour. If you pay the €7.50 admission, keep your ticket as proof you've paid for the palace entry, in case you decide to take a guided tour after you've wandered through Versailles by yourself.

Stand in the courtyard to orient yourself to Versailles' entrances:

Entrance A—State Apartments, Self-Guided Tour: If you don't have a Museum Pass and you want to tour the palace on your own (or with a €4 audioguide), join the line at entrance A. Enter the palace and take a one-way walk through the State Apartments from the King's Wing, through the Hall of Mirrors, and out via the Queen's and Nobles' Wing.

Entrance B-2: This entrance is for Museum Pass–holders who want to tour the palace on their own (following the €4 audioguide).

Entrance C—King's Private Apartments: If you lack a Museum Pass, enter here to tour Louis XIV's private bedroom, other rooms, and the Hall of Mirrors, with the help of a dry but informative audioguide (€4).

Entrance C-2: Same as C but for passholders.

Entrance D—Various Guided Tours: You can select a one-hour live tour from a variety of themes, such as the daily life of a king or the lives of such lesser-known nobles as the well-coiffed Madame de Pompadour (€4, join first English tour available). Or consider the 90-minute tour (€6) of the King's Private Apartments (Louis XV, Louis XVI, and Marie-Antoinette) and the chapel. This tour, which is the only way visitors can see the sumptuous Opera House, can be long depending on the quality of your guide.

For a live tour, make reservations immediately upon arrival, as tours can sell out by 13:00 (first tours generally begin at 10:00, last tours depart usually at 15:00 but as late as 16:00).

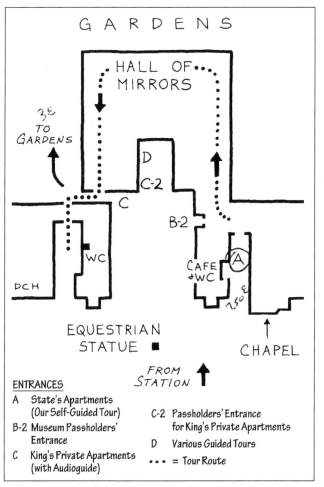

Entrances to Versailles

GARDENS

HALL OF
MIRRORS

TO
GARDENS

D

C-2

C

B-2

WC

CAFE
+WC

Ⓐ

DCH

EQUESTRIAN
STATUE ■

CHAPEL

FROM
STATION

ENTRANCES

A   State's Apartments
     (Our Self-Guided Tour)

B-2 Museum Passholders'
     Entrance

C   King's Private Apartments
     (with Audioguide)

C-2 Passholders' Entrance
     for King's Private Apartments

D   Various Guided Tours

••• = Tour Route

The Gardens: If you want to visit these first, go around the left side of the palace. The spacious gardens stretch for miles behind the palace, featuring landscaped plots, statues, bubbling fountains, a Grand Canal, and several smaller palaces, interesting both outside and in.

sights within Versailles, neither of these passes is worth considering. Of the two, the better value is the **Versailles Pass**, which covers your train fare from Paris and gives you priority access to these entrances: State Apartments, the King's Private Apartments, both Trianon Palaces, the gardens, and Les Grand Eaux Musicales (see "Fountain Spectacles," below; note that these run only on summer weekends). The pass also includes an audioguide (€21, sold at Paris train stations, RER stations that serve Versailles, and FNAC department stores). The **Versailles Passport** covers the same sights and services, except for the train fare from Paris (€20, sold at Versailles TI, listed in "Information," below).

Hours: The **palace** is open May–Sept Tue–Sun 9:00–18:30, Oct–April Tue–Sun 9:00–17:30, closed Mon (last entry 30 min before closing). The **Grand and Petit Trianon Palaces** are open April–Oct Tue–Sun 12:00–18:00, Nov–March Tue–Sun 12:00–17:00, closed Mon. The **gardens** are open daily from 7:00 (8:00 in winter) to sunset (as late as 21:30 or as early as 17:30).

In summer, Versailles is especially crowded around 10:00 and 13:00, and all day Tuesday and Sunday. Remember, the crowds gave Marie-Antoinette a pain in the neck, too, so relax and let them eat cake. For fewer crowds, go early or late: Either arrive by 9:00 (when the palace opens, touring the palace first, then the gardens) or after 15:30 (you'll get a reduced entry ticket but you'll probably miss the last guided tours of the day, which generally depart at 15:00). If you arrive midday, see the gardens first and the palace later, at 15:00. The gardens and palace are great late. On my last visit, at 18:00 I was the only tourist in the Hall of Mirrors...even on a Tuesday.

Information: A helpful TI is just past the Sofitel Hôtel on your walk from the RER station to the palace (see "Getting There," below; April–Sept Tue–Sun 9:00–19:00, Mon 10:00–18:00, Oct–March Tue–Sun 9:00–18:00, Mon 10:00–17:00, tel. 01 39 24 88 88, www.chateauversailles.fr). You'll also find information booths inside the château (at entrances A and B-2) and, during peak season, kiosks scattered around the courtyard. The useful brochure "Versailles Orientation Guide" explains your sightseeing options. A free checkroom is at entrance A.

Palace: To tour the palace on your own, join the line at entrance A if you need to pay admission. Those with a Versailles or Paris Museum Pass are allowed in through entrance B-2 without a wait. Enter the palace and take a one-way walk through the State Apartments from the King's Wing, through the Hall of Mirrors, and out via the Queen's and Nobles' Wing.

The Hall of Mirrors was the ultimate hall of the day—250 feet long, with 17 arched mirrors matching 17 windows with royal garden views, 24 gilded candelabra, eight busts of Roman emperors, and eight classical-style statues (7 are ancient originals). The ceiling is decorated with stories of Louis' triumphs. Imagine this place filled with silk gowns and powdered wigs, lit by thousands of candles. The mirrors—a luxury at the time—were a reflection of an era when aristocrats felt good about their looks and their fortunes. In another age altogether, this was the room in which the Treaty of Versailles was signed, ending World War I.

Before going downstairs at the end, take a stroll clockwise around the long room filled with the great battles of France murals. If you don't have *Rick Steves' Paris* or *Rick Steves' Best European City Walks & Museums* (buy in the United States), the guidebook called *The Châteaux, The Gardens, and Trianon* gives a room-by-room rundown.

Getting Around the Gardens: It's a 30-minute hike from the palace, down to the canal, past the two Trianon palaces to the Hamlet. The fast-looking, slow-moving tram for tired tourists leaves from behind the château (north side) and serves the Grand Canal and the Trianon palaces. You can hop on and off as you like (€5, 4/hr, 4 stops but not the Hamlet, commentary is nearly worthless). A horse carriage also departs from the north side of the palace. Or you can rent bikes near the Grand Canal (1 hr-€6).

Palace Gardens: The gardens offer a world of royal amusements.

Outside the palace is *l'orangerie*. Louis, the only person who could grow oranges in Paris, had a mobile orange grove that could be wheeled in and out of his greenhouses according to the weather. A promenade leads from the palace to the Grand Canal, an artificial lake that, in Louis' day, was a mini-sea with nine ships, including a 32-cannon warship. France's royalty used to float up and down the canal in Venetian gondolas.

While Louis cleverly used palace life at Versailles to "domesticate" his nobility, turning otherwise meddlesome nobles into groveling socialites, all this pomp and ceremony hampered the royal family as well. For an escape from the public life at Versailles, they built more intimate palaces as retreats in their garden. Before the Revolution there was plenty of space to retreat—the grounds were enclosed by a 25-mile-long fence.

The beautifully restored **Grand Trianon Palace** is as sumptuous as the main palace, but much smaller. With its pastel-pink colonnade and more human scale, this is a place you'd like to call home. The nearby **Petit Trianon**, which has a fine neoclassical exterior and an interior that can be skipped, was Marie-Antoinette's favorite residence (see "Cost" and "Hours," above).

You can almost see princesses bobbing gaily in the branches as you walk through the enchanting forest, past the white marble temple of love (1778) to the queen's fake-peasant **Hamlet** (*le Hameau;*

interior not tourable). Palace life really got to Marie-Antoinette. Sort of a back-to-basics queen, she retreated further and further from her blue-blooded reality. Her happiest days were spent at the Hamlet, under a bonnet, tending her perfumed sheep and her manicured gardens in a thatch-happy wonderland.

Fountain Spectacles: Classical music fills the king's backyard, and the garden's fountains are in full squirt, July–Sept on Sat and early April–early Oct on Sun (schedule for both days: 11:00–12:00 & 15:30–17:00 & 17:20–17:30). On these "spray days," the gardens cost €6 (not covered by Paris Museum Pass but covered by Versailles passes, ask for a map of fountains). Louis had his engineers literally reroute a river to fuel these fountains. Even by today's standards, they are impressive. Pick up the helpful brochure of the fountain show ("Les Grandes Eaux Musicales") at any information booth for a guide to the fountains. Also ask about the impressive *Les Fêtes de Nuit* nighttime spectacle (July–mid-Sept some Sat).

Equestrian Performances: The Academie du Spectacle Equestre (Equestrian Performance Academy) has brought the art of horseback riding back to Versailles. You can watch its rigorous training sessions every morning except Mon and Fri (€7, Tue–Thu 9:00–11:30, last entry at 11:00; Sat–Sun 10:00–12:00, last entry at 11:00). On Sat and Sun at 14:00, the same students parade their stuff to music without instructor interruptions (€15, 75 min) across the square from the château, at the stables (Grande Ecurie) next to the Poste. Buy tickets at the stables (not covered by any pass, tel. 01 39 02 07 14, www.acadequestre.fr).

Cafés: The cafeteria and WCs are next to door A. You'll find a sandwich kiosk and a decent restaurant are at the canal in the garden. For more recommendations, see page 162. A handy McDonald's is immediately across from the train station (WC without crowds).

Trip Length: Allow two hours for the palace and two for the gardens. Including two hours to cover your round-trip transit time, it's a six-hour day trip from Paris.

Getting There: Take the **RER-C train** (€6 round-trip, 30 min one-way) from any of these RER stops: Gare d'Austerlitz, St. Michel, Musée d'Orsay, Invalides, Pont de l'Alma, and Champ de Mars. Any train whose name starts with a V (e.g., "Vick") goes to Versailles; don't board other trains. Get off at the last stop (Versailles R.G. or "Rive Gauche"—not Versailles C.H., which is farther from the palace), and exit through the turnstiles by inserting your ticket. To reach the château, turn right out of the train station, then left at the first boulevard. It's a 10-minute walk to the palace.

Your Eurailpass covers this inexpensive trip, but it uses up a valuable "flexi" day. If you really want to use your railpass, consider seeing Versailles on your way into or out of Paris. To get free passage, show your railpass at an SCNF ticket window—for example, at the Invalides or Musée d'Orsay RER stop—and get a *contremarque de passage*. Keep this ticket to exit the system.

When returning to Paris from Versailles, look through the windows past the turnstiles for the departure board. Any train leaving Versailles serves all downtown Paris RER stops on the C line (they're marked on the schedule as stopping at *"toutes les gares jusqu'à Austerlitz,"* meaning "all stations up to Austerlitz").

Taxis for the 30-minute ride between Versailles and Paris cost about €25–30.

To reach Versailles from Paris by **car,** get on the *périphérique* freeway that circles Paris and take the toll-free autoroute A-13 toward Rouen. Follow signs into Versailles, then look for *château* signs and park in the huge pay lot in front of the palace. The drive takes about 30 minutes one-way.

Town of Versailles: After the palace closes and the tourists go, the prosperous, wholesome town of Versailles feels a long way from Paris. The central market thrives on place du Marché on Sunday, Tuesday, and Friday until 13:00 (leaving the RER station, turn right and walk 10 min). Consider the wisdom of picking up or dropping your rental car in Versailles rather than in Paris. In Versailles, the Hertz and Avis offices are at Gare des Chantiers (Versailles C.H., served by Paris' Montparnasse station). Versailles makes a fine home base; see Versailles accommodations and recommended restaurants under "Sleeping" (page 146) and "Eating" (page 162).

Chartres

Chartres and its cathedral make a ▲▲▲ day trip.

In 1194, a terrible fire destroyed the church at Chartres that housed the much-venerated veil of Mary. With almost unbelievably

good fortune, the monks found the veil miraculously preserved in the ashes. Money poured in for the building of a bigger and better cathedral—decorated with 2,000 carved figures and some of France's best stained glass. The cathedral feels too large for the city because it was designed to accommodate huge crowds of pilgrims. One of those pilgrims, an impressed Napoleon, declared after a visit in 1811: "Chartres is no place for an atheist." Auguste Rodin called it the "Acropolis of France." The cathedral's crypt can be visited only with a French tour.

Cost: Church entry free; costs €4.60 and 300 steps to climb north tower (free for kids).

Hours: Church open daily 8:30–19:30. Tower open Mon–Sat 9:30–12:00 & 14:00–17:30, Sun 13:00–18:30; closes at 17:00 daily in

Chartres

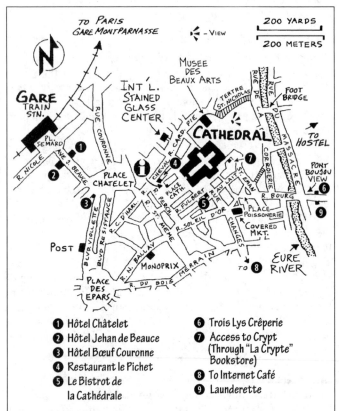

TO PARIS GARE MONTPARNASSE

← - VIEW

200 YARDS

200 METERS

GARE TRAIN STN.

MUSEE DES BEAUX ARTS

INT'L. STAINED GLASS CENTER

CATHEDRAL

FOOT BRIDGE

TO HOSTEL

PONT BOUJOU VIEW

PLACE CHATELET

PLACE POISSONERIE

COVERED MKT.

POST

MONOPRIX

PLACE DES EPARS

EURE RIVER

1. Hôtel Châtelet
2. Hôtel Jehan de Beauce
3. Hôtel Bœuf Couronne
4. Restaurant le Pichet
5. Le Bistrot de la Cathédrale
6. Trois Lys Crêperie
7. Access to Crypt (Through "La Crypte" Bookstore)
8. To Internet Café
9. Launderette

Sept–Oct and at 16:00 Nov–Feb (last entry 30 min before closing, entrance inside church after bookstore on left).

Information: The helpful TI offers a map and audioguide, both featuring a self-guided walking tour of the town of Chartres (April–Sept Mon–Sat 9:00–19:00, Sun 9:30–17:30, Oct–March Mon–Sat 10:00–18:00, Sun 10:00–13:00 & 14:30–16:30, located 100 yards in front of church, tel. 02 37 18 26 26). The church has two bookstores, one inside near the entrance, the other outside near the south porch (church tel. 02 37 21 22 07, www.diocese -chartres.com).

Tours: The fascinating English scholar, Malcolm Miller, moved here nearly 50 years ago, and has made the study this cathedral—and sharing its wonder through his guided walks—his life's work. His 75-minute tours (€10, offered Mon–Sat at 12:00 and 14:45, just show up) are worthwhile, even if you've taken my self-guided tour (below). Tours begin at the bookstore inside the church. He also offers private tours (tel. 02 37 28 15 58, fax 02 37 28 33 03, millerchartres @aol.com). For a detailed look at Chartres' windows, sculpture, and history, pick up Malcolm Miller's two guidebooks (sold at cathedral). The cathedral bookshop rents various **audioguide** tours.

Getting There: Chartres is a one-hour train trip from Paris' Gare Montparnasse (about €12 one-way, 10/day; figure on a round-trip total of 3 hrs from Paris to cathedral doorstep and back).

Sleeping in Chartres: The first two hotels face each other (200 yards straight out of train station, 300 yards below cathedral): **Hôtel Châtelet***** is comfortable, from its welcoming lobby to its spotless, spacious, well-furnished rooms (Sb-€57–71, Db-€63–78, extra person-€10, streetside rooms are cheaper, parking-€6, 6 avenue Jehan de Beauce, tel. 02 37 21 78 00, fax 02 37 36 23 01, www.hotelchatelet .com, hchatel@club-internet.fr). **Hôtel Jehan de Beauce**** is basic, clean, and quiet, with some tiny bathrooms (S-€33, D-€42, Ds-€45, Db-€56, Tb-€64, 19 avenue Jehan de Beauce, tel. 02 37 21 01 41, fax 02 37 21 59 10, jehandebeauce@club-internet.fr). **Hotel Boeuf Couronne**** is warmly run by Madame Vinsot, with 21 clean, simple rooms and a handy location (S-€27, Sb-€40–43, D-€30, Db-€50–57, 15 place Chatelet, tel. 02 37 18 06 06).

Eating in Chartres: **Le Pichet**, run by friendly Marie-Sylvie and Xavier, is reasonable and homey, with good daily specials (*menus* from €11, closed Tue–Wed, 19 rue du Cheval Blanc, near TI, tel. 02 37 21 08 35). **Le Bistrot de la Cathédrale** is fine for salads and basic bistro fare, but you'll pay for the view (*menus* from €15, daily, south side of cathedral at 1 cloître Notre-Dame, tel. 02 37 36 59 60). **Trois Lys Crêperie** makes cheap crêpes just across the river on pont Boujou (closed Mon, Porte Guillaume, tel. 02 37 28 42 02).

Giverny

Claude Monet spent 43 of his most creative years here (1883–1926). His gardens and home, a ▲ sight, are unfortunately split by a busy road and packed with tourists. Buy your ticket, explore the gardens, and take the underpass into Monet's famous lily-pad land. The path leads over the Japanese Bridge, under weeping willows, and past countless scenes that leave artists aching for an easel. Back on the other side, visit his more robust, structured garden and mildly inter-esting home. The jammed gift shop at the exit is Monet's actual skylit studio.

Cost and Hours: €5.50, €4 for gardens only, April–Oct Tue–Sun 9:30–18:00, last entry 17:30, closed Mon except holidays and Nov–March, tel. 02 32 51 28 21. While lines may be long and tour groups may trample the flowers, true fans still find magic in those lily pads. Minimize crowds by arriving by 9:15 (get in line, it opens at 9:30), during lunchtime, or after 16:00.

Nearby Sights: The American Art Museum (Musée d'Art

Paris Day Trips

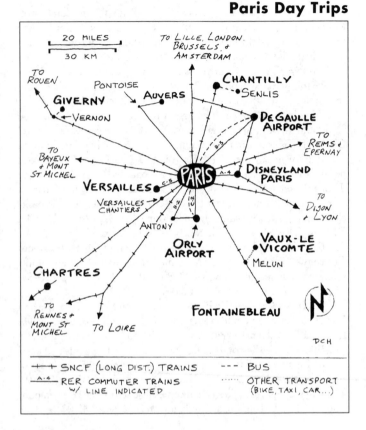

20 MILES
30 KM

TO LILLE, LONDON,
BRUSSELS, &
AMSTERDAM

TO
ROUEN

PONTOISE

GIVERNY
VERNON

AUVERS

CHANTILLY
SENLIS

DE GAULLE
AIRPORT

TO
REIMS &
EPERNAY

TO
BAYEUX
& MONT
ST MICHEL

B·5

PARIS

A·4

DISNEYLAND
PARIS

VERSAILLES
C·5

TO
DIJON
& LYON

VERSAILLES
CHANTIERS

ANTONY

ORLY
AIRPORT

VAUX-LE-
VICOMTE

MELUN

CHARTRES

N

TO
RENNES &
MONT ST
MICHEL

TO LOIRE

FONTAINEBLEAU

DCH

+++ SNCF (LONG DIST.) TRAINS   --- BUS
A·4 RER COMMUTER TRAINS   ...... OTHER TRANSPORT
    W/ LINE INDICATED   (BIKE, TAXI, CAR...)

Américain, turn left when leaving Monet's place and walk 100 yards) is devoted to American artists who followed Claude to Giverny (same price and hours as Monet's home). Monet and his garden had a great influence on American artists of his day. This bright, modern gallery—with a good but small Mary Cassatt section—is well-explained in English, though its most appealing feature might be its garden café (see below).

Getting There: Take the Rouen-bound train from Paris' Gare St. Lazare station to Vernon (about €22 round-trip, long gaps in service, know schedule before you go). From the Vernon train station to Monet's garden (4 miles one-way), you have four good options: by bus, taxi, bike, or on foot.

The Vernon–Giverny **bus** meets every train arriving from Paris for the 15-minute run to Giverny (no buses on Mon) and takes you back to every return train to Paris. If you miss the last bus, find others to share a taxi (see below). The stop to Giverny is in front of Vernon's train station, facing Café du Chemin de Fer (don't dally, the bus leaves soon after your train arrives). The ticket office at Monet's home in Giverny has bus schedules for the return trip. The bus stop for the return trip in the bus parking lot on the opposite side of the main road, by the roundabout. The stop is the first one on your right. Look for the white #18 bus marked "Vernon-Giverny Car."

If you take a **taxi**, allow €11 for up to three, €12 for four (tel. 06 07 34 36 68, tel. 06 76 08 50 78, or tel. 02 32 21 31 31). With buses meeting every train, taxis are unnecessary (unless you miss the bus). Taxis wait in front of station in Vernon.

You can rent a **bike** at Café du Chemin de Fer opposite the train station (€12, tel. 02 32 21 16 01), and follow a paved bike path *(piste cyclable)* that runs from near Vernon along an abandoned railroad right-of-way (figure about 30 min to Giverny). You'll likely get an easy-to-follow map to Giverny with your bike (in case you don't, leave the train station paralleling tracks to your right, take the first left and follow that to the river, cross the river, turn right and meet the bike trail). There's a lovely riverside park on the left side of the bridge after crossing the Seine (where you turn right for the bike path).

You can go on **foot** to Giverny, following the bike instructions above, and take a bus or taxi back.

Big tour companies do a Giverny day trip from Paris for around €60; ask at your hotel.

Sleeping and Eating in Giverny: To sleep two blocks from Monet's home, try the adorable **Hôtel La Musardière**** (Db-€54–72, Tb-€69–82, 132 rue Claude Monet, tel. 02 32 21 03 18, fax 02 32 21 60 00, iraymonde@aol.com). You'll find a café and sandwich stand near the entry to Monet's home, but the garden café at the overlooked American Art Museum is better—peaceful, and surrounded by gardens Monet would appreciate (salads-€9, picnics possible at the far end).

Disneyland Paris

Europe's Disneyland, a ▲▲ sight, is basically a modern remake of California's, with most of the same rides and smiles. The main differences are that Mickey Mouse speaks French, and you can buy wine with your lunch. My kids went ducky. It's easy to get to, and worth a day, if Paris is handier than Florida or California. Saturday, Sunday, Wednesday, public holidays, and any day in July and August are the most crowded. After dinner, crowds are gone.

Food is fun and not outrageously priced. (Still, many smuggle in a picnic.) The free FASTPASS system is a worthwhile timesaver (get

FASTPASS card at entry, good for 5 most popular rides, at ride insert card in machine to get a window of time to enter—often within about 45 min). You'll also save time by buying your tickets ahead (at airport TIs, over 100 Métro stations, or along the Champs-Elysées at the TI, Disney Store, or Virgin Megastore). Disney brochures are in every Paris hotel. For Disneyland information and reservations, call 01 60 30 60 30 (www.disneylandparis.com).

Walt Disney Studios: This zone, which opened in 2002 next to the original 10-year-old amusement park, has a Hollywood focus geared for an older crowd, with animation, special effects, and movie magic "rides." The Aerosmith Rock 'n' Roller Coaster is nothing special. The highlight is the Stunt Show Spectacular, filling a huge back-lot stadium five times a day for 45 minutes of car chases and thriller filming tips. An actual movie sequence is filmed with stunt drivers, audience bit players, and brash MTV-style hosts.

Cost: Disneyland Paris and Walt Disney Studios charge the same. You can pay separately for each or buy a combined ticket for both. A one-day pass to either park is €40 for adults and €30 for kids aged 3–11. For entry to both parks adults pay approximately €49 for one day, €89 for two days and €110 for three days. Kids ages 3–11 pay €39 for one day, €69 for two days and €84 for three days. Regular prices are discounted about 25 percent from November through March and promotions are offered occasionally (check www.disneylandparis.com). Kids under 3 are always free. The only budget deal (and, I think, the only way the Walt Disney Studios are worth visiting) is to pay for a full-price Walt Disney Studios ticket, which gets you into the Disneyland Park for free during the last three hours of that day.

Hours: Both parks are open April–June daily 9:00–20:00, July–Aug daily 9:00–23:00, and Sept–March Mon–Fri 10:00–20:00, Sat–Sun 9:00–20:00.

Sleeping at Disneyland: Most are better off sleeping in reality (Paris), though with direct buses and freeways to both airports, Disneyland makes a convenient first- or last-night stop. Seven different Disney-owned hotels offer accommodations at or near the park in all price ranges. Prices are impossible to pin down as they vary by season and by the "package deal" you choose (deals that include park entry are usually a better value). The cheapest is **Davy Crockett,** but you'll need a car. **Hôtel Santa Fe**** offers the best midrange value, with shuttle service to the park every 12 minutes. The most expensive is **Disneyland Hotel******, right at the park entry, about twice the price of the Santa Fe. To reserve any Disneyland hotel, call 01 60 30 60 30, fax 01 60 30 60 65, or check www.disneylandparis.com. The prices you'll be quoted include entry to the park.

Getting There: By **car,** Disneyland is about 40 minutes east of

Paris on the A-4 autoroute (direction Nancy/Metz, exit #14). Parking is €8 per day at the park.

By **RER,** the slick one-hour trip is the best way to Disneyland from downtown Paris. Take RER line A-4 to Marne-la-Vallée-Chessy (from Charles de Gaulle-Etoile, Auber, Châtelet-Les Halles, or Gare de Lyon stations, about €7.75 each way, hrly, drops you one hour later right in the park). The last train back to Paris leaves shortly after midnight. Be sure to get a ticket that is good on both the RER and Métro; when returning, remember to use your same RER ticket for your Métro connection in Paris.

Both airports have direct shuttle **buses** to Disneyland Paris (€13, daily 8:30–19:45, every 45 min).

TGV **trains** connect Disneyland directly with **Charles de Gaulle airport** (10 min), the **Loire Valley** (1.5 hrs, Tours-St. Pierre des Corps station, 15 min from Amboise), **Avignon** (3 hrs, TGV station), **Lyon** (2 hrs, Part Dieu station), and **Nice** (6 hrs, main station).

SHOPPING

Even staunch anti-shoppers may be tempted to partake in chic Paris. Wandering among the elegant and outrageous boutiques provides a break from the heavy halls of the Louvre, and, if you approach it right, a little cultural enlightenment.

Here are some tips for avoiding *faux pas* and making the most of the experience.

French Etiquette: Before you enter a Parisian store, remember the following points.

- In small stores, always greet the clerk by saying *"Bonjour,"* plus the appropriate title (*Madame, Mademoiselle,* or *Monsieur*). When leaving, say, *"Au revoir, Madame/Mademoiselle/Monsieur."*
- The customer is not always right. In fact, figure the clerk is doing you a favor by waiting on you.
- Except for in department stores, it's not normal for the customer to handle clothing. Ask first.
- Observe French shoppers. Then imitate.

Department Stores: Like cafés, department stores were invented here (surprisingly, not in America). Parisian department stores, monuments to a more relaxed and elegant era, begin with their spectacular perfume sections. Helpful information desks are usually nearby (pick up the handy store floor plan in English). Most stores have a good selection of souvenirs and toys at fair prices and reasonable restaurants; some have great view terraces. Choose from these four great Parisian department stores: Galeries Lafayette (behind old Opéra Garnier, Mo: Opéra), Printemps (next-door to Galeries Lafayette), Bon Marché (Mo: Sèvres-Babylone), and Samaritaine (near pont Neuf, Mo: Pont Neuf).

Boutiques: I enjoy window-shopping, pausing at cafés, and observing the rhythm of neighborhood life. While the shops are more intimate, sales clerks are more formal—mind your manners.

Here are four very different areas to explore:

A stroll from Sèvres-Babylone to St. Sulpice allows you to sample smart, classic clothing boutiques while enjoying one of Paris' prettier neighborhoods—for sustenance along the way, there's La Maison du Chocolat at 19 rue de Sèvres, selling handmade chocolates in exquisitely wrapped boxes.

The ritzy streets connecting place de la Madeleine and place Vendôme form a miracle mile of gourmet food shops, jewelry stores, four-star hotels, perfumeries, and exclusive clothing boutiques. Fauchon, on place de la Madeleine, is a bastion of over-the-top food products, hawking €7,000 bottles of Cognac (who buys this stuff?). Hédiard, at #21, across the square from Fauchon, is an older, more appealing, and accessible gourmet food shop. Next door, La Maison des Truffes sells black mushrooms for about €180 a pound, and white truffles from Italy for €2,500 a pound.

For more eclectic, avant-garde stores, peruse the artsy shops between the Pompidou Center and place des Vosges in the Marais (along rue Ste. Croix de la Bretonnerie and rue des Rosiers).

For a contemporary, more casual, and less frenetic shopping experience, and to see Paris' latest urban renewal project, take the Métro to Bercy Village, a once-thriving wine warehouse district that has been transformed into an outdoor shopping mall (Mo: Cour St. Emilion).

Flea Markets: Paris hosts several sprawling weekend flea markets (*marché aux puces,* mar-shay oh poos; literally translated, since *puce* is French for flea). These oversized garage sales date back to the Middle Ages, when middlemen would sell old, flea-infested clothes and discarded possessions of the wealthy at bargain prices to eager peasants. Today, some travelers find them claustrophobic, crowded, monster versions of those back home, though others find their French diamonds-in-the-rough and return happy.

The Puces St. Ouen (poos sahn-wahn) is the biggest and oldest of them all, with more than 2,000 vendors selling everything from flamingos to faucets (Sat 9:00–18:30, Sun–Mon 10:00–18:30, Mo: Porte de Clingancourt).

Street Markets: Several traffic-free street markets overflow with flowers, produce, fish vendors, and butchers, illustrating how most Parisians shopped before there were supermarkets and department stores. Good market streets include the rue Cler (Mo: Ecole Militaire), rue Montorgueil (Mo: Etienne Marcel), rue Mouffetard (Mo: Cardinal Lemoine or Censier-Daubenton), and rue Daguerre (Mo: Denfert-Rochereau). Browse these markets to collect a classy picnic (open daily except Sun afternoons and Mon, also closed for lunch 13:00–15:00).

Souvenir Shops: Avoid souvenir carts in front of famous monuments. Prices and selection are better in shops and department stores. The riverfront stalls near Notre-Dame sell a variety of used books, magazines, and tourist paraphernalia in the most romantic setting.

Whether you indulge in a new wardrobe, an artsy poster, or just one luscious pastry, you'll find that a shopping excursion provides a priceless slice of Parisian life.

NIGHTLIFE

Paris is brilliant after dark. Save energy from your day's sightseeing and get out at night. Whether it's a concert at Sainte-Chapelle, an

elevator up the Arc de Triomphe, or a late-night café, experience the City of Light when it's lit up. If a **Seine River cruise** sounds appealing, check out "Tours," on page 63.

Pariscope magazine (see "Tourist Information," page 55), offers a complete weekly listing of music, cinema, theater, opera, and other special events. *Paris Voice* newspaper, in English, has a monthly review of Paris entertainment (available at any English-language bookstore, French-American establishments, or the American Church, www.parisvoice.com).

Music

Jazz Clubs: With a lively mix of American, French, and international musicians, Paris has been an internationally acclaimed jazz capital since World War II. You'll pay €10–25 to enter a jazz club (1 drink may be included; if not, expect to pay €5–10 per drink; beer is cheapest). See *Pariscope* magazine under "Musique" for listings, or better, the American Church's *Paris Voice* paper for a good monthly review, or drop by the clubs to check out the calendars posted on their front doors. Music starts after 21:00 in most clubs. Some offer dinner concerts from about 20:30 on. Here are several good bets:

Caveau de la Huchette, a characteristic old jazz club, fills an ancient Latin Quarter cellar with live jazz and frenzied dancing every night (about €10 admission on weekdays, €14 on weekends, €6 drinks, Tue–Sun 21:30–2:30 or later, closed Mon, 5 rue de la Huchette, Mo: St. Michel, recorded info tel. 01 43 26 65 05, www.caveaudelahuchette.fr).

For a hotbed of late-night activity and jazz, go to the two-block-long rue des Lombards, at boulevard Sébastopol, midway between the river and the Pompidou Center (Mo: Châtelet). **Au Duc des Lombards,** right at the corner, is one of the most popular and respected jazz clubs in Paris, with concerts generally at 21:00 (42 rue des Lombards, tel. 01 42 33 22 88). **Le Sunside** offers more traditional jazz—Dixieland and big band—and fewer crowds, with concerts generally at 21:00 (60 rue des Lombards, tel. 01 40 26 21 25).

At the more down-to-earth and mellow **Le Cave du Franc Pinot,** you can enjoy a glass of chardonnay at the main-floor wine bar, then drop downstairs for a cool jazz scene. They have good dinner-and-jazz values as well—allow about €50 per person (closed Sun–Mon, located on Ile St. Louis where pont Marie meets the island, 1 quai de Bourbon, Mo: Pont Marie, tel. 01 46 33 60 64).

Classical Concerts: For classical music on any night, consult *Pariscope* magazine; the "Musique" section under "Concerts Classiques" lists concerts (both free and with fee). Look for posters at tourist-oriented churches. From March through November, these churches regularly host concerts: St. Sulpice, St. Germain-des-Prés, Ste. Madeleine, St. Eustache, St. Julien-le-Pauvre, and Sainte-Chapelle. It's worth the €15–23 entry for the pleasure of hearing Mozart while surrounded by the stained glass of the tiny Sainte-Chapelle (it's unheated—bring a sweater). Look also for daytime concerts in parks, such as the Luxembourg Garden. Even the Galeries Lafayette department store offers concerts. Many concerts are free *(entrée libre),* such as the Sunday atelier concert sponsored by the American Church (Sun 18:00, not every week, Sept–May, 65 quai d'Orsay, Mo: Invalides, RER: Pont de l'Alma, tel. 01 40 62 05 00).

Opera: Paris is home to two well-respected opera venues. The Opéra Bastille is the massive modern opera house that dominates place de la Bastille. Come here for state-of-the-art special effects and modern interpretations of classic ballets and operas. In the spirit of this everyman's opera, unsold seats are available at a big discount to seniors and students 15 minutes before the show (Mo: Bastille, tel. 01 43 43 96 96). The Opéra Garnier, Paris' first opera house, hosts opera and ballet performances. Come here for less expensive tickets and grand belle époque decor (Mo: Opéra, tel. 01 44 73 13 99). For tickets, call 01 44 73 13 00, go to the opera ticket offices (open 11:00–18:00), or best, reserve on the Web at www.opera-de-paris.fr (French only, for both opera houses).

After-Dark Bus Tours

Several companies offer evening tours of Paris. I've described two here. These trips are sold through your hotel (brochures in lobby) or directly at the offices listed below. You save no money by buying direct.

Paris Illumination Tours, run by Paris Vision, connect all the great illuminated sights of Paris with a 100-minute bus tour in 12 languages. The double-decker buses have huge windows, but the most desirable front seats are reserved for customers who've bought tickets for the overrated Moulin Rouge. Left-side seats are marginally better. Visibility is fine in the rain.

You'll stampede on with a United Nations of tourists, get an audioguide, and listen to a tape-recorded spiel, which is interesting but occasionally hard to hear. Uninspired as it is, this provides an entertaining first-night overview of the city at its floodlit and scenic best. Bring your city map to stay oriented as you go. You're always on the bus except for one five-minute cigarette break at the Eiffel Tower viewpoint (adults-€26, kids under 11 ride free, departures 19:00–21:30 depending on time of year, usually April–Oct only, departs from Paris Vision office at 214 rue de Rivoli, across the street from Mo: Tuileries, tel. 01 42 60 30 01, fax 01 42 86 95 36, www.parisvision.com).

Touringscope offers the same kind of bus tour but with live guides (they try to keep the different languages to no more than three). This smaller, "we try harder" company offers better service and if their big buses don't fill up, they'll send you in a more personal minivan (buses depart from 11 boulevard Haussmann, Mo: Opéra or Chausée d'Antin-La Fayette, tel. 01 53 34 11 94, www.touringscope.com).

SLEEPING

I've focused most of my recommendations on three safe, handy, and colorful neighborhoods: the village-like rue Cler (near the Eiffel Tower), the artsy and trendy Marais (near place de la Bastille), and the lively and Latin yet classy Luxembourg (on the Left Bank). Before reserving, read the descriptions of the three neighborhoods closely. Each offers different pros and cons, and your neighborhood is as important as your hotel for the success of your trip.

Reserve ahead for Paris—the sooner the better. Conventions clog Paris in September (worst), October, May, and June (very tough). In August, when Paris is quiet, some hotels offer lower rates to fill their rooms (if you're planning to visit Paris in the summer, the extra expense of an air-conditioned room can be money well spent). For advice on booking rooms, see "Making Reservations" in this book's introduction.

Old, characteristic, budget Parisian hotels have always been cramped. Retrofitted with elevators, toilets, and private showers (as most are today), they are even more cramped. Even three-star hotel rooms are small and often not worth the extra expense in Paris. Some hotels include the hotel tax (*taxe du séjour*, about €1 per person per day), though most will add this to your bill.

Recommended hotels have an elevator unless otherwise noted. Quad rooms usually have two double beds. Because rooms with double beds and showers are cheaper than rooms with twin beds and baths, room prices vary within each hotel.

Continental breakfasts run about €6–9, buffet breakfasts (baked goods, cereal, yogurt, and fruit) cost about €8–14. Café or picnic

Sleep Code

(€1 = about $1.20, country code: 33)
S = Single, **D** = Double/Twin, **T** = Triple, **Q** = Quad,
b = bathroom, **s** = shower only, **no CC** = Credit Cards not accepted, ***** = French hotel rating system (0-4 stars). For more information on the rating system, see "Sleeping" in this book's Introduction. Hotels with two or more stars are required to have an English-speaking staff. Nearly all hotels listed here will have someone who speaks English. You can assume a hotel takes credit cards unless you see "no CC" in the listing.

To help you sort easily through these listings, I've divided the rooms into three categories based on the price for a standard double room with bath:

$$$ **Higher Priced**—Most rooms €150 or more.
 $$ **Moderately Priced**—Most rooms between €100–150.
  $ **Lower Priced**—Most rooms €100 or less.

breakfasts are cheaper, but hotels usually give unlimited coffee.

Get advice from your hotel for safe parking (consider long-term parking at either airport—Orly is closer—and a taxi in). Garages are plentiful (€20–25/day, with special rates through some hotels). Meters are free in August. Self-serve launderettes are common; ask your hotelier for the nearest one (*"Où est un laverie automatique?"*, ooh ay uh lah-vay-ree auto-mah-teek).

Rue Cler

Rue Cler is a safe, tidy, village-like pedestrian street. It's so French that when I step out of my hotel in the morning, I feel like I must have been a poodle in a previous life. How such coziness lodged itself between the high-powered government district and the wealthy Eiffel Tower and Invalides areas, I'll never know. This is a neighborhood of wide, tree-lined boulevards, stately apartment buildings, and lots of Americans. The American Church, American Library, American University, and many of my readers call this area home.

Become a local at a rue Cler café for breakfast or join the afternoon crowd for *une bière pression* (a draft beer). On rue Cler, you can eat and browse your way through a street full of pastry shops, delis, cheese shops, and colorful outdoor produce stalls. Afternoon *boules* (lawn bowling) on the Esplanade des Invalides is a relaxing spectator sport (look for the dirt area to the upper right as you face Les Invalides). The manicured gardens behind the

The Rules of *Boules*

Throughout Paris—and particularly on Les Invalides' big "front lawn" near the rue Cler neighborhood—you'll see citizens playing *boules*.

Each player starts with three iron balls, with the object of getting them close to the target, a small wooden ball called a *cochonnet*. The first player tosses the *cochonnet* about 30 feet, then throws the first of his iron balls near the target. The next player takes a turn. As soon as a player's ball is closest, it's the other guy's turn. Once all balls have been thrown, the score is tallied—the player with the closest ball gets one point for each ball closer to the target than his opponent's. The loser gets zero. Games are generally to 15 points.

A regulation *boules* field is 10-by-43 feet, but the game is played everywhere—just scratch a throwing circle in the sand, toss the *cochonnet*, and you're off. Strategists can try to knock the opponent's balls out of position, knock the *cochonnet* itself out of position, or guard their best ball with the other two.

golden dome of Les Invalides are free, peaceful, and filled with flowers (at southwest corner of grounds, close at about 19:00). Take an evening stroll above the river through the parkway between pont de l'Alma and pont des Invalides.

For an after-dinner cruise on the Seine, it's a 15-minute walk to the river and the Bateaux-Mouches (see page 66). For a post-dinner cruise on foot, saunter into Champ de Mars park to admire the glowing Eiffel Tower.

Cross the Champ de Mars park to mix it up with bargain-hunters at the twice-weekly open-air market, **Marché Boulevard de Grenelle,** under the Métro a few blocks southwest of Champ de Mars park (Wed and Sun until 12:30, between Mo: Dupleix and Mo: La Motte-Picquet-Grenelle). The Epicerie de la Tour **grocery** is open until midnight (197 rue de Grenelle). Rue St. Dominique is the area's boutique-browsing street. **Cyber World Café** is at 20 rue de l'Exposition (open daily 12:00–22:00, Sun until 20:00, tel. 01 53 59 96 54).

Your neighborhood **TI** is at the Eiffel Tower (May–Sept daily 11:00–18:42, closed Oct–April, all-Paris TI tel. 08 36 68 31 12). There's a **post office** at the end of rue Cler on avenue de la Motte-Picquet, and a handy **SNCF train office** at 78 rue St. Dominique (Mon–Fri 9:00–19:00, Sat 10:00–12:30 & 14:00–18:00, closed Sun).

The **American Church and Franco-American Center** is the community center for Americans living in Paris, and should be one of your first stops if you're planning to stay awhile (reception open Mon–Sat 9:00–22:00, Sun 9:00–19:30, 65 quai d'Orsay,

Rue Cler Hotels

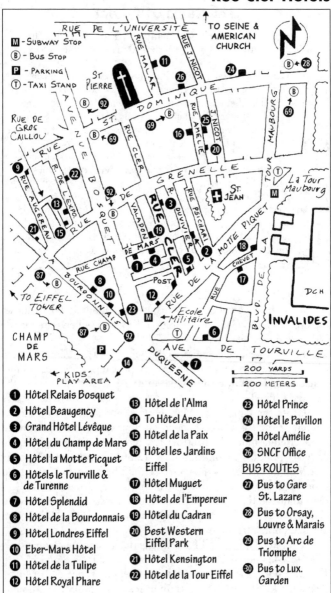

M – SUBWAY STOP
B – BUS STOP
P – PARKING
T – TAXI STAND

1 Hôtel Relais Bosquet
2 Hôtel Beaugency
3 Grand Hôtel Lévêque
4 Hôtel du Champ de Mars
5 Hôtel la Motte Picquet
6 Hôtels le Tourville & de Turenne
7 Hôtel Splendid
8 Hôtel de la Bourdonnais
9 Hôtel Londres Eiffel
10 Eber-Mars Hôtel
11 Hôtel de la Tulipe
12 Hôtel Royal Phare

13 Hôtel de l'Alma
14 To Hôtel Ares
15 Hôtel de la Paix
16 Hôtel les Jardins Eiffel
17 Hôtel Muguet
18 Hôtel de l'Empereur
19 Hôtel du Cadran
20 Best Western Eiffel Park
21 Hôtel Kensington
22 Hôtel de la Tour Eiffel

23 Hôtel Prince
24 Hôtel le Pavillon
25 Hôtel Amélie
26 SNCF Office

BUS ROUTES
27 Bus to Gare St. Lazare
28 Bus to Orsay, Louvre & Marais
29 Bus to Arc de Triomphe
30 Bus to Lux. Garden

tel. 01 40 62 05 00). Pick up a copy of *Paris Voice* for a monthly review of Paris entertainment, and *France–U.S.A. Contacts* for information on housing and employment through the community of 30,000 Americans living in Paris. The interdenominational services at 11:00 on Sunday, the coffee hour after church, and the free Sunday concerts (Sept–May 18:00, not every week) are a great way to make some friends and get a taste of émigré life in Paris.

Key **Métro** stops are Ecole Militaire, La Tour-Maubourg, and Invalides. The **RER-C** line runs from the Pont de l'Alma and Invalides stations, serving Versailles to the west; Auvers-sur-Oise to the north; and the Orsay Museum, Latin Quarter (St. Michel stop), and Austerlitz train station to the east.

Smart travelers take advantage of these helpful **bus routes** (see Rue Cler Hotels map, previous page, for stop locations): Line #69 runs along rue St. Dominique and serves Les Invalides, Orsay, Louvre, Marais, and Père Lachaise Cemetery. Line #63 runs along the river (the quai d'Orsay), serving the Latin Quarter along boulevard St. Germain to the east, and Trocadéro and the Marmottan Museum to the west. Line #92 runs along avenue Bosquet north to the Champs-Elysées and Arc de Triomphe (far better than the Métro) and south to the Montparnasse Tower. Line #87 runs on avenue de la Bourdonnais and serves St. Sulpice, Luxembourg Garden, and the Sèvres-Babylone shopping area (also more convenient than Métro for these destinations). Line #28 runs on boulevard de la Tour-Maubourg and serves Gare St. Lazare.

Sleeping in the Rue Cler Neighborhood

(7th *arrondissement*, Mo: Ecole Militaire or La Tour-Maubourg)
Rue Cler is the glue that holds this handsome neighborhood together. From here you can walk to the Eiffel Tower, Napoleon's Tomb, the Seine River, and the Orsay and Rodin museums. Hotels here are relatively spacious and a good value, considering the elegance of the neighborhood and the higher prices of the more cramped hotels in other central areas.

Many of my readers stay in this neighborhood. If you want to disappear into Paris, choose a hotel away from the rue Cler, or in the other neighborhoods I list. And if nightlife matters, sleep elsewhere. The first five hotels listed below are within Camembert-smelling distance of rue Cler; the others are within a 5- to 10-minute stroll.

The Heart of Rue Cler

$$$ Hôtel Relais Bosquet* is modern, spacious, and a bit upscale, with snazzy, air-conditioned rooms, electric darkness blinds, and big beds. Gerard and his staff are politely formal and friendly (standard Db-€150, spacious Db-€170, Sb- €20 less, ask about occasional promotional rates, extra bed-€20, parking-€14, 19 rue du Champ de Mars, tel. 01 47 05 25 45, fax 01 45 55 08 24, www.relaisbosquet .com, hotel@relaisbosquet.com).

$$$ **Hôtel la Motte Picquet***, at the end of rue Cler, is an elaborately decorated, plush place with 18 adorable and spendy rooms. Most face a busy street but the twins are on the quieter side (Sb-€115–125, standard Db-€130, bigger Db with air-con-€165, 30 avenue de la Motte-Picquet, tel. 01 47 05 09 57, fax 01 47 05 74 36, www.paris-hotel-mottepicquet.com, book@hotelmottepicquetparis .com).

$$ **Hôtel Beaugency***, on a quieter street a short block off rue Cler, has 30 small, cookie-cutter rooms, a helpful staff, and a lobby you can stretch out in (Sb-€106, Db-€125, Tb-€145, air-con, 21 rue Duvivier, tel. 01 47 05 01 63, fax 01 45 51 04 96, www.hotel -beaugency.com, infos@hotel-beaugency.com).

Warning: The next two hotels listed here are busy with my readers (reserve long in advance).

$ **Grand Hôtel Lévêque** is ideally located, with a helpful staff (Christophe and female Pascale SE), a singing maid, and a Starship *Enterprise* elevator. The simple but well-designed rooms have all the comforts, including air-conditioning and ceiling fans (S-€57, Db-€87–110, Tb-€125 for 2 adults and 1 child only, breakfast-€8, first breakfast free for readers of this book, 29 rue Cler, tel. 01 47 05 49 15, fax 01 45 50 49 36, www.hotel-leveque.com, info@hotel -leveque.com).

$ **Hôtel du Champ de Mars**, with charming pastel rooms and helpful English-speaking owners Françoise and Stephane, is a homier rue Cler option. This plush little hotel has a Provence-style, small-town feel from top to bottom. Rooms are small, but comfortable and an excellent value. Single rooms can work as tiny doubles (Sb-€70, Db-€76–85, Tb-€98, 30 yards off rue Cler at 7 rue du Champ de Mars, tel. 01 45 51 52 30, fax 01 45 51 64 36, www.hotel -du-champ-de-mars.com, stg@club-internet.fr).

Near Rue Cler, Close to Ecole Militaire Métro

The following listings are a 5- to 10-minute walk from rue Cler, near Métro stop Ecole Militaire or RER stop Pont de l'Alma.

$$$ **Hôtel le Tourville****** is the most classy and expensive of my rue Cler listings. This four-star place is surprisingly intimate, from its designer lobby and vaulted breakfast area to its pretty but small pastel rooms (small standard Db-€165, superior Db-€215, Db with private terrace-€240, junior suite for 3-4 people-€310–330, air-con, 16 avenue de Tourville, tel. 01 47 05 62 62, fax 01 47 05 43 90, www.hoteltourville.com, hotel@tourville.com).

$$$ **Hôtel de la Bourdonnais***** is a *très* Parisian place, mixing Old World elegance with professional service, comfortable public

spaces, and mostly spacious, traditionally decorated rooms (avoid the few *petite* rooms, Sb-€125, Db-€155, Tb-€175, Qb-€195, 5-person suite-€210, air-con, Internet access, 111 avenue de la Bourdonnais, tel. 01 47 05 45 42, fax 01 45 55 75 54, www.hotellabourdonnais.fr, otbourd@club-internet.fr).

$$ Hôtel Prince, across avenue Bosquet from the Ecole Militaire Métro stop, has good-enough rooms, air-conditioning, and reasonable rates (Sb-€76, Db-€90–120, Tb-€130, 66 avenue Bosquet, tel. 01 47 05 40 90, fax 01 47 53 06 62, www.hotel-paris-prince.com).

$ Eber-Mars Hôtel, on a busy street with oak-paneled public spaces, is a good midrange value with larger-than-average rooms and a beam-me-up-Jacques coffin-sized elevator (standard Db-€80, large Db-€95–115, Tb-€140, Qb-€160, pricey €10 breakfast, 117 avenue de la Bourdonnais, tel. 01 47 05 42 30, fax 01 47 05 45 91, www .hotelebermars.com, reservation@hotelebermars.com).

$ Hôtel Royal Phare is a simple place facing the busy Ecole Militaire Métro stop with a "we try harder" staff. The 34 rooms are unimaginative with pink-pastel decor; those on the courtyard are quietest (Sb-€68, Db-€72–82, Tb-€105, 40 avenue de la Motte-Picquet, tel. 01 47 05 57 30, fax 01 45 51 64 41, www.hotel-royalphare -paris.com, royalphare-hotel@wanadoo.fr).

$ Hôtel de Turenne, is a basic, well-located place with the cheapest air-conditioned rooms I found. While the rooms could use some work, the price is right. There are five truly single rooms and several connecting rooms good for families (Sb-€63, Db-€72–85, Tb-€100, extra bed-€10, 20 avenue de Tourville, tel. 01 47 05 99 92, fax 01 45 56 06 04, hotel.turenne.paris7@wanadoo.fr).

Near Rue Cler, Closer to Rue St. Dominique (and the Seine)

$$ Hôtel Londres Eiffel* is my closest listing to the Eiffel Tower and Champ de Mars park. It offers immaculate, warmly decorated rooms, cozy public spaces, Internet access, and air-conditioning. The helpful staff takes good care of their guests. It's less convenient to the Métro (10-min walk); handy bus #69 and the RER stop Pont de l'Alma are better options (Sb-€99–105, Db-€110–145, deluxe Db-€175, Tb-€165–195, extra bed-€20, 1 rue Augerau, tel. 01 45 51 63 02, fax 01 47 05 28 96, www.londres-eiffel.com, info@londres -eiffel.com).

$$ Hôtel de la Tulipe* is a unique place three blocks from rue Cler toward the river, with friendly Bernhard behind the desk. The smallish but artistically decorated rooms—each one different—come with little, stylish bathrooms and surround a seductive wood-beamed lounge and a peaceful, leafy courtyard (Db-€110–140, Tb-€180, 2-room suite-€250, no elevator, no air-con, 33 rue Malar, tel. 01 45 51 67 21, fax 01 47 53 96 37, www.paris-hotel-tulipe.com).

$ **Hôtel de l'Alma**** is a basic place but well-located on "restaurant row," with cheery rooms, small bathrooms, a *petite* courtyard, and reasonable rates (Sb-€85, Db-€95, includes breakfast, 32 rue de l'Exposition, tel. 01 47 05 45 70, fax 01 45 51 84 47, www.alma -paris-hotel.com, Carine SE).

Near Métro: La Tour-Maubourg

The next three listings are within two blocks of the intersection of avenue de la Motte-Picquet and boulevard de la Tour-Maubourg.

$$$ **Hôtel les Jardins Eiffel*****, on a quiet street, feels like a modern motel, but earns its three stars with professional service, its own parking garage, a spacious lobby, and 80 comfortable (if unimaginative), air-conditioned rooms—some with private balconies (ask for a room *avec petit balcon*). Even better: Readers of this book get free buffet breakfasts (Sb-€100–136, Db-€115–165, extra bed-€25–35 or free for a child, parking-€20/day, Internet access, 8 rue Amélie, tel. 01 47 05 46 21, fax 01 45 55 28 08, www.hoteljardinseiffel.com, paris@hoteljardinseiffel.com).

$$ **Hôtel Muguet****, a peaceful, stylish, and immaculate refuge, gives you three-star comfort for a two-star price. This delightful place offers 48 tasteful, air-conditioned rooms, a greenhouse lounge, and a small garden courtyard. The hands-on owner, Catherine, gives her guests a restful and secure home in Paris (Sb-€90, Db-€100–108, Tb-€140, 11 rue Chevert, tel. 01 47 05 05 93, fax 01 45 50 25 37, www.hotelmuguet.com, muguet@wanadoo.fr).

$ **Hôtel de l'Empereur**** lacks intimacy but is roomy and a fair value. Its 38 pleasant rooms come with real wood furniture, and all the comforts except air-conditioning. Streetside rooms have views but some noise; fifth-floor rooms have small balconies and Napoleonic views (Sb-€70–80, Db-€80–100, Tb-€120, Qb-€140, 2 rue Chevert, tel. 01 45 55 88 02, fax 01 45 51 88 54, www.hotelempereur.com, contact@hotelempereur.com).

The Other Side of Champ de Mars Park

To stay in a peaceful neighborhood with many qualities of the rue Cler area (in the 7th *arrondissement*), cross Champ de Mars park and enter the 15th *arrondissement*. While it's a 10- to 15-minute walk to rue Cler, you get more space for your money and fewer fellow Americans.

$$ **Hôtel Ares***** is handsome and situated on a quiet street a block toward the river from avenue de le Motte-Picquet. It has a classy lobby with elbow room, and pastel-soft rooms you can stretch out in (Sb-€115, Db-€135, Tb-€170, Qb-€200, between avenue de Suffren and boulevard de Grenelle—not to be confused with rue de Grenelle that crosses rue Cler, from the Métro follow rue d'Ouessant one block and turn right, 7 rue du Général de Larminat,

Mo: La Motte-Picquet–Grenelle, tel. 01 47 34 74 04, fax 01 47 34 48 56, www.paris-hotel-ares.com, aresotel@easynet.fr).

Lesser Values in the Rue Cler Area

Given this fine area, these are acceptable last choices.

$$$ Hôtel du Cadran***, while perfectly located, has a nice lobby but little charm in its tight and narrow rooms (Db-€152–170, air-con, 10 rue du Champ de Mars, tel. 01 40 62 67 00, fax 01 40 62 67 13, www.hotelducadran.com).

$$$ Hôtel Splendid*** is Art Deco modern, professional, and worth your while if you land one of its three suites with great Eiffel Tower views. Sixth-floor rooms have small terraces and sideways tower views, all rooms seem pricey and need sprucing up. Ask about their occasional promotional rates (Db-€134–165, Db with balcony and view-€180, Db suite-€200–230, 29 avenue de Tourville, tel. 01 45 51 24 77, fax 01 44 18 94 60, www.hotels-exclusive.com/hotels/splendid, splendid@club-internet.fr).

$$$ Best Western Eiffel Park***, is a dead-quiet, concrete business hotel with all the comforts, a friendly staff, 36 pleasant if unexceptional rooms, and a nifty and spacious rooftop terrace (Db-€135–185, occasional promotional rates, 17 bis rue Amélie, tel. 01 45 55 10 01, fax 01 47 05 28, 68, www.eiffelpark.com, reservation @eiffelpark.com).

$$ Hôtel Amélie**, in a skinny building, is a midrange possibility with no lobby, no elevator, and shabby halls but decent rooms (Db-€95–105, 5 rue Amélie, tel. 01 45 51 74 75, fax 01 45 56 93 55, www.hotelamelie.com, hotelamelie@wanadoo.fr).

$ Hôtel Kensington** has miniscule rooms and little personality, but is a fair value (Sb-€55, Db-€70–86, 79 avenue de la Bourdonnais, tel. 01 47 05 74 00, fax 01 47 05 25 81, www.hotel-kensington.com, hk@hotel-kensington.com).

$ Hôtel de la Tour Eiffel** is a modest little place with fairly priced rooms, but cheap furnishings and foam mattresses (Sb-€70, Db-€85, Tb-€105, 17 rue de l'Exposition, tel. 01 47 05 14 75, fax 01 47 53 99 46, hte7@wanadoo.fr).

$ Hôtel de la Paix **, located away from the fray on a quiet street, is a reasonable value but is poorly managed and asks for full payment up front (Sb-€68, Db-€98–110, Tb-€120, good breakfast, 19 rue du Gros-Caillou, tel. 01 45 51 86 17, fax 01 45 55 93 28, hotel.de.la.paix@wanadoo.fr).

$ Hôtel le Pavillon** is quiet, with basic rooms, no elevator, and cramped halls in a charming location (Sb-€80, Db-€90; Tb, Qb, or Quint/b-€135; 54 rue St. Dominique, tel. 01 45 51 42 87, fax 01 45 51 32 79, PatrickPavillon@aol.com).

Marais

Those interested in a more Soho/Greenwich Village locale should make the Marais their Parisian home. Only 15 years ago, it was a forgotten Parisian backwater, but now the Marais is one of Paris' most popular residential, tourist, and shopping areas. This is jumbled, medieval Paris at its finest, where classy stone mansions sit alongside trendy bars, antique shops, and fashion-conscious boutiques. The streets are a fascinating parade of artists, students, tourists, immigrants, and babies in strollers munching baguettes. The Marais is also known as a hub of the Parisian gay and lesbian scene. This area is *sans doute* livelier (and louder) than the rue Cler area.

In the Marais, you have these sights close at hand: Picasso Museum, Carnavalet Museum, Victor Hugo's House, Jewish Art and History Museum, and the Pompidou Center. You're also a manageable walk from Paris' two islands (Ile St. Louis and Ile de la Cité), home to Notre-Dame and the Sainte-Chapelle. The Opéra Bastille, Promenade Plantée park, place des Vosges (Paris' oldest square), Jewish Quarter (rue des Rosiers), and nightlife-packed rue de Lappe are also walkable. (Sight descriptions are listed in "Sights," page 78.)

The Marais has two good **open-air markets**: the sprawling Marché de la Bastille on place de la Bastille (Thu and Sun until 12:30) and the more intimate, very local Marché de la place d'Aligre (daily 9:00–12:00, a few blocks behind Opéra on place d'Aligre). Two little **grocery shops** are open until 23:00 on rue St. Antoine (near intersection with rue Castex).

The nearest **TI**s are in the Louvre (Wed–Mon 10:00–19:00, closed Tue) and Gare de Lyon (Mon–Sat 8:00–20:00, all-Paris TI tel. 08 36 68 31 12). Most banks and other services are on the main drag, rue de Rivoli, which becomes rue St. Antoine. For your Parisian Sears, find the **BHV** next to the Hôtel de Ville. Marais **post offices** are on rue Castex and on the corner of rue Pavée and rue des Francs Bourgeois. A rare **Internet café**, @aron, is at 3 rue des Ecouffes (tel. 01 42 71 05 07). The Marais is home to the friendliest English-language bookstore in Paris, Red Wheelbarrow Bookstore, with two stores (main store at 22 rue St. Paul, daily 10:00–19:00, Sun open at 14:00; children's bookstore at 13 rue Charles V, open Wed–Sun 10:00–19:00, closed Mon–Tue). These kind folks sell most of my books.

Métro service to the Marais neighborhood is excellent, with direct service to the Louvre, Champs-Elysées, Arc de Triomphe, La Défense (all on line 1), rue Cler area (line 8 from Bastille stop) and four major train stations: Gare de Lyon, Gare du Nord, Gare de l'Est, and Gare d'Austerlitz. Key Métro stops in the Marais are, from east to west: Bastille, St. Paul, and Hôtel de Ville (Sully-Morland, Pont Marie, and Rambuteau stops are also handy). There are also several helpful **bus routes**: Line #69 on rue St. Antoine takes you to the Louvre, Orsay, and Rodin museums, plus Napoleon's Tomb, and ends at the Eiffel Tower. Line #86 runs down boulevard Henri IV, crossing Ile St. Louis and serving the Latin Quarter along boulevard St. Germain. Line #87 follows a similar route but extends to the Eiffel Tower and rue Cler neighborhood. Line #96 runs on rues Turenne and François Miron and serves the Louvre and boulevard St. Germain (near Luxembourg Garden), ending at the Gare Montparnasse. Line #65 gets you to the Gare d'Austerlitz, Gare de l'Est, and Gare du Nord train stations from place de la Bastille.

You'll find **taxi stands** on place de la Bastille, on the north side of rue St. Antoine (where it meets rue Castex), and on the south side of rue St. Antoine (in front of St. Paul church).

Sleeping in the Marais Neighborhood
(4th *arrondissement*)
The Marais runs from the Pompidou Center to the Bastille (a 15-min walk), with most hotels located a few blocks north of the main east-west drag, the rue de Rivoli/rue St. Antoine. It's about 15 minutes on foot from any hotel in this area to Notre-Dame, Ile St. Louis, and the Latin Quarter. Strolling home (day or night) from Notre-Dame along the Ile St. Louis is marvelous.

$$ Hôtel des Chevaliers***, a pretty little boutique hotel one block northwest of place des Vosges, offers small, pleasant rooms with modern comforts, including air-conditioning. Eight of its 24 rooms are off the street and quiet—worth requesting (Sb-€125–135, Db-€140–150, 30 rue de Turenne, Mo: St. Paul, tel. 01 42 72 73 47, fax 01 42 72 54 10, info@hoteldeschevaliers.com).

$$ Hôtel Castex***, well-situated on a quiet street near the place de la Bastille, feels Spanish from the formal entry to the red-tiled floors and dark wood accents. A clever system of connecting rooms allows families total privacy between two rooms, each with its own bathroom. Rooms are narrow but tasteful and air-conditioned, and the elevator is big by Parisian standards. Your fourth night is free in August and from November through February—except around New Year's Eve (Sb-€95–115, Db-€120–140, Tb-€190–220, good €10 buffet breakfast is free through 2005 for readers of this book, just off place de la Bastille and rue St. Antoine, 5 rue Castex, Mo: Bastille, tel. 01 42 72 31 52, fax 01 42 72 57 91, www.castexhotel.com, info@castexhotel.com).

$$ Hôtel Bastille Spéria***, a short block off the place de la Bastille, offers business-type service. The 42 well-configured rooms are modern and comfortable with big beds and air-conditioning.

Walls are thin and the elevator operates at glacial speed but it's English-language-friendly, from the *International Herald Tribune*s in the lobby to the history of the Bastille posted in the elevator (Sb-€100, Db-€125–140, child's bed-€20, excellent buffet breakfast-€12.50, 1 rue de la Bastille, Mo: Bastille, tel. 01 42 72 04 01, fax 01 42 72 56 38, www.hotel-bastille-speria.com, info@hotel-bastille -speria.com).

$$ Hôtel St. Louis Marais** is a tiny, welcoming place, lost on a quiet residential street between the river and rue St. Antoine. The lobby is inviting and the 20 rooms are cozy but not air-conditioned (small Sb-€59, standard Sb-€91, small Db-€107, standard Db-€125, Tb-€140, no elevator but only three floors, ask about newer street-level annex rooms, bargain-priced parking-€12, 1 rue Charles V, Mo: Sully Morland, tel. 01 48 87 87 04, fax 01 48 87 33 26, www.saintlouismarais.com, slmarais@noos.fr).

$ Hôtel de 7ème Art**, two blocks south of rue St. Antoine toward the river, is a relaxed, Hollywood-nostalgia place, run by hip, friendly, young people, with a full-service café-bar and Charlie Chaplin murals. Its 23 rooms lack imagination, but are comfortable and a fair value. The large rooms are American-spacious (small Db-€80, standard Db-€90–105, large Db-€115–140, extra bed-€20, 20 rue St. Paul, Mo: St. Paul, tel. 01 44 54 85 00, fax 01 42 77 69 10).

$ Grand Hôtel Jeanne d'Arc**, a well-tended hotel with thoughtfully appointed rooms, is ideally located for (and very popular with) connoisseurs of the Marais. Rooms on the street can be noisy until the bars close. Sixth-floor rooms have a view, and corner rooms are wonderfully bright in the City of Light, though no rooms are air-conditioned. Reserve this place way ahead (Sb-€57–70, Db-€80, larger twin Db-€95, Tb-€113, good Qb-€130, 3 rue de Jarente, Mo: St. Paul, tel. 01 48 87 62 11, fax 01 48 87 37 31, www .hoteljeannedarc.com, information@hoteljeannedarc.com).

$ Hôtel Lyon-Mulhouse**, with half of its 40 pleasant rooms on a busy street off place de la Bastille, is a fair value. Its bigger, quieter rooms at the back are worth the extra euros (Sb-€65, Db-€70–75, twin Db-€85–90, Tb-€100, Qb-€120, no air-con, 8 boulevard Beaumarchais, Mo: Bastille, tel. 01 47 00 91 50, fax 01 47 00 06 31, hotelyonmulhouse@wanadoo.fr).

$ Hôtel Sévigné**, is a sharp little air-conditioned place with lavender halls, tidy, comfortable rooms at very fair prices, and an owner of few words (Sb-€64, Db-€74–86, Tb-€100, 2 rue Malher, Mo: St. Paul, tel. 01 42 72 76 17, fax 01 42 78 68 26, www.le -sevigne.com, contact@le-sevigne.com).

$ Hôtel Pointe Rivoli*, across from the St. Paul Métro stop, is a jumbled, treehouse of rooms in the thick of the Marais, with Paris' steepest stairs (no elevator) and modest rooms at reasonable rates (Sb-€70, Db-€80, Tb-€115, air-con promised for 2005 so rates may

Marais Hotels

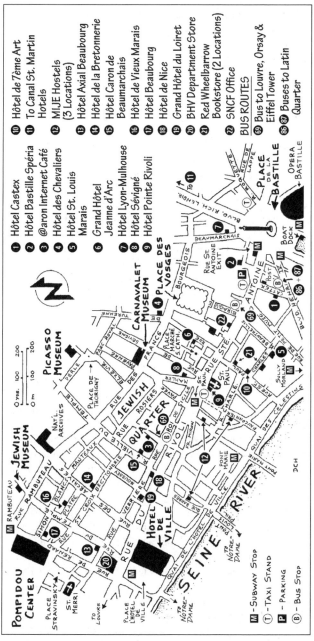

① Hôtel Castex
② Hôtel Bastille Spéria
③ @aron Internet Café
④ Hôtel des Chevaliers
⑤ Hôtel St. Louis Marais
⑥ Grand Hôtel Jeanne d'Arc
⑦ Hôtel Lyon-Mulhouse
⑧ Hôtel Sévigné
⑨ Hôtel Pointe Rivoli
⑩ Hôtel de 7ème Art
⑪ To Canal St. Martin Hotels
⑫ MIJE Hostels (3 Locations)
⑬ Hôtel Axial Beaubourg
⑭ Hôtel de la Bretonnerie
⑮ Hôtel Caron de Beaumarchais
⑯ Hôtel de Vieux Marais
⑰ Hôtel Beaubourg
⑱ Hôtel de Nice
⑲ Grand Hôtel du Loiret
⑳ BHV Department Store
㉑ Red Wheelbarrow Bookstore (2 Locations)
㉒ SNCF Office

BUS ROUTES
⑥⑨ Bus to Louvre, Orsay & Eiffel Tower
⑧⑥⑧⑦ Buses to Latin Quarter

Ⓜ – SUBWAY STOP
Ⓣ – TAXI STAND
🄿 – PARKING
Ⓑ – BUS STOP

increase, 125 rue St. Antoine, Mo: St. Paul, tel. 01 42 72 14 23, fax 01 42 72 51 11, pointerivoli@libertysurf.fr).

$ MIJE Youth Hostels: The Maison Internationale de la Jeunesse et des Etudiants (MIJE) runs three classy old residences, clustered a few blocks south of rue St. Antoine. Each is well-maintained with simple, clean, single-sex, one- to four-bed rooms for travelers of any age. None has an elevator or double beds, each has Internet access, and all rooms have showers. You can stay seven days maximum and prices given are per person and favor single travelers (2 people can find a double in a very simple hotel for similar rates). You can pay more to have your own room, or pay less and room with as many as three others (Sb-€43, Db-€33, Tb-€30, Qb-€28, no CC, includes breakfast but not towels, which you can get from a machine for €9; required membership card-€2.50 extra/person; rooms locked 12:00–15:00 and at 1:00). The hostels are: **MIJE Fourcy** (€11 dinners available to anyone with a membership card, 6 rue de Fourcy, just south of rue de Rivoli), **MIJE Fauconnier** (11 rue du Fauconnier), and the best, **MIJE Maubisson** (12 rue des Barres). They all share the same contact information (tel. 01 42 74 23 45, fax 01 40 27 81 64, www.mije.com) and Métro stop (St. Paul). Reservations are accepted, though you must arrive by noon or call the morning of arrival to confirm a later time.

Near the Pompidou Center

These hotels are farther west and closer to the Pompidou Center than to place de la Bastille. Métro stop Hôtel de Ville works well for all of these hotels, unless a closer stop is noted.

$$$ Hôtel Axial Beaubourg*,** a block from Hôtel de Ville toward the Pompidou Center, has a minimalist lobby and 28 pricey but plush rooms, many with wood beams. If you cancel with less than seven days' notice, you'll lose your one-night deposit (standard Db-€165, big Db-€200, air-con, 11 rue du Temple, tel. 01 42 72 72 22, fax 02 42 72 03 53, www.axialbeaubourg.com, infos @axialbeaubourg.com).

$$$ Hôtel Caron de Beaumarchais*** feels like a folk museum, with its 20 sweet little rooms and a lobby cluttered with bits from an elegant 18th-century Marais house. Short antique collectors love this place (small back-side Db-€145, larger Db on the front-€160, air-con, Internet access, 12 rue Vieille du Temple, tel. 01 42 72 34 12, fax 01 42 72 34 63, www.carondebeaumarchais.com, hotel @carondebeaumarchais.com).

$$$ Hôtel de la Bretonnerie*,** three blocks from the Hôtel de Ville, makes a fine Marais home. It has an on-the-ball staff, a big, welcoming lobby, elegant decor, and tastefully-appointed rooms with an antique, open-beam warmth (perfectly good standard "classic" Db-€110, bigger "charming" Db-€145, Db suite-€180, Tb-€170,

Tb suite-€205, Qb suite-€245, between rue Vieille du Temple and rue des Archives at 22 rue Ste. Croix de la Bretonnerie, tel. 01 48 87 77 63, fax 01 42 77 26 78, www.bretonnerie.com, hotel@bretonnerie .com, Francoise SE).

$$ Hôtel de Vieux Marais**** is tucked away on a quiet street two blocks east of the Pompidou Center and charges top euro in high season for its efficient rooms (Db-€115, €145 March-mid July, extra bed-€24, air-con, just off rue des Archives at 8 rue du Plâtre, Mo: Rambuteau or Hôtel de Ville, tel. 01 42 78 47 22, fax 01 42 78 34 32, www.vieuxmarais.com, hotel@vieuxmarais.com).

$$ Hôtel Beaubourg***** is a good three-star value on a quiet street in the shadow of the Pompidou Center. Its 28 rooms are wood-beam comfy and air-conditioned, and the inviting lounge is warm and pleasant (Db-€125–148, twins are considerably larger than doubles, includes breakfast, 11 rue Simon Le Franc, Mo: Rambuteau, tel. 01 42 74 34 24, fax 01 42 78 68 11, www.hotelbeaubourg.com, htlbeaubourg @hotellerie.net).

$$ Hôtel de Nice**,** on the Marais' busy main drag, is a turquoise-and-rose, "Marie-Antoinette does tie-dye" place. Its narrow halls are littered with paintings and covered with carpets, and its 23 non-air-conditioned rooms are filled with thoughtful touches and include tight bathrooms. Twin rooms, which cost the same as doubles, are larger and on the street side—but have effective double-paned windows (Sb-€74, Db-€105, Tb-€128, Qb-€140, extra bed-€20, 42 bis rue de Rivoli, tel. 01 42 78 55 29, fax 01 42 78 36 07, www.hoteldenice.com, contact@hoteldenice.com).

$ Grand Hôtel du Loiret**** is centrally-located, spartan, and basic, though the rooms are better than you might think (S-€48, Sb-€65, Db-€64–84, Tb-€95, 8 rue des Mauvais Garçons, tel. 01 48 87 77 00, fax 01 48 04 96 56, hotelduloiret@hotmail.com).

Near the Marais, on Ile St. Louis

The peaceful, residential character of this river-wrapped island, its brilliant location, and its homemade ice cream have drawn Americans for decades, allowing hotels to charge dearly for their rooms. There are no budget values here, but the island's coziness and proximity to the Marais, Notre-Dame, and the Latin Quarter compensate for higher rates. The hotels listed below are shown on the map on page 71. All are on the island's main drag, the rue St. Louis-en-l'Ile, where I list several restaurants (see page 158). Use Mo: Pont Marie or Sully-Morland.

$$$ Hôtel du Jeu de Paume****,** located in a 17th-century tennis center, is the most expensive hotel I list in Paris. When you enter its magnificent lobby, you'll understand why. Greet Scoop, the hotel dog, then ride the glass elevator for a half-timbered-treehouse experience, and marvel at the cozy lounges. The 30 quite comfortable rooms are carefully designed and *très* tasteful, though small for the price (you're paying for the location and public spaces). Most face a small garden and all are pin-drop peaceful (Sb-€160, standard Db-€225, larger Db-€240–270, deluxe Db-€295, Db suite-€480, 54 rue St. Louis-en-l'Ile, tel. 01 43 26 14 18, fax 01 40 46 02 76, www.jeudepaumehotel.com).

The following two hotels are owned by the same person. For both, if you must cancel, do so a week in advance or pay fees:

$$$ **Hôtel de Lutèce*** is the better, cozier value on the island, with a sit-a-while wood-paneled lobby, a fireplace, and warmly designed air-conditioned rooms. Twin rooms are larger and the same price as double rooms (Db-€162, Tb-€180, 65 rue St. Louis-en-l'Ile, tel. 01 43 26 23 52, fax 01 43 29 60 25, www.hotel-ile-saintlouis.com, lutece@hotel-ile-saintlouis.com).

$$$ **Hôtel des Deux Iles*** is brighter and more colorful with marginally smaller rooms (Db-€162, 59 rue St. Louis-en-l'Ile, tel. 01 43 26 13 35, fax 01 43 29 60 25, 2isles@hotel-ile-saintlouis.com).

Luxembourg

This neighborhood revolves around Paris' loveliest park and adds quick access to the city's best shopping streets and grandest café-hopping. Sleeping in the Luxembourg area is a true Left Bank experience. The Luxembourg Garden, boulevard St. Germain, Cluny Museum, and Latin Quarter are all within easy walking distance. Here you get the best of both worlds: youthful Left Bank energy and the classy trappings that surround the monumental Panthéon and St. Sulpice church.

Having the Luxembourg Garden at your back door allows strolls through meticulously-cared-for flowers, a great kids' play area, and a purifying escape from city traffic. Place St. Sulpice offers an elegant, pedestrian-friendly square and some of Paris' best boutiques. Sleeping in the Luxembourg area also puts several movie theaters at your fingertips (at Odéon Métro stop), as well as  lively cafés on the boulevard St. Germain, rue de Buci, place de la Sorbonne and place de la Contrescarpe, all of which buzz with action until late.

Admire the Panthéon and Sorbonne University from the outside, observe Daniel Roth play the magnificent organ at St. Sulpice church (see page 90), and peek inside the beautiful St. Etienne-du-Mont church. The colorful **street market** at the south end of rue Mouffetard is a worthwhile 10–15 minute walk down from these hotels (Tue–Sat 8:00–12:00 & 15:30–19:00, Sun 8:00–12:00, closed Mon, 5 blocks south of place de la Contrescarpe, Mo: Place Monge). The nearest **TI** is at the Louvre. Handy **Internet service** is between the Luxembourg Garden and Panthéon at 17 rue Soufflot (XS Arena, always open). The **Village Voice** bookstore carries a full selection of English-language books (including mine) and is near St. Sulpice (6 rue Princesse, tel. 01 46 33 36 47).

Métro lines #10 and #4 serve this area. Key stops are Cluny-La Sorbonne, Mabillon, Odéon and St. Sulpice. RER line B provides direct service to Charles de Gaulle airport and Gare du Nord trains from the Luxembourg station. Buses #63, #86, and #87 run eastbound through this area on boulevard St. Germain and westbound along rue des Ecoles, stopping on place St. Sulpice. Lines #63 and #87 provide a direct connection to the rue Cler area; Line #63 serves the Orsay, Invalides, Rodin and Marmottan museums. Lines #86 and #87 run to the Marais.

Sleeping in the Luxembourg Neighborhood

While it takes only 15 minutes to walk from one end of this neighborhood to the other, I've located the hotels by the key monument they are close to (St. Sulpice Church, the Odeon Theater, and the Panthéon). No hotel is farther than a 5-minute walk from the Luxembourg Garden.

Hotels Near St. Sulpice Church

(6th *arrondissement*)

These hotels are all within a block of St. Sulpice, and two blocks from the famous boulevard St. Germain. This is nirvana for boutique-minded shoppers. Métro stops St. Sulpice and Mabillon are equally close. See the map on page 141.

$$$ Hôtel Relais St. Sulpice***, on the small street just behind St. Sulpice church, feels like a cozy bar with a melt-in-your-chair lounge and 26 beautifully designed, air-conditioned rooms, most of which surround a leafy glass atrium. The dazzling breakfast room sits below the atrium near the sauna (Db-€170–180–195–210 depending on size, most Db-€170–180, beefy buffet breakfast-€12, 3 rue Garancière, tel. 01 46 33 99 00, fax 01 46 33 00 10, www.relais-saint-sulpice.com, relaisstsulpice@wanadoo.fr).

$$$ Hôtel la Perle*** is a pricey pearl in the thick of the lively rue des Canettes a block off place St. Sulpice. At this snappy, modern hotel, glass doors slide onto the traffic-free street, and a fun lobby built around a central bar and atrium greets you. Rooms are plush, air-conditioned, and wood-beamed (standard Db-€173, bigger Db-€195, luxury Db-€235, 14 rue des Canettes, tel. 01 43 29 10 10, fax 01 43 34 51 04, www.hotellaperle.com, booking @hotellaperle.com).

$$ Hôtel Bonaparte** sits between boutiques, a few steps from place St. Sulpice, on the smart rue Bonaparte. While the 29 air-conditioned rooms don't live up to the handsome entry, they are homey, comfortable, and generally spacious with big bathrooms, molded ceilings, and clashing bedspreads (Sb-€92–138, Db-€120, big Db-€154, Tb-€158, 61 rue Bonaparte, tel. 01 43 26 97 37, fax 01 46 33 57 67).

$$ **Hôtel le Récamier**** feels like grandma's house, tucked in the corner of place St. Sulpice. Flowery wallpaper, dark halls, and spotless, just-what-you-need rooms (with no TV!)—some with views of the square—make this a good, if somewhat pricey Paris refuge. How such a low-key place escaped the trendy style of other hotels in this chic area, I'll never know (S-€97, Sb-€110, D-€104, Db-€124–144, Tb-€176, Qb-€218, includes breakfast, 3 bis place St. Sulpice, tel. 01 43 26 04 89, fax 01 46 33 27 73, e-mail address? You need a computer first).

Near the Odéon Theater

These hotels are between the Odéon Métro stop and Luxembourg Garden (5 blocks east of St. Sulpice) and may have rooms when others don't. In addition to the Odéon Métro, the RER line B Luxembourg stop is a short walk away.

$$ **Hôtel Michelet Odéon**** sits shyly in a corner of place de l'Odéon, a block from the Luxembourg Garden. Most of the spacious, simple rooms have views and all have creaky floors (Db-€95–115, Tb-€135, Qb-€150, 6 place de l'Odéon, tel. 01 53 10 05 60, fax 01 46 34 55 35, www.hotelmicheletodeon.com, hotel @micheletodeon.com).

$$ **Grand Hôtel des Balcons**** has an inviting lobby and spick-and-span rooms with interesting colors and generous space. Some rooms have narrow balconies (Db-€100–120, big Db-€150, big Tb-€180, a block below the Odéon theater, 3 Casimir-Delavigne, tel. 01 46 34 78 50, fax 01 46 34 06 27, www.balcons .com, resa@balcons.com).

$$ **Hôtel Delavigne***** has a warm lobby and appealing rooms (Db-€115–130, Tb-€130–145, tel. 01 43 29 31 50, fax 01 43 29 78 56, 1 rue Casimir-Delavigne, www.hoteldelavigne.com, resa @hoteldelavigne.com).

Near the Panthéon

Use Métro: Cluny-La Sorbonne or RER-B: Luxembourg for the first five hotels listed. The first two wannabe-four-star hotels face the Panthéon's right transept and are owned by the same family (ask about their promotional rates, which may be available anytime, even during some summer weeks). The rates are high and the rooms aren't big, but the quality is tops.

$$$ **Hôtel du Panthéon***** welcomes you with a wood-beamed, cozy lobby and 32 country-French-cute rooms with air-conditioning and every possible comfort. Fifth-floor rooms have sliver balconies, but sixth-floor rooms have the best views (Sb/Db-€175–215–240,

Hotels and Restaurants near St. Sulpice and the Odéon Theatre

❶ Hôtel Relais St. Sulpice
❷ Hôtel la Perle
❸ Hôtel Bonaparte
❹ Hôtel le Récamier
❺ Hôtel Michelet Odéon
❻ Grand Hôtel des Balcons & Hôtel Delavigne
❼ Au Bon Saint-Pourcain
❽ Chez Diane
❾ Brasserie Fernand
❿ La Crêpe Rit du Clown
⓫ Chez Georges
⓬ Le Café de Flore & Les Deux Magots
⓭ Café Bonaparte
⓮ Café le Procope

Hotels and Restaurants near the Pantheon

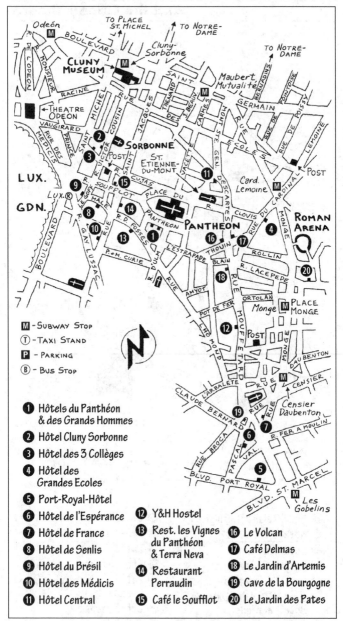

M – Subway Stop
T – Taxi Stand
P – Parking
B – Bus Stop

1. Hôtels du Panthéon & des Grands Hommes
2. Hôtel Cluny Sorbonne
3. Hôtel des 3 Collèges
4. Hôtel des Grandes Ecoles
5. Port-Royal-Hôtel
6. Hôtel de l'Espérance
7. Hôtel de France
8. Hôtel de Senlis
9. Hôtel du Brésil
10. Hôtel des Médicis
11. Hôtel Central
12. Y&H Hostel
13. Rest. les Vignes du Panthéon & Terra Neva
14. Restaurant Perraudin
15. Café le Soufflot
16. Le Volcan
17. Café Delmas
18. Le Jardin d'Artemis
19. Cave de la Bourgogne
20. Le Jardin des Pates

Tb-€200–225–244, price varies by season, highest price is for peak weeks, check Web site for specials, 19 place du Panthéon, tel. 01 43 54 32 95, fax 01 43 26 64 65, www.hoteldupantheon.com, hoteldupantheon@wanadoo.fr).

$$$ Hôtel des Grands Hommes*** was built to look good—and it does. The lobby is to be admired but not enjoyed, and the 31 rooms reflect an interior designer's dream. Rooms are generally tight but adorable, with great attention to detail and little expense spared. Fifth- and sixth-floor rooms have balconies; sixth-floor balconies, with grand views, are big enough to use. For more luxury, splurge for a suite (Sb/Db-€175–215–240, Db suite-€250–390, price varies by season and week, check Web site for deals, air-con, 17 place du Panthéon, tel. 01 46 34 19 60, fax 01 43 26 67 32, www.hoteldesgrandshommes .com, reservation@hoteldesgrandshommes.com).

$$ Hôtel des Grandes Ecoles*** is idyllic. A short alley leads to three buildings protecting a flower-filled garden courtyard, preserving a sense of tranquility that is rare in a city this size. Its 51 rooms are reasonably spacious and comfortable, many with large beds. This romantic place is deservedly popular, so call well in advance, though reservations are not accepted more than four months ahead (Db-€110–120, a few bigger rooms-€135, extra bed-€20, parking-€30, 75 rue du Cardinal Lemoine, Mo: Cardinal Lemoine, tel. 01 43 26 79 23, fax 01 43 25 28 15, www.hotel -grandes-ecoles.com, hotel.grandes.ecoles@wanadoo.fr, mellow Marie speaks some English, Maman does not).

$$ Hôtel des 3 Collèges** is a welcoming, well-run place with charm (Db-€90, bigger Db-€114–134, Tb-€150, 16 rue Cujas, tel. 01 43 54 67 30, fax 01 46 34 02 99, www.3colleges.com, hotel @3colleges.com).

$ Hôtel Cluny Sorbonne** is smartly managed, a good deal, and conveniently located across from the famous university, just below the Panthéon. Rooms are clean and comfortable with wood furnishings (standard Db-€85, big Db-€100, really big Db-€140, 8 rue Victor Cousin, tel. 01 43 54 66 66, fax 01 43 29 68 07, www.hotel-cluny.fr, cluny@club-internet.fr).

$ Hôtel de Senlis** is a fair deal, hiding quietly below the Panthéon, with modest rooms, carpeted walls, and metal closets. Most rooms have beamed ceilings, and all rooms could use a decorator with taste (Sb-€69, Db-€74–88, Tb-€95, Qb-€110, 7 rue Malebranche, Mo: Cluny-La Sorbonne, tel. 01 43 29 93 10, fax 01 43 29 00 24, www.hoteldesenlis.fr, hoteldesenlis@wanadoo.fr).

$ Hôtel du Brésil**, one block from Luxembourg Garden, has little character and some smoky rooms but reasonable rates, making it an acceptable choice. New family rooms are planned for 2005 (Sb-€68, Db-€74–85, 10 rue le Goff, RER-B: Luxembourg, tel. 01 43 54 76 11, fax 01 46 33 45 78, www.hoteldubresil.fr, hoteldubresil@wanadoo.fr).

$ Hôtel des Médicis is as cheap, stripped-down, and basic as it gets, with a soiled linoleum charm, a happy owner, and a great location. Request Jim Morrison's old room, if you dare (S-€16, D-€31–35, 214 rue St. Jacques, Mo: Cluny La Sorbonne or RER-B Luxembourg, tel. 01 43 54 14 66, hotelmedicis@aol.com, Denis SE).

$ Hôtel Central*, wedged between two cafés, has a smoky, dingy reception, a steep, slippery stairway, so-so beds, and basic-but-cheery-if-somewhat-mildewed rooms. To an optimist, this hotel defines unpretentiousness; to a pessimist, it's a dive with a charming location. Either way, it's cheap. All rooms have showers, but toilets are down the hall (Ss-€32–37, Ds-€45–50, no CC, no elevator, 6 rue Descartes, Mo: Cardinal Lemoine, tel. 01 46 33 57 93, sweet Pilar NSE).

$ Y&H Hostel is easygoing and English-speaking, with Internet access, kitchen facilities, and basic but acceptable hostel conditions (beds in 4-bed rooms-€23, beds in double rooms-€26, includes breakfast, sheets-€2.50, no CC, rooms closed 11:00–16:00 but reception stays open, 2:00 curfew, reservations require deposit, 80 rue Mouffetard, Mo: Place Monge, tel. 01 47 07 47 07, fax 01 47 07 22 24, www.youngandhappy.fr, smile@youngandhappy.fr).

At the Bottom of Rue Mouffetard

These places are away from the Seine and other tourists, in an appealing work-a-day area. They require a longer walk or Métro ride to sights but often have rooms when other places are booked up. The rue Mouffetard is the bohemian soul of this area, running south from its heart, place de la Contrescarpe, to rue de Bazeilles. Two thousand years ago it was the principal Roman road south to Italy. Today, this small, meandering street has a split personality. The lower half thrives in the daytime as a pedestrian shopping street. The upper half sleeps during the day but comes alive after dark, teeming with bars, restaurants, and nightlife. Use Métro stops Censier-Daubenton or Les Gobelins.

$ Port-Royal-Hôtel* has only one star, but don't let that fool you. This 46-room place is polished bottom to top and has been well-run by the same proud family for 67 years. You could eat off the floors of its spotless, comfy rooms. Ask for a room away from the street (S-€39–51, D-€51, big hall showers-€2.50, Db-€75, Tb-€89, no CC, requires cash deposit, climb stairs from rue Pascal to busy boulevard de Port-Royal, 8 boulevard de Port-Royal, Mo: Les Gobelins, tel. 01 43 31 70 06, fax 01 43 31 33 67, www.portroyalhotel.fr.st).

$ Hôtel de l'Espérance** is a solid two-star value. It's quiet, pink, fluffy, and comfortable, with thoughtfully appointed rooms, complete with canopy beds and a flamboyant owner (Sb-€70, Db-€78–86, 15 rue Pascal, Mo: Censier-Daubenton, tel. 01 47 07 10 99, fax 01 43 37 56 19, hotel.esperance@wanadoo.fr).

$ Hôtel de France** is set on a busy street, with adequately comfortable rooms, fair prices, and a charming owner, Madame Margo. The best and quietest rooms are *sur le cour* (on the courtyard), though streetside rooms are okay (Sb-€66, Db-€76–85, 108 rue Monge, Mo: Censier Daubenton, tel. 01 47 07 19 04, fax 01 43 36 62 34, hotel.de.fce@wanadoo.fr).

Sleeping Elsewhere in Paris

Near Notre-Dame

$ Hôtel Esmeralda*, built in 1640, is a creaky, musty, no-level-surface, no-straight-lines kind of place with 19 faded rooms. Step into a time tunnel and experience the Paris of starving artists (D-€35, Db-€65–85, Tb-€110, Qb-€120, top floor rooms have Notre-Dame views at no added cost, 4 rue St. Julien le Pauvre, Mo: St. Michel, tel. 01 43 54 19 20, fax 01 40 51 00 68).

Near Canal St. Martin

This is one of Paris' up-and-coming neighborhoods, just north of the Marais between place de la République and Canal St. Martin. The canal is the central feature of this unpretentious area, with pleasing walkways, arching footbridges and occasional boats plying its water. When the weather agrees, the entire neighborhood seems to descend on the canal in late afternoon, filling the cafés, parks, and benches. This neighborhood is convenient to the Gares du Nord and de l'Est (about 15 min on foot) and to the terrific Buttes-Chaumont park. There are no tourist sights around (except the canal). This area is the least touristy of those I list and its hotels are cheaper. For restaurant suggestions, see page 161. For nighttime fun, head over to rue Oberkampf and join the crowd. Use Métro République for these hotels.

$ Hôtel de la République**, a block toward the canal from the place de la République, is a well-run, welcoming place run by gentle Miguel. Rooms are sufficiently comfortable, with good natural light, showers instead of baths, and small balconies on the fifth floor (Sb-€50–61, Db-€60–71, Tb-€70–81, included buffet breakfast with this book, near place de la République, 31 rue Albert Thomas, tel. 01 42 39 19 03, fax 01 42 39 22 66, www.republiquehotel.com).

$ Hôtel Ibis**, barely off the place de la République toward the canal, is a good if less personal value, with air-conditioning and well-kept, white, bright rooms (Db-€79, Fri–Sun Db-€69, extra person-€10, 9 rue Léon Jouhaux, tel. 01 42 40 40 50, fax 01 42 40 11 12, h075@accor-hotels.com).

$ Budget Hôtel/Hostel Beauséjour is part two-star hotel, part four-beds-per-room hostel (also called the "Absolute Paris"). It's in the thick of this lively area, facing the canal, and filled with younger travelers. The rooms are industrial-strength clean and adequately comfortable (€22 each in 4-bed room with private bathroom, Db-€75, Tb-€90, includes breakfast, 1 rue de la Fontaine du Roi, tel. 01 47 00 47 00, fax 01 47 00 47 02, www.absolute-paris.com).

For Longer Stays

Staying a week or longer? Consider the advantages that come with renting a furnished apartment. Complete with a small, equipped kitchen and living room, this option is great for families. Among the many English-speaking organizations ready to help, the following have proven most reliable. Their Web sites are generally excellent and essential to understanding your options.

Paris Appartements Services rents studios and one-bedroom apartments in the Opéra, Louvre, and Marais neighborhoods (2 rue d'Argout, tel. 01 40 28 01 28, fax 01 40 28 92 01, www.paris -appartements-services.fr).

BridgeStreet Paris (formerly known as Apalachee Bay) is British-owned and offers an extensive range of carefully selected, furnished apartments (21 rue de Madrid, tel. 01 42 94 13 13, fax 01 42 94 83 01, www.bridgestreet.com).

Locaflat offers accommodations ranging from studios to five-room apartments (63 avenue de la Motte-Picquet, tel. 01 43 06 78 79, fax 01 40 56 99 69, www.locaflat.com).

Lodgis has studios from €400 per week and €900 euros per month (16 rue de la Folie Méricourt, tel. 01 48 07 11 06, www .lodgis.com).

Capitale Partners has studios to five-bedroom apartments (23 rue de la Boétie, Mo: St. Philippe du Roule, tel. 01 42 68 35 60, fax 01 42 68 35 61, www.capitalepartners.com).

Versailles

For a laid-back alternative to Paris within easy reach of the big city by RER train (5/hr, 30 min), Versailles, with easy, safe parking and reasonably priced hotels, can be a good overnight stop. Park in the château's main lot while looking for a hotel, or leave your car there overnight (free, 19:30–8:00). Get a map of Versailles at your hotel or at the TI.

Hôtel de France*, in an 18th-century townhouse, offers four-star value, with air-conditioned, appropriately royal rooms, a pleas-ant courtyard, comfy public spaces, a bar, and a restaurant (Db-€145, Tb-€180, Qb-€240, just off parking lot across from château, 5 rue Colbert, tel. 01 30 83 92 23, fax 01 30 83 92 24, www.hotelfrance -versailles.com, hotel-de-france-versailles@wanadoo.fr).

Hôtel le Cheval Rouge*, built in 1676 as Louis XIV's stables, now houses tourists. It's a block behind the place du Marché in a quaint corner of town on a large, quiet courtyard with free parking and sufficiently comfortable rooms (Sb-€66, Db-€70–85, Tb-€100,

Qb-€106, 18 rue André Chénier, tel. 01 39 50 03 03, fax 01 39 50 61 27, www.chevalrouge.fr.st, chevalrouge@club-internet.fr).

Hôtel Ibis Versailles** offers modern comfort, but no air-conditioning (Db-€72–82 weekday, cheaper weekend rates can't be reserved ahead, across from RER station, 4 avenue du Général de Gaulle, tel. 01 39 53 03 30, fax 01 39 50 06 31).

Hôtel du Palais, facing the RER station, has clean, sharp rooms—the cheapest I list in this area. Ask for a quiet room off the street (Db-€56, extra person-€11, piles of stairs, 6 place Lyautey, tel. 01 39 50 39 29, fax 01 39 50 80 41, hotelpalais@ifrance.com).

Hôtel d'Angleterre**, away from the frenzy, is a tranquil old place with smiling, Polish-born Madame Kutyla in control. Rooms are comfortable and spacious. Park nearby in the château lot (Db-€68–90, price rises with size of room, extra bed-€15, just below palace to the right as you exit, 2 rue de Fontenay, tel. 01 39 51 43 50, fax 01 39 51 45 63, hotel.angleterre.versailles@wanadoo.fr).

EATING

Paris is France's wine and cuisine melting pot. While it lacks a style of its own (only French onion soup is truly Parisian), it draws from the best of France. Paris could hold a gourmet Olympics and import nothing.

Picnic or go to bakeries for quick take-out lunches, or stop at a café for a lunch salad or *plat du jour,* but linger longer over dinner. Cafés are happy to serve a *plat du jour* (garnished plate of the day, about €10–16) or a chef-like salad (about €9) day or night, while restaurants expect you to enjoy a full dinner. Restaurants open for

dinner around 19:00, and small local favorites get crowded after 21:00. Most of the restaurants listed below accept credit cards.

To save piles of euros, review the budget eating tips in this book's introduction and consider dinner picnics (great take-out dishes available at charcuteries). My recommendations are centered around the same three great neighborhoods for which I list accommodations (above); you can come home exhausted after a busy day of sightseeing and have a good

selection of restaurants right around the corner. And evening is a fine time to explore any of these delightful neighborhoods, even if you're sleeping elsewhere.

Restaurants
If you are traveling outside of Paris, save your splurges for the countryside, where you'll enjoy regional cooking for less money. Many

---

Price Code

To help you choose among these listings, I've divided the restaurants into three categories, based on the price per person for a typical meal without wine.

    $$$ **Higher Priced**—Most meals €30 or more.
    $$ **Moderately Priced**—Most meals between €20–30.
    $ **Lower Priced**—Most meals under €20.

Parisian department stores have huge supermarkets hiding in the basement and top-floor cafeterias that offer affordable, low-risk, low-stress, what-you-see-is-what-you-get meals. The three neighborhoods highlighted in this book for sleeping in Paris are also pleasant areas to window-shop for just the right restaurant, as is the Ile St. Louis. Most restaurants we've listed in these areas have set-price *menus* between €15 and €30. In most cases, the few extra euros you pay are well-spent, and open up a variety of better choices. You decide.

Good Picnic Spots: For great people-watching, try the Pompidou Center (by the *Homage to Stravinsky* fountains), the elegant place des Vosges (closes at dusk), the gardens at the Rodin Museum, and Luxembourg Garden. The Palais Royal (across the street from the Louvre) is a good spot for a peaceful, royal picnic.

For a romantic picnic place, try the pedestrian bridge (pont des Arts) across from the Louvre, with its unmatched views and plentiful benches; the Champ de Mars park under the Eiffel Tower; and the western tip of Ile St. Louis, overlooking Ile de la Cité. Bring your own dinner feast, and then watch the riverboats and the Eiffel Tower light up the city for you.

In the Rue Cler Neighborhood

The rue Cler neighborhood caters to its residents. Its eateries, while not destination places, have an intimate charm. My favorites are small mom-and-pop places that love to serve traditional French food at good prices to a local clientele. You'll generally find great dinner *menus* for €20–30 and *plats du jour* for around €12–15. Eat early with tourists or late with locals.

Closer to Ecole Militaire, Between Rue de la Motte Picquet and Rue de Grenelle

$$$ **Le Bourdonnais**, boasting one Michelin star, is the neighborhood's intimate gourmet splurge. You'll find friendly but formal service in a plush and very subdued 10-table room. Micheline Coat, your hostess, will treat you well (€40 lunch *menu*, €63 dinner *menu*, daily, 113 avenue de la Bourdonnais, tel. 01 47 05 47 96).

Rue Cler Restaurants

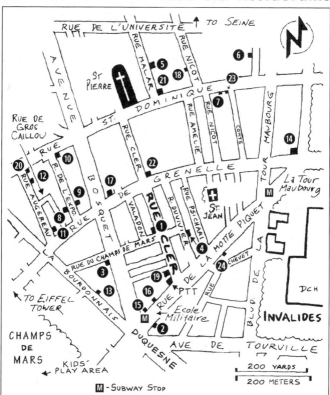

M – Subway Stop

1. Café du Marché
2. Le Comptoir du Septième
3. Café le Bosquet
4. Léo le Lion
5. L'Affriolé & L'Ami Jean
6. Au Petit Tonneau
7. Brasserie Thoumieux
8. Le P'tit Troquet & La Casa di Sergio
9. Restaurant la Serre
10. La Fontaine de Mars
11. La Varangue
12. Chez Agnès
13. Le Bourdonnais
14. Café de l'Esplanade
15. La Terrasse du 7eme
16. Fauchon Deli
17. Real McCoy
18. Pourjauran Bakery
19. Petite Brasserie PTT
20. Café Constant
21. Le Toulouse
22. Café la Roussillon
23. O'Brien's Pub
24. Le Florimond

$$$ Café de l'Esplanade, the latest buzz, is your opportunity to be surrounded by chic, yet older and sophisticated Parisians enjoying top-notch traditional cuisine as foreplay. There's not a tourist in sight. It's a sprawling place—half its tables, with well-stuffed chairs, fill a plush, living-room-like interior, and the other half are lined up outside under its elegant awning facing the street and car park. Dress competitively, as this is *the* place to be seen in the 7th *arrondissement* (€20 *plats du jour*, plan on €45 plus wine for dinner, open daily, reserve ahead—especially if you want a curbside table, non-smoking room in the back, bordering Les Invalides at 52 rue Fabert, tel. 01 47 05 38 80).

$$$ Léo le Lion—small, softly lit, and traditional, with velvet booths—is well respected by locals. Expect to spend €45 per person for fine à la carte choices and wine (closed Sun, 23 rue Duvivier, tel. 01 45 51 41 77).

$$$ Save **Le Florimond** for a special occasion. Locals come for classic French cuisine like grandma used to make, served with care in an intimate setting—and so should you. Since it's a neighborhood favorite, it's best to reserve ahead. Friendly English-speaking Laurent will take good care of you (€32 *menu*, closed Sun, good and reasonable wine selection, non-smoking, 19 avenue de la Motte Picquet, tel. 01 45 55 40 38).

$$$ Thoumieux, the neighborhood's classy, traditional Parisian brasserie, is a local institution and deservedly popular. It's big and dressy, with formal but good-natured waiters. They serve a €14 lunch *menu*, a €31–33 dinner *menu* (3 courses with wine), and really good *crème brûlée* (daily, 79 rue St. Dominique, tel. 01 47 05 49 75).

$$ La Terrasse du 7ème is a sprawling, happening café with outdoor seating (good for people-watching) and a living room-like interior with comfy love-seats. The owner is particular about his food—and it shows (daily until 02:00, no fixed-price *menu*, great *salade niçoise*, they'll make a vegetarian plate on request, at Ecole Militaire Métro stop, tel. 01 45 55 00 02).

$ Café du Marché, with the best seats, coffee, and prices on rue Cler, serves hearty €10 salads and good €11 *plats du jour* for lunch or dinner to a trendy, smoky, mainly French crowd. This easygoing café is ideal if you want a light dinner (good dinner salads) or a more substantial but simple meal. Arrive before 19:30; it's packed at 21:00. A chalkboard lists the plates of the day—each a meal (Mon–Sat 11:00–23:00, closes at 17:00 on Sun, at the corner of rue Cler and rue du Champ de Mars, at 38 rue Cler, tel. 01 47 05 51 27). In 2005, they plan to open a pasta restaurant next door.

$ Le Comptoir du Septième is owned by the Café du Marché folks and offers similar dishes and prices with better (but smoky) indoor seating (daily, 39 avenue de la Motte Picquet, at Ecole Militaire Métro stop, tel. 01 45 55 90 20).

$ Petite Brasserie PTT is popular with postal workers, offering traditional café fare at reasonable prices next to the PTT (post office) on rue Cler (closed Mon, opposite 53 rue Cler).

$ Café le Bosquet is a vintage Parisian brasserie with dressy waiters and a classic interior, or sidewalk tables on a busy street. Come here for a bowl of French onion soup, a salad, or a three-course *menu* (€18) and mix it up with waiters Didier and Antoine. Vegetarian dishes are possible—ask (closed Sun, many choices from a fun menu, the house red wine is plenty good, corner of rue du Champ de Mars and avenue Bosquet, at 46 avenue Bosquet, tel. 01 45 51 38 13).

Between Rue Grenelle and the River

$$$ Altitude 95 is in the Eiffel Tower, 95 meters (about 300 feet) above the ground (€21–31 lunches, €50 dinners, dinner seatings daily at 19:00 and 21:00, reserve well ahead for a view table; before you ascend to dine, drop by the booth between the north/*nord* and east/*est* pillars to buy your Eiffel Tower ticket and pick up a pass that enables you to skip the line; tel. 01 45 55 20 04, fax 01 47 05 94 40).

$$$ At L'Affriolé, you'll compete with young professionals for a table. This small and trendy place is well deserving of its rave reviews. Menu selections change daily, and the wine list is extensive, with some good bargains (€32 *menu*, closed Sun–Mon, 17 rue Malar, tel. 01 44 18 31 33).

$$$ Au Petit Tonneau is a souvenir of old Paris. Fun-loving owner-chef Madame Boyer prepares everything herself, wearing her tall chef's hat like a crown as she rules from her family-style kitchen. The small dining room is plain and doesn't look like it's changed in the 25 years she's been running the place. Her steaks and lamb are excellent (allow €28 for 2 courses, €35 3-course *menu*, open daily, can get smoky—come early, 20 rue Surcouf, tel. 01 47 05 09 01).

$$ Le P'tit Troquet is a petite place taking you back to Paris in the 1920s, gracefully and earnestly run by Dominique. The delicious three-course €29 *menu* comes with fun, traditional choices (closed Sun, 28 rue de l'Exposition, tel. 01 47 05 80 39).

$$ La Casa di Sergio is *the* place for gourmet Italian cuisine served family-style. Only Sergio could make me enthusiastic about Italian food in Paris. Sergio, a people-loving Sicilian, says he's waited his entire life to open a restaurant like this. Eating here involves a little trust...just sit down and let Sergio spoil you (€26–36 *menus*, open daily, 20 rue de l'Exposition, tel. 01 45 51 37 71).

$$ La Fontaine de Mars is a longtime favorite for locals, charmingly situated on a classic, tiny Parisian street and jumbled square. It's a happening scene, with tables jammed together for the serious business of good eating. Reserve in advance or risk eating upstairs without the fun street-level ambience (allow €40 per person with wine, open nightly, where rue de l'Exposition and rue St. Dominique meet, at 129 rue St. Dominique, tel. 01 47 05 46 44).

$$ Chez Agnès, the smallest restaurant listed in this book, is not for everyone. Small and flowery, it's a family-style place. Eccentric but sincere Agnès (with dog Gypsy at her side) does it all—in her minuscule kitchen, and serving, too—without a word of English. Don't come for a quick dinner; and don't come if you don't like dogs (€23 *menu*, closed Mon, 1 rue Augereau, tel. 01 45 51 06 04).

$$ L'Ami Jean is the place to go for excellent Basque specialties at fair prices—and everyone knows it. You must call ahead (try for an early reservation, when most Parisians won't dine), or join the crowd on the sidewalk and wait. The chef has made his reputation on the quality of his cuisine, not on the dark, simple decor (closed Sun–Mon, 27 rue Malar, tel. 01 47 05 86 89).

$ Café Constant is a tiny, two-level place that feels more like a small bistro, serving reasonably priced dishes in a lively setting. Though new, it has already established a loyal clientele (closed Sun, corner of rue Augereau and rue St. Dominique, next to recommended Hotel Londres Eiffel).

$ La Varangue is an entertaining one-man show featuring English-speaking Phillipe, who ran a French catering shop in Pennsylvania for three years, then returned to Paris to open his own place. He lives upstairs, and clearly has found his niche serving a Franco-American clientele who are all on a first-name basis. The food is cheap and basic (don't come here for a special dinner), the tables are few, and he opens early (at 17:30). Norman Rockwell would dig his tiny dining room (€10 *plats du jour* and a €15 *menu*, closed Sun, always a veggie option, 27 rue Augereau, tel. 01 47 05 51 22).

$ Le Toulouse is a cheap and easygoing food store-restaurant serving southwest French cuisine (featuring duck, *cassoulet*, and hearty salads) in a modern setting (closed Sun, 86 rue St Dominique, tel. 01 45 56 04 31).

$ Restaurant la Serre is reasonably priced and worth considering (*plats du jour* €11–15, closed Sun–Mon, good onion soup and duck specialties, 29 rue de l'Exposition, tel. 01 45 55 20 96, Margot).

Picnicking in Rue Cler

The rue Cler is a moveable feast that gives "fast food" a good name. The entire street is clogged with connoisseurs of good eating. Only the health-food store goes unnoticed. A festival of food, the street is lined with people whose lives seem to be devoted to their specialty: polished produce, rotisserie chicken, crêpes, or cheese.

For a magical picnic dinner at the Eiffel Tower, assemble it in no fewer than five shops on rue Cler and then go lounge on the best grass in Paris, with the dogs, Frisbees, a floodlit tower, and a cool breeze in the parc du Champ de Mars.

Asian delis (generically called *Traiteur Asie*) provide tasty, low-stress, low-price, takeout treats (€6 dinner plates, the one on rue Cler near rue du Champ de Mars has tables). There's a **Greek deli** with outdoor seats on rue Cler across from Grand Hôtel Lévêque. The elegant **Fauchon** *charcuterie* offers mouthwatering meals to go (open daily until 23:00, at Ecole Militaire Métro stop). **Real McCoy** is a little shop selling American food and sandwiches (closed Sun, 194 rue de Grenelle). There are small **late-night groceries** at 186 and 197 rue de Grenelle (open nightly until midnight).

Breakfast in Rue Cler
Café la Roussillon serves American breakfasts for €7.50 and a dynamite Sunday brunch for €15 (daily, at corner of rue de Grenelle and rue Cler, tel. 01 45 51 47 53). The **Pourjauran** bakery, offering great baguettes, hasn't changed in 70 years (20 rue Jean Nicot). The **bakery** at 112 rue St. Dominique is worth the detour, with classic decor and tables where you can enjoy your *café au lait* and croissant.

Nightlife in Rue Cler
This sleepy neighborhood is not the place for night owls, but there are a few notable exceptions. **Café du Marché** and its brother, **Le Comptoir du Septième** (both listed above), hop with a Franco-American crowd until about midnight, as does the flashier **Café la Roussillon** (nightly, at corner of rue de Grenelle and rue Cler). **O'Brien's Pub** is a relaxed Parisian rendition of an Irish pub (77 avenue St. Dominique).

In the Marais Neighborhood
The trendy Marais is filled with locals enjoying good food in colorful and atmospheric eateries. The scene is competitive and changes all the time. Here is an assortment of places—all handy to recommended hotels—that offer good food at reasonable prices, plus a memorable experience. For maximum ambience, go to the place des Vosges or place du Marché Ste. Catherine (several places listed below in each of these squares).

Dining on Romantic Place des Vosges
$$$ **Ma Bourgogne** is a good match for the classy place des Vosges, boasting a certain snob appeal. You'll sit under arcades in a whirlpool of Frenchness as bowtied and black-aproned waiters serve you traditional Burgundian specialties: steak, *coq au vin*, lots of French fries, escargot, and great red wine. Service at this institution comes with food but few smiles (€32 *menu*, open daily, dinner reservations smart, no CC, at northwest corner at #19, tel. 01 42 78 44 64).

$ **Café Hugo,** named for the square's most famous resident, sits across the square. It serves the same arcade ambience for less (standard café fare like onion soup, omelets, and salads for €6–10; €13 *plats du jour;* open daily).

$ **Nectarine**, next to Café Hugo, is a peaceful teahouse serving healthy salads, quiches, and inexpensive *plats du jour* both day and night. Its fun menu lets you mix and match omelets and crêpes (daily, 16 place des Vosges, tel. 01 42 77 23 78).

Near the Bastille
$$ **Brasserie Bofinger**, an institution for over a century, is famous for fish and traditional cuisine with Alsatian flair. You're surrounded by brisk, black-and-white-attired waiters in plush rooms reminiscent of the Roaring Twenties. The non-smoking room is best—under the grand 1919 *coupole*. You'll see boys shucking and stacking seafood platters out front before you enter. Their €33 three-course (with wine) *menu* is a good value (daily and nightly, reservations smart, 5 rue de la Bastille, don't be confused by the lesser "Petite" Bofinger across the street, tel. 01 42 72 87 82).

$$ **Chez Janou**, a Provençal bistro, tumbles out of its corner building and fills its broad sidewalk with happy eaters. At first glance, you know this is a find. But don't let the crowd intimidate you—inside and out, it's relaxed and charming. The style is French Mediterranean, with an emphasis on vegetables (€14 *plats du jour* that change with the season, open daily, two blocks beyond place des Vosges at 2 rue Roger Verlomme, tel. 01 42 72 28 41).

$$ **L'Impasse**, a relaxed bistro on a quiet alley, serves an enthusiastically French, €28 three-course *menu*. Françoise, a former dancer and artist, runs the place *con brio* (closed Sun, 4 impasse de Guéménée, tel. 01 42 72 08 45). Françoise promises anyone with this book a free glass of *byrrh*—it's pronounced "beer," but it's a French port-like drink. The restaurant is next to a self-serve launderette (open nightly until 21:30—clean your clothes while you dine).

$$ **Bistrot les Sans Culottes,** a zinc-bar classic on lively rue de Lappe, serves traditional French cuisine with a proper respect for fine wine (€25 3-course *menu*, closed Mon, 27 rue de Lappe, tel. 01 48 05 42 92). Stay out past your bedtime. Eat here. Then join the rue de Lappe party.

$ **Au Temps des Cerises**, a *très* local wine bar, is fun for its colorful lunch of cheese or cold meats with good wine (Mon–Fri until 20:00, closed Sat–Sun, at rue du Petit-Musc and rue de la Cerisaie).

$ **Vins des Pyrénées** is a younger, livelier place with fun ambience, inexpensive meals, some smoke, and a reasonable wine list (daily, 25 rue Beautreillis, tel. 01 42 72 64 94).

In the Heart of the Marais
$$$ **L'Excuse**, one of the neighborhood's top restaurants, is a good splurge for a romantic, dressy evening in a hushed atmosphere with lounge-lizard music. The elegant nouveau cuisine focuses on what's fresh, with plates that are petite but creative, and presented with

Marais Restaurants

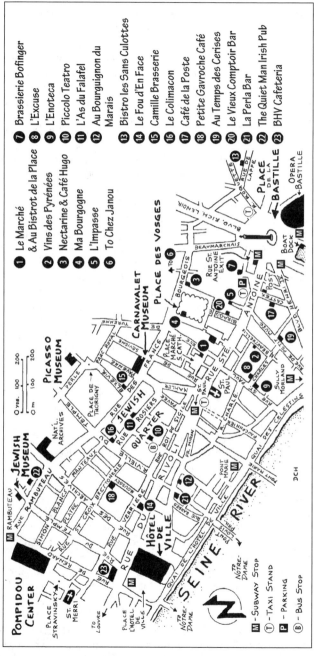

1 Le Marché & Au Bistrot de la Place
2 Vins des Pyrénées
3 Nectarine & Café Hugo
4 Ma Bourgogne
5 L'Impasse
6 To Chez Janou

7 Brasserie Bofinger
8 L'Excuse
9 L'Enoteca
10 Piccolo Teatro
11 L'As du Falafel
12 Au Bourguignon du Marais
13 Bistro les Sans Culottes
14 Le Fou d'En Face
15 Camille Brasserie
16 Le Colimacon
17 Café de la Poste
18 Petite Gavroche Café
19 Au Temps des Cerises
20 Le Vieux Comptoir Bar
21 La Perla Bar
22 The Quiet Man Irish Pub
23 BHV Cafeteria

M – Subway Stop
T – Taxi Stand
P – Parking
B – Bus Stop

panache (€37 *menu*, cheaper at lunch, closed Sun–Mon, reserve ahead, request downstairs—ideally by the window, 14 rue Charles V, tel. 01 42 77 98 97).

$$ *On place du Marché Ste. Catherine:* This tiny square, just off rue St. Antoine, is an international food festival cloaked in extremely Parisian, leafy-square ambience. On a balmy evening, this is clearly a neighborhood favorite, with five popular restaurants offering €20–30 meals. Survey the square and you'll find French-style bistros (Le Marché, Au Bistrot de la Place, both open daily), a fun Italian place (no outdoor tables), a popular Japanese/Korean restaurant, and a Russian eatery with an easy but adventurous menu. You'll eat under the trees surrounded by a futuristic-in-1800 planned residential quarter.

$$ L'Enoteca is a high-energy, half-timbered Italian wine bar–restaurant serving reasonable Italian cuisine (no pizza) with a tempting *antipasti* bar. It's a relaxed, open setting with busy, blue-aproned waiters serving two floors of local eaters (allow €30 for meals with wine, daily, across from L'Excuse at rue St. Paul and rue Charles V, 25 rue Charles V, tel. 01 42 78 91 44).

$ Camille, a traditional corner brasserie, is a neighborhood favorite with great indoor and sidewalk seating. White-aproned waiters serve €9 salads and very French *plats du jour* for €15 to a down-to-earth but sophisticated clientele (daily, 24 rue des Francs Bourgeois at corner of rue Elzévir, tel. 01 42 72 20 50).

$ Piccolo Teatro is where vegetarians should go for a good, inexpensive meal. Friendly British expatriate Rachel will take care of you (daily, near rue des Rosiers, 6 rue des Ecouffes, tel. 01 42 72 17 79).

$ L'As du Falafel serves inexpensive Jewish cuisine on plastic plates, with bustling ambience or to go (day and night until late, closed Sat, €6 "special falafel" is great, 34 rue des Rosiers).

$ Several hard-working **Chinese fast-food places** are along rue St. Antoine, great for a €6 meal.

Dining Closer to Hôtel de Ville

For restaurants near the Pompidou Center, see page 155.

$$$ Au Bourguignon du Marais, a small wine bar–bistro south of rue de Rivoli, is a place that wine-lovers shouldn't miss. Gentle English-speaking Jacques offers excellent Burgundy wines that blend well with his fine, though limited, selection of *plats du jour*. The escargots were the best I've had, and the dessert was...*délicieux* (allow €35–45 with wine, closed Sat–Sun, call by 19:00 to reserve, 52 rue Francois Miron, tel. 01 48 87 15 40).

$$ Le Fou d'En Face, with dynamite ambience inside and out, is a wine-focused restaurant run by an amiable fellow who loves his lot in life. It's on a small square barely off rue de Rivoli near the recommended Hôtel de Nice. Try the *pot-au-feu* (beef stew–€19), and test the superb wine selection (closed Sun, 3 rue du Bourg-Tibourg, tel. 01 48 87 03 75).

$$ Le Colimacon is a romantic little place twirled around its spiral stairs *(colimacon)*. They offer two-course (€18) or three-course (€23) *menus* of traditional cuisine, including *magret de canard aux fruits de saison*—duck breast with a sauce of seasonal fruit (closed Tue, reservations required, 44 rue Vieille du Temple, tel. 01 48 87 12 01).

$ BHV Department Store's fifth-floor cafeteria provides an escape from the busy streets below, nice views, and no-brainer, point-and-shoot cafeteria cuisine (Mon–Sat 11:30–18:00, closed Sun, at intersection of rue du Temple and rue de la Verrerie, one block from Hôtel de Ville).

$ Petite Gavroche is a charmingly basic place offering dirt-cheap French cooking (€9 *plats du jour*, 15 rue Ste. Croix de la Bretonnerie, tel. 01 48 87 74 26).

Picnicking in Marais

Picnic at peaceful place des Vosges (closes at dusk) or on the Ile St. Louis *quais* (see below). Stretch your euros at the basement super-market of the **Monoprix** department store (closed Sun, near place des Vosges on rue St. Antoine). Two small grocery shops are open until 23:00 on rue St. Antoine (near intersection with rue Castex).

Breakfast in Marais

For an incredibly cheap breakfast, try *Hilaire boulangerie-pâtisserie*, where the hotels buy their croissants (coffee machine-€0.70, cheap baby quiches, 1 block off place de la Bastille, corner of rue St. Antoine and rue de Lesdiguières).

Nightlife in Marais

The best scene is the dizzying array of wacky eateries, bars, and dance halls on rue de Lappe. This street is what the Latin Quarter wants to be. Just east of the stately place de la Bastille, it's one of the wildest night spots in Paris. Sitting amid the chaos like a van Gogh painting is the popular, time-warp **Bistrot les Sans Culottes** (see above).

Trendy cafés and bars—popular with gay men—also cluster on rue Vieille du Temple, rue des Archives, and rue Ste. Croix de la Bretonnerie (close at about 02:00). Rue de Rosiers bustles with youthful energy. **Le Vieux Comptoir** is tiny, lively, and just hip enough (off place des Vosges at 8 rue de Birague). **Vins des Pyrénées** is young and fun (see above). **La Perla** is full of Parisian yuppies in search of the perfect margarita (26 rue François Miron). The **Quiet Man** is a traditional Irish pub with happy hour from 16:00 to 20:00 (5 rue des Haudriettes).

Ile St. Louis

The Ile St. Louis is a romantic and peaceful place to window-shop for plenty of promising dinner possibilities. Cruise the island's main street for a variety of options, from cozy *crêperies* to Italian places (intimate pizzeria and upscale) to typical brasseries (several with fine outdoor seating facing the bridge to Ile de la Cité). After dinner, sample Paris' best sorbet. Then stroll across to the Ile de la Cité to see an illuminated Notre-Dame. All listings below line the island's main drag, the rue St. Louis-en-l'Ile (see map on page 71). Consider skipping dessert to enjoy a stroll licking the best ice cream in Paris.

$$$ **Le Tastevin** is a little mother-and-son-run place serving top-notch traditional French cuisine with white-tablecloth, candlelit elegance under heavy wooden beams. The *menus* start with three courses at about €30 and offer plenty of classic choices that change with the season to ensure freshness (daily, good wine list, 46 rue St. Louis-en-l'Ile, tel. 01 43 54 17 31; owner Madame Puisieux speaks just enough English, while her son tends the kitchen).

$$ **Nos Ancêtres les Gaulois** and **La Taverne du Sergeant Recruteur**, next door to each other on rue St. Louis-en-l'Ile, are famous for their rowdy, medieval cellar atmosphere. They serve all-you-can-eat buffets with straw baskets of raw veggies (cut whatever you like with your dagger), massive plates of pâté, a meat course, and all the wine you can stomach for €36–38. The food is just food; burping is encouraged. If you want to eat a lot, drink a lot of wine, and holler at your friends while receiving smart-aleck buccaneer service, these food fests can be fun. Nos Ancêtres les Gaulois, or "Our Ancestors the Gauls," has bigger tables and seems made-to-order for local stag parties (daily from 19:00, at #39, tel. 01 46 33 66 07). If you'd rather be surrounded by drunk tourists than locals, pick La Taverne du Sergeant Recruteur. The "Sergeant Recruiter" used to get young Parisians drunk and stuffed here, then sign them into the army (daily from 19:00, #41, tel. 01 43 54 75 42).

$$ **La Brasserie de l'Ile St. Louis** is situated at the prow of the island's ship as it faces Ile de la Cité, offering purely Alsatian cuisine (try the *choucroute garni* for €17), served in Franco-Germanic ambience with no-nonsense brasserie service (closed Wed, no reservations, 55 quai de Bourbon, tel. 01 43 54 02 59).

$ **Café Med**, closest to Notre-Dame at #77, is best for inexpensive salads, crêpes, and light €12 *menus* in a tight but cheery setting (daily, limited wine list, tel. 01 43 29 73 17, charming Eva SE). There's a similar *crêperie* just across the street.

Riverside Picnic

On sunny lunchtimes and balmy evenings, the *quai* on the Left Bank side of Ile St. Louis is lined with locals who have more class than money, spreading out tablecloths and even lighting candles for elegant picnics. Otherwise, it's a great walk for people-watching.

Ice-Cream Dessert
Half the people strolling Ile St. Louis are licking an ice cream cone, because this is the home of *les glaces Berthillon*. The original **Berthillon** shop, at 31 rue St. Louis-en-l'Ile, is marked by the line of salivating customers (closed Mon–Tue). It's so popular that the wealthy people who can afford to live on this fancy island complain about the congestion it causes. For a less-famous but at-least-as-tasty treat, the homemade Italian gelato a block away at **Amorino Gelati** is giving Berthillon competition (no line, bigger portions, easier to see what you want, and they offer little tastes—Berthillon doesn't need to, 47 rue St. Louis-en-l'Ile, tel. 01 44 07 48 08). Having some of each is a fine option.

In the Luxembourg Neighborhood
Sleeping in the Luxembourg neighborhood puts you near many exciting dining and after-hours options. Because my hotels for this area cluster around the Panthéon and St. Sulpice Church, I've organized restaurants the same way. Restaurants near the Panthéon tend to be calm, those around St. Sulpice more boisterous; it's a short walk from one area to the other. Anyone sleeping in this area is close to the inexpensive eateries that line the always-bustling rue Mouffetard. You're also within a 15-minute walk of the *grands cafés* of St. Germain and Montparnasse.

Near the Panthéon
For locations, see page 142.

$$ Les Vignes du Panthéon, on a quiet street a block from the Panthéon, is a homey, formal, traditional place with a zinc bar, original flooring, white tablecloths, and soft ambience. It serves a mostly local clientele and will make you feel you're truly in Paris (allow €28 for à la carte, closed Sun, English menu posted outside, 4 rue des Fossés St. Jacques, tel. 01 43 54 80 81).

$$ Terra Neva, a few doors up from Les Vignes du Panthéon, has a privileged position on a broad sidewalk along a peaceful street with views to the Panthéon's facade. Join the loyal clientele for Italian specialties. Two can easily split the big *antipasti* (ask for mozzarella with it), and each get a pasta main course for about €22 per person (closed Sun, limited and pricey wine list, 18 rue des Fossés St Jacques, tel. 01 43 54 83 09). The *other* Italian place across the street (one letter difference in name) serves more basic, cheaper pizzas and pastas.

$$ Restaurant Perraudin is a welcoming, family-run, red-checkered-tablecloth place. Gentle M. Rameau serves classic *cuisine bourgeoise* with an emphasis on Burgundian dishes. The decor is

classic turn-of-the-century, with big mirrors and old wood paneling (*bœuf bourguignon* is a specialty here, €28 *menus*, closed Sat–Sun, between the Panthéon and Luxembourg Garden at 157 rue St Jacques, tel. 01 46 33 15 75).

$ **Le Soufflot** is my favorite outdoor café between the Panthéon and Luxembourg Garden, with a nifty library-like interior and outdoor tables on a wide sidewalk with point-blank views of the Panthéon. The cuisine is café-classic: salads, omelets, and *plats du jour* (daily, a block below the Panthéon on the right side of rue Soufflot as you walk toward Luxembourg Garden, tel. 01 43 26 57 56).

$ **Le Volcan**, a few blocks behind the Panthéon, has a wood floor, wood-counter-cozy front room, and a reasonable menu with dinners from €16 (10 rue Thouin, tel. 01 46 33 38 33).

On Rue Mouffetard

$ **Café Delmas**, at the top of rue Mouffetard on picturesque place de la Contrescarpe, is *the* place to see and be seen. Come here for a before- or after-dinner drink on the broad outdoor terrace, or for typical café cuisine (salads-€12, *plats*-€15, great chocolate ice cream, open daily).

$ **Le Jardin d'Artemis** is one of the better values right on rue Mouffetard, serving traditional French specialties with a Greek touch in a cozy setting (no outside tables, €17–26 *menus*, closed Tue, 34 rue Mouffetard, tel. 01 45 35 17 47).

$ **Cave de la Bourgogne** serves reasonably-priced café fare at the bottom of rue Mouffetard, with picture-perfect tables on an raised terrace and a warm interior (specials listed on chalkboards, open daily, 144 rue Mouffetard).

$ **Le Jardin des Pates** is popular with less-strict vegetarians, serving pastas and salads at fair prices (daily, near Jardin des Plantes, 4 rue Lacépède, tel. 01 43 31 50 71).

Near St. Sulpice Church

For locations, see page 141.

$$$ **Au Bon Saint-Pourcain** is to be saved for a special night. Soft lights and a few outside tables greet passers-by, while those who duck inside become part of the club. Reserve ahead for this tiny place, which serves traditional cuisine, hiding on a quiet lane between St. Sulpice Church and the Luxembourg Garden (à la carte only, allow €45 per person with wine, daily, 10 bis rue Servandoni, tel. 01 43 54 93 63).

$$ **Chez Diane** is an antique bistro on the same street a block closer to Luxembourg Garden serving French classics with a light-hearted spirit (menus from €26, closed Sun, 25 rue Servandoni, tel. 01 46 33 12 06).

Rue des Canettes and Rue Guisarde: For an entirely different experience, roam the streets between the St. Sulpice Church and boulevard St. Germain, abounding with restaurants, *crêperies*, wine bars, and jazz haunts. Find rue des Canettes and rue Guisarde, and window-shop the many Franco-Italian places. Every place does a brisk business, and it's hard to distinguish one from the other. **Brasserie Fernand** is lined with tiny tables packed with folks enjoying €10–15 plates of traditional French food (closed Sun, 13 rue Guisarde, tel. 01 43 54 61 47). For crêpes, try **La Crêpe Rit du Clown** (Mon–Sat 12:00–23:00, closed Sun, 6 rue des Canettes, tel. 01 46 34 01 02). And for a bohemian pub with a cigarette-rolling gang surrounded by black-and-white photos of the artsy and revolutionary French Sixties, have a drink at **Chez Georges** (cheap drinks from time-warp menu upstairs, cool little street-side table nook; downstairs for mostly gay jazz dance cellar, open 14:00–2:00, closed Sun–Mon and in Aug, 11 rue des Canettes).

Elsewhere in Paris

Along the Canal St. Martin

Escape the popular tourist areas and enjoy a terrific canalside experience. Take the Métro to place de la République and walk down rue Beaurepaire to the Canal St. Martin. There you'll find two cafés that are as cool as it gets. They're both fun, with similarly reasonable prices; you decide: **$ Chez Plume** (canal ambience in and out, well-prepared food, €8 salads, €12-15 *plats*; daily, 71 quai de Valmy, tel. 01 42 41 30 47) or **$ La Marine** (closed Sun, 2 blocks to the right as you leave Chez Plume, 55 bis quai de Valmy, tel. 01 42 39 69 81).

Near Opéra Garnier

$ Bouillon Chartier is a noisy, old, classic eatery. It's named for the bouillon it served the neighborhood's poor workers back in 1896, when its calling was to provide an affordable warm meal for those folks. Workers used to eat *a la gamelle* (from a tin lunch box). That same spirit—complete with surly waiters and a cheap menu—survives today. With over 300 simple seats and 15 frantic waiters, you can still see the napkin drawers for its early regulars (€15 *menus*, daily 11:30–15:00 & 18:00–22:00, west of the Opéra Garnier near boulevard Poissonniere, 7 rue de Faubourg-Montmartre, Mo: Bonne-Nouvelle, tel. 01 47 70 86 29).

Montmartre

Montmartre is extremely touristy, with many mindless mobs following guides to cancan shows. But the ambience is undeniably fun, and an evening up here overlooking Paris is a quintessential experience in the City of Light. Along the touristy main drag (and just off it), several fun piano bars serve reasonable crêpes with great people-watching.

$$ Restaurant Chez Plumeau, just off the jam-packed place du Tertre, is a touristy yet cheery, moderately priced place with great seating on a tiny characteristic square (€28 *menu*, elaborate €15 salads, closed Wed, place du Calvaire, tel. 01 46 06 26 29).

$ **L'Eté en Pente Douce** hides under generous branches below the crowds on a classic neighborhood corner, with fine indoor and outdoor seating, €10 *plats du jour* and salads, veggie options, and good wines (daily, 23 rue Muller, many steps below Sacré-Cœur to the left as you leave, down the stairs below the WC, tel. 01 42 64 02 67).

Versailles

In the pleasant town center, around place du Marché Notre-Dame, you'll find a variety of reasonably priced restaurants, cafés, and a few cobbled lanes (market days Sun, Tue, and Fri until 13:00). The square is a 15-minute walk from the château (veer left when you leave château). From the place du Marché, consider shortcutting to Versailles' gardens by walking 10 minutes west down rue de la Paroisse. The château will be to your left after entering, and the main gardens, Trianon Palaces, and Hamlet straight ahead. The quickest way to the château's front door is along avenue de St. Cloud and rue Colbert.

The following restaurants serve good food and are open daily for lunch or dinner. The first two are located on or near place du Marché Notre-Dame. **La Bœuf à la Mode** is a bistro with traditional cuisine right on the square (2-course *menu*–€20, 3-course *menu*–€25, 4 rue au Pain, tel. 01 39 50 31 99). **A la Côte Bretonne** is the place to go for crêpes in a friendly, cozy setting (a few steps off the square on traffic-free rue des Deux Portes at #12, tel. 01 39 51 18 24).

Rue Satory, a pedestrian-friendly street lined with restaurants, is on the south side of the château near Hôtel d'Angleterre (10-min walk, angle right out of the château). **Le Limousin** is a warm, traditional restaurant on the corner nearest the château, with mostly meat dishes (€35–40 with wine, daily, lamb is a specialty, 4 rue de Satory, tel. 01 39 50 21 50).

TRANSPORTATION CONNECTIONS

Trains

Paris is Europe's rail hub, with six major train stations, each serving different regions: Gare de l'Est (eastbound trains), Gare du Nord (northern France and Europe), Gare St. Lazare (northwestern France), Gare d'Austerlitz (southwestern France and Europe), Gare de Lyon (southeastern France and Italy), and Gare Montparnasse (northwestern France and TGV service to France's southwest). Any train station can give you schedule information, make reservations, and sell tickets for any destination. Buying tickets is handier from an SNCF neighborhood office—including those at the Louvre,

Invalides, Orsay, Versailles, and airports—or at your neighborhood travel agency. It's worth the small fee. Look for SNCF signs in their window, which indicate they sell train tickets.

Schedules change by season, weekday, and weekend. Verify train schedules shown in this book (to study ahead on the Web, check http://bahn.hafas.de/bin/query.exe/en). The nationwide information line for train schedules and reservations is tel. 3635. Dial this four-digit number, then press "3" for reservations or ticket purchases when you get the message. Press 321 for Eurostar information or 322 for Thalys. This incredibly helpful, time-saving service costs €0.34 per minute from anywhere in France (ask for an English-speaking agent and hope for the best, allow 5 min per call). The time and energy you save easily justifies the telephone torture, particularly when making seat reservations (note that phoned reservations must be picked up at least 30 min prior to departure).

All six train stations have Métro, bus, and taxi service. All have banks or change offices, ATMs, information desks, telephones, cafés, newsstands, and clever pickpockets. Because of security concerns, not all have baggage check, though those with this service are identified below. Each station offers two types of rail service: long distance to other cities, called *Grandes Lignes* (major lines); and suburban service to outlying areas, called *banlieue* or RER. Both *banlieue* and RER trains serve outlying areas and the airports; the only difference is that *banlieue* lines are operated by SNCF (France's train system, called Transilien) and RER lines are operated by RATP (Paris' Métro and bus system). You may also see ticket windows identified as *Ile de France;* these are for Transilien (SNCF) trains serving destinations outside Paris in the Ile de France region (usually no longer than an hour from Paris).

Paris train stations can be intimidating, but if you slow down, take a deep breath, and ask for help, you'll find them manageable and efficient. Bring a pad of paper for clear communication at ticket/info windows. All stations have helpful *accueil* (information) booths; the bigger stations have roving helpers, usually in red vests. They're capable of answering rail questions more quickly than the information or ticket windows.

Station Overview

Here's an overview of Paris' major train stations. Métro and RER trains, as well as buses and taxis, are well-marked at every station. When arriving by Métro, follow signs for *Grandes Lignes*-SNCF to find the main tracks.

Gare du Nord

This vast station serves cities in northern France and international destinations north of Paris, including Copenhagen, Amsterdam, and

Paris Train Stations

Paris train stations & destinations

1 Gare St. Lazare: To Normandy (also Vernon/Giverny)

2 Gare Nord: To London, Brussels, Amsterdam & N. France
(also Chantilly & Auvers-sur-Oise)

3 Gare L'Est: To E. France, S. Germany, Switzerland & Austria

4 Gare du Lyon: To Italy & SE France
(also Fontainebleau & Melun/Vaux-le-Vicomte)

5 Gare d'Austerlitz: To SW France, Loire Valley & Spain

6 Gare Montparnasse: To SW France, Loire Valley,
Normandy & Brittany (also Chartres)

the Eurostar to London, as well as two of the day trips described in this book (Chantilly and Auvers-sur-Oise).

Arrive early to allow time to navigate this station. From the Métro, follow *Grandes Lignes* signs (main lines) and keep going up until you reach the tracks at street level. *Grandes Lignes* depart from tracks 3–21, suburban *(banlieue)* lines from tracks 30–36, and RER trains depart from tracks 37–44 (tracks 41–44 are 1 floor below). Glass train information booths *(accueil)* are scattered throughout the station and information-providing staff circulate to help (all rail staff are required to know English).

The tourist information kiosk opposite track 16 is a hotel reservation service for Accor chain hotels (they also have free Paris maps). Information booths for the **Thalys** (high-speed trains to Brussels and Amsterdam) are opposite track 8. All non-Eurostar ticket sales are opposite tracks 3–8. Passengers departing on **Eurostar** (London via Chunnel) must buy tickets and check in on the second level, opposite track 6. (Note: Britain's time zone is one hour earlier; times listed on Eurostar tickets are local times—Parisian time for departing Paris and the British time you'll arrive in London.) Monet-esque views over the trains and peaceful, air-conditioned cafés hide on the upper level, past the Eurostar ticket windows (find the cool view WCs down the steps in the café). Baggage check, taxis, and rental cars are at the far end, opposite track 3 and down the steps.

Key destinations served by Gare du Nord *Grandes Lignes:* **Brussels** (12/day, 1.5 hrs, see "To Brussels and Amsterdam by Thalys Train," page 168), **Bruges** (18/day, 2 hrs, change in Brussels, one direct), **Amsterdam** (10/day, 4 hrs, see "To Brussels and Amsterdam by Thalys Train," page 168), **Copenhagen** (1/day, 16 hrs, two night trains), **Koblenz** (6/day, 5 hrs, change in Köln), and **London** (Eurostar via Chunnel, 17/day, 3 hrs, tel. 08 36 35 35 39).

By *banlieue*/**RER lines**: **Chantilly-Gouvieux** (hrly, fewer on weekends, 35 min), **Charles de Gaulle Airport** (2/hr, 30 min, runs 5:30–23:00, track 4), **Auvers-sur-Oise** (2/hr, 1 hr, transfer at Pontoise).

Gare Montparnasse

This big and modern station covers three floors, serves lower Normandy and Brittany, and offers TGV service to the Loire Valley and southwestern France, as well as suburban service to Chartres. At street level, you'll find a bank, *banlieue* trains serving Chartres (you can also reach the *banlieue* trains from the second level), and ticket windows for Ile de France trains in the center, just past the escalators. Baggage check may re-open in 2005. (If this happens, it will be on the mezzanine between levels 1 and 2.)

Most services are provided on the second (top) level, where the *Grandes Lignes* arrive and depart. Ticket windows and an information booth are to the far left (with your back to glass exterior). *Banlieue* trains depart from tracks 10–19. The main rail information office is opposite track 15. Taxis and car rentals are to the far left as you leave the tracks. Air France buses to Orly and Charles de Gaulle airports stop in front of the station, down the escalators and outside.

Key destinations served by Gare Montparnasse: Chartres (20/day, 1 hr, *banlieue* lines), **Pontorson/Mont St. Michel** (5/day, 4.5 hrs, via Rennes, then take bus from Pontorson; or take train to Pontorson via Caen, then bus from Pontorson), **Dinan** (7/day, 4 hrs, change in Rennes and Dol), **Bordeaux** (14/day, 3.5 hrs), **Sarlat** (5/day, 6 hrs, change in Bordeaux, Libourne, or Souillac), **Toulouse** (11/day, 5 hrs, most require change, usually in Bordeaux), **Albi** (7/day, 6–7.5 hrs, change in Toulouse, also night train), **Carcassonne** (8/day, 6.5 hrs, most require changes in Toulouse and Bordeaux, direct trains take 10 hrs), and **Tours** (14/day, 1 hr).

Gare de Lyon

This huge and bewildering station offers TGV and regular service to southeastern France, Italy, and other international destinations (for more trains to Italy, see "Gare de Bercy," next page). Frequent *banlieue* trains serve Melun (near Vaux-le-Vicomte) and Fontainebleau (some depart from the main *Grandes Lignes* level, more frequent departures are from one level down, follow RER-D signs, and ask at any *accueil* or ticket window where the next departure leaves from). Don't leave this station without relaxing in Le Train Bleu Restaurant, up the stairs opposite track G.

Grande Lignes trains arrive and depart from one level, but are divided into two areas (tracks A-N and 5-23). They are connected by the long platform along tracks A and 5, and by the hallway adjacent to track A and opposite track 9. This hallway has all the services, including ticket windows, ticket information, banks, shops, and access to car rental. *Banlieue* ticket windows are just inside the hall adjacent to track A *(billets Ile de France)*. *Grandes Lignes* and *banlieue* lines share the same tracks. A tourist office (Mon–Sat 8:00–18:00, closed Sun) and a train information office are both opposite track L. From the RER or Métro, follow signs for *Grandes Lignes Arrivées* and take the escalator up to reach the platforms. Train information booths *(accueil)* are opposite tracks A and 11. Baggage check is down the stairs opposite track 13. Taxi stands are well-signed in front of the station and one floor below. For a quieter waiting area, follow *Consigne* (baggage check) signs down one floor from opposite track 13.

Air France buses to Montparnasse and Charles de Gaulle airport stop outside the main entrance to the station (opposite tracks A to L). Walk across the parking lot and the stop is opposite the European café (€11.50, 2/hr, normally at :15 and :45 after the hour).

Key destinations served by Gare de Lyon: Vaux-le-Vicomte (train to Melun, hrly, 30 min), **Fontainebleau** (nearly hrly, 45 min), **Beaune** (12/day, 2.5 hrs, most require change in Dijon), **Dijon** (15/day, 1.5 hrs), **Chamonix** (9/day, 9 hrs, change in Lyon and St. Gervais, 1 night train from Gare d'Austerlitz), **Annecy** (14/day, 4–7 hrs), **Lyon** (16/day, 2.5 hrs), **Avignon** (9/day in 2.5 hrs, 6/day in 4 hrs with change), **Arles** (14/day, 5 hrs, most with change in Marseille, Avignon, or Nîmes), **Nice** (14/day, 5.5–7 hrs, many with change in Marseille), **Venice** (3/day, 3/night, 11–15 hrs, most require changes), **Rome** (2/day, 5/night, 15–18 hrs, most require changes), and **Bern** (9/day, 5–11 hrs, most require changes, night train).

Gare de Bercy

This smaller station handles some night train service to Italy during renovation work at the Gare de Lyon (Mo: Bercy, one stop east of Gare de Lyon on line 14).

Gare de l'Est

This single-floor station (with underground Métro) serves eastern France and European points east of Paris. Train information booths are at tracks 1 and 26; the info booth at track 18 is for Transilien trains serving suburban areas; ticket windows are in the big hall opposite track 8; luggage storage *(Consigne)* is through the hall opposite track 12; Métro access is opposite track 18.

Key destinations served by Gare de l'Est: Colmar (12/day, 5.5 hrs, change in Strasbourg, Dijon, or Mulhouse), **Strasbourg** (14/day, 4.5 hrs, many require changes), **Reims** (12/day, 1.5 hrs), **Verdun** (5/day, 3 hrs, change in Metz or Chalon), **Munich** (5/day, 9 hrs, some require changes, night train), **Vienna** (7/day, 13–18 hrs, most require changes, night train), **Zürich** (10/day, 7 hrs, most require changes, night train), and **Prague** (2/day, 14 hrs, night train).

Gare St. Lazare

This relatively small station serves upper Normandy, including Rouen and Giverny. All trains arrive and depart one floor above street level. Follow signs to *Grandes Lignes* from the Métro to reach the tracks. Ticket windows are in the first hall at departure level. *Grandes Lignes* (main lines) depart from tracks 17–27; *banlieue* (suburban) trains depart from 1–16. The train information office *(accueil)* is opposite track 15. There's a post office (PTT) along track 27, and WCs are opposite track 19. There is no baggage check. You'll find many shops and services one floor below the departure level.

Key destinations served by Gare St. Lazare: Giverny (train to Vernon, 5/day, 45 min—then bus or taxi 10 min to Giverny), **Rouen** (15/day, 75 min), **Honfleur** (6/day, 3 hrs, via Lisieux, then bus), **Bayeux** (9/day, 2.5 hrs, some with change in Caen), and **Caen** (12/day, 2 hrs).

Gare d'Austerlitz

This small station provides non-TGV service to the Loire Valley, southwestern France, and Spain. All tracks are at street level. The information booth is opposite track 17, and all ticket sales are in the hall opposite track 10. Baggage check, WCs, and car rental are near track 27, along the side of the station, opposite track 21. To get to the Métro, you must walk outside and along either side of the station.

Key destinations served by Gare d'Austerlitz: Amboise (8/day in 2 hrs, 12/day in 1.5 hrs with change in St. Pierre-des-Corps), **Chamonix** (1 night train, day trains from Gare de Lyon) **Cahors** (7/day, 5–7 hrs, most with changes), **Barcelona** (1/day, 9 hrs, change in Montpellier, night trains), **Madrid** (2 night trains only, 13–16 hrs), and **Lisbon** (1/day, 24 hrs).

Buses

The main bus station is the Gare Routière du Paris-Gallieni (28 avenue du Général de Gaulle, in suburb of Bagnolet, Mo: Gallieni, tel. 01 49 72 51 51). Buses provide cheaper—if less comfortable and more time-consuming—transportation to major European cities. Eurolines' buses depart from here (tel. 08 36 69 52 52, www.eurolines.com). Eurolines has a couple of neighborhood offices: in the Latin Quarter (55 rue St. Jacques, tel. 01 43 54 11 99) and in Versailles (4 avenue des Sceaux, tel. 01 39 02 03 73).

To Brussels and Amsterdam by Thalys Train

The pricey Thalys train has the monopoly on the rail route (for a cheaper option, try the Eurolines bus; see above). Without a railpass, you'll pay about €80–100 second-class for the Paris–Amsterdam train (compared to €45 by bus) or about €60–80 second-class for the Paris–Brussels train (compared to €25 by bus). Even with a railpass, you need to pay for train reservations (second class-€14, first class-€30). Book at least a day ahead as seats are limited. Or hop on the bus, Gus.

To London by Eurostar Train

The fastest and most convenient way to get from the Eiffel Tower to Big Ben is by rail. Eurostar, a joint service of the Belgian, British, and French railways, is the speedy passenger train zips you (and up to 800 others in 18 sleek cars) from downtown Paris to downtown London (12–15/day, 2.5 hrs) faster and easier than flying. The actual tunnel crossing is a 20-minute, black, silent, 100-mile-per-hour non-event. Your ears won't even pop. Eurostar trains also run directly to London from Charles de Gaulle Airport (requires change in Lille) or Disneyland Paris (1/day direct, more often with transfer at Lille).

Eurostar Fares

Channel fares (essentially the same between London and Paris or Brussels) are reasonable but complicated. Prices vary depending on when you travel, whether you can live with restrictions, and whether you're eligible for any discounts (youth, seniors, and railpass-holders all qualify). Rates are lower for round trips and off-peak travel (midday, midweek, low-season, and low-interest). Fares are always changing. For specifics, visit www.ricksteves.com/eurostar.

As with airfares, the most expensive and flexible option is a **full-fare ticket** with no restrictions on refundability (even refundable after the departure date; for a one-way trip, figure around $345 in first class, $249 second class). A first-class ticket comes with a meal (a dinner departure nets you more grub than breakfast)—but it's not worth the extra expense.

Also like the airlines, **cheaper tickets** come with more restrictions—and are limited in number (so they sell out more quickly; for

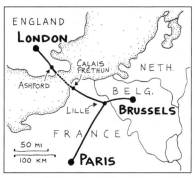

second-class, one-way tickets, figure $90–200). Non-full-fare tickets have severe restrictions on refundability (best-case scenario: you'll get 25 percent back, but with the cheapest options you'll get nothing). But several do allow you to change the specifics of your trip once before departure.

Those traveling with a railpass for Britain, France, or Belgium should look first at the **passholder** fare, an especially good value for one-way Eurostar trips (around $75).

Buying Eurostar Tickets

Refund and exchange restrictions are serious, so don't reserve until you're sure of your plans. If you're confident about the time and date of your crossing, order ahead from the United States. Only the most expensive ticket (full fare) is fully refundable, so if you want to have more flexibility, hold off—keeping in mind that the longer you wait, the more likely the cheapest tickets will sell out (you might end up having to pay for first class).

You can check and book fares by phone or online in the United States (order online at www.ricksteves.com/eurostar, prices listed in dollars; order by phone at U.S. tel. 800/EUROSTAR) or in France (French tel. 08 92 35 35 39, www.eurostar.com, prices listed in euros). These are different companies, often with slightly different prices and discount deals on similar tickets; if you order from the United States, check out both. (If you buy from a U.S. company, you'll pay for ticket delivery in the United States; if you book with the European company, you'll pick up your ticket at the train station.) In Europe, you can buy your Eurostar ticket at any major train station in any country, at neighborhood SNCF offices, or at any travel agency that handles train tickets (expect a booking fee).

Note that France's time zone is one hour later than Britain's. Times listed on tickets are local (Parisian time of departure and the British time of arrival in London).

Airports

Charles de Gaulle Airport

Paris' primary airport has two main terminals: T-1 and T-2, and two lesser terminals, T-3 and T-9. Air Canada, SAS, United, US Airways, KLM, Northwest, and Lufthansa all normally use T-1. Air France, British Airways, Continental, American, Alitalia, and KLM normally use T-2. Smaller airlines use T-3 and charter flights leave from T-9. Airlines sometimes switch terminals, so verify your terminal before flying. Terminals are connected every few minutes by a free *navette* (shuttle bus). The RER (Paris commuter train with links to the Metro) stops at T-2 and T-3 terminals, and the TGV (tay-zhay-vay, stands for *train à grande vitesse*) station is at T-2. There is no baggage storage at the airport. Beware of pickpockets on *navettes* between terminals and especially on RER trains. Do not take an unauthorized taxi from the men greeting you on arrival. Official taxi stands are well-signed.

Those flying to or from the United States will almost certainly use T-1 or T-2. Below is information for each terminal. For flight information, call 01 48 62 22 80. For the latest information on either of Paris' airports, check www.adp.fr.

Terminal 1 (T-1): This circular terminal has one main entry and covers three floors—arrival (*arrivées*, top floor), departure (*départs*, one floor down) and shops/boutiques (basement level). For information on getting to Paris, see "Transportation between Charles de Gaulle Airport and Paris," below.

Arrival level: You'll find a variety of services at these gates.

- Gate 36: Called *Meeting Point*, this gate has an ADP (a quasi-tourist office) that sells Museum Passes, offers free maps, and provides tourist/hotel information (daily 7:00–22:00). A nearby *Relay* store sells phone cards. To find the shuttle buses *(navettes)* for Terminal 2 and the RER trains to Paris, take the elevator down to level *(niveau)* 2, then walk outside (line #1 serves T-2 including the TGV station; line #2 goes directly to the RER station).
- Gate 34: Outside are Air France buses to Paris and Orly Airport.
- Gate 32: ATMs. Outside are Roissy Buses to Paris (buy tickets inside at gate 30 or from driver) and Disneyland Express buses.
- Gate 20: Taxis outside.

- Gate 16: A bank with lousy rates for currency exchange.
- Gates 10–24: Car-rental offices.

Departure level (*niveau* 3): This is limited to flight check-in, though you will find ADP information desks here. Those departing from T-1 will find restaurants, a PTT (post office), a pharmacy, boutiques, and a handy grocery store one floor below the ticketing desks (*niveau* 2 on the elevator).

Terminal 2 (T-2): This long, horseshoe-shaped terminal is dominated by Air France and divided into several sub-terminals (or halls), each identified by a letter. You can walk from one hall to the other. Halls are connected to the RER, the TGV station, and T-1 every five minutes via free *navettes* (shuttle buses, line #5 runs to T-1).

Here's where you should find these key carriers: Air France, Continental, and American Airlines—Hall A; British Airways—Hall B; Delta—Hall C; more Air France, KLM, and Alitalia—Hall F.

The RER and TGV stations are below the Sheraton Hotel (access by *navettes* or on foot). Stops for *navettes*, Air France buses, and Roissy Buses are all well-marked and near each Hall (see "Transportation between Charles de Gaulle Airport and Paris," below). ADP information desks are located near gate 5 in each Hall. Car-rental offices, post offices, pharmacies, and ATMs *(point d'argent)* are also well-signed.

Transportation between Charles de Gaulle Airport and Paris: Three efficient public-transportation routes, taxis, and airport shuttle vans link the airport's terminals with central Paris. All are well-marked, and stops are centrally located at all terminals. If you're carrying lots of baggage—or are just plain tired—airport shuttle vans or taxis are well worth the extra cost.

To get to the rue Cler area, the Roissy bus and Métro combination is the most convenient public transport route. To reach the Marais, your best option is the Air France bus to Gare de Lyon, with a quick trip on Métro line #1. Both routes are described below. For the Luxembourg area, take RER-B to the Luxembourg stop. All your options into Paris are well-marked, but if you have trouble, ask any airport employee.

RER trains stop near T-1 and at T-2, cost €8, and run every 15 minutes, with stops in central Paris at Gare du Nord, Châtelet-Les Halles, St. Michel, and Luxembourg. When coming from Paris to the airport, T-1 is the first RER stop at Charles de Gaulle; T-2 is the second stop. Beware of pickpockets preying on jet-lagged tourists on these trains; wear your moneybelt. The other transportation options described below have far fewer theft problems.

Roissy Buses run every 15 minutes to Paris' Opéra Garnier (€8.50, 40–60 min). You'll arrive at a bus stop on rue Scribe at the American Express office, on the left side of the Opéra building. To get to the Métro entrance, turn left out of the bus, heading towards the front of the Opéra. For rue Cler hotels, take the #8 Métro line (direction: Balard) to La Tour Maubourg or Ecole Militaire. For hotels in the Marais neighborhood, take the same #8 line (direction: Créteil Préfecture) to the Bastille stop.

Air France bus routes serve central Paris about every 15–30 minutes (to Arc de Triomphe and Porte Maillot-€10, 40 min; to Montparnasse Tower/train station-€11.50, 60 min; or to the Gare de Lyon station-€11.50, 40 min). To reach Marais hotels from Gare de Lyon, take Métro line 1 (direction La Défense) to the Bastille, St. Paul, or Hôtel de Ville stops.

Taxis will run €40–50 with bags, more if traffic is bad. If taking a cab to the airport, ask your hotel to call for you (the night before if you must leave early) and specify that you want a real taxi *(un taxi normal)* and not a limo-service that costs €20 more. Remember, you pay a bit more on Sundays, before 7:00, and after 19:00.

Airport shuttles offer a less stressful trip between either of Paris' airports and downtown, ideal for single travelers or families of four or more (taxis are limited to three). Reserve from home and they'll meet you at the airport. Airport shuttles cost about €20–30 for one person, €30–40 for two, and €40–52 for three. Some offer deals if you do a round trip and most are more expensive at night (20:00–6:00). Plan on a 30-minute wait if you ask them to pick you up at the airport. Be clear on where and how you are to meet your driver. If you're planning to use an airport shuttle service to get from Paris to the airport, book your trip at least a day in advance (most hoteliers will make the call for you).

Choose between three options: **Golden Air**—among the most reliable of the many shuttles—with €18 one-way trips to or from Charles de Gaulle and a 10-percent discount for my readers (tel. 01 34 10 12 92, fax 01 34 10 93 89, www.paris-airport-shuttle -limousine.com, goldenair@goldenair.net), **Airport Connection** (tel. 01 44 18 36 02, fax 01 45 55 85 19, www.airport-connection.com), and **Paris Airports Service** (tel. 01 55 98 10 80, fax 01 55 98 10 89, www.parisairportservice.com).

Sleeping at or near Charles de Gaulle Airport: **Hôtel Ibis****, outside the RER Roissy Rail station at T-3 (the first RER stop coming from Paris), offers standard and predictable accommodations (Db-€80–90, near *navette* stop, free shuttle bus to all terminals, tel. 01 49 19 19 19, fax 01 49 19 19 21, www.ibishotel.com, h1404@accor-hotels.com). **Novotel***** is next door and the next step up (Db-€125–160, tel. 01 49 19 27 27, fax 01 49 19 27 99, www.novotel.com).

The small village of Roissy, which gave its name to the airport (Roissy Charles de Gaulle), has better-value chain hotels with shuttle service to the airport (6/hr, 10 min). There, you'll also find a real village to shop for your last Parisian dinner or an early-morning café breakfast. Choose from **Hotel Campanile** (Db-€65, tel. 01 34 29 80 40, fax 01 34 29 80 39, www.campanile.fr, roissy@campanile.fr) or **Hotel Kyriad** (Db-€85, tel. 01 34 29 00 00, fax 01 34 29 00 11, www.kyriad.fr, roissy@bleumarine.fr).

To avoid rush-hour traffic, drivers can consider sleeping north of Paris in the pleasant medieval town of **Senlis** (15 min north of airport) at **Hostellerie de la Porte Bellon** (Db-€60–75, central at 51 rue Bellon, near rue de la République, tel. 03 44 53 03 05, fax 03 44 53 29 94).

Orly Airport

This airport feels small. Orly has two terminals: Sud (south) and Ouest (west). International flights arrive at Sud. Arriving in Orly, you'll exit Sud's baggage claim (near gate H) and see signs directing you to city transportation, car rental, and so on. Turn left to enter the main terminal area, and you'll find exchange offices with bad rates, an ATM, the ADP (a quasi-tourist office that offers free city maps and basic sightseeing information, open until 23:00), and an SNCF rail desk (until 18:00, sells train tickets and even Eurailpasses, next to ADP). Downstairs are a sandwich bar, WCs, a bank (same bad rates), a newsstand (buy a phone card), and a post office with great rates for cash or American Express traveler's checks. Car-rental offices are located in the parking lot in front of the terminal. For flight info on any airline serving Orly, call 01 49 75 15 15. For information on either of Paris' airports, visit www.adp.fr.

Transportation between Orly Airport and Paris: Several efficient public transportation routes, taxis, and a couple of airport shuttle services link Orly with central Paris. The gate locations listed below apply to Orly Sud, but the same transportation services are available from both terminals.

The **Air France bus** (outside gate K) runs to Paris' Invalides Métro stop (€8, 4/hr, 30 min) and is handy for those staying in or near the rue Cler neighborhood (from Invalides bus stop, take the Métro two stops to Ecole Militaire to reach recommended hotels, see RER train info, next page).

Bus #285 (also called Jetbus, outside gate H, €5.30, 4/hr) is the quickest way to the Paris subway and the best way to the Marais and Luxembourg neighborhoods. Take Jetbus to the Villejuif Louis Aragon Métro stop and buy a *carnet* (book) of 10 Métro tickets. To reach the Marais neighborhood, take the Métro to the Sully Morland stop. For the Luxembourg area, take the same train to the Censier-Daubenton or Place Monge stops. If you're going to the airport, make sure before you board the Métro that your train is heading to Villejuif Louis Aragon (not Mairie d'Ivry), as the route splits at the end of the line.

The **Orlybus** (outside gate H, €6, 3/hr) takes you to the

Denfert-Rochereau RER-B line and the Métro, offering subway access to central Paris, including the Latin Quarter and Notre-Dame Cathedral, as well as the Gare du Nord train station.

These routes provide access to Paris via **RER trains**: an ADP shuttle bus takes you to RER-C, with connections to Gare d'Austerlitz, St. Michel/Notre-Dame, Musée d'Orsay, Invalides, and Pont de l'Alma stations (outside gate G, 4/hr, €5.50). The **Orlyval trains** are overpriced (€9) and require a transfer at the Antony stop to reach RER-B (serving Luxembourg, Châtelet-Les Halles, St. Michel, and Gare du Nord stations in central Paris).

Taxis are to the far right as you leave the terminal, at gate M. Allow €25–35 with bags for a taxi into central Paris.

Airport shuttle minivans are ideal for single travelers or families of four or more (see "Charles de Gaulle Airport," above, for the companies to contact; from Orly, figure about €23/1 person, €30/2 people, less for larger groups and kids).

Sleeping near Orly Airport: Two chain hotels, owned by the same company, are your best option near Orly. **Hôtel Ibis**** is reasonable, basic, and close by (Db-€60, tel. 01 56 70 50 60, fax 01 56 70 50 70, www.ibishotel.com, h1413@accor-hotels.com). **Hôtel Mercure***** provides more comfort for a higher price (Db-€120–135, tel. 01 49 75 15 50, fax 01 49 75 15 51, h1246@accor-hotels.com). Both have free shuttles to the terminal.

NORMANDY

Apple orchards, dramatic coastlines, half-timbered towns, and thatched roofs punctuate the green, rolling hills of Normandy. Parisians call Normandy "the 21st *arrondissement*." It's their escape—the nearest beach. Brits call this area close enough for a weekend away.

Despite the peacefulness of present-day Normandy, the region's history is full of war. It was founded by Viking Norsemen who invaded from the north, settled here in the 9th century, and gave Normandy its name. A couple hundred years later, William the Conqueror invaded England from Normandy. His victory is commemorated in a remarkable tapestry at Bayeux. A few hundred years after that, France's greatest cheerleader, Joan of Arc (Jeanne d'Arc), was convicted of heresy in Rouen and burned at the stake by the English, against whom she rallied  France during the Hundred Years' War. And in 1944, Normandy hosted a World War II battle that changed the course of history.

The rugged, rainy coast of Normandy harbors not only WWII bunkers, but also charming fishing villages, such as little Honfleur. And, on the border of Brittany, the almost surreal island abbey of Mont St. Michel rises serene and majestic, oblivious to the tides of tourists.

Planning Your Time

Rouen, Honfleur, the D-Day beaches, and Mont St. Michel all merit overnight visits. If you're driving between Paris and Honfleur, Giverny (see page 115) or Rouen (sights closed Tue) are easy stops;

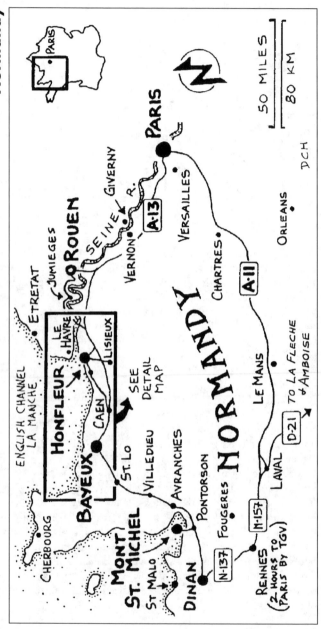

Camembert Cheese

This cheap, soft, white, Brie-like cheese is sold all over France (and America) in distinctive round, wooden containers. Camembert has been known for its cheese for 500 years, but local legend has it that today's cheese got its start in the French Revolution, when a priest on the run was taken in by Marie Harel, a Camembert farmer. He repaid the favor by giving her the secret formula from his own hometown—Brie.

From cow to customer, it takes about three weeks to make. High-fat milk from Norman cows is curdled with rennet, ladled into round five-inch molds, sprinkled with *penicillium camemberti* bacteria, and left to dry. In the first three days, the cheese goes from the cow's body temperature to room temperature to refrigerator cool (50 degrees).

Two weeks later, the ripened and aged cheese is wrapped in wooden bands and labeled for market. Like wines, Camembert cheese is controlled by government regulations and must bear the "A.O.C." *(Appellation d'Origine Contrôlée)* stamp of approval.

by train, they're best as day trips from Paris. The WWII memorial museum in Caen works well as a stop between Honfleur and Bayeux (and the D-Day beaches). Mont St. Michel is best seen early or late to avoid the masses of midday tourists. Dinan, only a 40-minute drive from Mont St. Michel (one hour by train), offers an enchanting introduction to Brittany. Some enjoy Mont St. Michel as a day trip from Dinan.

Getting Around Normandy

This region is great by car. Trains from Paris serve Rouen, Caen, Bayeux, Mont St. Michel (via Pontorson), and Dinan. But service between these sights can be frustrating. Plan ahead. Buses make Giverny (covered in Paris chapter), Honfleur, Arromanches, and Mont St. Michel accessible to train stations in nearby towns, though Sundays have little if any bus service. Mont St. Michel is a headache by train, except from Paris.

Cuisine Scene in Normandy

Known as the land of the four Cs (Calvados, Camembert—see sidebar above—cider, and *crème*), Normandy specializes in cream sauces, organ meats (sweetbreads, tripe, and kidneys—"the gizzard salads" are great), and seafood *(fruits de mer)*. Dairy products are big here. Local cheeses are Camembert (mild to very strong), Brillat-Savarin (buttery), Livarot (spicy and pungent), Pavé d'Auge (spicy and tangy), and Pont l'Evêque (earthy flavor). Normandy is famous for its powerful Calvados apple brandy, Benedictine brandy (made by local monks), and three kinds of alcoholic apple ciders (*cidre* can be *doux*—sweet, *brut*—dry, or *bouche*—sparkling, and the strongest). Also look for *poiret*, a tasty pear cider.

Remember, restaurants serve only during lunch (11:30–14:00) and dinner (19:00–21:00, later in bigger cities); cafés serve food throughout the day.

Rouen

This 2,000-year-old city of 100,000 people mixes dazzling Gothic architecture, charming half-timbered houses, and contemporary bustle like no other in France. Busy Rouen (roo-ohn) is France's fifth-largest port and Europe's biggest food exporter (mostly wheat and grain).

Rouen is nothing new. It was a regional capital during Roman times, and France's second largest city in medieval times (with 40,000 residents—only Paris had more). In the 9th century, the Normans made the town their capital. William the Conqueror called it home before moving to England. Rouen walked a political tightrope between England and France for centuries. An English base during the Hundred Years' War, it was the place where Joan of Arc was burned in 1431. Rouen's historic wealth was based on its wool industry and trade—for centuries, it was the last bridge across the Seine River before the Atlantic. In April 1944, as America and Britain weakened German control of Normandy before the D-Day landings, Allied bombers destroyed 50 percent of Rouen. While the industrial suburbs were devastated, most of the historic core survived, keeping Rouen a pedestrian's delight. And on summer evenings, a sound-and-light show transforms Notre-Dame Cathedral's facade into the changing colors of Monet's Impressionist canvas.

Planning Your Time

Rouen, with convenient connections to Paris (hrly, 75-min trains from Gare St. Lazare), makes an easy day trip if you want a dose of a much smaller—yet lively—French city. Considering the easy Paris connection and Rouen's ideal location in Normandy, drivers can save money and headaches by seeing Paris, then taking the train to Rouen to pick up a rental car (see "Car Rental" under "Helpful Hints," next page).

ORIENTATION

While Paris embraces the Seine, Rouen ignores it. The area we're most interested in is bounded by the river to the south, the Museum of Fine Arts (esplanade Marcel Duchamp) to the north, rue de la République to the east, and the place du Vieux Marché to the west.

It's a 20-minute walk from the train station to the river. Everything of interest is within a 10-minute walk of Notre-Dame Cathedral.

Tourist Information

The TI faces the cathedral. Pick up their good English walking tour flier, a map with information on Rouen's museums, and for drivers, a brochure on the Route of the Ancient Abbeys—described below (May–Sept Mon–Sat 9:00–19:00, Sun 9:30–12:30 & 14:00–18:00; Oct–April Mon–Sat 9:00–18:00, Sun 10:00–13:00, tel. 02 32 08 32 40).

A small American Express office in the TI changes money (closed during lunch year-round, tel. 02 35 89 48 60).

Arrival in Rouen

By Train: Rue Jeanne d'Arc cuts down from Rouen's train station (baggage check available) through the town center to the Seine River. Walk from the station down rue Jeanne d'Arc to rue du Gros Horloge. This pedestrian mall in the medieval center connects the open-air market and Joan of Arc Church (to your right) with the Notre-Dame Cathedral (to your left, starting point of my self-guided "Introductory Walking Tour of Rouen," page 181). Rouen's new subway whisks you from the train station to the Palais de la Justice in one stop (€1.30), one block above rue du Gros Horloge.

By Car: Follow signs to *Centre-Ville* (city center) and the *Rive Droite* (right bank). You can park for free overnight along the river (metered until 19:00), or in one of many underground lots. *Parking la Vieille Tour*, just below the cathedral, is handy (€9/day). If you get turned around (likely because of the narrow, one-way streets), aim for the cathedral spires.

Helpful Hints

Market Days: The best open-air market is on place St. Marc, a few blocks east of St. Maclou Church (Tue, Fri–Sun); the next best is on place du Vieux Marché, by Joan of Arc Church (daily except Mon). Markets are open roughly 8:00 to 13:00.

Internet Access: Consider **Place Net** (€4/hr, Mon–Sat 11:00–24:00, Sun 14:00–24:00, 37 rue de la République, tel. 02 32 78 02 22).

English Bookstore: ABC Books has nothing but English-language books, some American and mostly British (Tue–Sat 10:00–18:00, closed Sun–Mon, south of Eglise St. Ouen at 11 rue des Faulx, tel. 02 35 71 08 67, abcbookshop@wanadoo.fr).

Laundry: Try **Lav-pratic Laverie** (daily 8:00–20:00, no attendant and no English—completely coin-operated and automated from central control box, 43 rue de la République, near recommended hotels and next to Internet café).

Car Rental: Hertz is across from the train station (Mon–Fri

Rouen

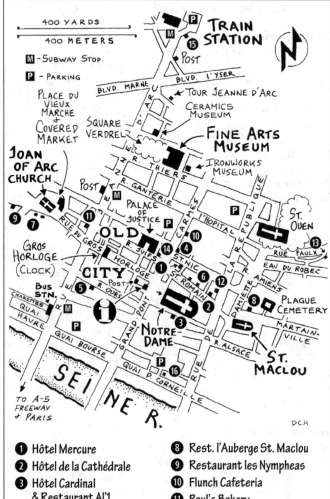

1 Hôtel Mercure
2 Hôtel de la Cathédrale
3 Hôtel Cardinal
  & Restaurant Al'1
4 Hôtel des Arcades
5 Chambre d'Hote Aunay
6 Crêperie le St. Romain
  & Fayencerie Augy China Shop
7 Rests. le Terre-Neuvas
  & le Maupassant
8 Rest. l'Auberge St. Maclou
9 Restaurant les Nympheas
10 Flunch Cafeteria
11 Paul's Bakery
12 Internet Café & Launderette
13 ABC Books
14 SNCF Office
15 Hertz
16 Europcar

8:00–9:00, Sat 8:00–12:00 & 14:00–18:00, closed Sun, 130 rue Jeanne d'Arc, tel. 02 35 70 70 71). **Europcar** is on the river below the cathedral (Mon–Sat 8:00–12:00 & 14:00–19:00, closed Sun, 17 quai Pierre Corneille, tel. 02 32 08 39 09, fax 02 32 08 39 00). Figure about €70 for one day (includes 250 kilometers/155 miles—that's plenty) or two days for €130 (includes 500 kilometers/310 miles).

Taxi: Call 02 35 88 50 50.

SNCF Train Office: To avoid a 15-minute walk to the station, get info and train tickets at the office in town (corner of rue aux Juifs and rue Eugène Boudin, Mon–Sat 10:00–19:00, closed Sun).

Introductory Walking Tour of Rouen

To see the essential Rouen sights, take the short historic walk described below (note that many sights are closed 12:00–14:00). You'll start at the cathedral square (and TI), walk four blocks east to the plague cemetery, and return by walking six blocks west of Notre-Dame Cathedral to Joan of Arc Church, where you'll find several recommended restaurants. To begin, stand in front of the cathedral.

▲▲**Notre-Dame Cathedral (Cathédrale Notre-Dame)**—You're seeing essentially what Claude Monet saw (from an apartment he rented here in the early 1890s) as he painted 20 different studies of this cathedral's frilly Gothic facade at various times of day. Using the physical building only as a rack upon which to hang light, mist, dusk, and shadows, Monet was capturing "impressions." (One of the paintings is in Rouen's Museum of Fine Arts, and four others are at the Orsay Museum in Paris.)

Enter the cathedral (Tue–Sun 8:00–18:00, Mon 14:00–18:00, closed Mon mornings and during Mass), stand at the back, and look down the **nave**. This is a classic Gothic nave—four stories of pointed-arch arcades, the top one filled with windows to help light the interior. Today—with the original colored glass (destroyed mostly in World War II) replaced by clear glass—the interior is lighter than intended. Why such a big cathedral in a small town? Until the 1700s, Rouen was the second city of France—rich from its wool trade and its booming port.

Next, circle counterclockwise three-quarters of the way around the church along the ambulatory (the side aisle that leads behind the high altar) before exiting via the left transept. The side chapels and windows are described in English; they come from an assortment of centuries and styles—bold blues and reds are generally from the 13th century. Photos halfway down on the right show WWII bomb damage.

Passing an iron gate near the high altar (closed during Mass—but often open on the opposite side even during Mass), you come to several important Norman **tombs**, dating from when Rouen was the Norman capital. The first tomb is of Rollo—the first duke of

Normandy in 933 (and great-great-great-great grandfather of William the Conqueror, seventh duke of Normandy, c. 1028). As first duke, he was chief of the first gang of Vikings (the original "Normans") who decided to actually settle here. Called "the father of Normandy," Rollo died at the age of 80, but is portrayed on his tomb as if he looks 33 (as was the fashion, because Jesus died at that age). Because of later pillage and plunder, only Rollo's femur is inside the tomb. And speaking of body parts, the next tomb contains only the heart of Richard the Lionhearted (the rest of his body lies in the Abbey of Fontevraud, described in the Loire Valley chapter). A descendant of the duke who conquered the English, this Norman was both a king of the English and the 12th duke of Normandy.

Circle behind the altar. Look back above the entry to see a rare black-and-white rose window (its medieval colored glass is long gone).

A small photo on the wall across the nave from Rollo's tomb shows the mess that resulted when a violent 1999 storm blew the spire off the roof, sending it crashing to the cathedral floor. Looking directly above Rollo's femur, you can see the patchwork in the ceiling. Perhaps this might be a good time to exit. Pass through the small iron gate, turn right, and leave through the side door (north transept).

Stepping outside, look back at the **facade.** The fine carved tympanum (the area over the door) shows a graphic Last Judgment. Jesus stands between the saved (on the left) and the damned (on the right). Notice the devil grasping a miser, who clutches a bag of coins. Look for the hellish hot tub, where even a bishop (pointy hat) is eternally in hot water.

Most of the facade has been cleaned—blasted with jets of water—but the fine limestone carving is still black. It's too delicate to survive the hosing, and instead awaits a more expensive laser cleaning.

From this courtyard, a gate deposits you on a charming street, rue St. Romain. Turn right and walk downhill on...

Rue St. Romain—This street has half-timbered buildings and lanes worth a look. Peek into the flowery pastel shop run by Rouen's last hatmaker. Nearby, you can look through an arch back at the cathedral's spire. Made of cast iron in the late 1800s—about the same time Eiffel was building his tower in Paris—the spire is, at 490 feet, the tallest in France. You can also see the former location of the missing smaller (green) spire—downed in that 1999 storm. Farther down the street, just past the Mormon church (read the French), a skinny and very picturesque half-timbered side lane (rue des Chanoines) leads left. And beyond that, a shop shows off a traditional art form in action...

Faïencerie Augy—Monsieur Augy welcomes potential shoppers to browse his studio/gallery/shop and see Rouen's clay "china" being made the traditional way. (When you enter the shop, say, *"Bonjour, Monsieur Augy"*; oh-zhee). First, the clay is molded and fired. Then

The Hundred Years' War
(1336–1453)

It would take a hundred years to explain all the causes, battles, and political maneuverings of this century-plus of warfare between France and England, but here goes:

In 1300, before the era of the modern nation-state, the borders between France and England were fuzzy. French-speaking kings had ruled England, English kings owned the south of France, and English merchants dominated trade in the north. Dukes and lords in both countries were aligned more along family lines than by national identity. When the French king died without a male heir (1328), both France and England claimed the crown, and the battle was on.

England invaded the more populous country (1345) and—thanks to skilled archers using armor-penetrating longbows—won big battles at Crécy (1346) and Poitiers (1356). Despite a truce, roving bands of English mercenaries stayed behind and paid themselves by looting French villages. The French responded with guerrilla tactics.

In 1415, the English took still more territory, with Henry V's big victory at Agincourt. But rallied by the heavenly visions of young Joan of Arc, the French slowly drove the invaders out. Paris was liberated in 1436, and when Bordeaux fell to French forces (1453), the fighting ended without a treaty.

it's dipped in white enamel, dried, lovingly hand-painted, and fired a second time. Rouen was the first city in France to make faience, earthenware with colored glazes. In the 1700s, the town had 18 factories churning out the popular product (Mon 10:00–18:00, Tue–Sat 9:00–19:00, closed Sun, 29 rue St. Romain, tel. 02 35 88 77 47, VAT tax refunds nearly pay for the shipping). For much more faience, visit the local Museum of Ceramics (see page 187). Rue St. Romain leads to the very fancy...

St. Maclou Church—This church's bowed facade is textbook Flamboyant Gothic. Notice the flame-like tracery decorating its gable. Since this was built at the very end of the Gothic age—and construction took many years—the doors are from the next age: Renaissance (c. 1550). The interior is of no great importance (Mon–Sat 10:00–17:00, Sun 10:30–17:30).

Leaving the church, turn right, then take another right (giving the boys on the corner a wide berth) and wander past a fine wall of half-timbered buildings fronting rue Martainville to the end of St. Maclou Church.

Half-Timbered Buildings—Because the local stone, a chalky limestone from the cliffs of the Seine River, was of poor quality (your thumbnail is stronger), and because local oak was plentiful, half-timbered buildings became a Rouen forte during the 14th to the 19th centuries. Cantilevered floors were standard until the early 1500s. These top-heavy designs made sense: City land was limited, property taxes were based on ground-floor square footage, and the cantilevering minimized unsupported spans on upper floors. The oak beams provided the structural skeleton of the building, which was then filled in with a mix of clay, straw, pebbles...or whatever was available.

A block farther down, at 186 rue Martainville, a covered lane leads to the...

Plague Cemetery (Aître St. Maclou)—During the great plagues of the Middle Ages, as many as two-thirds of the people in this parish died. Just taking care of the corpses was an overwhelming task for the decimated community. This half-timbered courtyard (c. 1520) was a mass grave and ossuary where the bodies were "processed." Bodies would be dumped into the grave (where the well is now) and drenched in liquid lime to speed decomposition. Later, the bones would be stacked in alcoves above the colonnades that line this courtyard. Notice the ghoulish carvings (c. 1560s)—gravediggers' tools, skulls, crossbones, and characters doing the "dance of death." In this *danse macabre*, Death, the great equalizer, grabs people of all social classes (free, mid-March–Oct daily 9:00–19:00, Nov–mid-March closes at 18:00). The place is now an art school. Peek in on the young artists. As you leave, find the dried black cat (died c. 1520, in tiny glass case to the left of the door). To overcome evil, it was buried during the building's construction.

Farther down rue Martainville, at place St. Marc, a colorful produce market blooms (Tue and Fri–Sun until 13:00). Otherwise, turn right upon leaving the boneyard and hike back up to Notre-Dame Cathedral. As it passes the cathedral, rue du Gros Horloge—the town's main shopping street since Roman times—leads to Rouen's...

Big Clock (Gros Horloge)—The impressive Renaissance public clock (1528), le Gros Horloge (groh oar-lohzh), decorates the former city hall. In the 16th century, an hour hand offered ample precision; minute hands only became necessary in a later, faster-paced age. The lamb at the end of the hour hand is a reminder that wool rules (and is the source of Rouen's wealth). The town medallion features the sacrificial lamb (with both religious and business significance). But the artistic highlight fills the underside of the arch (walk under and stretch your back) with the good shepherd and lots of sheep.

Continue walking downhill and cross the busy rue Jeanne d'Arc. (The train station is on your right, the bridge over the Seine is on your left, and the new Métro line is under your feet.) Fifty yards past the medieval McDonald's, Les Larmes de Jeanne d'Arc de

Joan of Arc
(1412-1431)

The cross-dressing teenager who rallied French soldiers to drive out English invaders was born the illiterate daughter of a humble farmer. One summer day, in her dad's garden, 13-year-old Joan heard a heavenly voice accompanied by bright light. It was the first of several saints (including Michael, Margaret, and Catherine) to talk to her during her short life.

In 1429, the young girl was instructed by the voices to save France from the English. Dressed in men's clothing, she traveled to see the king and predicted that the French armies would be defeated near Orleans—they were. King Charles VII equipped her with an ancient sword and a banner saying "Jesus, Maria," and sent her to rally the troops.

Soon, "the Maid" *(la Pucelle)* was bivouacking amid rough soldiers, riding with them into battle, and suffering an arrow to the chest, while liberating the town of Orleans. On July 17, 1429, she held her banner high in the cathedral of Reims as Charles was officially proclaimed king of a resurgent France.

Joan and company next tried to retake Paris (1429), but the English held on. She suffered a crossbow wound through the thigh, and her reputation of invincibility was tarnished. During a battle at Compiegne (1430), she was captured and turned over to the English for 10,000 pounds. In Rouen, they chained her by the neck inside an iron cage while the local French authorities (allied with the English) plotted against her. The Inquisition—insisting that Joan's voices were "false and diabolical"—tried and sentenced her as a witch and heretic.

On May 30, 1431, Joan of Arc was tied to a stake on Rouen's old market square (Place du Vieux Marché). She yelled, "Rouen! Rouen! Must I die here?" Then they lit the fire; she fixed her eyes on a crucifix and died chanting, "Jesus, Jesus, Jesus."

After her death, her place in history was slowly rehabilitated. French authorities proclaimed her trial illegal (1455), prominent writers and artists were inspired by her, and the Catholic Church finally beatified (1909) and canonized her (1920) as St. Joan of Arc.

Rouen (a chocolate shop at #163) would love to tempt you with its chocolate-covered almond "tears *(larmes)* of Joan of Arc." While you must resist touching the chocolate fountain, you are welcome to taste a tear. One is free; a small bag costs €7. The street continues to...

Place du Vieux Marché—The old market square, surrounded by fine old half-timbered buildings and plenty of good eateries, has a covered produce market, a park commemorating Joan of Arc's burning, and a modern church in her name. The market leads to the garden, where a tall aluminum cross marks the spot where Rouen publicly punished and executed people. The pillories stood here, and during the Revolution, the town's guillotine made 800 people "a foot shorter at the top." In 1431, Joan of Arc—only 19 years old—was burned. As the flames engulfed her, an English soldier said, "Oh my God, we've killed a saint." (Nearly 500 years later, Joan was canonized, and the soldier was proven right.) A waxy **Joan of Arc Museum** on the square tells the story of this inspirational teenager of supreme faith who, after hearing voices for several years, won the confidence of her countrymen, was given an army, and rallied the French against their English invaders. Those touched by her story will enjoy this humble museum (€4, English descriptions, mid-April–Sept daily 9:30–19:00, Oct–mid-April daily 10:00–12:00 & 14:00–18:00, 33 place du Vieux Marché). Between the museum and the church are ruins of a 15th-century church that stood on this spot and was destroyed during the French Revolution.

▲**Joan of Arc Church (Eglise Jeanne d'Arc)**—The modern church is a tribute to Joan of Arc, who was canonized in 1920 and later became the patron saint of France. The church, completed in 1979, feels Scandinavian inside and out—reminding us again of Normandy's Nordic roots. Sumptuous 16th-century windows, salvaged from a church lost in World War II, have been worked into the soft architectural lines, and with a ship's-hull vaulting, the church is a delightful place—reminiscent of the churches of Le Corbusier (€0.40 English pamphlet, Sun–Thu 10:00–12:30 & 14:00–18:00, Fri–Sat 14:00–18:00, WC 30 yards from church doors).

SIGHTS

In Rouen

These three museums are within a block of each other, closed on Tuesdays, and never crowded, and they can all be visited with a €5.40 combo-ticket.

▲**Museum of Fine Arts (Musée des Beaux-Arts)**—Paintings from many periods are beautifully displayed in this museum, including works by Michelangelo da Caravaggio, Peter Paul Rubens, Paolo Veronese, Jan Steen, Théodore Géricault, Jean-Auguste-Dominique Ingres, Eugène Delacroix, and the Impressionists. Don't miss Monet's painting of Rouen's Notre-Dame Cathedral, and the room dedicated to Géricault. Pick up the museum map at the ticket desk. Key rooms have excellent English descriptions on small, portable boards, and even have clever foldaway stools. The €2.30 audioguide is good, but spotty in its coverage (€3, Wed–Mon 10:00–18:00, 17th-century rooms close 13:00–14:00, closed Tue, 26 bis rue Jean Lecanuet, 3 blocks below train station, tel. 02 35 71 28 40).

Museum of Ironworks (Musée le Secq des Tournelles)—This deconsecrated Gothic church houses iron objects, many of them more than 1,500 years old. Locks, keys, tools, coffee grinders—virtually anything made out of iron is on display (€2.30, Wed–Mon 10:00–13:00 & 14:00–18:00, closed Tue, no English explanations, behind Musée des Beaux-Arts, 2 rue Jacques Villon, tel. 02 35 88 42 92).

Museum of Ceramics—Rouen's famous faience, or earthenware, dating from the 16th to the 18th centuries, fills this fine old mansion. Unfortunately, there is not a word of English to make things meaningful to Americans (same hours and cost as Museum of Ironworks, above; 1 rue Faucon, tel. 02 35 07 31 74).

Near Rouen

The Route of the Ancient Abbeys (La Route des Anciennes Abbayes)—This route is punctuated with abbeys, apples, Seine River views, and pastoral scenery. Drivers follow D-982, west of Rouen. Without a car, it's more difficult: Bus #30A goes to Jumièges, with a change in Duclair (€5, 1 hr, about 4/day July–Aug; 1/day in winter—leave Rouen 11:00, arrive Jumièges 12:05, return from Jumièges 13:50; depart from Rouen's bus station at 9 rue Jeanne d'Arc, tel. 08 25 07 60 27).

Drivers can stop to admire the Romanesque church at the **Abbey of St. Georges de Boscherville** (but skip the abbey grounds). The romantically ruined **Abbey of Jumièges** is *the* sight to visit on this route (follow the river on D-65 from Duclair for a more scenic approach). Founded in 654, it was destroyed by Vikings and rebuilt by William the Conqueror, only to be torn down again by French revolutionaries (€4.60, mid-April–mid-Sept daily 9:30–19:00, mid-Sept–mid-April daily 9:30–13:00 & 14:30–17:30, helpful English handout, or more detailed booklet for €6). **Auberge des Ruines,** across the street, makes a good if pricey lunch stop. A cheaper option is **Auberge du Bac,** just across from the ferry *(bac)* crossing *(menus* from €13, terrace seating, closed Tue–Wed, tel. 02 35 37 24 16). Cross the Seine between Jumièges and Honfleur on the €1.70 car ferry just down the road from the abbey (follow signs to Bac), at Duclair, or on one of three suspension bridges.

SLEEPING

These hotels are perfectly central, within two blocks of Notre-Dame Cathedral; directions are given from the cathedral. Because Rouen is busy with business travelers on workdays and quiet on weekends, the TI offers a *"bon weekend"* plan, where participating hotels offer two weekend nights (Fri, Sat, or Sun) for the price of one. While this sounds good in theory, it's hard to cash in on it in practice. Free rooms must be claimed at the time of reservation. If you walk into the TI without hotel reservations, ask for the *"bon weekend"* deal at

Sleep Code

(€1 = about $1.20, country code: 33)
S = Single, **D** = Double/Twin, **T** = Triple, **Q** = Quad, **b** = bathroom, **s** = shower only, **no CC** = Credit Cards not accepted, **SE** = Speaks English, **NSE** = No English, * = French hotel rating system (0–4 stars). You can assume a hotel takes credit cards unless you see "no CC" in the listing.

To help you sort easily through these listings, I've divided the rooms into three categories based on the price for a standard double room with bath:

$$$ **Higher Priced**—Most rooms €90 or more
$$ **Moderately Priced**—Most rooms between €60–90.
$ **Lower Priced**—Most rooms €60 or less.

that time. If you book ahead with a hotel, request the deal directly from the hotel. Again, don't get your hopes up.

$$$ Hôtel Mercure***, ideally situated a block north of the cathedral, is a sprawling business hotel with a professional staff, vast lobby, bar, and 125 rooms loaded with modern comforts (Sb-€99, Db-€105, suite-€170, elevator, air-con, parking garage-€10/day, 7 rue Croix de Fer, tel. 02 35 52 69 52, fax 02 35 89 41 46, www .mercure.com, h1301@accor-hotels.com, SE).

$$ Hôtel de la Cathédrale** welcomes you with a flowery, umbrella-filled courtyard; a cozy, wood-beamed breakfast room; and characteristic rooms, some with hardwood floors (Sb-€49–59, Db-€59–69, Tb-€85, Qb-€100, extra bed-€10, breakfast buffet-€7.50, Internet access-€6/hr, elevator, overnight parking-€5, 24-hr parking-€10, 12 rue St. Romain, a block from St. Maclou church, tel. 02 35 71 57 95, fax 02 35 70 15 54, www.hotel-de-la-cathedrale.fr, friendly Nathalie and Christelle SE).

$$ Hôtel Cardinal**, offering the same good quality and value as Hôtel de la Cathédrale, is run by Madame Picard and her English-speaking daughter, Sandrine. Nearly all of its spotless, comfortable rooms look right onto the cathedral; some have private balconies, and a few are ideal for families (Sb-€44–58, small Db-€52, big Db-€66, Tb-€79, Qb-€87, extra bed-€11, good breakfast buffet-€7, elevator, 1 place de la Cathédrale, tel. 02 35 70 24 42, fax 02 35 89 75 14, hotelcardinal.rouen@wanadoo.fr).

$ Hôtel des Arcades*, two short blocks north of the cathedral, is a safe budget option with sufficiently spacious, comfortable rooms and a friendly French welcome (D-€27, D with toilet only-€32, Db-€42, 52 rue des Carmes, tel. 02 35 70 10 30, fax 02 35 70 08 91, www.hotel-des-arcades.fr, hotel-des-arcades@wanadoo.fr).

$ *Chambre d'Hôte:* Monsieur Philippe Aunay rents two rooms in his 17th-century half-timbered home. A cross between a museum and a rummage sale, it's like sleeping at your eccentric grandma's house. One room comes with a piano, bathtub, and shower. The other is a three-room mini-apartment complete with a small kitchen and two bathrooms (Sb-€36, Db-€52, Tb-€78, Qb-€104, apartment for 5-€140, includes breakfast, no CC, 45 rue aux Ours, no sign, push buzzer, tel. 02 35 70 99 68, SE enough).

EATING

Restaurant Al'1, on a leafy square under the facade of the cathedral, is the place for a hearty salad (enormous €9 salads, Mon–Fri 12:00–15:30 & 19:00–22:00, closed Sat–Sun, indoor/outdoor seating, slick and efficient service, 3 place de la Cathédrale).

Crêperie le St. Romain, between the cathedral and St. Maclou Church, is a good budget option. It's run by a welcoming, eager-to-please owner who serves filling €7 crêpes with small salads (lunch Tue–Sat, dinner Thu–Sat, closed Sun–Mon, 52 rue St. Romain, tel. 02 35 88 90 36).

Two of Rouen's best moderately priced restaurants face place du Vieux Marché across from Joan of Arc Church. **Le Terre-Neuvas** is best for seafood (*menus* from €17, daily, 3 place du Vieux Marché, tel. 02 35 71 58 21). **Le Maupassant** is a jolly place with an outdoor terrace and three lively floors filled with red velvet booths and appreciative locals; it's famous for its *moelleux au chocolate*, melted chocolate over ice cream and cake (regional *menus* from €17, daily, 39 place du Vieux Marché, tel. 02 35 07 56 90).

L'Auberge St. Maclou, in a red-timbered building next to St. Maclou Church, is quiet and intimate, offering reasonable regional *menus* from €13 (closed Mon year-round and on Sun July–Feb, 222 rue St. Martainville, tel. 02 35 71 06 67).

Restaurant les Nymphéas is your chance to dress up for white-tablecloth elegance and extremely attentive service, and yet still not go broke. Named for Monet's water lilies, the restaurant carries an ambience more modern than ye olde, but it does offer the option of women's menus (without prices), a throwback to an earlier time when ladies weren't supposed to know what their dates were paying. The €32 *menu* offers four fine courses with plenty of choices. Expect to pay €20 for half a bottle of wine (dinner from 19:30, closed Sun–Mon, reservations smart, a block beyond place du Vieux Marché at 7 rue de la Pie, tel. 02 35 89 26 69). Only French is spoken in this formal setting, adding a touch of adventure to the experience.

Flunch hangs at the other end of the extreme—not a tablecloth or candle in sight. Here, you'll find family-friendly, cheap, point-and-shoot, cafeteria-style meals in a fast-food setting (€4 salad bar;

menu with salad bar, main course, and drink for €8; good kids' menu, open until 22:00, a block from cathedral at 66 rue des Carmes, tel. 02 35 71 81 81).

For **picnics**, try the morning open-air markets (closed Mon, see "Helpful Hints," page 179) or any small grocery store. Several late-night mini-markets are on rue de la République between rue St. Romain and rue de l'Hôpital (open until 24:00). **Monoprix** also has a large supermarket in the back of the store (Mon–Sat 8:30–21:00, closed Sun, on rue du Gros Horloge).

Rouen's **best bakery** is Paul's. It's always jammed, and a joy even if you're only looking (corner of rue Jeanne d'Arc and rue Rollon, a block above rue du Gros Horloge).

TRANSPORTATION CONNECTIONS

Rouen is well-served by trains from Paris, through Amiens to other points north, and through Caen to other destinations west and south.

From Rouen by train to: Paris' Gare St. Lazare (15/day, 75 min), **Bayeux** (3/day, 3.5 hrs, change in Caen), **Pontorson-Mont St. Michel** (5/day, 7 hrs, via Paris, change train stations from St. Lazare to Montparnasse, then TGV to Rennes, then 1.75-hr bus to Mont St. Michel; see Mont St. Michel's "Transportation Connections," page 226).

By train and bus to: Honfleur (5/day, 1.5 hrs, train to Le Havre, then 30-min, €8 bus over pont de Normandie to Honfleur—Le Havre's bus station is right next to the train station, making connections easy; or train to Caen, 3/day, 2.5 hrs, then bus #20 to Honfleur—take either the express bus, 2/day, 1 hr, €15, or the longer, more scenic *par la côte*, 8/day, 2 hr, €12).

Honfleur

Honfleur (ohn-flur) escaped the bombs of World War II, and feels as picturesque as it looks. Gazing at its cozy harbor lined with skinny, soaring houses, it's easy to overlook the historic importance of this port. For over a thousand years, sailors have enjoyed Honfleur's ideal location, where the Seine River meets the  English Channel. William the Conqueror received supplies shipped from Honfleur. And Samuel de Champlain sailed from here in 1608 to North America, where he discovered the St. Lawrence River and founded Quebec City. The town was also a favorite of 19th-century

Impressionists: Eugène Boudin (boo-dan) lived and painted here, attracting Monet and others from Paris. In some ways, modern art was born in the fine light of idyllic Honfleur.

Today's Honfleur, long eclipsed by the gargantuan port of Le Havre just across the Seine, happily uses its past as a bar stool and sits on it.

ORIENTATION

All of Honfleur's appealing streets and activities are within a short stroll of its old port (Vieux Bassin). The Seine River flows just east of the center, the hills of the Côte de Grâce form its western limit, and rue de la République slices north-south through the center to the port.

Tourist Information

The TI is in the left end of the flashy glass public library (Mediathéque) on quai le Paulmier, two blocks from the Vieux Bassin toward Le Havre. Their town map is useless. The €8.50 **museum pass** saves money only if you visit at least three museums (Easter–June and Sept–Oct Mon–Sat 10:00–12:30 & 14:00–18:30, Sun 10:00–17:00; July–Aug until 19:00 Mon–Sat with no midday closing; Nov–Easter Mon–Sat 10:00–12:30 & 14:00–18:00, closed Sun, tel. 02 31 89 23 30, www.ot-honfleur.fr). From May to mid-October, guided visits of Honfleur are offered on Mondays at 15:00 (€6, 90 min, smart to reserve, call TI).

Arrival in Honfleur

By Bus: Get off at the small station, called the *gare routière*, near the TI (useful information counter, confirm your departure, see "Transportation Connections," page 199). To reach the TI, old town, and port, walk five minutes up quai le Paulmier (with Hôtel Moderne on your left).

By Car: Follow *Centre-Ville* signs and park as close to the port (Vieux Bassin) as possible to unload your bags. Parking is tight in Honfleur, especially on summer and holiday weekends. The vast Parking du Bassin is close (across from TI), but charges €10 per day (€1.50/hr). For an extra five-minute walk, you can park all day for €2 at the metered Parking Privilégié (follow parking signs at round-about near river, park at far end, and cross gray swivel bridge on foot for quick access to port). Street meters are free from 19:00 to 9:00, and your hotel may have helpful parking suggestions. If you're driving into town and on a budget, note that there are cheaper alternatives to the impressive but expensive (€5) toll bridge, pont de Normandie, connecting Rouen and Honfleur. The bridges a few miles east of pont de Normandie cost €1.50–2.50, and pont de Bretonne is sometimes free.

Honfleur

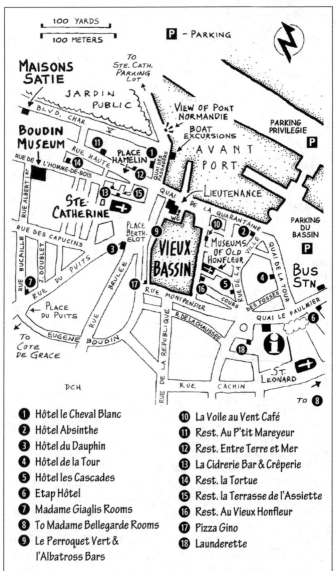

1 Hôtel le Cheval Blanc

2 Hôtel Absinthe

3 Hôtel du Dauphin

4 Hôtel de la Tour

5 Hôtel les Cascades

6 Etap Hôtel

7 Madame Giaglis Rooms

8 To Madame Bellegarde Rooms

9 Le Perroquet Vert & l'Albatross Bars

10 La Voile au Vent Café

11 Rest. Au P'tit Mareyeur

12 Rest. Entre Terre et Mer

13 La Cidrerie Bar & Crêperie

14 Rest. la Tortue

15 Rest. la Terrasse de l'Assiette

16 Rest. Au Vieux Honfleur

17 Pizza Gino

18 Launderette

Helpful Hints

Saturday Market: The area around St. Catherine Church becomes a colorful open-air market every Saturday morning (9:00–12:30).

Laundry: A good launderette, **Lavomatique**, is a block behind and toward the port from the TI (daily 7:00–20:00, 4 rue Notre-Dame).

SIGHTS

Old Basin (Vieux Bassin)—Stand at the riverside of Honfleur's square harbor (with your back to the river) and survey the town. The word Honfleur is Scandinavian, meaning the shelter *(fleur)* of Hon (a Norse settler). Eventually, the harbor was fortified by a wall with two gates (the one surviving gate is on your right) and a narrow boat passage protected by a chain. Just in front of the old barrel-vaulted entry to the town, you can see a bronze bust of Champlain—the explorer who sailed with an Honfleur crew to make his discoveries in Canada. The harbor, once filled with fishing boats, is now home to local yachts. Turn around to see various tour and fishing boats and the sleek suspension bridge, pont de Normandie (described below) in the distance. Fisherfolk catch flatfish, scallops, and tiny shrimps.

On the left, you may see a fisherman's wife—like Linda—selling *crevettes* (shrimp). You can buy them *cuites* (cooked) or *vivantes* (alive and wiggly). Linda is happy to let you sample one (rip off the cute little head and tail, and pop the middle into your mouth—*délicieuse!*) or buy a cupful to go (€1.50, daily in season).

Walk around the basin (to the left) past the old-time carousel, where you're likely to see an artist sitting at an easel, as Boudin and Monet did. Many consider this spot the birthplace of Impressionism. Artists still set up easels on this side of the basin to catch the light playing on the line of buildings, slates, timbers, geraniums, clouds, and reflections in the water. Monet came here to visit the artist Boudin, a hometown boy, and the battle cry of the Impressionists— "Out of the studio and into the light!"—was born.

▲▲St. Catherine Church (Eglise Ste. Catherine)—Looking at this church, it seems that if you could turn it over, it would float. That's because it was built by a community of sailors and fishermen in a region with plenty of boatbuilders and no cathedral architects. Sit down inside. When the first nave was built in 1466, it was immediately apparent that more space was needed—so the second was built in 1497. Because it felt too much like a market hall, side aisles were added. Notice the oak pillars. Since each had to be the same thickness, and trees come in different sizes, some are full length and others are supported by stone bases. In the last months of World War II, a bomb fell through the roof—but didn't explode. The pipe organ is popular for concerts, and the modern pews are designed to flip so that you can face the music. Take a close look at the many medieval instruments carved into the railing below the organ—a 16th-century combo band in wood.

The church's bell tower was built not atop the church, but across the square—to lighten the load of the wooden church's roof, and to minimize fire hazards. The church is free; the tower—a tiny museum with a few church artifacts—is not worth the €2 (tower and church open 9:00–18:30 daily in summer, off-season daily 9:00–12:00 & 14:00–18:00).

▲**Eugène Boudin Museum**—This pleasant, airy museum houses three interesting floors of exhibits: first floor—Norman folk costumes; second floor—the Boudin collection; and third floor—the Hambourg and Rachet collection. Pick up a map at the ticket counter.

First Floor: Monsieur and Madame Louveau (see their photo as you enter) gave Honfleur this quality collection of local traditional costumes. The hats, blouses, and shoes are supported by paintings that place them in an understandable historical and cultural context. Of special interest are the lace bonnets, typical of 19th-century Normandy. You could name a woman's village by her style of bonnet. The dolls are not toys for tots, but marketing tools for traveling clothing merchants—designed to show off the latest fashions.

Second Floor: After walking through a temporary exhibition hall on your left, you come to a fine gallery of 19th-century paintings arranged chronologically, from Romanticism through Realism to Impressionism. Upon showing their work in Paris, Normandy artists—such as Eugène Boudin (1824–1898)—created enough of a stir that Normandy came into vogue; many Parisian artists (including Monet and other early Impressionists) traveled to Honfleur to tune in to the action. Boudin himself made a big impression on the father of Impressionism. This collection of his paintings—which he gave to his hometown—provides a good study of the evolution from realistic portrayals of subjects (outlines colored in, like a coloring book) to masses of colors catching light (Impressionism). Boudin's beach scenes, showing aristocrats taking a healthy saltwater dip, helped fuel that trend. His skies were good enough to earn him the nickname "King of Skies."

Third Floor: In 1988, André Hambourg and his wife, Nicole Rachet, donated their art to this museum. The collection is enjoyably Impressionistic, but from the mid-20th century.

Cost and Hours: €5, mid-March–Sept Wed–Mon 10:00–12:00 & 14:00–18:00; Oct–mid-March Sat–Sun 10:00–12:00 & 14:30–17:00 and weekday afternoons only; closed Tue year-round and Jan–mid-Feb, elevator, no photos, rue de l'Homme de Bois, tel. 02 31 89 54 00.

▲**Maisons Satie**—The museum, housed in composer Erik Satie's birthplace, presents his music in a creative and enjoyable way. Upon

Eugène Boudin
(1824–1898)

Born in Honfleur, Boudin was the son of a harbor pilot. As an amateur teenage artist, he got work in an art supplies store that catered to famous artists from Paris (such as Jean-Baptiste-Camille Corot and Jean-François Millet) who came to paint the seaside. Boudin studied art in Paris, but kept his hometown roots. Thanks to his Paris connections, Boudin's work was exhibited at the Salon.

At age 30, Boudin met the teenaged Claude Monet. Monet had grown up in nearby Le Havre, and, like Boudin, sketched the world around him—beaches, boats, and small-town life. Boudin encouraged him to don a scarf, set up his easel outdoors, and paint the scene exactly as he saw it. (Today, we say: "Well, duh!" But "open-air" painting was unorthodox for artists trained to thoroughly study their subjects in the perfect lighting of a controlled studio setting.) Boudin taught Monet not so much technique as the courage to follow his artistic instincts.

In the 1860s and 1870s, Boudin spent summers at his farm (St. Siméon) on the outskirts of Honfleur, hosting Monet, Manet, and others. They taught Boudin the Impressionist techniques of using bright colors and building a figure with many individual brushstrokes. Boudin adapted those "strokes" to build figures with "patches" of color. In 1874, when the Impressionists held their renegade exhibition in Paris—Boudin was in it.

---

entry, you get a headset. As you wander from room to room, infrared signals transmit bits of Satie's music, along with a first-person story, to your headphones. As if you're living as an artist in 1920s Paris, you'll drift past winged pears, strangers in the window, and small girls with green eyes. (If you like what you hear…don't move; the infrared transmission is sensitive, and the soundtrack switches every few feet.) The finale—performed by you—is the Laboratory of Emotions. For a relaxing sit, enjoy the 12-minute movie (4/hr, time of next showing marked on door) showing modern dance springing from Satie's collaboration with Picasso types (€5, Wed–Mon May–Sept 10:00–19:00, Oct–April 11:00–18:00, closed Tue year-round and Jan–mid-Feb, free English audioguide, 5-min walk from harbor at 67 boulevard Charles V).

Museums of Old Honfleur—Two side-by-side museums combine to paint a picture of daily life in Honfleur since the Middle Ages. The curator creatively supports the artifacts with paintings, making the cultural context clearer. The **Museum of the Navy (Musée de la Marine)** fills a small 15th-century church (facing Vieux Bassin) with an interesting collection of ship models and marine paraphernalia.

The **Museum of Ethnographie and Norman Popular Art (Musée d'Ethnographie et d'Art Populaire)**, located in the old prison and courthouse on a very quaint old lane, re-creates typical rooms from various eras and crams them with objects of daily life (€4 for both or €3 each, both open April–June and Sept Tue–Sun 10:00–12:00 & 14:00–18:00, closed Mon; July–Aug daily 10:00–13:00 & 14:30–18:30; Oct–mid-Nov Sat–Sun 10:00–12:00 & 14:00–18:00 and weekday afternoons only, closed on Mon; ask for English explanation pages).

Boat Excursions—Boats to pont de Normandie (see below) depart from in front of Hôtel le Cheval Blanc (adult-€6.50, child-€5, run Easter–Nov, usually 10:30–17:30, 50 min, tel. 02 31 89 41 80). Any trip like this away from town includes two boring stops through the locks. The tour boat *Calypso* gives 40-minute trips around Honfleur's harbor (€4, no stops for locks).

Côte de Grâce Walk—For good exercise and a bird's-eye view of Honfleur and pont de Normandie, take the steep, 15-minute walk up to the Côte de Grâce viewpoint (from St. Catherine Church, walk past Hôtel du Dauphin and up rue Brûlée, turn right on rue Eugène Boudin, then turn left at the top and climb la Rampe du Mont Joli; best in early morning or at sunset).

▲Normandy Bridge (Pont de Normandie)—The 1.25-mile-long pont de Normandie is the longest cable-stayed bridge in the Western world. This is a key piece of a super-freeway that links the Atlantic ports from Belgium to Spain (€5–11). View the bridge from Honfleur (better from an excursion boat or above the town on Côte de Grâce viewpoint, and best at night, when bridge is floodlit) and consider visiting the free Exhibition Hall (under tollbooth on Le Havre side, daily 8:00–19:00). The Seine finishes its winding 500-mile journey here. From its source, it drops only 1,500 feet. It flows so slowly that in certain places, a stiff breeze can send it flowing upstream.

SLEEPING

(€1 = about 1.20, country code: 33)
Honfleur is busy on weekends, holidays, and in the summer. English is widely spoken. The lower room rates listed below are for off-season (generally Oct–May).

$$$ Hôtel le Cheval Blanc*** is a waterfront splurge in an old, half-timbered building with port views from most of the 32 pleasant rooms, many with queen-size beds, and a rare (in this town) elevator (Sb-€55–78, Db-€70–200, most Db-about €122, family rooms available, includes good buffet breakfast and taxes, must cancel with at least one week's notice or lose deposit, 2 quai des Passagers, tel. 02 31 81 65 00, fax 02 31 89 52 80, lecheval.blanc@wanadoo.fr, Madame Dubois).

$$$ Hôtel Absinthe* offers seven cushy rooms in a tastefully restored hotel behind the restaurant Le Bistro du Port. Whirlpool tubs, wood-beamed decor, and a cozy lounge with a fireplace make this worthwhile (Db-€93–126, Db suite-€220, extra bed-€24, 1 rue de la Ville; if no receptionist, keys available in Absinthe restaurant across alley; tel. 02 31 89 23 23, fax 02 31 89 53 60, www.absinthe.fr).

$$ Hôtel du Dauphin** is Honfleur's best midrange bet, with a family feel, a homey lounge/breakfast room, many stairs, and an Escher-esque floor plan. The rooms—some with open-beam ceilings, some with street noise—are all comfortable (Sb-€59, Db-€49–66, Tb-€75–110; pay-as-you-go breakfast upgrades include cereal, yogurt, or fruit at €1 apiece and freshly squeezed juice for €2; coin-operated Internet access, a stone's throw from church at 10 place Pierre Berthelot, tel. 02 31 89 15 53, fax 02 31 89 92 06, www.hotel-du-dauphin.com, hotel.dudauphin@wanadoo.fr, friendly Valerie SE).

$$ Hôtel de la Tour*, a basic hotel near the parking lots, has 48 efficient rooms, little personality, and a strange staff (Sb-€46–66, Db-€55–86, loft family room-€80–110, elevator, 3 quai de la Tour, near bus terminal and TI, tel. 02 31 89 21 22, fax 02 31 89 53 51, www.hoteldelatourhonfleur.com, hoteldelatourhonfleur@wanadoo.fr).

**$ Hôtel les Cascades*, while a bit musty with squishy beds, is still a good budget option. It's well-located across from the TI and above a restaurant (Db-€32–53, third person-€8, fourth person-€10, room 17 is best, dinner may be required on weekends and in summer, facing rue Montpensier at 17 place Thiers, tel. 02 31 89 05 83, fax 02 31 89 32 13, Melanie SE).

$ Etap Hôtel is modern, efficient, and tight, with cheap, antiseptically clean rooms (Sb-€27–32, €5–10 for each extra person, breakfast-€4, 24-hour room-renting automat when reception is closed, elevator, across from bus station and main parking lot on rue des Vases, tel. 02 31 89 71 70, fax 02 31 89 77 88).

Chambres d'Hôte

The TI has a long list of Honfleur's many *chambres d'hôte* (rooms in private homes), but most are too far from the town center. The following two, each a short walk from the center, are fine values.

$$ Gregarious Madame Giaglis (Lilliane) is the stage director of an utterly delightful bed-and-breakfast with five rooms surrounding a perfectly Norman courtyard, small terrace, and garden. The rooms—as cheery as the owner—are big, with firm beds and a separate sitting area (Db-€60–70, no CC, 200 yards up rue Brûlée from St. Catherine Church at 74 rue du Puit, tel. 06 22 34 78 94, www.giaglis.com, giaglis@wanadoo.fr).

$ Gentle Madame Bellegarde offers comfortable rooms in her traditional home (Db-€31–36, family-friendly Tb with kitchenette and great bathroom view-€55, 54 rue St. Léonard, 10-min uphill walk from TI, 3 blocks up from St. Leonard Church in non-touristy part of Honfleur, look for sign in window, tel. 02 31 89 06 52).

EATING

Eat seafood here, but be careful. Honfleur's many restaurants serve primarily a tourist clientele, so quality varies wildly. Trust my suggestions and consider your hotelier's opinion. It's a tough choice between the hard-to-resist waterfront tables of the many look-alike places lining Vieux Bassin, and those with more solid reputations that are on small side streets. If it's even close to sunny, skip your hotel breakfast and enjoy ambience for a cheaper price by eating on the port, where several cafés offer *petit déjeuner* for about €6; **L'Albatross** is good. Views are best from the lower side of the port, towards Le Havre. **La Voile au Vent**, with great views, is the only all-day café on this side.

A few doors separate two of Honfleur's best moderately priced restaurants (reserve ahead): **Au P'tit Mareyeur** is warm, intimate, and all about seafood (€19 *menu*, try the *bouillabaisse honfleuraise*, closed Mon–Tue and Jan, 4 place Hamelin, tel. 02 31 98 84 23); **Entre Terre et Mer** has outdoor seating and a brighter, fancier interior with a good range of regional dishes (*menus* from €20, closed Wed except July–Aug, 12 place Hamelin, tel. 02 31 89 70 60). Across the street and in an alcove, **La Cidrerie** is a cozy cider bar with fresh crêpes, Calvados, and an inviting atmosphere (closed Tue–Wed, set back on cathedral side of place Hamelin at #26).

La Tortue, between the port and Boudin Museum, serves good €16 and €22 *menus* in a snug living-room setting. The chef makes everything fresh *à la commande,* so service can be slow (closed Tue off-season, 36 rue de l'Homme de Bois, tel. 02 31 89 04 93).

La Terrasse de l'Assiette is a high-end, dress-up affair in an elegant half-timbered building (€25–45 *menus*, just across from church toward the water, reservations smart, 8 place Ste. Catherine, tel. 02 31 89 31 33).

At the port, your best bet is **Au Vieux Honfleur**, which sits serenely by the harbor. It offers comfortable indoor dining and outdoor tables with views, with a locally respected cuisine (*menus* from €28, daily, 13 quai St. Etienne, tel. 02 31 89 15 31). **Pizza Gino**, also at the port, has mediocre pizza and no character, but it's open daily until late and has waterfront tables (average pizza-€10, tel. 02 31 89 99 86).

Nightlife in Honfleur centers on the old port. Two bar-cafés sit 50 yards apart on the side of the port with taller buildings, dividing Honfleur's after-hours clientele by age: **Le Perroquet Vert** entertains a fortysomething crowd, while **L'Albatross** is clearly Generation X.

TRANSPORTATION CONNECTIONS

Buses connect Honfleur with Le Havre, Caen, Deauville, and Lisieux, where you'll catch a train to other points. While train and bus service are usually coordinated, ask at Honfleur's bus station for the best connection for your trip (information desk open Mon–Fri 9:00–12:15 & 14:30–18:30, Sat 9:15–12:15, open Sun 9:15–12:15 only in summer, tel. 02 31 89 28 41). Railpass-holders will save money by connecting through the nearest city, as bus fares increase with distance.

From Honfleur by bus and/or train to: Caen (bus #20: express 2/day, 1 hr, €15; more scenic *par la côte* 8/day, 2 hrs, €12), **Bayeux** (5/day, 3 hrs, 1-hr bus #50 to Lisieux then 1-hr train, or via more frequent 2-hr buses to Caen, then 30-min train), **Rouen** (3/day, 2 hrs, #20 or #50 bus over pont de Normandie to Le Havre, then train to Rouen; or in 3 hrs via Caen), **Paris**' Gare St. Lazare (5/day, 3 hrs; 1-hr bus to Lisieux or Deauville, then 2-hr train to Paris; buses from Honfleur meet most Paris trains).

Bayeux

Only six miles from the D-Day beaches, Bayeux was the first city liberated after the landing. Incredibly, the town was spared the bombs of World War II. After a local convent chaplain made sure London knew that this was not a German headquarters and of no strategic importance, a scheduled bombing raid was canceled—making Bayeux the closest city to the D-Day landing site not destroyed. Even without its famous tapestry and proximity to the D-Day beaches, Bayeux would be worth a visit for its pleasant town center and awe-inspiring cathedral, beautifully illuminated at night. Bayeux makes a good home base for visiting the area's sights, particularly if you lack a car.

ORIENTATION

Tourist Information

The TI is two blocks north of the cathedral on the street that connects place St. Patrice and the tapestry (on the small bridge, pont St. Jean). Pick up a town map, the excellent *D-Day Landings and the Battle of Normandy* brochure, bus schedules to the beaches, and regional information (June–Aug Mon–Sat 9:00–19:00, Sun 9:00–13:00 & 14:00–18:00; Sept–May Mon–Sat 9:30–12:30 & 14:00–17:30, Sun 10:00–12:30 & 14:00–17:30 but closed Sun Nov–March, Internet access, on pont St. Jean leading to pedestrian street rue St. Jean, tel. 02 31 51 28 28, www.bayeux-tourism.com).

Walking Tours: For a self-guided walking tour, pick up the brochure at the TI called *Discover Old Bayeux*, follow the numbers, and look for the tourist information plaques with English translations at many sights.

Tours in English of old Bayeux are offered in July and August, and sometimes off-season (€4, 90 min, call for times, tel. 02 31 92 14 21).

Arrival in Bayeux

Navigating Bayeux is a breeze. By car, look for the cathedral spires and follow the signs to *Centre-Ville*, then *Tapisserie*. On foot, it's a 20-minute walk from the train station to the tapestry and 15 minutes from the tapestry to place St. Patrice (recommended hotels and Sat market). Allow €6 for a taxi from the train station to any recommended hotel or sight in Bayeux.

Helpful Hints

Market Days: The Saturday open-air market (on place St. Patrice) is much larger than the Wednesday market (on pedestrian rue St. Jean). Both end by 13:00.

Internet Access: You can get online at the TI, but you'll need to buy a special card (€5/30 min, see above for hours and location). The Internet café **Microsimplus** is also a good choice (67 rue des Bouchers, next to launderette, tel. 02 31 22 06 02).

Laundry: Two launderettes are near place St. Patrice—one at 4 rue St. Patrice, the other at 69 rue des Bouchers (both open daily 7:00–21:00).

Bike Rental: Try **Cycles 14** (€15/day, on ring road at boulevard Winston Churchill at the eastern corner of town, tel. 02 31 92 27 75) or ask at the TI.

Car Rental: Bayeux offers few choices (you'll do better in the bigger city of Caen). **Hertz** is at the Shell station on the ring road at the town's eastern limit (boulevard du 6 Juin, tel. 02 31 92 25 33, fax 02 31 22 88 27). **Scauto** is handier, just below the train station at the BP gas station (tel. 02 31 51 18 51, fax 02 31 51 18 30).

SIGHTS

▲▲▲**Bayeux Tapestry**—Actually made of wool embroidered onto linen cloth, this document—precious to historians—is a 70-yard cartoon. The tapestry tells the story of William the Conqueror's rise from duke of Normandy to king of England and shows his victory over Harold at the Battle of Hastings in 1066. Long and skinny, it was designed to hang in the nave of Bayeux cathedral.

Your visit consists of separate parts, explaining the basic story of the battle three times—which was about right for me: First (after noting the time of the next movie showing at the top of the steps), you'll walk through a room full of mood-setting images into a room

Bayeux

1. Hôtel le Lion d'Or
2. Hôtel le Bayeux
3. Hôtel d'Argouges
4. Hôtel Mogador
5. Hôtel de la Gare
6. La Chaumière Deli
7. Rest. la Table du Terroir
8. Rest. le Pommier
9. Rest. l'Assiette Normande
10. Rest. le Petit Normand
11. Lace Conservatory & le Petit Bistro
12. Baron Gérard Museum
13. Launderettes (2 locations)
14. Internet Café

that contains a reproduction of the tapestry, with extensive explanations. Then you'll continue to a room showing Norman culture and the impact it ultimately had on England. Next, a 15-minute A/V show in the cinema (up one flight) gives a relaxing dramatization of the battle. Finally, you'll see the real McCoy: the tapestry itself. Before entering, pick up the headphones (worth the wait and included in the entry ticket), which give a top-notch, fast-moving, 20-minute, scene-by-scene narration complete with period music. If you lose your place, you'll find subtitles in Latin.

Remember, this is Norman propaganda—the English (the bad guys, referred to as *les goddamns*, after a phrase the French kept hearing them say) are shown with mustaches and long hair; the French (*les* good guys) are clean-cut and clean shaven—with even the backs of their heads shaved for a better helmet fit.

Cost and Hours: €7.40 includes audioguide, mid-March–mid-Oct daily 9:00–18:30, May–Aug daily 9:00–19:00, mid-Oct–mid-March daily 9:30–12:30 & 14:00–18:00, tel. 02 31 51 25 50). Arrive by 9:00 or late in the day to avoid crowds. When buying your ticket, find out the English film times. To minimize congestion in the actual tapestry hall, try to see the 15-minute film first, exit the way you entered, and backtrack to see the reproduction before the original tapestry (cinemagoers pile into the original tapestry room after each film). Because of the exhibit's generous English descriptions, the €2 English guide booklet is worthwhile only as a souvenir.

▲▲Bayeux Cathedral—This massive building dominates Bayeux. As you approach, notice its two towers—originally Romanesque, capped later with tall Gothic spires. The little rectangular stone house atop one tower was the watchman's home, from which he'd keep an eye out for incoming English troops during the Hundred Years' War...and for Germans five centuries later. Bayeux was liberated on D-Day plus one, June 7. About the only casualty was the German lookout—shot while doing just that from the window of this house. The west facade is structurally Romanesque, but with a decorative Gothic "curtain" added.

Walk inside. The view of the **nave** from the top of the steps shows a fun mix of Romanesque and Gothic. Historians believe the Bayeux Tapestry originally hung here. Imagine it proudly circling the Norman congregation, draped around the nave from the arches. The nave's huge, round lower arches are Romanesque (11th century) and decorated with the same zigzag pattern that characterizes this "Norman" art in England. The nave is so brightly lighted because of the huge windows above, in the Gothic half of the nave. The glass was originally richly colored (see the rare surviving 13th-century bits in the high central window above the altar). The finest example of 13th-century "Norman" Gothic is in the choir (the fancy area behind the central altar). Each of the columns is decorated with Romanesque

Bayeux History—The Battle of Hastings

Because of this pivotal battle, the most memorable date of the Middle Ages is 1066. England's King Edward was about to die without an heir. The big question: Who would succeed him—Harold, an English nobleman and the king's brother-in-law, or William, duke of Normandy and the king's cousin? Edward chose William and sent Harold to Normandy to give William the news. On the journey, Harold was captured. To win his release, he promised he would be loyal to William and not contest the decision. To test his loyalty, William sent Harold to battle for him in Brittany. Harold was successful, and William knighted him. To further test his loyalty, William had Harold swear on the relics of the Bayeux cathedral that when Edward died, he would allow William to ascend the throne. Harold returned to England, Edward died, and Harold grabbed the throne. William, known as William the Bastard, invaded England to claim the throne he reasoned was rightfully his. Harold met him in southern England at the town of Hastings, where their forces fought a fierce 14-hour battle. Harold was killed, and his Saxon forces were routed. William—now "the Conqueror"—marched to London, claimed his throne, and became king of England as well as duke of Normandy.

The advent of a Norman king of England muddied the political waters and set in motion 400 years of conflict between England and France—not to be resolved until the end of the Hundred Years' War (around 1450).

The Norman conquest of England brought England into the European mainstream (but still no euros). The Normans established a strong central English government. They brought with them the Romanesque style of architecture (e.g., the Tower of London and Durham Cathedral) that the English call "Norman." Historians speculate that had William not succeeded, England would have remained on the fringe of Europe (like Scandinavia), and French culture (and language) would have prevailed in the New World. Hmmm.

carvings. But those carvings lie under a Gothic-style stone exterior (with characteristic tall, thin lines adding a graceful verticality to the overall feel of the interior).

For maximum 1066 atmosphere, step into the crypt (below central altar), which was used originally as a safe spot for the cathedral's relics. The crypt shows two interesting columns with fine Romanesque carving. During a reinforcement of the nave, these two columns were replaced. Workers removed the Gothic veneer and discovered their true inner Romanesque beauty (free, Sept–June daily 8:30–18:00, July–Aug daily 8:30–19:00). The cathedral is beautifully illuminated after dark.

Lace Conservatory (Conservatoire de la Dentelle)—Notable for its carved 15th-century facade, the Adam and Eve house (find Adam, Eve, and the snake) offers a free chance to watch workers design and weave intricate lace, just as artisans did in the 1600s. You can also see examples of lace from the past (free, daily 10:00–12:30 & 14:00–18:00, across from cathedral entrance, tel. 02 31 92 73 80).

Baron Gérard Museum—The museum, housed in Hôtel du Doyen outside the cathedral's south transept, has a modest painting gallery and a collection of porcelain and lace (free with ticket to tapestry or €2.60, daily 10:00–12:30 & 14:00–18:00, July–Aug until 19:00 with no midday closing).

▲**Battle of Normandy Memorial Museum (Musée Memorial de la Bataille de Normandie)**—Providing a good overview of the Battle of Normandy, the museum features tanks, jeeps, uniforms, and countless informative displays, plus an enlightening 30-minute film (€5.50, May–mid-Sept daily 9:30–18:30, mid-Sept–April daily 10:00–12:30 & 14:00–18:00, on Bayeux's ring road, 20 min on foot from center, tel. 02 31 51 46 90, www.normandiememoire.com).

SLEEPING

(€1 = about 1.20, country code: 33)
Hotels are a good value here. Drivers should also see "Sleeping" under Arromanches, page 215.

Near the Tapestry

$$$ **Hôtel le Lion d'Or***** is Bayeux's close-to-classy, Old World hotel, with a palm-tree-lined courtyard, easy parking, professional service, and an elegant restaurant (small Db-€83, Db-€111–138, Tb-€158–176, includes buffet breakfast, no elevator, 71 rue St. Jean, tel. 02 31 92 06 90, fax 02 31 22 15 64, www.liondor-bayeux.fr, lion.d-or.bayeux@wanadoo.fr).

$ **Hôtel le Bayeux****, run by amiable Monsieur and Madame Lamontagne, has long halls, bright colors, and 29 super clean, modern rooms at great rates (Db-€45–59, Tb-€58–67, Qb-€74, some family rooms available with bunk beds, non-smoking rooms available, a block from cathedral's right transept at 9 rue Tardif, easy parking, tel. 02 31 92 70 08, fax 02 31 21 15 74).

Near Place St. Patrice

These two excellent hotels are just off the big place St. Patrice (easy parking), a 10-minute walk up rue St. Martin from the TI.

$$ **Hôtel d'Argouges**** greets travelers with a flowery court-yard and three-plus-star comfort at two-star prices. Every one of the 28 rooms (all with new beds) is warmly decorated and meticulously cared for by the formal owners, Monsieur and Madame Ropartz.

Named for its builder, Lord d'Argouges, this tranquil retreat has a château-like feel, with classy public lounges and a lovely private garden (Sb-€51, Db-€65–77, fine family suites-€90–126, deluxe mega-suite for up to five-€200, extra bed-€15, pay-as-you-go breakfast, free parking, just off huge place St. Patrice at 21 rue St. Patrice, tel. 02 31 92 88 86, fax 02 31 92 69 16, dargouges@aol.com).

$ **Hôtel Mogador**** is a sure two-star bet, with welcoming Monsieur Mencaroni at the helm. Choose between cozy, wood-beamed rooms on the busy square or quiet, more modern rooms off the street (Sb-€38, Db-€43–48, Tb-€56, Qb-€69, good breakfast-€6, 20 rue Alain Chartier/place St. Patrice, tel. 02 31 92 24 58, fax 02 31 92 24 85, hotel.mogador@wanadoo.fr, SE).

Near the Station
$ The unpredictable **Hôtel de la Gare*** is a basic, simple option for desperate train travelers (D-€24, Db-€40, no CC, 26 place de la Gare, tel. 02 31 92 10 70, fax 02 31 51 95 99).

EATING

It's easy to dine inexpensively in Bayeux. Rue St. Jean is lined with *crêperies*, simple restaurants, and the best *charcuterie* (deli) in town, **La Chaumière** (closed 13:00–15:00, Sun afternoons, and Mon; otherwise open until 19:30, salads and quiches to go, across from Hôtel Churchill).

La Table du Terroir is run by a butcher, so meat is tops in this fun, traditional place where clients share monastic, meet-your-neighbor, plank tables (lunch *menu* with no choice-€11, dinner *menus* from €16, closed Sun–Mon, a short block off rue St. Jean at 42 rue St. Jean, tel. 02 31 92 05 53).

Hôtel le Lion d'Or, where locals go for a special meal, has a big dining room that's hunting-lodge elegant and accustomed to foreigners (€21 and €31 *menus*, closed Mon; see Bayeux—"Sleeping," above).

L'Assiette Normande, run by a young, friendly couple, is small and simple (*menus* from €10, closed Mon–Tue, 3 rue des Chanoines, tel. 02 31 22 04 61).

Near the Cathedral
Le Petit Bistro is aptly named, with six intimate tables opposite the cathedral entry at 2 rue Bienvenue (*menus* from €19, closed Sun–Mon, tel. 02 31 51 85 40).

Le Pommier, a block away, is an easygoing place with a good variety of reasonable choices served with ambience, inside or out (*plats du jour*-€9, *menus* from €13, closed Tue–Wed, 38 rue des Cuisiniers, tel. 02 31 21 52 10).

Le Petit Normand, just below the cathedral, is popular with locals and *très raisonnable* (*menus* from €17, open daily, 21 rue Larcher, tel. 02 31 22 88 86).

TRANSPORTATION CONNECTIONS

From Bayeux by train to: Paris' Gare St. Lazare (9/day, 2.5 hrs, 3 require change in Caen), **Amboise** (4/day, 5 hrs, change in Caen and Tours, or Paris-Montparnasse and Tours-St. Pierre des Corps), **Rouen** (3/day, 3 hrs, change in Caen), **Caen** (10/day, 15 min), **Honfleur** (5/day, 2.5 hrs; train to Lisieux or Caen, then bus to Honfleur; trip is quicker via Caen; for bus information, call 02 31 89 28 41), **Pontorson-Mont St. Michel** (2/day, one at about 7:45, the other at about 17:00, 2 hrs to Pontorson with bus to Mont St. Michel; see Mont St. Michel's "Transportation Connections," page 226).

By bus to the D-Day beaches: Bus Verts du Calvados serves the area (TI has schedules, tel. 08 10 21 42 14), with stops in Bayeux at place St. Patrice and at the train station. Line #75 runs to Arromanches (3/day in summer, 1/day off-season, 20 min), and line #70 serves the American Cemetery (2–4/day, 35 min). Bus Verts also runs a summer line connecting key sights (TI has schedule).

D-Day Beaches

Along the 75 miles of Atlantic coast north of Bayeux, stretching from Ste. Marie-du-Mont to Ouistreham, you'll find WWII museums, monuments, cemeteries, and battle remains left in tribute to the courage of the British, Canadian, and American armies who successfully carried out the largest military operation in history. It was on these beautiful beaches, at the crack of dawn on June 6, 1944, that the Allies finally gained a foothold in France, and Nazi Europe began to crumble.

> *"The first 24 hours of the invasion will be decisive.... The fate of Germany depends on the outcome.... For the Allies, as well as Germany, it will be the longest day."*
> —Field Marshal Erwin Rommel to his aide, April 22, 1944 (from the movie *The Longest Day*)

Getting Around the D-Day Beaches

On Your Own: A car is ideal, particularly for three or more people. If you have a railpass and an avid interest in World War II, consider stowing your pass and **renting a car** for a day or two to do this area efficiently and properly (see Bayeux "Helpful Hints," page 200, for car and bike rental; the Bayeux TI has more information). Park in monitored locations at the sights, as break-ins have been a problem, particularly at the American Cemetery. To mix in some exercise, you can also bike between the sights. **Buses** link Bayeux, the coastal town of Arromanches, and the most impressive sights of D-Day (*Jour J* in French); see "Transportation Connections," previous page.

By Taxi: Taxi minivans shuttle up to seven people between the key sights at surprisingly fair rates. Approximate prices per taxi (not per person) are: €20 from Bayeux to Arromanches, €35 round-trip with one-hour wait time; €30 from Bayeux to the American Cemetery, €45 round-trip with one-hour wait time; and €65 round-trip for the American Cemetery and Pointe du Hoc with two hours total wait time at the sights (other combinations possible, 50 percent surcharge after 19:00 and on Sun, taxi tel. 02 31 92 92 40).

By Tour: Several companies offer excursions to the D-Day beaches from Bayeux or Caen (€31–35/4 hrs, €60–70/full day). These companies cover virtually the same sights: **Battlebus,** which departs from Bayeux, gets the best reviews from historians (tel. 02 31 22 28 82, www.battlebus.fr, tours@battlebs.fr). **Victory Tours,** run by friendly Roel, is less formal and very informative. Since it offers only one minivan that seats eight, it's best to reserve in advance (departs from Bayeux only, tel. 02 31 51 98 14, mobile 06 75 12 88 28, fax 02 31 51 07 01, www.lignerolles.homestead.com). **Normandy Sightseeing Tours** advertises "licensed guides" and uses minivans and, if needed, 50-person buses for its tours (€35–45 for half-day departures from Bayeux daily at 8:30 and 12:50, reserve by phone with CC, tel. 02 31 51 70 52, fax 02 31 51 74 74, www .normandywebguide.com, francois.gauthron@wanadoo.fr). Another option from Bayeux is **Normandy Tours** (tel. 02 31 92 10 70, fax 02 31 51 95 99). **Salient Tours** advertises "expert British guides" and offers 9:00 departures from Caen and 14:30 departures from Bayeux (each lasts 3.5 hrs); the Caen departures cover only the British sector (including Arromanches), while Bayeux departures cover only the American sector (tel. 06 76 38 96 89). The Caen Memorial Museum offers tours of the D-Day beaches in combination with a visit to their museum (described below).

Caen

WWII bombs destroyed most of the city, but today's Caen (pop. 115,000) bristles with confidence, students, and a well-restored old city. Eurailers find Caen practical as a home base, with frequent train connections to Paris, buses to Honfleur and the Caen Memorial Museum, and minivan excursions to the D-Day beaches.

The **TI** is on place St. Pierre, 10 blocks across the canal from the train station. Pick up a map (€0.30) and free visitor's guide filled with practical information (June–Sept Mon–Sat 9:00–19:00,

Countdown to D-Day

1939 On September 1, Adolf Hitler invades Poland, sparking World War II.

1940 Germany's "Blitzkrieg" ("lightning war") quickly overwhelms France, Nazis goose-step down the avenue des Champs-Elysées, and the country is divided into Occupied France (the north) and Vichy France (the south, ruled by right-wing French). Just like that, virtually the entire continent is fascist.

1941 The Allies (Britain, the United States, the Soviet Union, and others) peck away at the fringes of "fortress Europe." The Soviets repel Hitler's invasion at Moscow, while the Brits (with American aid) battle German U-boats for control of the seas.

1942 Three crucial battles—at Stalingrad, El-Alamein, and Guadalcanal—weaken the German forces and their ally, Japan. The victorious tank battle at El-Alamein in the deserts of north Africa soon gives the Allies a jumping-off point (Tunis) for the first assault on the Continent.

1943 150,000 Americans and Brits, under the command of George Patton and Bernard ("Monty") Montgomery, land in Sicily and begin working their way north through Italy. Meanwhile, Germany has to fend off tenacious Soviets on their eastern front.

1944 On June 6, 1944, the Allies launch "Operation Overlord," better known as D-Day. Three million Allies and six million tons of materiel had been amassed in England in preparation for the biggest fleet-led invasion in history—across the Channel to France, then eastward to Berlin. The Germans, hunkered down in northern France,

Sun 9:00–17:00; Oct–May Mon–Sat 9:00–13:00 & 14:00–19:00, Sun 9:00–13:00 & 14:00–17:00; from train station, walk up avenue du 6 Juin, drivers follow signs for *Parking Château*, tel. 02 31 27 14 14).

The looming château, built by William the Conqueror in 1060, sits across the street from the TI. West of the TI, modern rue St. Pierre is a popular shopping area and pedestrian zone. To the east of the TI, the more historic Vagueux quarter has many restaurants and cafés in half-timbered buildings.

knew an invasion was imminent, but the Allies kept it top secret. On the night of June 5, 150,000 soldiers boarded ships and planes, not knowing where they were headed until they were underway. Each one carried a note from General Dwight D. Eisenhower: "The tide has turned. The free men of the world are marching together to victory."

At 6:30 in the morning on June 6, 1944, Americans spilled out of troop transports into the cold waters off a beach in Normandy, code-named Omaha. The weather was bad, seas were rough, and the prep bombing had failed. The soldiers, many seeing their first action, were dazed and confused. Nazi machine guns pinned them against the sea. Slowly, they crawled up the beach on their stomachs. A thousand died. They held on until the next wave of transports arrived.

All day long, Allied confusion did battle with German indecision—the Nazis never really counterattacked, thinking D-Day was just a ruse, not the main invasion. By day's end, the Allies had taken several beaches along the Normandy coast and began building artificial harbors, providing a tiny port-of-entry for the reconquest of Europe. The stage was set for a quick and easy end to the war. Right.

1945   After liberating Paris (August 26, 1944), the Allied march on Berlin bogs down, hit by poor supply lines, bad weather, and the surprising German counter-punch at the Battle of the Bulge. Finally, in the spring, Soviet soldiers take Berlin, Hitler shoots himself, and—after five long years of war—Europe is free.

SIGHTS

▲▲▲**Caen Memorial Museum (Le Mémorial de Caen)**—Caen (kehn), the modern capital of lower Normandy, has the best WWII museum in France. Officially named the "The Caen Memorial, A Museum for Peace" *(Le Mémorial de Caen, un musée pour la paix)*, it effectively puts the Battle of Normandy in a broader context. Your visit has numerous parts: the lead-up to World War II, the actual Battle of Normandy, two video presentations, the Cold War, and the

D-Day Beaches

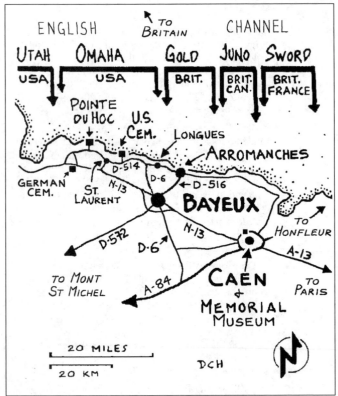

ENGLISH   TO BRITAIN   CHANNEL

UTAH   OMAHA   GOLD   JUNO   SWORD

USA   USA   BRIT.   BRIT. CAN.   BRIT. FRANCE

POINTE DU HOC   U.S. CEM.   LONGUES

ARROMANCHES

GERMAN CEM.   ST. LAURENT   N-13   D-514   D-6   ← D-516

BAYEUX

TO HONFLEUR

D-572   D-6   N-13   A-13

TO MONT ST MICHEL   A-84   CAEN + MEMORIAL MUSEUM   TO PARIS

20 MILES

20 KM

DCH

N

ongoing fight for peace (Nobel Prize Gallery and Peace Gardens). In addition, a special exhibition called "D-Day Words" presents the daily life of troops during the campaign by drawing on rough letters and diaries written during the summer of 1944. Opened in 2004 as part of the 60th anniversary of the D-Day landing, the exhibit becomes a permanent fixture of the memorial in 2005.

The museum is brilliant. Begin with a downward spiral stroll, tracing (almost psychoanalyzing) the path Europe followed from the end of World War I to the rise of fascism to World War II.

The lower level gives a thorough look at how World War II was fought—from General Charles de Gaulle's London radio broadcasts to Hitler's early missiles to wartime fashion to the D-Day landings.

You then see two powerful movies. *Jour J (D-Day)* is a 30-minute film that shows the build-up to D-Day itself, and the successful campaign from there to Berlin (every 40 min from 10:00 to 19:00, works in any language, pick up schedule as you enter). While snippets come from the movie *The Longest Day*, most of the film consists of footage from actual battle scenes. The second movie, *Espérance (Hope)*, is a thrilling sweep through the pains and triumphs of the 20th century (on the half hour, 20 min, also good in all languages).

The new Cold War wing sets the scene with audio testimonies and photos of European cities destroyed during World War II. It continues with a helpful overview of the bipolar world that followed the war, with fascinating insights into the psychological battle waged by the Soviet Union and the United States for the hearts and minds of their people until the fall of communism. The wing concludes with the Hall of Peace, which has a space-age design that encourages contemplation of a different future. The museum is the only place outside of the United States that displays remains from the 9/11 attacks (you can see them at the end of the building, through the glass windows). The newly opened British Gardens, inaugurated June 5, 2004, by Prince Charles, are located east of the Hall for Peace Building.

The next section of the museum celebrates the irrepressible human spirit in the Gallery of Nobel Peace Prizewinners. It honors the courageous and too-often-inconspicuous work of people such as Andrei Sakharov, Elie Wiesel, and Desmond Tutu, who understand that peace is more than an absence of war.

The finale is a walk through the U.S. Armed Forces Memorial Garden. I was bothered by the mindless laughing of lighthearted children unable to appreciate their blessings. Then I read on the pavement: "From the heart of our land flows the blood of our youth, given to you in the name of freedom." Then their laughter made me happy.

Cost and Hours: €18, free for all veterans and kids under 10. The museum is open daily 9:00–19:00 (mid-July–Aug until 20:00, Nov–Feb closes at 18:00, ticket office closes 75 min before museum, tel. 02 31 06 06 44—as in June 6, 1944, fax 02 31 06 06 70, www .memorial-caen.fr).

Allow a minimum of 2.5 hours for your visit, including an hour for videos. You could easily spend all day here; remember that tickets are valid for 24 hours if you want to return the next day. There are no guided tours. Free supervised babysitting is offered for children under 10 (for whom exhibits may be too graphic). The museum has a large gift shop with plenty of books in English, an all-day cafeteria, and a restaurant with a garden-side terrace (lunch only, located in the Cold War wing). Picnicking in the gardens is also an option.

Tours: The museum runs eight-person minivan guided tours of the D-Day beaches. Tours include entry to Caen Memorial Museum and four-hour tours of the D-Day beaches, including Longues-sur-Mer, Arromanches, Omaha Beach, the American Cemetery, and Pointe du Hoc (€56-morning tour, €67-afternoon tour, both cover same sights though afternoon tour is a bit longer, includes an English information book, daily April–Sept 9:00 & 14:00, Oct–March 13:00 only, pickup from museum or Caen train station; contact museum for details, reservations, and advance payment; www.memorial-caen.fr, resa@memorial-caen.fr).

Getting to the Museum: Finding the memorial is quick and easy for drivers. It's just off the ring-road freeway *(périphérique nord)* in Caen *(sortie #7, look for signs to Mémorial).*

By train, Caen is two hours from Paris (14/day) and 15 minutes from Bayeux (10/day). At Caen's train station, take the new tramway from in front of the station to the Eglise St. Pierre stop, then take bus #2 (3/hr) to *le Mémorial.* Taxis cost about €10 one-way from the station.

SLEEPING

(€1.20 = about $1, country code: 33)
Hôtel de France**, a three-minute walk from Caen's train station, has plain but sleepable rooms (Db-€42–50, 10 rue de la Gare, turn right out of train station, right on first main street, and you'll see signs, tel. 02 31 52 16 99, fax 02 31 83 23 16).

Hôtel du Havre** is a basic, fair deal (Ss-€31, Sb-€39, Ds-€35, Db-€43, Tb-€52, family room-€57, 10-min walk from station up avenue du 6 Juin, left on rue du Havre to #11, tel. 02 31 86 19 80, fax 02 31 38 87 67, www.hotelduhavre.com, resa@hotelduhavre.com, Madame Fiault, some SE).

Arromanches

This small town was ground zero for the D-Day invasion. Almost overnight, it sprouted the immense Port Winston, which enabled the Allies to establish a foothold in Normandy from whence to begin their victorious push to Berlin and end World War II. Today, you'll find a fine museum, an evocative beach and bluff, and a delightful little town that offers a pleasant cocktail of war memories, cotton candy, and beachfront trinket shops. The population of tiny Arromanches just reached 500 people (about the same as on June 6, 1944).

The **TI** is across the parking lot from the D-Day Landing Museum on rue Colonel René Michel (May–Sept daily 10:00–13:00 & 14:00–18:00, Oct–April closed 12:00–14:00 & at 17:00, Internet access in summer only, tel. 02 31 21 47 56, www.arromanches.com).

There's a supermarket (above the town by the parking lot), a post office, and an ATM (near the museum). Arromanches and Bayeux are connected by five buses a day in the summer (#75), two a day off-season (#74, 30-min ride). To get a taxi, you'll need to call the Bayeux taxi service (tel. 02 31 92 92 40).

SIGHTS

In Arromanches

▲▲Port Winston and the D-Day Landing Museum (Musée du Débarquement)—The first-ever prefab harbor was created by the British in Arromanches. Since it was Churchill's brainchild, it was named Port Winston. Walk along the seaside promenade and imagine the building of this port. Seventeen old ships crossed the English Channel under their own steam and were sunk by their crews bow to stern, forming the first shelter. Then 115 football-field-sized cement blocks (called "Mulberries") were towed across the channel and sunk, creating a four-mile-long breakwater 1.5 miles offshore—a port the size of Dover, England. Then, seven floating steel "pierheads" with extendable legs were set up and linked to shore by four mile-long floating roads made of concrete pontoons. Anti-aircraft guns were set up on the pontoons. Within six days, 54,000 vehicles, 326,000 troops, and 110,000 tons of goods had been delivered. An Allied toehold on Normandy was secure. Eleven months later, Hitler was dead and the war was over.

The D-Day Landing Museum, which faces the still visible remains of the temporary harbor, provides an instructive hour to those who are interested. With models, maps, mementos, and two short audiovisual shows, this low-tech exhibit tells the story of this incredible undertaking. One video (8 min, ground floor) recalls D-Day. The other (15 min, upstairs) features the construction of the temporary port—ask for English times (€6, pick up English flier at door, May–Aug daily 9:00–19:00, Sept daily 9:00–18:00, Feb–April & Oct–Dec daily 9:30–12:30 & 13:30–17:30, closed Jan, tel. 02 31 22 34 31, www.normandy1944.com).

Hike 10 minutes to the top of the bluff behind the museum for the view from the *Arromanches 360°* theater (€1.50 for parking) and ponder how, from this makeshift harbor, the liberation of Europe commenced. Inside, *The Price of Freedom* offers D-Day footage in a noisy montage of videos on its 360-degree screen (€4, 2 shows/hr, 20 min, last showing at 18:40, tel. 02 31 22 30 30).

But the most thought-provoking experience in town is simply to wander the beach among the concrete and rusted litter of the battle, and be thankful that all you hear are birds and surf.

Near Arromanches

▲Longues-sur-Mer Gun Battery—Several German bunkers, guns intact, are left guarding against seaborne attacks on the city of Arromanches (free, €5 booklet helpful, skip the €5.50 tour, follow signs for *Batterie* in Longues-sur-Mer). Walk to the observation post for a great view over the channel (located between Arromanches and Port-en-Bessin; turn right at signal in Longues-sur-Mer). You can walk 15 minutes or drive down to the water by continuing on the small road past the parking lot. From Longues-sur-Mer and the beaches below, there are dramatic coastal views, including about the best look you can get of the remains of Port Winston at Arromanches.

▲▲▲WWII Normandy American Cemetery and Memorial at St. Laurent—Crowning a bluff just above Omaha Beach and the eye of the D-Day storm, nearly 10,000 brilliant white-marble crosses and Stars of David glow in memory of Americans who gave their lives to free Europe on the beaches below.

First, stop by the Visitors' Office to pick up an English information sheet. Read the 1956 letter from the French president (on the wall above the fireplace), which eloquently expresses the feeling of gratitude the French still have for the United States. The attendant at the computer terminal has a database that can provide ready access to the story of any serviceman who died in Normandy.

Walk past the memorial and cemetery to the bluff that overlooks the piece of Normandy beach called "that embattled shore—portal of freedom." It's quiet and peaceful today, but imagine the horrific carnage of June 6, 1944.

Walk back to the memorial, where you'll see giant reliefs of the Battle for Normandy and the Battle for Europe etched on the walls. Behind that is the semicircular Garden of the Missing, with the names of 1,557 soldiers who were never found.

Finally, wander among the peaceful and poignant sea of crosses. Notice the names, home states, and dates of death inscribed on each. Immediately after the war, all the dead were buried in temporary cemeteries. In the mid-1950s, the families of the soldiers decided whether their loved ones should remain with their comrades or be brought home. Officers were disproportionately left here. Their families knew they'd want to be buried with the men they fought and died with.

France has given the United States permanent free use of this 172-acre site. It is immaculately maintained by the American Battle Monuments Commission (free, daily 9:00–17:00, park carefully, breakins have been a problem, tel. 02 31 51 62 00, www.abmc.gov/no.htm).

▲German Military Cemetery—To ponder German losses, drop by this somber, thought-provoking resting place of 21,000 German soldiers. While the American Cemetery is the focus of American travelers, visitors here speak in hushed German. The site is glum, with two graves per simple marker and dark crosses that huddle together in groups of five. It's just south of Pointe du Hoc (right off N-13 in village of La Cambe, 3.5 miles west of Bayeux; follow signs to *Cimetière Allemand,* April–Oct daily 8:00–19:00, Nov–March closes at 17:30, tel. 02 31 22 70 76).

▲▲**Pointe du Hoc Ranger Monument**—During the D-Day invasion, 225 U.S. Army Rangers attempted a castle-style assault of the German-occupied cliffs by using grappling hooks and ladders borrowed from London fire departments. Only 90 servicemen survived. German bunkers and bomb craters remain as they were found (20 min by car west of American Cemetery in St. Laurent, just past Vierville-sur-Mer, daily 9:00–17:00, tel. 02 31 51 62 00, www.abmc .gov/ph.htm). A museum dedicated to the Rangers is in nearby Grandcamp-Maisy.

SLEEPING

(€1 = about 1.20, country code: 33)

In Arromanches

Arromanches, with its pinwheels and seagulls, has a salty beach-town ambience that makes it a good overnight stop. For evening fun, try the cheery bar at **Hôtel d'Arromanches-Restaurant "Le Pappagall"** (see below), or, for more of a nightclub scene, have a drink at **Pub Marie Celeste**, around the corner on rue de la Poste.

$$ Friendly **Hôtel d'Arromanches-Restaurant "Le Pappagall"**** is a reasonable value, with nine smartly appointed rooms, tight stairways and halls, a fun bar, and a cheery restaurant (Db-€62–69, Tb-€83–90, includes breakfast, 2 rue Colonel René Michel, 14117 Arromanches, tel. 02 31 22 36 26, fax 02 31 22 23 29, www .hoteldarromanches.fr, hoteldarromanche@ifrance.com, Alain and Rosa SE).

$$ **Hôtel de la Marine**** is equally good and offers beach views from most of its 28 comfy enough rooms and its elegant restaurant (Db-€61–72, Tb-€76–118, family rooms for up to five-€125, restaurant *menus* from €19, quai du Canada, tel. 02 31 22 34 19, fax 02 31 22 98 80, hotel.de.la.marine@wanadoo.fr, Madame and Monsieur Durand SE).

Near Arromanches

Chambres d'hôte litter the coast (the TIs in Bayeux and Arromanches have long lists).

$ **André and Madeleine Sebires**' working farmhouse, with four homey and cheap rooms and a pleasant garden, is worth the effort to track down. It's in tiny Ryes (between Bayeux and Arromanches) at Ferme du Clos Neuf—and tough to find. Try these directions from

Arromanches: Take D-87, enter Ryes and pass the church on the left; then, at the first junction, turn right onto rue de la Forge (look for the faded *Chambres* signs) and continue until you cross a tiny bridge. Turn right just after the bridge onto rue de la Triangle, and follow that road until you see a small sign on right to Le Clos Neuf. Park near the tractors. If the Sebires prove too elusive, call from Ryes and they'll come get you (Sb-€28, Db-€33, Tb-€40, includes breakfast, tel. 02 31 22 32 34, emmanuelle.sebire@wanadoo.fr, NSE except when daughter Emmanuelle is there on the weekends).

Mont St. Michel

For more than a thousand years, the distant silhouette of this island abbey sent pilgrims' spirits soaring. Today, it does the same for tourists. Mont St. Michel, among the top four pilgrimage sites in Christendom through the ages, floats like a mirage on the horizon—though it does show up on film. Today, 3.5 million visitors—far more tourists than pilgrims—flood the single street of the tiny island each year.

ORIENTATION

Mont St. Michel is connected by a two-mile causeway to the mainland and surrounded by a vast mudflat. Your visit features a one-street village that winds up to the fortified abbey. Between 10:00 and 16:00, tourists trample the dreamscape (as earnest pilgrims did 800 years ago). A ramble on the ramparts offers mudflat views and an escape from the tourist zone. While four tacky history-in-wax museums tempt visitors, the only worthwhile sight is the abbey itself, at the summit of the island.

Daytime Mont St. Michel is a touristy gauntlet—worth a stop, but a short one will do. The tourist tide recedes late each afternoon. On nights from autumn through spring, the island stands serene, its floodlit abbey towering above a sleepy village.

Arrive late and depart early if you can. The abbey interior should be open until midnight from May through September (off-season until 22:00). To avoid the human traffic jam on the main drag, follow the detour path up or down the mount, described below under "The Village Below the Abbey."

Tourist Information
The overwhelmed TI (and €0.35 WC) is to your left as you enter Mont St. Michel's gates. They have listings of *chambres d'hôte* (B&Bs

on the nearby mainland), English tour times for the abbey, bus schedules, and the tide table *(Horaires des Marées)*, which is essential if you plan to explore the mudflats outside Mont St. Michel (July–Aug daily 9:00–19:00, Sept and April–June daily 9:00–12:30 & 14:00–18:30, Oct–March daily 9:00–12:00 & 14:00–18:00, tel. 02 33 60 14 30, www.ot-montsaintmichel.com). A post office (PTT) and ATM are 50 yards beyond the TI.

Tides: The tides here rise over 50 feet—the largest and most dangerous in Europe. High tides *(grandes marées)* lap against the tourist-office door (where you'll find tide hours posted).

Arrival in Mont St. Michel

By Train: The nearest train station is in Pontorson (called Pontorson-Mont St. Michel), with an easy bus connection to Mont St. Michel (6 buses/day, 16/day in summer, 15 min). Most trains that arrive in Pontorson are met by a bus waiting to take passengers to Mont St. Michel (winter evening trains may not have a bus connection; call Couriers Bretons for all bus information in this region—tel. 02 99 19 70 70).

Taxis from Pontorson to Mont St. Michel (or vice versa) cost about €14 (€20 after 19:00 and on weekends/holidays, try to share a cab, taxi tel. 02 33 60 26 89).

By Car: Drive in slowly on the causeway: Watch out for fine views and crossing sheep. Park in the pay lot near the base of the island. Very high tides rise to the edge of the causeway, which leaves the causeway open...but any cars parked below it are left underwater. Relatively safe parking is available at the foot of Mont St. Michel; you will be instructed where to park under high-tide conditions (€4, don't leave any luggage visible in your car). There's plenty of parking, except midday in high season. Jot down your parking sector and plan on a 10-minute walk to the island from your car (15 minutes with luggage to your hotel).

If you'll be continuing by car to Dinan in Brittany, see page 238 for a scenic coastal route from Dinan to Mont St. Michel (to reverse the directions and go from Mont St. Michel to Dinan, just drive backwards).

SIGHTS

Mont St. Michel

These sights are listed in the order you approach them from the mainland.

The Bay of Mont St. Michel—The vast Bay of Mont St. Michel, which turns into a mudflat at low tide, has long played a key role. Since the 6th century, hermit monks in search of solitude lived here. The word "hermit" comes from an ancient Greek word

Mont St. Michel Area

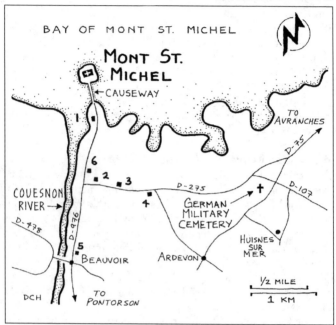

BAY OF MONT ST. MICHEL

MONT ST. MICHEL

←CAUSEWAY

TO AVRANCHES

D-75

COUESNON RIVER →

1

6

2

3

D-275

4

D-476

D-478

GERMAN MILITARY CEMETERY

D-107

5

BEAUVOIR

ARDEVON

HUISNES SUR MER

DCH

TO PONTORSON

½ MILE

1 KM

meaning "desert." The next best thing to a desert in this part of Europe was the sea. Imagine the "desert" this bay provided as the first monk climbed the rock to get close to God. Add to that the mythic tide, which sends the surf speeding eight miles in and out with each tide cycle. Long before the causeway was built, when Mont St. Michel was an island, pilgrims would approach across the mudflat, aware that the tide swept in "at the speed of a galloping horse" (well, maybe a trotting horse...12 mph, or about 2 feet per second).

Quicksand was another peril. But the real danger for adventurers today is the thoroughly disorienting fog and the fact that the sea can encircle unwary hikers. (Bring a mobile phone.) Braving these devilish risks for centuries, pilgrims kept their eyes on the spire crowned by their protector, St. Michael, and eventually reached their spiritual goal.

The Causeway—In 1878, a causeway was built, which let pilgrims come and go without hip boots, regardless of the tide. While this increased the flow of visitors, it stopped the flow of water around the island. The result: This part of the bay has silted up, and Mont St. Michel is no longer an island. A new bridge and dam *(barrage)* on the Couesnon will be built in the next few years, allowing the water to circulate—so Mont St. Michel will once again be an island (with a shuttle bus or train to zip visitors between the island and a distant car park). However, these plans have been already in the making for several years, and work may or may not begin in 2005.

The Village Below the Abbey—Mont St. Michel's main street (rue Principale, or "Grande Rue"), lined with shops and hotels leading to the abbey, is grotesquely touristy. It is some consolation to remember that, even in the Middle Ages, this was a commercial gauntlet, with stalls selling souvenir medallions, candles, and fast food. With only 30 full-time residents, the village lives solely for tourists. After the TI, check the tide warnings posted on the wall and pass through the imposing doors. Before the drawbridge, on your left, peek through the door of Restaurant la Mère Poulard. The original Madame

Poulard (the maid of an abbey architect who married the village baker) made quick and tasty omelettes here. They were popular for pilgrims who needed to beat the tide to get out in pre-causeway days and—even at the rip-off price of €23—they're a hit with tourists today. Pop in for a minute, just to enjoy the show as old-time-costumed cooks beat omelettes.

As you pass through the old drawbridge, you hit the main (and only) street and begin your trudge through the crowds uphill past several gimmicky museums to the abbey (all island hotel receptions are located on this street). Or, if the abbey's your goal, you can miss the crowds by climbing the first steps on your right after the drawbridge and following the ramparts in either direction up and up to the abbey (quieter if you go right). Public WCs are next to the TI, halfway up, and at the abbey entrance.

You can attend Mass at the tiny St. Pierre church (Thu & Sun at 11:00, opposite Hôtel la Vielle Auberge).

▲▲Abbey of Mont St. Michel—Mont St. Michel has been an important pilgrimage center since A.D. 708, when the bishop of Avranches heard the voice of Archangel Michael saying, "Build here and build high." With brilliant foresight, Michael reassured the bishop, "If you build it...they will come." Today's abbey is built on the remains of a Romanesque church, which was built on the remains of a Carolingian church. St. Michael, whose gilded statue decorates the top of the spire, was the patron saint of many French kings, making this a favored sight for French royalty through the ages. St. Michael was particularly popular in Counter-Reformation times, as the Church employed his warlike image in the fight against Protestant heresy.

While this abbey has 1,200 years of history, much of its story was lost when its archives were taken to St. Lô for safety during World War II—only to be destroyed during the D-Day fighting. As

Mont St. Michel

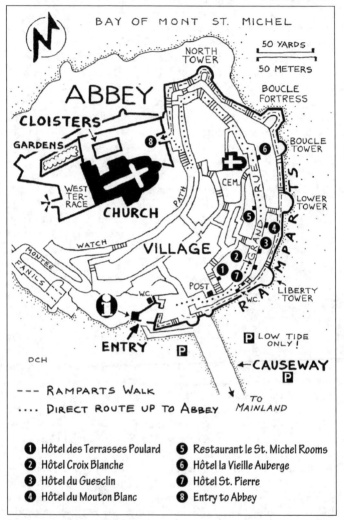

BAY OF MONT ST. MICHEL

NORTH TOWER

50 YARDS
50 METERS

BOUCLE FORTRESS

ABBEY

CLOISTERS

GARDENS

BOUCLE TOWER

WEST TER-RACE

CEM.

LOWER TOWER

CHURCH

RUE GRANDE

RAMPARTS

WATCH

VILLAGE

MONTEE FANILS

PATH

POST

W.C.

W.C.

LIBERTY TOWER

ENTRY

DCH

P

LOW TIDE ONLY!

←CAUSEWAY
P

--- RAMPARTS WALK
.... DIRECT ROUTE UP TO ABBEY

TO MAINLAND

❶ Hôtel des Terrasses Poulard
❷ Hôtel Croix Blanche
❸ Hôtel du Guesclin
❹ Hôtel du Mouton Blanc
❺ Restaurant le St. Michel Rooms
❻ Hôtel la Vieille Auberge
❼ Hôtel St. Pierre
❽ Entry to Abbey

you climb the stairs, imagine the centuries of pilgrims and monks who have worn down the edges of these same stone steps.

Cost and Hours: €7, May–Aug daily 9:00–19:00, Sept–April daily 9:30–18:00, last entry one hour before closing, closes at 16:00 in winter (tel. 02 33 89 80 00). Buy your ticket to the abbey and keep climbing. Allow 20 minutes to climb at a steady pace from the TI. You'll find no English explanations in the abbey. You can rent an **audioguide** (€4, €5.50 for 2) or take the 75-minute English-language **tour** (free, tip requested, 4–6 tours/day, first tour usually at 10:00, last at 16:00, confirm tour times at TI, meet at top terrace in front of church, groups can be large). The abbey might be open on Saturday evenings in summer—ask. Mass is held daily at 12:15 in the abbey church, except on Mondays.

Self-Guided Tour: Tour the abbey by following a one-way route. Keep climbing to the ticket booths and turnstile, then climb some more. Pass a public WC and a room that has interesting models of the abbey through the ages and a guides' desk (posting the time of the next tour), and finally to the...

West Terrace: A fire destroyed the west end of the church in 1776, leaving this fine view terrace. The original extent of the church can be seen in the pavement stones (as well as the stonecutter numbers, generally not exposed like this—a reminder that they were paid by the piece). The buildings of Mont St. Michel are made of granite stones quarried from the Isles of Chausey (visible on a clear day, 20 miles away). Tidal power was ingeniously harnessed to load, unload, and even transport the stones as barges hitched a ride with each incoming tide.

As you survey the Bay of Mont St. Michel, notice the polder land—farmland reclaimed by Normans in the 19th century with the help of Dutch engineers. The lines of trees mark strips of land used in the process. Today, this reclaimed land is covered by salt-loving plants and grazed by sheep whose salty meat is considered a local treat. You're standing 240 feet above sea level at the summit of what was an island called "the big tomb." The small island just farther out is "the little tomb."

Survey the bay stretching from Normandy to Brittany. The river below marks the historic border between the two lands. Brittany and Normandy have long vied for Mont St. Michel. In fact, the river used to pass Mont St. Michel on the other side, making the abbey part of Brittany. Today, it's just barely—but thoroughly—part of Normandy. Now head back into the...

Abbey Church: Sit on a pew near the front of the church, under the little statue of the Archangel Michael (with the spear to defeat dragons and evil, and the scales to evaluate your soul). Monks built the church on the tip of this rock so as to be as close to heaven as possible. The downside: There wasn't enough level ground to support a sizable abbey and church. The solution: Four immense crypts were built under the church to create a platform supporting each of its wings. While most of the church is Romanesque (round arches, 11th century), the apse behind the altar was built later and is Gothic (and, therefore, filled with much more light). In 1421, the crypt that supported the apse collapsed, taking its end of the church with it. Almost none of the original windows survive (victims of fires, storms, lightning, and the Revolution). Just outside the church, you'll find the...

Cloisters: A standard feature of an abbey, this was the peaceful zone connecting various rooms where monks could tend their gardens (food and herbs for medicine), meditate, and read the Bible. The great view window is enjoyable today (what's the tide doing?), but it was of no use to the monks. The more secluded a monk could be, the closer he was to God. (A cloister, by definition, is an enclosed place.) Notice the carved frieze featuring various plants and heightening the Garden-of-Eden ambience the cloister offered the monks. The statues of various saints carved among the columns were defaced—literally—by French Revolutionary troops. Continue on the tour to the...

Refectory: This was the dining hall where the monks consumed both food and the word of God in silence, as one monk read in a monotone from the Bible during meals (pulpit on the right near the far end). The monks gathered as a family here in one undivided space under one big arch—an impressive engineering feat in its day. The abbot ate at the head table; guests sat at the table in the middle. The clever columns are thin but very deep, thus allowing maximum light while offering maximum support. From 966 until 2001, this was a Benedictine abbey. In 2001, the last three Benedictine monks checked out, and a new order of monks from Paris took over. Stairs lead down to the...

Guests' Hall: St. Benedict wrote that guests should be welcomed according to their status. That meant that when the king (or other VIPs) visited, they were wined and dined without a hint of monastic austerity. This room was once brilliantly painted, with gold stars on a blue sky across the ceiling and a floor of glazed red and green tiles—all bathed in glorious sunlight made divine as it passed through a filter of stained glass. The painting of this room was said to be the model for Sainte-Chapelle in Paris. The big double fireplace served as a kitchen, kept out of sight by hanging tapestries. Hike the stairs to the...

Hall of the Grand Pillars: As the huge abbey was perched on a pointy rock, four sturdy crypts like this were built to prop it up. You're standing under the Gothic portion of the abbey church. This was the crypt that collapsed in 1421. Notice the immensity of the columns (15 feet around) in the new crypt, rebuilt with a determination not to fall again. To see what kind of crypt collapsed, walk on to the...

Crypt of St. Martin: This simple, 11th-century, Romanesque vault has only a tiny window for light, since the walls needed to be solid and fat to support the buildings above. Next, you'll find the...

Ossuary (identifiable by its big treadwheel): The monks celebrated death as well as life. This part of the abbey housed the hospital, morgue, and ossuary. Because the abbey graveyard was small, it was routinely emptied, and the bones were stacked here.

During the Revolution, monasticism was abolished and the church property was taken by the atheistic government. From 1793 to 1863, Mont St. Michel was used as an Alcatraz-type prison—its first inmates were 300 priests who refused to renounce their vows. (Victor Hugo complained that using such a place as a prison was like keeping a toad in a reliquary.) The big treadwheel—the kind that did heavy lifting for big building projects throughout the Middle Ages—is from the decades when the abbey was a prison. Teams of six prisoners marched two abreast in the wheel—hamster-style—powering two-ton loads of stone and supplies up Mont St. Michel. Spin the rollers of the sled next to the wheel. Look down the steep ramp. While you're here, notice the parking lot and the crowds below. When the tide is very high, careless drivers can become carless drivers. A few years ago, a Scottish bus driver (oblivious to the time and tide but very busy in a hotel room) lost his bus...destroyed by a salty bath. Local police tethered it to the lot so it wouldn't float away.

Finish your visit by walking through the Promenade of the Monks, under more Gothic vaults, through the shop, past an impressive model of the spire-crowning statue of St. Michael, and down into the garden. From here, look up at the miracle of medieval engineering.

The "Merveille": This was an immense building project—a marvel back in 1220. Three levels of buildings were created: one for security, one for feasting, and one for serenity. It was a medieval skyscraper, built to support the cloisters at church level. (Remember looking out of those top windows earlier?) The vision was even grander. The place where you're standing was to be built up in similar fashion to support a further expansion of the church. But the money ran out, and the project was abandoned. Stairs lead from here back into the village. But to avoid the crowds, once you hit the stairs you climbed on your way up, scale a few stairs on your left (marked *Chemin des Ramparts*), turn right, and hike down via the...

Ramparts: Mont St. Michel is ringed by a fine example of 15th-century fortifications. They were built to defend against a new weapon—the cannon. They were low, rather than tall—to make a smaller target—and connected by protected passageways, which enabled soldiers to zip quickly to whichever zone was under attack. The five-sided Boucle Tower (1481) is designed with no blind angles, so defenders can protect it and the nearby walls in all directions. While the English took all of Normandy, they never took this well-fortified island. Because of its stubborn success against the English in the Hundred Years' War, Mont St. Michel became a symbol of French national identity.

After dark, the island is magically floodlit. Views from the ramparts are sublime. For the best view, exit the island and walk out on the causeway a few hundred yards.

▲▲**Stroll Around Mont St. Michel**—To resurrect that Mont St. Michel dreamscape and evade all those tacky tourist stalls, you can walk out on the mudflats around the island. At low tide, it's reasonably dry and a great memory-maker. This can be extremely hazardous, so be sure to double-check the tides. Remember the scene from the Bayeux tapestry where Harold rescues Normans from the quicksand? It happened somewhere in this bay. You may notice groups hiking in from the muddy horizon. The TI advises against going out at all. Attempting this without a local guide is reckless.

Near Mont St. Michel

German Military Cemetery (Cimetière Militaire Allemand)—

Located three miles from Mont St. Michel near tiny Huisnes-sur-Mer, this somber but thoughtfully presented cemetery-mortuary houses the remains of 12,000 German soldiers and offers insight into their lives with letters they sent home (English translations). From the lookout, there are sensational views over Mont St. Michel.

SLEEPING

(€1 = about $1.20, country code: 33)

Sleeping on the island, inside the walls, is the best way to experience Mont St. Michel, though drivers should also consider the *chambres d'hôtes* listed below. There are eight small hotels on the island, three of which are family-run with a greater interest in your stay. Many hotels feel tired, and their staff seem burned out. While some pad their profits by requesting guests to buy dinner from their restaurant, *requiring* it is illegal. Several are closed from November until Easter. Because most visitors only day-trip here, finding a room is generally no problem.

Mont St. Michel

When a price range is given for rooms, the higher-priced rooms generally have bay views.

$$$ **Hôtel des Terrasses Poulard*****, 50 yards after the TI, rents the most polished and overpriced rooms on the island (Db-€105–165, tel. 02 33 60 14 09, fax 02 33 60 37 31, www.terrasses-poulard.com).

The following hotels are listed in order of altitude (the first are lowest on the island and closest to parking).

$$ **Hôtel St. Pierre** and **Hôtel Croix Blanche*****, owned by the same company, sit side by side, each with comfortable rooms, some with good views. St. Pierre is fancier, with a good breakfast buffet; Croix Blanche has an Internet station (Db-€84–105, Tb-€120, Qb-€118–127, tel. 02 33 60 14 03, fax 02 33 48 59 82, www.auberge-saint-pierre.fr).

$$ Hôtel du Guesclin** is family-run and *très traditionnel*, with a well-respected restaurant and good, clean rooms at competitive rates. Beware the disagreeable owner, whose retirement is well overdue (Db-€43–74, Tb-€87, tel. 02 33 60 14 10, fax 02 33 60 45 81).

$$ Hôtel du Mouton Blanc** is company-owned, but has decent, generally cozy rooms and a young, helpful staff (Db-€66, Tb/Qb-€82–98, tel. 02 33 60 14 08, fax 02 33 60 05 62).

$$ Hôtel la Vieille Auberge** is family-run by entrepreneurial Nadine (SE) and her Old World mother-in-law, Madame. Their 11 rooms are among the best for the price, and the four rooms with large view terraces are my pick for the island—but don't let Madame talk you into more room than you need. Arrive by 17:00 or lose your reservation (Db-€70, Db with view-€80, my favorite Db with view and terrace-€123 in an annex farther up, extra bed-€16, hotel is closed on Wed except July–Aug, tel. 02 33 60 14 34, fax 02 33 70 87 04).

$ Restaurant le St. Michel, across from Hôtel du Mouton Blanc, rents six rooms in a nearby annex and is the best budget value on the island. It's run by lighthearted Patricia, Philippe, and Frédéric, all of whom speak English (Ds-€46, Db-€54–56 depending on view, extra person-€10, no dinner requirements but a good restaurant, tel. & fax 02 33 60 14 37, www.lesaintmichelridel.com).

The Mainland

Modern hotels gather at the mainland end of the causeway, and they have soulless but cheaper rooms with easy parking and many tour groups. Motel Vert (see below) rents bikes, offering easy access to the island.

$$ Friendly Hôtel de la Digue*** is the best and most convenient place to stay on the mainland. Most rooms are spacious and well-equipped. Ask for one of the four rooms with private terrace on the riverside: *une chambre avec petit balcon sur la Couesnon*. You can dine with a partial view of Mont St. Michel at their restaurant (small Db-€61–66, spacious Db-€73–80, Tb-€84, Qb-€95, good breakfast-€8.60, tel. 02 33 60 14 02, fax 02 33 60 37 59, www.ladigue.fr). From here, it's a wonderful 20-minute walk to Mont St. Michel.

$$ Motel Vert is musty-smelling and huge (112 rooms), but it's close, cheap, and works in a pinch (Db-€48–58, Tb-€59–70, Qb-€71–81, bike rental, tel. 02 33 60 09 33, fax 02 33 60 20 02).

Chambres d'Hôte

Simply great values, these converted farmhouses are near the village of Ardevon, a few minutes' drive from the island toward Avranches.

$ La Jacotière, charming Madame Brault's stone farmhouse, is closest (walkable to the causeway), with six immaculate, modern rooms and great views of Mont St. Michel from her picnic-perfect garden (Db-€38, studio with view-€42, extra bed-€10, tel. 02 33 60 22 94, fax 02 33 60 20 48, la.jacotiere@wanadoo.fr, Claudine SE).

$ Equally charming **Madame Audienne**'s stone farmhouse, with two wings (each with five rooms) is about one mile farther away from Mont St. Michel. Like Mama, the older wing feels a wee bit tired, but has more character; and, like daughter Estelle (SE), the modern wing is young and bright, with spacious, tiled rooms and modern facilities. Most rooms have good views of Mont St. Michel, better from Estelle's wing (Sb-€25, Db-€35, Tb-€45, Qb-€55, includes breakfast, no CC, tel. & fax 02 33 48 28 89).

Between Ardevon and Pontorson: $$ **Les Vieilles Digues,** two miles toward Pontorson, has seven beautifully furnished, spotless, and homey rooms, all with exterior entrances but no views (D-€48, Db-€60, Tb-€64–76, includes breakfast, easy parking, tel. 02 33 58 55 30, fax 02 33 58 83 09, danielle.tchen@wanadoo.fr, SE).

Pontorson

Train travelers could sleep in dismal Pontorson, a 15-minute drive from Mont St. Michel. $ **Hôtel Vauban**** , across from the train station, is quiet and comfortable (D-€32, Db-€39–51, Tb-€54, 2 boulevard Clémenceau, tel. 02 33 60 03 84, fax 02 33 60 35 48).

EATING

Puffy omelettes *(omelette montoise)* are Mont St. Michel's specialty. Also look for mussels (best with *crème fraîche*) and seafood platters, locally raised lamb (a saltwater-grass diet gives the meat a unique taste), and Muscadet wine (dry, cheap, and white).

Patricia and Philippe run the lighthearted and reasonable **Restaurant le St. Michel** (good omelettes and mussels, tel. 02 33 60 14 37), across from Hôtel du Mouton Blanc.

For lunch, try the *moules à la crème fraîche* (mussels with cream) at the recommended **Hôtel la Vieille Auberge** (closes at 19:00, no dinner service).

The **supermarket**, on the mainland near Hôtel de la Digue, has what you need for a romantic picnic (daily 8:30–20:00), though you can buy sandwiches, salads, and drinks to-go on the island. Picnic in the small park below the abbey (to the left as you look up at the abbey).

TRANSPORTATION CONNECTIONS

The nearest train station is in **Pontorson** (called Pontorson-Mont St. Michel), connected with Mont St. Michel by bus (6–16/day, 15) or taxi (€14–20, tel. 02 33 60 26 89). For more information, see page 217.

From Pontorson by train to: Paris (2/day, 5 hrs, transfer in Caen or Rennes), **Bayeux** (2/day, 2.5 hrs), **Dinan** (3/day, 2 hrs, transfer in Dol), **St. Malo** (3/day, 1.5 hrs, transfer in Dol, direct bus from Mont St. Michel also available, see below), **Amboise** (4/day, 7 hrs, transfers in Rennes, Le Mans, and Tours' main station).

From Mont St. Michel by bus to: St. Malo (2–3/day, 75 min direct), **Rennes** (4/day, 1.75 hrs). Rennes has connections to many destinations, including the fastest route to **Paris** (4/day, 4 hrs includes bus to Rennes and TGV to Paris).

BRITTANY

The Couesnon River, barely west of Mont St. Michel, marks the border between Normandy and Brittany. The peninsula of Brittany is rugged, with an isolated interior, a well-discovered coast, strong Celtic ties, and a passion for crêpes (locally called *galettes* when they are savory and *crêpes* when they are sweet) and *cidre* (alcoholic apple

cider served in bowls). This region of independent-minded locals is linguistically and culturally different from Normandy and, for that matter, the rest of France.

In 1491, Brittany's Duchess Anne was forced to marry the French king, and Brittany became part of France—allowing France to overcome the independence of this feisty province. Brittany lost its freedom, but, with Anne as queen, gained certain rights (such as free roads—even today, 500 years later, Brittany highways come with no tolls...unique in France).

Locals take great pride in their distinct Breton culture. In Brittany, music stores sell more Celtic music than anything else. It's hard to imagine that this music was forbidden as recently as the 1980s. During a more repressive time, many of today's big pop stars were underground artists. In fact, in the recent past, a child would lose French citizenship if christened with a Celtic name.

But the freckled locals are now free to wave their flag, sing their songs, and speak their language (there's a Breton TV station and radio station). Like their Irish counterparts, Bretons—many with red hair—are chatty, their music is alive with struggles against an oppressor, and the sea forms an integral part of their identity. The coastal route from Mont St. Michel through the town of Cancale (famous for oysters; good lunch stop), Pointe du Grouin (fabulous ocean views), and the historic walled city of St. Malo gives a good introduction to this province.

Cuisine Scene in Brittany

While the endless coastline suggests otherwise, there is more than seafood to this rugged Celtic land. Crêpes are to Bretons what pasta is to Italians: a basic, reasonably priced, daily necessity. *Galettes* are savory buckwheat crêpes, commonly filled with ham, cheese, eggs, mushrooms, spinach, seafood, or a combination.

Oysters *(huîtres)* are the second food of Brittany and are available all year. Mussels, clams, and scallops are often served as main courses. Look for crêpes with scallops and *moules marinières* (mussels steamed in white wine, parsley, and shallots).

Farmers compete with fishermen for the hearts of locals by growing fresh vegetables, such as peas, beans, and cauliflower.

For dessert, look for *far breton,* a traditional custard often served with prunes. Dessert crêpes, made with white flour, are served with a variety of toppings.

Cider is the locally produced drink. Order *une bolée de cidre* (a traditional bowl of hard apple cider) with your crêpes.

Remember, restaurants serve only during lunch (11:30–14:00) and dinner (19:00–21:00, later in bigger cities); cafés serve food throughout the day.

Dinan

If you have time for only one stop in Brittany, do Dinan. Its hefty ramparts bundle its half-timbered and cobbled quaintness into Brittany's best medieval town center. While it has a touristic icing—plenty of *crêperies,* shops selling Brittany kitsch, and colorful flags—it is clearly a work-a-day Breton town filled with people who appreciate the beautiful place they call home. This delightfully preserved ancient city (which escaped the bombs of World War II) is peaceful and conveniently located (about a 40-min drive from Mont St. Michel).

ORIENTATION

Dinan's old city, contained within its medieval ramparts, climbs steeply uphill east to west from the Rance River and its small port to huge place du Guesclin. There you'll find lots of parking and the TI. Place des Merciers is ground zero for most activities in Dinan.

Tourist Information

Pick up a free map and bus and train schedules, and ask about walking tours of Dinan and boat trips on the Rance River; skip their overpriced tourist magazine (mid-June–mid-Sept Mon–Sat 9:00–19:00, Sun 10:00–12:30 & 14:30–18:00; mid-Sept–mid-June Mon–Sat 9:00–12:30 & 14:00–18:00, closed Sun; just off place du Guesclin near Château de Dinan on 9 rue du Château, tel. 02 96 87 69 76, www.dinan-tourisme.com).

Walking Tours: The TI offers 90-minute walking tours of old Dinan in French and English (€5, 3/week July–Aug, usually in afternoon, get details at TI).

Arrival in Dinan

By Train: To get to the town center from Dinan's Old World train station (no lockers or baggage check), either call a taxi (see "Helpful Hints," below) or walk 20 minutes (left out of train station, right at Hôtel Europa up rue Carnot, right on rue Thiers, then left across big place Duclos-Pinot, passing on the left of Café de la Mairie to reach the old center). For the TI, go to the right of the café, following rue du Marchix to place du Guesclin. The TI is on the far end of the square on your right.

By Bus: Dinan's main bus stop is in front of the post office on place Duclos-Pinot, five minutes from the center (for directions, see "By Train," above).

By Car: Dinan is confusing for drivers; follow *Centre-Ville* signs to *la gare* (train station). From there, follow the walking route described above (see "By Train") to reach the massive place du Guesclin (free parking except July–Sept and on Thu market days). Check with your hotelier before leaving your car overnight on place du Guesclin; they will tow it before 8:00 on market or festival days.

Helpful Hints

Market Days: On Thursday, a big open-air market is held on place du Guesclin (8:00–13:00). In July and August, Wednesday is flea-market day on place St. Sauveur.

Supermarkets: Groceries are upstairs in the **Monoprix** at 7 rue du Marchix (Mon–Sat 9:00–19:30, closed Sun). On Sundays, try **Super U** on place Duclos-Pinot (Mon–Sat 7:00–19:00, Sun 9:00–13:00).

Picnic-Perfect Park: The lovely Jardin Anglais hides behind the big church of St. Sauveur.

Internet Access: Try **Arospace Cyber Café** (€1.50/15 min, Tue–Sat 10:00–12:30 & 14:00–19:00, closed Sun–Mon, near place du Guesclin at 9 rue de la Chaux, tel. 02 96 87 14 85).

Laundry: **Pressing-Laverie's** charming owner, Madame Philippot, does your laundry in a few hours (Mon 14:00–19:00, Tue–Sat

Dinan

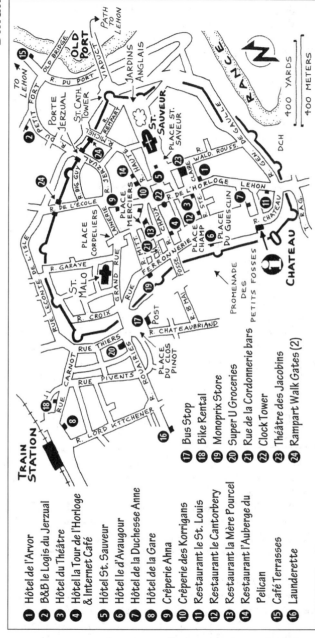

1 Hôtel de l'Arvor
2 B&B le Logis du Jerzual
3 Hôtel du Théâtre
4 Hôtel la Tour de l'Horloge & Internet Café
5 Hôtel St. Sauveur
6 Hôtel le d'Avaugour
7 Hôtel de la Duchesse Anne
8 Hôtel de la Gare
9 Crêperie Ahna
10 Crêperie des Korrigans
11 Restaurant le St. Louis
12 Restaurant le Cantorbery
13 Restaurant la Mère Pourcel
14 Restaurant l'Auberge du Pelican
15 Café Terrasses
16 Launderette
17 Bus Stop
18 Bike Rental
19 Monoprix Store
20 Super U Groceries
21 Rue de la Cordonnerie bars
22 Clock Tower
23 Théâtre des Jacobins
24 Rampart Walk Gates (2)

8:30–19:00, closed 12:00–13:45 Tue and Thu and all day Sun, €7.50/wash and dry, about 4 blocks from train station at 19 rue de Brest, tel. 02 96 39 71 35).

Bike Rental: Peugeot Cycles Scardin is a block from the train station at 30 rue Carnot (€13/half day, Tue–Sat 9:00–12:00 & 14:00–19:00, closed Sun–Mon, tel. 02 96 39 21 94).

Car Rental: Consider **Europcar** (48 rue de Brest, tel. 02 96 85 07 51) or the less central **Hertz** (Garage Galivel, Z. A. Bel Air, tel. 02 96 39 44 20).

Taxi: Call tel. 02 96 39 74 16, mobile 06 07 49 95 31 or 06 08 00 80 90 (8-seat minivans available).

Introductory Dinan Walking Tour

Frankly, I wouldn't go through a turnstile in Dinan. The attraction here is the town itself. Enjoy the old town center, ramble around the ramparts, and check out the old riverfront harbor. Here are some ideas, laced together as a quick walk starting at place du Guesclin (gek-lahn). As you wander, notice the pride locals take in their Breton culture.

Place du Guesclin: This sprawling town square is named after the 14th-century local knight who became a great French military leader, famous for victories over England. For 700 years, merchants have filled this square to sell their produce and crafts (in modern times, Thu 8:00–13:00). The TI and some impressive fortifications are just beyond the square. The *donjon* (keep) and nearby walls are all that's left of Dinan's once massive castle. The museum (no English) and the view from the top are both disappointing. From the statue of Guesclin, rue Ste. Claire leads to...

Théâtre des Jacobins: Fronting a pleasant little square, the theater was once one of the many convents that dominated the town. In fact, in medieval times, a third of Dinan consisted of convents—not uncommon in Brittany, which remains the most Catholic part of France. As you walk down rue de l'Horloge toward the clock tower, you'll see on your left...

Nobody's Tombstone: The tombstone without a head is a town mascot. It's actually a prefab tombstone, made during the Hundred Years' War, when there was more death than money in France. A portrait bust would be attached to this generic body for a proper, yet economic, burial. Continue to the...

Clock Tower: The old town spins around this clock tower, which has long symbolized the power of the town's merchants. The tower comes with a mediocre little museum and 160 steps (the last few on a ladder) to a fine city view. Warning: Plug your ears on the quarter hour, when the bells ring (€2.70, July–Aug daily 10:00–18:30, April–June and Sept daily 14:00–18:00 only, closed off-season). Across from the tower, a bakery sells *ker-y-pom* (€1.50), traditional

Breton shortbread biscuits with butter, honey, and an apple-pie filling. When warm, they're the best-tasting treat in town. Past the tower, take the first left into Dinan's historic commercial center, the place des Merciers.

Old Town Center: These arcaded, half-timbered buildings are Dinan's oldest and most charming. They date from the time when property taxes were based on the square footage of the ground floor. To provide shelter from both the taxes and the rain, buildings started with small ground floors, then expanded outward with their upper floors. Medieval shopkeepers would sell goods in front of their homes under the shelter of leaning walls. Picturesque rue de la Cordonnerie is a fine example of a medieval lane, with overhanging buildings whose roofs nearly touch. After a disastrous 18th-century fire, a law required that the traditional thatch be replaced by safer slate.

Best Town View: Walk past Dinan's basilica, St. Sauveur (of little sightseeing importance), through a pleasant English garden, and to Ste. Catherine's tower for a great view of the river valley below the town. From here, you'll enjoy a commanding view of the old port and the Rance River (described below). From Ste. Catherine's tower, take the first right on rue du Rempart and another right on rue Michel, then look for the iron gate on the left side of the bend in the road with the sign *Chemin de Ronde* (open 8:00–21:00). The gate leads to the best stretch of the...

Ramparts: For the best look at Dinan's impressive fortified wall, hike from the Jerzual gate past the Governor's tower to St. Malo's tower. As you exit the ramparts, walk through the gate at St. Malo, then turn left on rue de l'Ecole—which brings you back to the center of town.

While the old port town was destroyed repeatedly, these ramparts were never taken by force. (They were taken, however, by siege.) If an attacker got by the *contrescarpe* (second outer wall) and through the moat, he could be pummeled by nasty things dropped through the holes lining the ramparts. Venture out on the Governor's tower to see how the cannon slots enabled defenders to shoot in all directions. Today, the ramparts seem to guard only the town's residential charm—gardens, wells, and homey backyards.

When you're done exploring the ramparts, you can follow the steep and scenic rue du Jerzual (cobblestones are slippery when wet, and it's a slow, 10-min walk down; remember, what goes down must come back up) from the old town center under the medieval gate *(Porte du Jerzual)* down to the...

Old Port: This was the birthplace of Dinan a thousand years ago. It was once an exportation and fishing port connected to the sea—15 miles away—by the Rance River. By taxing river traffic, the town grew. The tiny Old Bridge *(Vieux Pont)* dates to the 15th century. But because this location was so exposed, the townsfolk later retreated to the bluff behind its current fortifications. Notice the viaduct built in 1850 to send traffic around the town and alleviate congestion. Until then, the main road crossed the tiny Old Bridge and went up the steep rue du Jerzual through Dinan—which is where you can head, now that our walk is finished, unless you want to spend more time exploring the Rance River (see below).

SIGHTS

▲**Rance River Valley**—The best thing about Dinan's port is the access it provides to dreamy riverside paths that meander along the gentle Rance Valley. You can walk, bike, or boat in either interesting direction.

On Foot: For a breath of fresh Brittany air, cross the Old Bridge in Dinan's port, turn right, and walk the level river trail for 30 minutes to the pristine little village of Léhon. Visitors are greeted by a proud 9th-century abbey and church (where you might see weddings), flowery cobbled lanes, and **La Marmite de l'Abbaye** café/restaurant (lunch salads, wood-fire-grilled meats for lunch and dinner, and drinks in between, July–Aug daily, Sept–June closed Mon and maybe Tue, tel. 02 96 87 39 39). The château ruins perched above the village are off-limits.

By Bike: For bike rental, see "Helpful Hints," above. Cyclists can follow the "On Foot" route, above, then cross Léhon's bridge and continue along the canal as far as they can pedal, passing Breton cows, cute little lock houses, sublime scenery, and other nature-lovers. The villages of Evran and Treverien are both within reach (allow 45 min from Dinan to Evran, 25 min more to Treverien). By turning left rather than right at Dinan's port (and staying on the Dinan side of the river), bikers can join the parade of ocean-bound boats. It's a breezy and level 30-minute ride past rock faces, corn-fields, and slate-roofed homes to the picturesque Port de Lyvet (cross small dam to reach village, trail ends a short distance beyond). **Le Ty-Corentin** café/restaurant is perfectly positioned in the port (open daily for lunch, dinner, or a refreshing drink, closed Wed off-season, tel. 02 96 83 21 10).

By Boat: Boats depart from Dinan's port at the bottom of rue du Jerzual 50 feet to the left of Old Bridge on the Dinan side (schedules depend on tides, get details at TI). The one-hour cruise on the *Jaman IV* boat comes with a live English-speaking guide, plenty of scenery, and a chance to go through a lock (€9, cruises April–Oct, 2–5 boats/day, closed Tue except July–Aug, tel. 02 96 39 28 41). A longer cruise with the **Compagnie Corsaire** (a slow and very scenic 2.5 hrs one-way) goes to St. Malo (one-way-€18, April–Sept, tel. 08 25 16 81 20). Enjoy St. Malo, then take the bus back, but make sure to get bus schedules before you leave Dinan.

Sleep Code

(€1 = $1.20, country code: 33)

S = Single, **D** = Double/Twin, **T** = Triple, **Q** = Quad, **b** = bathroom, **s** = shower only, **no CC** = Credit Cards not accepted, **SE** = Speaks English, **NSE** = No English, * = French hotel rating system (0–4 stars). You can assume a hotel takes credit cards unless you see "no CC" in the listing.

To help you sort easily through these listings, I've divided the rooms into three categories based on the price for a standard double room with bath:

$$$ **Higher Priced**—Most rooms €90 or more.
$$ **Moderately Priced**—Most rooms between €60–90.
$ **Lower Priced**—Most rooms €60 or less.

Musée du Rail—Train buffs can wax nostalgic over the 1:87-scale railroad model displaying trains from many periods (€4, June–mid-Sept daily 14:00–18:00, closed mid-Sept–May, at train station, tel. 02 96 39 53 48).

SLEEPING

Weekends and summers are busy. Dinan likes its nightlife, so be careful of loud rooms over bars, particularly on lively weekends.

In the Old Center

$$ Hôtel de l'Arvor**, ideally located a block off place du Guesclin, has 24 modern, adequately maintained rooms (with so-so beds) behind an old stone facade (standard Db-€47, larger Db-€62, Tb-€64–75, elevator, 5 rue Pavie, tel. 02 96 39 21 22, fax 02 96 39 83 09, hotel-arvor@wanadoo.fr).

$$ Chambres d'Hôtes Le Logis du Jerzual is a haven of calm in an old building with terraced gardens, just up from the port off a characteristic street (a long, steep climb below the main town). The rooms are wonderfully furnished with antiques, fine carpets, and canopied beds (Sb-€45, Db-€60–75, extra bed-€15, includes breakfast, tel. 02 96 85 46 54, fax 02 96 39 46 94, ronsseray@wanadoo.fr, delightful Sylvie SE). Drive up rue du Petit Fort from the port (it's well-signed) and drop your bags. Parking is nearby.

$ Hôtel du Théâtre, with the cheapest rooms in this book, sits across from Hôtel de l'Arvor above a small café. Its six no-star rooms are clean and cheery, though some can be smoky (S-€16, D-€22, Db-€28–38, Tb-€38, no CC, 2 rue Ste. Claire, tel. 02 96 39 06 91, reserved but friendly Michel NSE).

$ **Hôtel la Tour de l'Horloge****, an 18th-century manor house burrowed deep in the center, rents 12 modern rooms with little personality but fair rates. Rooms fronting the bar-lined rue de la Chaux can be noisy (Sb-€44, Db-€48–57, Tb-€69, Qb-€81, 5 rue de la Chaux, tel. 02 96 39 96 92, fax 02 96 85 06 99, hiliotel @wanadoo.fr, SE).

$ **Hôtel St. Sauveur** rents six sharp rooms in a 15th-century home over a fun pub (with pool table) on an atmospheric square near the basilica (Db-€49, Tb-€59, extra bed-€9, 19 place St. Sauveur, tel. 02 96 85 30 20, fax 02 96 87 91 66, run by Monsieur and Madame Gourvenac).

On Place du Guesclin

These hotels offer the easiest, closest parking on place du Guesclin (except on Wed night, since Thu is market day).

$$$ **Hôtel le d'Avaugour*****, facing a busy street, is Dinan's best and priciest hotel, with an efficient staff (SE) and a backyard garden oasis near the town's medieval wall. The wood-furnished rooms have great beds and all the modern hotel comforts (prices vary greatly by season, rooms over garden are best, street side Db-€90–170, garden side Db-€120–220, third person-€30, suites available, elevator, big buffet breakfast-€11, 1 place du Champ, tel. 02 96 39 07 49, fax 02 96 85 43 04, www.avaugourhotel.com, avaugour.hotel@wanadoo.fr).

$ **Hôtel de la Duchesse Anne***, run by friendly Giles, offers reasonable comfort, a small bar, and a *crêperie* (Ss/Ds-€38, Db-€44–48, Tb-€58, Qb-€72, includes breakfast, 10 place du Guesclin, tel. 02 96 39 09 43, fax 02 96 87 57 26).

Near the Train Station

$ **Hôtel de la Gare*** faces the station and offers the complete Breton experience, with *charmant* Laurence and Claude (who both love Americans), a local café hangout, and surprisingly quiet, clean, and comfortable rooms for a bargain. Don't let the hallways scare you (D-€24, Ds-€27, Db/Tb/Qb-€40, place de la Gare, tel. 02 96 39 04 57, fax 02 96 39 02 29).

Near Dinan

Overlooking the Rance River, $$ **Le Manoir de Rigourdaine****, run by adorable Patrick and Anne-France Van Valenberg, is a well-renovated farmhouse with old beams everywhere, generous public spaces, a fireplace in the reception area, immaculate grounds, a pool table, and simple, clean, comfortable rooms. Some rooms have exterior entries and loft beds (Sb-€52–68, Db-€52–76, Tb-€75–91, Qb-€90–98, no CC, route de Langrolay, 15 min north of Dinan off N-176 in village of Plouër-sur-Rance, tel. 02 96 86 89 96, fax 02 96 86 92 46, www.hotel-rigourdaine.fr, hotel.rigourdaine.fr@wanadoo.fr).

EATING

Dinan has good restaurants for every budget. Since *galettes* (crêpes) are the specialty, *crêperies* are a good and inexpensive choice, available on every corner. Crêpes with ham are too salty; I prefer the crêpes with scallops and cream.

Crêperie Ahna is one of the best. It's also a cozy place with more than just crêpes: Try the *pierrades*—meat dishes grilled on hot stones (7 rue de la Poissonnerie, closed Sun and several weeks during Nov–March, tel. 02 96 39 09 13). **Crêperie des Korrigans** is similarly good and cheap (€10 for 3 courses of crêpes, closed Tue, 17 rue de l'Apport, tel. 02 96 87 56 75).

If not in the mood for crepes, try **Le St. Louis,** where the firelight flickers on wood beams and white tablecloths (€18 *menu*, last lunch seating 13:30, last dinner seating 21:15; closed Sun night, all day Mon, and Wed off-season; great salad bar and dessert buffet, hidden 2 blocks behind place du Guesclin at 9 rue de Léhon, reservations smart, tel. 02 96 39 89 50, charming Marie-Claire SE).

Le Cantorbery is a warm place (literally), where meats are grilled in the dining room's fireplace *à la tradition,* and the seafood is *très* tasty (*menus* from €22, closed Wed and Sun off-season, just off place du Guesclin at 6 rue Ste. Claire, tel. 02 96 39 02 52).

If you want the best, **La Mère Pourcel**, with dressy service and refined cuisine served beneath medieval but elegant 15th-century beams, is my Dinan splurge (dinner *menus* from €28, €21 lunch *menus*, closed Sun–Mon off-season, 3 place des Merciers, tel. 02 96 39 03 80).

For fine seafood at reasonable prices, try **L'Auberge du Pelican** (closed Mon and Thu, indoor and outdoor tables, just off place St. Sauveur at 3 rue Haute-Voie, tel. 02 96 39 47 05).

You'll find several cozy restaurants in the old port (long, steep walk down rue du Jerzual); **Café Terrasses** sits right on the river, has *menus* from €15, and serves late. Consider a drink on its riverfront terrace (daily, tel. 02 96 39 09 60).

Nightlife: So many lively bars line the narrow, pedestrian-friendly **rue de la Cordonnerie** that the street is nicknamed "rue de la Soif" (Street of Thirst). When the weather is good, you can sit outside at the long, wooden tables and strike up a conversation with a friendly Breton.

TRANSPORTATION CONNECTIONS

From Dinan by train to: Paris' Gare Montparnasse (6/day, 4 hrs, change in Dol and Rennes), **Pontorson-Mont St. Michel** (3/day, 1–2 hrs, change in Dol, then bus or taxi from Pontorson, best connection is 12:45 departure from Dinan), **St. Malo** (3/day, 1 hr, change in Dol, bus is better, see below), **Amboise** (6/day, 5–6 hrs, via Rennes, then

TGV to Paris with no station change needed in Paris; or cross-country via Rennes, Le Mans, and Tours (2/day, 5–6 hrs).

By bus to: St. Malo (3–4/day, 50 min, faster and better than trains, as bus stops in both cities are more central), **Mont St. Michel** (3/day, 2 hrs, change in St. Malo).

MORE SIGHTS NEAR DINAN

▲▲**Scenic Drive between Dinan and Mont St. Michel**—Dinan is ideally situated for a quick taste-of-Brittany driving tour that samples a bit of the rugged peninsula's coast. If you're connecting Dinan and Mont St. Michel and aren't pressed for time, link the two with a worthwhile little detour (these directions are from Dinan to Mont St. Michel, but this can be done just as easily in reverse order).

Drive north to St. Malo (described below), then take the scenic drive hugging the coast east on D-201 to Pointe du Grouin, where the appropriately named Emerald Coast (Côte d'Emeraude) begins. Drive as far as you can, past Hôtel du Grouin, park your car (WCs there), and continue on foot. Pass the *semaphore du grouin* (signal station), where paths lead in all directions. Take a stroll and breathe in the sea air. The big rock to your right is L'Ile des Landes, an island that was earmarked for a fort during the French Revolution. The fort was never built, and the island remains home to thousands of birds.

Return to your car and leave Pointe du Grouin, following signs to Cancale, Brittany's appealing oyster capital. Its harbor *(le port)* is lined with restaurants, all offering oysters and mussels. Upon arrival in Cancale, follow signs *par la cote* to arrive on the port side, where there are plenty of restaurants to choose from. Slurp oysters here.

Cancale is a 45-minute drive from Mont St. Michel. The best views of the abbey island are from Cancale. Head out of Cancale toward Mont St. Michel on D-155, then D-797, and drive along *la Route de la Baie*, which skirts the bay and passes heavy-stone villages, windmills, flocks of sheep, and shops selling fresh oysters and mussels *(huitres et moules)*. In the bay, you'll see oyster beds and, at low-tide, grounded boats quietly waiting for the sea to return. On a clear day, look for Mont St. Michel in the distance. On a foggy day, look harder.

▲**St. Malo**—Come here to experience *the* Breton beach resort. The old center has an eerie, almost claustrophobic feeling, thanks to its tall, dark, stone buildings. The town feels better up top on the walls. Walk the impressive ramparts that circle the old city. It's about a half mile all the way around, with stair access at each door *(porte)*. Walk as far out on the beaches as the tides allow, then return to sample seafood—there's a seemingly limitless supply of restaurants and cafés. St. Malo is a zoo best avoided in summer. But if you're game, it's an easy 45-minute drive, or a one-hour bus or train ride, from Mont St. Michel or Dinan—a handy day trip. The **TI** is across from the old city gate on esplanade St. Vincent (maps-€0.50, April–Sept Mon–Sat 9:00–12:30 & 13:30–18:30, Sun 10:00–12:30 & 14:30–18:00; July–Aug no lunch closing; Oct–March closes at 18:00; tel. 08 25 16 02 00, www.st-malo-tourisme.com).

To get to St. Malo by **car**, follow signs for *St. Malo par la côte.* You will pass through extensive sprawl before reaching the town center; follow *Centre-Ville* signs to the old center, and then to the *Office de Tourisme*, which is directly across from the entrance gate *(Porte St. Vincent)* to the old town *(Intra-Muros)*. Park your car there and walk in.

St. Malo's **bus stop** and **TI** are at esplanade St. Vincent, across from the old city gate of the same name. A ferry runs between St. Malo and Dinard.

▲**Dinard**—This upscale old resort comes with a kid-friendly beach and plenty of old-time, Coney Island–style, beach-promenade ambience (2 buses/day from Dinan). The small passenger-only **ferry** to St. Malo provides the most scenic arrival (departs from below Promenade du Clair de Lune at Embarcadère).

The **TI,** between the casino and place de la République parking lot, is at 2 boulevard Féart (from place de la République, walk toward the water, take your first right, and then another right on boulevard Féart, tel. 02 99 46 94 12).

Dinard is a 10- to 20-minute drive from St. Malo (leaving St. Malo, follow signs through the unappealing port for *Barrage de la Rance,* then in Dinard, follow *Centre-Ville* signs, and park on place de la République).

▲**Fougères**—This very Breton city is a memorable stop for drivers traveling between the Loire châteaux and Mont St. Michel. Fougères has one of Europe's largest medieval castles, a fine city center, and a panoramic park viewpoint (from St. Léonard Church in Jardin Public). Try one of the café/*crêperies* near the castle, such as the tempting Crêperie des Remparts, one block uphill from the castle. Pick up a city map and castle description in English at the castle entrance. The interior is grass and walls.

The **TI** is on place Aristide Briand (from the château, walk in opposite direction of parking lot, up rue de la Pinterie, tel. 02 99 94 12 20).

THE LOIRE

The Loire River, which glides gently east to west across France and separates north from south, gives its name to this popular tourist region. The Loire Valley is carpeted with fertile fields, crisscrossed by rivers and streams, and studded with hundreds of castles and palaces in all shapes and sizes. The medieval castles highlight the area's strategic value during the Hundred Years' War (for information on the war, see page 183).

Renaissance palaces replaced medieval castles when a "valley address" became a must among hunt-crazy royalty and the rich. Today, the Loire Valley has a split personality: It's one of France's most important agricultural regions, but also a burgeoning bedroom community of Paris, thanks to the TGV bullet trains that link France's capital with this pastoral area in an hour.

In the Loire region, you'll pass many little vegetable gardens along the rivers. These are community gardens given to residents by the French government after World War II, when food was scarce and land was plentiful (and cheap). It took years for the food supply system to be reorganized, given the structural damage to railways, roads, and farms. While community gardens were the policy throughout France, they are more numerous and more visible in this region.

Planning Your Time

Many travelers find the Loire a good first or last stop on their French odyssey (5 TGV trains/day connect Paris' Charles de Gaulle airport in 1 hr with the city of Tours, which has car rental agencies at the station).

Use Amboise (good for Eurailers or drivers) or Chenonceaux (good for drivers) as a home base for touring the famous châteaux east of Tours: Chenonceau, Blois, Chambord, Chaumont-sur-Loire,

The Loire Valley

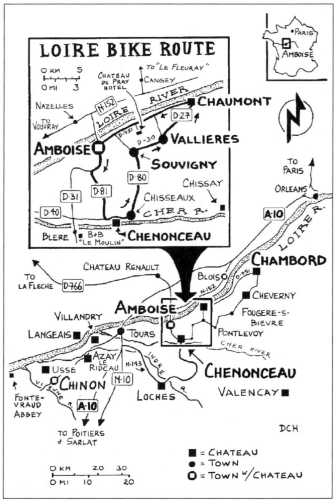

and Cheverny. Use Chinon or Azay-le-Rideau as your home base to visit the châteaux west of Tours: Chinon, Azay-le-Rideau, Langeais, and Villandry.

A day and a half is sufficient to sample the best châteaux. Don't go overboard. Two châteaux, possibly three (if you're a big person), make up the recommended daily dosage. Famous châteaux are least crowded early and late in the day. Most open around 9:00 and close between 18:00 and 19:00. During the off-season, many close from 12:00 to 14:00 and at 17:00.

Drivers: If you have only a day, consider this plan: Visit

Chenonceau (in the town of Chenonceaux) early, when crowds are smaller, spend midday at Chambord, and enjoy Cheverny late (the hunting dogs are fed at 17:00).

If arriving by car, try to see one château on your way in (e.g., Chambord if arriving from the north, Langeais or Villandry from the west, or Azay-le-Rideau from the south). If arriving by train from Paris, consider a stop in Blois and the bus excursion to Chambord and Cheverny (see "Getting Around the Loire Valley," below), or go directly to Amboise and try to visit Château du Clos-Lucé that afternoon.

If you're driving to the Dordogne from the Loire, the A-20 autoroute via Limoges (near Oradour-sur-Glane) is fastest and toll-free until Brive-la-Gaillarde.

Without Wheels: Many find the Loire manageable as a day trip from Paris (see "By Guided Minibus Tour," below). A good, one-day minivan-tour plan for those with no car and tight budget is to catch the once-per-day bus from Amboise to Chenonceaux (see "Getting Around the Loire Valley," below), tour Chenonceau, then spend the afternoon enjoying Amboise, its château, and Leonardo's last home at Clos-Lucé.

Getting Around the Loire Valley

By Train: With easy access from Amboise, the big city of Tours is the transport hub for train travelers. It has two important train stations and a bus station with service to several châteaux. The main train station is called Tours SNCF, and the smaller TGV station is St. Pierre-des-Corps. Check the schedules carefully, as service is sparse on some lines. The châteaux of Chenonceau, Langeais, Chinon, and Azay-le-Rideau have some train and/or bus service from Tours' main station (although Chenonceau is better by bus or bike from Amboise).

By Bus: There's one bus per day from **Amboise to Chenonceaux** (one-way-€1.10, daily except Sun; departs Amboise about 10:50, 15-min trip, returns from Chenonceaux at about 12:35, allowing you about 80 min at the château; in summer, there's also an afternoon departure at about 14:50, with a return from Chenonceaux at about 17:10; stop is across from post office, look for the green & yellow sign at bus stop, or ask at TI). From the city of **Tours to Amboise**, buses are cheaper than trains (€2.10, 8/day, none on Sun). Buses from Amboise to Chenonceaux or Tours are operated by Compagnie Touraine Fil Vert (tel. 02 47 05 30 49, www.touraine-filvert.com—in French only).

From mid-May through August, a handy **excursion bus from the Blois train station** (20 min by frequent train from Amboise) serves Chambord and Cheverny, giving you 90 minutes at each château (€10 includes bus fare and discounts on château entries, buy tickets from TI or bus driver; departs Blois station at 9:10, returns at 13:10; or departs Blois at 13:20, returns at 18:00, look for bus marked "Chambord/Cheverny" in front of the restaurant at Blois station). When combined with a visit to the château in Blois, this makes a good, full day. For details, call the Blois TI at 02 54 90 41 41 (also see "Blois" on page 258).

Touraine Evasion offers the same service as the above excursion bus from Blois, but **from Amboise** and in a minibus. You'll visit Chambord and Cheverny and enjoy drive-by views of Chaumont and Blois châteaux (€29 includes reduced admission prices at châteaux, runs year-round, minimal commentary, leaves from Amboise TI at 14:00, returns at 18:15, tel. 06 07 39 13 31 fax. 02 47 44 31 10, www.tourevasion.com).

By Guided Minibus Tour: Pascal Accolay runs **Acco-Dispo**, a small, personal minibus company with good all-day château tours from Amboise and Tours. Costs vary with the itinerary (€32/half-day, €50/day). English is the primary language. While on the road, you'll get a fun and enthusiastic running commentary covering each château's background, as well as the region's contemporary scene, but you're on your own at each château—and you pay the admission fee. All-day tours depart 8:30–10:30 (varies by itinerary); afternoon tours depart 13:20–13:50. Both return to Amboise around 18:30. Several tours are available; most include Chenonceau, and some include a wine-tasting. Reserve two to three days ahead if possible; groups are small, ranging from two to eight château-hoppers. (Day-trippers from Paris find this service convenient; after a 1-hr TGV ride to Tours, they're met near the central station and returned there at day's end.) Acco-Dispo also runs multi-day tours of the Loire and Brittany (daily, free hotel pickups, 18 rue des Vallées in Amboise, tel. 06 82 00 64 51 or 02 47 30 54 12, fax 02 47 23 15 73, www.accodispo-tours.com).

St. Eloi Excursions are an Acco-Dispo knock-off (same prices, comparable tour offerings, reserve at TI or your hotel, tel. 02 47 32 83 47, fax 02 47 32 83 80, www.saint-eloi.com).

By Taxi: A taxi from Amboise to Chenonceaux costs about €20. Your hotel can call one for you. The meter doesn't start until you do (see "Helpful Hints" under "Amboise," page 246).

By Rental Car: You can rent cars at either of Tours' train stations and in Amboise (also see "Helpful Hints" under "Amboise," page 246).

By Bike: Cycling options are endless in the Loire where the elevation gain is generally manageable (still, many find even the shortest rides exhausting and too time-consuming). Amboise, Blois, and Chinon make the best bike bases. From Amboise, allow an hour to Chenonceaux, but be warned: The first two miles are uphill. Serious bikers can ride to Chaumont in 90 minutes and connect Amboise,

Chenonceaux, and Chaumont with an all-day 37-mile pedal (see Loire Valley map in this chapter for details). Cycling from Blois to Chambord is a manageable 75-minute, one-way ride, but adding Cheverny makes a grueling, full-day, 30-mile round-trip. Most can do the pleasant bike ride from Chinon to Ussé (though you encounter a very big hill when leaving Chinon), and some will find the energy to continue on to Langeais. Only those in top condition will enjoy biking farther to Villandry (see "Chinon," page 264). Call the Blois TI (tel. 02 54 90 41 41) or see "Amboise," below for bike-rental information.

Cuisine Scene in the Loire Valley

Here in "the garden of France," food produced locally is delicious. Loire Valley rivers yield fresh trout *(truite)*, salmon *(saumon)*, and smelt *(éperlau)*, which are often served fried *(friture)*. *Rillettes*, a stringy pile of cooked and whipped pork, makes for a cheap, mouth-watering sandwich spread (use lots of mustard and add a baby pickle, called a *cornichon*). The area's fine goat cheeses include Crottin de Chavignol *(crottin* means horse dung, which is what this cheese, when aged, resembles), Saint-Maure Fermier (soft and creamy), and Selles-sur-Cher (mild). For dessert, try a delicious *tarte tatin* (upside-down caramel-apple tart).

The best and most expensive white wines are the Sancerres, made in the less touristed, western edge of the Loire. Less expensive, but still tasty, are Touraine Sauvignons and the sweeter Vouvrays, whose grapes are grown near Amboise. Vouvray is also famous for its light and refreshing sparkling wines. The better reds come from Chinon and Bourgeuil.

Remember, restaurants serve only during lunch (11:30–14:00) and dinner (19:00–21:00, later in bigger cities); cafés serve food throughout the day.

Amboise

Straddling the widest part of the Loire, the town of Amboise slumbers in the shadow of its hilltop château. A castle has overlooked the Loire from Amboise since Roman times. Leonardo da Vinci retired here...just one more fine idea.

As the royal residence of François I (r. 1515–1547), Amboise wielded far more importance than you'd imagine from a lazy walk down the pleasant, pedestrian-only commercial zone at the base of the palace. In fact, its 14,000 residents are quite conservative, giving the town "an attitude"—as if no one told them they're no longer the second capital of France. The locals are the kind who keep their wealth to themselves; consequently, many fine mansions hide behind nondescript facades. There's even a Royalist element here (and the duke of Paris, the guy who'd be king if there was one, lives here).

The half-mile-long "Golden Island" is the only island in the Loire substantial enough to be flood-proof and have permanent buildings (including a soccer stadium and a 13th-century church). This was important historically as the place where northern and southern France, divided by the longest river in the country, came together. Truces were made here. The Loire marked the farthest north that the Moors conquered as they pushed through Europe from Morocco (Loire means "impassable" in Arabic). Today, this region still divides the country (for example, weather forecasters say "north of the Loire...and south of the Loire").

With or without a car, Amboise is an ideal small-town home base for exploring the best of château country.

ORIENTATION

Amboise (pop. 11,000) covers both sides of the Loire and an island in the middle. The train station is on the north side of the river, but nearly everything else is on the south (château) side, including the TI.

Pedestrian-friendly rue Nationale leads from the base of Château d'Amboise through the town center and past the clock tower—once part of the town wall—to the striking Romanesque Church of St. Denis.

Tourist Information

The information-packed TI is in the round building on the riverbank at quai du Général de Gaulle (June and Sept Mon–Sat 9:30–13:00 & 14:00–18:30, Sun 10:00–13:00 & 15:00–18:00; July–Aug Mon–Sat 9:00–20:00, Sun 10:00–18:00; Oct–May Mon–Sat 10:00–13:00 & 14:00–18:00, Sun 10:00–13:00, tel. 02 47 57 09 28, www.amboise-valdeloire.com). Skip their hard-to-read map and ask for the English tourist booklet called *Amboise Valley* which includes a map, a self-guided walking tour, and some sightseeing information. They sell maps of bike routes for €2. In summer, ask about the sound-and-light shows. The TI can reserve a room for you in a hotel or *chambre d'hôte* (for a €2.50 fee), but first peruse the photo album of regional *chambres d'hôte*. Their free service, SOS Chambres d'Hôtes, can tell you what rooms are still available (tel. 02 47 23 27 42).

Arrival in Amboise

By Train: Amboise's train station, with a post office and taxi stand, is birds-chirping peaceful (tel. 02 47 23 18 23). Turn left out of the station, make a quick right, and walk down rue de Nazelles five minutes to the bridge, which leads you over the Loire River into town. Within three blocks of the station, you'll find a recommended hotel, B&B, and bike-rental shop.

By Car: Drivers set their sights on the flag-festooned château that caps the hill. Most recommended accommodations and restaurants cluster just downriver (west). Warning: If driving through Amboise with the river on your left, note that some streets on your right have the right-of-way when merging. Free parking is available near the TI under the triple row of trees—or ask your hotelier for parking advice.

Helpful Hints

Market Days: Open-air markets are held on Friday (smaller, food only) and Sunday (bigger) in the parking lot behind the TI on the river (both 8:30–13:00).

Supermarket: Marché Plus is across from the TI (Mon–Sat 7:00–21:00, Sun 9:00–13:00).

Chocolate Fantasy: An essential and historic stop for chocoholics is **Bigot Pâtisserie & Chocolatier** (one block off river, where place Michel Debré meets rue Nationale).

Internet Access: Playconnect Cyber C@fe has great rates, but odd hours (€1/15 min, Mon 13:00–22:00, Tue and Thu 10:00–22:00, Fri–Sat 10:00–24:00, Sun 15:00–22:00, closed Wed, 119 rue Nationale, tel. 02 47 57 18 04).

Bookstore: Maison de la Presse has a small selection of English novels and a good selection of maps and English guidebooks—such as Michelin's *Châteaux of the Loire* Green Guide (English versions cost €14, about 30 percent off U.S. price; across from TI at 5 quai du Général de Gaulle).

Bike Rental: You can rent a bike (roughly €11/half-day, €14/day, leave your passport or a photocopy) at either of these reliable places: **Locacycle** (daily 9:00–12:30 & 14:00–19:00, can return full-day rentals the next morning, near TI at 2 rue Jean-Jacques Rousseau, tel. 02 47 57 00 28, some English spoken) or **Cycles Richard** (closed 12:00–14:30 and all day Sun–Mon, located on train-station side of river, just past bridge at 2 rue de Nazelles, tel. 02 47 57 01 79, NSE).

Car Rental: Avis is expensive (about €82/day with 150 kilometers/90 miles free, across from Amboise TI, tel. 02 47 23 21 11). **Garage Jourdain** costs about half that price (approx. €47/day with 100 kilometers/60 miles free, downriver from TI at 105 route de Tours, tel. 02 47 57 17 92, fax 02 47 57 77 50). Both have similar hours (closed Mon–Fri 12:00–14:00 and at 18:00, at 17:00 on Sat, and all day Sun).

Taxi: Call 02 47 57 01 54 (allow €20 to Chenonceaux).

Laundry: The handy coin-op **Lav'centre** is just across the street from the TI and up allée du Sergent Turpin at #9 (daily 7:00–21:00, Oct–May until 20:00, about €7/load, English instructions). The door locks at closing time; leave beforehand, or you'll trigger the alarm.

Amboise

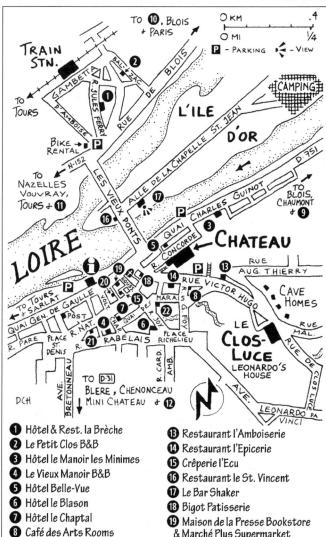

1. Hôtel & Rest. la Brèche
2. Le Petit Clos B&B
3. Hôtel le Manoir les Minimes
4. Le Vieux Manoir B&B
5. Hôtel Belle-Vue
6. Hôtel le Blason
7. Hôtel le Chaptal
8. Café des Arts Rooms
9. To Château de Pray
10. To Hôtel le Fleuray
11. To Château de Nazelles B&B
12. To Le Moulin du Fief Gentil B&B & La Chevalerie B&B
13. Restaurant l'Amboiserie
14. Restaurant l'Epicerie
15. Crêperie l'Ecu
16. Restaurant le St. Vincent
17. Le Bar Shaker
18. Bigot Patisserie
19. Maison de la Presse Bookstore & Marché Plus Supermarket
20. Launderette
21. Internet Café
22. Katia Frain B&B

SIGHTS

▲▲**Château du Clos-Lucé**—In 1516, Leonardo da Vinci packed his bags (and several of his favorite paintings, including the *Mona Lisa*) and left an imploding Rome for better working conditions in the Loire Valley. He accepted the position of engineer, architect, and painter to the French king. This "House of Light" is the plush palace where he spent his last three years. France's Renaissance king François I set Leonardo up here just so he could enjoy his intellectual company. François I was 22 when his 65-year-old mentor moved in. There's a touching sketch in Leonardo's bedroom of François I comforting his genius pal on his deathbed. The house was built in 1450—just within the protective walls of the town—as a guest house to the château. While it hosted VIPs before and after Leonardo, today it thoughtfully re-creates (with adequate English information) the everyday atmosphere Leonardo enjoyed as he lived here—pursuing his passions to the very end.

The ground floor is filled with sketches recording the storm patterns of Leonardo's brain and models of his remarkable inventions (inspired by designs occurring in nature and built according to his notes). It's hard to imagine that this Roman candle of creativity died nearly 500 years ago. In the model room, notice the entry to the long tunnel that connects this house with the château. The garden café is reasonable and appropriately meditative; above it is a French-only video about Leonardo. The visit finishes with a stroll through the park grounds where you'll find life-size models of his inventions (€11 entry, less in winter, April–June and Oct daily 9:00–19:00, July–Aug daily 9:00–20:00, Feb–March and Nov–Dec daily 9:00–18:00, Jan daily 10:00–17:00, follow the free and fine English handout, tel. 02 47 57 62 88 or 02 47 57 00 73, www.vinci-closluce.com). It's a 15-minute walk from the TI, up past troglodyte homes (unsafe parking lot at Clos-Lucé).

Château d'Amboise—This royal residence was built during the reign of three kings, and part of it was designed by Leonardo da Vinci. The king who did most of the building (Charles VIII) is famous for accidentally killing himself by walking into a doorjamb on his way to a tennis match (seriously). Later occupants were more careful. François I brought the Renaissance here in 1516 (through Leonardo da Vinci). While the English handout helps, no room stands out as exceptionally furnished or compelling, and this place pales when compared to other area châteaux. But the grand views over Amboise and the river almost merit the entry fee.

After climbing the flower-lined ramp, your first stop is the lacy, petite chapel where Leonardo da Vinci is supposedly buried. This flamboyant little Gothic chapel comes with two fireplaces "to comfort the king" and a plaque "evoking the final resting place" of

Leonardo. Where he's actually buried, no one seems to know.

Views of rooftops and the Loire River follow you through red-brick rooms lined with high-backed chairs and massive stone fireplaces. At stop #2 ("the Sentry Walk"), plans show the château's original size. The bulky horsemen's tower climbs 130 feet in five spirals—designed for a mounted soldier in a hurry. As you leave the tower, hang a sharp right and walk on the outside passage around the same tower; mind the gargoyle's big mouths above.

Best château views are from the garden terraces farther upriver past the royal croquet set. You can exit the way you entered, or follow signs through the bookshop and down through the spiralling tower (€7.50, April–June and Oct daily 9:00–18:00, July–Aug daily 9:00–19:00, off-season closes 12:00-14:00 and at 17:00, tel. 02 47 57 00 98, www.chateau-amboise.tm.fr).

▲**Château d'Amboise Sound-and-Light Show**—If you're into S&L, this is considered one of the best shows of its kind in the area. While it's entirely in French, you can buy the English booklet for €5. Volunteer locals from toddlers to pensioners recreate the life of François I with costumes, jugglers, impressive light displays, and fireworks. Dress warmly, and be prepared for a long show (adults-€13–16, kids ages 6–14-€7, Wed and Sat end of June–Aug 22:30–24:00, starts 22:00 in Aug, get details at TI or call 02 47 57 14 47, www.renaissance-amboise.com). The ticket window is on the ramp to the château and opens at 20:30. While you may feel locked in, you're welcome to leave at any time.

Mini-Châteaux—This five-acre park on the edge of Amboise (on the route to Chenonceaux) shows all the Loire châteaux in 1:25-scale models, forested with 600 bonsai trees and laced together by a model TGV train. For children, it's a great introduction to the real châteaux they'll be visiting. The English brochure is essential (adult-€12, kids ages 4–16-€8, April–June and Sept daily 10:00–18:00, July–Aug daily 10:00–20:00, off-season closes at 17:00, last ticket sold 1 hr before closing, tel. 02 47 23 44 44).

You'll find other kid-oriented attractions at Mini-Châteaux; skip the donkey show, but consider playing a round of mini-golf and feeding the fish in the moat (a great way to get rid of that old baguette).

Caveau des Vignerons—This small cave offers free tastings of regional wines, cheeses, and foie gras they may have for sale (mid-March–mid-Nov 10:00–19:00, under Château d'Amboise across from recommended l'Epicerie restaurant, tel. 02 47 57 23 69).

Wine-Tasting in Nearby Vouvray—Jean-Pierre Laisement, a local vintner, welcomes visitors to his Caves Laisement winery for a fun wine-tasting and a look around his place. His elderly mother serves, while his truffle dog, Razor, looks on. Telephone before dropping in to be sure Monsieur Laisement is at home (9 miles toward Tours from Amboise off RN 152 near Les Patys, 15 rue de la Vallée

Coquette, Vouvray, tel. 02 47 52 74 47). For tips on wine-tasting, see "French Wine-Tasting 101" on page 46.

SLEEPING

Amboise is busy in the summer, but there are lots of hotels and *chambres d'hôte* in and around the city; the TI can help with reservations.

In the Center
$$$ Le Manoir les Minimes**, a renovated 17th-century mansion with 15 rooms, feels over the top, with precious furniture, but it works for those seeking luxury in Amboise. Rooms are large and modern (standard Db-€80–110, larger Db-€100–125, deluxe Db-€125–170, 3–4-person suites-€195–240, extra bed-€20, air-con, Internet access, 34 quai Charles Guinot, 3 blocks upriver from bridge, tel. 02 47 30 40 40, fax 02 47 30 40 77, www.manoirlesminimes.com, minimes @wanadoo.fr).

$$$ Le Vieux Manoir is an entirely different high-end splurge. American expats Gloria and Bob Belknap have lovingly restored this secluded but central one-time convent with an attention to detail that Martha Stewart would envy. The atrium-like breakfast room opens to manicured gardens, the public spaces are American-cozy, and the six bedrooms would make an antique collector drool. The Belknaps are also a wealth of information (Db-€125–175, includes hearty breakfast, air-con planned for 2005; ask about the 2-room, 2-floor apartment with full kitchen; easy parking, 13 rue Rabelais, tel. & fax 02 47 30 41 27, www.le-vieux-manoir.com).

$$ Hôtel Belle-Vue* overlooks the river where the bridge hits town. This basic hotel has spacious public rooms, dark halls, and effective double-paned windows, but needs a face-lift. Half its simple rooms have views of the château; four come with huge shared terraces (Db-€62–72, Tb-€79–88, Qb-€103, includes buffet breakfast, elevator, 12 quai Charles Guinot, tel. 02 47 57 02 26, fax 02 47 30 51 23).

$ Katia Frain may be the most engaging person in Amboise. Her family-oriented *chambres* in a historic building on a busy road are a good value, but can be stuffy if it's hot. Katia and her husband teach music and welcome you to relax in their artsy garden (Db-€45, big Tb-€60, Qb-€75, Quint/b-€90, includes breakfast, 14 quai des Marais, tel. 02 47 30 46 51, vianney.frain@wanadoo.fr, SE).

$ Hôtel le Blason** is a old, half-timbered building five blocks from the river on a busy street. Its 28 rooms are small, bright, and modern, with double-paned windows (Sb-€45, Db-€50–55, Tb-€65, Qb-€75, quieter rooms in back and on top floor, some with air-con, parking nearby, 11 place Richelieu, tel. 02 47 23 22 41, fax 02 47 57 56 18, www.leblason.fr, leblason@hotel-leblason.com).

Sleep Code

(€1 = about $1.20, country code: 33)
S = Single, **D** = Double/Twin, **T** = Triple, **Q** = Quad,
b = bathroom, **s** = shower only, **no CC** = Credit Cards not
accepted, **SE** = Speaks English, **NSE** = No English, * = French
hotel rating system (0–4 stars). You can assume a hotel takes
credit cards unless you see "no CC" in the listing.

To help you sort easily through these listings, I've divided
the rooms into three categories based on the price for a standard
double room with bath:

$$$ **Higher Priced**—Most rooms €90 or more.
$$ **Moderately Priced**—Most rooms between €60–90.
$ **Lower Priced**—Most rooms €60 or less.

$ **Hôtel le Chaptal*** offers one-star comfort with its cheap, *très*
frumpy rooms. With marginal beds and old carpets, the place needs
attention, but its prices are fair (Db-€39–44, Tb-€45–50, Qb-€50,
13 rue Chaptal, tel. 02 47 57 14 46, fax 02 47 57 67 83, NSE). In
summer, they request that you dine in their cheery, inexpensive
dining room.

$ **Café des Arts,** a popular hangout with locals, rents seven
simple rooms above the loud, smoky bar. It's a step up from a youth
hostel, but barely. Rooms are linoleum-floored and come with
modern bunk beds for a good price (S-€20, D-€33, T-€47, Q-€58,
up to 6 people possible, across from château exit at 32 rue Victor
Hugo, tel. & fax 02 47 57 25 04).

Near the Train Station

$$ **Hôtel la Brèche**, a tired little refuge, has 14 adequate rooms
with paper-thin walls and small bathrooms. Many rooms overlook
the peaceful garden; those on the street are generally larger. Half-
pension, required in the summer, gets you a dinner that includes a
good salad bar and dessert buffet for an extra €12 per person. Box
lunches are also available for €8 (S-€40, Sb-€53, D-€51, Db-€64,
Tb-€77, Qb-€87–93, includes breakfast, a few good family rooms,
table tennis, 15-min walk from city center and 2-min walk from sta-
tion, 26 rue Jules Ferry, tel. 02 47 57 00 79, fax 02 47 57 65 49,
www.labreche-amboise.com, info@labreche-amboise.com).

$ **Le Petit Clos** *chambre d'hôte* has three cheery, cottage-style,
ground-floor rooms off a quiet, picnic-perfect, private garden. Sweet
Madame Roullet and her just-as-sweet husband, Dominique, speak
a leetle English. This place is immaculate, as Madame was a nurse in
her other life (Db-€56, family suite for up to 5-€120, no CC,

includes big, farm-fresh breakfast with homemade everything, easy parking in garden, turn left out of train station and follow tracks 200 yards to rue Balzac and turn right, it's at #7, tel. 02 47 57 43 52).

Near Amboise

The area around Amboise is replete with good-value accommodations in every shape, size, and price range. A list follows of those that justify the detour. (For more accommodations, drivers could also check out "Sleeping" in Chenonceaux, page 257.)

$$$ **Château de Pray****, a 750-year-old fortified castle, retains hints of its medieval origins behind its Renaissance elegance. The dining room is splendid, and the chef talented (€41–60 *menus*, reservations required). The pool lies below the château, which has a modern annex (Db in annex-€95–110, smaller Db in main building-€105–120, larger Db-€130–170, extra bed-€32, 3-min drive upriver from Amboise, toward Chaumont on D-751, look for turnoff just after passing under bridge, tel. 02 47 57 23 67, fax 02 47 57 32 50, http://praycastel.online.fr, chateau.depray@wanadoo.fr).

$$$ **Hôtel Le Fleuray** is a lovingly restored French farmhouse wrapped in a peaceful country setting about a 15-minute drive northeast of Amboise. It's warmly operated by owners Hazel and Peter Newington. She runs the kitchen, while he handles the hotel details. Their two friendly children, Jordan and Cassie, make good helpers. All rooms are bright-floral-print pretty, with those in the outbuildings—overlooking the heated swimming pool—a bit larger and better for families. The restaurant serves average cuisine (Db-€72–110, *menus* from €28, tel. 02 47 56 09 25, fax 02 47 56 93 97, www.lefleurayhotel.com, lefleurayhotel@wanadoo.fr). From Amboise, take the N-152 about five miles toward Blois, turn left on D-74 toward Cangey, and follow signs another five miles past Fleuray. From the A-10, take exit 18 and follow the signs.

$$$ **Château de Nazelles** *chambre d'hôte* is for those who want a château hotel experience *sans* pretension. Young, friendly, and English-speaking Monsieur and Madame Fructus have tastefully restored this seven-room, 16th-century hillside castle, once home to the original builder of Chenonceau. The two special troglodyte rooms come with garden views and rock-walled bathrooms. In summer, the old orangerie serves as a basic kitchen for picnics or barbecues in the garden. Trails to the forest above, a cliff-sculpted pool, and lush gardens with views over Amboise are all included (Db-€90–110, comes with breakfast, tel. & fax 02 47 30 53 79, www.chateau -nazelles.com). From Amboise, take N-152 toward Tours, turn right on D-5, then left in Nazelles-Négron on D-1 and quickly veer right above the post office (PTT) to 16 rue Tue-la-Soif. Look for the sign on your left and enter through the archway on the right.

$$ **Le Moulin du Fief Gentil**, a beautifully renovated

16th-century mill house, offers a lovely experience 15 minutes from Amboise and Chenonceaux. You get four acres and a backyard pond (fishing possible in summer), smartly decorated rooms, and a splendid common living room. If Ann is cooking, splurge for dinner (Db-€74–99, 2-room apartment-€120, includes breakfast, 4-course dinner-€25/person, no CC, tel. 02 47 30 32 51, mobile 06 64 82 37 18, www.fiefgentil.com, florence.heurtebise@wanadoo.fr). It's located on the edge of Bléré; from Bléré, follow signs toward Luzille.

$ At **La Chevalerie**, closer to Amboise, Martine Aleksic rents four bargain *chambres* that are family-friendly in every way—total seclusion in a farm setting, with a swingset, tiny fishing pond, common kitchens, and connecting rooms all offered with a warm reception (Db-€40, Tb-€55, Qb-€70, no CC, in La Croix-en-Touraine, from Amboise take D-31 toward Bléré and look for sign on your left after about 2.5 miles, tel. 02 47 57 83 64).

EATING

Amboise is filled with inexpensive and forgettable restaurants. Those nearest the château are busy with tourists, but offer good enough value.

L'Amboiserie is a budget option, with a large selection of basic dishes (crêpes, salads, meats) and a pleasant, umbrella-dotted upstairs terrace (daily, closed mid-Nov–mid-Feb, 7 rue Victor Hugo, tel. 02 47 30 50 40).

L'Epicerie, a romantic's choice, serves traditional cuisine under a wood-beam ceiling at fair prices (tasty €20 *menu*, daily, 46 place Michel Debré, tel. 02 47 57 08 94).

Crêperie L'Ecu is good and quiet (closed Sun night and all day Mon, indoor/outdoor seating, near pedestrian street rue Nationale, 7 rue Corneille, tel. 02 47 30 58 95).

In any weather, **Hôtel La Brèche**'s simple restaurant, with its outdoor terrace, is a decent value, with a salad bar and dessert buffet (daily, see "Sleeping," above, near train station); the walk home includes a floodlit château.

Le St. Vincent is where local hoteliers send their discerning clients (on the island, across from Château d'Amboise). The cheery interior is Provençal yellow and blue, with a van Gogh motif. Even more importantly, the food is fresh, tasty, and beautifully presented (fine discounted lunch menu, dinner *menus* from €20, daily, 7 rue Commire, reservations smart, especially for a view window table for 2, tel. 02 47 30 49 49). Across the street, **Le Bar Shaker** offers scenic cocktails and outdoor tables with late-night château views.

Eating near Amboise: Drivers should consider making the three-minute drive to **Château de Pray** for a royal experience—but reserve first (see "Near Amboise" under "Sleeping," above).

TRANSPORTATION CONNECTIONS

Twelve 15-minute trains link Amboise daily to the regional train hub of St. Pierre-des-Corps (suburban Tours). From there, you'll find reasonable connections to distant points (including the TGV to Paris-Montparnasse). Transferring in Paris can be the fastest way to reach many French destinations, even in the south.

From Amboise by train to: Paris (20/day, 1.5 hrs, 8/day direct to Paris-Austerlitz and 12/day to Paris-Montparnasse with change at St. Pierre-de-Corps), **Sarlat** (4/day, 5–6 hrs, change at St. Pierre-des-Corps, then TGV to Libourne or Bordeaux-St. Jean, then train through Bordeaux vineyards to Sarlat), **Blois** (14/day, 20 min), **Limoges** (near Oradour-sur-Glane, 9/day, 4 hrs, change at St. Pierre-des-Corps and Vierzon or at Les Aubrais-Orléans and Vierzon, then tricky bus connection from Limoges to Oradour-sur-Glane), **Pontorson-Mont St. Michel** (4/day, 7 hrs, changes at Tours main station, Caen, then bus from Pontorson; or via Paris TGV with changes at St. Pierre-des-Corps, Paris-Montparnasse, then bus from Rennes, 4/day, 7 hrs), **Bayeux** (9/day, 5–6 hrs, changes in Caen and Tours, or at Paris-Montparnasse and St. Pierre-des-Corps).

By bus to: Chenonceaux (1/day, 15 min, departs Amboise about 10:50 from bus stop across from post office on route de Montrichard, returns from Chenonceaux at 12:35, in summer an afternoon departure from Amboise at about 14:50 with a return from Chenonceaux about 17:10).

Chenonceaux

This quiet, sleepy village—with a knockout château—makes a good home base for drivers. Note that Chenonceaux is the name of the town, and Chenonceau (no "x") is the name of the château, but they're pronounced the same: shuh-non-so.

The small **TI** is on the main road from Amboise as you enter the village (summer 10:00–13:00 & 14:00–19:00, closed Sun except July–Aug, shorter hours off-season, tel. 02 47 23 94 45). Warning: Because this parking lot is not patrolled, don't leave any luggage visible in your car.

Chenonceau, rated ▲▲▲, is the toast of the Loire. This 16th-century Renaissance palace arches gracefully over the Cher River. Understandably popular, Chenonceau is the third-most-visited château in France (after Versailles and Fontainebleau). To beat the crowds, arrive at 8:45 or after 17:00, and plan on a 15-minute walk from the parking lot to the château.

While earlier châteaux were built for defensive purposes,

Chenonceau was the first great pleasure palace. Nicknamed **"the château of the ladies,"** it housed many famous women over the centuries. The original builder's wife oversaw the construction of the main part of the château. In 1547, King Henry II gave the château to his mistress, Diane de Poitiers. She added an arched bridge across the river to access the hunting grounds. She enjoyed her lovely retreat until Henry II died (pierced in a jousting tournament in Paris) and his vengeful wife, Catherine de Médicis, unceremoniously kicked her out (and into the château of Chaumont). Catherine added the three-story structure on Diane's bridge. She died before completing her vision of a matching château on the far side of the river, but not before turning Chenonceau into *the* place to see and be seen by local aristocracy. (Note that whenever you see a split coat of arms, it belongs to a woman—half her husband's and half her father's.)

Approaching Chenonceau, you'll cross three moats and two drawbridges and pass an old round tower, which predates the main building. Notice the tower's fine limestone veneer, added so the top would better fit the new château.

The main château's original oak door greets you with Fs (for François I, who ruled 1515–1547), his fire-breathing salamander emblem, and coats of arms. The knocker is high enough to be used by visitors on horseback. The smaller door within the larger one could be for two purposes: To slip in after curfew, and to enter during winter without letting out all the heat.

The interior is fascinating—but only if you take full advantage of the excellent 20-page booklet given out at the entry. Follow that, but notice the few details described below as well:

In the **guard room**, the fine original tiles survive best near the walls. While the tapestries kept the room cozy, they also functioned to tell news or recent history (to the king's liking, of course).

The finely detailed **chapel** survived the vandalism of the Revolution because the fast-thinking lady of the palace filled it with firewood. Angry masses were supplied with mallets and instructions to smash everything royal and religious. While this room was both, all they saw was stacked wood. The hatch door provided a quick path to the kitchen and an escape boat downstairs. The windows, blown out during World War II, are replacements from the 1950s.

The centerpiece of the **bedroom of Diane de Poitiers** is a portrait of Catherine de Médicis. After the queen booted out the mistress, she placed her own portrait over the fireplace, but she never used the bedroom of her husband's mistress. The 16th-century tapestries here are among the finest in France. Each one took an average of 60 worker-years to make. Study the complex compositions of the *Triumph of Charity* and the violent *Triumph of Force*.

The **gallery,** at 200 feet long, spanned the river with three stories—the upper stories house double-decker ballrooms and guest rooms. Notice how differently the slate and limestone of the checkered floor wear after 500 years. Imagine grand banquets here. Catherine, a contemporary of Queen Elizabeth I of England, wanted to rule with style. She threw wild parties and employed her ladies to circulate and soak up all the political gossip possible from the well-lubricated Kennedys and Rockefellers of her realm. Parties included grand fireworks displays and mock naval battles in the river. For a quick walk outside (and more good palace views), cross the bridge, pick up a reentry ticket, take your stroll (you're across the river from the château), then show your reentry ticket when you return. (Chenonceau, which marked the border between free and Nazi France in World War II, was the scene of dramatic prisoner swaps.)

Back inside the gallery, the staircase leading **upstairs** wowed royal guests. It was the first non-spiral staircase they'd seen...quite a treat in the 16th century. The upper gallery usually contains a temporary modern-art exhibit. Small side rooms on the upper floor show fascinating old architectural sketches of the château. The walls, 20 feet thick, were honeycombed with the flues of 224 fireplaces and passages for servants to do their pleasure-providing work unseen. There was no need for plumbing. Servants fetched, carried, and dumped everything pipes do today. The balcony here provides fine views of the gardens— originally functional with vegetables and herbs. The estate is still full of wild boar and deer—the primary dishes of past centuries.

The state-of-the-art (in the 16th century) **kitchen** is not to be missed. It was in the basement because heat rises (helping heat the palace), and near water to fight the inevitable kitchen fires. Beyond the fine servants' dining room, there's a landing bay for goods to be ferried in and out. In 1916, the château was a hospital for France's countless wounded soldiers—with a hundred beds lining its gallery. The slick kitchen is from that time.

Cost and Hours: €8, mid-March–mid-Sept daily 9:00–19:00, earlier closing off-season, tel. 02 47 23 90 07, www.chenonceau.com. There are two different iPod **audioguides**: The 45-min tour is sufficient for most; the 90-min tour is overkill (€2 for either). Pay for the audioguide when buying your ticket before entering the château grounds; you won't have a second chance to pay where you actually pick up the audioguide. Chenonceau's crowds are the worst in the Loire—arrive early or late.

In summer, rental **rowboats** offer an idyllic way to savor graceful château views (€2/30 min, 10:00–19:00, 4 persons/boat). Ask about nighttime sound-and-light shows in July and August (€5 fee doesn't include château, 22:00–23:30).

The château stables (in front of the grand entry) house **La Galerie des Dames-Musée de Cires**, which puts a waxy face on the juicy history of the château. It's well-described in English and offers a good introduction before you sightsee (€3). Next door is a modern, pricey cafeteria. Fancy meals are served in the orangerie behind the stables.

SLEEPING

(€1 = about $1.20, country code: 33)
$$ Hôtel la Roseraie* enchants with its 17 delightfully decorated, country-classy rooms, while English-speaking Laurent and Sophie try their best to spoil you (Db-€57–95, a few grand family rooms-€76–125, apartment-€180, some rooms with air-con, free parking, heated pool, wood-beamed dining room for which I dress up to splurge for a fine dinner, €23–37 *menus*, non-smoking restaurant, located dead center on main drag at 7 rue du Dr. Bretonneau, hard-to-read sign, tel. 02 47 23 90 09, fax 02 47 23 91 59, www.charmingroseraie.com).

$$ Relais Chenonceaux*, across from Hôtel La Roseraie, has a flowery patio and modern, wood-finished rooms, but the reception lacks a certain *je ne sais quoi* (Db-€46–68, Tb-€63–74, Qb-€80–94, tel. 02 47 23 98 11, fax 02 47 23 84 07, www.chenonceaux.com).

$ Hostel du Roy** offers 33 simple rooms, a quiet garden courtyard, and an average restaurant (Db-€40–48, Tb-€51–55, Qb-€59, 9 rue du Dr. Bretonneau, 5-min walk to château, tel. 02 47 23 90 17, fax 02 47 23 89 81, www.hostelduroy.com, Nathalie SE).

EATING

For a splurge, try **Hôtel la Roseraie** (listed above). **Au Gâteau Breton** is good, friendly, and reasonably priced for lunch or dinner (closed Tue–Wed evenings, 16 rue du Dr. Bretonneau, tel. 02 47 23 90 14).

TRANSPORTATION CONNECTIONS

From Chenonceaux by train to: Tours (3/day, 30 min).
By bus to: Amboise (1/day, 15 min, departs Chenonceaux at about 12:35, and in summer also at about 17:10).

More Châteaux East of Tours

To explore the following châteaux, use either Amboise (page 244) or Chenonceaux (page 254) as your home base. For tips on transportation, See "Getting Around the Loire Valley" on page 242.

The region between the Loire and Paris, known as the Beauce, is the breadbasket of France, with fertile soil and a temperate climate. (It has almost no snow, nor need for summer air-conditioning.) Because this rich land was vulnerable from attacks from the west (by those pesky dukes of Anjou), the first châteaux were defensive. Later, when the country was more established and the kings lived in the neighborhood, these were the palaces of France's rich and powerful.

Blois

Blois, rated ▲▲, is a good urban stop in this mostly rural region. It has quick access to Chambord (bus or car, see "Getting Around the Loire Valley," page 242), a fresh coat of paint, dolled-up pedestrian areas, and a dynamite château.

The **TI** is just across from the château entrance. Save time to explore the center of Blois (blwah) by using the TI's handy walking-tour brochure; the brown and purple routes are best (May–Sept Tue–Sat 9:00–19:00, Sun–Mon 10:00–19:00; Oct–April Mon 10:00–12:30 & 14:00–18:00, Tue–Sat from 9:00, Sun 9:30–12:30, 23 place du Château, tel. 02 54 90 41 41). Train travelers can walk 15 minutes to the TI and château; drivers can follow signs to *Centre-Ville*, then pull into *Parking du Château* (30 min free, then €0.60/hr).

Château Royal, unlike other châteaux, is right in the city center, without a nearby forest, river, or lake. It's an easy walk from the train station, near ample underground parking, and just above the TI. Pick up an English brochure and read the English displays at this well-presented castle. This château, home to Louis XII and François I, is where Catherine de Médicis spent her last night (see page 255). Begin in the courtyard, where four different wings, ranging from Gothic to neoclassical, surround you and underscore the importance of this château over many centuries. Your visit to the interior begins in the dazzling Hall of the Estates-General, continues to a great display of gargoyles and models in a small lapidary museum, then up through several gorgeously tiled and decorated royal rooms, and ends in a fine arts museum with a 16th-century who's-who portrait gallery and interesting ironworks room (château entry-€6.50, May–Sept daily 9:00–18:00, July–Aug daily 9:00–19:00, Oct–April daily 9:00–12:30 & 14:00–17:30, occasional English tours, sound-and-light show many evenings mid-April–Sept, €9.50 or €12 combo-ticket with daytime château entry, €15 gets you both plus the House of Magic).

The House of Magic, home of Jean-Eugène Robert-Houdin, the illusionist whose name was adopted by Harry Houdini, offers an interesting but overpriced history of illusion and magic (€7.50, Tue–Sun 10:00–18:00, often closes during lunch, closed Mon except July–Aug, tel. 02 54 55 26 26).

If you're stopping in Blois around lunchtime, plan on eating at **Le Marignan** on a breezy, traffic-free square in front of the château (daily, good salads, fast service, 5 place du Château, tel. 02 54 74 73 15). At the top of the hour, you can watch the stately mansion opposite the château become "the dragon house," as monsters crane their long necks out its many windows.

Chambord

Chambord, rated ▲▲▲, has 440 rooms and 365 fireplaces. This place is big. It's surrounded by Europe's largest enclosed forest park—a game preserve defined by a 20-mile-long wall and teeming

with wild deer and boar. Chambord (shamb-bor), which began as a simple hunting lodge for bored Blois counts, became a monument to the royal sport and duty of hunting. (Apparently, hunting was considered important to keep the animal population under control and the vital forests healthy.) Starting in 1518, François I, using 1,800 workmen over 15 years, created this "weekend retreat" (leaving his signature salamander symbol everywhere).

François I was an absolute monarch—with an emphasis on absolute. In 32 years of rule (1515–1547), he never called the Estates-General (a rudimentary parliament in *ancien régime* France). This grand hunting palace was another way to show off his power. Charles V—the Holy Roman Emperor and most powerful man of the age—was invited here and thoroughly wowed.

The château, six times the size of most, consists of a keep in the shape of a Greek cross, with four towers and two wings surrounded by stables. It has three floors: first floor—reception rooms; second floor—royal apartments; third floor—now a hunting museum; and rooftop—a hunt-viewing terrace. Because hunting visibility is best after autumn leaves fall, Chambord was a winter palace. Only 80 of Chambord's rooms are open to the public—and that's plenty. Here are the highlights:

From the ground floor reception rooms (nothing much to see), climb the monumental **double-spiral staircase,** which was likely inspired by Leonardo da Vinci, who died just as construction was starting. Allowing people to go up and down without passing each other (look up the center from the ground floor), it's a masterpiece of the French Renaissance.

On the second floor, with its marvelously decorated vaulted ceilings, are the royal apartments in the **king's wing**, including François I and Louis XIV's bedrooms. The rooms devoted to the **Count of Chambord**—the final owner of the château—are interesting. This 19th-century count, last of the French Bourbons, was next in line to be the king when France decided it didn't need one. He was raring to rule. You'll see his coronation outfits and even souvenirs from the coronation that never happened. Notice his boyhood collection of little guns, including a working mini-cannon.

The third floor, a series of ballrooms that once hosted post-hunt parties, is now a museum with finely crafted **hunting weapons and exhibits** on myths and legends, and traditions and techniques from the 16th, 17th, and 18th centuries.

The **rooftop**, a pincushion of spires and chimneys, was a viewing terrace for the ladies to enjoy the spectacle of their ego-pumping hunters. On hunt day, a line of beaters would fan out and work inward from the distant walls, flushing wild game to the center, where the king and his buddies waited. To see what happens when you put 365 fireplaces in your house, just count the chimneys (used to heat the place in winter even today—check out all the firewood lying around). Notice the lantern tower of the tallest spire, which glowed with a nighttime torch when the king was in. From the rooftop, view the fine king's wing—marked by FRF *(François Roi de France)* and bristling with fleurs-de-lis.

This château requires helpful information to make it come alive. The brochure is useless. Better options are the free 90-minute English **tour** (€4, daily at 12:30, maybe more often in high season) or the **audioguide** (€4, second earphone-€1.50).

Cost and Hours: €7, April–Sept daily 9:00–18:15, Oct–March daily 9:00–17:15 (last entry is 30 min before closing, but you'll need more time there anyway; tel. 02 54 50 40 00). In July and August, the château is open evenings with music and mood lighting (€12, or €14 for a day-and-night ticket, dusk-24:00 except Sun).

Also look for **horse-riding demonstrations** (€7.50, May–Sept daily at 11:45, July–Aug and weekends at 16:00 or 17:00, tel. 02 54 20 31 01, www.chambord-horse-show.fr).

The Town: Chambord's TI, next to the souvenir shops, has information on bike rentals and *chambres d'hôte* (tel. 02 54 20 34 86). One daily 40-minute bus connects Chambord with Blois' train station on weekdays (€3.50), but the Blois excursion bus is better (€10, departs Blois at 9:10 & 13:20; for more info, see "Getting Around the Loire Valley," page 242).

Sleeping near Chambord: To wake up with Chambord outside your window, try $$ **Hôtel du Grand St. Michel****. It comes with a faded, Old World, hunting-lodge atmosphere, an elegant dining room (€19 and €25 *menus*), and a chance to roam the château grounds after the peasants have been run out (Db-€61, big Db with view of château-€81—worth the extra cost, Tb-€72, breakfast-€8, tel. 02 54 20 31 31, fax 02 54 20 36 40).

Cheverny

Rated ▲▲▲, this stately hunting palace is the most lavishly furnished of all the Loire châteaux. Those who complain that the Loire châteaux have stark and barren interiors missed Cheverny (shuh-vayr-nee). Because the palace was built and decorated from 1604 to

1634 and is immaculately preserved, it offers a unique architectural harmony and unity of style. From the start, this château has been in the Hurault family, and Hurault pride shows in its flawless preservation and intimate feel. The viscount's family still lives on the third floor—you'll see some family photos. Cheverny was spared by the French Revolution; the owners were popular then, as today, even among the village farmers.

Walking across the finely manicured grounds, you approach the gleaming château, with its row of Roman emperors—Julius Caesar in the center. The fine English flier at the door describes the interior beautifully. The private apartments upstairs were occupied until

1985 and show the French art of living. In the bedroom—literally fit for a king—study the fun ceiling art, especially the "boys will be boys" cupids. You'll find a Raphael painting, a grandfather clock with a second hand that's been ticking for 250 years, a family tree going back to 1490, and a letter of thanks from George Washington to this family for their help in

booting out the English. The attic of the orangerie out back was filled with treasures from the Louvre during World War II, including the *Mona Lisa*.

Barking dogs remind visitors that the viscount still loves to hunt. The **kennel** (200 yards in front of the château, signs to *Chenil*) is especially interesting at dinnertime, when the 70 hounds are fed (April–mid-Sept at 17:00, mid-Sept–March at 15:00, except Tue,

Sat, and Sun). The dogs—half English foxhound and half French *Poitou*—are bred to have big feet and lots of stamina. They're fed once a day. The feeding is a spectacle that demonstrates their strict training. Before chow time, the hungry dogs are let out. They fill the little kennel rooftop and watch the trainer bring in troughs stacked with delectable raw meat. He opens the gate, and they gather enthusiastically around the food and yelp hysterically. Only when the trainer says to eat do these finely trained hounds dig in. You can see the dogs at any time, but the feeding show is worth planning for. The adjacent trophy room is stuffed with over a thousand antlers and the heads of five wild boar.

Cost and Hours: €6.10, April–Sept daily 9:15–18:15, July–Aug daily 9:15–18:45, Oct daily 9:45–17:30, Nov–March daily 9:45–17:00 (tel. 02 54 79 96 29, www.chateau-cheverny.fr). Pick up the English self-guided tour brochure inside the château, not where you buy your ticket.

The Town: Cheverny has a small grocery and several cafés. The town is easy to reach from Blois by excursion bus (see "Getting Around the Loire," page 242.)

Fougères-sur-Bièvre

This feudal castle of Fougères-sur-Bièvre (foo-zher soor bee-eh-vruh) is worth a look, even if you don't go inside. Located a few minutes from Cheverny on the way to Chenonceaux and Amboise, it's right in the village (constructed for defense, not hunting) and was built over the small river (unlimited water supply during sieges). It has been completely renovated, and, while there are no furnishings, you'll see models of castle-construction techniques. Contemplate the impressive roof structure, gaze through loopholes, stand over dropholes in the main tower (hot oil, anyone?), and ponder two medieval latrines that demonstrate how little toilet technology has changed in 800 years. Posters throughout (French only) describe modern renovation techniques (€4.60, under 18-free, May–mid-Sept daily 9:30–12:00 & 14:00–18:00; mid-Sept–April closes at 16:30, closed Tue; helpful English handout, tel. 02 54 20 27 18).

Chaumont-sur-Loire

A castle has been located on this spot since the 11th century. The first priority here was defense. You'll appreciate the strategic location on the long climb up from the village below.

The Chaumont château you see today, rated ▲▲, was built mostly in the 15th and 16th centuries. Catherine de Médicis forced

Diane de Poitiers to swap Chenonceau for Chaumont (show-mon); you'll see tidbits about both women inside. Louis XVI, Marie-Antoinette, Voltaire, and Benjamin Franklin all spent time here.

Today's château offers a good look at the best defense design in 1500 (on a cliff with a dry moat, big and small drawbridges with classic ramparts, loopholes for archers, and machicolations—holes for rocks and hot oil against attackers). The entry is littered with various coats of arms. As you enter, take a close look at the two drawbridges.

Inside, the heavy defensive feel is replaced with palatial luxury. Around 1700, a more stable age, the fourth wing was taken down to give the terrace a fine river-valley view. The 165-foot-deep well is fun for echoes. Study the entertaining spouts and decor on the courtyard walls.

Your walk through the palace—restored mostly in the 19th century—is poorly described in the flier you'll pick up as you enter. Here's more helpful information on what you'll see.

The case of **ceramic portrait busts** date from 1770, when the lord of the house had a tradition of welcoming guests by having their portrait sketched, then giving them a ceramic bust made from this sketch when they departed. Find Ben Franklin's medallion.

The **dining room**'s fanciful limestone fireplace is finely carved. Find the food (frog legs, snails, goats for cheese), the maid with the billows, and even the sculptor with a hammer and chisel at the top.

The treasury box in the **guard room** upstairs is a fine example of 1600 locksmithing. The lord's wealth could be locked up here as safely as possible in those days, with a false keyhole, no handles, and even an extra box inside for diamonds.

The **bedroom** has a private balcony that overlooks the chapel, handy when the lord wanted to go to church on a bad hair day. The sentimental glass, from 1880, shows scenes from the castle's history. The tiny balcony window has an original etching of Catherine de Médicis' favorite nephew. Gaze at him and imagine the elegance of 16th-century court life. Catherine de Médicis, who missed her native Florence, brought a touch of Italy to all her châteaux. As you leave, appreciate the nifty central handrail on the spiral staircase.

The **stables** were entirely rebuilt in the 1880s. The medallion above the door reads *pour l'avenir* ("for the future"), which shows off a real commitment to horse technology. Inside, circle clockwise. Notice the deluxe horse stalls—padded with bins and bowls for hay, oats, and water, and complete with a strategically placed drainage ditch. The horses were named for Greek gods and great châteaux. The horse gear was rigorously maintained for the safety of carriage passengers. The covered alcove is where the horse and carriage were prepared for the prince. And the former kiln was redesigned to be a room for training the horses.

The estate is a **tree garden**, set off by a fine lawn. Trees were imported from throughout the Mediterranean world to be enjoyed—and to fend off any erosion on this strategic bluff.

Cost and Hours: €6.10, includes stables; May–mid-Sept daily 9:30–18:30, April and late Sept daily 10:30–17:30, Oct–March daily 10:00–17:00 (last entry 30 min before closing, ticket office sometimes closes during lunch off-season, English handout available, tel. 02 54 51 26 26).

Drivers can save a 10-minute uphill hike by driving up and around to park (free) at the higher *Annex du Château* entrance.

Loches and Valançay

The overlooked town of Loches (lohsh), located about 30 minutes south of Amboise, would be my choice for the best Loire home base if it were more central. This pretty town sits on the region's loveliest river, the Indre, and offers an appealing mix of medieval monuments, stroll-worthy streets, and fewer tourists. Its château, which dominates the skyline, is worth a short visit. The Wednesday street market is small but lively. For an overnight stay, consider **Hôtel George Sand*****, next to the river, with a well-respected restaurant, idyllic terrace, and rustic, comfortable rooms (Db-€48–85, a few large Db-€110, no elevator, 300 yards south of TI at 39 rue Quintefol, tel. 02 47 59 39 74, fax 02 47 91 55 75, www.hotelrestaurant-georgesand.com).

The nearby Renaissance château of **Valançay** (vah-lahn-say) is a massive, luxuriously furnished structure with echoes of Talleyrand (Napoleon's prime minister), lovely gardens, and many kid-friendly summer events, such as fencing demonstrations (€8.50, April–Nov daily 9:30–18:00, July–Aug daily 9:30–19:30, closed Dec–Feb, audioguide available, tel. 02 54 00 10 66).

Chinon

This pleasing town straddles the Vienne River and hides its ancient cobbles under a historic castle. Chinon (shee-non) is best known today for its popular red wines (tasting opportunities abound), but for me, it makes the best home base for seeing the sights west of Tours: Azay-le-Rideau, Villandry, Langeais, Ussé, and the Abbey of Fontevraud.

Everything of interest to travelers is between the château and the river. The **TI** has *chambres d'hôte* listings, wine-tasting details (wine-route maps available for the serious taster), and a handy, English-language, self-guided tour of the town (May–Sept daily 10:00–19:00, Oct–April Mon–Sat 10:00–12:00 & 14:00–18:00, closed Sun, in village center on place Hofheim, tel. 02 47 93 17 85, www.chinon.com). You'll find free public WCs around the back of the TI.

Helpful Hints

Supermarket: Shoppi is across from the Hôtel de Ville on place du Général de Gaulle (closes for lunch 13:00–15:00 and on Sun afternoon).

Internet Access: Try **Le Ménestral** bar, just off place Jeanne d'Arc (tel. 02 47 93 07 20).

Laundry: On quai Charles VII near the bridge, you'll find **Salon Laverie** at #7 (daily 7:00–21:00).

SIGHTS

▲▲**Château de Chinon**—Don't underestimate this crumbled castle, especially if you're looking for a stark medieval comparison to châteaux of the lavish hunting-lodge variety. Henry II of England and Eleanor of Aquitaine loved this place, and it was here that Joan of Arc first encouraged Charles VII to take the throne. It's a steep walk up from the town of Chinon, but the views are sensational. What remains of this 12th-century castle is well-presented in English by tour-on-your-own pamphlets or, even better, with unusually good group tours (5/day in summer, 4/day in winter, free with entry ticket, call château for hours). Start in the "exposition room" with a short, automated history of the château (every other show in English), and end at the impressive *donjon* (keep), which houses a three-floor museum about Joan of Arc. For information broadcast in English on a loudspeaker, press the English button by the exit door of each room. Enjoy the stunning views from the top of the château (€6, April–Sept daily 9:00–19:00, Oct–March daily 9:30–17:00, tel. 02 47 93 13 45).

Wine-Tasting—Just across from the château, **Couly-Dutheil** offers free tasting of their Chinon wines. Their Le Clos de l'Echo boutique is named for their finest wine, made from the grapes in the vineyard behind the building (May–Oct daily 10:00–19:00, closed Nov–April, route de Tours, from château entrance, walk down small street to your left and cross the road, tel. 02 47 81 20 86, SE).

SLEEPING

(€1 = about $1.20, country code: 33)

Hotels are a good value in Chinon. If you sleep here, walk out to the river after dark for a floodlit view of the château walls.

$$ Hôtel Diderot**, an appealing 18th-century manor house on the eastern edge of town, offers comfortable rooms surrounding a peaceful courtyard. Ground-floor rooms are a bit dark but have private patios. There are a few good family rooms. Breakfast includes a rainbow of Laurent's homemade jams (Sb-€41–52, Db-€51–71, extra bed-€13, breakfast-€6.60, 4 rue Buffon, tel. 02 47 93 18 87,

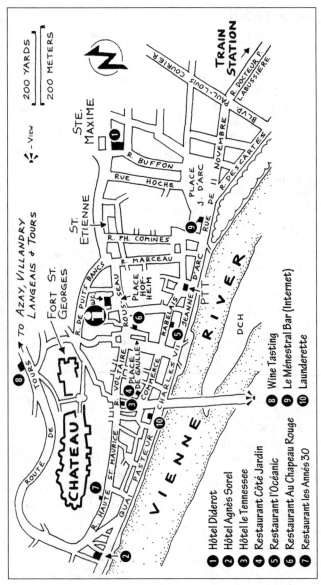

Chinon

200 YARDS
200 METERS

— VIEW

TRAIN STATION

STE. MAXIME

R. BUFFON

RUE HOCHE

ST. ETIENNE

PLACE J. D'ARC

R. PH. COMINES

R. MARCEAU

PLACE HOFHEIM

R. DE PUITS BANCS

FORT ST. GEORGES

TO AZAY, VILLANDRY LANGEAIS + TOURS

ROUTE DE TOURS

CHATEAU

R. HAUTE ST. MAURICE

QUAI PASTEUR

R. VOLTAIRE

PLACE DE GAULLE

R. COMMERCE

R. CHARLES VII

R. RABELAIS

JEANNE D'ARC

RUE DE II NOVEMBRE

R. DES CARTES

BLVD PAUL-LOUIS COURIER

R. DOCTEUR P. LABUSSIERE

VIENNE RIVER

PTT

DCH

● 1 Hôtel Diderot
● 2 Hôtel Agnès Sorel
● 3 Hôtelle Tennessee
● 4 Restaurant Côté Jardin
● 5 Restaurant l'Océanic
● 6 Restaurant Au Chapeau Rouge
● 7 Restaurant les Années 30
● 8 Wine Tasting
● 9 Le Ménestral Bar (Internet)
● 10 Launderette

fax 02 47 93 37 10, www.hoteldiderot.com, friendly Rachel, Laurent, and Françoise SE).

$$ Hôtel Agnès Sorel, a 10-minute walk west of the TI, is intimate and cozy, with friendly owners and 10 traditionally furnished rooms. A few have river views, and four rooms are in an annex surrounding a flowery courtyard (Db-€48–72, Db suite-€93, T/Qb suite-€112, 4 quai Pasteur, tel. 02 47 93 04 37, fax 02 47 93 06 37, www.agnes-sorel.com, info@agnes-sorel.com).

$ Le Tennessee, with clean, linoleum-floored rooms above a café in the town center, is this town's best budget value, with no stars, no fluff, lots of stairs—and an owner with an attitude (Db-€33, 11 rue Voltaire, tel. 02 47 93 02 85, fax 02 47 98 43 72).

EATING

Côté Jardin is inexpensive and a good deal. Enjoy the outdoor terrace (through the back of the restaurant), or the non-smoking inside (*menus* from €12, closed Sun–Mon, rue du Commerce, tel. 02 47 93 10 97).

Les Années 30 welcomes you with consistently good, classic French cuisine (*menus* from €25, closed Wed year-round and Tue–Wed in winter, 78 rue Voltaire, tel. 02 47 93 37 18).

L'Océanic, where locals go for good seafood, offers the best wine-list in town (*menus* from €21, closed Sun–Mon, 13 rue Rabelais, tel. 02 47 93 44 55).

Au Chapeau Rouge is the most expensive and chic of my listings, with *menus* from €28 (closed Sun, 49 place du Général de Gaulle, tel. 02 47 98 08 08).

For an experience and a meal you won't soon forget, drive 15 minutes to Villandry and dine at the farmhouse **Domaine de la Giraudière.** Have your hotel reserve a table for you (€13–25 *menus*, daily 12:00–15:00 & 19:30–21:00, closed mid-Nov–mid-March, half-mile from château toward Druye, tel. 02 47 50 08 60, fax 02 47 50 06 60).

More Châteaux West of Tours

For information on your transportation options, see "Getting Around the Loire Valley" on page 242.

Azay-le-Rideau

Most famous for its romantic, reflecting-pond setting, serene ▲-worthy Azay-le-Rideau (ah-zay luh ree-doh) sits in a beautiful park. The château's interior is far more interesting if you rent the €4.50

audioguide (€6.10 entry, April–Oct daily 9:30–18:00, until 19:00 in summer; Nov–March 9:00–12:30 & 14:00–17:30, last entry 45 min before closing, tel. 02 47 45 42 04).

Azay-le-Rideau's **TI** is behind Hôtel le Grand Monarque on place de l'Europe (April–Oct daily 9:00–13:00 & 14:00–18:00; Nov–March Tue–Sat 14:00–18:00, closed Sun–Mon, tel. 02 57 45 44 40).

The town's appealing center may convince you to set up here. If you do, **Hôtel Biencourt**** is ideally located near the château, with light, airy rooms in a restored convent (Db-€47–52, open March–mid-Nov, 7 rue de Balzac, Azay-le-Rideau, tel. 02 47 45 20 75, fax 02 47 45 91 73, biencourt@infonie.fr, Emmanuelle and Cédric SE). Eat at the small, central, and easygoing **Ridelloise** (*menus* from €10, daily, 34–36 rue Nationale, tel. 02 47 45 46 53). **Restaurant les Grottes,** a bit more expensive, serves creative cuisine in a cave (€15 and €23 *menus*, 23 rue Pineau, closed Thu year-round and Wed off-season, tel. 02 47 45 21 04).

Langeais

This epitome of medieval castles, complete with a moat, drawbridge, lavish defenses, and turrets, is elegantly furnished and has basic English descriptions in each room. Langeais (lahn-zhay), worth ▲▲ and providing a good feudal contrast to the other more playful châteaux, is the area's fourth-most-interesting castle after Chenonceau, Chambord, and Cheverny (€7, April–mid-Oct daily 9:30–18:30, until 20:00 in summer but last entry at 19:00; mid-Oct–March daily 10:00–17:30, tel. 02 47 96 72 60; frequent train service from Tours).

Villandry

Villandry (vee-lahn-dree) is an unremarkable château worth ▲ (▲▲▲ for gardeners), but it has the Loire's best gardens, immaculately maintained and arranged in elaborate geometric patterns. The garden viewpoint behind the château is terrific. The 10-acre, Italian Renaissance–style garden (designed c. 1530) is full of symbolism that's explained in the flier you pick up as you enter. Even the herb and vegetable sections are artistic. This was the home that France's minister of finance built in 1536. The château interior is forgettable, but the château ticket gives you a 10-minute *Four Seasons of Villandry* slide show (with period music) that offers a look at the gardens throughout the year (€7.50, €5 for gardens only, April–Sept daily 9:00–19:00, March and Oct daily 9:00–18:00, Nov–Feb 9:00–17:00, tel. 02 47 50 02 09, www.chateauvillandry.com). Consider combining your visit with a meal at the nearby **Domaine de la Giraudière** (see "Eating" in Chinon, page 267).

Ussé

This château, famous as the "*Sleeping Beauty* castle," is worth a quick photo stop for its fairy-tale turrets and gardens, but don't bother touring it. The best view, with reflections and a golden-slipper picnic spot, is from just across the bridge.

Abbaye Royale de Fontevraud

Located a 15-minute drive west of Chinon, the Abbaye Royale de Fontevraud (fohn-tuh-vroh) is a well-presented 12th-century abbey, worth ▲, which housed nuns and monks and was run by powerful women. The tombs of England's Henry II, Eleanor of Aquitaine, and Richard the Lionhearted are in the beautifully austere church. Don't miss the one-of-a-kind medieval kitchen (€6.50, June–Sept daily 9:00–18:30, April–May and Oct daily 10:00–18:00, Nov–March daily 10:00–17:30, 4 English tours/day June–Sept, or tour it alone using the informative handout and the few English descriptions, tel. 02 41 51 71 41, www.abbaye-fontevraud.com).

DORDOGNE

The Dordogne River Valley is a dreamy blend of natural and man-made beauty. Walnut orchards, tobacco plants, and cornfields carpet the valley, while stone fortresses stand guard on cliffs above. During much of the on-again, off-again Hundred Years' War, this lazy river separated Britain and France. Today's Dordogne carries more tourists than goods, and the region struggles to manage its popularity.

The joys of the region include rock-sculpted villages, fertile farms surrounding I-could-retire-here cottages, film-gobbling vistas, relaxed canoe rides, and a local cuisine worth loosening your belt for. But what draws most to this region is its amazing concentration of prehistoric artifacts. The Dordogne region is littered with limestone caves, many of which are decorated with prehistoric artwork. The caves of Font-de-Gaume and Pech Merle have the greatest ancient cave paintings (15,000 years old) still open to the public.

Planning Your Time

You'll want two days to explore this magnificent region. Your sight-seeing obligations are prehistoric cave art, the Dordogne River Valley, the town of Sarlat, and, if you have a bit more time, the less traveled Lot River Valley (best done when heading to or from the south)—or, if wine matters, St. Emilion, two hours to the west. You'll need a full roll of film for the riverfront villages and medieval castles, a waterproof camera for your canoe trip, and a bib to drool on as you gaze at 15,000-year-old art. Call well in advance to reserve a ticket to view the cave art at Grotte de Font-de-Gaume (easier at Pech Merle caves), or ask your hotel for help when you reserve your room (see page 292). This area is inundated with tourists in August.

A good way to organize your **first day** would be a morning in Sarlat (ideally during market day) and an afternoon canoe trip, with time at the day's end to explore Beynac and/or Castelnaud. If it's not market day in Sarlat, do the canoe trip first thing (9:00ish), and you'll have the river and castles to yourself. The brilliant views from Castlenaud castle and Domme are best in the morning; visit Beynac's castle late in the day for the best light.

For part or most of a **second day**, drivers can begin with a tour of a Cro-Magnon cave (several listed in "Cro-Magnon Caves," page 290), then explore the less traveled Vézère River connecting Les Eyzies-de-Tayac, La Roque St. Christophe, the village of St. Leon, and then the Lascaux II cave at Montignac (canoes also available on the Vézère River). Train travelers with a second day should take one of the minivan or taxi excursions described in "Getting Around the Dordogne," below.

With a **third day** and a car, head upriver to explore Rocamadour, Gouffre de Padirac, and storybook villages such as Carennac, Autoire, and Loubressac. With good preparation, train travelers can fit in more stops (see Sarlat's "Transportation Connections," page 283).

As you drive in or out the day before or after (connecting the Dordogne with the Loire and Carcassonne), break long drives with stops in Oradour-sur-Glane and Collonges-la-Rouge to the north (the A-20 autoroute from Brive-la-Gaillarde is currently free and provides quick access to Oradour-sur-Glane and the Loire Valley), and by all means cruise the Lot Valley on your way south (from Cahors to Cajarc). If you're heading west, take time to sample the Bordeaux wine region's prettiest town, St. Emilion.

Choosing a Home Base

It's not an easy decision; there are many good choices. My hotel recommendations cluster in the golden triangle formed by Sarlat, Beynac, and La Roque-Gageac. It's a gorgeous area, central to sightseeing and replete with good values.

Sarlat is the only practical solution for non-drivers, and the best for urban types. Beynac is my favorite village; La Roque-Gageac (5 min away by car) is also appealing and has the best midrange hotel. But if you drive only five more minutes upriver, Domme has the best view hotel. For a grand château hotel experience that won't break the bank, sleep near the Lascaux caves at Château de la Fleunie (30 min north of Sarlat). If you'd rather frolic on a real farm, sleep near Les Eyzies-de-Tayac at Ferme Veyret. Remember, air-conditioning and buffet breakfasts are rare in this traditionally French area.

Getting Around the Dordogne

This region is a joy with a car, but tough without one. You could rent a car or a bike (in Sarlat or Les Eyzies-de-Tayac), take a minivan excursion (see below), or go to Beynac and toss your itinerary into the Dordogne River.

By Bike or Moped: Bikers find the Dordogne beautiful, but darn hilly, with busy main roads. Consider a moped, if you dare. Rent bikes and mopeds in Sarlat (see "Helpful Hints," page 276). A Dordogne Valley scenic loop ride is described in "Along the Dordogne River," page 288.

By Train: Service is sparse. Trains run from Sarlat to the Font-de-Gaume caves in Les Eyzies-de-Tayac (transfer in Le Buisson, 30-min walk from station to caves), but leave you in Les Eyzies-de-Tayac all day. Consider a taxi back (see below).

By Car: Roads are small, slow, and scenic. There is no autoroute near Sarlat, so you'll need more time than usual to get in to, out of, and around this relatively remote region. You can rent a car in Sarlat (see "Helpful Hints," page 276), though bigger cites, such as Bordeaux and Brive-la-Gaillarde, offer more choices and better deals.

By Custom Taxi/Minivan Excursions: You have two good options. **Allô-Philippe Taxi** is run by friendly Philippe, who speaks English and has a comfortable vehicle with leather interior and raised seats for better viewing. Philippe will custom-design your tour, help with cave reservations, and give running commentary on his region during your excursion. Many pickup locations are possible, including Bordeaux's airport and remote train stations (€29/hr for up to 7 people, but 6 is more comfortable, tours year-round, book early, tel. 05 53 59 39 65, mobile 06 08 57 30 10, http://allophilippetaxi .monsite.wanadoo.fr, allophilippetaxi@orange.fr).

Decouverte et Loisirs is run by equally friendly Christine, who offers minivan tours with several fixed itineraries in French and English for one to eight people (€29–50 per person, tel. 05 65 37 19 00, mobile 06 22 70 13 76, decouverte.loisirs@wanadoo.fr). While her fixed tours don't include Font-de-Gaume, she's happy to structure a tour that does, and to make the necessary reservations for you if you book with her early enough.

By Taxi: For taxi service from Sarlat to Beynac or La Roque-Gageac, allow €16–18 (€25 at night); from Sarlat to Les Eyzies-de-Tayac, allow €30 one-way (€45 at night and on Sun) or €60 round-trip.

Cuisine Scene in the Dordogne River Valley

Gourmets flock to this area for its geese, ducks, and wild mushrooms. The geese produce (involuntarily) the region's famous foie gras (they're force-fed, denied exercise, and slaughtered for their livers). Foie gras tastes like butter and costs like gold. The duck specialty is *confit de canard* (duck meat preserved in its own fat—sounds terrible, but tastes great). *Pommes de terre sarladaises* are mouthwatering, thinly sliced potatoes fried in duck fat and commonly served with *confit de canard*. Wild truffles are dirty black mushrooms that farmers traditionally locate with sniffing pigs and then charge a fortune for (€457 per kilo, $190 per pound). Native cheeses are Cabécou (a silver-dollar-sized, pungent, nutty-flavored goat cheese) and Echourgnac

Heart of the Dordogne

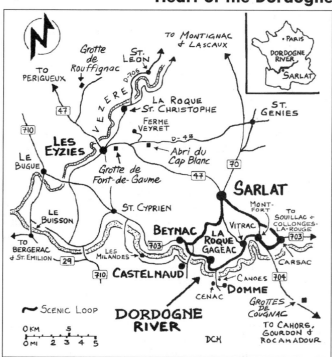

(made by local Trappist monks). You'll find walnuts *(noix)* in salads, cakes, and liqueurs. Wines to sample are Bergerac (red and white), Pecharmant (red, must be at least four years old), Cahors (a full-bodied red), and Monbazillac (sweet dessert wine). The *vin de noix* (sweet walnut liqueur) is perfect before dinner.

Remember, restaurants serve only during lunch (11:30–14:00) and dinner (19:00–21:00, later in bigger cities); cafés serve food throughout the day.

Dordogne Market Days

Market days are a big deal in rural France, and nowhere more than in the Dordogne (see "Market Day," page 43). I've listed good market days below for every day of the week, so there's no excuse for drivers not to experience a market in the Dordogne. Here's what to look for:

Strawberries *(fraises):* Everyone in France knows the best strawberries come from this region. Available from April to

November, they're gorgeous, and they smell even better than they look. Buy *une barquette* (small basket) and keep the leftovers for breakfast. Look also for *fraises des bois*, the tiny, sweet, and less visually appealing strawberries found in nearby forests.

Cheese *(fromages):* The region is famous for its Cabécou cheese (see above), though often you'll also find Auvergne cheeses (St. Nectaire and Cantal are the most common) from just east of the Dordogne (usually in big rounds).

Truffles *(truffes):* Often only the bigger markets will have these ugly, jet-black mushrooms on display. Truffle season is our off-season (Nov–Feb), when you'll find them at every market. Those you see displayed at other times are sterilized. On Sarlat market days, there's usually a guy in the center of la place de la Liberté with a photo of his grandfather and his truffle-hunting dog.

Anything with walnuts *(aux noix): Pain aux noix* are thick-as-a-brick bread loaves chock-full of walnuts. *Moutarde de noix* is walnut mustard. *Confiture de noix* is a walnut spread for hors d'oeuvres. *Gâteaux de noix* are tasty cakes studded with walnuts. *Liqueur de noix* is a marvelous creamy liqueur, great over ice or blended with a local white wine.

Goose liver pâté (foie gras): This spread is made from geese (better) and ducks (still good), or from a mix of the two. You'll see two basic forms: *entier* and *bloc*. Both are 100 percent foie gras; *entier* is a piece cut right from the product, *bloc* has been whipped to make it easier to spread. Foie gras is best accompanied by a sweet white wine (like the locally produced Monbazillac or Sauterne from Bordeaux). You can bring the unopened tins back into the United States, *pas de problème*.

Dried sausages *(saucissons secs):* Long tables piled high with dried sausages covered in herbs or stuffed with local goodies are a common sight in French markets. You'll always be offered a mouth-watering sample. Some of the variations you will see: *porc, canard* (duck), *fumé* (smoked), *à l'ail* (garlic), *cendré* (rolled in ashes), *aux myrtilles* (with blueberries), *sanglier* (wild boar), and even *âne* (donkey)—and of course, *aux noix* (with walnuts).

Olive oil *(huile d'olive):* You'll find stylish bottles of oil flavored with walnuts, chestnuts *(châtaignes)*, and hazelnuts *(noisettes)*—good for cooking, ideal on salads, and great as gifts.

Olives and nuts *(olives et noix):* These interlopers from Provence find their way to every market in France.

Liqueurs: While they're not made in this region, Armagnac, Cognac, and other southwestern fruit-flavored liquors are often available from a seller or two. Philippe (not the same as taxi-guide Philippe) makes it to many of the area markets (he's usually in Sarlat for Wed and Sat markets); try his *liqueur de pomme verte* and *crème de myrtilles*. His family has been distilling these creations for over 200 years.

Dordogne Market Schedule

The best markets are in Sarlat (Sat and Wed, in that order), followed by the markets in Cahors on Saturday, St. Cyprien on Sunday, and Le Bugue on Tuesday. Markets usually shut down by 13:00.

Sunday:	St. Cyprien (lively market, 10 min west of Beynac), Montignac (near Lascaux), and St. Genies (a tiny, intimate market with few tourists; halfway between Sarlat and Montignac)
Monday:	Les Eyzies-de-Tayac (Font-de-Gaume caves are here), and a tiny one in Beynac
Tuesday:	Cénac (canoe float begins here), Le Bugue (great market 20 min west of Beynac)
Wednesday:	Sarlat (bustling market)
Thursday:	Domme
Friday:	Souillac (transfer point to Cahors, Carcassonne)
Saturday:	Sarlat and Cahors (both are excellent)

Sarlat

Sarlat (sar-lah) is a pedestrian-filled banquet of a town, scenically set amid forested hills. There are no blockbuster sights here, just a seductive tangle of traffic-free, golden cobblestone alleys peppered with beautiful buildings and stuffed with foie gras stores (geese hate Sarlat). The town is warmly lit at night and perfect for after-dinner strolls. Sarlat is just the right size—large enough to have a theater with four screens, and small enough so that everything is an easy meander from the town center. This pretty town is almost too popular for its own good, and struggles to keep its head above the waves of shopping tourists.

ORIENTATION

Rue de la République slices like an arrow through the circular old town. Sarlat's smaller half has few shops and many quiet lanes; all of the action lies east of rue de la République. Get yourself lost.

Tourist Information

The English-speaking TI is on rue Tourny, 50 yards to the right of the cathedral as you face it. Ask for an English version of the free city map, *chambres d'hôte* listings, brochures on most regional sights, and the useful *Guide Pratique* booklet if you need car, bike, and canoe rental information (April–Oct Mon–Sat 9:00–19:00, Sun 10:00–12:00 & 14:00–18:00; Nov–March Mon–Sat 9:00–12:00 & 14:00–19:00, closed Sun, tel. 05 53 31 45 45, www.ot-sarlat -perigord.fr—in French only). For €2, the TI reserves hotels or *chambres d'hôte* (in person only). They also sell the well-done, laminated *City of Sarlat* walking tour map for €5 (as well as maps for Domme and Beynac castle).

Arrival in Sarlat

By Train: Train travelers have a mostly downhill, 20-minute walk to the town center (consider a taxi, about €8, see "Helpful Hints," below). To walk into town, turn left out of the train station and follow the *Centre-Ville* sign down avenue de la Gare as it curves downhill, then turn right at the bottom on avenue Thiers.

By Car: Sarlat's limited access funnels cars through narrow streets, which creates long backups at busy times. Parking can be a headache, particularly on market days. Try parking along avenue Gambetta in the north end of town, or in one of the signed lots along the ring road.

Helpful Hints

Market Days: Sarlat has been an important market town since the Middle Ages. Outdoor markets thrive on Wednesday morning and all day Saturday (see "Dordogne Market Days" and "Dordogne Market Schedule," above). Saturday's market is best in the morning (produce and food vendors leave at noon), and seems to swallow the entire town.

Internet Access: La Taverne du Web is open daily (Tue–Sat 11:00–21:00, Sun–Mon 14:00–20:00, longer hours July–Aug, 17 avenue Gambetta, tel. 05 53 30 80 77).

Laundry: A launderette is across from the recommended Hôtel la Couleuvrine (self-serve daily 8:00–22:00, or leave and pick up Mon–Fri only 8:00–12:00 & 14:00–18:00, 10 place de la Bouquerie).

Bike Rental: Friendly Englishman **Joel Caine** offers free delivery and pickup, provides maps, and can help you plan your route (€17/day, helmet-€2, daily 10:00–18:00, call the day before to reserve delivery, tel. 06 08 94 42 01). Your cheapest option is **Peugeot-Cycles Sarladais,** but they don't deliver (€12/day, 36 avenue Thiers, tel. 05 53 28 51 87, fax 05 53 28 50 08). **Budget** car rental also rents bikes and scooters (listed below).

Car Rental: Consider **Europcar** (Le Pontet, place de Lattre de Tassigny, tel. 05 53 30 30 40, fax 05 53 31 10 39) or **Budget** (Centre Commercial du Pontet, tel. 05 53 28 10 21, fax 05 53 28 10 92).

Taxi: Call Philippe of **Allô-Philippe Taxi** (tel. 05 53 59 39 65, mobile 06 08 57 30 10) or **Taxi Sarlat** (tel. 05 53 59 02 43, mobile 06 80 08 65 05).

Introductory Walking Tour of Sarlat

If you'd like a map to help you follow the route, either use the TI's free map (with a microscopic-print walking tour) or buy the informative, four-panel, laminated *City of Sarlat* map (€5 at many shops).

Place du Peyrou: Start in front of the cathedral on place du Peyrou. An 8th-century Benedictine abbey once stood where the cathedral does today, and provided the stability for Sarlat to develop into an important trading city during the Middle Ages. Unlike other castle-protected villages you'll visit in this area, this abbey town grew up without natural or man-made defenses. The building to your right is the old Bishop's Palace, built right into the cathedral, providing a short commute for the bishop and looking *molto* Italian, with the top-floor loggia (notice the building on the opposite side of the square with a similar loggia). Sarlat saw its zenith about 1450–1550, after the Hundred Years' War (see sidebar on page 183), when Renaissance style was the fashion and Italian architects were in high demand. Many of Sarlat's most impressive buildings date from this prosperous era, such as that beautiful house on your left. It was the home of Etienne de la Boëtie (lah bow-ess-ee), a 16th-century radical who spoke and wrote against the rule of tyrants, and who remains a local favorite. Notice how the nearby house arches over the small street, a common practice to maximize buildable space in the Middle Ages. The **cathedral** itself began as an abbey church, and today shows an eclectic mix of styles with almost no exterior decoration. It was dedicated to St. Sacerdos, a bishop from nearby Limoges whose claim to fame was curing leprosy. Walk inside. The interior is freshly cleaned. A column on the right shows a long list of hometown boys who gave their lives for France in World War I.

Lantern of the Dead (Lanterne des Morts): Exit the cathedral via the right transept into what were once the abbey's cloisters. Snoop through two quiet courtyards and then turn left at the café, making your way toward the rear of the cathedral. Climb the steps to the bullet-shaped building, the Lantern of the Dead. Tradition has it that a flame glowed from this tower, identifying the location of a cemetery where big shots were buried in the Middle Ages. It looks more like a medieval spaceship to me.

You'll see dark stone roofs on many buildings. Called *lauzes* in French, these flat limestone rocks (gathered by farmers clearing their fields) were common in this area and made into cheap, durable roofing material. The roofs last about 200 years and weigh about 100 pounds per square foot. The unusually steep pitch of the *lauzes* roofs in this region help disperse the weight over a greater area. Notice in comparison the flatness of the Roman-tiled roofs of the church's chapels closest to you. Over time, most *lauzes* roofs have been replaced by more practical roofing materials, but Sarlat retains a great number of stone-roofed homes today.

Sarlat

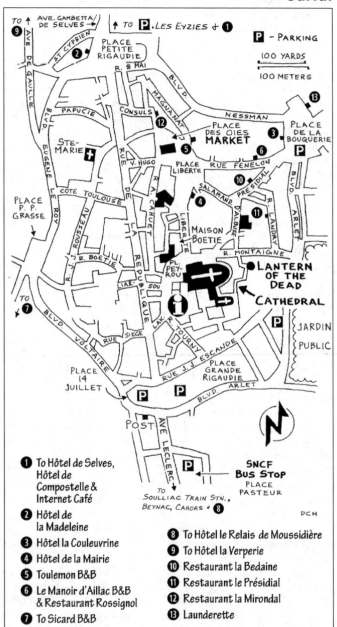

P – PARKING

100 YARDS
100 METERS

❶ To Hôtel de Selves, Hôtel de Compostelle & Internet Café
❷ Hôtel de la Madeleine
❸ Hôtel la Couleuvrine
❹ Hôtel de la Mairie
❺ Toulemon B&B
❻ Le Manoir d'Aillac B&B & Restaurant Rossignol
❼ To Sicard B&B
❽ To Hôtel le Relais de Moussidière
❾ To Hôtel la Verperie
❿ Restaurant la Bedaine
⓫ Restaurant le Présidial
⓬ Restaurant la Mirondal
⓭ Launderette

DCH

Exit right (facing the cathedral), past that adorable house. Cross one street, then turn left on impasse de la Vielle Poste, make a quick right on rue d'Albusse, and then take a left on rue de la Salamandre (street of the salamander). Peer in that Gothic-framed doorway just below on your right. Spiral stairways like these were replaced with grand Renaissance stairs when income and space permitted. Locals like to say that Sarlat is a Renaissance city built on medieval foundations. Step back now and notice the tower that housed the staircase; it looks almost like an afterthought. You'll see many staircase towers like this in Sarlat—some round, some octagonal. Continue downhill until you reach...

Place de la Liberté: This has been Sarlat's main market square since the Middle Ages. The café in front of you is the best place to people-watch. Sarlat's pretty town hall stands behind you. The tallest building to the right, with that clear glass, Gothic-framed window, was the church of Ste. Marie; it's now a daily indoor market (open to the public). Those huge, gray doors would make Boeing envious—they weigh seven tons and are opened with big hand cranks. Walk toward the church and take the steps just to its right. The tan lad has the best view over place de la Liberté. Veer left behind him, down the ramp into a postcard-perfect square...

Place des Oies (Square of the Geese): Feathers fly when geese are traded here on market days (Nov–March Sat). It's serious business that's been happening here since the Middle Ages. Trophy homes surround this cute little square on all sides. On the right lived a wealthy merchant. His tower was a sign of prestige—the bigger the better. Walk to the building with the Gothic window frame opposite the tower home. Enter the wooden doorway a few doors to the right (if open) and admire the massive Renaissance stairway. These stairways consumed huge building space, requiring a big house and a bigger income. Spiral stairs were far more space-efficient, even back then. Continue working your way down the rue des Consuls and enter the straight-as-an-arrow rue de la République.

Rue de la République: This awful thoroughfare dates from the mid-1800s, when blasting big roads through medieval cities was the fashion. It wasn't until 1963 that Sarlat's other streets would become off-limits to cars, thanks to France's minister of culture at the time, André Malraux, whose *Loi Malraux* served to preserve and restore important monuments and neighborhoods throughout France. Eager to protect the country's architectural heritage, private investors, cities, and regions worked together to create traffic-free zones and rebuild crumbling buildings. Without this law, Sarlat might well have "efficient" roads like rue de la République crisscrossing its old center.

SLEEPING

In Sarlat

Even with summer crowds, Sarlat is the train traveler's best home base. Note that in July and August several hotels require half pension.

The following hotels are central, except for Hôtel de Selves and Hôtel de Compostelle.

$$$ Hôtel de Selves***, a 10-minute walk down avenue Gambetta from the old city, is big and modern, with 40 rooms, good beds, and pastel decor surrounding a swimming pool and pretty garden (Db-€73, bigger Db-€90, Db with balcony-€98, extra bed-€22, some non-smoking rooms, air-con, sauna, elevator, garage-€8/day, 93 avenue de Selves, tel. 05 53 31 50 00, fax 05 53 31 23 52, www.selves-sarlat.com, hotel@selves-sarlat.com).

$$$ Hôtel de la Madeleine*** has formal service, elegant lounges, and 39 mostly fine, air-conditioned rooms (higher prices for larger rooms, usually with bathtubs; less expensive rooms are on third floor, square-side, with smaller bathrooms, showers, and a motel-like feel; Sb-€66–81, Db-€76–92, Tb-€106, Qb-€122, less off-season, elevator, Internet access, garage-€6/day, at north end of ring road at 1 place de la Petite Rigaudie, tel. 05 53 59 10 41, fax 05 53 31 03 62, www.hoteldelamadeleine-sarlat.com, hotel.madeleine@wanadoo.fr, SE).

$$ Hôtel de Compostelle**, a 10-minute walk down avenue Gambetta from Hôtel de la Madeleine, offers modern rooms and a few good family suites, but little character (Db-€52–62, Db with air-con-€66, Tb-€80–90, Qb-€104–124 for 4–6 people, elevator, 64 avenue de Selves, tel. 05 53 59 08 53, fax 05 53 30 31 65, hotel .compostelle@wanadoo.fr).

$ Hôtel de la Mairie** plays second fiddle to its café. It's young and basic, but well-located, with big rooms right on the main square. Rooms #3 and #6 have the best views (Ds-€40, Db-€45–55, Tb-€60–70, Qb-€75, place de la Liberté, best to reserve by phone, check in at café, tel. 05 53 59 05 71, fax 05 53 59 59 95).

$ Hôtel la Couleuvrine** has plenty of medieval atmosphere, small but mostly cozy rooms, and a good location across from the launderette and near the park. Families enjoy *les chambres familles*— #19 and #20 are in the tower—and a few rooms have private terraces (Db-€44–53, Tb-€66–70, elevator, on ring road at 1 place de la Bouquerie, tel. 05 53 59 27 80, fax 05 53 31 26 83, www.la -couleuvrine.com, lacouleuvrine@wanadoo.fr, Olivier, Isabelle, and Ingride SE). Half pension is encouraged at busy periods and in summer (figure €50–55 per person for room, breakfast, and a good dinner in an elegant restaurant). The hotel also has a nice little wine bar with good choices by the glass.

Sleep Code

(€1= about $1.20, country code: 33)
S = Single, **D** = Double/Twin, **T** = Triple, **Q** = Quad, **b** = bathroom, **s** = shower only, **no CC** = Credit Cards not accepted, **SE** = Speaks English, **NSE** = No English, * = French hotel rating system (0–4 stars). You can assume a hotel takes credit cards unless you see "no CC" in the listing.

To help you sort easily through these listings, I've divided the rooms into three categories based on the price for a standard double room with bath:

$$$ **Higher Priced**—Most rooms €90 or more.
$$ **Moderately Priced**—Most rooms between €60–90.
$ **Lower Priced**—Most rooms €60 or less.

Chambres d'Hôte: These three *chambres d'hôte* are all central and compare well with the hotels listed above.

$ Friendly, English-speaking **Pierre-Henri Toulemon** and French-speaking **Diane** have three large rooms with an independent entry in a 17th-century home, a few steps from the main square (Db-€37–45, €8/per extra person up to 5, no CC, no deposit required, simply call 1–2 days ahead to confirm your approximate arrival time, Diane gives massages at her parlor below, 4 rue Magnanat, look for big steps from northeast corner of place de la Liberté, tel. 05 53 31 26 60, mobile 06 08 67 76 90, www .toulemon.com, p-h.toulemon@wanadoo.fr).

$ **Le Manoir d'Aillac,** a grand mansion, has three stone-and-wood furnished rooms with a separate entry. It's owned by the Paulsens, German refugees who lived in New Jersey for nine years (Db-€48–58, open mid-May or early June through mid-Sept, walk through courtyard next to Rossignol restaurant at 13 rue Fénelon, tel. 05 53 59 02 63, josef.paulsen@wanadoo.fr, SE).

$ The traditional **Sicards** offer three nice rooms in a newer home barely off the ring road on the southeastern edge of the old town, a five-minute walk from the TI. The common terrace has nice views over Sarlat (Sb-€30, Db-€32, Tb-€38, no CC, easy parking, Le Pignol, rue Louis Arlet, tel. 05 53 59 14 28, NSE).

Near Sarlat

Many golden stone hotels (with easy parking) surround Sarlat for those who prefer to be close by, yet semirural.

$$$ **Hôtel le Relais de Moussidière***, a five-minute drive below Sarlat off the road to Domme/Beynac, offers affordable luxury in a lovely, lush setting, with 35 rooms, a huge pool, private terraces,

and an almost tropical feel. Friendly husband-and-wife team Dominique and Dominique (no kidding) love Americans and run the place with enthusiasm. Faye Dunaway stayed here for a month in 1999 while filming *The Messenger: The Story of Joan of Arc* in Beynac (fine standard Db-€124, bigger Db-€154, includes buffet breakfast, air-con, in Moussidière Basse, leave Sarlat to the south, direction Bergerac, watch for sign on left just after Citroën garage, tel. 05 53 28 28 74, fax 05 53 28 25 11, www.hotel-moussidiere .com, contact@hotel-moussidiere.com).

$$ **Hôtel la Verperie**** (Green Fields), aptly named, sits barely above Sarlat, surrounded by a parklike setting. Ideal for budget-minded families, the hotel has 25 rooms, a pool, table tennis, swings, restaurant, affordable rates, and adequate comfort in the bungalow-like rooms, each with a simple terrace (Db-€60, Tb-€73, Qb-€94, half pension requested in high season: €54/adult per day, €30/child ages 3–12, an easy 15-min walk west of the city, look for brown signs to La Verperie when arriving in Sarlat from Les Eyzies or Montignac, tel. 05 53 59 00 20, fax 05 53 28 58 94, www.laverperie .com, hotellaverperie@wanadoo.fr).

EATING

Sarlat is packed with restaurants that cater mostly to tourists, all serving local specialties, some of which are pretty tasty. Enjoy a light meal outdoors at a café on the main square, place de la Liberté, or try one of these eateries:

Hôtel La Coulevrine offers ambience with heavy wood beams and white tablecloths, plus a reliable regional cuisine (*menus* from €23, daily, see "Sleeping," above).

At **Le Présidial,** Sarlat's most romantic splurge, dine in the garden or inside this historic mansion and enjoy a memorable meal (lunch *menus* from €20, dinner *menus* from €26, closed Sun, rue Landry, reservations smart, tel. 05 53 28 92 47). Even if you don't eat here, pop in for a peek into the splendid courtyard.

La Mirondal, on a small lane, is a good bet for a simpler meal, with indoor and outdoor tables (daily, reasonable salads, *plats du jour,* and *menus,* a block off rue de la République at 7 rue des Consuls, tel. 05 53 29 53 89).

La Bedaine relies on tourist trade, but is a cute little place tucked away on small street below Le Présdial. Dine at tables inside or out, and choose from many *menu* options starting at €13 (daily, 4 rue du Présdial, tel. 05 53 59 44 07).

Drivers can go to Beynac or La Roque-Gageac for a beautiful setting and excellent value (see "Eating" under Beynac-Cazenac, page 287).

TRANSPORTATION CONNECTIONS

Sarlat's TI has train schedules. Souillac and Périgueux are the train hubs for points within the greater region. For all destinations below, you can go west via the Libourne/Bordeaux line (transferring in either city, depending on your connection), or east via SNCF bus to Souillac (covered by railpass). I've listed the fastest path in each case. Sarlat train info: tel. 05 53 59 00 21.

From Sarlat by train to: Paris (7/day, allow 6 hrs; 3/day with change in Libourne or Bordeaux-St. Jean, then TGV; and 4/day via bus to Souillac then train with possible change in Brive-la-Gaillarde), **Amboise** (3/day, 5 hrs, via Libourne or Bordeaux-St. Jean, then TGV to St. Pierre-des-Corps, then local train to Amboise), **Limoges/Oradour-sur-Glane** (difficult trip, 5/day, 3–4 hrs; 3/day via bus to Souillac and train to Limoges, then bus to Oradour-sur-Glane; 2/day with change in Le Buisson and Périgueux), **Cahors** (5/day, 2–3 hrs, bus to Souillac, then train to Cahors), **Albi** and **Carcassonne** (2/day, 4.5 hrs with changes in Le Buisson, Agen, and Toulouse; 3/day, 6–7 hrs via bus to Souillac, then train with changes possible in Brive-la-Gaillarde and Toulouse), **St. Emilion** (4/day, 2 hrs via Libourne, then bus or taxi).

To Beynac: Beynac is accessible only by taxi (about €18) or bike (best rented in Sarlat). See Sarlat's "Helpful Hints," above, for specifics.

Beynac-Cazenac

The feudal village of Beynac (bay-nak) tumbles down a steep hill from its hulking castle to the river far below, and sees fewer tourists than its big brother, Sarlat. You'll have the Dordogne River at your doorstep and a perfectly preserved medieval village winding, like a sepia-toned film set, from the beach to the castle above. The flood-lit village is always open for evening strollers. Some of the film *Chocolat* was filmed here, which adds to Beynac's popularity with tourists (for another *Chocolat* setting, see "Flavigny-sur-Ozerain" on page 562 in the Burgundy chapter).

ORIENTATION

A too-busy road separates Beynac from its river. The village climbs steeply uphill from there to the château.

A trail follows the river toward Castelnaud (begins across from Hôtel Bonnet), with great views back toward Beynac (ideal at night) and, for able route finders, a healthy one-hour hike to Castelnaud. Find time to walk at least a few hundred yards along this trail for the view to Beynac; the light is best in the morning.

There's a cute little market on Monday mornings on the river parking lot.

Tourist Information

The TI is across from the recommended Hôtel du Château (daily 9:30–12:30 & 14:00–17:30, tel. & fax 05 53 29 43 08, www.perigord .tm.fr—in French only). Pick up the *Plan de Beynac* in English for a simple, self-guided walking tour. A few steps down from the TI is the post office (with an ATM).

Arrival in Beynac

Drivers pay to park at different lots located on the river, way up at the castle (follow signs to Château de Beynac), or halfway between. The same parking ticket works up at the château if you decide against the climb.

SIGHTS

▲Château de Beynac—This brooding, cliff-clinging castle soars 500 feet above the Dordogne River. During the Hundred Years' War (see sidebar on page 183), the castle of Beynac housed the French, while the British set up across the river at Castelnaud. From the condition of the castles, it looks like France won. This sparsely furnished castle is most interesting for the valley views but still manages to evoke a powerful medieval feel—these castles never had much furniture in any case. Stone oil lamps light the way; swords, spears and crossbows keep you honest; and the two stone WCs keep your kids entertained. Notice the list across from the ticket window showing Beynac et Ses Barons (*croisade* means crusade, and *Coeur de Lion* means Lionheart). It's best to tour the château on your own from 12:15 to 13:45 (though the light is better at the end of the day); otherwise, you must go with a free French-speaking guide who will normally give some information in English if you ask. Pick up the English translation; the guide may let you wander on your own (€7, April–Oct 10:00–18:30, Nov–March until 16:00 or 17:00, depending on weather and whim, last tour departs 45 min before closing, tel. 05 53 29 50 40).

▲River Valley View—If you pass on the castle, don't skip the view from the top of the village over several castles and the river far below. Walk outside the village at the top (parking available), turn right— passing the little cemetery, and walk about 75 yards. There are better views if you stay on the higher path to the left. The light glows at the end of the day.

River Cruise Trips—Boats leave from Beynac's riverside parking lot and give a mildly interesting, relaxing 50-minute cruise of the Dordogne, with written English explanations (€6.50, children under 12 free in morning, departures nearly hourly 10:00–12:30 &

14:00–18:00 Easter–Oct, more frequent July–Aug, tel. 05 53 28 51 15).
Foie Gras in the Making—You can witness (evenings only) the force-feeding *(la gavage)* of geese at many places. Look for *Gavage* signs, but beware: It's hard for the squeamish to watch, and you're expected to buy. A small tin of blended duck-and-goose foie gras costs about €5; for pure goose, it's €30. Friendly Madame Gauthier's farm offers a look at the *gavage* and is down the road behind Château de Beynac (park there, or walk 10 min from château through parking lot and away from river—you'll see signs, demonstrations 18:00–19:30, tel. 05 53 29 51 45).

SLEEPING

(€1 = about $1.20, country code: 33)

In Beynac

Those with a car should sleep in or near Beynac. With hotel pickup services and taxis, even those without a car may find Beynac worth the trouble. The tiny Beynac TI posts a listing on its door of all accommodations, with prices and current availability. You must pay to park in the riverfront lot between 10:00 and 19:00. Leave nothing in your car at night, as theft is a problem.

$$ **Hôtel du Château****, on the river at Beynac's only intersection, is run by friendly Sarissa and Christophe, a French-Dutch couple with baby Timon (tee-moan) and dog Max. The 18 reasonably priced rooms are bright and clean, with fluffy linens. Some have terraces facing the river, and others are family-friendly (Sb-€40–50, Db-€45–60, price range is from low to high season, swimming pool, Internet access, tel. 05 53 29 19 20, fax 05 53 28 55 56, www .hotelduchateau-dordogne.com, info@hotelduchateau-dordogne .com, SE).

$ **Hôtel Bonnet**** offers sufficient but inconsistent comfort in 20 spacious rooms (some are sharp, others need sharpening) on the eastern edge of town. Many rooms have river views (with some street noise, though windows are double-paned). Their restaurant feels like a hunting lodge; reserve a table by the window for river views (Db-€48–55, Tb-€58–62, Qb-€60–68, peaceful backyard garden, free parking or €4 in their garage, tel. 05 53 29 50 01, fax 05 53 29 83 74, hbonnet@free.fr, SE).

$ **Hostellerie Maleville**, with a riverfront reception near Beynac's main intersection, has little personality but rents 12 clean and quiet rooms in an annex up the street at their **Hôtel Pontet**** (Db-€52, Tb-€62, Qb-€70, includes use of pool at their other hotel in nearby Vézac, check in at Hostellerie Maleville, tel. 05 53 29 50 06, fax 05 53 28 52, www.hostellerie-maleville.com, hostellerie .maleville@wanadoo.fr).

$ Le Café de la Rivière, next door to Hostellerie Maleville, has three airy, pleasant and non-smoking rooms above a garden café: two with river views and some road noise, and one quieter room in the back with village views (Db-€36–47, 2-night min, air-con, tel. 05 53 28 35 49, cafe-de-la-riviere@wanadoo.fr, Hamish and Xanthe SE).

$ Chambres Residence Versailles does its name justice, with five immaculate and spacious rooms that Louis would have appreciated, laundry facilities, a quiet terrace and garden, and, best of all, the welcoming Fleurys, Jean-Claude and Françoise, who speak just enough English (Db-€50–55, 3 rooms have fine views, all with big beds, includes large English breakfast, no CC, route du Château, tel. & fax 05 53 29 35 06, www.residence-versailles.com, contact @residence-versailles.com). With the river on your right, take the small road—wedged between the hill and Hôtel Bonnet—for a half mile, turn right when you see the sign that points left to *le Château*, and continue 100 yards, then take a right down a steep driveway.

Upriver from Beynac

In Vézac: **$$ Château Nineyrol,** relaxed and welcoming, is run by Brit expats Anne and Phil Penfold, who are as excited about this region as you are. Ideally situated between Beynac and La Roque-Gageac at the foot of the bridge leading to Castlenaud, their place has four guest rooms with personality: one big room (sleeps up to four) and three smallish doubles (rooms with views come with light road noise). Enjoy the large pool and terrace with views to Castlenaud castle (Db/Tb-€60–80, Qb-€70–80, includes breakfast, 2-night minimum, bikes and laundry service available, Anne cooks a nice dinner with wine-€25, tel. 05 53 30 46 01, www.nineyrol.com, nineyrol@wanadoo.fr).

$ Relais des 5 Châteaux**, also in Vézac, is in the open valley barely outside Beynac on the road to Sarlat. It's polished and modern, with a good restaurant and a pool (Db-€53, tel. 05 53 30 30 72, fax 05 53 30 30 08, 5chateaux@perigord.com).

In La Roque-Gageac: **$$ Hôtel Belle Etoile****, located on the river in the center of La Roque-Gageac, is the best-run two-star hotel-restaurant in the region. Hostess Danielle (SE) and chef Régis (ray-geez)—who greets every diner—make the ideal team and have hired a loyal staff. The restaurant is how I discovered this place—it's where locals go for a fine meal (*menus* start at €22, closed Mon, closed Wed at lunch). Rooms are comfy, cozy, and well-maintained; most have river views. The hotel is closed from October through March (non-riverview Db-€48, riverview Db-€64 or €74 for better view, I like the €64 rooms, reserve private parking ahead, tel. 05 53 29 51 44, fax 05 53 29 45 63, hotel.belle-etoile@wanadoo.fr).

In Domme: The splendid **$$$ Hôtel l'Esplanade*****, in the touristy hilltop village of Domme (see page 288), has the best view rooms in the Dordogne and a well-respected, though pricey, restaurant (Db with view-€72–104, Db with view and balcony-€130, extra person-€17, air-con, reserve early for a dinner terrace table with commanding view, €30–80 *menus*, tel. 05 53 28 31 41, fax 05 53 28 49 92, esplanade.domme@wanadoo.fr).

In Cénac: Below Domme, in unassuming little Cénac, you can stay at $ **Chambres d'Hôte La Touille**, a newer home owned by charming Serge and Myreille. They take great pride in their five comfortable rooms, each with an independent entry and access to a picnic-perfect garden. The €5 breakfast includes Myreille's home-baked pastries (D-€31, Db-€36, Tb-€45, no CC, route de l'Eglise, Cénac St. Julien, 200 yards on right after crossing bridge to Cénac, follow green signs, tel. 05 53 28 35 25, mobile 06 76 22 28 62, sbarry.latouille@wanadoo.fr, NSE).

EATING

You have a variety of good choices in and near Beynac.

In Beynac

At **Le Café de la Rivière**, next door to Hostellerie Maleville, cheerful Hamish and Xanthe serve low-stress, less traditional food on a lovely terrace with valley views (daily, good veggie options, air-con, tel. 05 53 28 35 49).

La Petite Tonnelle is an intimate, welcoming place with a village-view terrace and two charming interior rooms. It serves the best €16 *menu* I've had in this area, as well as great desserts—try the crème brûlée (daily, 100 yards from river on road to castle, book ahead if possible, tel. 05 53 29 95 18).

At **Hôtel du Château**, you'll dine well in air-conditioned comfort, with personal service, generous servings, and reasonable prices (*menus* from €17, closed Sun).

Hôtel Bonnet, at the other end of Beynac, has the town's most appealing rustic dining room and a generally good €18 *menu* (see "Sleeping," above).

Taverne des Remparts sits high above the town and serves up simple meals or just coffee; I can't imagine leaving Beynac without relaxing at their view-perfect café, best at night (closed Mon, tel. 05 53 29 57 76, across from castle, Jerome and Sophie SE).

Near Beynac

Hôtel Belle Etoile, a few minutes' drive upriver in La Roque-Gageac, is a lovely place that serves an excellent dinner in a romantic setting. The cuisine is classic French, with an emphasis on regional cuisine. Servings are not huge, but the quality is (*menus* from €22, see under "Sleeping—Upriver from Beynac," above).

Along the Dordogne River

▲▲▲Dordogne Valley Scenic Loop Ride or Drive—The most scenic stretch of the Dordogne lies between Carsac and Beynac. From Sarlat, follow signs toward Cahors and Carsac, then veer right to Eglise de Carsac (visit this tiny Romanesque church if it's open). From Carsac, follow the river via Montfort (photo-op stop mandatory), La Roque-Gageac, and Beynac. Bikers, note that the round-trip from Sarlat totals about 28 miles. Less ambitious bikers will find the 18-mile loop ride from Sarlat to La Roque-Gageac to Beynac and back to Sarlat sufficient. This trip works just as well from Beynac. Here are the key sights you'll encounter on this drive.

Carsac—High atop a bluff over the Dordogne River looms the imposing **Montfort Castle,** a one-time home to Simon de Montfort, the military leader of the Cathar Crusades (see "The Cathars" sidebar, page 340.)

Domme—You'll see views up to this *bastide* (fortified village) as you near La Roque-Gageac. The only reason to climb the hill to this over-boutiqued, soulless town is for the truly magnificent valley view. Turn your back on the trinkets and take in the sensational view with your drink or simple lunch at **Belvedere Café** (dinners also served, tel. 05 53 31 12 01), or, better, stay at the splendid **Hôtel l'Esplanade**, with the best view rooms in the Dordogne (see under "Sleeping—Upriver from Beynac," above).

▲La Roque-Gageac—A few minutes upriver from Beynac, "La Roque" (the rock), as the locals call this village, looks sculpted out of its rock between the river and the cliffs. This village is understandably popular and lively with day-trippers, but is tranquil at night. It's a linear place, leaving road traffic and pedestrians competing for the same riverfront space. Get off the road and wander up the narrow tangle of lanes that seem to disappear into the cliffs, and find the viewpoint overlooking the Castlenaud castle. The sky-high **Fort Troglodyte** is a good energy-burner, but offers little more than views (€4, daily 10:00–19:00, borrow written English explanation).

La Roque was once a thriving port, exporting Limousin oak to Bordeaux for wine barrels. Find the old ramp that leads down to the river. Life in "the rock" can be dicey, as three floods have risen 10 feet above street level and occasional rock avalanches have wreaked havoc from above.

The small **TI** is in a parking lot at the east end of town, across from the public WCs (Easter–Sept daily 10:00–12:00 & 14:00–18:00, closed off-season, tel. 05 53 29 17 01).

You can rent a canoe here and float to the stop for Beynac, about 150 yards from town (see "Dordogne Canoe Trips," below). Two companies offer one-hour **boat cruises** from La Roque-Gageac

The Dordogne Region

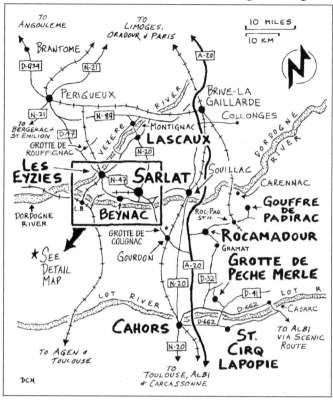

down the Dordogne; look for their kiosks near the parking lot. Pretend you're Johnny Depp riding to Beynac to find Juliette Binoche (€8, 2/hr, April–Nov daily, tel. 05 53 29 40 44).

For a good hotel with a great restaurant, try **Hôtel Belle Etoile**** (see listing on page 286).

▲▲**Castelnaud**—Château de Beynac's crumbling rival looks a little less mighty, but the inside packs a medieval punch. In this carefully prepared castle-museum, every room has a story to tell. Several rooms display weaponry and artifacts from the Hundred Years' War, and others have videos, interactive computers (in English), and castle models. Some are slice-and-dice-of-life rooms, like the kitchen. It's all designed to teach you about battles and daily castle life. The upper courtyard comes with a well 150 feet deep (drop a pebble), and the rampart views are as unbeatable as the siege tools outside the walls are formidable (€6.50, May–June and Sept daily 10:00–19:00, July–Aug daily 9:00–20:00, Oct and Feb–April daily 10:00–18:00, Nov–Jan daily 14:00–17:00, last entry 1 hr before closing, excellent and essential English *Guide-Book*-€1.50, ask about English tours in summer; from the river, it's a steep 20-min hike through a pleasant peasant village, the €2 car park is a hilly drive but gets you closer, tel. 05 53 31 30 00). There's a view café (la Taverne) just below, and a fun medieval gift shop at the entrance. Come in the morning when the light maximizes the terrific views.

You can stop at Castelnaud on your canoe trip, or take a one-hour hike from Beynac along a riverside path (difficult to follow, it hugs the river as it passes through campgrounds and farms, determined walkers do fine).

▲▲▲**Dordogne Canoe Trips**—For a refreshing break from the car or train, explore the riverside castles and villages of the Dordogne by canoe or open kayak. Countless outfits rent plastic two-person canoes (and 1-person kayaks) and will pick you up at an agreed-upon spot (even in Sarlat, if your group is large enough or business is slow).

The most scenic section is from above La Roque-Gageac to below Beynac (figure about 3 hrs), but there are good shorter segments as well. If Beynac is your home base, make sure the rental allows you to get out near Beynac (note that dropoffs in Beynac proper are not allowed; the stop is 150 yards from town). Rentals at **Dordogne Randonées** cost about €24 (includes shuttle); two can paddle the best two-hour stretch from Cénac to near Beynac (coming from Sarlat or Beynac, reach their office by taking the first left after crossing the bridge to Cénac, tel. 05 53 28 22 01, randodordogne @wanadoo.fr). In La Roque-Gageac, **Canoe-Dordogne** rents canoes for the equally appealing two-hour float to Château des Milandes (€24, tel. 05 53 29 58 50). It's OK if you're a complete novice—the only whitewater you'll encounter will be your partner frothing at the views. You'll get a life vest and, for a few extra euros, a watertight bucket. Beach your boat wherever you want to take a break. The best stops are the villages of La Roque-Gageac, Castelnaud, and Beynac.

▲▲**Hot-Air Balloons (Montgolfiers)**—Balloon rides offer the best views of this glorious region's castles, rivers, and hill towns, but for a price (€180-230 per person). **Montgolfiere du Perigord** is based in La Roque-Gageac (tel. 05 53 28 18 58, www.perigordballoons.com) and **Périgord Dordogne Montgolfieres** is closer to Beynac in St. Cyprien (tel. 05 53 29 20 56, www.perigord-dordogne-montgolfieres.com).

Cro-Magnon Caves

Les-Eyzies-de-Tayac
This town is the overrun, touristy hub of a cluster of historic caves, castles, and rivers, and merits a stop only for its National Museum of Prehistory and Font-de-Gaume Cave (described below). Train

travelers wanting to see the museum and Font-de-Gaume will find Les Eyzies a practical place to sleep. Drivers interested in a fun-farm experience will also like Les Eyzies (see "Sleeping in and near Les-Eyzies-de-Tayac," below).

The **TI** rents bikes (July–Aug Mon–Sat 9:00–19:00, Sun 10:00–12:00 & 14:00–18:00; Sept–June Mon–Sat 9:00–12:00 & 14:00–18:00, Sun 10:00–12:00 & 14:00–17:00; tel. 05 53 06 97 05, fax 05 53 06 90 79, www.leseyzies.com). The train station is a level 500 yards from the town center (turn right out of the station).

Sleeping in and near Les Eyzies-de-Tayac: **$$ Auberge Veyret,** a 10-minute drive from Les Eyzies, is as real a farm experience as it gets. Mama greets you with a huge smile and nary a word of English, son cooks, and daughter and husband do everything else. The rooms are spotless and furnished like grandma's, but with modern conveniences like hair dryers. You'll be expected to dine here—and you'd be a fool not to, as dinner includes everything from aperitif to digestif, with five courses in between and wine throughout (Db-€47 per person, includes breakfast and dinner, large pool, beefy cows, plump pigs, en route to Abri du Cap Blanc, look for yellow signs, tel. 05 53 29 68 44, fax 05 53 31 58 28, www.perigord .com/auberge-veyret, auberge-vyret@perigord.com).

$ Madame Bauchet owns the closest rooms to the train station, and they're a good, clean value (Db-€32–36, Tb-€44, Qb-€44, 200 yards from the station left at 40 avenue de la Préhistoire, tel. 05 53 06 97 71, bauchetgerard@wanadoo.fr.)

SIGHTS

National Museum of Prehistory (Musée National de Préhistoire)—The long-awaited opening of this museum's new home took place in late summer 2004. It houses over 18,000 prehistoric artifacts found in this region and takes you through our collective prehistory, starting 3.5 million years ago. This should make a good first stop in your prehistory lesson (English explanations should be provided). Appropriately located on a cliff ledge (across from Les Eyzies-de-Tayac's TI), the museum has a sleek, linear design intended to blend into the cliffs and provide a progressive, learning experience for visitors. Among the prehistoric artifacts are everyday tools, impressively sculpted clay bison, and a variety of human and animal skeletons dating from 50,000 B.C. (€6, July–Aug daily 9:30–18:30, mid-March–June and Sept–mid-Nov Wed–Mon 9:30–12:00 & 14:00–17:30, closed Tue except July-Aug, www.leseyzies.com/musee-prehistoire).

Caves near Les Eyzies-de-Tayac

The first four cave sights listed below are within an easy 25-minute drive of Les Eyzies-de-Tayac. Except for Rouffignac, all are also

Prehistoric Caves

There are four caves in this region with original cave paintings that tourists can still admire:

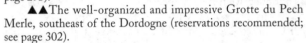

▲▲▲The top-quality Grotte de Font-de-Gaume (reservations recommended, see below).

▲▲The deep Grotte de Rouffignac (no reservations needed, but arrive early; see page 293).

▲▲The well-organized and impressive Grotte du Pech Merle, southeast of the Dordogne (reservations recommended; see page 302).

▲The smaller, less touristed but interesting Grotte de Cougnac (reservations possible; see page 298).

(The famous Lascaux II, rated ▲▲, is a copy of the original cave. Reservations are recommended; see page 297.)

Tips on Visiting Caves

1. Book your visit way ahead if possible. Ask about tours. A limited number of English tours is possible, though never certain, at each of the caves.
2. Read "Cave Art 101" (pages 294–296) to gain a better understanding of what you'll see.
3. Dress warmly, even if it's hot outside. Tours can last up to an hour, and the caves are about 50ºF.
4. Arrive early if you have a tour scheduled.
5. While on tour, lag behind the group to have the paintings to yourself for a few moments.
6. Watch your head!
7. No photos, no day packs, no big purses, and no strollers are allowed. You can check these on site.

within 30 minutes of Sarlat, as are the caves at Lascaux II and Grotte de Cougnac.

▲▲▲**Grotte de Font-de-Gaume**—Even if you're not a connoisseur of Cro-Magnon art, you'll dig this cave. It's the last cave in Europe with prehistoric (polychrome) painting still open to the public, and its turnstile days are numbered (the number of daily visitors allowable was reduced by 40 percent in 2003, because heavy-breathing tourist hordes damage the art by raising and lowering the temperature and humidity levels). On a carefully guided and controlled 330-foot walk, you'll see about 20 red-and-black bison—often in elegant motion—painted with a moving sensitivity. Your guide, with a laser pointer and great reverence, will trace the faded outline of the bison and explain how, 15,000 years ago, cave dwellers used local minerals and the rock's natural contour to give the paintings dimension. The paintings were discovered in 1901 by the village schoolteacher.

Visits are limited to 180 persons per day in groups of 12; 130 tickets are set aside daily for those with advance reservations (no reservations taken for Sun). Summertime spots get booked up to three weeks ahead (reserve by phone, even from the United States, English is understood, e-mail coming soon). The remaining 50 tickets are sold first come, first served (all 180 available on Sun), beginning at 9:30—line up early to get a ticket and time slot (Sept–June arrive by 9:00, July–Aug by 8:30). Ask if an English tour is possible (not guaranteed), and arrive 30 minutes before the tour starts or lose your place. You'll find your visit interesting even with a French-speaking guide, but ask for the English brochure and read through the books in the gift shop before you go (€6.20, mid-May–mid-Sept Sun–Fri 9:30–17:30, mid-Sept–mid-May Sun–Fri 9:30–12:30 & 14:00–17:30, closed Sat, last departure 90 min before closing, no photography or large bags, tel. 05 53 06 86 00, fax 05 53 35 26 18).

Drivers who can't get a parking spot here (or who want to see completely different caves) should try the caves at Rouffignac (see below), or aim for the more remote Grotte du Pech Merle, about 30 minutes east of Cahors (see page 302).

▲▲**Abri du Cap Blanc**—In this prehistoric cave (just up the road from Grotte de Font-de-Gaume), early artists used the rock's natural contours to add dimension to their sculpture. The small museum, with English explanations, will prepare you, and the useful English handout will guide you. Look for places where the artists smoothed or roughened the surfaces to add depth. In this single stone room, your French-speaking guide will spend 30 minutes explaining 14,000-year-old carvings. Impressive as these are, their subtle majesty is lost on some people. Free 45-minute tours leave on the half hour (€6, daily April–Oct 10:00–12:00 & 14:00–18:00, July–Aug 10:00–19:00 and no midday closing, closed Nov–March, no photos, park at lot and walk 200 yards down, tel. 05 53 59 21 74). The sight is well-signed, two miles after Grotte de Font-de-Gaume on the road to Sarlat.

▲▲**Grotte de Rouffignac**—This is the second-best cave in the area after Grotte de Font-de-Gaume, and is very different. Dress warmly; the visit lasts 60 minutes and extends about a half mile into the cool hillside.

In this extensive cave, a French-speaking guide escorts you on a funky open tram, stopping to point out engravings of mammoths (done with wood sticks) and prehistoric bear scratches (done with claws). You'll also break for mesmerizing black-outlined paintings of rhinos, bison, horses, mammoths, and reindeer. The most interesting stop is at the end, as you descend from the tram into a vault of

Cave Art 101

To fully appreciate the Dordogne region's prehistoric cave art—famous throughout the world for its remarkably modern-looking technique, beauty, and mystery—it's best to familiarize yourself with the artists and their style of painting.

From 18,000 to 10,000 B.C., long before Stonehenge, before the pyramids, before metalworking, farming, and domesticated dogs, back when mammoths and saber-toothed cats still roamed the earth, prehistoric people painted deep inside limestone caverns in southern France and northern Spain. These are not crude doodles with a charcoal-tipped stick. They're sophisticated, costly, time-consuming engineering projects planned and executed by dedicated artists supported by a unified and stable culture—The Magdalenians.

The Magdalenians (c. 18,000–10,000 B.C.): These hunter-gatherers of the Upper Paleolithic period (40,000–10,000 B.C.) were driven south by the Second Ice Age. (Historians named them after the Madeline archaeological site.) The Magdalenians flourished in southern France and northern Spain for some eight millennia, long enough to chronicle the evolution and extinction of several animal species. (Think: Egypt lasted a mere 3,000 years; Rome lasted 1,000; America less than 250 so far.)

Physically, the people were Cro-Magnons. Unlike hulking, beetle-browed Neanderthals, Cro-Magnons were fully developed Homo sapiens who could blend into our modern population. We know these people by the possessions found in their settlements: stone axes, flint arrowheads, bone needles for making clothes, musical instruments, and cave paintings and sculpture. Many objects are beautifully decorated.

The Magdalenians did not live in the deep limestone caverns they painted (which are cold and inaccessible). Many did live in the shallow cliffside caves of La Roque St. Cristophe, which were continuously inhabited from prehistoric times until the Middle Ages.

The Paintings: Though there are dozens of caves painted over a span of more than 8,000 years, they're all surprisingly similar. These Stone Age hunters painted the animals they hunted—bison or bulls (especially at Lascaux and Font-de-Gaume), horses, deer, reindeer, ibex (mountain goats), wolves, bears, and cats, plus animals that are now extinct—mammoths (the engravings at Rouffignac), woolly rhinoceros (Font-de-Gaume), and wild oxen.

Besides animals, you'll see geometric and abstract designs, such as circles, squiggles, and hash marks. There's scarcely a *Homo sapiens* in sight (except the famous "fallen hunter" at Lascaux), but there are human handprints traced on the wall by blowing paint through a hollow bone tube around the hand. The hunter-gatherers painted the animals they hunted...but none of the plants they gathered.

Style: The animals stand in profile, with unnaturally big bodies and small limbs and heads. Black, red, and yellow dominate (with some white, brown, and violet). The thick black outlines are often wavy, suggesting the animal in motion. Except for a few friezes showing a conga line of animals running across the cave wall, there is no apparent order or composition. Some paintings are simply superimposed atop others. The artists had clearly mastered the animals' anatomy, but they chose to simplify the outlines and distort the heads and limbs for effect, always painting in the distinct Magdalenian style.

Many of the cave paintings are on a Sistine Chapel–size scale. The "canvas" was huge: Lascaux's main caverns are more than a football field long; Font-de-Gaume is 430 feet long; and Rouffignac meanders six miles deep. The figures are monumental (bulls at Lascaux are 16 feet high). All are painted high up on walls and ceilings, like the woolly rhinoceros of Font-de-Gaume.

Techniques: Besides painting the animals, these early artists also engraved them on the wall by laboriously scratching outlines into the rock with a flint blade, many following the rock's natural contour. A typical animal might be made using several techniques—an engraved outline that follows the natural contour, reinforced with thick outline paint, then colored in.

The paints were mixed from natural pigments dissolved in cave water and oil (animal or vegetable). At Lascaux, archaeologists have found more than 150 different minerals on hand to mix paints. Even basic black might be a mix of manganese dioxide, ground quartz, and a calcium phosphate that had to be made by heating bone to 700 degrees Fahrenheit, then grinding it.

No paintbrushes have been found, so artists probably used a sponge-like material made from animal skin and fat. They may have used moss or hair, or maybe even finger-painted with globs of pure pigment. Once they'd drawn the outlines, they filled it in with spray paint—either spit out from the mouth or blown through hollow bone tubes.

Imagine the engineering problems of painting one of these caves, and you can appreciate how sophisticated these "primitive" people were. First, you'd have to haul all your materials into a cold, pitch-black, not-easily-accessible place. Assistants erected scaffolding to reach ceilings and high walls, ground up minerals with a mortar and pestle, mixed paints, tended the torches and oil lamps, prepared the "paintbrushes," laid out major outlines with a connect-the-dots series of points...then stepped aside for Magdalenian Michelangelos to ascend the scaffolding and create.

Why? No one knows the purpose of the cave paintings. Interestingly, the sites the artists chose were deliberately awe-inspiring, out of the way, and special. They knew their work here would last for untold generations, as had the paintings that came before theirs. Here are some theories of what this first human art might mean:

It's no mystery that hunters would paint animals, the source of

Continued on next page

"Cave Art 101," continued from previous page

their existence. The first scholar to study the caves, Abbe Henri Breuil, thought the painted animals were magic symbols made by hunters to increase the supply of game. Or perhaps hunters thought that if you could "master" an animal by painting it, you could later master it in battle. Some scholars think the paintings teach the art of hunting, but there's very little apparent hunting technique shown. Did they worship animals? The paintings definitely depict an animal-centered (rather than a human-centered) universe.

The paintings may have a religious purpose, and some of the caverns are large and special enough that rituals and ceremonies could have been held there. But the paintings show no priests, sacrifices, rituals, or ceremonies. Scholars writing on primitive art in other parts of the world speculate that art was made by shamans in a religious or drug-induced trance, but France's paintings are very methodical.

The order of paintings on the walls seems random. Could it be that the caves are a painted collage of the history of the Magdalenians, with each successive generation adding their distinct animal or symbol to the collage, putting it in just the right place that established their place in history?

The fact that styles and subject matter changed so little over the millennia might imply that the artists purposely chose time-less images to relate their generation with those before and after. Or they simply lived in a stable culture that did not value innovation. Or these people were too primitive to invent new techqniues and topics.

Maybe the paintings are simply the result of the universal human drive to create, and these caverns were Europe's first art galleries, bringing the first tourists.

Very likely, there is no single meaning that applies to all the paintings in all the caves. Prehistoric art may be as varied in meaning as current art.

Picture how a Magdalenian would have viewed these paintings: You'd be guided by someone into a cold, echoing, and otherworldly chamber. In the darkness, someone would light torches and lamps, and suddenly the animals would flicker to life, appearing to run around the cave, like a prehistoric movie. In front of you, a bull would appear, behind you a mammoth (which you'd never seen in the flesh), and overhead a symbol that might have tied the whole experience together. You'd be amazed that an artist could capture the real world and reproduce it on a wall. Whatever the purpose—religious, aesthetic, or just plain fun—there's no doubt the effect was (and is) thrilling.

Today, you can visit the caves and share a common experience with a caveman. Feel a bond with these long-gone people...or stand in awe at how different they were from us. Ultimately, the paintings are as mysterious as the human species.

black-and-white ceiling paintings where the animals float above you (notice the original level of the floor through the end of this cave; the artists had to crawl into the cave and draw while lying on their backs). The horse is amazing.

The guides usually make time to answer questions in English, but normally lead the tour in French; call ahead and ask about English tours (€6, April–Nov daily 10:00–11:30 & 14:00–17:00, July–Aug daily 9:00–11:30 & 14:00–18:00, closed Dec–March, no reservations, tours leave about every 30 min in high season, tel. 05 53 05 41 71). The best strategy is to arrive a little before opening time in early morning and take the first tour. Afternoons are busier, summer afternoons are downright ugly, and Saturdays are relatively quiet. It's well-signed from the route between Les Eyzies-de-Tayac and Périgueux; allow 25 minutes from Les Eyzies-de-Tayac.

La Roque St. Christophe—Like hanging gardens over the Vézère River, these extensive, cliff-hugging ledges and caves (no paintings) were inhabited from 50,000 years ago to the Middle Ages, and help paint a picture of life before written history. They'll pique your interest with their sheer size, multiple levels, and stunning setting. Buy the well-done, essential €2 English handout for a self-guided visit (€6, March–Oct daily 10:00–18:30, Nov–Feb daily 11:00–17:00, last entry 45 min before closing, lots of steps, 5 miles north of Les Eyzies-de-Tayac, follow signs to Montignac, tel. 05 53 50 70 45).

St. Léon-sur-Vézère, just north of La Roque St. Christophe (toward Lascaux), makes a fine lunch or coffee stop and a welcome break from the prehistoric stuff. Wander the unspoiled lanes of the village and find **Déjeuner sur l'Herbe** café for an inexpensive, rich, and relaxed riverfront eating experience (closed Mon, delicious *tartes* and salads, ideal for families, next to St. Léon's church).

▲▲**Lascaux II**—The region's—and the world's—most famous cave paintings are at Lascaux, 14 miles north of Sarlat and Les Eyzies-de-Tayac. In the interest of preservation, these caves are closed. But the adjacent Lascaux II copy caves are impressive in everything but authenticity. At Lascaux II, the reindeer, horses, and bulls of Lascaux I are painstakingly reproduced by top artists using the same dyes, tools, and techniques their predecessors did 15,000 years ago. While most are more impressed seeing the real thing available at other caves, anyone into caveman art will appreciate the thoughtful explanations, providing they get an English tour (it's worth planning your schedule around English tour times). Come here for your cave art introduction, then visit the caves with original paintings I've listed. Crowds diminish the experience, as 40 people per tour are hustled through the two-room cave reproductions, though the paintings are astonishing.

Unless visiting October to March, you must buy your ticket before coming to Lascaux; the ticket office is next to the TI in Montignac, five minutes away by car. Deep blue signs direct drivers to *La Billeterie* in Montignac (follow signs for *Centre-Ville*, then look for *La Billeterie*); Lascaux is well-signed from there. In July and August, tours are usually sold out by 13:00, so get there early (€8, April–Sept daily 9:30–18:30, July–Aug daily 9:00–20:00, Oct–Dec and Feb–March Tue–Sun 10:00–12:00 & 14:00–17:30, closed Jan; call ahead for English tour times, 40 min, 4–6/day July–Aug, usually 2/day off-season, call 05 53 51 96 23). Pleasant Montignac is worth a wander if you have time to kill.

Sleeping near Lascaux: The **Château de la Fleunie***** offers regal 15th-century château accommodations, surrounded by pastures and mountain goats, the biggest private pool I've seen in France, tennis courts, and a restaurant with *beaucoup d'ambiance* (modern annex with terrace Db-€80, in the château Db-€70–90, most at €90, Tb-€110, tower room for two-€140, *menus* from €26, 10-min drive north of Montignac on road to Brive-la-Gaillarde, in Condat-sur-Vézère, tel. 05 53 51 32 74, fax 05 53 50 58 98, www.lafleunie.com, lafleunie@free.fr).

▲**Grotte de Cougnac**—Located 19 miles south of Sarlat, this less touristy cave is handy for drivers. The cave offers impressive rock formations and a more intimate look at Cro-Magnon cave art. It's three miles north of Gourdon, just off D-704, near the cute village of Payrignac (€6, May–June and Sept daily 10:00–11:30 & 14:30–17:00, July–Aug daily 10:00–18:00, April and Oct daily 14:30–17:00, closed Nov–March, English book available, 70-min tours, some in English, call ahead, tel. 05 65 41 47 54).

North of the Dordogne

▲▲▲**Oradour-sur-Glane**—Located two hours north of Sarlat and 15 miles west of Limoges, this is one of the most powerful sights in France. French schoolchildren know this town well. Most make a pilgrimage here. *La Ville Martyr,* as it is known, was machine-gunned and burned on June 10, 1944, by Nazi troops. The Nazis were either seeking revenge for the killing of one of their officers (by French Resistance fighters in a neighboring village) or simply terrorizing the populace in preparation for the upcoming Allied invasion (this was 4 days after D-Day). With cool attention to detail, the Nazis methodically rounded up the entire population of 642 townspeople. The women and children were herded into the town church, where they were tear-gassed and machine-gunned. Plaques mark the place where the town's men were grouped and executed. The town was then set on fire, its victims left under a blanket of ashes. Today, the ghost town, left untouched for nearly 60 years, greets every pilgrim who enters with only one English word: Remember.

Start at the **underground museum** (Centre de la Mémoire),

which provides a good social and political context for the event (with English explanations), including home videos of locals before the attack and disturbing footage of the actual event. Don't miss the 12-minute film with English audioguide translations (€6, daily mid-May–mid-Sept 9:00–19:00, closes 17:00–18:00 off-season, closes entirely mid-Dec–Jan, tel. 05 55 43 04 30, www.oradour.org). Then, with hushed visitors, walk the length of Oradour's main street, past gutted, charred buildings in the shade of lush trees, to the underground memorial on the market square (rusted toys, broken crucifixes, town mementos under glass). The plaques on the buildings tell us the names and occupations of the people who lived there. Visit the cemetery where most lives ended on June 10, 1944, and finish at the church, with its bullet-pocked altar (entry to Oradour village is free, same hours as the museum).

Public transport here is a challenge. Four daily buses connect Limoges with Oradour in 20 minutes (10-min walk from Limoges train station to bus stop on place Winston Churchill). Consider a taxi. Limoges is a stop on an alternative train route between Amboise and Sarlat.

Mortemart—With a car and extra time, visit this nontouristy village (15-min drive northwest of Oradour-sur-Glane on D-675). You'll find a medieval market hall, a few cafés, and a sweet château (good picnic benches behind). **Hôtel Relais**** offers five rooms over a well-respected restaurant (Db-€47, Tb-€61, *menus* from €16, restaurant closed Tue–Wed, tel. & fax 05 55 68 12 09).

▲**Collonges-la-Rouge**—Connoisseurs of beautiful villages need to visit this deep red sandstone and slate-roofed village that curls down a friendly hill. Collonges-la-Rouge is a scenic 15-minute drive east of the A-20 autoroute (exit at Noailles), just south of Brive-la-Gaillarde and about a 50-minute drive from Sarlat.

The **TI** (near the top of town, tel. 05 55 25 32 25) has a brochure with English explanations and information on other nearby worth-a-wander villages. Don't miss the church's Moorish entry, wavy floor, and holy dome. Like all adorable villages, Collonges-la-Rouge has plenty of shops and is busy at midday from June through September.

Southeast Dordogne Region

Some find this remote, less visited section of the Dordogne even more beautiful than the area around Sarlat. Follow the Dordogne upriver east from Souillac to connect these *charmant* villages: Martel, Carennac, Loubressac, Autoire, and the impressively situated Château de Castelnau-Bretenoux (worthwhile inside and out). Just below are the Tom Sawyer–like Gouffre de Padirac and the cliff-hanging Rocamadour.

Rocamadour (▲▲ after dark)—One hour east of Sarlat, the dramatic rock-face setting and medieval charm of this historic pilgrimage town can be trampled daily by hordes of tourists. Those who arrive late and spend the night enjoy fewer crowds and a floodlit fantasy. Those who come only during the day might wonder why they did, as there's little to do here except to climb the steps as pilgrims did (and some still do), or cheat and take the elevator to a few churches and stare at the view.

If you're spending the night, don't miss the views of illuminated Rocamadour after dark from the opposite side of the valley. Without a car, take the cheesy but convenient **Petit-Train** (€5, round-trip 30 min with recorded English commentary, 2 trips/evening, times depend on season, check at the TI or call tel. 05 65 33 67 84). If you're walking at night, wear light-colored or reflective clothing or take a flashlight, as there is minimal lighting and no shoulder on the road.

Rocamadour has three basic levels: the bottom-level pedestrian street, with shops and restaurants; the chapel level, at 216 steps up (or elevator, see below), with a snazzy Museum of Sacred Art (€5, excellent English handout, tel. 05 65 33 23 30); and the very top level, with its private château. To reach the top, walk the Stations of the Cross *(chemin de croix)* from the chapel level, or take the elevator *(ascenseur inclinée*, €2.50, €4 round-trip, skip the €2.60 view from the château ramparts). Eight hundred years ago, there were even more tourists climbing these steps, as this was an important stop on the famous pilgrimage route to Santiago de Compostela in Spain. In 1244, the stairs attracted St. Louis, a Crusades-bound king (who built Sainte-Chapelle in Paris).

There are two **TI**s: the glassy TI that you come to first in l'Hospitalet above Rocamadour (May–Sept daily 10:00–12:30 & 14:00–18:30, stays open at lunch July–Aug, fewer hours off-season), and another down in La Cité Medievale on the level pedestrian street (July–Aug daily 9:30–19:30, otherwise daily 10:00–12:30 & 14:00–18:30, tel. 05 65 33 22 00). Ask about occasional English tours of the chapels.

Trains (transfer in Brive-la-Gaillarde) leave you about three miles from the village (€10 taxi, tel. 05 65 33 63 10). Drivers can approach Rocamadour in two ways: Park at the top (then walk down a series of switchbacks on the Stations of the Cross or take the elevator down—€4 round-trip, follow signs to Parking Château), or drive below the cliff to the bottom of the village (then walk or take the elevator up—€2 round-trip).

Sleeping in and near Rocamadour: Every hotel has a restaurant where they'd like you to dine. **Hôtel des Pèlerins****, near the western end of the pedestrian street in La Cité Medievale, has immaculate, comfortable rooms; the best have balconies and face the valley

Southeast Dordogne Region

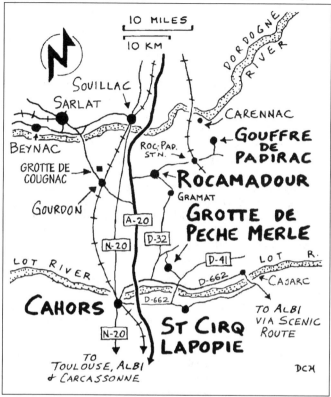

(Sb-€39–48, Db-€45, Db with view and balcony-€57, Tb-€61, tel. 05 65 33 62 14, fax 05 65 33 72 10, www.terminus-des-pelerins.com, owner Geneviève is friendly and helpful).

Moulin de Fresquet is a sublime *chambre d'hôte* five miles from Rocamadour. Gracious Gérard has restored an ancient mill, complete with five antique-furnished rooms, outdoor terraces, and a duck pond—with ducks for pets, not for dinner. If Gérard's wife Claude is cooking, eat here (Db-€57–76, Tb-€91, Qb-€97, includes breakfast, dinner-€21, in Gramat, tel. 05 65 38 70 60, mobile 06 08 85 09 21, fax 05 65 33 60 13, www.moulindefresquet.com, moulindefresquet @ifrance.com, SE).

▲▲**Gouffre de Padirac**—Twenty minutes from Rocamadour is the fascinating sinkhole of Padirac with its underground river (lots of stalagmites and stalactites, but no cave art). If the line is long (often in summer), buy the cheapest English-language booklet on the caves and read it while you wait in line, and you'll be well-briefed to follow the 90-minute French-language tour through this huge system of caverns. Choose between a series of three elevators or 15 minutes of stairs down to the bottom. From here, you'll take a subterranean gondola ride (ask for the English-translation leaflet) and continue the rest of the visit on the other side by foot (many steps) to underground lakes and calcite wonders. Dress warmly (€8, April–Oct daily 9:00–12:00 & 14:00–18:00, long lines at 14:00; no lunch closing July–Aug, closed Nov–March, day trips organized from Rocamadour TI, tel. 05 65 33 64 56, www.gouffre-de-padirac.com).

▲▲▲**Lot River Valley**—Ninety minutes south of the Dordogne, the overlooked Lot River meanders under stubborn cliffs, past tempting villages, and through a stunningly beautiful valley. The fortified bridge at Cahors, prehistoric cave paintings at Grotte du Pech Merle, and the breathtaking town of St. Cirq Lapopie are remarkable sights in this valley—each within a half hour of the others. These all are worthwhile for drivers connecting the Dordogne with Albi or Carcassonne, or as a long day trip from Sarlat. With extra time, spend a night in St. Cirq Lapopie (see below), since it makes a good base for visiting the area. With more time, continue upriver to Cajarc (those going to or coming from the south can scenically connect with Albi via Villefranche-de-Rouergue and Cordes-sur-Ciel).

Pont Valentré at Cahors—One of Europe's finest medieval monuments, this fortified bridge was built in 1308 to keep the English out of Cahors. It worked. Learn the story of the devil on the center tower. The steep trail on the non-city side leads to great views (keep climbing, avoid branch trails, be careful if the trail is wet) and was once part of the pilgrimage route to Santiago de Compostela. Just past the city-side end of the bridge is **Le Cèdre**, a wine shop/café/souvenir stand with delightful owners; say *bonjour* to Marie-Danielle and Jean-Claude, and ask to sample Cahors' black wine and foie gras (duck is cheaper than goose and just as tasty). They have reasonable salads and sandwiches, and can ship wine to the United States. If you need an urban fix, stroll the pedestrian-friendly alleys between Cahors' cathedral and the river.

▲▲**Grotte du Pech Merle**—This cave, about 30 minutes east of Cahors, with its prehistoric paintings of mammoths, bison, and horses, rivals the better-known cave art at Grotte de Font-de-Gaume. Pech Merle is easier to view, as more people per day are allowed in (700), but that also makes the cave a bit less special. Still, it has great cave art with interesting stalactite and stalagmite formations. I liked the mud-preserved Cro-Magnon footprint. Call to reserve a time (English spoken), and ask about rare English tours. Start at the museum with a 20-minute film subtitled in English, then descend to the caves. If you can't join an English tour, ask for the English translation booklet. In summer, arrive by 9:30 or call to reserve a spot four to five days in advance. It's best to call before you arrive in any season, as private groups can fill the caves' quota (€7, Easter–Oct daily

9:30–12:00 & 13:30–17:00, closes earlier off-season, tel. 05 65 31 27 05, fax 05 65 31 20 47, www.pechmerle.com).

▲▲**St. Cirq Lapopie**—Beg, borrow, or steal a night in St. Cirq Lapopie (san seer lah-poh-pee). Thirty minutes from Cahors (well-signed) and clinging to a ledge 600 feet above the Lot River, this spectacularly situated village knows only two directions—straight up and way down. And while you need to be careful of weekend and summer crowds, St. Cirq Lapopie has not been blemished by too many boutiques and remains pin-drop peaceful after hours. Wander the rambling footpaths and uneven lanes, find the best light for your memories, and just appreciate where you are. You'll find superb picnic perches, a few galleries, and several restaurants. Views from the bottom and top of the village justify the effort. The first views of St. Cirq are impressive enough to justify the detour. Pass on the free parking *(Parking Gratuit)* that's too far below; you'll find handy lots halfway up (€2, exact change required) and all the way at the top (great views from here). Pull over for photo stops as you climb.

The **TI** is located across from the recommended Auberge du Sombral (May–Sept daily 10:00–13:00 & 14:00–18:30, closed Mon–Tue off-season, tel. 05 65 31 29 06). St. Cirq Lapopie has 18 rooms, none of which are open off-season (mid-Nov–March), and eight of which are at the oh-so-cozy and central **Auberge du Sombral****, run with panache by Madame Haldeveled (Sb-€50, Db with shower-€65, Db with tub-€72, tel. 05 65 31 26 08, fax 05 65 30 26 37, phone better than fax, she has English-speaking staff). **Hôtel de la Pelissaria*****, at the lower end of the village, has 10 creatively appointed rooms, most of which cascade down the hill amid terraced gardens and postcard views to the main village (standard Db-€72, bigger Db-€104, superior Db-€115, tiny pool, tel. 05 65 31 25 14, fax 05 65 30 25 52, http://perso.wanadoo.fr/hoteldelapelissaria, hoteldelapelissaria@wanadoo.fr). For dinner, try **L'Oustal**, just below the towering church (€15 and €31 *menus*, €15 *plats du jour*, tel. 05 65 31 20 17).

St. Emilion and Bordeaux Wine Country

Two hours due west of Sarlat and just 40 minutes from Bordeaux, St. Emilion is another pretty face just waiting to flirt with you. Carved like an amphitheater in the bowl of a limestone hill, St. Emilion's manicured streets connect a few picture-perfect squares and scads of well-stocked wine shops. There's little to do in this town of 300 well-heeled residents other than enjoy the setting, and, of course, sample the local product. Wine has been good to St. Emilion, though it accounts for barely five percent of Bordeaux's famous red-wine production (about 60 percent of the grapes you see are Merlot). From the staff of St. Emilion's well-organized TI to the surprisingly friendly wine shops, everyone here speaks English. Sunday is market day in St. Emilion.

Tourist Information

The TI is at the top of the town on place des Créneaux, across from the high church belltower. It's located in a one-time abbey and connected to nice cloisters. It has everything you need, including free public WCs, Internet access, bike rental (and recommended bike routes), wine-tasting excursions, good information on St. Emilion's few sights, and a long list of *chambres d'hôte* (mid-June–mid-Sept daily 9:30–19:00, July–Aug daily 9:30–20:00, mid-Sept–May daily 9:30–12:30 & 13:45–18:30, Nov–March closes at 18:00, place Pioceau, tel. 05 57 24 72 90, fax 05 57 55 28 29, www.saint-emilion -tourisme.com).

Arrival in St. Emilion

While there is a train station near St. Emilion, it's a 20-minute walk from town, with no taxis and scant trains. Get off in Libourne (5 miles away, with good train service and easy car rental near the station). From here, you can catch a cab (€15, tel. 06 07 63 62 56 or 06 09 35 78 39) or take an infrequent bus to St. Emilion (2/day) from the bus station *(gare routière)* next to the train station.

Drivers can pay to park at the lower end of the town or park for free along the wall above the town (paid parking also available above town).

SIGHTS

Underground Tours of St. Emilion—The TI offers frequent and reasonably interesting 45-minute tours with three stops: the catacombs (sorry, no bones); the underground Monolithic church, which literally rocks; and Trinity Chapel (€5.50). Learn who St. Emilion was, and be impressed that it took dedicated Benedictine monks 300 years to dig this Monolithic church out of one big rock (9th–12th centuries). You'll also learn that there are between 90 and 125 miles of underground tunnels in the St. Emilion area, originally dug as quarries. Today, they're ideal for wine storage. The tour is mandatory if you want to see these sights, but there's usually just one or two tours a day in English (though the English handout given on French tours is thorough). I'd skip it if time's limited and you can't get an English tour.

Views over St. Emilion—You can climb the **bell tower** in front of the TI for a fine view (€1, get key at TI in exchange for an ID, 9:30–12:30 & 13:45–19:00, no midday closure in summer, closes at 18:00 Oct–March), though the view is better from the **Tour du Donjon** several blocks below (also €1, same hours).

Wine-Tasting—Of course, St. Emilion's primary sightseeing is for your palate. You can sample tasty homemade macaroons at many shops. And while the TI offers various €9 "tasting initations," including a guided bus excursion to the vineyards (in English and French, includes a tasting, usually departs TI at 14:30 or 15:30), the many **wine shops** offer the best and easiest way to sample the array of local wines (see "French Wine-Tasting 101" on page 46). Small shops typically greet visitors with a central tasting table, maps of the vineyards, and several open bottles (most shops open 10:00–19:00, 20:00 in summer). And while it's hard to distinguish these classy wine stores from each other, you'll be pleasantly surprised at the welcoming attitude and passion shopkeepers show for their wines (remember, everyone here speaks English). Americans may represent only about 15 percent of the visitors, but we buy 40 percent of their wine. While it is hoped that you will buy (particularly if you taste many wines), and shipping is easy (except to California and Texas), there is no pressure or fee for the tastings. You can start at **Cercle des Oenophiles** on rue Guadat and ask to visit the nearby cellars with over 400,000 stored bottles of wine (tel. 05 57 74 45 55).

SLEEPING

(€1 = about $1.20, country code: 33)
There are no cheap accommodations in St. Emilion; prices skyrocket during the VinExpo festival at the end of June and during harvest time at the end of September. To save money, consider a *chambre d'hôte* nearby. Both of my hotel recommendations are well located at the top of the town, within a block of each other. My *chambre d'hôte* is one mile from the town center.

$$$ **Au Logis des Remparts***** is *très* snazzy, with mod rooms, a pool, and a garden overlooking the vineyards (standard Db-€72–90, nicer rooms with bathtubs and garden views Db-€100–115, suites-€135, easy parking, tel. 05 57 24 70 43, fax 05 57 74 47 44, logis-des-remparts@wanadoo.fr).

$$ **L'Auberge de la Commanderie**** has welcoming owners and 16 sharp rooms. Those in the main building have funky, bright paintings that don't appeal to everyone; the annex has some family-friendly rooms (standard Db-€65–80, bigger Db-€95–105, Tb-€90–105, two-room apartment for up to four-€125, free parking, closed Jan–Feb, tel. 05 57 24 70 19, fax 05 57 74 44 53, www.aubergedelacommanderie .com, contact@aubergedelacommanderie.com.)

$ **Madame Favard** rents four traditional rooms in a wine *domaine* cradled by vineyards and within knocking distance of St.

Emilion's doorstep (Sb-€47–52, Db-€51–57, Tb-€67–72, includes breakfast, no CC, washer/dryer, bikes available, from the top of St. Emilion follow D-243 toward Libourne, at 1 mile turn left at signs to Château Meylet, tel. 05 57 24 68 85, chateaumeylet@free.fr).

EATING

Skip the cafés lining the street by the TI, and find the cafés on the melt-in-your-chair place du Marché. **Amelia-Canta** is the best spot on this square, with café fare, salads, and veggie options (€15–38 *menus*, daily March–Nov, tel. 05 57 74 48 03).

Logis de la Cadène, sitting just above the place du Marché, has romantically set tables inside or out, (*menus* from €21, closed Sun–Mon, reserve ahead, tel. 05 57 24 71 40).

BASQUE COUNTRY
(Le Pays Basque—Euskadi)

Two hours southwest of Bordeaux and far off most Americans' radar screens lies an ancient, free-spirited corner of Europe. In Basque country, bright white chalet-style homes with deep-red-and-green shutters scatter across lush rolling hills; the Pyrénées mountains soar high above the Atlantic; and surfers and sardines share the waves. Insulated from mainstream Europe for centuries, this plucky region has maintained its spirit while split between Spain and France. An easily crossed border separates the French Pays Basque from the Spanish País Vasco, thus allowing you to sample both sides from a single base. Central, cozy, and manageable St. Jean-de-Luz makes the ideal place for exploring the best of the French region, and fun-loving San Sebastián is a great home base for the Spanish Basque lands.

The French and Spanish Basque regions share a common language (Euskera), flag (like a Union Jack, but white, red, and green), and cuisine. But they have taken different routes since the French Revolution. The Revolution "tamed" French Basque ideas of independence 130 years before Spain's Generalissimo Franco did the same to his separatist-minded Basques.

Language is the key to this unique culture; locals say that Euskera, which is absolutely unrelated to any other language, dates back to Neolithic times. Euskera, with its seemingly-impossible-to-pronounce words filled with k's and z's (rest rooms in Basque are *gizonak* for men and *emakumeak* for women), suddenly makes speaking French seem easy. Look for Basque street signs, menus, and signs in shops. Proud of their language and culture, many locals can switch effortlessly from Euskera to Spanish or French.

Today, the Basque lands are undergoing a 21st-century renaissance, with brilliant revitalization occurring in long ignored cities like Bayonne, dazzling architecture replacing rusted industries in

Bilbao, and enthusiastic visitors rejuvenating the resorts of San Sebastián and Biarritz.

The Basque terrorist organization, ETA (which stands for "Basque Homeland and Freedom"), is primarily active on the Spanish side of the border and is supported by a minority of the population. They focus their anger on political targets and go largely unnoticed by tourists.

Planning Your Time

Allow two full days to sample French and Spanish Basque country. Most of your sightseeing will be cultural and scenic, as only two sights merit the entry fee (the Museum of Basque Culture in Bayonne and the Guggenheim modern art museum in Bilbao).

On the French side, you'll want to save time for the easygoing beach resort of St. Jean-de-Luz, the striking capital city of Bayonne, and the villages that curl up in the protective arms of the Pyrénées foothills, such as Aïnhoa, Sare, and St. Jean-Pied-de-Port.

Barely across the border, little Hondarribia offers a quick peek into Spain. Just 30 minutes deeper is the glittering resort of San Sebastián, and an hour beyond that, Bilbao. Near Bilbao is the Basque port town of Lekeitio, lively in summer and sleepy off-season.

Getting Around the Basque Country

Just 80 miles separates the two Basque capitals, Spanish Bilbao and French Bayonne. Freeways, trains, and buses provide convenient connections between Bayonne, St. Jean-de-Luz, San Sebastián, and, to a lesser extent, Bilbao.

By Bus and Train: Trains link St. Jean-de-Luz with Bayonne (25 min), St. Jean-Pied-de-Port (90 min, transfer in Bayonne), San Sebastián (1 hr, transfer in Hendaye; faster by bus: 2/day direct, 45 min), and Hondarribia (1 hr, transfer to bus in Hendaye). Excursion tours provide the easiest public-transport access to Bilbao's Guggenheim. Buses serve many pretty Basque villages.

By Car: From St. Jean-de-Luz, drivers can zip on the autoroute to San Sebastián (30 min) and Bilbao (90 min). The curving coastal route from San Sebastián to Bilbao takes you (carsick) through Zarautz, Getaria, Ondarroa, Lekeitio, and Guernica. For a good sampling of traditional Basque villages, connect St. Jean-de-Luz connect Sare, Aïnhoa, Cambo-les-Bains, and St. Jean-Pied-de-Port.

Cuisine Scene in Basque Country

Mixing influences from the mountains, sea, Spain, and France, Basque food is reason enough to visit the region. The local cuisine—dominated by seafood, tomatoes, and red peppers—offers some spicy dishes, unusual in France. The red peppers hanging from homes in small villages end up in *piperade*, a dish that combines peppers,

Basque Country

tomatoes, garlic, ham, and eggs. Don't leave without trying *ttoro* (tchoo-roh), a seafood stew that is Basque's answer to bouillabaisse and cioppino. Look for anything *basquaise* (cooked with tomato, eggplant, red pepper, and garlic), such as *thon* (tuna) or *poulet* (chicken). *Marmitako* is a hearty tuna stew. Local cheeses come from Pyrenean sheep's milk *(pur brebis)*, and the local ham *(jambon de Bayonne)* is famous throughout France. Hard apple cider is the locally made beverage, but the region's wine, Irouleguy, isn't worth its price.

St. Jean-de-Luz
(Donibane Lohizune)

St. Jean-de-Luz (san zhahn-duh-looz) sits happily off the beaten path, cradled between its small port and gentle bay. Pastry shops serve Basque specialties, and shops sell berets. Ice-cream lickers meet traffic-free streets, while soft, sandy beaches tempt travelers to toss their speedy itineraries into the bay. The knobby little mountain La Rhune towers above the happy scene.

The town has precious little of sightseeing importance. But it's a fine base for exploring the Basque country, and a relaxing beach and port town that provides the most enjoyable dose of Basque culture in France.

ORIENTATION

St. Jean-de-Luz's old city lies between the train tracks, the Nivelle River, and the Atlantic. The main traffic-free street, rue Gambetta, channels walkers through the center, halfway between the train tracks and the ocean. The small town of Ciboure, across the river, holds nothing of interest to us.

The only sight worth entering is the church where Louis XIV and Marie-Thérèse tied the royal knot (Eglise St. Jean-Baptiste, described below). St. Jean-de-Luz is best appreciated along its pedestrian streets, lively squares, and golden, sandy beaches. The park at the far eastern end of the beachfront promenade at Pointe Ste. Barbe makes a good walking destination, with views and walking trails.

Tourist Information: The helpful TI is in a small, red-roofed building a block off the port and three blocks from the train station, on place du Maréchal Foch (Sept–June Mon–Sat 9:00–12:30 & 14:30–18:30, Sun 10:00–13:00, July–Aug Mon–Sat 9:00–19:30, Sun 10:00–13:00 & 15:00–19:00, tel. 05 59 26 03 16, www.saint-jean -de-luz.com).

Arrival in St. Jean-de-Luz

By Train or Bus: From the station, cross boulevard Commandant Passicot (or take the pedestrian underpass), then walk left along this busy street. Stay straight around the traffic circle and carry on along avenue de Verdun to the TI, just across the second traffic circle.

By Car: Follow signs for *Centre-Ville*, then *Gare* and *Office de Tourisme*. Parking (except on some peak summer days) is relatively easy. Hotels can advise you.

By Plane: The nearest airport is in Biarritz, 10 miles to the northeast. The tiny airport is easy to navigate, with a useful TI desk. The 20-minute taxi ride into St. Jean-de-Luz runs about €30 (the bus costs only €3, but the bus stop is a 300-yard walk from the terminal, and schedules are sparse). Airport info: tel. 05 59 43 83 83, www.biarritz.aeroport.fr.

Helpful Hints

Market Days: Tuesday and Friday mornings (and summer Saturdays, too), the farmers' market spills through the streets from the market *(Les Halles)* and seems to give everyone a stiff dose of "life is good."

Internet Access: It's at 8 boulevard Thiers (Mon–Fri 9:00–12:30 & 14:00–18:00, closed Sat–Sun, near east end of rue Gambetta, tel. 05 59 51 22 50).

Laundry: Laverie du Port is across from the TI at 5 place du Maréchal Foch (daily 7:00–21:00, self-serve and full-service, €10 per full-service load).

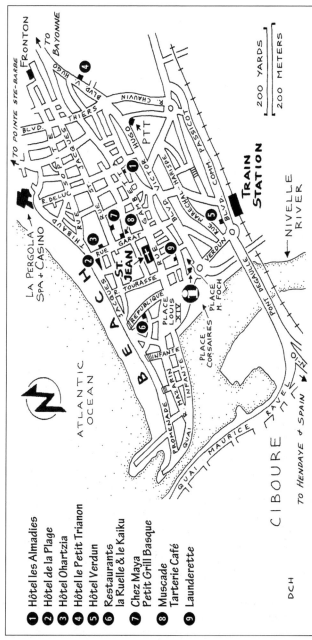

St. Jean-de-Luz

1 Hôtel les Almadies
2 Hôtel de la Plage
3 Hôtel Ohartzia
4 Hôtel le Petit Trianon
5 Hôtel Verdun
6 Restaurants
   la Ruelle & le Kaiku
7 Chez Maya
   Petit Grill Basque
8 Muscade
   Tarterie Café
9 Launderette

Car Rental: Avis is handiest, at the train station (Mon–Sat 8:00–12:00 & 14:00–18:00, closed Sun, tel. 05 59 26 76 66, fax 05 55 26 19 42).

Introductory Walking Tour of St. Jean-de-Luz

To get a feel for the town, take this self-guided tour. You'll start at the port and make your way to the historic church. Allow about one hour for this level, two-mile walk.

Port: From the TI, check out the little working port (pleasure craft are in the next port over). While fishing boats used to catch lots of whales, now they take in cod, sardines, tuna, and anchovies, and take out tourists (two boats advertise today's and tomorrow's mini-Atlantic cruises, summer only). St. Jean-de-Luz feels cute and non-threatening now, but in the 17th century, it was home to the Basque Corsairs. With the French government's blessing, these pirates, who worked the sea—and enriched the town—moored here. Facing the port is...

Place Louis XIV: The town's main square, named for the king who was married here, is a hub of action (the bandstand features traditional Basque music on summer Wednesdays at 21:00). Facing the square is the City Hall (Herriko Etxea) and the "House of Louis XIV" (in which he lived for 40 festive days in 1660). His visit is memorialized by a small black equestrian statue (a miniature of the huge one that marks the center of the Versailles courtyard). Opposite the port on the far side of the square is...

Rue de la République: From Place Louis XIV, this historic lane—lined with mostly edible temptations—leads to the beach. Facing the square, the shop Macarons Adam still bakes (according to the family recipe) the macaroons Louis XIV enjoyed during his visit. You can try one (€0.70), or sample a less historic *gâteau basque* (€1.50). Farther down rue de la République, you'll find the Pierre Oteiza shop, stacked with rustic Basque cheeses and meats from mountain villages (with a few samples generally out for the tasting). You'll likely eat on this lane tonight. Kaiku, the town's top restaurant, fills the oldest building in St. Jean-de-Luz (with its characteristic lookout tower), dating from the 1500s. Continue to the...

Beach: A high embankment protects the town from storm waters, but generally the Grande Plage—which is lovingly groomed daily—is the peaceful haunt of sun-seekers and happy children. Walk the elevated promenade (to the right). Various tableaux tell history in French. Storms routinely knocked down buildings (with a particularly disastrous one in 1749) until Napoleon III built the three breakwaters in the 1800s.

Stroll past the Art Deco–style La Pergola, which houses a casino and the Hélianthal spa center (entrance around back) and overlooks the beach. Anyone in a white robe strolling the beach is from the spa. Beyond La Pergola is the neo-Romantic Grand Hôtel

(c. 1900), with an inviting terrace for a coffee break.

Rue Gambetta: From here, circle back to your starting point inland along the town's lively pedestrian shopping street. Just before Place Louis XIV, you'll see the town's main church.

Church (Eglise St. Jean-Baptiste): The marriage of Louis XIV and Marie-Thérèse put St. Jean-de-Luz on the map to stay, and this church is where it all took place. The ultimate in political marriages, the knot tied between Louis XIV and Marie-Thérèse in 1660 also cinched a reconciliation deal between Europe's two most powerful countries. The king of Spain, Philip IV (who built the El Escorial Palace), gave his daughter in marriage to the king of France (who built Versailles). This marriage united Europe's two largest palaces, which helped wrap up a hundred years of hostility and forged an alliance that enabled both to focus attention on other matters (like England). Little St. Jean-de-Luz was selected for its 15 minutes of fame because it was roughly halfway between Madrid and Paris, and virtually on the France-Spain border. The wedding cleared out both Versailles and El Escorial palaces, as anyone who was anyone attended this glamorous event.

The church, centered on the pedestrian street rue Gambetta, seems modest enough from the exterior...but step inside (daily 8:00–12:00 & 14:00–18:00). As the local expertise was in shipbuilding, the ceiling is like the hull of a ship turned upside down. The dark wood balconies running along the nave—segregating the men from the women and children (until the 1960s)—were typical of Basque churches. The number of levels depended on the importance of the church, and this church, with three levels, is the largest Basque church in France. The three-foot-long paddle-wheel ship hanging in the center was a gift from Napoleon III's wife, Eugènie. It's a model of a ship she had been on that had almost sunk just off-shore. The 1670 Baroque altar, which feels Spanish, features 20 French saints. Locals call it the finest in Basque country. Drop €1 in the box to see it light up. The 17th-century organ is still used for concerts (the place has great acoustics). As you leave the church, turn left and find the bricked-up doorway—the church's original entrance. It was sealed after the royal marriage (shown on the wall to the right in a photo of a painting) to symbolize a permanent closing of the door on troubles between France and Spain.

Cultural Events

Various activities enliven St. Jean-de-Luz and crank up the Basque flavor. If you're in town at the right time, consider sampling a few of the local events.

***Pelota* Matches**—In the traditional Basque game of *pelota* (which Americans know as jai alai), players in white pants and red scarves or shirts use a long, hook-shaped racket (called a *txistera*) to whip a ball (smaller and far bouncier than a baseball) back and forth off walls at more than 150 miles per hour. This men's-only game can also be played bare-handed (ouch) or with a glove, and with a wall at one or both ends of the court. You'll see *fronton* courts, which resemble handball courts, in every town. The players are not professional, but betting on them is common. The TI in St. Jean-de-Luz sells tickets and has a schedule of matches throughout the area; you're more likely to find a match in summer (21:00, almost daily July–mid-Sept; afternoon matches sometimes on Sun and occasionally on Sat). The matches on Wednesdays and Fridays often come with Basque folk-loric halftime shows.

Concerts—There's traditional Basque music in the bandstand on the main square on Wednesdays in July and August (21:00).

SLEEPING

Hotels are a good value. The higher prices are for peak season (generally June–Sept). In winter, some prices drop below those I've listed. Most hoteliers speak English. Breakfast costs extra. Those wanting to eat and sleep cheaply will do better just over the border, in San Sebastián.

$$$ Hôtel de la Plage*** has the best location, right on the ocean. Its 22 rooms, many with ocean views, were beautifully renovated from the studs out in 2003, leaving it with lively yellow-and-blue nautical decor (Db-€70–106, ocean view Db-€86–134, higher prices are for rooms with seaview balcony or terrace, peak-season prices include breakfast, off-season breakfast-€8, family rooms, air-con, elevator, garage-€9, 33 rue Garrat, tel. 05 59 51 03 44, fax 05 59 51 03 48, www.hoteldelaplage.com, pg214@dial.oleane.com, run by friendly Fabian).

$$$ Hôtel les Almadies***, on the main pedestrian street, is a boutique hotel with seven flawless rooms, comfy public spaces with clever modern touches, a pleasant breakfast terrace, and an owner who cares (Sb/Db-€90–105, child's bed-€20, buffet breakfast-€10, 58 rue Gambetta, tel. 05 59 85 34 48, fax 05 59 26 12 42, www.hotel-les-almadies.com, hotel.lesalmadies@wanadoo.fr, Monsieur and Madame Hargous will charm you with their Franglish).

$$ Hôtel Ohartzia**, one block off the beach, is comfortable, clean, and characteristic, with the most charming facade I've seen. It comes with 17 well-cared-for rooms, generous and homey public spaces, sloping floors, and a bird-chirping, flower-petaled garden (Aug–Sept Db-€75–84, Oct–July Db-€59–68, extra bed-€15, rooms with showers cost €6 less than baths, peaceful at 28 rue Garat, tel. 05 59 26 00 06, fax 05 59 26 74 75, www.hotel-ohartzia.com, hotel.ohartzia@wanadoo.fr). Their desk is technically open only 8:00–20:00, but it's usually staffed longer in-season.

Sleep Code

(€1 = about $1.20, country code: 33)
S = Single, **D** = Double/Twin, **T** = Triple, **Q** = Quad,
b = bathroom, **s** = shower only, **no CC** = Credit Cards not
accepted, **SE** = Speaks English, **NSE** = No English, ***** = French
hotel rating system (0–4 stars). You can assume a hotel takes
credit cards unless you see "no CC" in the listing.

To help you sort easily through these listings, I've divided
the rooms into three categories based on the price for a standard
double room with bath:

   $$$ **Higher Priced**—Most rooms €90 or more.
    $$ **Moderately Priced**—Most rooms between €60–90.
     $ **Lower Priced**—Most rooms €60 or less.

$ Hôtel le Petit Trianon**, on a major street, is well-run,
simple, and traditional, with 30 worn but nicely appointed rooms.
To get a room over the quieter courtyard, ask for *coté cours* (coat-ay
coor; Db-€45–72, rooms with no TV are cheaper, garage-€9, 56
boulevard Victor Hugo, tel. 05 59 26 11 90, fax 05 59 26 14 10,
http://perso.wanadoo.fr/lepetittrianon, lepetittrianon@wanadoo.fr).

$ Hôtel Verdun, a bleak little 11-room place above a dreary
restaurant, faces the train station and offers the only cheap beds in
town (D-€23–38, Ds-€26–42, Db-€30–49, top prices are for
July–Sept, 13 avenue de Verdun, tel. 05 59 26 02 55, Henry SE).
It's often full in the off-season, when it houses people who have
come here to do seasonal labor.

EATING

St. Jean-de-Luz restaurants are known for offering good-value,
high-quality cuisine. You can find a wide variety of eateries in the
old center. For forgettable food with unforgettable views, choose
from several places overlooking the beach. For something fast and
cheap to go, try the crêpe stands on rue Gambetta. For a salad or
tart—sweet or savory—consider **Muscade Tarterie** (20 rue Garat).

The traffic-free rue de la République, which runs from place
Louis XIV to the ocean promenade, is lined with hardworking
restaurants (two of which are recommended below). You'll find
places empty at 19:30 and packed at 20:30. Making a reservation,
especially on weekends or in summer, is wise. Consider a fun night
of bar-hopping for dinner in San Sebastián (about an hour away in
Spain) if you're not otherwise going into Spain.

La Ruelle serves good, traditionally Basque cuisine—mostly
seafood—in two tight little rooms jam-packed with tables, happy

eaters, and kitschy Basque decor. Andre and his playful staff obviously enjoy their work, which gives this popular spot a relaxed and fun ambience. Portions are huge; their €15 *ttoro* seafood stew easily feeds two (*menus* from €20, closed Mon–Tue Oct–May, 19 rue de la République, tel. 05 59 26 37 80).

Le Kaiku is *the* gastronomic experience in town, with a chef who studied with Alain Ducasse (famous for his restaurants in Paris and Monaco). They serve modern cuisine, specializing in "wild" (rather than farmed) seafood. The place is dressy, but offers a good time (*menus* from €34, closed Tue–Wed, 17 rue de la République, tel. 05 59 26 13 20).

Chez Maya Petit Grill Basque serves good traditional Basque cuisine. Their *ttoro* was a highlight of my day. They have a €19 *menu*, but à la carte is more interesting (open from 12:15 and from 19:15, closed Wed, 2 rue St. Jacques, tel. 05 59 26 80 76).

TRANSPORTATION CONNECTIONS

The train station in St. Jean-de-Luz is called St. Jean-de-Luz-Ciboure. Its clever departure board displays lights next to any trains leaving today. Buses leave from the green building next door. Bus and rail service are reduced on Sundays and off-season.

From St. Jean-de-Luz by train to: Bayonne (12/day, 25 min), **St. Jean-Pied-de-Port** (8/day, 90 min, transfer in Bayonne), **Paris** (4 direct/day, 5.5 hrs), **Bordeaux** (12/day, 2 hrs), **Sarlat** (4/day, 4 hrs, transfer in Bordeaux), **Carcassonne** (5/day, 6 hrs, transfers likely in Bayonne and Toulouse).

By train to San Sebastián: You'll take the 10-minute train to the French border town of Hendaye (Gare SNCF stop; €4.20, about 10/day). Leave the Hendaye station to the right and look for the light-blue Eusko Tren building, where you'll catch the commuter train into San Sebastián (€1.25, every 30 min at :03 and :33 after the hour, 7:00–22:00). This milk-run train is known as the Topo train, since it goes underground part of the time (*topo* means mole). If there's no convenient train to Hendaye, take a bus to the Hendaye train station to catch the Eusko Tren.

By bus to San Sebastián: 2/day direct, 45 min (info in Spain tel. 902-101-210).

By taxi to San Sebastián: This option is convenient, but costs around €60 (tel. 05 59 26 10 11).

By excursion bus: The TI has information and sells tickets for these two popular day-trip excursions—**Guggenheim Bilbao** (2/week, Easter–mid-Oct only, departs 13:00 from bus terminal next to train station, returns 19:30, about €30 round-trip, includes admission, ask at TI) and **Pamplona** (during Running of the Bulls, 2/day, 1 hr, leaves around 19:30 and returns in the morning).

Villages in the French Basque Country

Use St. Jean-de-Luz as your base to visit the Basque sights described below.

Traditional villages among the green hills, with buildings colored like the Basque flag, offer the best glimpse at Basque culture. Cheese, hard cider, and *pelota* players are the primary products of these villages, which attract few foreigners, but many French summer visitors. Most of these villages have welcomed pilgrims bound for Santiago de Compostela since the Middle Ages. Today's hikers lace together local villages or head into the Pyrénées. The most appealing villages lie in the foothills of the Pyrénées, spared from beach-scene development.

Sare, which sits at the base of the towering mountain La Rhune, is among the most picturesque—and touristed. It's easily reached from St. Jean-de-Luz by bus or car. A small train takes tourists from the town to the top of La Rhune for fantastic views (great only if it's clear, crowded on weekends and in the summer).

Aïnhoa, farther up, is a one-street town that sees fewer tourists. Its chunks of fortified walls and gates mingle with red-and-white half-timbered buildings. The 14th-century church and *fronton* court share center stage. Find the Chapelle de Notre-Dame d'Aranazau for a fine village view.

St. Jean-Pied-de-Port is the most popular of all (1 hr from Bayonne by scenic train, 70 min by car from St. Jean-de-Luz, and just 10 min to Spain; TI tel. 05 59 37 03 57). This walled town is famous as the final stopover in France for Santiago-bound pilgrims, who gathered here to cross the Pyrénées together and continue their march through Spain. You'll find scallop shells—the symbol of St. Jacques (French for James)—etched on walls throughout the town. This place is packed in the summer (come early or late). Find the main drag, rue de la Citadelle, with its pastel-pink buildings, and stroll it as pilgrims have for over 1,000 years. Climb to la Citadelle for views, but skip the €3 Bishop's Prison (Prison des Evêques).

Bayonne
(Baiona)

To feel the urban pulse of French Basque country, visit Bayonne. This work-a-day capital of the French Basque lands has been modestly but honestly nicknamed "your anchor in the Basque Country" by its tourist board. With frequent, fast train connections with St. Jean-de-Luz (hrly, 25 min), Bayonne makes an easy, half-day side-trip.

Come here to browse through Bayonne's characteristic, well-worn, yet lively old town, and to admire its impressive Museum of Basque Culture. Known for establishing Europe's first whaling industry and for inventing the bayonet, Bayonne is more famous today for its ham *(jambon de Bayonne)* and chocolate.

Bayonne's two rivers, Adour and Nive, divide the city into three parts: St. Esprit, with the train station, and the more interesting Grand Bayonne and Petit Bayonne, which together make up the old town.

In pretty Grand Bayonne, tall, slender buildings climb above cobbled streets, and are decorated in Basque fashion with green and red shutters. Make sure to stroll the streets around the cathedral and along banks of the smaller Nive river, where you'll find the market *(Les Halles)*.

Tourist Information: The TI is a block off the mighty Adour River, on the northeastern edge of Grand Bayonne in a modern parking lot (Mon–Fri 9:00–18:30, Sat 10:00–18:00, closed Sun except 10:00–13:00 in July–Aug, place des Basques, tel. 05 59 46 01 46). They have very little in English other than a map.

Arrival in Bayonne

By Train: The TI and Grand Bayonne are a 10-minute walk from the train station. From the station, walk straight out, cross the traffic circle, and then cross the imposing bridge (pont St. Esprit). Once past the big Adour River, continue across a smaller bridge (pont Mayou), which spans the smaller Nive River. Stop on pont Mayou to orient yourself: You just left Petit Bayonne (left side of Nive River). Ahead of you is Grand Bayonne (spires of cathedral straight ahead, TI a few blocks to the right). The Museum of Basque Culture is in Petit Bayonne, facing the next bridge up the Nive River.

By Car: Drivers should follow signs for the *Office de Tourisme* and park there.

SIGHTS

Cathédrale Ste. Marie, bankrolled by the whaling community, sits dead center in Grand Bayonne and is worth a peek.

With no more whales to catch, Bayonne turned to producing mouth-watering chocolates and marzipan; look for shops on the arcaded **rue du pont Neuf** (running between the cathedral and the Adour River).

The ramparts, while open for walking, do not allow access to either of Bayonne's castles—both are closed to the public.

The superb **Museum of Basque Culture** (Musée Basque, in Petit Bayonne, facing the Nive River at pont Marengo) explains French Basque culture from cradle to grave—in French, Euskera, and Spanish. The only English you'll read is "do not touch" (unless you buy their English booklet for €5). Videos take you into the traditional Basque villages and sit you in the front row of traditional festivals (€5.50, May–Oct Tue–Sun 10:00–18:30, Nov–April Tue–Sun 10:00–12:30 & 14:00–18:00, always closed Mon, ticket office closed an hour early, tel. 05 59 46 61 90).

Spanish Basque Country
(País Vasco)

A short dash into Spain is now a breeze, thanks to the euro currency and lack of border checks.

Phones: Spain's telephone country code is 34. Remember that French phone cards and stamps will not work in Spain.

Hours: Most Spanish sights and stores close from about 13:00 to 16:00, and dinner doesn't begin until 21:00 (though tapas appetizers are always available).

San Sebastián
(Donostia)

Shimmering above the breathtaking bay of La Concha, elegant and prosperous San Sebastián has a favored location, with golden beaches capped by twin peaks at either end, and a cute little island in the center. A delightful beachfront promenade runs the length of

the bay, with an intriguing old town at one end and a smart shopping district in the center. It has 180,000 residents, and almost that many tourists in high season (July–Sept). With a romantic setting, the soaring statue of Christ gazing over the city, and the late-night lively old town, San Sebastián has a Rio de Janeiro aura.

While there's no compelling museum to visit, the scenic city provides a pleasant Basque-flavored introduction to Spain.

In 1845, Queen Isabel II's doctor recommended she treat her skin problems by bathing here in the sea. Her visit attracted Spain's aristocracy, and soon the city was on the map as a seaside resort. By the turn of the 20th century, Donostia was the toast of the belle époque, and a leading resort for Europe's beautiful people. Before World War I, Queen María Cristina summered here and held court in her Miramar Palace, overlooking the crescent beach. Hotels, casinos, and theaters flourished. Even Franco enjoyed 35 summers in a place he was sure to call by its Spanish name, not its Basque name, Donostia.

Key Spanish Phrases

Good day.	*Buenos días.*	**bway**-nohs **dee**-ahs
Mr./Mrs.	*Señor/Señora*	sayn-**yor**/ sayn-**yor**-ah
Please.	*Por favor.*	por fah-**bor**
Thank you.	*Muchas gracias.*	**moo**-chahs **grah**-thee-ahs
coffee with milk	*café con leche*	kah-**feh** kohn **lay**-chay
sandwich	*bocadillo*	boh-kah-**dee**-yoh
Where is...?	*¿Donde está...?*	**dohn**-day ay-**stah**
Tourist office	*Turismo*	too-**rees**-moh
City center	*Centro ciudad*	**thehn**-troh thee-oo-**dahd**

Planning Your Time

San Sebastián is worth a day. Stroll the two-mile-long promenade and scout the place you'll grab to work on a tan. The promenade leads to a funicular that lifts you to the Monte Igueldo viewpoint (described below). After exploring the old town and port, head up to the hill of Monte Urgull. A big part of any visit to San Sebastián is enjoying the tapas in bars in the old town.

ORIENTATION

The San Sebastián we're interested in surrounds the Bay of Concha (Bahía de la Concha), and can be divided into three areas: Playa de la Concha (best beaches), the shopping district (called *centro romántico*), and the skinny streets of the grid-planned old town (called *parte vieja*, to the north of the shopping district). *Centro romántico*, just east of Playa de la Concha, has beautiful turn-of-the-20th-century architecture, but no real sights.

It's all bookended by mini-mountains: Monte Urgull to the north and east, Monte Igueldo to the south and west. The River *(Río)* Urumea divides central San Sebastián from the district called Gros (with a lively night scene and surfing beach).

Tourist Information: The TI, which lies on the boulevard between the shopping area and old city, a block from the river, has complete information on city and regional sights. Pick up the excellent town booklet, which has English descriptions of the three walking tours—the Old Quarter/Monte Urgull walk is best. Skip the San Sebastián Card (€10 for 2 days of free bus transport, plus minor sightseeing discounts). The TI also has bus and train schedules (June–Sept Mon–Sat 8:00–20:00, Sun 10:00–14:00 &

15:30–19:00; Oct–May Mon–Sat 9:00–13:30 & 15:30–19:00, Sun 10:00–14:00, just off Zurriola bridge at Calle Reina Regente 3, tel. 943-481-166).

Arrival in San Sebastián

By Train: If you're coming on a regional Topo train from Hendaye on the French border, get off at the Eusko Tren station (end of the line, called Amara). It's a level 15-minute walk to the center. Exit the station and walk across the long plaza, then walk eight blocks down Calle Easo to reach the beach. The old town will be ahead to your right, Playa de la Concha to your left. To speed things up, catch bus #26 or #28 along Calle Easo—headed in the same direction you are—and take it to the Boulevard stop, near the TI at the bottom of the old town.

By Bus: If you're arriving by bus from Hondarribia, hop off at pretty Plaza de Gipuzkoa (first stop after crossing the river, in shopping area, near TI). To reach the TI, walk down Legazpi, cross Alameda del Boulevard, and turn right.

By Car: Coming from France, it's best to park at the station in Hendaye and take the frequent, cheap Topo trains, since navigating and parking in San Sebastián are tricky. If you do drive into San Sebastián, take the Amara freeway exit, follow Centro Ciudad signs into the city center, and park in a pay lot (many are well-signed). If turning in or picking up a rental car, **Hertz** (Zubieta 5, tel. 943-461-084) and **Avis** (Triunfo 2, tel. 943-461-556) are near Hotel Niza, and **Europcar** is at the main train station (tel. 943-322-304).

Helpful Hints

Useful Phone Numbers: For the **police,** dial 943-481-320. For flight information, call San Sebastián's **airport** (in Hondarribia, 12 miles away) at tel. 943-668-500.

Internet Access: There are several places in the old town; the handiest is **Donosti-NET** (daily 9:00–23:00, 2 locations a block apart—Calle Embeltrán 2 and Calle San Jerónimo 8, tel. 943-429-497). They also sell cheap phone cards for calling home.

Bookstore: Bilintx, near several recommended restaurants in the old town, has a wide selection, including some guidebooks in English (daily, but closed for siesta 14:00–16:00, Fermín Calbetón 21, tel. 943-420-080).

Getting Around San Sebastián

You'll do better finding a taxi stand rather than trying to hail one (€3 drop charge, €0.50 per kilometer, you can call a cab at tel. 943-464-646 or tel. 943-404-040).

At Alameda del Boulevard, along the bottom edge of the old town, you'll find a handy taxi stand and a line of public buses ready to take you anywhere in town; tell any driver your destination, and

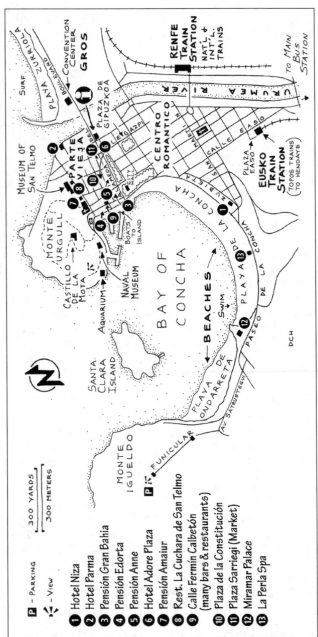

San Sebastián

P – PARKING
✓̇ – VIEW

❶ Hotel Niza
❷ Hotel Parma
❸ Pensión Gran Bahia
❹ Pensión Edorta
❺ Pensión Anne
❻ Hotel Adore Plaza
❼ Pensión Amaiur
❽ Rest. La Cuchara de San Telmo
❾ Calle Fermín Calbetón
    (many bars & restaurants)
❿ Plaza de la Constitución
⓫ Plaza Sarriegi (Market)
⓬ Miramar Palace
⓭ La Perla Spa

he'll tell you the number of the bus to catch (€1, pay driver).

Some handy bus routes: #26 or #28 connects the bus and Eusko Tren stations to the TI (get off at "Boulevard"); #16 takes you from the Boulevard/TI, along Playa de la Concha, to the base of the Monte Igueldo funicular.

A "txu-txu" tourist train and a hop-on, hop-off bus tour are also available, but they're not necessary in this little and lazy city.

SIGHTS

The Beach

▲▲La Concha Beach and Promenade—The shell-shaped Playa de La Concha, the pride of San Sebastián, has one of Europe's most appealing stretches of sand. Lined with a two-mile-long promenade, it allows even backpackers to feel aristocratic. While pretty empty

off-season, its shores are packed with sunbathers in summer. But year-round, it's surprisingly devoid of eateries and money-grubbing businesses. *Cabinas* provide lockers, showers, and shade for a fee. There are free showers, too. The Miramar palace and park, which divides the crescent in the middle, was where Queen María Cristina held court when she summered here. Her royal changing rooms are used today as inviting cafés, restaurants, and a fancy spa (see "La Perla Spa," below). For a century, the characteristic and lovingly painted wrought-iron balustrade that stretches the length of the promenade has been a symbol of the city; it shows up on everything from jewelry to headboards.

La Perla Spa—The spa attracts a less royal crowd today, and appeals mostly to visitors interested in sampling "the curative properties of the sea." For €17.50, you can enjoy its Thalasso Fitness Circuit—105 minutes of intensive relaxation, featuring a hydrotherapy pool, relaxation pool, panoramic whirlpool tub, cold water pools, seawater steam sauna, dry sauna, and relaxation area. For those seriously into spas, they offer much more, from Dead Sea mud wraps to massages to day-long "personalized programs" (daily 8:00–22:00, caps and towels rented/sold, bring or buy a swimsuit, on the beach at the center of the crescent, Paseo de La Concha, tel. 943-458-856).

Old Town (Parte Vieja)

Huddling securely in the shadow of its once-protective Monte Urgull, the old town (worth ▲▲) is where San Sebastián was born about a thousand years ago. This grid plan of streets hides heavy Baroque and Gothic churches, surprise plazas, and fun little shops (venerable pastry shops, rugged produce markets, Basque independence souvenir shops, seafood-to-go delis, and even "THC shops" for the latest from the decriminalized marijuana scene in Spain—adults are allowed to grow two plants). Be sure to wander out to the port to see the fishing industry in action. The old town's main square, Plaza de la Constitución (where bullfights used to be held—notice the seat numbering on the balconies) features inviting café tables spilling from all corners. The highlight of the old town is its incredibly lively tapas (*pintxos*, PEEN-chohs) bars. (See "Eating," page 327.)

Museum of San Telmo (Museo San Telmo)—Displayed in rooms around the peaceful cloister of a former Dominican monastery, this humble museum has a few exhibits on Basque folk life and a small collection of 19th- and 20th-century paintings by Basque artists that offer an interesting peek into the spirit, faces, and natural beauty of this fiercely independent region (free, other featured artists include El Greco and Rubens, minimal English information, Tue–Sat 10:30–13:30 & 16:00–19:30, Sun 10:30–14:00, closed Mon, Plaza Zuloaga 1, tel. 943-481-580).

The Port

At the west end of the old town, protected by Monte Urgull, is the port. To reach the first three sights, take the passage through the wall at the appropriately-named Calle Puerto, and jog right along the level, portside Paseo del Muelle. You'll pass fishing boats unloading the catch of the day (while hungry locals look on), salty sailors' pubs, and fisherfolk mending nets. The trails to Monte Urgull are just above this scene, near Santa María Church (or climb up the stairs next to the aquarium).

Cruise—Small boats cruise from the old town's port to the island in the bay (Isla Santa Clara), where you can hike the trails and have lunch at the lone café (€2.60 round-trip, every 30 min 10:00–20:00, June–Sept only).

▲Aquarium—San Sebastián's impressive aquarium exhibits include a history of the sea, fascinating models showing various drift-netting techniques, a petting tank filled with nervous fish, a huge whale skeleton, and a 45-foot-long tunnel that allows you to look up at floppy rays and menacing sharks (€9, €5 for kids under 13, April–June daily 10:00–20:00, July–Aug daily 10:00–21:00, Sept–March Mon–Fri 10:00–19:00, Sat–Sun 10:00–20:00, ongoing renovations may close some exhibits, Paseo del Muelle 34, tel. 943-440-099).

Naval Museum (Museo Naval)—Located at the port, the museum shows two floors of the seafaring city's history and provides a link between the Basque culture and the sea (borrow the English translation booklet, entry-€1.20, Tue–Sat 10:00–13:30 &

16:00–19:30, Sun 11:00–14:00, closed Mon, just before aquarium at Paseo del Muelle 24, tel. 943-430-051).

▲**Monte Urgull**—The once mighty castle (Castillo de la Mota) atop this hill deterred most attackers, allowing the city to prosper in the Middle Ages. The museum of San Sebastián history, located within the castle, is mildly interesting. The best views from the hill are not from the statue of Christ, but from the ramparts on the left side as you face the hill, just above the port's aquarium. Café El Polvorin, nestled in the park, is a friendly place with salads, sandwiches, and good sangria. The path is technically open only during daytime (May–Sept daily 8:00–21:00, Oct–April daily 8:00–19:00). Why are some of the directional signs defaced? Because you're in *El País Vasco*, not Spain—and to remind you, some proud Basque has spray-painted over the Spanish.

Other Sights

Monte Igueldo—For commanding city views (if you ignore the tacky amusements on top), ride the funicular up Monte Igueldo, a mirror image of Monte Urgull. The views into the distant green mountains, along the coast, and over San Sebastián are sensational day or night. The entrance to the funicular is behind the tennis club on the far western end of Playa de Ondarreta, which extends from Playa de la Concha to the west (€1.60, July–mid-Sept daily 10:00–22:00, April–June and mid-Sept–Oct daily 11:00–20:00, Nov–March Mon–Fri 11:00–16:00, Sat–Sun 11:00–20:00, closed Wed). If you drive here, you'll pay €1.30 to enter.

Kursaal Conference Center—These two Lego-like boxes (just east and across the river from the old town) mark the spot of what was once a grand casino, torn down by Franco to discourage gambling. While many locals wanted to rebuild it as it once was—in a similar style to the turn-of-the-20th-century buildings in the *centro romántico*—this design, by Rafael Moneo, won instead. The complex is supposed to resemble the angular rocks that make up the town's breakwater. Though the Kursaal has a similarly stark, postmodern style, it's no match for Frank Gehry's Guggenheim in Bilbao (despite what some competitive and deliriously proud San Sebastián residents would have you believe). The Kursaal houses a theater, conference facilities, some gift shops and travel agencies, and a good restaurant (with tapas and a fine €13 lunch *menu*).

SLEEPING

Unless otherwise noted, assume breakfast is not included; you'll have plenty of *churrerías* and cafeterias to choose from in the old town.

$$$ **Hotel Niza,** set on the western edge of Playa de la Concha, is understandably often booked long in advance. Half of its 40 rooms

(some with balconies) overlook the bay. From its chandeliered and plush lounge, a classic elevator takes you to its comfortable, pastel rooms with wedding-cake molding (Db-€103–118, view rooms cost the same—requests with reservation considered...but no promises, only street-side rooms have air-con, extra bed-€19, buffet breakfast with sea view-€8, elevator, parking-€12/day, Zubieta 56, tel. 943-426-663, fax 943-441-251, www.hotelniza.com, reservas@hotelniza .com, SE). The cheap and cheery restaurant downstairs serves good pizzas and salads.

$$$ **Hotel Parma,** a business-class place with 27 fine rooms and family-run attention to detail and service, stands on the edge of the old town, away from the bar-scene noise, overlooking the river and a surfing beach (Sb-€54–72, very quiet internal Db-€79–109, view Db-€97–120, breakfast-€6 or €7 in high season, modern lounge, air-con, Paseo de Salamanca 10, tel. 943-428-893, fax 943-424-082, www.hotelparma.com, hotelparma@hotelparma.com, Iñaki Azurza SE).

$$ **Pensión Gran Bahía** offers 10 classy rooms a cut above other old-town *pensiones*. You'll enjoy the rich, dark wood floors polished to a slippery shine. Teresa (NSE) has a big personality and lots of rules, but is justifiably proud of her fine *pensión* (June–Sept Db-€85, Tb-€118; off-season Db-€49, Tb-€73; prices soft off-season, 7 percent tax not included, air-con, tries to be non-smoking, Embeltran 16, tel. 943-420-216, fax 943-428-276, www.paisvasco .com/granbahia—in Spanish, granbahia@mixmail.com).

$$ **Pensión Edorta** elegantly mixes wood, brick, and color into 12 stylish rooms (S-€30–50, D-€40–60, Sb/Db-€60–80, extra bed-€20–25, elevator, Calle Puerto 15, tel. 943-423-773, fax 943-433-570, www.pensionedorta.com, info@pensionedorta.com).

$ **Pensión Anne** is a tiny, well-run place on a relatively quiet lane in the old town, with six rooms sharing two bathrooms. Its simple rooms are bright and clean but have no sinks (S-€24–38, D-€30–48, Db-€45–60, Esterlines 15, tel. 943-421-438, www.pensionanne .com, pensionanne@yahoo.es, Anne SE).

$ **Adore Plaza,** run by the same folks, offers similar good-value rooms overlooking the old town's centerpiece, Plaza de la Constitución. Seven rooms—including four with views of the plaza—share four bathrooms (D-€45–60, higher prices are for plaza-view rooms, Db has similar prices but without views, beds in 4-bed room with lockers-€15–25 per person, Plaza de la Constitución 6, tel. & fax 943-422-270, www.adoreplaza.com, adoreplaza@yahoo.es, Miren SE)

$ **Pensión Amaiur,** a popular hangout with the *Let's Go* crowd, is a cheap and inviting option buried deep in the old town. Flowery Virginia (SE) gives the place a homey warmth and provides backpackers with a clean and colorful home. Her 13 rooms share seven bathrooms (S-€24–35, D-€38–50, quiet windowless D-€33–45,

T-€51–72, Q-€66–85, kitchen facilities, Internet access, family room, next to Santa María church, Calle 31 de Agosto 44, tel. 943-429-654, www.pensionamaiur.com, amaiur@telefonica.net).

EATING

On menus, you'll see *bacalao* (salted cod), best when cooked *à la bizkaina* (with tomatoes, onions, and roasted peppers); *merluza* (hake, a light white fish prepared in a variety of ways); and *chipirones en su tinta* (squid served in their own black ink). Carnivores will find plenty of lamb (try *chuletas*, massive lamb chops). Local brews include *sidra* (hard apple cider), *txacoli* (tax-oh-lee, a local, light, sparkling white wine—often theatrically poured from high above the glass for aeration), and *izarra* (herbal-flavored brandy). Spanish wine is generally served by the glass; *crianza* spends two years in oak kegs and is *con cuerpo* (full-bodied).

Bar-Hopping

Txiquiteo is the word for hopping from bar to bar, enjoying characteristically small sandwiches and tiny snacks *(pintxos)* and glasses of local wine. Local competition drives small bars to lay out the most appealing array of *pintxos*. San Sebastián's old town provides the ideal backdrop for tapas-hopping. The selection is amazing. Later in the evening, the best spreads get picked over (20:00 is prime time). I'd poke into a dozen or so bars to survey the scene, and go back to the ones with the liveliest crowds. Places most serious about their food don't have the TV on. Calle Fermín Calbetón has the best concentration of bars (don't miss Bar Goiz Argi, see below). San Jerónimo and 31 de Agosto are also good. For a little grander ambience, consider the bars on Plaza de la Constitución.

Bar Goiz Argi serves its tiny dishes with pride and attitude. Advertising *pinxos calientes*, they cook each treat for you, allowing you a montage of petite gourmet snacks; try their *tartaleta de txangurro* (spider-crab spread on bread). Wash it all down with a glass of whichever wine you like. Open bottles are clearly priced and displayed on the shelf. While it's not on their menu, they can whip up a good salad *(ensalada)* by request, so you can call this an entire meal. You stand at the bar, since there are no chairs (closed Mon–Tue, Fermín Calbetón 4, tel. 943-425-204).

For top-end tapas, seek out two more bars—each packed with locals, rather than tourists: **Ganbara Bar** serves the typical little sandwich *pintxos,* but also heaps piles of peppers and mushrooms—whatever's in season—on its bar and sautées tasty *raciones* for a steep price (see the dry-erase board, San Jerónimo 21, tel. 943-422-575, closed Mon). **La Cuchara de San Telmo**—with cooks taught by a big-name Basque chef—is a cramped place that devotes as much space to its thriving kitchen as its bar. It has nothing pre-cooked and on the bar. You order your mini-gourmet plates with a spirit of adventure from the constantly changing blackboard (*pintxos* go for €2–3, closed Mon, tucked away on a lonely alley behind Museum of San Telmo at 31 de Agosto 28, tel. 943-420-840).

Restaurants, Picnics, and *Churros*

For modern Basque cuisine in a dark and traditional setting, try **Bodégon Alejandro** (3-course *menu*-€28, from 13:00 and 21:00, closed Sun–Mon, no dinner Tue, in the thick of the old town on Calle Fermín Calbetón 4, tel. 943-427-158). **Casa Urola**, a block away, is *the* place in the old town for a good, traditional, sit-down Basque meal (more expensive, reservations smart from 13:00 and 20:00, Calle Fermín Calbetón 20, tel. 943-423-424).

For seafood with a view, check out the half-dozen hard-working, local-feeling restaurants that line the harbor on the way to the aquarium.

For **picnics**, drop by one of the countless tiny grocery stores or the Bretxa public market at Plaza Sarriegi (down the modern escalator), near the TI. Then head for the beach or up Monte Urgull.

Santa Lucía, a '50s-style Basque diner, is ideal for a cheap old-town breakfast or *churros* break. Photos of 20 different breakfasts decorate the walls, and plates of fresh *churros* with sugar keep patrons happy (daily 8:00–22:00, Calle Puerto 6, tel. 943-425-019). Grease is liberally applied to the grill...from a squeeze bottle. To counteract this place's heart-attack potential, get a glass of OJ, fresh-squeezed by a clever machine.

TRANSPORTATION CONNECTIONS

All Paris, Barcelona, and Madrid trains require reservations. To connect with the SNCF French rail system, you'll save time using San Sebastián's smaller Eusko Tren station (tel. 902-543-210).

From San Sebastián by train to: Bilbao (hrly, 2.75 hrs—bus is much better option), **Barcelona** (1/day, 8.5 hrs; 1/night except Sat, 10 hrs), **Madrid** (3/day, 6–8.5 hrs; 1/night, 10.5 hr), **Hendaye/French border** (2/hr, 30 min, departs Eusko Tren station at :15 and :45 after the hour 7:15–21:45), **Paris** (get to Hendaye via the Eusko station—see above, then 4/day, 5.5 hrs, or 8.5-hr night train).

By bus to: Bilbao (2/hr, 1/hr on weekends, 6:30–22:00, 70 min, get €8 ticket from office, departs San Sebastián's main bus station on Plaza Pío XII, on the river three blocks below Eusko Tren station, bus tel. 902-101-210; once in Bilbao, buses leave you a 30-minute walk or quick tram ride from the museum), **Hondarribia** (3/hr, 1 hr, buy ticket from driver, many bus stops, most central is on Plaza de Gipuzkoa in shopping area), **St. Jean-de-Luz**, France

(2 direct 45-min buses daily, 9:00 and 14:30, €4, runs only 1/week off-season, from Plaza Pío XII, tel. 902-101-210).

Hondarribia

For a taste of small-town País Vasco, dip into this enchanting, seldom visited town. Much smaller and easier to manage than San Sebastián, and also closer to France (across the Bay of Txingudi from Hendaye), Hondarribia allows travelers a stress-free opportunity to

enjoy Basque culture. While it's easy to think of this as a border town (between France and Spain), culturally it's in the middle of Basque country.

The town comes in two parts: the lower port town and the historic, balcony-lined streets of the hilly and walled upper town. The **TI** is located between the two parts, two blocks up from the port on Jabier Ugarte 6 (Mon–Fri 9:00–13:30 & 16:00–18:30, Sat 10:00–14:00, closed Sun, tel. 943-645-458). You can follow their self-guided tour of the old town (English brochure available) or just lose yourself within the walls. Explore the plazas of the upper city.

Today, Charles V's odd, squat castle is a *parador* (Db-€170, Plaza de Armas 14, tel. 943-645-500, fax 943-642-153, hondarribia @parador.es). Tourists are allowed to have sangria in the *muy* cool bar, though the terraces are for guests only. In the modern lower town, straight shopping streets serve a local clientele and a pleasant walkway takes strollers along the beach.

TRANSPORTATION CONNECTIONS

From Hondarribia by bus to: San Sebastián (3/hr, 45 min to go 12 miles), **Hendaye/French border** (2/hr, 20 min, June–Sept only). A bus stop in Hondarribia is across from the post office, one block below the TI.

By boat to: Hendaye (4/hr, 15 min, €1.40, runs about 11:00–19:00 or until dark).

Bilbao

In the last five years, the cultural and economic capital of the País Vasco, Bilbao (pop. 500,000), has seen a transformation like no other Spanish city. Entire sectors of the industrial city's long-depressed port have been cleared away to allow construction of a new opera house, convention center, and the stunning Guggenheim Museum. Still, the city will always be a Marseille-like port; for most, it's worth a visit only for its incredible modern art museum.

Tourist Information: Bilbao's handiest TI is across from the Guggenheim (July–Aug Mon–Sat 10:00–15:00 & 16:00–19:00, Sun 10:00–15:00; Sept–June Tue–Fri 11:00–14:30 & 15:30–18:00, Sat 11:00–15:00 & 16:00–19:00, Sun 11:00–14:00, closed Mon; Avenida Abandoibarra 2, central TI tel. 944-795-760, www.bilbao .net). If you're interested in anything besides the Guggenheim, pick up a map, the bimonthly *Bilbao Guide* newsletter, and the museum's brochure (describing museums dedicated to everything from Basques and bullfighting to Holy Week processionals).

Arrival in Bilbao

By Train: Bilbao's **Renfe station** (trains from most parts of Spain) is on the river in central Bilbao. Ask for a city map at the train information office. To reach the tram to the Guggenheim, use the exit marked Hurtado de Amézaga, and go right to find the BBK bank. Go inside, find the *Automatikoa* door on the right, and buy your €1 ticket at the green machine marked Abando. Leave the bank, continuing right around the corner, and take a tram marked "San Mamés" (headed in the direction you just came from).

Trains coming from San Sebastián arrive at the riverside **Atxuri station**, southeast of the museum. Buy and validate your ticket, hop on a tram, and follow the river to the Guggenheim stop.

By Bus: Buses stop at the **Termibus station** on the western edge of downtown, about a mile southwest of the museum. Take a tram (direction: Atxuri) to Guggenheim.

By Car: Parking at the museum itself is a hassle; the closest option is the garage two blocks in front (Calle Iparraguirre 18). But to avoid stressful city traffic and frustrating one-ways, the best plan is this: Use the expressway exit marked *Centro*, following signs to Guggenheim. You'll pass the long train station on your right; continue straight through the traffic circle, veer left at the river, and park at the big garage (called Pío Baroja). Walk 10 minutes to the museum, or hop on the tram (direction: San Mamés).

SIGHTS

Guggenheim Bilbao

While the collection of art in this ▲▲▲ museum is no better than that in Europe's other great modern art museums, the building itself—designed by Frank Gehry and opened in 1997—is the reason why so many travelers happily splice Bilbao into their itineraries.

Gehry's triumph offers a fascinating look at 21st-century architecture. Using cutting-edge technologies, unusual materials, and

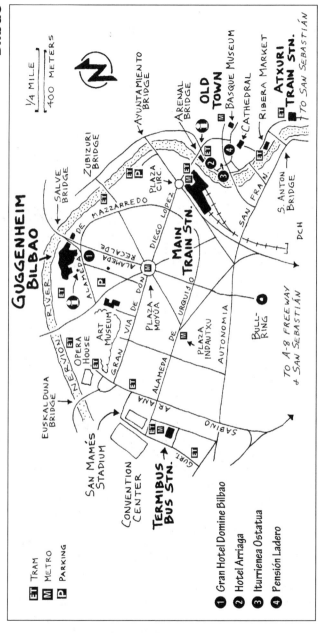

Bilbao

daring forms, he created a piece of sculpture that smoothly integrates with its environment and serves as the perfect stage for some of today's best art.

This limestone and titanium building looks like a huge, silvery fish, connecting the city with its river. Gehry meshed many visions. To him, the building's multiple forms jostle like a loose crate of bottles. They also evoke sails heading out to sea. Gehry keeps returning to his fish motif, reminding visitors that, as a boy, he was inspired by carp...even taking them into the bathtub with him. The building's skin—shiny, metallic, fish-like scales—is made of thin titanium, carefully created to give just the desired color and reflective quality.

A great way to really enjoy the exterior is to take a circular stroll up and down each side of the river along the handsome promenade and over the two modern pedestrian bridges.

Guarding the **main entrance** is artist Jeff Koons' 42-foot-tall West Highland Terrier. Its 60,000 plants and flowers, chosen to blossom in concert, grow through steel mesh. A joyful structure, it brings viewers back to their child-hood...perhaps evoking humankind's relation-ship to God...or maybe it's just another notorious Koons hoax. One thing is clear: It answers to "Puppy."

Inside, just beyond the turnstile, you come upon the **atrium**. This is clearly the heart of the building, pumping visitors from vari-ous rooms on three levels out and back. The architect invites you to caress the sensual curves of the walls. Only the floor is straight. Notice the sheets of glass, overlapping like scales on a fish, making the elevator shaft. The various glass and limestone panels are each unique, designed and shaped by a computer—as will likely be stan-dard in constructing the great buildings of the future.

From the atrium, step out onto the riverside **terrace**. The shal-low pool lets the river lick at the foundations of the building. Notice the museum's commitment to public spaces: On the right, a grand public staircase leads under a big green bridge to a tower designed to wrap the bridge into the museum's grand scheme.

As you enter, pick up the English brochure explaining the architecture and the monthly bulletin detailing the art currently on display. Because this museum is part of the Guggenheim "family" of museums, the collection perpetually rotates among the sister Guggenheim galleries in New York, Venice, and Berlin. The best approach to your visit is simply to immerse yourself in a modern art happening, rather than to count on seeing a particular piece or a spe-cific artist's works. Gehry designed the vast **ground floor** mainly to show off the often huge modern art installations. Computer-controlled lighting adjusts for different exhibits. Surfaces are clean and bare, so you can focus on the art.

Cost, Hours, Location: Entry price varies, depending on exhibit, generally €8–10; July–Aug daily 10:00–20:00, Sept–June Tue–Sun 10:00–20:00, closed Mon (tram stop: Guggenheim, Avenida Abandoibarra 2, tel. 944-359-080, www.guggenheim -bilbao.es). No photos are allowed. There's a handy café on site.

Tours: The museum offers excellent audioguides (sometimes included with admission, sometimes a few euros extra), which give descriptions of current exhibits and fascinating information about the building's architecture. For the schedule of guided tours in English, call 944-359-080.

Getting There: Thanks to a perfectly planned new tram system (Eusko Tran), getting to the museum is a snap. From any point of entry, simply buy a €1 single-ride ticket at a user-friendly green machine, hop on a tram, and head for the Guggenheim stop (only 1 line, so you can't get lost, trams come every 10–15 min, www .euskotran.es). When you buy your ticket, validate it at the machine (follow the red arrow), since you can't do it once on board.

The new Metro system, designed by prominent architect Lord Norman Foster, is a work of art...but not practical for most visitors. If you get lost, ask: "*¿Dónde está el museo Guggenheim?*" (dohn-day ay-stah el moo-say-oo Guggenheim).

SLEEPING

(€1 = about $1.20, country code: 34)
Bilbao merits an overnight stay. Even those who are only interested in the Guggenheim find that there's much more to this historic yet quickly changing city. Here are a few options. The first one is across from the Guggenheim, the others are in the Old Town (Casco Viejo), which offers a bustling, pedestrians-only Old World ambience and lots of dining options. To reach this district, turn right out of the train station and follow the tram tracks across the river. The seven percent tax is not included in the prices listed below.

$$$ Gran Hotel Domine Bilbao is *the* place for wealthy modern art fans looking for a handy splurge. It's right across the street from the Guggenheim, with decor clearly inspired by Gehry's masterpiece. Its 135 plush rooms are all postmodern class (standard Db-€200–230, super-swanky "executive" Db-€230–260, but prices very soft; ask about promotional rates, especially on weekends, when you'll pay closer to €155–€170; elevator, Alameda Mazarredo 61, tel 944-253-300, fax 944-253-301, www.granhoteldominebilbao.com, recepcion@granhoteldominebilbao.com, SE).

$ Hotel Arriaga offers 21 old-fashioned but well-maintained rooms (Sb-€48, Db-€60–64, extra bed-€11, some rooms overlook a busy street—request a quiet back room, Calle Ribera 3, tel. 944-790-001, fax 944-790-516). As you cross the bridge from the station, it's just behind the big theater of the same name.

$ **Iturrienea Ostatua**, on a quiet pedestrian street in the old town, has 21 rooms packed with brick, stone, and antiques (Sb-€46, Db-€55–60, Tb-€73, breakfast-€4, Santa María Kalea 14, tel. 944-161-500, fax 944-158-929). From the station, cross the bridge and go past the big theater. Turn left, up quaint Santa María Kalea, when the river bends.

$ **Pensión Ladero** is a fine budget option in the old town. They don't accept reservations, but you can call when you arrive to check availability (S-€20, D-€32, T-€40–45, up 4 flights of stairs; 7 rooms share 1 bathroom up a very tight spiral staircase, but 14 rooms use the other 3 bathrooms on the main floor; no CC, Lotería 1, tel. 944-150-932, SE). You'll find the pensión just before the big church at the center of the old town. This is a better value than the more prominent Pensión Roquefer across the street.

TRANSPORTATION CONNECTIONS

From Bilbao by bus to: San Sebastián (2/hr, 6:00–22:30, 70 min, departs Bilbao's Termibus station, arrives in San Sebastián at Plaza Pío XII).

Lekeitio

A small fishing port with an idyllic harbor and a fine beach, Lekeitio is an hour by bus from Bilbao and an easy stop for drivers. It's protected from the Bay of Biscay by a sand spit that leads to the lush and rugged little San Nicolás Island. Hake boats fly their Basque flags and proud Basque locals black out the Spanish translations on street signs.

Lekeitio is a teeming resort during July and August (when its population of 7,000 triples as big-city Basque folks move in to their vacation condos), and it's a sleepy backwater the rest of the year. It's isolated from the modern rat race by its location down a long, windy little road.

While sights are humble here, the 15th-century St. Mary's Parish Church is a good example of Basque Gothic with an impressive altarpiece. The town's back lanes are reminiscent of old days when fishing was the only industry. Fisherwomen sell their husbands' catches each morning from about 10:30 at the tiny Plaza Arranegi market (a block off the harbor). The golden crescent beach is as inviting as the sand bar, which—at low tide—challenges you to join the seagulls out on San Nicolás Island.

The **TI** faces the fish market next to the harbor (mid-June–mid-Sept daily 10:00–14:00 & 16:00–20:00; off-season Tue–Sat 10:30–13:30 & 16:00–19:00, Sun 10:00–14:00, closed Mon; tel. 946-844-017). While buses connect Lekeitio with Bilbao hourly (and San Sebastián 4/day), this stop is most logical for those with a car.

The TI recommends Lekeitio as a base for car explorations of the area (coastal and medieval hill villages). The nearby town of **Guernica** ("Gernika" in Euskera, 9 miles toward Bilbao) is near and dear to Basques and pacifists alike for good reason. This is the site of the Gernikako Arbola (oak tree of Guernica), which marked the ancient assembly point where the Lords of Bizkaia (Basque leaders) met through the ages to assert their people's freedom. Long the symbolic heart of Basque separatism, this was a natural target for Franco in the Spanish Civil War. His buddy Hitler agreed to use Guernica as a kind of target practice in 1937. This historic "first air raid"—a prelude to the horrific aerial bombings of World War II—was made famous by Picasso's epic work, *Guernica* (now in Madrid).

Sleeping in Lekeitio: **$ Emperatriz Zita Hotel** is the obvious best bet for your beach-town break. It's named for Empress Zita (who lived here in exile after her Hapsburg family lost World War I and were booted from Vienna). While Zita's mansion burned down, this 1930s rebuild still has a belle époque aristocratic charm, solid classy furniture in 42 spacious rooms, real hardwood floors, and an elegant spa in the basement. Located on the beach a few steps from the harbor, with handy parking and a view restaurant, it's a fine value (Sb-€40–50, Db-€55–68, Db suite-€85–100, views—ask for *vistas del mar*—are worth the extra euros, high prices are for July–Aug, third bed-€19, breakfast-€7, elevator, Santa Elena Etorbidea, tel. 946-842-655, fax 946-243-500, www.aisiahoteles.com—in Spanish, ezita@saviat.net). Room prices include a thermal seawater pool and whirlpool tub; the full-service spa is available at reasonable prices.

Eating in Lekeitio: Although it's sleepy in the off-season, the harbor promenade is made-to-order in summer for a slow meal or a tapas crawl. For fancy seafood, the local favorite is **Restaurante Zapirain** (€20 plates, Igualdegi 3, tel. 946-840-255). *Txangurro* (baked and stuffed crabs) is a specialty worth asking for.

LANGUEDOC

From the 10th to the 13th centuries, this mighty and independent region controlled most of southern France. The ultimate in mean-spirited crusades against the Albigensians (or Cathars) began here in 1208, igniting Languedoc's meltdown and eventual incorporation into the state of France.

The name *languedoc* comes from the *langue* (language) its people spoke: *Langue d'oc* ("language of Oc," *Oc* for the way they said "yes") was the dialect of southern France; *langue d'oïl* was the dialect of northern France (where *oïl*, later to become *oui*, was the way of saying "yes"). Languedoc's language faded with its power.

The Moors, Charlemagne, and the Spanish have all called this area home. The Spanish influence remains in this region, where proud restaurant owners offer paella, and the siesta is still respected.

While sharing many of the same attributes as Provence (climate, wind, grapes, and sea), this sunny, intoxicating, southwest-ernmost region of France is allocated little time by most travelers. Lacking Provence's cachet and sophistication, Languedoc feels more real. Pay homage to Henri de Toulouse-Lautrec in Albi; spend a night in Europe's greatest fortress city, Carcassonne; scamper up to a remote Cathar castle; and sift through sand in Collioure. That wind you feel is called *la tramontane* (trah-mon-tah-nyuh), Languedoc's version of Provence's mistral.

Planning Your Time

Albi makes a good day or overnight stop between the Dordogne region and Carcassonne. Plan your arrival at Carcassonne carefully: If you arrive late in the afternoon, spend the night, and leave by noon the next day, you'll miss the day-trippers. Collioure is your Mediterranean beach-town vacation from your vacation. To find the Cathar castle ruins and Minerve, you'll need wheels of your own and

Languedoc

a good map. If you're driving, the most exciting Cathar castles—
Peyrepertuse and Quéribus—work well as stops between Carcassonne
and Collioure. And if nature beckons, the Gorges du Tarn makes an
idyllic joyride east of Albi. No matter what kind of transportation you
use, Languedoc is a logical stop between the Dordogne and Provence,
or on the way to Barcelona, which is just over the border.

Getting Around Languedoc

Albi, Carcassonne, and Collioure are all accessible by train, but a car
is essential for seeing the remote sights. Pick up your rental car in
Albi or Carcassonne, and buy the Michelin Local maps #344 and
#338. Roads can be pencil-thin, and traffic slow.

East of Montauban, the D-115 highway to Bruniquel connects with D-964 via Castelnau-de-Montmiral, providing a reasonably fast and scenic route to Albi. With more time, follow D-926 from Caussade to D-5 to St. Antonin-Noble-Val. From there, follow D-115 and D-964 to Bruniquel, then Castelnau-de-Montmiral, and on to Albi (see "Near Albi—Route of the Bastides," page 342).

Drivers continuing north should consider these beautiful but slower drives: through the Lot River Valley via Villefranche-de-Rouergue and Cajarc (see "Southeast of the Dordogne," page 302), or along the Route of the Bastides (see page 342).

Cuisine Scene in Languedoc

Hearty peasant cooking and full-bodied red wines are Languedoc's tasty trademarks. Be adventurous. Cassoulet, an old Roman concoction of goose, duck, pork, mutton, sausage, and white beans, is the main-course specialty. You'll also see *cargolade*, a satisfying stew of snail, lamb, and sausage. Local cheeses are Roquefort and Pelardon (a nutty-tasting goat cheese). Corbières, Minervois, and Côtes du Roussillon are the area's good-value red wines. The locals distill a fine brandy, Armagnac, which tastes just like cognac and costs less.

Remember, restaurants serve only during lunch (11:30–14:00) and dinner (19:00–21:00, later in bigger cities); cafés serve food throughout the day.

Albi

Those coming to see the cathedral and the Toulouse-Lautrec Museum will be pleasantly surprised by Albi's sienna-toned bricks, half-timbered buildings, and many traffic-free streets. Lost in the Dordogne-to-Carcassonne shuffle and overshadowed by its big brother Toulouse, unpretentious Albi awaits your visit with minimal tourist trappings.

Albi's cathedral is home base. All sights, pedestrian streets, and hotels fan out from here, and nothing is more than a 10-minute walk away. The Tarn river hides below and behind the cathedral.

Tourist Information: The helpful TI is on the square in front of the cathedral, next to the Toulouse-Lautrec Museum (July–Aug Mon–Sat 9:00–19:30, Sept–June Mon–Sat 9:00–12:30 & 14:00–18:00, Sun all year 10:30–12:30 & 14:00–18:30, tel. 05 63 49 48 80). Pick up a map of the city center with the walking tour brochure and get the map of *La Route des Bastides* (hill towns near Albi).

Arrival in Albi

By Train: There are two stations in Albi; you want *Albi-Ville* (no baggage check). It's a level, 15-minute walk to the town center. Take the second left out of the station onto avenue Maréchal Joffre, walking past Hôtel Terminus, and then take another left on avenue du Général de Gaulle. Go straight across place Lapérouse and find the traffic-free street that leads into the city center. This turns into rue Ste. Cécile and leads to the recommended hotels and the cathedral.

By Car: Follow signs to *Centre-Ville* and *Cathédrale,* and park as close to the cathedral as you can (parking at or near place Lapérouse works well for me).

Helpful Hints

Market Day: It's on Saturday morning on place Lapérouse (until 12:30).

Internet Access: Ludi.com is at 62 rue Sére de Riviere (tel. 05 63 43 34 24).

Taxi: Call **Albi Taxi Radio** at 05 63 54 85 03.

Car Rental: Europcar is closest to the train station (24 avenue François Verdier, walk 1 long block down avenue Général Leclerc from the station and turn right, tel. 05 63 48 88 33). All others require a taxi ride.

SIGHTS

In Albi

The TI's English walking tour brochure gives you several interesting routes to follow (the purple *circuit pourpre* is best). You'll find English information posted on walls at key points along the way. Along the way, you'll see the...

▲▲▲**St. Cécile Cathedral (Cathédrale Ste. Cécile)**—This massive 13th-century cathedral was the nail in the Albigensian coffin. Built after the Cathar crusades were successfully accomplished, the cathedral made it clear who was in charge. The imposing exterior and the stunning interior drive home the message of the Catholic (read: "universal") Church in a way that would have stuck with any medieval worshipper. This place oozes power. The cathedral looks less like a church and more like the fortress it was, a central feature of the town's defensive walls. Notice how high the windows are (out of stone-tossing range). The extravagant porch looks like the afterthought it was. The interior is an explosion of colors and geometric shapes framing a vivid *Last Judgment.* Inspect it closely. There was no confusion here: If you were bad, you were in for a lousy retirement. Even with the gaping hole that was cut from it to make room for a newer pipe organ, the point is clear (June–Sept daily 9:00–18:30, Oct–May daily 9:00–12:00 & 14:30–18:30, €3 headsets provide an excellent 1-hour, self-guided tour). The choir is worth the €1 admission. In summer, the sound-and-light show—Son et Lumière Spectacle—is worth staying up for (€4.75, at 22:00, ask at TI).

The Cathars

The Cathars were a heretical group of Christians who grew in numbers from the 11th through the 13th centuries under tolerant rule in Languedoc. They saw life as a battle between good (the spiritual) and bad (the material), and they considered material things evil and of the devil. While others called them "Cathars" (from the Greek word for "pure") or "Albigenses" (for their main city, Albi), they called themselves simply "friends of God." Cathars focused on the teachings of St. John, and recognized only baptism as a sacrament. Because they believed in reincarnation, they were vegetarians.

Travelers encounter traces of the Cathars in their Languedoc sightseeing because of the Albigensian Crusades (1209–1240s). The king of France wanted to consolidate his grip on southern France. The pope needed to make a strong point that the only acceptable Christianity was Roman-style. Both found self-serving reasons to wage a genocidal war against the Cathars, who never amounted to more than 10 percent of the local population and coexisted happily with their non-Cathar neighbors. After a terrible generation of torture and mass burnings, the Cathars were wiped out. There were over five million victims in this tragedy (Cathar and others). The last Cathar was burned in 1321.

Today, tourists find haunting castle ruins (once Cathar strongholds) high in the Pyrénées, and eat hearty *salade Cathar*.

▲▲**Toulouse-Lautrec Museum (Musée Toulouse-Lautrec)**—The Palais de la Berbie (once the fortified home of the archbishop) has the world's best collection of Henri de Toulouse-Lautrec's paintings, posters, and sketches. The artist, crippled from youth and therefore on the fringe of society, had an affinity for people who didn't quite fit in. He painted the dregs of Parisian society because they were his world. His famous Parisian nightlife posters are here. The top floor houses a so-so collection of contemporary art, with a few works by Bonnard, Vuillard, Vlaminck, and Matisse (€4.50, audioguide-€3, April–May daily 10:00–12:00 & 14:00–18:00; June and Sept daily from 9:00 with lunch break; July–Aug daily 9:00–18:00; Oct–March Wed–Mon 10:00–12:00 & 14:00–17:00, closed Tue, tel. 05 63 49 48 70). The pretty gardens below have fine views.

St. Salvy Church and Cloister (Église St. Salvi et Cloître)—This is an OK church with fine cloisters. Delicate arches surround an enclosed courtyard, providing a peaceful interlude from the shoppers that fill the pedestrian streets (open all day).

Market Hall (Marché Couvert)—This quiet Art Nouveau market is good for picnic-gathering and people-watching (Tue–Sun until 13:00, closed Mon, 2 blocks from cathedral).

Albi

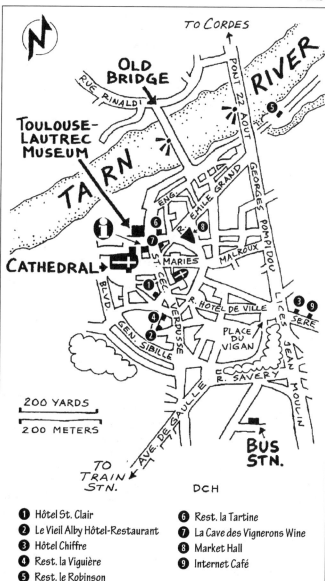

1. Hôtel St. Clair
2. Le Vieil Alby Hôtel-Restaurant
3. Hôtel Chiffre
4. Rest. la Viguière
5. Rest. le Robinson
6. Rest. la Tartine
7. La Cave des Vignerons Wine
8. Market Hall
9. Internet Café

Near Albi

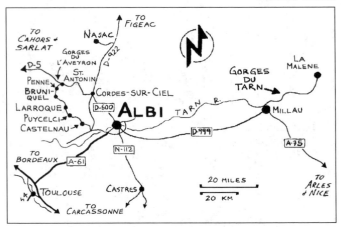

City Views—For great views of Albi and the Tarn River, walk or drive past the cathedral down to either of these bridges: the pont Vieux or the newer and higher pont 22 Août 1944.

La Cave des Vignerons (Confidences du Terroir)—This wine cave presents regional wines in an appealing setting (Mon–Sat 10:00–13:00 & 14:00–19:00, closed Sun, across from cathedral, 1 place Ste-Cécile, where rue des Fargues meets the square, tel. 05 63 54 05 78).

Near Albi

▲**Route of the Bastides**—The hilly terrain north of Albi was tailor-made for medieval villages to organize around for defensive purposes. Here, hundreds of fortified villages *(bastides)* spill over hill-tops, above rivers, and between wheat fields and forests, creating a worthwhile detour for drivers. *Bastides* were the medieval product of community efforts organized by local religious or military leaders. Most were built during the Hundred Years' War (see sidebar on page 183) in an effort to establish a foothold for French or British rule in this hotly contested region. Unlike other French hill towns, *bastides* were not the product of a safe haven provided by a castle. They were a premeditated effort by a community to collectively construct houses as a planned defensive unit, *sans* castle. They were usually designed with grid streets around a single central square.

Connect these *bastides* as a day trip from Albi, or as you drive between Albi and the Dordogne. From Albi, cross the pont 22 Août 1944 bridge and follow signs to Cordes-sur-Ciel (allow 30 min). The view of Cordes as you approach is memorable, but that's as close as I'd get (see below). From Cordes, follow signs to St. Antonin Noble-Val, an appealing, flat "hill town" on the river, with few tourists. Then pass vertical little Penne, Bruniquel (my favorite *bastide*, signed from St. Antonin-Noble-Val), Larroque, Puycelci, and finally, Castelnau-de-Montmiral (with a fine main square), before returning to Albi. Each of these places is worth exploring if you have the time. If continuing north to the Dordogne, leave Albi on N-88 to Gaillac, then follow D-964 to Castelnau-de-Montmiral and on to Bruniquel. Then either head directly to Caussade and Cahors, or continue scenically north on D-115 to St. Antonin Noble-Val through the Gorges de l'Aveyron. From St. Antonin, follow D-5 and D-926 to Caussade, then take N-20 to Cahors.

Cordes-sur-Ciel—It's hard to resist this brilliantly situated hill town just 15 miles north of Albi, but I would. Enjoy the fantastic view on the road from Albi, but go no closer. Cordes, once an important Cathar base, has slipped over the boutique-filled edge to the point where it's hard to find the medieval town, and it's jammed on weekends and in the summer. It's a brutal, 30-minute walk up to the town from the lower parking spots (blue-lined spaces are free for the first hour, then €1 buys 2 hours; parking lot costs €2.50). If you must go, take the frequent *navette* shuttle bus (round-trip-€2, 4/hr, buy ticket at parking meter or from driver, departs from place Jeanne Ramel-Cals, next to lower TI). Trains get you as far as Cordes-Vindrac, where a taxi-bus will shuttle you three miles to Cordes (Mon–Sat-€5, Sun-€8, tel. 05 63 56 14 80).

Cordes has two **TI**s, one at the base of the hill town and another in the center (daily 10:30–12:30 & 14:00–18:00, no midday closing in summer, tel. 05 63 56 00 52). The rustic **Hostellerie de Vieux Cordes***** at the top is the only reason to come here. Rooms are cozy and a good value, and several have valley views (standard Db-€48–58, bigger Db-€70, fine restaurant, 21 rue St. Michel, tel. 05 63 53 79 20, fax 05 63 56 02 47, vieux.cordes@thuries.fr).

Gorges du Tarn—Adventure-lovers can canoe, hike, or drive the stunning Tarn River gorge by heading east from Albi to Millau, then following the gorge all the way to St. Enimie. Roads are slow but spectacular.

The best base for canoeing is from tiny La Malène (25 miles northeast of Millau). In La Malène, **Company Canoë 2000** rents what you need to run the mellow river (down the path to the right of bridge, tel. 04 66 48 57 71); the seven- or 11-kilometer trips have the best views. Take your lunch and picnic along the way. If you don't want to canoe but still want the unbeatable views from the river, take a Batelier boat (leaves from bridge, seats 5–6 people, ask for a boatman who speaks a leetle English).

Sleeping in La Malène: Stay at the simple but comfortable **Auberge de l'Emarcadère** (Db-€46, Tb-€52, tel. 04 66 48 51 03, fax 04 66 48 58 94) or in the country-luxurious **Manoir de Montesquiou,** run entirely by one family: Dad runs the hotel, Mom is the head chef, the three sisters serve your meals, and son-in-law Greg runs the bar

(Db-€68–106, suites fit for a queen-€131–139, extra bed-€16, you'll be expected to dine at its great restaurant-€28, tel. 04 66 48 51 12, fax 04 66 48 50 47, www.manoir-montesquiou.com).

SLEEPING

Here are three good choices in Albi.

$$ Hôtel Chiffre* is a safe bet with minimal personality but all the comforts, including an elevator and air-conditioning (Db-€80, near place du Vigan at 50 rue Séré-de-Rivières, tel. 06 63 48 58 48, fax 05 63 47 20 61, www.hotelchiffre.com).

$ Hôtel St. Clair, as central as you can get, has a small, flowered courtyard and rooms split between two buildings. The four bright, modern, and air-conditioned rooms in the annex are comfortable; the 11 *très* traditional rooms in the main building are cheap but need upgrading. It's run by the animated, English-speaking Michèle, who offers a wealth of information and opinions (Db-€42–60, Tb-€55–65; 3 parking spaces-€8/day, must reserve in advance; hotel is 2 blocks from cathedral in pedestrian zone at 8 rue St. Clair, tel. 05 63 54 25 66, fax 05 63 47 27 58, http://andrieu .michele.free.fr, micheleandrieu@hotmail.com).

$ Le Vieil Alby Hôtel-Restaurant, in the heart of Albi's pedestrian area, has modern, well-maintained, and non-smoking rooms, and is run by helpful, English-speaking Monsieur Sicard (Sb/Db-€45–60, Tb-€50–65, copious breakfast-€7, garage-€7/day, 25 rue Toulouse-Lautrec, tel. 05 63 54 14 69, fax 05 63 54 96 75).

EATING

Albi is filled with reasonable restaurants that serve a rich local cuisine, but be careful of the popular organ-meat dishes like *tripes* (cow intestines), *andouillette* (sausages made from pig intestines), *fois de veau* (calf liver), and *tête de veau* (calf's head). Choose a restaurant or select from one of the many cafés on the lively place du Vigan. For a more traditional restaurant experience, find rue Toulouse-Lautrec (2 blocks from Hôtel St. Clair).

La Viguière is the place to go for a fine meal, served in an elegant interior or on a pleasant courtyard. The cuisine is classic French with a dash of local specialties thrown in (*menus*-€16–39, 7 rue Toulouse-Lautrec, tel. 05 63 54 76 44).

Le Vieil Alby Hôtel-Restaurant, with dull decor, is a solid value with a focus on local cuisine (*menus*-€16–25, closed Sun, 25 rue Toulouse-Lautrec).

Le Robinson provides a fun experience but not necessarily the best food. From the point where lices Georges Pompidou (*lices* refers to the no-man's land along a wall) meets the river, take the path that

Sleep Code

(€1 = about $1.20, country code: 33)
S = Single, **D** = Double/Twin, **T** = Triple, **Q** = Quad,
b = bathroom, **s** = shower only, **no CC** = Credit Cards not
accepted, **SE** = Speaks English, **NSE** = No English, * = French
hotel rating system (0–4 stars). You can assume a hotel takes
credit cards unless you see "no CC" in the listing.

To help you sort easily through these listings, I've divided
the rooms into three categories based on the price for a standard
double room with bath:

$$$ **Higher Priced**—Most rooms €90 or more.
  $$ **Moderately Priced**—Most rooms between €60–90.
   $ **Lower Priced**—Most rooms €60 or less.

leads down to this vine-strewn haven (*menus*-€17–31, open April–
Oct, closed Mon, 142 rue Edouard Branly, tel. 05 63 46 15 69).

La Tartine restaurant-bar, across from the TI, offers salads and
various plates for €7.50, *menus* at €12 and €23, and a large terrace
(daily, tel. 05 63 54 50 60).

TRANSPORTATION CONNECTIONS

You'll connect to just about any destination through Toulouse.

From Albi by train to: Toulouse (11/day, 70 min), **Carcassonne**
(9/day, 2.5 hrs, change in Toulouse), **Sarlat** (2/day in 4.5 hrs with
changes in Toulouse, Agen, and Le Buisson; or 3/day in 6–7 hrs via
Souillac with changes possible in Brive-la-Gaillarde and Toulouse,
then bus from Souillac), **Paris** (7/day, 6–7.5 hrs, change in Toulouse,
then TGV night train).

Carcassonne

Medieval Carcassonne is a 13th-century world of towers, turrets, and
cobblestone alleys. It's Europe's ultimate walled fortress city—
packed with too many tourists. At 10:00, the salespeople stand at
the doors of their main-street shops, their gauntlet of tacky temptations poised and ready for their daily ration of customers. But early,
late, or off-season, a quieter Carcassonne is an evocative playground
for any medievalist. Forget midday...spend the night.

Locals like to believe that Carcassonne got its name this way:
1,200 years ago, Charlemagne and his troops besieged this fortress-
town (then called La Cité) for several years. A cunning townsperson

named Madame Carcas saved the town. Just as food was running out, she fed the last bits of grain to the last pig and tossed him over the wall. Splat. Charlemagne's bored and frustrated forces, amazed that the town still had enough food to throw fat party pigs over the wall, decided they would never succeed in starving the people out. They ended the siege, and the city was saved. Madame Carcas *sonne*-d (sounded) the long-awaited victory bells, and La Cité had a new name: Carcas-sonne. Historians, however, suspect that Carcassonne is a Frenchified version of the town's original name (Carcas).

As a teenager on my first visit to Carcassonne, I wrote this in my journal: "Before me lies Carcassonne, the perfect medieval city. Like a fish that everyone thought was extinct, somehow Europe's greatest Romanesque fortress city has survived the centuries. I was supposed to be gone yesterday, but here I sit imprisoned by choice—curled in a cranny on top of the wall. The wind blows away the sounds of today, and my imagination 'medievals' me. The moat is one foot over and 100 feet down. Small plants and moss upholster my throne." Let this place make you a kid on a rampart.

ORIENTATION

Contemporary Carcassonne is neatly divided into two cities: The magnificent La Cité (fortified old city, with 200 full-time residents taking care of lots more tourists) and the lively Ville Basse (modern lower city). Two bridges connect the two parts, the busy pont Neuf and the traffic-free pont Vieux, both with great views.

Tourist Information: Carcassonne has two handy TIs: a kiosk office across from the train station, and a more complete office in La Cité. The **La Cité TI** is just to your right as you enter the main gate, called porte Narbonnaise (April–Oct daily 9:00–18:00, until 19:00 July–Sept, until 17:00 Nov–March). The tower opposite this TI has information on walking tours of the walls, a good book selection, and a fine wood model of La Cité (notice that no house rises above the fortified walls). Pick up the map of La Cité and the one-page history in English, and ask about festivals. The **train station TI** is across the canal from the station in the round kiosk (daily April–Oct 14:00–18:00, July–Aug 9:00–18:00, closed Nov–March).

Carcassonne Overview

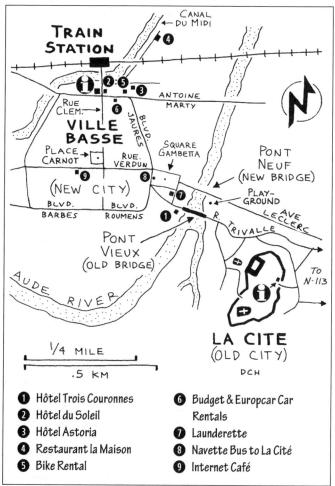

- **1** Hôtel Trois Couronnes
- **2** Hôtel du Soleil
- **3** Hôtel Astoria
- **4** Restaurant la Maison
- **5** Bike Rental
- **6** Budget & Europcar Car Rentals
- **7** Launderette
- **8** Navette Bus to La Cité
- **9** Internet Café

Arrival in Carcassonne

By Train: There is no baggage check in Carcassonne. The train station is located in the Ville Basse, a 30-minute walk from La Cité. You have three choices for reaching La Cité: taxi, walk to the shuttle bus stop, or walk the whole way. Taxis charge €7 for the short but worthwhile trip to La Cité (taxi stand is 1 block across canal in front of station). A *navette* shuttle bus whisks you from square Gambetta to La Cité, though it requires a 15-minute walk from the station (€1, 4/hr, mid-June–mid-Oct daily 9:30–19:30, ticket good for round-trip, so hang onto it). In the off-season, catch bus #2 from the same stop (€1 one-way, 2/hr). If you wonder why the *navette* can't pick up closer to the station, ask a taxi driver. As long as you're not in a hurry, the 15-minute walk to the shuttle stop is pleasant, crossing Carcassonne's appealing lower city via traffic-free streets and passing the lively place Carnot (good cafés, busy market on Tue, Thu, and Sat). Walk straight out of the station, cross the canal and busy road and keep straight on rue Clemenceau for about seven blocks. Turn left just after place Carnot on rue de Verdun, walk three blocks and turn right on the big square Gambetta. The stop is just to the right; look for signs for *La Navette*.

If you're walking all the way to La Cité, continue across the square, turn right at Hôtel Ibis, then left across pont Vieux, following *La Cité* signs up rue Trivalle to rue Nadaud.

By Car: Use the *Carcassonne Est* exit from the autoroute, then carefully follow signs to *La Cité*. You'll come to a large parking lot (€3.70/24 hrs) and a drawbridge (Narbonne Gate, or porte Narbonnaise) at the walled city's entrance. If staying inside the walls, show your reservation (verbal assurances won't do) and park free in the outside lot, then drive into the city after 18:00. Theft is common—leave nothing in your car at night.

Helpful Hints

Market Days: The lovely place Carnot in Ville Basse hosts a non-touristy open market Tuesday, Thursday, and Saturday mornings. The *navette* shuttle bus (described above) works well for this trip.

Internet Access: Most hotels in La Cité have Internet access; you'll also find several places in the Ville Basse (try **Alerte Rouge,** 73 rue de Verdun, tel. 04 68 25 20 39).

Laundry: Try **Laverie Express** (daily 8:00–22:00, 5 square Gambetta, from La Cité, cross pont Vieux and turn right, it's at Hôtel Ibis).

Bike Rental: Espace 11 is about three blocks from the train station (Tue–Sat 9:00–12:00 & 14:00–19:00, closed Sun–Mon, cross canal, turn left, then turn right at first street, and find the little gas pump at 3 route Minervoise, tel. 04 68 25 28 18). Canalfront rides are a fun and level way to spin your wheels. The friendly owner can suggest good destinations.

Car Rental: Avis is at the station (tel. 04 68 25 05 84). **Hertz, Budget**, and **Europcar** are two blocks straight out of the station, on boulevard Omer Sarraut (Europcar is at #5, tel. 04 68 25 25 09).

Taxi: Call 04 68 71 50 50 or 04 68 71 36 36.

Chauffeur Guide: Lydia Bercial, a licensed local guide with a comfy new van, does private city and countryside tours. She speaks excellent English and teaches with a good mix of expertise, charm, and enthusiasm. Given the difficulty of exploring the region by public transportation and gaining an understanding of Cathar country

Carcassonne's La Cité

100 YARDS

100 METERS

DCH

••• MEDIEVAL
WALL WALK

❶ Hôtel de la Cité & Barbican Rest.

❷ Hôtels le Donjon & des Remparts

❸ Chambres le Grand Puits

❹ Youth Hostel

❺ Hôtel Montmorency

❻ To Hôtel Mercure

❼ Hôtel Espace Cité

❽ Restaurant la Comte Roger

❾ Restaurant le Jardin
   de la Tour

❿ Restaurant l'Auberge
   des Lices

⓫ Rest. l'Auberge
   du Grand Puits

⓬ Le Bar à Vins Café
   & Jazz Bar

⓭ Cellier des Vignerons
   Wine Bar

and its dramatic castles, Lydia's services can be a real boon (1-hour city walk: €15/person, €45 for 3–7; half-day bus tours: €40/person, €100 for 3–7; all-day bus tours: €60/person, €150 for 3–7; tel. 04 68 47 03 65, l.bercial@libertysurf.fr).

Introductory Walking Tour:
The Medieval Walls and La Cité

While the tourists shuffle up the main street, this walk, rated ▲▲▲, introduces you to the city with history and wonder, rather than tour groups and plastic swords. We'll sneak into the town on the other side of the wall...through the back door.

Start outside La Cité's main gate, Narbonne Gate (porte Narbonnaise). You're welcomed by a contemporary-looking bust of Madame Carcas—which is actually modeled after a 16th-century original of the town's legendary first lady (for her story, see page 346). Then cross the bridge to...

Narbonne Gate: Pause on the drawbridge and survey this immense fortification. When forces from northern France finally conquered Carcassonne, it was a strategic prize. Not taking any chances, they evicted the residents, whom they allowed to settle in the lower town (Ville Basse)—as long as they stayed across the river. (While called "new," this lower town actually dates from the 13th century.) La Cité remained a French military garrison until the 18th century.

The drawbridge was made crooked to slow any attackers' rush to the main gate. (It's just as effective today with tourists.) After crossing the drawbridge, lose the crowds and follow the cobbled path to the left and uphill between the walls *(les lices)*. The only reason to continue straight is to visit the TI—just inside the next gate to the right, with fine Gothic vaulting and a medieval cistern. At the first short set of stairs, climb to the outer-wall walkway and find a seat.

Wall View: These massive walls—nearly two miles around, with 52 towers—defended an important site near the intersection of the north–south, east–west trade routes. People have occupied this spot since Neolithic times. The Romans built Carcassonne's first wall, upon which the bigger medieval wall was constructed. Identify the ancient Roman bits by finding the smaller rocks mixed with narrow stripes of red bricks (and no arrow slits). The outer wall was not built until the 1300s.

Look over the wall and down at the moat below. Like most medieval moats, it was never filled with water (or even alligators). A ditch like this—which was originally even deeper—effectively stopped attacking forces from rolling up against the wall in their mobile towers and spilling into the city. Another enemy tactic was to "undermine" (tunnel underneath) the wall, causing a section to cave in. Notice the small, square holes along the ramparts. Wooden extensions of the ramparts (which we'll see later at the castle) once plugged into these holes, so that townsfolk could drop nasty things on anyone tunneling in. In peacetime, the area between the two walls was used for medieval tournaments, jousting practice, and markets.

During La Cité's golden age, the 1100s, independent rulers with open minds allowed Jews and Cathars to live and prosper within the walls, while troubadours wrote poems of ideal love. This liberal attitude made for a rich intellectual life, but also proved to be La Cité's downfall. The Crusades aimed to rid France of the dangerous Cathar movement, which led to Carcassonne's defeat and eventual incorporation into the kingdom of France

The walls of this majestic fortress were partially reconstructed in 1855 as part of a program to restore France's important monuments. The tidy crenellations and the pointy tower roofs are generally 19th-century. As you continue your wall walk to higher elevations, the lack of guardrails becomes apparent. This would never happen in the United States; in France, if you fall, it's your own darn fault (so be careful). Also, notice the lights embedded in the walls. This fortress, like most important French monuments, is beautifully illuminated every night, despite the significant cost of electricity (for directions to a good nighttime view, see "Sights— Walk to Pont Vieux," page 353).

Keep working your way around the walls, and finish with the five Roman towers just before you return to the starting point. Walking the entire circle between the inner and outer gate is a delightful 20-minute stroll, but for this tour, we'll enter La Cité at the first entrance possible, the...

Inner Wall Gate: The wall has the same four gates it had in Roman times. Before entering, notice the squat tower on the outer wall—this was a "barbican" (placed opposite each inner gate for extra protection). Barbicans were always semicircular—open on the inside to expose anyone who breached the outer defenses. Invading today is far easier than in the good old days. As you leave the square gate room to finally enter the town, look up, and you'll see various slots and holes used for dumping things on intruders, a slot for the portcullis (the big iron grate), the frame for a heavy wooden door, and more of the same.

Once safely inside, look back up at the inner wall tower. If it's open, climb it. It's the only section of the inner wall you can climb without a tour, and the tower-top bookstore is good.

St. Nazaire Church (Basilique St. Nazaire): This was a cathedral until the 18th century, when the bishop moved to the lower town. Today, due to the depopulation of the basically-dead-except-for-tourism Cité, it's not even a functioning parish church. Notice the Romanesque arches of the nave and the delicately vaulted Gothic arches over the altar and transepts. After its successful conquest of this region in the 13th-century Albigensian crusades, France set out to destroy all the Romanesque churches and replace them with Gothic ones—symbolically asserting its northern rule with this more northern style of church. With the start of the Hundred Years' War in 1317, the expensive demolition was abandoned. Today, the Romanesque remainder survives, and the destroyed section has been rebuilt Gothic, which makes it one of the best examples of Gothic architecture in southern France. When the lights are off (as they often are), the interior, lit only by candles and 14th-century stained glass, is evocatively medieval (daily 9:00–11:45 & 13:45–18:00).

Hôtel de la Cité: Located across from St. Nazaire, this posh hotel sits where the Bishop's Palace did 700 years ago. Today, it's a worthwhile detour to see how the privileged few travel. You're free to wander, so find the library-cozy bar and consider a pricey post-dinner drink. Then find the rear garden, and turn right for super wall views that you can't see from anywhere else.

From here, follow the main road (rue St. Louis) several blocks past the post office to a castle-view terrace on your left.

Château Comtal: Carcassonne's third layer of defense, while originally built in 1125, was completely redesigned in later reconstructions. From this fine viewpoint, you can see the wooden rampart extensions that once encircled the entire city wall. (Notice the empty peg holes to the left of the bridge.) When *Robin Hood: Prince of Thieves,* starring Kevin Costner, was filmed here in 1990, the entire city was turned into a film set. Locals enjoyed playing bit parts and seeing their château labeled "Nottingham Castle" in the fanciful film.

The castle is open to the public and offers an exhibit on the reconstruction, a modest museum, and a guided walk (generally in French, with an English-language flier for translation) that gives you a 30-minute romp on the inner wall and up a tower—but no more info than you already have (€6.20, April–Sept daily 9:30–18:30, Oct–March daily 9:30–17:00).

Place du Château: This busy little square, 50 yards away, opposite the entrance to the castle, sports a modest statue remembering the man who saved the city from deterioration and neglect in the 19th century. The bronze model circling the base of the statue shows Carcassonne's walls as they looked before the 1855 reconstruction by Eugène Viollet-le-Duc. Just uphill is the town's lively restaurant square (place Marcou), and straight down the tiny main drag is the Narbonne Gate, where you began this walk.

SIGHTS

▲▲▲**Night Wall Walk**—Save post-dinner energy for a don't-miss walk around the same walls you visited today. The effect at night is mesmerizing. With a little imagination, the embedded lights become torches and unfamiliar voices the enemy. Combine this with a walk to pont Vieux (see below) and you can do no better. The best route is a partial circumnavigation clockwise between the walls. Start at the Narbonne Gate, following my "Introductory Walking Tour: The Medieval Walls and La Cité" (above), and continue until the Inner Gate. Don't enter the through the Inner Gate, but continue your walk between the walls around La Cité. You'll soon come to a ramp leading down after passing through a straight passage behind Château Comtal; look for a hard left at the bottom of a cobbled decline just where the path rises back up. This ramp leads down to rue de la Barbacanne, where you'll turn right to reach the pont Vieux. Return from the pont Vieux by reversing the directions given below.

▲▲▲**Walk to Pont Vieux**—For a brilliant view up to the floodlit walls of Carcassonne, hike 10 minutes down to the traffic-free "old bridge," the pont Vieux (of course, that means it's 20 min back up). As you exit the Narbonne Gate, go left down the ramp, join rue Nadaud, turn left at the bottom, pass Hôtel du Pont Vieux, and you're there.

Consider a return attack through La Cité's back door (the path is shorter but steeper than the route you took down): From the pont Vieux, walk right on rue de la Barbacanne past the hideous neon discothèque, take the second left past a small church, and join the path.

▲**Summer Festivals**—Carcassonne becomes colorfully medieval during many special events each July and August. Highlights are the *spectacle équestre* (jousting matches) and July 14 (Bastille Day) fireworks. The TI has details.

Cellier des Vignerons—Duck into this snappy wine bar to pick up the free "Great Wines which Express the Languedoc" pamphlet and to sample a good selection of local wines. Christiane—who represents the small vintners of the Languedoc—generally has at least three local wines open for tasting (€5, free if you buy). Prices are reasonable, and you'll need something to drink on the ramparts tonight (loose hours, usually until 19:00, often until 24:00 in summer, 13 rue du Grand Puits, tel. 06 07 13 26 41). If it's hot, linger at the end of her counter in the full blast of the air-conditioner.

Canal du Midi—Completed in 1681, this sleepy, 155-mile canal connects France's Mediterranean and Atlantic coasts. The canal runs right in front of the train station in Carcassonne. Before railways, Canal du Midi was jammed with commercial traffic. Today, it's busy with pleasure craft. Look for the slow-moving hotel barges strewn with tanned and well-fed vacationers. The TI has information on half-day cruises from Carcassonne. Consider a relaxed bike ride along biking along the canal's level towpath (for bike rental, see "Helpful Hints," above, or ask at TI).

SLEEPING

(€1 = about $1.20, country code: 33)

In Carcassonne's La Cité

Sleep in or near the old walls. In the summer, when La Cité is jammed with tourists, consider sleeping in quieter Caunes-Minervois (see "Near Carcassonne," page 356). Two hotels, a B&B, and a hostel offer rooms inside the walls. See Hôtel du Soleil and Hôtel Astoria for lodgings near the train station. Top prices listed are for July and August, when the place is packed. At other times of year, prices drop and there are generally plenty of rooms. Breakfast is typically not included.

$$$ **Hôtel de la Cité****** offers 61 rooms with deluxe everything, wrapped in an old stone building next to St. Nazaire Church. Peaceful gardens, a swimming pool, sumptuous public spaces, an elegant restaurant (€60–75 *menus*), and reliable luxury are yours—for a price (Db-€315–415, suites-€440–650, extra adult-€55, 20 percent winter discount, air-con, garage-€15/day, place de l'Église, tel. 04 68 71 98 71, fax 04 68 71 50 15, www.hoteldelacite.orient-express .com, reservations@hoteldelacite.com).

$$$ **Hôtel le Donjon*****, a Best Western, offers 62 tight but well-appointed rooms, a busy but mood-setting lobby, and a great location inside the walls (Ds-€80–95, bigger Db-€106–150, Tb-€95–113, bigger Tb-€125–165, breakfast buffet-€10, private parking-€10, air-con, elevator, 2 rue Comte Roger, tel. 04 68 11 23 00, fax 04 68 25 06 60, www.hotel-donjon.fr, hotel.donjon.best.western-donjon @wanadoo.fr). I prefer their independent annex—**Hôtel des Remparts**—because the rooms are a bit bigger, the prices are the same, it's quieter, and parking is easier, though it has no elevator (only 2 floors) and no breakfast room (have breakfast at Hôtel le Donjon).

$ **Chambres le Grand Puits**, across from Hôtel des Remparts, is a splendid value, with one cute double room and two cavernous apartment-like rooms that could sleep five, with kitchenette, private terrace, and nice personal touches. Inquire in the small boutique, and say *bonjour* to happy-go-lucky Madame Cordonnier (Sb-€37–44, Db-€44–54, Tb-€54–59, Qb-€58–69, includes self-serve breakfast, no CC, 8 place du Grand Puits, tel. & fax 04 68 25 16 67, http ://legrandpuits.free.fr).

$ The **Auberge de Jeunesse** (youth hostel) is big, clean, and well-run, with an outdoor garden courtyard, self-service kitchen, TV room, bar, washer/dryer, Internet station, and a welcoming ambience. If you ever wanted to bunk down in a hostel, do it here—all ages are welcome. Only summer is tight; reserve ahead. Non-members pay €3 extra (dorm bed-€16, 4–6 in a room, includes sheets and breakfast, open all day, rue du Vicomte

Trencavel, tel. 04 68 25 23 16, fax 04 68 71 14 84, www.fuaj.org or www.hostelbooking.com, carcassonne@fuaj.org).

Near La Cité

$$$ Hôtel des Trois Couronnes*** offers 40 terrific rooms with a view of La Cité, wrapped in an unappealing concrete shell. It's well-located: just across pont Vieux, with a grassy parkway in front, 15 minutes on foot from La Cité and the station. Stay here only if you can get a view room (Sb with view-€82, Db with view-€98, parking garage-€8, elevator, air-con, 2 rue des Trois Couronnes, tel. 04 68 25 36 10, fax 04 68 25 92 92, www.hotel-destroiscouronnes.com, hotel3couronnes@wanadoo.fr).

$$ At Hôtel Montmorency**, Cécile, Stephane, and dog Opus are perfect hosts and offer the best value in Carcassonne, with comfortable rooms knocking at the door of La Cité's drawbridge. Gaze at the city walls from the stylish swimming pool (heated all year), whirlpool tub, or terrace tables. While the main building has 15 old, basic rooms (cheaper, no air-con), the 20 rooms in the annex building are sharp, with warm colors, firm beds, and air-conditioning (Db annex-€62 with shower, €70 with bath, Tb-€84, small Db main building-€46, big Db main building-€70, Tb-€70; swanky new 4-star rooms by the pool with private terraces, vaulted ceilings and the works-€180; family deals, free Internet access, disabled-access room, free parking, 2 rue Camille Saint-Saëns, tel. 04 68 11 96 70, fax 04 68 11 96 79, www.lemontmorency.com, le.montmorency@wanadoo.fr).

Decent Last Resorts near La Cité

$$$ Hôtel Mercure**,** which hides behind the parking lots and Hôtel Montmorency, is a five-minute walk to La Cité. It has 61 snug but comfy, air-conditioned rooms, a refreshing garden, a good-sized pool, big elevators, a bar-lounge, and a restaurant. A few rooms have views of La Cité (small Db-€94, moderate Db-€97, big Db-€155, Tb-€170, free parking, 18 rue Camille Saint-Saëns, tel. 04 68 11 92 82, fax 04 68 71 11 45, h1622@accor-hotels.com).

$$ Hôtel Espace Cité**, two blocks downhill from Hôtel Montmorency, is sterile and shiny, with small rooms, but it's handy for drivers (Db-€62, Tb-€75, air-con, 132 rue Trivalle, tel. 04 68 25 24 24, fax 04 68 25 17 17, www.hotelespacecite.fr, infos @hotelespacecite.fr).

At the Train Station

$$ Hôtel du Soleil***, just across from the train station, is turn-of-the-century grand, and worth ducking inside for its lobby alone. The rooms are roomy and comfortable, with high ceilings (standard Db-€80–144, superior Db-€98–180, includes breakfast, elevator, 2 avenue Maréchal Joffre, tel. 04 68 25 25 00, fax 04 68 72 53 09).

$ **Hôtel Astoria*** offers the cheapest hotel beds that I list. From the train station, walk across the canal, turn left, and go two blocks. The tiled rooms are basic, modern, clean, and perfectly sleepable, and the owners are helpful. Call ahead—it's popular (D-€23, Ds-€28, Db-€37–44, 18 rue Tourtel, tel. 04 68 25 31 38, fax 04 68 71 34 14, hotel-astoria@wanadoo.fr).

Near Carcassonne

To experience unspoiled, tranquil Languedoc, sleep surrounded by vineyards a 25-minute drive from Carcassonne, in the unspoiled village of Caunes-Minervois. Comfortably nestled in the foothills of the Montagne Noire, Caunes-Minervois offers an 8th-century abbey (complete with Internet access), two cafés, a good pizzeria, a few wineries, and very few tourists. Two of my hotel recommendations sit side by side in the heart of the village, and their owners are eager to help you explore their region. To sleep in the country, but closer to Carcassonne, consider La Ferme de la Sauzette, just five minutes south of La Cité on D-142.

$ At **L'Ancienne Boulangerie**, Americans Terry and Lois Link take good care of you. The rooms are thoughtfully designed, the beds are tops, and the breakfast terrace will slow your pulse. Ask about Terry's guidebook, *Adapter Kit: France—A Traveler's Tools for Living Like a Local* (S-€25, Sb-€40, D-€40, Db-€60, lofty family room-€60 per couple, €10 per child, includes breakfast, rue St. Genes, tel. 04 68 78 01 32, ancienneboulangerie@free.fr). They also offer weekly rentals of four countryside apartments with pool (€360–590/week, price varies by size and season).

$ **Hôtel d'Alibert****, a wonderfully Old-World place with traditionally French rooms, is run by Frédéric with relaxed panache (large Db-€48–63, extra person-€10, place de la Mairie, tel. 04 68 78 00 54, frederic.dalibert@wanadoo.fr). Don't skip a meal in his terrific restaurant (closed Sun–Mon).

$$ At **La Ferme de la Sauzette,** British Diana and Chris warmly welcome travelers in their cottage-like farmhouse with five antiqued rooms and the possibility of a home-cooked dinner (Sb-€55–66, Db-€62–73, Tb-€81, 2-night min June–Sept, dinner with wine-€28, no CC; take D-42, then D-142 south from Carcassonne for 3 miles to Cazilhac, Sauzette is on the left, 2 miles from Cazilhac town hall—*mairie*—along D-56 in direction of Villefloure; tel. 04 68 79 81 32, fax 04 68 79 65 99, www.lasauzette.com, info@lasauzette.com).

EATING

In La Cité

Skip the touristy joints that line the main drag. For a better (though still touristy) alternative, take your pick from a food circus of eateries on a leafy courtyard—often with strolling musicians in the summer—on lively place Marcou (just inside the front gate and up to the left).

Hôtel de la Cité's **Barbican Restaurant** owns Carcassonne's only Michelin star (€60–75 meals, see "Hotel de la Cité" on page 354). While cassoulet is the traditional must, gourmet salads provide a light yet rich alternative.

La Comte Roger's quiet elegance seems out of place in this raucous, overrun town. For half the price of the Barbican, you can celebrate a special occasion memorably. Ask for a table on the peaceful courtyard, and book ahead (€29–39 *menus*, closed Sun–Mon, 14 rue St. Louis, tel. 04 68 11 93 40).

Le Jardin de la Tour is a good bet for reliable cuisine and friendly service at midrange prices. The tranquil rear garden tables look up to the château, while in the summer, a tent covers the bustling front-door tapas terrace. The interior rooms are always ramshackle medieval plush, and English-speaking Elody somehow oversees it all (basic *menu*-€20, €28 for traditional extravaganza, hearty €15 cassoulet will stuff you, daily in summer, closed off-season Sun–Mon, hidden entrance next to L'Écu d'Or restaurant, 11 rue Porte d'Aude, tel. 04 68 25 71 24).

L'Auberge des Lices, hidden down a small lane, relies on local business and honest service to survive. It has a pretty interior and a pleasant outdoor courtyard (*menus*-€16 and €23, closed Wed, 3 rue R. Trencavel, tel. 04 68 72 34 07).

At inexpensive **L'Auberge du Grand Puits,** you'll sit in a flimsy chair to eat a copious meal served by a lighthearted staff (many choices, their €14 *menu* would fill two, open daily, great music, 1 place des Grands Puits, tel. 04 68 71 27 88, cool Jerome SE).

Le Bar à Vins is tucked away in a leafy garden just inside the wall, but away from the crowds. It serves an enticing selection of open wines and €10 tapas—open-faced sandwiches, along with a meal-sized variety plate of ham, cheese, fish, and *chorizo* (€2 per glass of wine, mid-June–mid-Sept daily 10:00–24:00, closes earlier off-season, 6 rue du Plô, tel. 04 68 47 38 38).

Picnics can be gathered at the small *magasin d'alimentation* (grocery) on the main drag (generally open until 19:30). For your beggar's banquet, picnic on the city walls. For fast, cheap, hot food, look for places on the main drag that have quiche and pizza to go.

In the lower city, the canalfront **La Maison** is *the* place to go. Mouthwatering cuisine like grandma made, a funky decor, and friendly owners await (*menus* from €22, closed Sun–Mon; leaving the train station, cross the canal, turn left and follow the canal 5 min on foot to 48 route Minervoise; tel. 04 68 72 52 20).

NIGHTLIFE

For relief from all the medieval kitsch, you can savor a drink in four-star country club ambience at the **Hôtel de la Cité** bar (€7 for a glass of wine or beer). To enjoy the liveliest square with lots of tourists and strolling musicians, sip a drink or nibble a dessert on place Marcou. To be a medieval poet, share a bottle of wine in your own private niche, somewhere remote on the ramparts. **Cellier des Vignerons** is sometimes open later (see "Sights," page 353). And **Le Bar à Vins** offers jazz, good wines by the glass (€2), and a young crowd enjoying a garden in the moonshadow of the wall...without any tourists (described above, daily, 6 rue du Plô, tel. 04 68 47 38 38).

TRANSPORTATION CONNECTIONS

From Carcassonne by train to: Sarlat (2/day in 4.5 hrs, with changes in Toulouse, Agen, and Le Buisson; or 3/day in 6–7 hrs via Souillac, with changes possible in Brive-la-Gaillarde and Toulouse, then bus from Souillac), **Arles** (6/day, 3 hrs, 3 require changes in Narbonne and Nîmes or Avignon), **Nice** (6/day, 6–9 hrs, fastest via change in Marseille), **Paris**' Gare Montparnasse (8/day, a few direct in 10 hrs or in 6.5 hrs by TGV, with changes in Toulouse and possibly Bordeaux), **Toulouse** (hrly, 1 hr), **Barcelona** (3/day, 5 hrs, change in Narbonne and Port Bou, the border town).

SIGHTS NEAR CARCASSONNE

The land around Carcassonne is littered with romantically ruined castles, lost abbeys, and photogenic hill towns. The ruined castles of Peyrepertuse and Quéribus make good stops between Carcassonne and Collioure (allow 2 hours from Carcassonne on narrow, winding roads). The Abbey of Fontfroide and gorge-village of Minerve work well for Provence-bound travelers. While public transportation is hopeless, taxis capable of seating six cost €150–200 for a day-long excursion (taxi tel. 04 68 71 50 50). Even better, contact local guide Lydia Bercial, who runs private minivan tours at reasonable rates (see page 348, tel. 04 68 47 03 65, l.bercial@libertysurf.fr).

▲▲▲**Châteaux of Hautes Corbières**—Two hours south of Carcassonne, in the scenic foothills of the Pyrénées, lies a series of surreal, mountain-capping castle ruins. Like a Maginot Line of the 13th century, these sky-high castles were strategically located between France and the Spanish kingdom of Roussillon. As you can see by flipping through the picture books in Carcassonne tourist shops, these castles' crumbled ruins are an impressive contrast to the restored walls of La Cité. Bring a good map (lots of tiny roads) and sturdy

Carcassone Area

walking shoes—prepare for a climb, and be wary of slick stones.

The most spectacular is the château of **Peyrepertuse**. The ruins seem to grow right out from the narrow splinter of cliff. The views are so sensational, you feel you can reach out and touch Spain. Let your imagination soar, but watch your step as you try to reconstruct this eagle's nest (€4, April–Oct daily 9:00–19:00, until 20:30 June–Sept, Nov–March daily 10:00–17:00, tel. 04 68 45 40 55). Canyon-lovers will enjoy the detour to the nearby and narrow **Gorges de Galamus**, just north of St. Paul de Fenouillet. Closer to D-117, **Quéribus** towers above (steep hike) and is famous as the last Cathar castle to fall. It was left useless after 1659, when the border between France and Spain was moved further south into the high Pyrénées (€4, get English pamphlet, April–Sept daily 9:30–19:00, Oct and March daily 10:00–18:00, Nov–Feb daily 10:00–17:00).

Châteaux of Lastours—Ten miles north of Carcassonne, these four ruined castles cap a barren hilltop and offer drivers a handy, if less impressive, look at the region's Cathar castles. From Carcassonne, follow signs to Mazamet, then Conques-sur-Orbiel, then Lastours. In Lastours, park at the lot as you enter the village, then walk to the old factory (look for *Accueil* signs) to the slick ticket office (get the English information). It's a 20-minute uphill walk to the castles, which were the inheritance of four sons from their father, a ruler who wanted to treat each son equally. Drive high to the belvedere for a panorama overlooking the castles (€4 for access to castles and belvedere viewpoint, April–Sept daily 10:00–18:00, Oct daily 10:00–17:00, closed Nov–March).

▲**Abbaye de Fontfroide**—Hidden in the Corbières mountains, this beautiful abbey is a worthwhile detour just six miles south of Narbonne (exit 38 from A-9 autoroute). Founded in 1093, this once powerful Cistercian abbey worked the front lines against the spread of Catharism. The assassination of one of its monks unleashed the terrible Albigensian Crusades. Today's abbey is privately owned and well-restored; it has 3,000 roses, sublime cloisters, a massive church, and a monk's dormitory, all amid total isolation. Call ahead for English tours, or visit on a French-only tour with printed English explanations (€7.50, April–Oct daily 10:00–12:15 & 13:45–17:30, July–Aug 9:30–18:00, Nov–March 10:00–12:00 & 14:00–16:00, hourly tours, tel. 04 68 45 18 31).

▲**Minerve**—A one-time Cathar hideout, spectacular Minerve is sculpted out of a deep canyon that provided a natural defense. But strong as it was, it didn't keep out the pope's army. The village was razed during the vicious Albigensian Crusades. The view from the small parking lot alone (€2) justifies the detour. Cross the bridge on foot, then wander into the village to its upper end and a ruined tower. A path leads down to the river from here (watch your step as you descend); you can reenter the village from the riverbed at its lower end.

Minerve has two pleasant cafés, one hotel, an intriguing museum of prehistory, a few wine shops—and not much more. Stay here and melt into southern France (almost literally, if it's summer); you won't regret it. Sleep and eat at the friendly and cozy **Relais Chantovent** (Sb-€340, Db-€39–47, Tb-€52, Qb-€50, tel. 04 68 91 14 18, fax 04 68 91 81 99). People travel great distances to dine here (*menus* from €17, closed Sun–Mon), so reserve early. The **Café de la Place** provides the perfect break and has a pool for anyone's use (€3, tel. 05 68 91 22 94).

Minerve is between Carcassonne and Béziers, nine miles northeast of Olonzac and 40 minutes by car from Carcassonne. It's a good stop between Provence and Carcassonne. In the mood for wine-tasting? Stop at **Domaine de Pech d'André** and visit my friends Monsieur and Madame Remaury. They offer a good selection and an exquisite setting in which to sample the local product (coming from Minerve, it's just past Azillanet, look for Domaine signs on your left, tel. 04 68 91 22 66, a leetle Engleesh spoken).

Collioure

Surrounded by less appealing resorts, lovely Collioure is blessed with a privileged climate and a romantic setting. By Mediterranean standards, this seaside village should be overrun—it has everything. Like an ice-cream shop, Collioure offers 31 flavors of pastel houses and six petite, scooped-out, pebbled beaches sprinkled with visitors. This sweet scene, capped by a winking lighthouse, sits under a once mighty castle in the shade of the Pyrénées. Evenings are best in Collioure—as the sky darkens, yellow lamps reflect warm pastels and deep blues.

Just 15 miles from the Spanish border, Collioure (Cottlieure in Catalan) shares a common history and independent attitude with its Catalan siblings on the other side of the border. Happily French yet proudly Catalan, it sports the yellow and red flag, street names in French and Catalan, and business names with *el* and *las,* rather than *le* and *les.* Sixty years ago, most villagers spoke Catalan, and today the language is enjoying a resurgence as Collioure rediscovers its roots.

Come here to unwind and regroup. Even with its crowds of vacationers in peak season (July and August are jammed), Collioure is what many look for when they head to the Riviera—a sunny, relaxing splash in the Mediterranean.

Leave your ambition at the station. Enjoy a slow coffee on le Med, lose yourself in the old town's streets, compare the *gelati* shops on rue Vauban, and snuggle into a pebble-sand beach (waterproof shoes are helpful). And if you're with car, don't miss a drive into the hills above Collioure (described below).

ORIENTATION

Most of Collioure's shopping, sights, and hotels are in the old town, across the drainage channel from Château Royal. There are good views of the old town from across the bay near the recommended Hôtel Boramar, and brilliant views from the hills above.

Tourist Information: The TI hides behind the main beachfront cafés at 5 place du 18 Juin. Ask about hikes in the area (June–Sept Mon–Sat 9:00–12:00 & 14:00–19:00, Oct–May Tue–Sat 9:00–12:00 & 14:00–18:00, Mon 14:00–18:00, closed Sun except July–Aug, tel. 04 68 82 15 47, www.collioure.com).

Arrival in Collioure

By Train: Walk out of the station, turn right, and follow the road downhill for about 10 minutes until you see Hôtel Fregate (hotels are listed from this point). The station ticket office has irregular hours; if they're open, pick up a schedule for any Spain side-trips or for your next destination.

By Car: Collioure is 16 miles south of Perpignan. Take the *Perpignan-Sud Sortie* from the autoroute and follow signs to Argelès-sur-Mer, then Collioure. Parking is tricky, and almost impossible in summer. Arrive early or late for easiest (and free) parking. Follow Collioure *Centre-Ville* signs and look for any spots available as you head to the train station (Gare SNCF). There's a big, handy pay lot (Parking Glacis) that you reach by following signs to *Centre-Ville*, then drive down rue de la République and stay right at the bottom through a metered lot; find the ramp (and gate) near the château (€1.30/hr, €8/24 hrs). Ask your hotel for parking suggestions, and take everything out of the car.

Helpful Hints

Market Days: Markets are held on Wednesday and Sunday mornings on place Maréchal Leclerc, across from Hôtel Fregate.

Internet Access: The TI offers access using a prepaid French *télécarte* (for information on how to use it, see page 30.

Launderette: Laverie 3L will do your laundry while you do your relaxing (July–Aug daily 9:00–19:00, otherwise daily 9:00–12:00 & 15:00–18:00, at roundabout at 28 rue de la République, tel. 04 68 98 04 17; the sign tells you to drop laundry next door at Immosud). There's also a **self-serve launderette** a block away (daily 7:00–21:00, across from bike shop, next to 10 rue de Gaulle).

Car Rental: National Car is located in Garage Renault, opposite the launderette on rue de la République (tel. 04 68 82 08 34).

Taxi: Call 04 68 82 27 80 or 04 68 82 09 30.

SIGHTS

There's no important sight here except what lies on the beach and the views over Collioure, described below. Indulge in a long seaside lunch, inspect the intriguing art galleries, catch up on your postcards, and maybe take a hike. Don't be surprised to see French Marines playing commando in their rafts; Collioure's bay caters to more than sun-loving tourists.

Collioure in a Nutshell

Walk out to the jetty's end, past the church, and past the little chapel with the Matisse poster. Take in the pretty scene. Collioure has been

Collioure

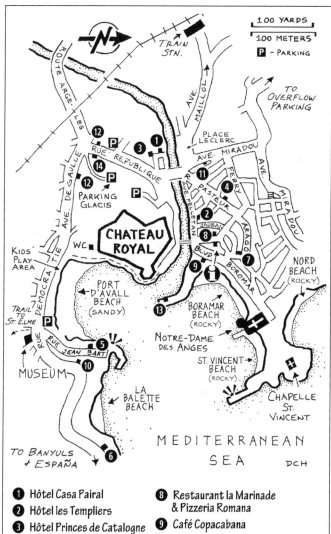

1 Hôtel Casa Pairal
2 Hôtel les Templiers
3 Hôtel Princes de Catalogne
4 Peroneille's Chambres
5 Hôtel Boramar
6 Hôtel les Caranques
7 Restaurant le Tremail
8 Restaurant la Marinade
   & Pizzeria Romana
9 Café Copacabana
10 Restaurant la Neptune
11 Les Caves du Roussillon Wine Shop
12 Launderettes (2 locations)
13 Promenade sur Mer Boat
14 Car Rental

a popular place since long before your visit. For more than 2,500 years, people have fought to own its enviable position on the Mediterranean and at the foot of the Pyrénées. The mountains that rise behind Collioure provide a natural defense, while its port gives it a commercial edge. This combination made Collioure an irresistible target. A string of forts defended Collioure's landlocked side. To the left, you can see the still-standing Fort St. Elme (built by powerful Spanish king Charles V, the same guy who built El Escorial near Madrid). The 2,100-foot-high observation tower of Madeloc stands straight ahead, and scattered ruins crown several other hilltops. Collioure's medieval town gathers between its church and château, sandwiched defensively and spiritually between the two. The town was batted back and forth between the French and Spanish for centuries (locals just wanted to be left alone—as Catalans). It was Spanish for nearly 400 years before becoming definitively French in 1659 (thank Louis XIV). More recently, Collioure was rediscovered, after decades of neglect, by artists who were drawn to the colorful houses and lovely setting. Matisse, Derain, Picasso, Braque, Dufy, and Chagall all spent time here. In fact, you're likely to recognize Collioure in paintings in many museums in Europe.

Royal Castle (Château Royal)—The 800-year-old castle, built over Roman ruins, served as home over the years to Majorcan kings, Crusaders, Dominican monks, and Louis XIV (who had the final say on the appearance we see now). Today, it serves tourists, offering great rampart walks, views, and mildly interesting local history exhibits (€4, June–Sept daily 10:00–18:00, Oct–May daily 9:00–17:00, last entry 45 min before closing).

Our Lady of the Angels Church (Notre-Dame des Anges)—This waterfront church is worth a gander—after all, how many times can you hear waves crashing while attending church? Supporting a guiding light (in more than one way), its foundations are built into the sea, and its one-of-a-kind lighthouse-bell tower helped sailors return home safely. The highlight is its over-the-top golden altar, unusual in France but typical of Catalan churches across the border. Drop €1 in the box to the left of the altar: lights, cameras, wow! (Daily 9:00–12:00 & 14:00–18:00.)

Path of Fauvism (Chemin du Fauvisme)—As you stroll Collioure's waterfront, notice occasional prints hanging on the walls. You're on the "Chemin du Fauvisme," where you'll find copies of André Derain's and Henri Matisse's works, inspired by their stays in Collioure in 1905. But as with Arles and Vincent van Gogh, there are no original paintings of theirs left here for the public to enjoy. However, the museum in Céret has a good collection (page 366), as does the recommended Hôtel les Templiers (page 367).

Beaches (Plages)—You'll usually find the best sand-to-stone ratio at plage St. Vincent and at plage de Port d'Avall (paddleboat/kayak rental-€11/hr, when open). The tiny plage de la Balette is quietest, with views of Collioure.

Wine-Tasting—Collioure and the surrounding area produce well-respected wines, and many shops offer relaxed tastings of the sweet Banyuls and Collioure reds and rosés. Try **Les Caves du Roussillon,** with a solid selection from many wineries and good prices (daily 10:00–13:00 & 15:00–20:00, next to Hôtel Fregate at 6 place Maréchal Leclerc).

Cruise—Consider a **Promenade sur Mer** boat excursion (€7, 1-hr Mediterranean cruise toward Spain and back, 5/day Easter–Sept weather permitting, leaves from breakwater near château, great views but commentary in French only, tel. 04 68 81 43 88).

Views Over Collioure

The three views described below offer different perspectives of this lovely area.

Stone Windmill—Stone steps lead 10 minutes up behind Collioure's museum to a 13th-century windmill with magnificent views that are positively dreamy at sunset. Find the museum behind Hôtel Triton, walk through its backyard, and follow the paved path marked with yellow dashes. Bring your own beverage.

▲**Hike to Fort St. Elme**—This vertical hike (1 hr each way) is best done early or late (no shade) and is worth the sweat, even if you don't make it to the top (trail starts from windmill described above). You can't miss the square castle lurking high above Collioure. The view from the top is sensational, though the privately owned castle is not open to the public.

Cheaters can do it by car by driving to Port Vendres, then following the small road from its train station.

▲▲▲**Drive/Hike Through Vineyards to Madeloc Tower (Tour de Madeloc)**—Check your vertigo at the hotel, fasten your seatbelt, and take this drive-and-hike combination high above Collioure. The narrow road, hairpin turns, and absence of guardrails only add to the experience, as Collioure shrinks to Lego size and the clouds get ever closer. Leave Collioure toward Perpignan, and look for signs to *Tour de Madeloc* at the roundabout above the town. Climb through impossibly steep and rocky terraced vineyards following *Tour* and *Balcon de Madeloc* signs. After about 20 minutes, you'll come to a fork in the road; you'll see a paved path (with a "Do Not Enter" sign that applies to cars) and a road leading downhill (the sign identifies it as *La Route des Vignobles*—The Route of the Vineyards). Park at the fork in the road, and walk 10–15 minutes up the paved path to the first ruined structure (the *Balcon*). The views everywhere are magnificent—to the Pyrénées on one side, and the beach towns of Port Vendres and Collioure on the other (scenic picnic tables provided). While this satisfies most, you can continue hiking up and up the tiny road to *la Tour* (the Tower) and commune with the gods, if you're a task-oriented type who must complete the mission. Allow an hour at a slow yet steady pace along the splintered ridge top, and you'll reach the eagle's-nest setting of this ancient tower, now fitted with communication devices. There's no shade, so do this hike early or late in the day. Once you're back down among mortals, you can return to Collioure following La Route des Vignobles to Banyuls sur Mer, then take coastal N-114 to Collioure and your hotel.

Near Collioure

Day Trip to Spain—The 15-mile, 40-minute coastal drive via the Col de Banyuls into Spain is beautiful and well worth the countless curves, even if you don't venture past the border.

Train travelers can day-trip to Spain, either to Barcelona (3 hrs one-way, 4/day) or, closer, to Figueres (1.5 hrs) and its Salvador Dalí museum (€9, July–Sept daily 9:00–19:45, April–June and Oct–Dec daily 10:30–17:45, Jan–March Tue–Sun 10:30–17:45, closed Mon, tel. 972-677-500). Get train schedules at the station.

Céret—Twenty-five windy miles inland, this enchanting town awaits, featuring fountains and mountains at its front door, and an excellent modern art museum with works by some of Collioure's more famous visitors, including Pablo Picasso, Joan Miró, Marc Chagall, and Matisse (€8, mid-June–mid-Sept daily 10:00–19:00, otherwise 10:00–18:00, tel. 04 68 87 27 76). This makes a fine day trip from Collioure (allow 50 min to Céret by car, or take a train to nearby Perpignan and a bus from there, get details at TI).

SLEEPING

(€1 = about $1.20, country code: 33)
Collioure has a good range of hotels at favorable rates. You have two good choices for your hotel's location: central, in the old town (closer to train station); or across the bay, with views of the old town (10-min walk from old town, with easier parking).

In the Old Town

Directions to the following places are given from the big Hôtel Fregate, at the entrance to the old town, a five-minute walk down from the train station. Price ranges reflect low versus high season.

$$$ **Casa Pairal*****, opposite Hôtel Fregate, is Mediterranean-elegant and Collioure's best splurge. Enter to the sounds of a fountain gurgling in the flowery courtyard; recline on lounges in the garden or by the pool. Rooms are quiet, comfortable, well-designed, and air-conditioned (small Db-€74–82, pleasant Db-€98–125, big Db-€118–140, extra bed-€24, good buffet breakfast-€10, parking-€8, impasse des Palmiers, tel. 04 68 82 05 81, fax 04 68 82 52 10,

www.hotel-casa-pairal.com, reserve ahead for room and parking).

$$ Hôtel les Templiers**, in the thick of things in the old town, has wall-to-wall paintings squeezed in every available space, a perennially popular café-bar, and fine-value rooms. The paintings were payments in kind and thank-yous from artists who have stayed here—find the black and white photo in the bar of the hotel's owner with Pablo Picasso. The rooms are either new and modern, or older with character. Some have views, and all have air-conditioning (standard Db-€55–64, bigger Db-€65–78, ask about connecting family rooms, pass on their annex rooms unless they're next to main hotel block, a block toward beach from Hôtel Fregate along drainage canal at 12 quai de l'Amirauté, tel. 04 68 98 31 10, fax 04 68 98 01 24, www.hotel-templiers.com).

$$ Princes de Catalogne*** offers American-style comfort and spacious rooms with air-conditioning. Get a room on the quieter mountain side—*côté montagne* (coat-ay mon-tan-yah; Db-€62–70, extra person-€12, next to Casa Pairal, rue des Palmiers, tel. 04 68 98 30 00, fax 04 68 98 30 31, www.hotel-princescatalogne.com).

$ Monsieur and Madame **Peroneille's Chambres,** on the pedestrian street two blocks past Hôtel Fregate, are the cheapest rooms in the old town. Rooms are simple, clean, and mostly spacious. The more serious Monsieur (who speaks Catalan) and bubbly Madame are both 80 years old and have rented these rooms for more than 30 years without learning a word of English—so don't hold your breath (Sb-€32, D-€40, Db-€45, Tb-€65, Qb-€70, no CC, 20 rue Pasteur, tel. 04 68 82 15 31, fax 04 68 82 35 94). The rooms in the main building *(la maison principale)* are better than the cheaper rooms in the annex, but both are fine. Ask to see the rooftop terrace.

Across the Bay

$$ Hôtel les Caranques**, a few curves toward Spain from Collioure's center, tumbles down the cliffs and showcases million-dollar sea views from each of its spotless, white rooms (most with balconies beyond slick sliding glass doors). Enjoy the various view terraces with mod plastic furniture, and the four-star breakfast room panorama. This idyllic place, run by gentle Monsieur Sarrazin, is a steal (D-€42, Db-€60–74, most are €65 and great, route de Port Vendres, 30-min walk from train station, tel. 04 68 82 06 68, fax 04 68 82 00 92, www.les-caranques.com, contact@les-caranques.com SE).

$$ Hôtel Boramar**, which faces Collioure's center across the bay, is understated and modest, but well-maintained. Get a room with a terrace facing the sea and smile, or sleep elsewhere (Db without view-€50, Db with view-€60-65, Tb with view-€70, rue Jean Bart, tel. 04 68 82 07 06, no fax, no e-mail, no reason).

EATING

Try the local wine and eat anything Catalan, including the fish and anchovies (hand-filleted, as no machine has ever been able to accomplish this precise task).

All restaurants listed have indoor and outdoor tables, and all but the last are in the old town (the first four are within 50 yards of each other). Your task is to decide whether you want to eat well or with a view. Several delicious *gelati* shops fuel after-dinner strollers with the perfect last course. If you're traveling off-season, call ahead, since many restaurants here are closed December through February.

Café Copacabana, on the main beach (Boramar), offers big salads and a few seafood dishes in its sandy café. Skip their sidewalk-bound restaurant (which has a bigger selection but smaller view) and find a red sway-back chair beachside. The quality is good enough, considering the view, and it's family-friendly—kids can play on the beach while you dine (daily mid-March–mid Dec, plage du Boramar, tel. 04 68 82 06 74, best at sunset).

Le Tremail is *the* place to go for contemporary seafood and Catalan specialties served outside or in. It's a small, friendly, popular place one block from the bay, where rue Arago and rue Mailly meet. Reserve ahead if you can (*menus*-€22–34, closed Mon–Tue and Jan, 16 bis rue Mailly, tel. 04 68 82 16 10).

La Marinade, across from the TI, is a consistently good bet for seafood served in a fun outdoor setting (*menus*-€18 and €23, closed Mon and Nov–Feb, 14 place du 18 Juin, tel. 04 68 82 09 76).

Pizzeria Romana, next to La Marinade, is an appealing and lively place serving cheap pizza, good salads, and more (daily, good tables inside or out, 6 place du 18 Juin).

La Neptune, across the bay, dishes up top seafood and views of Collioure to discerning diners. Dress up a bit, cross the bay, and ask for a table with a view (*menus* from €30, closed Tue–Wed, 9 route de Port Vendres, tel. 04 68 82 02 27).

Small places sell a variety of meals to go (*à emporter;* ah em-pohr-tay) for budget-minded romantics wanting to dine on the bay.

For post-dinner fun, head to one of the bayfront cafés on plage Boramar, or try the recommended **Hôtel les Templiers** and get down with the locals (daily, 12 quai de l'Amirauté, tel. 04 68 98 31 10).

TRANSPORTATION CONNECTIONS

From Collioure by train to: Carcassonne (9/day, 2 hrs, 6 require change in Narbonne), **Paris** (5/day, 6 hrs, changes in Perpignan or Montpellier and Lyon, then TGV to Gare Montparnasse, one direct train to Gare d'Austerlitz in 10 hrs, and a handy night train), **Barcelona** (4/day, 3 hrs, change in Cerbère), **Figueres,** Spain (2/day,

1.5 hrs, transfer in Cerbère), **Avignon/Arles** (7/day, 3.5 hrs, many transfer points possible). Consider handy night trains to Paris, key Italy destinations, and Geneva, Switzerland. The train station's ticket office closes at 17:45 (tel. 04 68 82 05 89).

PROVENCE

This magnificent region is shaped like a giant wedge of quiche. From its sunburned crust, fanning out along the Mediterranean coast from Nîmes to Nice, it stretches north along the Rhône Valley to Orange. The Romans were here in force and left many ruins—some of the best anywhere. Seven popes; great artists such as van Gogh, Cézanne, and Picasso; and author Peter Mayle all enjoyed their years in Provence. The region offers a splendid recipe of arid climate (except for occasional vicious winds, known as the mistral), captivating cities, exciting hill towns, dramatic scenery, and oceans of vineyards.

Explore the ghost town that is ancient Les Baux and see France's greatest Roman ruin, Pont du Gard. Spend your starry, starry nights where van Gogh did, in Arles. Uncover its Roman past, then find the linger-longer squares and café corners that inspired Vincent. Youthful but classy Avignon bustles in the shadow of its brooding pope's palace. It's a short hop from Arles or Avignon into the splendid scenery and villages of the Côtes du Rhône and Luberon regions that make Provence so popular today.

Planning Your Time

Make Arles or Avignon your sightseeing base, particularly if you have no car. Arles has a blue-collar quality and good-value hotels, while Avignon (three times larger than Arles) feels sophisticated and offers more nightlife and shopping. Italophiles prefer smaller Arles, while poodles pick urban Avignon.

To measure the pulse of Provence, spend at least one night in a smaller town. Vaison la Romaine is ideal for those heading to/from the north, and Isle-sur-la-Sorgue is centrally located between Avignon and the Luberon. Most destinations are accessible by public transit.

Provence

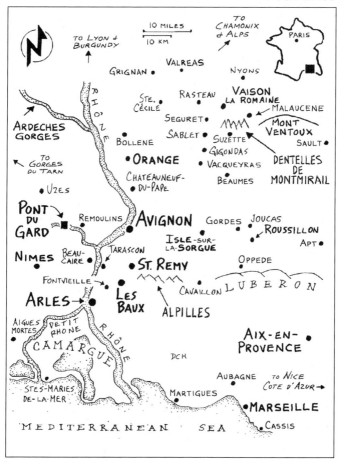

You'll want a full day for sightseeing in Arles (best on Wed or Sat, when the morning market rages), a half day for Avignon, and a day or two for the villages and sights in the countryside.

Getting Around Provence

By Car: The yellow Michelin map of this region is essential for drivers. Avignon (population 100,000) is a headache for drivers; Arles (population 35,000) is easier, though it still requires go-cart driving skills. Park only in well-watched spaces, and leave nothing in your car. For one of Provence's most scenic drives, follow my day-trip route of the Côtes du Rhône wine villages. If you're heading north from Provence, consider a three-hour detour through the spectacular Ardèche Gorges (see page 427).

By Train or Bus: Travelers relying on public transportation will find their choices limited. Public transit is good between cities and decent to some towns, but marginal at best to the villages.

Frequent trains link Avignon and Arles (about 30 min between each). Orange is easy from Avignon by train. Buses connect smaller towns, but Les Baux can be reached only by taxi or tour.

Isle-sur-la-Sorgue and St. Rémy offer the most accessible small-town experiences. From Avignon, Isle-sur-la-Sorgue is an easy hop by train or bus. St. Rémy and the Pont du Gard—and to a lesser extent, Vaison la Romaine and some Côtes du Rhône villages—are also connected by bus from Avignon.

Tours of Provence

It's possible to take half-day or full-day excursions to most of the sights described in this book from Arles or (better) Avignon. Local TIs have brochures on all of these excursions and can help you make a reservation. Here are two options:

Visit Provence—This tour company, based in Avignon, offers a great variety of half-day or full-day guided tours in eight-seat minivans (€50/half day, €100/day). For example, a half-day tour to both the Châteauneuf-du-Pape vineyards, with wine-tasting, and to Orange (includes Triumphal Arch, Roman Theater, and audioguide for Theater) costs €50. Other day trips include: Les Baux/Arles and St. Rémy/Les Baux/Pont du Gard. Not all tours include entry fees for sights, but reservations are required for all. Ask about their cheaper large-coach excursions (tel. 04 90 14 70 00, www.provence -reservation.com).

Lieutaud—This company operates cheap, unguided, big-bus excursions from Arles and Avignon to many hard-to-reach places at a fraction of the price you'd pay for a taxi. Different half-day and full-day trips are available every day, but no admission fees are included. Here are a few examples: Pont du Gard (€15/half-day, runs twice weekly, usually Tue and Thu); Vaison la Romaine and Orange (€19/half-day, 1 weekly, usually Mon); St. Rémy Wednesday morning market (€15/half-day); and Nîmes, Arles, and the Camargue (€28/day, usually Fri). They also offer weekly excursions to Les Baux or the Luberon, including Gordes and Roussillon (tel. 04 90 86 36 75, www.cars-lieutaud.fr).

Cuisine Scene in Provence

The almost extravagant use of garlic, olive oil, herbs, and tomatoes makes Provence's cuisine France's liveliest. To sample it, order anything *à la Provençale*. Among the area's spicy specialties are ratatouille (a thick mixture of vegetables in an herb-flavored tomato sauce), *brandade* (a salt cod, garlic, and cream mousse), aioli (a garlicky mayonnaise, often served atop fresh vegetables), tapenade

Le Mistral

Provence lives with its vicious mistral winds, which blow 30 to 60 miles per hour, about 100 days out of the year. Locals say it blows in multiples of threes: three, six, or nine days in a row. *Le mistral* clears people off the streets and turns lively cities into virtual ghost towns. You'll likely spend a few hours taking refuge—or searching for cover.

When *le mistral* blows, it's everywhere, and you can't escape. Peter Mayle said it could blow the ears off a donkey. Locals say it ruins crops, shutters, and roofs (look for the stones holding tiles in place on many homes). They'll also tell you that this pernicious wind has driven many crazy (including young Vincent van Gogh). A weak version of the wind is called a *mistralet*.

Le mistral starts above the Alps and Massif Central Mountains and gathers steam as it heads south, gaining momentum as it screams over the Rhône Valley (which acts like a funnel between the Alps and Pyrénées) before exhausting itself as it hits the Mediterranean. While this wind rattles shutters throughout the Riviera and Provence, it's strongest over the Rhône Valley...so Avignon, Arles, and the Côtes du Rhône villages bear its brunt. While wiping the dust from your eyes, remember the good news: *Le mistral* brings clear skies.

(a paste of pureed olives, capers, anchovies, herbs, and sometimes tuna), *soupe au pistou* (vegetable soup with basil, garlic, and cheese), and *soupe à l'ail* (garlic soup). Look also for *riz Camarguaise* (rice from the Camargue) and *taureau* (bull meat). Banon (wrapped in chestnut leaves) and Picodon (nutty taste) are the native cheeses. The region's sheep's milk cheese, Brousse, is creamy and fresh. Provence also produces some of France's great wines at relatively reasonable prices. Look for Gigondas, Sablet, Côtes du Rhône, and Côte de Provence. If you like rosé, try the Tavel. This is the place to splurge for a bottle of Châteauneuf-du-Pape.

Remember, restaurants serve only during lunch (11:30–14:00) and dinner (19:00–21:00, later in bigger cities); cafés serve food throughout the day.

Provence Market Days

Provençal market days offer France's most colorful and tantalizing outdoor shopping. The best markets are on Monday in Cavaillon,

Tuesday in Vaison la Romaine, Wednesday in St. Rémy, Thursday in Nyons, Friday in Lourmarin, Saturday in Arles, Uzès, and Apt, and, best of all, Sunday in Isle-sur-la-Sorgue. Crowds and parking problems abound at these popular events—arrive by 9:00, or, even better, sleep in the town the night before.

Monday: Cavaillon, Bedoin (between Vaison la Romaine and Mont Ventoux)

Tuesday: Vaison la Romaine, Tarascon, and Gordes

Wednesday: St. Rémy, Arles, and Malaucene (near Vaison la Romaine)

Thursday: Nyons, Beaucaire, Vacqueyras, and Isle-sur-la-Sorgue

Friday: Lourmarin, Remoulins (near Pont du Gard), Bonnieux (smaller but fun), and Châteauneuf-du-Pape

Saturday: Arles, Uzès, and Apt

Sunday: Isle-sur-la-Sorgue, Mausanne (near Les Baux), and Beaucaire

Arles

By helping Julius Caesar defeat Marseille, Arles (pronounced arl) earned the imperial nod and was made an important port city. With the first bridge over the Rhône River, Arles was a key stop on the Roman road from Italy to Spain, the Via Domitia. After reigning as the seat of an important archbishop and a trading center for centuries, the city became a sleepy place of little importance in the 1700s. Vincent van Gogh settled here a hundred years ago, but left only a chunk of his ear (now gone). American bombers destroyed much of Arles in World War II, as the townsfolk hid out in its underground Roman galleries. Today, Arles thrives again, with its evocative Roman ruins, an eclectic assortment of museums, made-for-ice-cream pedestrian zones, and squares that play hide-and-seek with visitors. It's an understandably popular home base from which to explore France's trendy Provence region.

ORIENTATION

Arles faces the Mediterranean and turns its back on Paris. While the town is built along the Rhône, it completely ignores the river (the part of Arles most damaged by Allied bombers in World War II, and therefore the least charming today).

Landmarks hide in Arles' medieval tangle of narrow, winding streets. Virtually everything is close—but first-time visitors can walk forever to get there. Hotels have good, free city maps, and Arles provides helpful street-corner signs that point you toward sights and hotels. Racing cars enjoy Arles' medieval lanes, turning sidewalks into tightropes and pedestrians into leaping targets.

Tourist Information

The main TI is on the ring road, esplanade Charles de Gaulle (April–Sept daily 9:00–18:45, Oct–March Mon–Sat 9:00–17:45, Sun 10:30–14:30, tel. 04 90 18 41 20). There's also a TI at the train station (open year-round, Mon–Sat 9:00–13:00, closed Sun). Both charge €1 to reserve hotel rooms. Pick up the good city map, note the bus schedules, and get English information on nearby destinations such as the Camargue wildlife area. Ask about bullfights and bus excursions to regional sights (see "Helpful Hints," below). Ask if buses to Les Baux have been reinstated.

Excursions from Arles: The TI can book bus excursions to many destinations that require a car to reach. These are the best half-day excursions I saw: Pont du Gard and Les Baux for €50, Luberon villages for €50, and Camargue for €36. An all-day trip to the lavender fields is offered in summer for €100 (go only in late June–July, when fields are blooming). See "Tours of Provence," page 372.

Arrival in Arles

By Train and Bus: The train and bus stations are next to each other on the river, a 10-minute walk from the town center (baggage storage not available). Get what you need at the train station TI before leaving. To reach the old town, turn left out of either station and walk 10 blocks, or take bus #3 from the shelter right across from the train station (2/hr, €0.80, buy ticket from driver). Taxis generally do not wait at either station, but you can summon one by asking the TI or calling 04 90 96 90 03 (rates are fixed, allow €8–10 to any hotel I list).

By Car: Follow signs to *Centre-Ville*, then follow signs toward Gare SNCF (train station). You'll come to a huge roundabout (place Lamartine) with a Monoprix department store to the right. Park along the city wall or in nearby lots; pay attention to No Parking signs on Wednesday and Saturday until 13:00 (violators will be towed to make way for Arles' huge outdoor produce markets). Some hotels have limited parking. Theft is a big problem; leave nothing in your car. From place Lamartine, walk into the city between the two stumpy towers.

Helpful Hints

Market Days: The big days are Wednesday and Saturday (see listing on previous page).

Supermarket: A big, handy **Monoprix** supermarket/department store is on place Lamartine (Mon–Sat 8:30–19:25, closed Sun).

Internet Access: Cyber City is central (daily 10:00–22:00, 41 rue du Quatre Septembre, tel. 04 90 96 87 76).

Laundry: One launderette is at 12 rue Portagnel; another is nearby at 6 rue de la Cavalerie, near place Voltaire (both daily 7:00–21:00, you can stay later to finish if you're already inside, English instructions).

Bike Rental: Try the **Peugeot** store (15 rue du Pont, tel. 04 90 96 03 77). While Vaison la Romaine and Isle-sur-la-Sorgue make better biking bases, rides to Les Baux (20 miles round-trip, very steep climb) or into the Camargue (40 miles round-trip, forget it in the wind) are possible from Arles—provided you're in great shape.

Car Rental: **Avis** is at the train station (tel. 04 90 96 82 42), **Europcar** and **Hertz** are downtown (2 bis avenue Victor Hugo, Europcar tel. 04 90 93 23 24, Hertz tel. 04 90 96 75 23), and **National** is just off place Lamartine toward the station (4 avenue Paulin Talabot, tel. 04 90 93 02 17).

Local Guide: Jacqueline Neujean, an excellent guide, knows Arles like the back of her hand (2 hrs/€90, tel. 04 90 98 47 51).

Cooking Courses: Friendly American **Madeleine** organizes a fun variety of wine appreciation and cooking courses from her B&B in the city center. See Maison d'Hôtes en Provence under "Sleeping," in Arles section (page 389).

Serious Coffee or Tea: Recharge at **Café de la Major** (closed Sun, near Forum Square at 7 bis rue Réattu, tel. 04 90 96 14 15).

Public Pools: Arles has three public pools (indoor and outdoor). Ask at the TI or your hotel.

Getting Around Arles

Everything's within walking distance. Only the Ancient History Museum requires a long walk (you can take the bus instead, €0.80, details in sight listing, below). The elevated riverside walk provides Rhône views and a direct (if odorous) route to the Ancient History Museum, with an easy return to the train station. Keep your head up for *Starry Night* memories, but eyes down for decorations by dogs with poorly trained owners.

Arles' **taxis** charge a set fee of about €8, but only the Ancient History Museum is worth a taxi ride (figure €30 each way to Les Baux, tel. 04 90 96 90 03).

SIGHTS AND ACTIVITIES

The worthwhile **monument pass** *(le pass monuments)* covers Arles' many sights and is valid for one week (adults-€13.50, under 18-€12, sold at each sight). Otherwise, it's €3–4 per sight and €5.50 for the Ancient History Museum. While any sight is worth a few minutes, many aren't worth the individual admission. Start at the Ancient History Museum for a helpful overview, then dive into the sights

Arles Sights

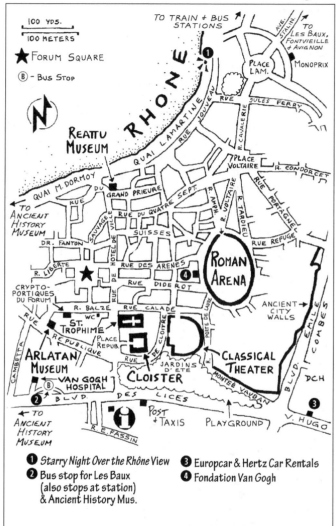

100 YDS.
100 METERS

★ FORUM SQUARE

Ⓑ - BUS STOP

TO TRAIN + BUS STATIONS

AVE. STALIN.

TO Les Baux, Fontvieille + Avignon

PLACE LAM.

MONOPRIX

N

RHONE

REATTU MUSEUM

RUE JOUVEAU

RUE LAMARTINE

RUE JULES FERRY

R. CAVALERIE

PLACE VOLTAIRE

R. CONDORCET

QUAI LAMARTINE

QUAI M. DORMOY

DU

GRAND PRIEURE

RUE SAUVAGE

R. AMPH.

R. VOLTAIRE

RUE TARDIEU

RUE PORTAGNEL

TO ANCIENT HISTORY MUSEUM

RUE

RUE DU QUATRE SEPT.

SUISSES

RUE REFUGE

DR. FANTON

RUE DE HOTEL DE VILLE

RUE DES ARENES

ROMAN ARENA

R. LIBERTE

RUE DIDEROT

ANCIENT CITY WALLS

CRYPTO-PORTIQUES DU FORUM

R. BALZE

RUE CALADE

POSTE DE LURE

RUE

WC

ST. TROPHIME

RUE DE CLOITRE

EMILE COMBES

RUE REPUBLIQUE

PLACE REPUB.

CLASSICAL THEATER

DCH

ARLATAN MUSEUM

RUE DE

JARDINS D'ETE

BLVD.

R. CAMBETTA

VAN GOGH HOSPITAL

Ⓑ

CLOISTER

MONTEE VAUBAN

B L V D.   D E S   L I C E S

TO ANCIENT HISTORY MUSEUM

POST + TAXIS

PLAYGROUND

V. HUGO

R. E. FASSIN

❶ *Starry Night Over the Rhône* View
❷ Bus stop for Les Baux (also stops at station) & Ancient History Mus.

❸ Europcar & Hertz Car Rentals
❹ Fondation Van Gogh

(ideally in the order described below). Remember, many begin closing rooms 30 minutes early.

▲▲▲**Ancient History Museum (Musée de l'Arles Antique)**—Begin your town visit here—it's Roman Arles 101. Models and original sculptures (with meager help from the English brochure) re-create the Roman city, making work-a-day life and culture easier to imagine.

You're greeted by an impressive row of pagan and early-Christian sarcophagi (2nd through 5th centuries). These would have lined the Via Aurelia outside the town wall. Pagan sarcophagi show simple slice-of-Roman-life scenes, while the Christian ones feature Bible stories. In the early days of the Church, Jesus was often portrayed beardless and as the good shepherd, with a lamb over his shoulder.

Next, you'll find models of every Roman structure in Arles you can visit today. These are the highlight for me, as they breathe a little life into buildings as they looked 2,000 years ago. Find the Forum model, and commit it to memory for when you visit the real thing later. Check out the pontoon bridge (over the widest, and therefore slowest, part of the river), find the arena (with its moveable stadium cover, which sheltered spectators

from sun or rain), and locate Arles' chariot racecourse (where you are now). While virtually nothing is left of the racecourse (a.k.a. circus), the model shows that it must have rivaled Rome's Circus Maximus. Looking at the model, you can see that an emphasis on sports—with huge stadiums at the edge of town—is not unique to modern America. The model of the entire city puts it all together, illustrating how little Arles seems to have changed over two millennia—warehouses still on the opposite side of the river, and houses clustered around the city center.

All of the statues are original, except for the greatest—the *Venus of Arles*—which Louis XIV took a liking to and had moved to Versailles. It's now in the Louvre (and, as locals say, "When it's in Paris...bye-bye"). Jewelry, fine metal and glass artifacts, and well-crafted mosaic floors make it clear that Roman Arles was a city of art and culture.

Built at the site of the chariot racecourse (the arc of which is built into the parking lot), this air-conditioned, all-on-one-floor museum is a 25-minute walk from Arles along the river, or a bus ride with a short walk (€5.50, March–Oct daily 9:00–19:00, Nov–Feb daily 10:00–17:00, tel. 04 90 18 88 88, www.arles -antique.org—in French only).

Bus #1 gets you within a five-minute walk. Catch the bus in downtown Arles on boulevard des Lices (€0.80, pay driver, runs every 20 min, daily except Sun); to find the museum, exit left off the bus and then keep right, passing Hôtel Mercure. To return by bus, cross the bridge in front of museum and keep right, passing Hôtel Mercure; the bus stop (look for glass shelter) will be on your left across from the next roundabout; you want direction: Trebon.

To reach the museum by foot from the city center, turn left at the river and take the riverside path to the big modern building just past the new bridge. The museum can call a taxi for your return (allow €8–10).

▲▲Forum Square (Place du Forum)—Named for the Roman forum that once stood here, this square was the political and religious center of Roman Arles. Still lively, this café-crammed square is popular for a *pastis*. The bistros on the square, while no place for a fine dinner, can put together a good enough salad or *plat du jour*—and when you sprinkle on the ambience, that's €10 well spent.

At the corner of Grand Hôtel Nord-Pinus, a plaque shows how the Romans built a foundation of galleries to make the main square level. The two columns are all that survive of a temple. Steps leading to the entrance are buried (the Roman street level was about 20 feet below you).

The statue on the square is of Frédéric Mistral. This popular poet, who wrote in the local dialect rather than French, was a champion of Provençal culture. After receiving the Nobel Prize in Literature in 1904, Mistral used his prize money to preserve and display the folk identity of Provence. He founded the regional folk museum (see Arlatan Museum, below) at a time when France was rapidly centralizing. (The famous local mistral—literally, "master"—wind has nothing to do with his name.)

The bright-yellow café is famous as the subject of one of Vincent van Gogh's first works in Arles. While his painting showed the café in a brilliant yellow from the glow of gas lamps, the facade was bare limestone, just like the other cafés on this square. The café's current owners have painted it to match van Gogh's version...and to cash in on the Vincent-crazed hordes who pay way too much to eat or drink here.

Cryptoportiques du Forum—The only Baroque church in Arles (admire the wooden ceiling) provides a dramatic entry to this underground system of arches and vaults that supported the southern end of the Roman Forum (and hid French resistance fighters during World War II). The galleries of arches demonstrate the extent to which Roman engineers would go to follow standard city plans: If the land doesn't suit the blueprint, change the land. While remarkable, there's not much to it beyond the initial "Oh, wow!" (€3.50, May–Sept daily 9:00–12:00 & 14:00–18:00, April and Oct daily 9:00–11:30 & 14:00–17:30, Nov–March daily 10:00–11:30 & 14:00–16:30, leave Forum Square with Grand Hôtel Nord-Pinus on your right and turn right on rue Balze.)

▲▲St. Trophime Church, Cloisters, and Republic Square (Place de la République)—This church, named after a 3rd-century bishop of Arles and located on a fun square, sports the finest Romanesque main entrance (west portal) I've seen anywhere. Get a good view of it from...

Republic Square: This square used to be called "place Royale"... until the French Revolution. The obelisk was the centerpiece of

Arles' Roman Circus. The lions at its base are the symbol of the city, whose slogan is "far from the anger of the lion." This is a popular gathering place for young Arlesians at night. Find a seat and watch the peasants—pilgrims, locals, and street musicians. There's nothing new about this scene.

Tympanum (on church facade): Like a Roman triumphal arch, the church trumpets the promise of Judgment Day. The tympanum (the semicircular area above the door) is filled with Christian symbolism. Christ sits in majesty, surrounded by symbols of the four evangelists: Matthew—the winged man, Mark—the winged lion, Luke—the ox, and John—the eagle. The 12 apostles are lined up below Jesus. It's Judgment Day...some are saved, and others aren't.

Notice the condemned (on the right)—a chain gang doing a sad bunny-hop over the fires of hell. For them, the tune trumpeted by the three angels at the very top is not a happy one. Below the chain gang, St. Stephen is being stoned to death, with his soul leaving through his mouth and instantly being welcomed by angels. Ride the exquisite detail back to a simpler age. In an illiterate medieval world, long before the vivid images of our Technicolor time, this was a neon billboard over the town square. (A chart just inside the church on the right helps explain the carvings.)

Inside St. Trophime: The tall, 12th-century Romanesque nave is decorated by a set of tapestries showing scenes from the life of Mary (17th century, from French town of Aubusson). Immediately to the left of the entry, a chapel is built on an early-Christian sarcophagus from Roman Arles (from around A.D. 300). On its right side, the three Magi give gifts to baby Jesus, and a frieze below shows the flight to Egypt. Under the left transept, another Roman sarcophagus shows Jews hopping over the Red Sea as they leave Egypt. Amble around the Gothic apse and check out the relic chapel. This church is a stop on the ancient pilgrimage route to Santiago de Compostela in northwest Spain. For 800 years, pilgrims on their way to Santiago have paused here. Even today, modern-day pilgrimages are advertised near the church's entry (church entry is free, May–Sept daily 9:00–18:30, March–April and Oct daily 9:00–17:30, Nov–Feb daily 10:00–16:30).

The adjacent **cloisters** are the best in Provence (enter from square, through courtyard to right of church). Enjoy the sculpted capitals of the rounded 12th-century Romanesque columns and the pointed 14th-century Gothic columns. The second floor offers only a view of the cloisters from above (€3.50, same hours as church).

To get to the next sight, the Classical Theater, face the church, walk left, then take the first right on rue de la Calade.

Classical Theater (Théâtre Antique)—Precious little survives from this Roman theater, which served as a handy town quarry throughout the Middle Ages. Walk to a center aisle and pull up a stone seat. Built in the 1st century B.C., this theater seated 10,000. To appreciate its original size, look to the upper left side of the tower and find the protrusion that supported the highest of three seating levels. Today, 3,000 can attend events in this restored facility. Two lonely Corinthian columns look out from the stage over the audience. The orchestra section is defined by a semicircular pattern in the stone. Stepping up onto the left side of the stage and look down to the narrow channel that allowed the curtain to disappear below, like magic. Go backstage and browse through broken bits of Rome, and loop back to the entry behind the grass (€3, you can see much of the theater by peeking through the fence for free, May–Sept daily 9:00–11:30 & 14:00–18:30, April and Oct daily 9:00–11:30 & 14:00–17:30, Nov–March 10:00–11:30 & 14:00–16:30). A block uphill is the...

▲▲▲Roman Arena (Amphithéâtre)—Nearly 2,000 years ago, gladiators fought wild animals here to the delight of 20,000 screaming fans. Today, local daredevils fight wild bulls. In Roman times, games were free (sponsored by city bigwigs) and fans were seated by

social class. The many exits allowed for rapid dispersal after the games—fights would break out among frenzied fans if they couldn't leave quickly. Through medieval times and until the early 1800s, the arches were bricked up, and the stadium became a fortified town—with 200 humble homes crammed within its circular defenses. Three of the medieval towers survive (the one above the ticket booth is open and rewards those who climb it with a good view). To see two still-sealed arches, complete with cute medieval window frames, turn right as you leave, walk to the Andaluz restaurant, and look back (€4, May–Sept daily 9:00–18:00, March–April and Oct daily 9:00–17:30, and Nov–Feb daily 10:00–16:30). Bullfight posters around the Arena advertise upcoming spectacles.

Turn left out of the arena and find...

▲▲Fondation Van Gogh—Refreshing to any art lover, and especially interesting to van Gogh fans, this small gallery features pieces by major contemporary artists and pays homage to Vincent through thought-provoking interpretations of his works. Many pieces are explained in English by the artists. The black-and-white photographs (both art and shots of places Vincent painted) complement the paintings (€7, not covered by monument pass, great collection of van Gogh prints and postcards for sale in free entry area,

Van Gogh in Arles

"The whole future of art is to be found in the south of France."
—Vincent van Gogh, 1888

Vincent was 35 years old when he arrived in Arles in 1888, and it was here that he discovered the light that would forever change him. Coming from the gray skies and flatlands of the Netherlands and Paris, he was bowled over by everything Provençal—jagged peaks, gnarled olive trees, brilliant sunflowers, and the furious wind. Van Gogh worked in a flurry in Arles, producing more paintings than at any other period in his too-brief career— over 200 in just a few months. (The fact that locals pronounced his name "vahn-saw van gog" had nothing to do with his psychological struggles here.)

Sadly, none of van Gogh's paintings remain in Arles—but you can still visit the places that inspired him. Around downtown Arles, you'll find 17 steel-and-concrete van Gogh **"easels"** that mark places

April–mid-Oct daily 10:30-20:00, mid-Oct–March Tue–Sun 11:00–17:00, closed Mon, facing Roman Arena at 24 bis rond-point des Arènes, tel. 04 90 49 94 04, www.fondationvangogh-arles.org).

▲**Arlatan Museum (Musée Arlaten/Museon Arlaten)**—Built on the remains of the Roman Forum (see the courtyard), this museum houses the treasures of daily Provençal life. It was given to Arles by Nobel Prize winner Frédéric Mistral (see Forum Square, above). Mistral's vision was to give locals an appreciation of their cultural roots, presented in tableaux that unschooled villagers could understand—"a veritable poem for the ordinary people who cannot read." Even though there are no English descriptions, the museum offers a unique and intimate look at local folk culture from the 18th and 19th centuries.

A one-way route takes you through 30 rooms. The first few rooms display folk costumes chronologically until about 1900, when traditional dress was replaced by the modern nondescript norm. You'll then see fine freestanding wedding armoires (given to brides by parents, filled with essentials to begin a new home). Finely crafted wooden cages—called *panetières*—hung from walls and kept bread away from mice. *Santons* were popular figurines, giving nativity scenes a Provençal look. The second floor shows local history, and a large room covers lifestyles of residents of the marshy Camargue. A fascinating case shows antique Coursa Provençal bullfighting memorabilia, including a stuffed champion bull named Lion, who died of old age.

The last two rooms are the collection's pride and joy. In one, a

Vincent painted, including the *Café at Night* on Forum Square. Each comes with a photo of the actual painting (see photo at left) and provides fans with a fun opportunity to compare the scene then and now. The TI has a €1 brochure that locates all the easels.

The **hospital** where Vincent was sent to treat his self-inflicted ear wound is today a cultural center (called *Espace Van Gogh* and *Mediathèque*). It surrounds a garden that the artist loved (and the only flower garden I've seen in Arles). Only the courtyard is open to the public; find the "easel" to see what Vincent painted here (free, near the Arlatan Museum on rue President Wilson). Vincent was sent from here to the mental institution in nearby St. Rémy (see page 416) before Dr. Paul Gachet invited him to Auvers-sur-Oise, near Paris.

From place Lamartine, walk to the river, then look toward the town to find where Vincent set his easel for this ***Starry Night over the Rhône*** painting, where stars boil above the skyline of Arles. Riverfront cafés that once stood here were destroyed by bridge-seeking bombs in World War II, as was the bridge whose remains you see on your right.

rich mom is shown with her newborn. Her friends visit with gifts representing four physical and moral qualities hoped for in a new baby—good as bread, full as an egg, wise as salt, and straight as a match. The cradle is fully stocked with everything needed to raise an infant in 1888.

The next room shows "the great supper"—a traditional feast served on Christmas Eve before midnight Mass. It's 1860, and everything on the table is locally produced. Traditionally, 13 sweets—for Jesus and the 12 apostles—were served. Grandma and grandpa warm themselves in front of the fireplace; grandpa pours wine on a log for good luck in the coming year (€4, pick up excellent English brochure, April–Sept daily 9:30–12:30 & 14:00–18:00, Oct–March daily until 17:00, 29 rue de la République, tel. 04 90 96 08 23).

Réattu Museum (Musée Réattu)—Housed in a beautiful 15th-century mansion, this mildly interesting, mostly modern art collection includes 57 Picasso drawings (some two-sided, and all done in a flurry of creativity—I liked the bullfights best), a room of Henri Rousseau's Camargue watercolors, and an unfinished painting by the neoclassical artist Jacques Réattu, none with English explanations (€4, extra for special exhibits, May–Sept daily 9:00–12:00 & 14:00–18:30; March–April and Oct until 17:00; Nov–Feb daily 13:00–17:00; 10 rue du Grand Prieuré, tel. 04 90 96 37 68).

▲▲Wednesday and Saturday Markets—Twice a week in the morning, Arles' ring road erupts into an open-air market of fish, flowers, produce, and you-name-it. The Wednesday market runs along boulevard Emile Combes, between place Lamartine and Avenue Victor Hugo; the segment nearer place Lamartine is all about food, the upper half is about clothing, tablecloths, purses, etc.... The Saturday market is along boulevard des Lices near the TI. Join in, buy flowers, try the olives, sample some wine, and swat a pickpocket; both markets are open until 12:00. On the first Wednesday of the month, it's a grand flea market.

Much of the market has a North African feel, thanks to the Algerians and Moroccans who live in Arles. They came to do the lowly city jobs that locals didn't want, and now mostly do the region's labor-intensive agricultural jobs (picking olives, harvesting fruit, and working in local greenhouses).

▲▲**Bullfights (Courses Camarguaises)**—Occupy the same seats fans have used for nearly 2,000 years, and take in Arles' most memorable experience—a bullfight *à la provençale* in the ancient arena. These are more sporting than bloody Spanish bullfights. The bulls of Arles (who, locals stress, "die of old age") are billed even more boldly than their human foes in the posters. A bull has a ribbon *(cocarde)* above its forehead, laced between its horns. The bullfighter, with a special hook, has 15 minutes to snare the ribbon. Local businessmen encourage  a fighter by hollering out how much money they'll pay for the *cocarde*. If the bull pulls a good stunt, the band plays the famous "Toreador Song" from *Carmen*. The following day, newspapers have reports on the fight, including how many *Carmens* the bull earned.

Three classes of bullfights—determined by the experience of the fighters—are advertised in posters: The *course de protection* is for rookie bullfighters. The *trophée de l'Avenir* comes with better fighters. And the *trophée des As* features top professionals. During Easter and the fall rice harvest festival (Féria du Riz), the arena hosts actual Spanish bullfights (look for *corrida*) with outfits, swords, spikes, and the whole gory shebang (tickets €5–10, Easter–Oct on Sat, Sun, and holidays). Don't pass on a chance to see *Toro Piscine*, a silly spectacle for warm summer evenings where the bull ends up in a swimming pool (uh huh, get more details at TI). Nearby villages stage bullfights in small wooden bullrings nearly every weekend; the TI has the latest schedule.

Near Arles

The Camargue—Knocking on Arles' doorstep, this is one of the few truly "wild" areas of France, where pink flamingos, wild bulls, and the famous white horses wander freely amid rice fields, lagoons, and mosquitoes. It's a ▲▲▲ sight for nature-lovers, but boring for

Sights near Arles

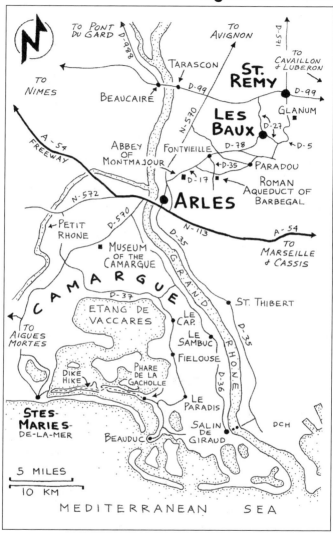

others. The D-37 that skirts the Etang de Vaccarès lagoon has some of the best views.

The **Museum of the Camargue (Musée Camarguais)** describes the natural features and traditions of the Camargue (some English information) and has a two-mile nature trail. It's eight miles from Arles on D-570 toward Stes-Maries-de-la-Mer; at the Mas du Pont de Rousty farmhouse, look for signs (€5, May–Sept daily 9:15–7:45; Oct–April Wed–Mon 10:15–16:45, closed Tue; tel. 04 90 97 10 82).

To venture farther into the Camargue after you pass the museum, follow D-37 toward Salin de Giraud and Le Sambuc as it skirts the Etang de Vaccarès lagoon; turn right onto the tiny road at Villeneuve and find La Capelière and Fielouse, then drive to Le Paradis and see how far you can get on the road that heads to the right. A slow dirt road ultimately leads to Beauduc (the end of the Camargue's world). Find Salin de Giraud, cross the Grande Rhône River by ferry, then return to Arles on the D-35. For public transportation options, see "Transportation Connections" for Arles, page 391.

From **Stes-Maries-de-la-Mer**, a seaside village at the far side of the Camargue, you can take a horse, jeep, or bike into the wilderness. The **TI** has a long list of options (April–Sept daily 9:00–19:00, until 20:00 in summer, Oct–March daily 9:00–17:00, 5 avenue Van Gogh, tel. 04 90 97 82 55, www.saintesmaries.com). For **horses**, contact the Association Camarguaise de Tourisme Equestre, which represents many places (€13–16/1 hr, €40/half day, €60–80/day, just outside Stes-Maries-de-la-Mer on the road from Arles, Route d'Arles, tel. 04 90 97 58 45, elevage.parc@wanadoo.fr). You can rent **bikes** and get advice on the best route at Le Vélo (19 rue de la République in Stes-Maries-de-la-Mer, tel. 04 90 97 74 56). **Jeep** excursions run €25 for 2.5 hours; Camargue Safaris Gallon has offices in Stes-Maries-de-la-Mer and Arles, with departures from either office (in Stes-Maries-de-la-Mer at 22 avenue Van Gogh, tel. 04 90 97 86 93; in Arles at 38 avenue Edouard Herriot, tel. 04 90 93 60 31, fax 04 90 96 31 55).

SLEEPING

Hotels are a great value here; many are air-conditioned, though few have elevators.

$$$ Hôtel d'Arlatan*** , built over the site of a Roman basilica, is classy in every sense of the word. It has sumptuous public spaces, a tranquil terrace, a designer pool, a turtle pond, and antique-filled rooms, most with high, wood-beamed ceilings and stone walls. In the lobby of this 15th-century building, a glass floor looks down into Roman ruins (standard Db-€88, bigger Db-€105–125, still bigger Db-€145, Db/Qb suites-€180–250, excellent buffet breakfast-€11, air-con, elevator, parking-€11, 26 rue Sauvage, 1 block below Forum Square, tel. 04 90 93 56 66, fax 04 90 49 68 45, www.hotel -arlatan.fr, hotel-arlatan@wanadoo.fr, SE).

The next three hotels are worthy of three stars; each is an exceptional deal:

$$ Hôtel de l'Amphithéâtre**, a carefully decorated boutique hotel, is just steps from the Roman Arena. Public spaces are very sharp, with a museum quality, and the owners pay attention to every detail of your stay. The Belvedere room for €140 has the best view over Arles

Sleep Code

(€1 = about $1.20, country code: 33)

S = Single, **D** = Double/Twin, **T** = Triple, **Q** = Quad, **b** = bathroom, **s** = shower only, no **CC** = Credit Cards not accepted, **SE** = Speaks English, **NSE** = No English, * = French hotel rating system (0–4 stars). Unless otherwise noted, credit cards are accepted.

To help you sort easily through these listings, I've divided the rooms into three categories based on the price for a standard double room with bath:

$$$ **Higher Priced**—Most rooms €90 or more.
$$ **Moderately Priced**—Most rooms between €60–90.
$ **Lower Priced**—Most rooms €60 or less.

I've seen (Db-€52–72, superior Db-€82, Tb-€92, Qb-€120, air-con, elevator, parking-€5, 5 rue Diderot, one block from Arena, tel. 04 90 96 10 30, fax 04 90 93 98 69, www.hotelamphitheatre.fr, contact @hotelamphitheatre.fr, helpful Fabrice and Denis SE).

$$ Hôtel du Musée** is a quiet, delightful manor-home hideaway with 20 comfortable, air-conditioned rooms, a flowery two-tiered courtyard, and a snazzy art-gallery lounge. The rooms in the new section are worth the few extra euros and steps. Claude and English-speaking Laurence are gracious owners. The price ranges listed are for rooms in the old (lower rates) or new buildings (Sb-€43–50, Db-€55–65, Tb-€65–80, Qb-€80, buffet breakfast-€7, elevator, parking-€7, 11 rue du Grand Prieuré, follow signs to Réattu Museum, tel. 04 90 93 88 88, fax 04 90 49 98 15, www .hoteldumusee.com.fr, contact@hoteldumusee.com.fr).

$$ Hôtel Calendal**, located between the Roman Arena and Classical Theater, is Provençal chic and does everything right, with smartly appointed rooms—some with views overlooking the Arena—surrounding a large, palm-shaded courtyard. They even have my Provence video on DVD in the lobby. Enjoy the great buffet breakfast (€8), the salad-and-pasta-bar lunch buffet (€14), and the seductive ambience. Price ranges reflect room size (Db facing street-€45–70, Db facing garden-€72–85, Db with balcony-€90–100, air-con, Internet access, reserve ahead for parking-€10, 5 rue Porte de Laure, just above Arena, tel. 04 90 96 11 89, fax 04 90 96 05 84, www.lecalendal.com, contact@lecalendal.com, SE).

$$ Hôtel de la Muette**, with eager-to-please owners (NSE), is a good choice when the places listed above are full. Located in a quiet corner of Arles, the place is well-kept, with stone walls, wood beams, and air conditioning (Db-€55–60, Tb-€60–70, Qb-€80, no

Arles Hotels and Restaurants

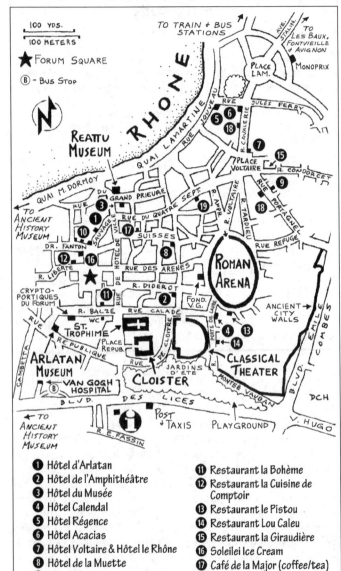

1. Hôtel d'Arlatan
2. Hôtel de l'Amphithéâtre
3. Hôtel du Musée
4. Hôtel Calendal
5. Hôtel Régence
6. Hôtel Acacias
7. Hôtel Voltaire & Hôtel le Rhône
8. Hôtel de la Muette
9. Maison d'Hotes en Provence
10. Restaurants le 16, Au Bryn du Thym & La Paillotte
11. Restaurant la Bohème
12. Restaurant la Cuisine de Comptoir
13. Restaurant le Pistou
14. Restaurant Lou Caleu
15. Restaurant la Giraudière
16. Soleilei Ice Cream
17. Café de la Major (coffee/tea)
18. Launderettes (2 locations)
19. Internet Café

elevator, 15 rue de Suisses, tel. 04 90 96 15 30, fax 04 90 49 73 16, http//perso.wanadoo.fr/hotel-muette, hotel.muette@wanadoo.fr).

$$ Maison d'Hôtes en Provence, run by engaging American Madeleine and her soft-spoken French husband, Erique, combines an interesting B&B experience—four spacious and funky but comfortable rooms—with optional Provençal cooking workshops. Foodies should check out their Web site for its appealing and affordable range of gourmet classes (Db-€65, extra person-€15, good family room, across from launderette at 11 rue Portagnel, tel. & fax 04 90 49 69 20, www.cuisineprovencale.com, actvedel@wanadoo.fr).

$ Hôtel Régence**, one of the best deals in Arles, has a riverfront location, immaculate and comfortable rooms, good beds, safe parking, and easy access to the train station (Db-€35–48, Tb-€40–57, Qb-€60–67, choose riverview or quieter courtyard rooms, most with shower, air-con, no elevator but only two floors, excellent buffet breakfast-€5, Internet access, 5 rue Marius Jouveau, from place Lamartine, turn right immediately after passing between towers, tel. 04 90 96 39 85, fax 04 90 96 67 64, www.hotel-regence.com, contact @hotel-regence.com, the gentle Nouvions speak some English).

$ Hôtel Acacias**, just off place Lamartine inside the old city walls, is a modern, pastel paradise, with smallish, reasonably priced rooms with all the comforts, including cable TV and hairdryers (Db-€46–55, Tb-€61–79, Qb-€78–87, buffet breakfast-€6, air-con, elevator, 1 rue Marius Jouveau, tel. 04 90 96 37 88, fax 04 90 96 32 51, www.hotel-acacias.com, contact@hotel-acacias.com, Christophe and Sylvie SE).

$ Hôtel Voltaire* rents 12 small and spartan rooms with ceiling fans and nifty balconies overlooking a caffeine-stained square. It's perfect for starving artists, a block below the arena. Smiling owner Mr. Ferran (fur-ran) loves the States (his dream is to travel there), and hopes you'll add to his postcard collection. He also serves daily lunch and dinner; see "Eating," below (D-€28, Ds-€30, Db-€36, 1 place Voltaire, tel. 04 90 96 49 18, fax 04 90 96 45 49, levoltaire@aol.com).

$ Hôtel le Rhône* greets you with neon yellow outside and hardworking owners inside—Benedicte and Hervé, refugees from northern France. Their 11 cute, spotless little rooms are decorated with cheery colors (D-€26, Ds-€31, Db-€38–40, some rooms have balconies over the square, 11 place Voltaire, tel. 04 90 96 43 70, fax 04 90 93 87 03, hotellerhone@wanadoo.fr).

EATING

You can dine well in Arles on a modest budget—in fact, it's hard to blow a lot on dinner here (all my listings have *menus* for €22 or less). The bad news is that restaurants here change regularly, so double-check my suggestions. All restaurants listed have outdoor seating, except La Bohème. Before dinner, go local on Forum Square and enjoy a *pastis*. This anise-based apéritif is served straight in a glass with ice, plus a carafe of water—dilute to taste.

On or near Forum Square

Great atmosphere and mediocre food at fair prices await on Forum Square. A half block below the Forum on rue du Dr. Fanton lies a lineup of these three tempting places:

Le 16, with warm ambience inside and out, is ideal for a fresh salad or one-course dinner. It offers a daily *plat du jour* and seasonal *menu* (closed Sat–Sun, just below Forum Square on 16 rue du Dr. Fanton, tel. 04 90 93 77 36).

La Paillotte, a few doors down, has rosy tablecloths under wood-beamed comfort inside, a nice terrace outside, and fine regional cuisine at affordable prices (€15–21 *menus*, closed Wed, 28 rue Dr. Fanton, tel. 04 90 96 33 15).

Au Bryn du Thym, almost next door, is reliable and specializes in traditional Provençal cuisine. Arrive early for an outdoor table (€19 *menu*, closed Tue, 22 rue Dr. Fanton, tel. 04 90 49 95 96).

La Bohème seems lost a block above Forum Square. Here you dine under a long, vaulted ceiling with good budget options (€14 vegetarian *menu*, €18 Provençal *menu*, closed Sun–Mon, 6 rue Balze, tel. 04 90 18 58 92).

La Cuisine de Comptoir (marked CDC) is the place urbanites go to lose that Provençal décor and pretend they're in Paris. It's a cool little bistro serving light *tartine* dinners (dishes served over toasted bread) at inexpensive prices (closed Sun, just off Forum Square's lower end at 10 rue de la Liberté, tel. 04 90 96 86 28).

Near the Roman Arena

For about the same price as on Forum Square, you can enjoy regional cuisine with a point-blank view of the arena. Of the two restaurants sitting side by side, I prefer **Le Pistou.** Arrive early to get an outdoor table with a view (*menus* from €18, closed Tue, at top of Arena, 30 rond-point des Arènes, tel. 04 90 18 20 92).

On the same block as the recommended Hôtel Calendal lies a mini-restaurant row, with several reasonable options. **Lou Caleu** is the best (though not cheapest), with very Provençal cuisine and *menus* at €18 and €26 (closed Mon, 27 rue Porte de Laure, tel. 04 90 49 71 77).

La Giraudière, a few blocks below the Arena on place Voltaire, is mauve and pretty and offers reliable regional cuisine under a heavy-beamed ceiling. Come here to dine inside, and show this book to get a free *kir* (€22–35 *menus*, closed Tue, air-con, tel. 04 90 93 27 52).

The recommended **Hôtel Calendal** hosts an all-you-can-eat salad-and-pasta bar (daily 12:00–16:00 for €14); the selection is as good as the quality. Retreat from the city and enjoy a healthy lunch in the hotel's palm-shaded garden.

The recommended **Hôtel Voltaire** serves a nothing-fancy three-course dinner (or lunch) for €11 and hearty salads for €8–10 (try *salade Fermiere*) daily on place Voltaire.

Dessert

For the best ice cream in Arles, find **Soleilei**, with all-natural ingredients and unusual flavors, such as *fadoli* (olive oil; daily, across from recommended La Vitamine restaurant at 9 rue du Dr. Fanton).

TRANSPORTATION CONNECTIONS

From Arles by bus to: Nîmes (5/day, 1 hr), **St. Rémy** (6/day, 45 min), **Camargue/Stes-Maries-de-la-Mer** (5/day Mon–Sat, 4/day Sun, 1 hr). There are two bus stops in Arles: the Centre-Ville stop is at 16 boulevard Clemenceau (2 blocks below main TI, next to Café le Wilson); the other is at the train station. Bus info: tel. 04 90 49 38 01 (NSE). Ask about buses to **Les Baux** (it's possible they will be reinstated by the time you read this).

From Arles by train to: Paris (17/day, two direct TGVs in 4 hrs, 15 with transfer in Avignon in 5 hrs), **Avignon Centre-Ville** (11/day, 20 min, afternoon gaps), **Avignon TGV** (2/hr, 20 min, take SNCF bus), **Nîmes** (9/day, 25 min), **Orange** (4/day direct, 35 min, more with transfer in Avignon), **Aix-en-Provence Centre-Ville** (10/day, 2 hrs, requires at least one transfer in Marseille), **Marseille** (20/day, 1 hr), **Carcassonne** (6/day, 3 hrs, 3 with transfer in Narbonne), **Beaune** (10/day, 4.5 hrs, 9 with transfer in Nîmes or Avignon and Lyon), **Nice** (11/day, 4 hrs, 10 with transfer in Marseille), **Barcelona** (2/day, 6 hrs, transfer in Montpellier), **Italy** (3/day, transfer in Marseille and Nice; from Arles, it's 4.5 hrs to Ventimiglia on the border, 8 hrs to Milan, 9.5 hrs to Cinque Terre, 11 hrs to Florence, and 13 hrs to Venice or Rome).

Avignon

Famous for its nursery rhyme, medieval bridge, and brooding Palace of the Popes, contemporary Avignon (ah-veen-yohn) bustles and prospers behind its mighty walls. During the 68 years (1309–1377) that Avignon starred as the Franco Vaticano, it grew from a quiet village into the thriving city it remains today. With its large student population and fashionable shops, today's Avignon is an intriguing blend of youthful spirit and urban sophistication. Street performers entertain the international crowds who fill Avignon's ubiquitous cafés and trendy boutiques. If you're here in July, be prepared for the rollicking theater festival (be sure to reserve your hotel months in advance). Clean, sharp, and popular with tourists, Avignon is more impressive for its outdoor ambience than for its museums and monuments. See the Palace of the Popes, then explore the city's thriving streets and beautiful vistas from the parc des Rochers des Doms.

ORIENTATION

The cours Jean Jaurès, which turns into rue de la République, runs straight from the train station to place de l'Horloge and the Palace of the Popes, splitting Avignon in two. The larger eastern half is where the action is. Climb to the parc des Rochers des Doms for a fine view, enjoy the people scene on place de l'Horloge, meander the backstreets (see "Discovering Avignon's Backstreets," page 398), and lose yourself in a quiet square. Avignon's shopping district fills the traffic-free streets where rue de la République meets place de l'Horloge.

Tourist Information

The main TI is between the train station and the old town, at 41 cours Jean Jaurès (April–Oct Mon–Sat 9:00–18:00, Sun 9:00–17:00; Nov–March Mon–Fri 9:00–18:00, Sat 9:00–17:00, Sun 10:00–12:00; longer hours during July festival, tel. 04 32 74 32 74, www.avignon -tourisme.com). Other branch offices may be open at either in the Palace of the Popes or at the St. Bénezet Bridge (rue Ferruce, but slow, with just one person working).

At any TI, get the good tear-off map and pick up the free and handy *Guide Pratique* (info on car and bike rental, hotels, and museums) as well as their Avignon "passion" map and guide, which includes several good (but tricky-to-follow) walking tours. It comes with the free **Avignon Passion Pass** (valid 15 days). Get the pass stamped when you pay full price at your first sight, and then receive reductions at the others; for example, €2 less at Palace of the Popes and €3 less at Petit Palais.

The TI offers informative English-language **walking tours** of Avignon (€10, €7 with Avignon Passion Pass; April–Oct Tue, Thu, and Sat at 10:00; Nov–March on Sat only, depart from the main TI, 2 hrs). They also have information on bus excursions to popular regional sights, including the wine route, Luberon, and Camargue.

The TI can book **excursions** to many destinations that require a car. Also see "Tours of Provence," page 372.

Arrival in Avignon

By Train: Avignon has two stations, the TGV and Centre-Ville (connected by frequent €1.10 shuttle bus). Avignon's new space-age TGV train station—located away from the center—is big news. While it makes Paris a zippy three-hour ride away, locals say it benefits rich Parisians the most. As Provence is now within easy weekend striking distance of the French capital, rural homes are being gobbled up by urbanites at inflated prices that locals can't afford.

Arrival at the TGV Station (Gare TGV): There is no baggage check here, though you can check your bags at the Centre-Ville station (see below). For the shuttle bus *(navette)* to the center of town, go out the north exit *(sortie nord),* down the stairs, and to the left. Look for the shuttle bus or the stop marked Avignon Centre (€1.10, 3/hr, buy tickets at info booth or from the driver). It drops you close to the other station (Centre-Ville). To reach the city center from the bus stop, walk through the city walls onto cours Jean Jaurès (TI is three blocks down at #41).

A taxi from the station to downtown Avignon costs €12.

If you want to rent a car at the TGV station, take the south exit *(sortie sud)* to find the *location de voitures.*

From Downtown Avignon to the TGV Station: The bus stop for the shuttle bus to the station is just in front of the main post office *(poste principal,* across from the main station on cours Président Kennedy). When a market fills that street, the bus waits on the east side of cours Jean Jaurès.

Arrival at Centre-Ville Station (Gare Avignon Centre-Ville): All non-TGV trains serve the central station. You can check bags here (exit the station to the left, look for *consignes* sign, May–Sept 6:00–22:00, Oct–April 7:00–19:00). The bus station *(gare routière)* is 100 yards to the right of the Centre-Ville station as you leave it (beyond and below Ibis Hôtel). From Centre-Ville station, walk through the city walls onto cours Jean Jaurès. The TI is three blocks down at #41.

By Car: Drivers entering Avignon should follow *Centre-Ville* and *Gare SNCF* (train station) signs. Park either near the walls for free (on boulevard Saint-Roch near Porte de la République), or, more securely, in a parking garage or a lot (€4/half-day, €7/day). The Palace of the Popes is just inside the walls where the "ruined" St. Bénezet Bridge meets the city, and there's a TI in season. Leave nothing in your car. Hotels have advice for smart overnight parking.

Helpful Hints

Book Ahead for July: During the July theater festival, rooms are rare—reserve very early, or stay in Arles (page 386) or St. Rémy (page 417).

Internet Access: Consider **Webzone** (daily 14:00–24:00, 25 rue Carnot), or ask your hotelier for the nearest Internet café.

Avignon Sights

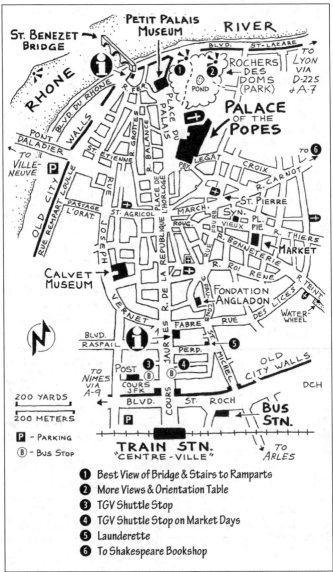

1. Best View of Bridge & Stairs to Ramparts
2. More Views & Orientation Table
3. TGV Shuttle Stop
4. TGV Shuttle Stop on Market Days
5. Launderette
6. To Shakespeare Bookshop

English Bookstore: Try **Shakespeare Bookshop** (Tue–Sat 9:30–12:30 & 14:00–18:30, closed Mon, 155 rue Carreterie, in Avignon's northeast corner, tel. 04 90 27 38 50).

Launderette: The launderette at 66 place des Corps-Saints (where rue Agricol Perdiguier ends) is near most hotels (daily 7:00–20:00).

Bike Rental: Consider **Provence Bike** at the bus station *(gare routière)* for bikes and scooters (52 boulevard St. Roch, tel. 04 90 27 92 61, www.provence-bike.com).

Car Rental: The TGV station has the most car-rental agencies (open long hours daily); the Centre-Ville station has fewer companies and shorter hours.

Tourist Trains: Two little trains, designed for tired tourists, leave regularly from the Palace of the Popes (mid-March–mid-Oct daily 10:00–19:00). One does a town tour (€7, 2/hr, 45 min, English commentary) and the other choo-choos you sweat-free to the top of the park, high above the river (€2, schedule depends on demand, no commentary).

Commanding City Views: Walk or drive across the Daladier Bridge (pont Daladier) for a great view of Avignon and the Rhône River. You can see other great views from the top of Parc des Rochers des Doms and from the end of the famous broken bridge, St. Bénezet (pont St. Bénezet).

SIGHTS

I've listed sights in the best order to visit, and have added a short walking tour of Avignon's backstreets to get you beyond the surface. Entries are listed at full price and also with the discount card (Avignon Passion Pass). Start your tour where the Romans did, on place de l'Horloge, and find a seat on a stone bench in front of City Hall (Hôtel de Ville).

Place de l'Horloge—The square, which was the town forum during Roman times and the market square through the Middle Ages, is Avignon's café square. (Restaurants here come with a fun ambience, but they also have high prices and low-quality meals.) Named for a medieval clock tower that the City Hall now hides, this square's present popularity arrived with the trains in 1854. Walk a few steps to the center and look down the main drag, rue de la République. When trains arrived in Avignon, proud city fathers wanted a direct, impressive way to link the new station to the heart of the city (just like in Paris)—so they plowed over homes to create the rue de la République, and widened place de l'Horloge.

Walk past the merry-go-round (public WCs behind), veer right, walk into Palace Square, and then walk uphill past the Palace of the Popes and enter...

Palace Square (Place du Palais)—This grand square surrounds the forbidding Palace of the Popes, the Petit Palais, and the cathedral.

In the 1300s, the Vatican moved the entire headquarters of the Catholic Church to Avignon. The Church bought Avignon and gave it a complete face-lift. Along with clearing out vast spaces like this square, and building this three-acre palace, the Church erected more than three miles of protective wall, with 39 towers, "appropriate" housing for cardinals (read: mansions), and residences for the entire Vatican bureaucracy. The city was Europe's largest construction zone. Avignon's population grew from 6,000 to 25,000 in short order. (Today, 13,000 people live within the walls.) The limits of pre-pope Avignon are outlined on the TI map. Rue Joseph Vernet, rue Henri Fabre, rue des Lices, and rue Philonarde all follow the route of the city's earlier defensive wall.

The Petit Palais (Little Palace) seals the uphill end of the square and was built for a cardinal; today, it houses medieval paintings (museum described below). The church to the left of the Palace of the Popes is Avignon's cathedral. It predates the Church's purchase of Avignon by 200 years. Its small size reflects Avignon's modest, pre-pope population. The gilded Mary was added in 1859.

Notice the stumps in front of the Conservatoire National de Musique. Nicknamed "*bites,*" slang for the male anatomy, they effectively keep cars from double-parking in areas designed for people. Many of the metal ones slide up and down by remote control to let privileged cars come and go.

Petit Palace Museum (Musée du Petit Palais)—This palace displays the Church's collection of medieval Italian painting and sculpture. All 350 paintings deal with Christian themes. A visit here before going to the Palace of the Popes helps furnish and people that otherwise barren building (€6, €3 with Avignon Passion Pass, Oct–May Wed–Mon 9:30–13:00 & 14:00–17:30; June–Sept Wed–Mon 10:00–13:00 & 14:00–18:00, closed Tue year-round; at north end of the Palace Square, tel. 04 90 86 44 58).

▲▲Park (Parc des Rochers des Doms), Ramparts, and St. Bénezet Bridge (Pont St. Bénezet)—With a short loop, you can enjoy a park, hike to a commanding river view, walk a bit of the wall, and visit Avignon's beloved broken bridge.

Park: Hike (or catch the tourist train, see "Helpful Hints," above) from the Palace of the Popes to the rocky top where Avignon was first settled. While the park itself is a delight, with many lookout points, don't miss the climax—a grand view of the Rhône River Valley and the broken bridge. On the largest terrace in the north side of the park, an orientation table explains the view; all around the terrace, several tableaux provide a little history in English.

On a clear day, the tallest peak you see is Mont Ventoux ("windy mountain"). St. André Fortress (across the river) was built by the French in 1360, shortly after the Pope moved to Avignon, to counter the papal incursion into this part of Europe. The fortress was in the kingdom of France. Avignon's famous bridge was a key border crossing, with towers on either end—one French and one Vatican.

To find the highest view, where all the teenage lovers hang out, climb the rocky stairs behind the fountain on the north side of the park (watch your step). In the center of the park, you'll also find a small café and public WCs.

Ramparts: From the viewpoint closest to the bridge, find the stairs leading down onto the only bit of the rampart you can walk on. When the pope came in the 1360s, small Avignon had no town wall...so he built one (restored in the 19th century).

St. Bénezet Bridge: This bridge, whose construction and location were inspired by a shepherd's religious vision, is the "pont d'Avignon" of nursery-rhyme fame. The ditty (which you've probably been humming all day) dates back to the 15th century: *Sur le pont d'Avignon / on y danse, on y danse / sur le pont d'Avignon / on y danse tout en rond* ("On the bridge of Avignon, we dance there, we dance there, on the bridge of Avignon, we dance there all in a circle").

But the bridge is a big deal even outside of its kiddie-tune fame. This was the only bridge crossing the mighty Rhône in the Middle Ages, until it was knocked down by a flood. While only four arches

survive today, the bridge was huge: Imagine a 22-arch, 3,000-foot-long bridge extending from Vatican territory to the lonely Tower of Philip the Fair, which marked the beginning of France. A Romanesque **chapel** on the bridge is dedicated to St. Bénezet. While there's not much to actually see on the bridge, the audioguide included in the €4 combo-ticket (available with the Palace of the Popes admission) tells a good story. It's also just fun to be in the breezy middle of the river, with a fine city view (April–Oct daily 9:00–19:00, July until 21:00, Aug–Sept until 20:00, Nov–March daily 9:30–17:45, last ticket sold 30 min before closing, tel. 04 90 27 51 16).

As you exit down the stairs, dip into the tiny and free museum, **Musée du Pont,** for some bridge history (daily 9:00–22:00, €0.50 WCs in same courtyard).

To get to the Palace of the Popes from here, exit the courtyard to the right and follow rue Ferruce straight ahead (don't take a right on rue Ferruce toward the river). After a block, look for the brown signs leading you left under the passageway, and up the stairs to the Palace Square.

▲Palace of the Popes (Palais des Papes)—In 1309, a French pope was elected (Pope Clement V). At the urging of the French king, His Holiness decided he'd had enough of unholy Italy. So, he loaded up his carts and moved to Avignon for a steady rule under a supportive king. The Catholic Church literally bought Avignon (then a two-bit town), and popes resided here until 1403. From 1378 on, there were twin popes, one in Rome and one in Avignon, causing a schism in the Catholic Church that wasn't fully resolved until 1417.

The papal palace is tourable. The included audioguide leads you through the one-way route and does a decent job of overcoming the lack of furnishings, teaching the basic history while allowing you to tour this largely empty palace at your own pace. As you wander, remember that this palace—the biggest surviving Gothic palace in Europe—was built to accommodate 500 people as the administrative center of the Vatican and home of the pope (you'll walk through his personal quarters, frescoed with happy hunting scenes). In the Napoleonic age, the palace was a barracks, housing 1,800 soldiers. You can see cuts in the wall where high ceilings gave way to floor beams.

The film auditorium shows a continuous 20-minute video in French that features images of the papal court, both in the Vatican and in Avignon. Nearby, a staircase leads to the tower for a view and windswept café.

A room at the end of the tour is dedicated to the region's wines, of which the pope was a fan. Sniff Le Nez du Vin (54 tiny bottles designed to develop your "nose"). Châteauneuf-du-Pape is a nearby village where the pope summered in the 1320s. Its famous wine is a direct descendant of his wine. You're welcome to taste some here (free, or split the €6 tasters' deal, which comes with a souvenir tasting cup).

You'll exit to the rear of the palace, where my backstreets walking tour begins (below). To return to the Palace Square, make two rights after exiting (€10, €8 with Avignon Passion Pass, combo-ticket available with St. Bénezet Bridge, April–Oct daily 9:00–19:00, July daily until 21:00, Aug–Sept daily until 20:00, Nov–March daily 9:30–17:45, last entry one hour before closing, tel. 04 90 27 50 74, www.palais-des-papes.com).

▲▲**Discovering Avignon's Backstreets**—Use the map in this book or the TI map to navigate this easy, level, 30-minute walk. This self-guided tour begins in the small square behind the Palace of the Popes, where visitors exit. (If you skipped the interior of the Palace of the Popes, walk down the Palace Square with the palace to your left, and take the first left down the narrow, cobbled rue Peyrolerie; notice how it was cut through the rock. You'll pop out into a small square behind the Palace of the Popes. Veer left and you're ready to go.)

Hôtel la Mirande: Located on the square, Avignon's finest hotel welcomes visitors. Find the atrium lounge and consider a coffee break amid the understated luxury (afternoon tea with a pastry, €15, is served 15:00–18:00). Inspect the royal lounge and dining room (recommended on page 405); cooking courses are offered in the basement below. Rooms start at €300.

Turn left out of the hotel and left again on rue Peyrolerie (Street of Coppersmiths), then take your first right on rue des Ciseaux d'Or. On the small square ahead, you'll find the...

Church of St. Pierre: The original chestnut doors were carved in 1551, when tales of New World discoveries raced across Europe (notice the Indian headdress). The fine Annunciation (lower left) shows Gabriel giving Mary the exciting news in impressive Renaissance 3-D.

Follow the alley to the left, which turned into a tunnel when it was covered with housing as the town's population grew. It leads into what was the cloister of St. Pierre (place des Châtaignes), named for chestnut trees, but now replaced by plane trees. Continue around the church.

With the church on your right, cross busy place Carnot to the Banque Chaix. The building opposite, with its beams showing, is a rare vestige from the Middle Ages. Notice how the building widens the higher it gets. A medieval loophole based taxes on ground-floor area—everything above was tax-free. Walking left down the pedestrian street, rue des Fourbisseurs (Street of Animal Furriers), notice how the top floors almost meet. Fire was a constant danger in the Middle Ages, as flames leapt easily from one home to the next. In fact, the lookout guard's primary responsibility was watching for fires, not the enemy. Virtually all of Avignon's medieval homes have been replaced by safer structures.

Turn left on traffic-free rue du Vieux Sextier (Street of the Balance, for weighing items); another left under the first arch leads to...

Avignon's Synagogue: Jews first came to Avignon with the diaspora of the 1st century. Avignon's Jews were nicknamed "the Pope's Jews" because of the protection that the Pope offered to Jews expelled from France. While this synagogue dates from 1220s, in Revolutionary times it was completely rebuilt in a neoclassical, Greek-temple style by a non-Jewish architect. This is the only synagogue under a rotunda that you'll see anywhere. The ark holding the Torah is in the east, next to a list of Jews deported from here to Auschwitz in 1942, after Vichy France was gobbled up by the Nazis. To visit the synagogue, press the buzzer, and friendly Rabbi Moshe Aman will be your guide (Mon–Thu 10:00–12:00 & 15:00–17:00, Fri 10:00–12:00, closed Sat–Sun).

From here, retrace your steps to rue du Vieux Sextier. Cross it, then go through the arch and down the yellow alley. Turn left on rue

de la Bonneterie ("street of hosiery"), which leads to the big, boxy...

Market (Les Halles): In 1970, the open-air market was replaced by this modern one, which may be ugly, but provides plenty of parking upstairs. Step inside for a sensual experience of organic breads, olives, and festival-of-mold cheeses. The rue des Temptations cuts down the center. The cafés and cheese shops are on the left—as far as possible from the stinky fish stall on the right (Tue–Sun until 13:00, closed Mon).

Continue on five minutes from Les Halles, on rue de la Bonneterie, which eventually becomes...

Rue des Teinturiers: This Street of the Dyers is Avignon's headquarters for all that's hip. You'll pass the Gray Penitents chapel. The facade shows the GPs, who dressed up in robes and pointy hoods to do their anonymous good deeds back in the 13th century (long before the KKK dressed this way).

You'll see the work of amateur sculptors, who have carved whimsical car barriers out of limestone. Earthy cafés, galleries, and a small stream (a branch of the Sorgue River) with waterwheels line this tie-dyed street. This was the cloth industry's dyeing and textile center in the 1800s. Those stylish Provençal fabrics and patterns you see for sale everywhere started here, after a pattern imported from China.

Waterwheel: At the waterwheel, imagine the Sorgue River, which hits the mighty Rhône here in Avignon, being broken into several canals in order to turn 23 such wheels. Around 1800, this powered the town's industries. The little cogwheel above the big one could be shoved into place, kicking another machine into gear behind the wall.

Across from the wheel at #41, **La Cave Breysse** would love to serve you a fragrant glass of regional wine (€2.50 per glass). Choose from the blackboard by the bar that lists all the bottles open today. You're welcome to take it out and sit by the canal (wine with salads and lunch plates, flexible hours, normally Tue–Sat 11:00–15:00, wine only Tue–Sat 18:00–22:30, closed Sun–Mon, Christine Savory and Tim Sweet SE).

To get back to the real world, double back on rue des Teinturiers, turning left on rue des Lices, which traces the first medieval wall—*lices* is the no-man's-land along a wall. You'll pass a four-story arcaded building that was a home for the poor in the 1600s, an army barracks in the 1800s, a fine arts school in the 1900s, and a deluxe condominium today (much of this neighborhood is going high-class residential). Eventually, you'll return to rue de la République, Avignon's main drag.

More Sights

Fondation Angladon-Dubrujeaud—This museum mixes a small but enjoyable collection of art from Post-Impressionists (including Paul Cézanne, Vincent van Gogh, Honoré Daumier, Edgar Degas, and Pablo Picasso) with re-created art studios and furnishings from many periods. It's a quiet place with a few superb paintings (€6, €4 with Avignon Passion Pass, Tue–Sun 13:00–18:00, closed Mon year-round and Tue in winter, 5 rue Laboureur, tel. 04 90 82 29 03, www.angladon.com).

Calvet Museum (Musée Calvet)—This museum impressively displays its wide-ranging collection, covering prehistory to 20th-century art with no English information. You'll find everything from Neolithic artifacts to medieval tapestries to porcelain plates to Impressionist paintings (€6, €3 with Avignon Passion Pass, Wed–Mon 10:00–13:00 & 14:00–18:00, closed Tue, on quieter west half of town at 65 rue Joseph Vernet; its antiquities collection is a few blocks away at 27 rue de la République—same hours and ticket; tel. 04 90 86 33 84).

Near Avignon in Villeneuve-lès-Avignon

▲Tower of Philip the Fair (Tour Philippe-le-Bel)—Built to protect access to St. Bénezet Bridge in 1307, this massive tower offers the best view over Avignon and the Rhône basin. It's best late in the day (€1.60, €0.90 with Avignon Passion Pass, April–Sept daily 10:00–12:30 & 14:00–18:30; Oct–Nov and March Tue–Sun 10:00–12:00 & 14:00–17:00, closed Mon and Dec–Feb; tel. 04 32 70 08 57). To reach the tower from Avignon, you can drive (5 min, cross Daladier Bridge, follow signs to Villeneuve-lès-Avignon); take a boat (Bateau-Bus departs from Mireio Embarcadère near Daladier Bridge); or take bus #11 (2/hr, catch bus across from Centre-Ville train station, in front of post office on cours Président Kennedy).

SLEEPING

Hotel values are distinctly better in Arles, though these are all solid values. Avignon is particularly popular during its July festival, when you must book ahead and can expect inflated prices. (Note that only a few hotels have elevators; specifically, the first three listed near place de l'Horloge.)

Near Centre-Ville Station

The next three listings are a 10-minute walk from the main train station; turn right off cours Jean Jaurès on rue Agricol Perdiguier.

$$ **Hôtel Colbert**** is a fine midrange bet. Parisian escapees Patrice and Annie, who both speak English, are your hosts. They care for this restored manor house, and it shows, from the peaceful patio to the warm room decor throughout (Sb-€43–53, Db-€60–70, Tb-€70–90, air-con, 7 rue Agricol Perdiguier, tel. 04 90 86 20 20, fax 04 90 85 97 00, www.lecolbert-hotel.com, colbert.hotel@wanadoo.fr).

At $$ **Hôtel le Splendid***, ever-smiling Madame Prel-Lemoine rents 17 cheery rooms with good beds, ceiling fans, and small bathrooms (Sb-€42–45, Db-€54–64, 17 rue Agricol Perdiguier, tel. 04 90 86 14 46, fax 04 90 85 38 55, www.avignon-splendid-hotel.com, contact@avignon-splendid-hotel.com).

$ **Hôtel du Parc***, across the street at #18, is a little less sharp, but cheaper than Hôtel le Splendid, with entertaining Avignon native Madame Rous thrown in for free. Rooms have pretty stone walls; the best overlook the park. Madame bakes all her own bread and pastry for breakfast (S-€28, Ss-€35, D-€35, Ds-€44, Db-€48, Tb-€65, no TVs or phones, tel. 04 90 82 71 55, fax 04 90 85 64 86, hotel.du.parc.84@wanadoo.fr).

In the Center, near Place de l'Horloge

At $$$ **Hôtel d'Europe******, you can be a vagabond in the palace at Avignon's most prestigious address—if you get one of the 15 surprisingly reasonable "standard rooms." Enter into a fountain-filled courtyard, linger in the lounges, and enjoy every comfort. The hotel is located on handsome place Crillon, near the river (standard Db-€134, spacious Db standard-€164, first-class Db-€224, deluxe Db-€312, superior Db-€420, breakfast-€25, elevator, Internet access, garage-€16, 12 place Crillon, near Daladier Bridge, tel. 04 90 14 76 76, fax 04 90 14 76 71, www.heurope.com, reservations@heurope.com, SE).

$$$ **Hôtel Mercure Cité des Papes***** is a modern hotel chain within spitting distance of the Palace of the Popes. It has 73 smartly designed, smallish rooms, musty halls, air-conditioning, elevators, and all the comforts (Db-€113–130, extra bed-€14, many rooms have views over place de l'Horloge, 1 rue Jean Vilar, tel. 04 90 80 93 00, fax 04 90 80 93 01, h1952@accor-hotels.com, SE).

$$$**Hôtel Pont d'Avignon***** is nearby, just inside the walls, near St. Bénezet Bridge (87 rooms, same chain, same price, rue Ferruce, tel. 04 90 80 93 93, fax 04 90 80 93 94, h0549@accor-hotels.com, SE).

$$ **Hôtel de Blauvac**** and friendly owner Veronica offer 16 mostly spacious, high-ceilinged rooms (many with an additional upstairs loft) and a sky-high atrium. It's a grand old manor home near the pedestrian zone (Sb-€60–70, Db-€65–75, Tb €80–90, Qb-€95, €10 less off-season, 11 rue de la Bancasse, 1 block off rue de la République, tel. 04 90 86 34 11, fax 04 90 86 27 41, www.hotel-blauvac.com, blauvac@aol.com).

Avignon Hotels and Restaurants

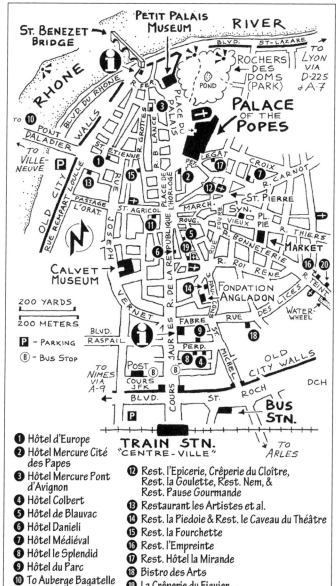

1 Hôtel d'Europe
2 Hôtel Mercure Cité des Papes
3 Hôtel Mercure Pont d'Avignon
4 Hôtel Colbert
5 Hôtel de Blauvac
6 Hôtel Danieli
7 Hôtel Médiéval
8 Hôtel le Splendid
9 Hôtel du Parc
10 To Auberge Bagatelle
11 Villa Agapè

12 Rest. l'Epicerie, Crêperie du Cloître, Rest. la Goulette, Rest. Nem, & Rest. Pause Gourmande
13 Restaurant les Artistes et al.
14 Rest. la Piedoie & Rest. le Caveau du Théâtre
15 Rest. la Fourchette
16 Rest. l'Empreinte
17 Rest. Hôtel la Mirande
18 Bistro des Arts
19 La Crêperie du Figuier
20 La Cave Breysse Wine Bar

$$ **Hôtel Danieli**** is a Hello-Dolly fluffball of a place that rents 29 colorful and comfortable rooms on the main drag. It has air-conditioning and lots of tour groups (Sb-€61–73, Db-€72–85, Tb-€83–100, Qb-€100–120, elevator, 17 rue de la République, tel. 04 90 86 46 82, fax 04 90 27 09 24, www.hotel-danieli-avignon.com, contact@hotel-danieli-avignon.com, kind owner Madame Shogol SE).

$$ **Hôtel Médiéval**** is burrowed deep a few blocks from the St. Pierre church in a massive stone mansion with a small flower-filled garden. The 34 unimaginative yet adequate rooms have firm beds (Db-€56–70, Tb-€79, kitchenettes available but require 3-day minimum stay, 15 rue Petite Saunerie, 5 blocks east of place de l'Horloge, behind Church of St. Pierre, tel. 04 90 86 11 06, fax 04 90 82 08 64, hotel.medieval@wanadoo.fr).

Chambre d'Hôte

$$$ **Villa Agapè**, just off busy place de l'Horloge, right in the center of town, is an oasis of calm and good taste. Run by helpful Madame de La Pommeraye, the villa has three handsomely decorated rooms, a peaceful courtyard, and a soaking pool to boot (Db-€100–140, extra person-€30, includes breakfast, 2-night minimum in high season; from place de l'Horloge, walk one block toward the TI and train sation and turn right on rue St. Agricol, it's on the left above the pharmacy, ring buzzer, 13 rue St. Agricol; tel. 04 90 85 21 22, fax 06 07 98 71 30, www.villa-agape.com, michele@villa-agape.com). For a week-long stay, ask about renting her entire house, where you get Madame's room, study, kitchen, and everything.

Sleeping Cheaply near Avignon

$ **Auberge Bagatelle's hostel/campground** offers dirt-cheap beds, a lively atmosphere, a busy pool, a café, a grocery store, a launderette, great views of Avignon, and campers for neighbors (dorm bed-€12, D-€25, across Daladier Bridge on the island l'Ile de la Barthelasse, bus #10 from main post office, tel. 04 90 86 30 39, fax 04 90 27 16 23, camping.bagatelle@wanadoo.fr).

EATING

Skip the overpriced places on place de l'Horloge (Les Domaines and La Civette near the carousel are the least of evils here), and find a more intimate location for your dinner. Avignon has many delightful squares filled with tables ready to seat you.

Near the Church of St. Pierre

This church has enclosed squares on both sides, offering outdoor yet intimate ambience.

L'Epicerie is charmingly located and popular, with the highest-quality cuisine around St. Pierre church, including a good selection of à la carte items (€20 main dishes, closed Sun, cozy interior good in bad weather, 10 place St. Pierre, tel. 04 90 82 74 22).

Pass under the arch by L'Epicerie restaurant and enter enchanting place des Châtaignes, filled with the tables of four restaurants: **Crêperie du Cloître** (big salad and main-course crêpe for about €13, closed Sun–Mon); **Restaurant la Goulette** (Tunisian specialties, *tagine* or couscous-€17, closed Mon); **Restaurant Nem,** tucked in the corner of the square (Vietnamese, family-run, *menus* from €10, closed Tue–Wed); and **Pause Gourmande** (lunch only, *plats du jour*-€7, always a veggie choice, closed Sun).

Crillon Square (Place Crillon)

This large, open square just off the river provides more atmosphere than quality. Several cafés offer inexpensive bistro fare with *menus* from €14, *plats* from €12, and many tables to choose from. **Restaurant les Artistes** is one of several (daily, 21 place Crillon, tel. 04 90 82 23 54).

Elsewhere in Avignon

Bistro des Arts, with a colorful interior and pleasant service, is a good choice for Provençal dishes (daily, 24 rue des Lices, tel. 04 90 85 67 21).

La Crêperie du Figuier has good crêpes and salads that won't break the bank (dinner crêpe or salad for €11, closed Sun, 3 rue du Figuier, tel. 04 90 82 60 67).

At **La Piedoie,** a few blocks northeast of the TI, eager-to-please owner-chef Thierry Piedoie serves fine traditional and Provençal dishes in an intimate, elegant setting (€36 *menu*, closed Wed, interior seating only, 26 rue des Trois Faucons, tel. 04 90 86 51 53).

Le Caveau du Théâtre is the antithesis of its neighbor, La Piedoie, with wild posters decorating a carefree interior. Wine and good-value dishes are the specialties (€13 *plats*, €18 *menus*, fun ambience for free, closed Sun, 16 rue des Trois Faucons, tel. 04 90 82 60 91).

La Fourchette is cozy, indoor-only, traditional, and well-respected. It's a block from place de l'Horloge toward the river (*menus* from €29, closed Sat–Sun, 17 rue Racine, tel. 04 90 85 20 93).

L'Empreinte is good for North African cuisine in a trendy location (copious couscous for €11–16, takeout and veggie options available, daily, 33 rue des Teinturiers, tel. 04 32 76 31 84).

Hôtel la Mirande is the ultimate Avignon splurge. Reserve ahead here for understated elegance and Avignon's top cuisine (€28 lunch *menu*, €50 dinner *menu*, €85 tasting *menu*, closed Tue–Wed, behind Palace of the Popes, 4 place de la Mirande, tel. 04 90 86 93 93, fax 04 90 86 26 85, www.la-mirande.fr).

TRANSPORTATION CONNECTIONS

Trains

Remember, there are two train stations in Avignon: the new suburban TGV station and the Centre-Ville station in the city center (€1.10 shuttle buses connect to both stations, 3/hr, 10 min). Only the Centre-Ville station has baggage check. Car rental is available at both stations (better at TGV). Some cities are served both by slower local trains from the Centre-Ville station and by faster TGV trains from the TGV station; I've listed the most convenient stations for each trip.

From Avignon's Centre-Ville station to: Arles (12/day, 20 min), **Orange** (10/day, 15 min), **Nîmes** (14/day, 30 min), **Isle-sur-la-Sorgue** (6/day, 30 min), **Lyon** (10/day, 2 hrs), **Carcassonne** (8/day, 7 with transfer in Narbonne, 3 hrs), **Barcelona** (2/day, 6 hrs, transfer in Montpellier).

From Avignon's TGV station to: Arles (2/hr, by SNCF bus, 30 min), **Nice** (10/day, 4 hrs, a few direct, most require transfer in Marseille), **Marseille** (10/day, 70 min), **Aix-en-Provence TGV** (10/day, 75 min), **Lyon** (12/day, 1.5 hrs, also from Centre-Ville station—see above), **Paris'** Gare de Lyon (14/day, 3 with transfer in Lyon, 2.5 hrs), **Paris'** Charles de Gaulle airport (7/day, 3 hrs).

Buses

The bus station (*gare routière*, tel. 04 90 82 07 35) is just past and below the Ibis Hôtel to the right as you exit the train station (information desk open Mon–Fri 10:15–13:00 & 14:00–18:00, Sat 8:00–12:00, closed Sun). Nearly all buses leave from this station. The biggest exception is the SNCF bus service that runs from the Avignon TGV station to Arles (10/day, 30 min). The Avignon TI has schedules. Service is reduced or nonexistent on Sunday and holidays.

From Avignon by bus to: Pont du Gard (5/day in summer, 3/day off-season, 40 min), **St. Rémy** (6/day, 45 min, handy way to visit its Wed market); **Isle-sur-la-Sorgue** (5/day, 45 min); **Vaison la Romaine** (2–3/day during school year, called *période scolaire*, 1/day otherwise and 1/day from TGV station, 90 min).

More Sights in Provence:
Pont du Gard, Les Baux, St. Rémy, and Orange

A car is a dream come true here. Below I've described key sights and a full-day excursion deep into the countryside (even better done as an overnight; see "Côtes du Rhône Villages: Self-Guided Driving Tour," page 429). Les Baux and St. Rémy work well by car from

Avignon or Arles. The town of Orange ties in tidily with a trip to the Côtes du Rhône villages. The Pont du Gard is a short hop west of Avignon and on the way to/from Languedoc for drivers. Travelers relying on public transportation will find their choices very limited. St. Rémy (page 438) and Isle-sur-la-Sorgue (page 414) are the most accessible small towns.

Pont du Gard

Throughout the ancient world, aqueducts were like flags of stone that heralded the greatness of Rome. A visit to this sight still works to proclaim the wonders of that age. This perfectly preserved Roman aqueduct was built as *the* critical link of a 30-mile canal that, by dropping one inch for every 350 feet, supplied nine million gallons of water per day (about 100 gallons per second) to Nîmes—one of ancient Europe's largest cities. Though most of the aqueduct is on or below the ground, at the Pont du Gard it spans a canyon on a massive bridge—one of the most remarkable surviving Roman ruins anywhere.

Getting to the Pont du Gard

By Bus: Buses run to Pont du Gard (Rive Gauche) from Avignon (5/day summer, 3/day off-season, 40 min.

Bus stops are at the traffic roundabout 300 yards from the Pont du Gard. The stop from Avignon and to Nîmes is on the opposite side of the roundabout from the Pont du Gard; the stop from Nîmes and to Avignon is on the same side as the Pont du Gard, just to the left as you enter the traffic circle. Make sure you're waiting for the bus on the correct side of the traffic circle.

By Car: Pont du Gard is an easy 25-minute drive due west of Avignon (follow signs to Nîmes) and 45 minutes northwest of Arles (via Tarascon). The Rive Gauche parking is off D-981, which leads from Remoulins to Uzès. (Parking is also available on the Rive Droite side, but it's farther away from the museum.)

ORIENTATION

There are two riversides to the Pont du Gard: the left and right banks (Rive Gauche and Rive Droite). Park on the Rive Gauche, where you'll find the museums, ticket booth, cafeteria, WC, and shops—all built into a modern plaza. You'll see the aqueduct in two parts: first, a fine new museum complex, then the actual river gorge spanned by the ancient bridge.

Cost: While it's free to see the aqueduct itself, the various optional activities each have a cost: parking (€5), museum (€6), informative 25-minute film (€3, see below), and a kids' space called Ludo (€4.50, scratch-and-sniff experience in English of various aspects of Roman life and the importance of water). The new extensive outdoor *garrigue* natural area, featuring historic crops and landscapes of the Mediterranean, is free (though €4 gets you a helpful English booklet). All are designed to give the sight more meaning—and they do—but for most visitors, only the museum

is worth paying for. The €10 combo-ticket—which covers all sights and parking—is best for drivers. If you get the combo-ticket, check the movie schedule; the 25-minute film is silly, but offers good information in a flirtatious French style...and a cool, entertaining, and cushy break. During summer months, a free sound-and-light show plays at night against the Pont du Gard.

Hours: The museum is open daily (Easter–Nov 9:30–19:00, mid-June–Aug until 21:30, Dec–Easter until 18:00, closed most of Jan, tel. 08 20 09 33 30). The aqueduct itself is free and open until 22:00 (same hours as parking lot).

Canoe Rental: Consider seeing the Pont du Gard by canoe. Collias Canoes will pick you up at the Pont du Gard (or elsewhere, if prearranged) and shuttle you to the town of Collias. You'll float down the river to the nearby town of Remoulins, where they'll pick you up and take you back to the Pont du Gard (2-person canoe-€27, usually 2 hrs, though you can take as long as you like, tel. 04 66 22 85 54, SE).

SIGHTS

▲**Museum**—This state-of-the-art museum's multimedia approach (well-described in English) shows how water was an essential part of the Roman "art of living." You'll see examples of lead pipes, faucets, and siphons; walk through a rock quarry; learn how they moved those huge rocks into place; and learn how those massive arches were made. While actual artifacts from the aqueduct on display are few, the exhibit shows the immensity of the undertaking, as well as the payoff. Imagine the excitement as this extravagant supply of water finally tumbled into Nîmes. A relaxing highlight is the scenic video helicopter ride along the entire 30-mile course of the structure, from its start at Uzès all the way to the Castellum in Nîmes.

▲▲▲**Viewing the Aqueduct**—A parklike path leads to the aqueduct. Until a few years ago, this was an actual road—adjacent to the aqueduct—that has spanned the river since 1743. Before you cross the bridge, pass under it and hike 350 feet along the riverbank for a grand viewpoint from which to study the second-highest standing Roman structure (Rome's Colosseum is 2 yards taller).

This was the biggest bridge in the whole 30-mile-long aqueduct. It seems exceptional because it is: The arches are twice the width of standard aqueducts, and the main arch is the largest the Romans ever built—80 feet (so it wouldn't get its feet wet). The bridge is about 160 feet high, and was originally about 1,100 feet long. Today, 12 arches are missing, reducing the length to 790 feet.

While the distance from the source (in Uzès) to Nîmes was only 12 miles as the eagle flew, engineers chose the most economical route, winding and zigzagging 30 miles. The water made the trip in 24 hours with a drop of only 40 feet. Ninety percent of the aqueduct is on or under the ground, but a few river canyons like this required bridges. A stone lid hides a four-foot-wide, six-foot-tall chamber lined with waterproof mortar that carried a stream for over 400 years. For 150 years, this system provided Nîmes with good drinking water. Expert as the Romans were, they miscalculated the backup caused by a downstream corner, and had to add the thin extra layer you can see just under the lid to make the channel deeper.

The bridge and the river below provide great fun for holiday-goers. While parents suntan on inviting rocks, kids splash into the gorge from under the aqueduct. Some daredevils actually jump from the aqueduct itself—not knowing that crazy winds scrambled by the structure cause painful belly flops, and sometimes even accidental death. For the most refreshing view, float flat on your back under the structure (bring a swimsuit and sandals for the rocks).

The appearance of the entire gorge changed in 2002, when a huge flood flushed lots of greenery downstream. Those floodwaters put Roman provisions to the test. Notice the triangular-shaped buttresses at the lower level—designed to split and divert the force of any flood *around* the feet of the arches, rather than *into* them. The 2002 floodwaters reached the top of those buttresses. Anxious park rangers winced at the sounds of trees crashing onto the ancient stones...but the arches stood strong.

The stones that jut out—giving the aqueduct a rough, unfinished appearance—supported the original scaffolding. The protuberances were left, rather than cut off, in anticipation of future repair needs. The lips under the arches supported the wooden templates that allowed the stones of the round arches to rest on something until the all-important keystone was dropped into place. Each stone weighs four to six tons. The structure stands with no mortar—taking full advantage of the innovative Roman arch, made strong by gravity.

Hike over the bridge for a closer look. Across the river, a high trail (marked Panorama) leads upstream and offers commanding views. On the exhibit side of the structure, a trail marked Accès l'Aqueduc leads up to surviving stretches of the aqueduct. For a peaceful walk alongside the top of the aqueduct (where it's on land and no longer a bridge), follow the red-and-yellow markings. Remains of this part are scant because of medieval cannibalization—frugal builders couldn't resist the pre-cut stones as they constructed local churches. The ancient quarry (about a third of a mile downstream on the exhibit side) may open in 2005.

Les Baux

Crowning the rugged Alpilles (ahl-pee) Mountains, this rock-capping castle town is a memorable place to visit. Even with the tourist crowds, the place evokes a strong community that lived a rugged life—thankful more for their top-notch fortifications than their dramatic views. While mobbed with tourists through most of the day, the town is a more peaceful scene for those arriving by 9:00 or after 17:00. Sunsets are dramatic, and nights in Les Baux-de-Provence are pin-drop peaceful. After dark, the castle is closed—but beautifully illuminated.

Les Baux is actually two visits in one: castle ruins on an almost lunar landscape, and, below, a medieval town packed with shops, cafés, and tourist knickknacks. See the castle, then savor or blitz the lower town on your way out. There's no free parking; get as close to the top as you can, and pay €4 (good for 3 days, take ticket and pay at machine next to telephone and bakery about 30 steps below town entry).

One cobbled street leads into town, where you're greeted first by the **TI** (April–Sept daily 9:00–19:00, Oct–March 9:00–12:00 & 13:00–18:00, in Hôtel de Ville, tel. 04 90 54 34 39). The main drag leads directly to the castle (15-min uphill walk).

Getting to Les Baux

By Bus: Longtime bus service with Arles was canceled in 2004 for "local political reasons." It might be reinstated—someday—ask. Consider taking a bus to St. Rémy (about €4 from Arles or Avignon), and then a taxi from there (figure €15 one-way). This allows you to combine two worthwhile stops while saving euros.

By Taxi: Figure €30 for a taxi one-way from Arles (tel. 06 80 27 60 92).

By Foot: Les Baux is a beautiful three-hour hike from St. Rémy; see "Hike to Les Baux" on page 417.

By Car: Les Baux is a 20-minute drive from Arles. From Arles, follow signs to Avignon, then Les Baux. Drivers can combine Les Baux with St. Rémy (15 min away).

Les Baux

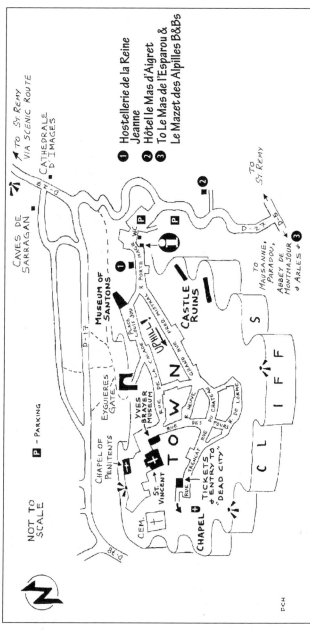

TO ST REMY VIA SCENIC ROUTE

CATHEDRALE D'IMAGES

CAVES DE SARRAGAN

D-17

NOT TO SCALE

🅿 - PARKING

N

PCH

MUSEUM OF SANTONS

Eyguieres Gate

TOWN

UPHILL

R PORTE MAGE

PLACE LOUIS JOU

RUE DE LA CALADE

GRAND RUE

RUE FRED MISTRAL

CASTLE RUINS

CHAPEL OF PENITENTS

YVES BRAYER MUSEUM

ST. VINCENT

CEM.

CHAPEL

TICKETS & ENTRY TO "DEAD CITY"

RUE TRANCAT

RUE NEUVE

RUE DES...

RUE DU CHATEAU

RUE DU FOURS

RUE DE L'ORME

CLIFFS

WC

🅿

🅿

TO ST REMY

D-27

D-5

TO MAUSANNE, PARADOU, ABBEY DE MONTMAJOUR & ARLES + 3

1 Hostellerie de la Reine Jeanne
2 Hôtel le Mas d'Aigret
3 To Le Mas de l'Esparou & Le Mazet des Alpilles B&Bs

SIGHTS

The Castle Ruins

Many of the ancient walls of Les Baux's striking castle still stand in testament to the proud past of this village. The climbing is fun, the views are sensational, and the mistral wind just might blow your socks off. Buy your ticket in the old olive-mill room, and study the museum exhibits (models of the town in the 13th and 16th centuries, interesting photos showing the town before tourism and today). Pick up the informative and included audioguide.

A 12th-century regional powerhouse, Les Baux was razed in 1632 by a paranoid Louis XIII, who was afraid of these troublemaking upstarts. The sun-bleached "dead city" ruins are carved into, out of, and on top of a rock 650 feet above the valley floor. As you wander out on the wind-blown field past kid-thrilling medieval siege weaponry, try to imagine 6,000 people living behind stone walls on this cliff. Notice the water-catchment system (a slanted field that caught rain water and drained it into a cistern—necessary during a siege). In the little chapel across from the museum, the slideshow ("Van Gogh, Gauguin, and Cézanne: Painting in the Land of the Olive Trees") provides a relaxing 10-minute interlude. Early July through late August, medieval events take place in the open area (visitors' crossbow shooting range might be continued in 2005, check at TI as you enter; castle entry-€7, Easter–Oct daily 9:00–19:00, July–Aug until 20:00, Nov–Easter daily 9:30–17:00).

Lower Town

You can shop and eat your way back to your car or the bus station through the new town. Or you can take your first left, go downhill, and check out these minor but fun sights as you descend from the castle:

Yves Brayer Museum (Musée Yves Brayer)—This is an appealing exhibit of paintings (van Gogh–like Expressionism, without the tumult) by Yves Brayer, who spent his final years in the 1970s here in Les Baux (€4, daily 10:00–12:30 & 14:00–18:30).

Downhill, around the corner, is...

St. Vincent Church—This 12th-century Romanesque church was built short and wide to fit the terrain. The center chapel on the right houses the town's traditional Provençal processional chariot. Each Christmas Eve a ram pulled this cart—holding a lamb, symbolizing Jesus, and surrounded by candles—to this church.

In front of the church is the old-town "laundry"—with a

pig-snout faucet and 14th-century stone washing surface with drains designed for short women.

Around the corner, toward a great view, is the...

Chapel of Penitents—Notice the nativity scene painted by Yves Brayer, which shows the local legend that Jesus was born in Les Baux.

Staying left as you round the old laundry and heading downhill, you'll pass plenty of cafés with wonderful views. You'll see the town's fortified wall and one of its two gates. Farther below, you'll come to the...

Museum of Santons—The museum displays a collection of *santons*, popular folk figurines, which decorate local Christmas mangers (free entry). Notice how the nativity scene proves once again that Jesus was born in Les Baux. These painted clay dolls show off local dress and traditions. Find the old couple leaning into *le mistral* wind.

Near Les Baux

A half mile beyond Les Baux, D-27 leads to dramatic views of the hill town, with pullouts and walking trails at the pass, and two sights that fill cool, cavernous caves in former limestone quarries that date back to the Middle Ages. (The limestone is easy to cut, but gets hard and nicely polished when exposed to the weather.)

Caves de Sarragan—Occupied by the Sarragan Winery (which invites you in for a taste), the best views of Les Baux can be seen from its parking lot. While this place looks like it's designed for groups, the friendly, English-speaking staff welcomes individuals (free, April–Sept daily 10:00–12:00 & 14:00–19:00, Oct–March until 18:00, tel. 04 90 54 33 58).

Cathédrale d'Images—In a similar cave nearby, it offers a mesmerizing sound-and-slide show. Its 48 projectors flash countless images set to music on the quarry walls as visitors wander around, immersed in the year's theme (€7, daily 10:00–18:00). The D-27 continues to St. Rémy and makes a good loop if you return via D-5 from St. Rémy.

Speaking of quarries, in 1821, the rocks and soil of the area were discovered to contain an important mineral for the making of aluminum. It was named after the town—bauxite.

SLEEPING

In or near Les Baux

$$$ Le Mas d'Aigret*** crouches barely past Les Baux on the road to St. Rémy. Lie on your back and stare up at the castle walls rising beyond your swimming pool in this mini-oasis. Most of the average-sized, artfully designed rooms have private terraces and views over the valley, and the restaurant is troglodyte-chic (non-view Db-€100, larger Db with balcony-€135, Tb-€175, prices include breakfast, air-con, some daytime road noise with view rooms, €30 *menu* at restaurant, tel. 04 90 54 20 00, fax 04 90 54 44 00, www.masdaigret .com, contact@masdaigret.com, SE).

$$ Le Mas de l'Esparou *chambre d'hôte*, a few minutes below Les Baux, is welcoming and kid-friendly, with three spacious rooms, squishy mattresses, a swimming pool, table tennis, and distant views of Les Baux. Jacqueline loves her job, and her lack of English only makes her more animated. Monsieur Roux painted the artwork in your room and has a gallery in Les Baux (Db-€62, extra person-about €16, no CC, between Les Baux and Maussane les Alpilles on D-5, look for white sign with green lettering, tel. & fax 04 90 54 41 32, NSE).

$ Hostellerie de la Reine Jeanne**, an exceptional value, offers comfy rooms 150 feet to your right after the main entry to the live city, where you can watch the sun set and rise from Les Baux (standard Ds-€47, standard Db-€51, Db with view deck-€63, cavernous family suite-€92, air-con in some rooms, ask for *chambre avec terrasse*, good *menus* from €20, tel. 04 90 54 32 06, fax 04 90 54 32 33, www.la-reinejeanne.com, reine.jeanne@wanadoo.fr, affable Alain SE).

$ Le Mazet des Alpilles is a small home with three tidy air-conditioned rooms, just outside the unspoiled village of Paradou, five minutes below Les Baux. It may have space when others don't (Db-€53, ask for largest room, child's bed available, no CC, follow brown signs from D-17, in Paradou look for route de Brunelly, tel. 04 90 54 45 89, fax 04 90 54 44 66, lemazet@wanadoo.fr, charming Annick speaks just enough English).

St. Rémy

Sophisticated and sassy, St. Rémy-de-Provence gave birth to Nostradamus and cared for a distraught artist. A few minutes from the town center, you can visit the once thriving Roman city called Glanum, the mental ward where Vincent van Gogh was sent after lopping off his lobe, and an art center dedicated to his memory. Best of all, elbow your way  through its raucous Wednesday market (until 12:30). A racecourse-like ring road hems in a pedestrian-friendly center that's well-stocked with fine foods and the latest Provençal fashions.

The **TI** on place Jean Jaurès is two blocks toward Les Baux from the ring road (Mon–Sat 9:30–12:30 & 14:00–19:00, Sun 10:00–12:00 & 15:00–17:00, tel. 04 90 92 05 22). Parking in St. Rémy is tricky and always comes with a fee; it's easiest at the TI lot. From the TI, it's a 15-minute walk to Glanum and Clinique St. Paul (van Gogh's mental hospital).

St. Rémy Area

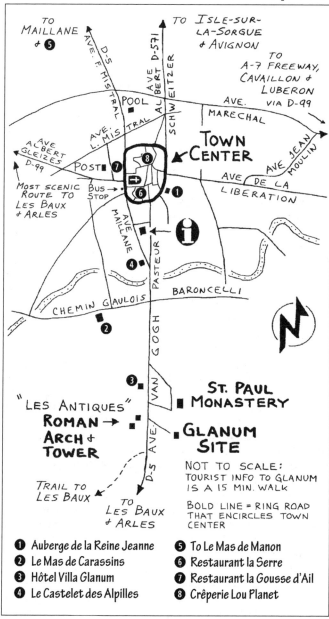

TO MAILLANE &

TO ISLE-SUR-LA-SORGUE & AVIGNON

TO A-7 FREEWAY, CAVAILLON & LUBERON VIA D-99

AVE. F. MISTRAL

D-5

AVE. ALBERT D-571

SCHWEITZER

POOL

AVE. MARECHAL

AVE. L. MISTRAL

AVE. ALBERT GLEIZES D-99

TOWN CENTER

AVE JEAN MOULIN

POST

MOST SCENIC ROUTE TO LES BAUX & ARLES

BUS STOP

AVE. DE LA LIBERATION

AVE MAILLANE

VAN GOGH PASTEUR

BARONCELLI

CHEMIN GAULOIS

N

"LES ANTIQUES" ROMAN → ARCH & TOWER

VAN GOGH

D-5 AVE.

ST. PAUL MONASTERY

GLANUM SITE

NOT TO SCALE: TOURIST INFO TO GLANUM IS A 15 MIN. WALK

TRAIL TO LES BAUX

TO LES BAUX & ARLES

BOLD LINE = RING ROAD THAT ENCIRCLES TOWN CENTER

❶ Auberge de la Reine Jeanne
❷ Le Mas de Carassins
❸ Hôtel Villa Glanum
❹ Le Castelet des Alpilles
❺ To Le Mas de Manon
❻ Restaurant la Serre
❼ Restaurant la Gousse d'Ail
❽ Crêperie Lou Planet

Getting to St. Rémy

By Bus: Buses run from Arles and Avignon to St. Rémy (6/day, 45 min). If arriving at St. Rémy by bus, get off on the ring road, just before the turnoff to Les Baux and the TI.

By Taxi: From Les Baux, figure on €15; from Avignon, allow €40 (tel. 06 80 27 60 92).

By Car: A spectacular 15-minute drive along D-27, over the hills and through the woods, separates St. Rémy and Les Baux. Coming from Les Baux, find D-27 by passing Cathédrale d'Images. If you're driving from St. Rémy to Les Baux, follow signs for Tarascon, and you'll see the D-27 turnoff to Les Baux in a few miles.

SIGHTS

▲**Glanum**—These crumbling stones are the foundations of a Roman market town, located at the crossroads of two ancient trade routes between Italy and Spain. This important town had grand villas and temples, a basilica, a forum, a wooden dam, aqueducts, and more. A massive Roman arch and tower stand proud and lonely near the ruins' parking lot. The arch marked the entry into Glanum, and the tower is a memorial to the grandsons of Emperor Caesar Augustus. The setting is stunning, though shadeless, and the small museum at the entry sets the stage well. While the ruins are, well, ruined, they remind us of the range and prosperity of the Roman Empire. Along with other Roman monuments in Provence, they allow us to paint a more complete picture of Roman life (the city is estimated to have been 7 times as large as the ruins you see). The English handout is helpful, but consider buying one of the two English booklets (one has better photos, the other provides much better background). Inside the ruins, signs give basic English explanations at key locations, and the view from the belvedere justifies the effort (€6, May–Aug daily 9:00–19:00, Sept–April daily 10:30–17:00).

St. Paul Monastery (Le Monastère St. Paul de Mausole)—Just below Glanum is the still-functioning mental hospital (Valetudo, formerly called Clinique St. Paul) that treated Vincent van Gogh from 1889 to 1890. Pay €3.50 and enter Vincent's temporarily peaceful world: a small chapel, intimate cloisters, and a re-creation of his room. You'll find limited information in English about Vincent's life. Amazingly, he painted 150 works in his 53 weeks here—none of which remain anywhere nearby today. The contrast between the utter simplicity of his room (and his life) and the multimillion-dollar value of his paintings today is jarring. The site is managed by Valetudo, a center specializing in art therapy (April–Oct daily 9:30–19:00, Nov–March daily 10:15–16:45). Outside the complex, dirt trails lead to Vincent's favorite footpaths with (sometimes vandalized) copies of his paintings located where he painted them.

Food Lovers' Guide to St. Rémy—Wednesday is market day in St. Rémy, but you don't have to fast until then. Foodies will appreciate the three shops that gather on the ringroad in St. Rémy, near the turnoff to Les Baux.

Start at Olive-Huiles du Monde, where you can saddle up to a wine-bar-like setting and sample the best olive oil in this area; also check out the fine display of other products made from olive oil (daily 10:00–13:00 & 15:00–19:00, 16 boulevard Victor Hugo).

Le Petit Duc, across the road, offers a remarkable introduction to antique cookies. Let friendly owner Anne, who speaks English, take you on a tour (daily 10:00–13:00 & 15:00–19:00, 7 boulevard Victor Hugo).

Just one whiff of Joel Durand's chocolate will lure chocoholics inside. Ask for a sample, and learn the letter-coded system (daily 10:00–19:00, 3 boulevard Victor Hugo, next door to Le Petit Duc).

Centre d'Art Présence Vincent van Gogh—Here you'll find a permanent tribute to the painter (including some reproductions), as well as rotating exhibits reflecting the enormous influence of his work on contemporary artists (€3.50, Tue–Sun 10:30–12:30 & 14:30–18:30, closed Mon, inside the ring road on rue Estrine, tel. 04 90 92 34 72).

Hike to Les Baux—These directions will help you find your way on the lovely three-hour hike from St. Rémy to Les Baux (for more details, ask at TI). Start from the signposted slope opposite the Glanum entry. Follow the goat path up into the mountain, and arrive at the chimney. Go down the iron ladder, and you'll come to a lake. Walk around the lake on the left-hand side, turning left along the Mas de Gros cart track. A mile later, turn right on Sentier des Crêtes and follow the yellow markings to Les Baux. You'll end on the paved road in Val d'Enfer.

SLEEPING

(€1 = about $1.20, country code: 33)

$$$ Le Mas de Carassins***, a 15-minute walk from the center, is impeccably run by friendly Paris refugees Michel and Pierre. Luxury is affordable here. They pay attention to every aspect of the hotel, from the generously sized pool and gardens to the muted room decor to the optional €26 weekday-only dinner (standard Db-€98, bigger Db-€115, deluxe Db-€120, suite-€165, extra bed-€15, aircon, table tennis, look for signs 200 yards toward Les Baux from TI, 1 Chemin Gaulois, tel. 04 90 92 15 48, fax 04 90 92 63 47, www.hoteldescarassins.com, info@hoteldescarassins.com).

$$ Le Castelet des Alpilles*** is a slightly tired and Old World place, but the location is good (a few blocks toward Les Baux from the TI), the price is fair, and the rooms are plenty comfortable. Rooms are generally big and airy, and the balcony rooms have views of the Alpilles (Db-€65, Db with air-con and view balcony-€87, 6 place Mireille, tel. 04 90 92 07 31, fax 04 90 92 52 03, www.castelet-alpilles.com, hotel.castel.alpilles@wanadoo.fr).

\$\$ Hôtel Villa Glanum**, right across from the Glanum ruins, with some traffic noise, is a 15-minute walk from the town center. Rooms are small and unimaginative, yet adequate. The best rooms, which come with higher rates, are in bungalows around the pretty pool (Db-€62–82, Tb-€85–100, Qb-€105–120, cheaper off-season, 46 avenue van Gogh, tel. 04 90 92 03 59, fax 04 90 92 00 08, www.villaglanum.com, villa.glanum@wanadoo.fr).

\$\$ Auberge de la Reine Jeanne** is more central, if less personal. The 11 traditionally decorated, spotless, and spacious rooms (with big beds) take a backseat to the popular restaurant. Some rooms overlook a courtyard filled with tables and umbrellas (Db-€59–68, Tb/Qb-€76, €25 *menu* in fine restaurant, on right side of ring road a few blocks after you enter from Les Baux, 12 boulevard Mirabeau, tel. 04 90 92 15 33, fax 04 90 92 49 65, aubergereinejeanne@wanadoo.fr).

\$\$ Le Mas de Manon *chambre d'hôte* has rooms two miles from St. Rémy, off a bamboo-lined lane in a lush locale. Salty owners Marie-Odile (SE) and Claude (forget it) run this restored farmhouse, with modern rooms at fair prices. A stay here includes all the comforts and a pretty little garden (Db-€60, includes breakfast, no CC, leave St. Rémy toward Maillane on D-5 and look for signs after 2 miles, Chemin des Lones, tel. & fax 04 32 60 09 86, mobile 06 09 44 92 22, masdemanon@libertysurf.fr).

EATING

St. Rémy is packed with fine restaurants, each trying to outdo the others. Join the evening strollers and compare. To dine well in an interior courtyard packed with plants, try **La Serre,** where everything from bread to pâté is homemade (€22 *menu*, closed Mon, a block from where the road to Les Baux meets the ringroad in the old center, 8 rue de la Commune, tel. 04 90 92 37 21).

La Gousse d'Ail is no secret, but even so, it's a reliable and warm place for a mini-splurge (*menus* from €30, on the ring road just after the turnoff to Maillane at 6 boulevard Marceau, closed Thu, tel. 04 90 92 16 87).

Crêperie Lou Planet, on pleasant place Favier, is cheap and peaceful (daily until 20:00, behind Hôtel de Ville).

Orange

Orange is notable for its Roman arch and grand theater. The town, while otherwise insignificant, has more than its share of Roman monuments, because it was an important city in ancient times—strategically situated on the Via Agrippa connecting Lyon and Arles. It was actually founded as a nice place for Roman army officers to enjoy their retirement. Even in Roman times, career military men retired after only 20 years. Does the emperor want thousands of well-trained, relatively young guys hanging around Rome? No way. What to do? "How about a nice place in the south of France...?"

Tourist Information: The TI is opposite the Roman Theater's stage wall (daily 10:00–13:00 & 14:15–18:00, place des Frères Mounet, tel. 04 90 34 70 88).

Arrival in Orange

By Train: Orange's **train station** (no baggage check, though if you ask nicely at Accueil, they might keep your bags up to 2 hours) is a 15-minute walk from the Roman Theater (or a €7 taxi ride, tel. 06 09 32 57 71): Walk straight out of the station down avenue Frédéric Mistral, merge left onto Orange's main shopping street (rue de la République), then turn left on rue Caristie and you'll run into the stage wall.

By Bus: Buses from Avignon, Vaison la Romaine, and other wine villages arrive at the big square, place Pourtoules. To reach the Roman Theater, walk toward the hill and turn right at the end of place Pourtoules.

By Car: Drivers follow *Centre-Ville* signs, then *Théâtre Antique* signs, and park as close to the Roman Theater's huge wall as possible. (Parking Théâtre Antique is large and close to the theater, with another TI nearby).

SIGHTS

▲**Roman "Arc de Triomphe"**—Technically, the only real Roman arches of triumph are in Rome's Forum, built to commemorate various emperors' victories. The great Roman arch of Orange is actually a municipal arch erected (around A.D. 19) to commemorate a general, named Germanicus, who protected the town. The 60-foot-tall arch is on a noisy traffic circle (north of city center on avenue Arc de Triomphe).

▲▲**Roman Theater (Théâtre Antique)**—Orange's ancient theater is the best-preserved in existence, and the only one in Europe with its acoustic wall still standing (two others in Asia Minor also survive).

After you enter (to the right of the actual theater), you'll see a huge dig—the site of the Temple to the Cult of the Emperor.

Climb the steep stairs to the top of the theater to appreciate the acoustics (eavesdrop on people by the stage) and contemplate the idea that, 2,000 years ago, Orange residents enjoyed grand spectacles with high-tech sound and lighting effects—such as simulated thunder, lightning, and rain.

This is the standard Roman theater design: a semicircular orchestra, a half circle of theater seats, and a small stage with a high back wall—originally covered with a marble veneer and colorfully painted. A huge awning could be unfurled from the 130-foot-tall stage wall to provide shade.

A grandiose Caesar overlooks everything. If it seems like you've seen this statue before, you probably have. Countless sculptures identical to this one were mass-produced in Rome and shipped throughout the empire to grace buildings like this theater for propaganda purposes. To save money on shipping and handling, only the heads of these statues were changed with each new ruler. The permanent body wears a breastplate emblazoned with the imperial griffin (body of a lion, head and wings of an eagle) that only the emperor could wear. When a new emperor came to power, new heads were made in Rome and shipped off throughout the empire to replace the pop-off heads on all these statues. (Imagine John Kerry's head on George W. Bush's body. Now pop off Kerry's head and pop on anybody else's.)

Archaeologists believe that a puny, vanquished Celt was included at the knee of the emperor and touching his ruler's robe respectfully—a show of humble subservience to the emperor. It's interesting to consider how an effective propaganda machine can con the masses into being impressed by their leader.

The horn has blown. It's time to grab your seat: row two, number 30. Sitting down, you're comforted by the "EQ GIII" carved into the seat (Equitas Gradus #3...three rows for the Equestrian order.) You're not comforted by the hard limestone bench (thinking it'll probably last 2,000 years). The theater is filled with 10,000 people. Thankfully, you mix only with your class (the nouveau riche—merchants, tradesmen, and city big shots). The people above you are the working-class, and way up in the "chicken roost" section are the scum of the earth—slaves, beggars, prostitutes, and youth hostelers. Scanning the orchestra section (where the super-rich sit on real chairs), you notice the town dignitaries hosting some visiting VIPs.

Okay, time to worship. They're parading a bust of the emperor from its sacred home in the adjacent temple around the stage. Next is the ritual animal sacrifice, called *la pompa* (so fancy, future generations will use that word for anything full of such...pomp). Finally, you settle in for an all-day series of spectacles and dramatic entertainment. All eyes are on the big stage door in the middle—where the Julia Roberts and Jack Nicholsons of the day will appear. (Lesser actors come out of the side doors.)

The play is good, but many come for the halftime shows—jugglers, acrobats, and strip-tease dancers. In Roman times, the theater was a festival of immorality. An ancient writer commented, "The vanquished take their revenge on us by giving us their vices through the theater."

With an audience of 10,000 and no amplification, acoustics were very important. At the top of the side walls, a slanted line of stones marks the position of a long-gone roof—not to protect from the weather, but to project the voices of the actors into the crowd. For further help, actors wore masks with leather caricature mouths that functioned as megaphones.

The Roman Theater was all part of the "give them bread and circuses" approach to winning the support of the masses (not unlike today's philosophy of "give them tax cuts and Fox News Channel"). The spectacle grew from 65 days of games per year, when the theater was first built (and when Rome was at its height), to about 180 days each year by the time Rome finally fell.

Cost and Hours: Your ticket includes a worthwhile audioguide and entrance to the small museum across the street. Pop in to see a few theater details and a rare grid used as the official property-ownership registry; each square represented a 120-acre plot of land (theater entry-€7.50, April–Sept daily 9:00–19:00, until 20:00 in summer, closes at 18:00 or 17:00 off-season, tel. 04 90 51 17 60). Vagabonds wanting to see the theater for free can hike up nearby stairs (*escalier est* off of rue Pourtoules is closest) to view it from the bluff high above.

TRANSPORTATION CONNECTIONS

From Orange by train to: Avignon (10/day, 15 min), **Arles** (4/day direct, 35 min, more with transfer in Avignon), **Lyon** (16/day, 2 hrs).

By bus to: Vaison la Romaine (2–3/day, 45 min), **Avignon** (hrly, 55 min). Buses to Vaison la Romaine and other wine villages depart from the big square, place Pourtoules (turn right out of the Roman Theater and right again on rue Pourtoules).

Villages of the Côtes du Rhône

The sunny Côtes du Rhône wine road—one of France's best—starts at Avignon's doorstep and winds north through an appealingly rugged, mountainous landscape carpeted with vines, peppered with warm stone villages, and presided over by the Vesuvius-like Mont

Ventoux. The wines of the Côtes du Rhône (grown on the *côtes*, or hillsides, of the Rhône Valley) are easy on the palate and on your budget. But this hospitable place offers more than famous wine— its hill-capping villages inspire travel posters, and its vistas are fantastic. Yes, there are good opportunities for enjoyable wine-tasting, but there is also a soul to this area...if you take the time to look.

Planning Your Time

Vaison la Romaine is the small hub of this region, offering limited bus connections with Avignon and Orange, bike rental, and a mini-Pompeii in the town center. Nearby, you can visit the world's best-preserved Roman Theater in Orange, drive to the top of Mont Ventoux, follow my self-guided driving tour of Côtes du Rhône villages and wineries, and pedal to nearby villages for a breath of fresh air. The Dentelles de Montmirail mountains are laced with a variety of exciting trails, ideal for hikers.

Two nights make a good start for exploring this area. Drivers should head for the hills (read the "Côtes du Rhône Villages: Self-Guided Driving Tour," below, before deciding where to stay). Those without wheels find that Vaison la Romaine makes an easier home base.

Getting Around the Côtes du Rhône

By Bus: Buses run to the Côtes du Rhône from Avignon and Orange (2–3/day, 45 min from Orange, 90 min from Avignon) and connect several wine villages (including Gigondas, Sablet, and Beaumes-de-Venise) with Vaison la Romaine and Nyons to the north.

By Train: Trains get you as far as Orange (from Avignon: 10/day, 15 min), from which buses make the 45-minute trip to Vaison la Romaine (2–3/day).

By Car: Pick up the Michelin local map #332 to navigate (landmarks like Dentelles de Montmirail and Mont Ventoux make it easier to get your bearings). If you're connecting the Côtes du Rhône with the Luberon, consider doing it scenically via Mont Ventoux (follow signs to Malaucène, then to Mont Ventoux, allowing 2 hrs to Roussillon). This route is one of the most spectacular in Provence.

By Tour: Lieutaud offers big-bus excursions to Vaison la Romaine and Orange (see page 372).

Vaison la Romaine

With quick access to vineyards, villages, and Mont Ventoux, this lively little town of 6,000 makes a great base for exploring the Côtes du Rhône region by car or bike. You get two villages for the price of one: Vaison la Romaine's "modern" lower city is like a mini-Arles, with worthwhile Roman ruins, a lone pedestrian street, and too many cars. The car-free medieval hill town looms above, with meandering cobbled lanes, a dash of art galleries and cafés, and a ruined castle (good view from its base).

ORIENTATION

The city is split in two by the Ouvèze River. The Roman bridge connects the newer city (Ville-Basse) with the hill-capping medieval city (Ville-Haute).

Tourist Information: The superb TI is in the newer city, between the two Roman ruin sites, at place du Chanoine Sautel (May–Sept Mon–Sat 9:00–12:00 & 14:00–18:45, Sun 9:00–12:00; Oct–April Mon–Sat 9:00–12:30 & 14:00–17:45, closed Sun; tel. 04 90 36 02 11, www.vaison-la-romaine.com). Say *bonjour* to *charmante* and ever-so-patient Valerie, ask about festivals and evening programs, get bus schedules, and pick up information on walks and bike rides from Vaison la Romaine. Also ask about the Nocturiales, nighttime sound-and-light visits to the Roman ruins (summers only).

Arrival in Vaison la Romaine

By Bus: The unmarked bus stop to Orange and Avignon is in front of the Cave la Romaine winery. Buses from Orange or Avignon drop you across the street (2–3/day, 45 min from Orange, 90 min from Avignon). Tell the driver you want the stop for the Office de Tourisme. When you get off the bus, walk five minutes down avenue Général de Gaulle to reach the TI and hotels.

By Car: Follow signs to *Centre-Ville*, then *Office de Tourisme*; park free across from the TI.

Helpful Hints

Market Day: Sleep in Vaison la Romaine on Monday night, and you'll wake to an amazing Tuesday market. But be warned: Mondays are quiet, and the town's two best restaurants are closed. If you do spend a Monday night, avoid parking at market sites.

Internet Café: Le Cyber Café de Net & Cie is on the outskirts of town (Mon–Fri 9:00–19:00, Sat 9:00–12:00 & 14:00–18:00, closed Sun, 30 ZA de l'Ouvèze, across from cemetery and Renault shop, tel. 04 90 28 97 41).

Launderette: The self-service **Laverie la Lavandière** is on cours Taulignan near avenue Victor Hugo (daily 8:00–20:00). The friendly owners (who work next door at the dry cleaner) will do your laundry while you sightsee—when you pick it up, thank them with a small tip.

Bike Rental: Try **Mag 2 Roues**, near the TI on cours Taulignan (tel. 04 90 28 80 46).

Vaison la Romaine

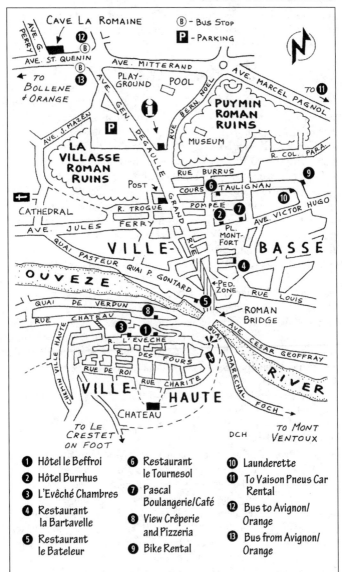

1. Hôtel le Beffroi
2. Hôtel Burrhus
3. L'Evêché Chambres
4. Restaurant la Bartavelle
5. Restaurant le Bateleur
6. Restaurant le Tournesol
7. Pascal Boulangerie/Café
8. View Crêperie and Pizzeria
9. Bike Rental
10. Launderette
11. To Vaison Pneus Car Rental
12. Bus to Avignon/Orange
13. Bus from Avignon/Orange

Car Rental: Try **Vaison Pneus** (avenue Marcel Pagnol, tel. 04 90 28 89 81).

Taxi: To call a taxi, dial 04 90 46 81 36 or 06 82 93 68 42.

Local Guide: Let sincere **Anna-Marie Melard** bring those Roman ruins to life for you (€35 for a tour of the ruins, tel. 04 90 36 50 48).

SIGHTS AND ACTIVITIES

In Vaison la Romaine

Roman Ruins—Ancient Vaison la Romaine had a treaty that gave it the preferred "federated" relationship with Rome (rather than

simply being a colony). This, along with a healthy farm economy (olives and vineyards), made it a most prosperous place—as a close look at its sprawling ruins indicates. Two thousand years ago, about 6,000 people called Vaison home. When the barbarians arrived, the Romans were forced out, and the Vaison townspeople fled into the hills. The town has only recently reached the same population as during its Roman era—that's mind-boggling.

Vaison la Romaine's Roman ruins are split by a modern road into two sites: Puymin and La Villasse. Each is well-presented, offering a good picture of life during the Roman Empire (€7, price includes both sets of ruins, plus the cloister at the Notre-Dame de Nazareth Cathedral; June–Sept daily 9:30–18:00, Oct–March daily 10:00–12:30 & 14:00–18:00, Nov–Feb daily 10:00–16:00, English tours about once a week in summer, check with TI). Visit **Puymin** first. The brief but helpful English flier explains the site (pick it up when you pay). Inside the site, climb the hill to the museum (exhibits explained in English loaner booklet). Behind the museum is a 6,000-seat theater (just enough seats for the number of residents). Nearest the entry are the scant but impressive remains of a sprawling mansion. Back across the modern road in **La Villasse**, you'll explore a "street of shops" and the foundations of more houses.

Lower Town (Ville-Basse)—Vaison la Romaine's nondescript modern town stretches out from its car-littered main square, place Montfort. The cafés grab the north side of the square, conveniently sheltered from the prevailing mistral wind, and they enjoy the generous shade of the ubiquitous *platane* trees (cut back each year to form a leafy canopy). A few blocks away, the stout Notre-Dame de Nazareth Cathedral, with an evocative cloister, is a good example of Provençal Romanesque (cloister entry covered by €7 Roman ruins ticket—see above). The pedestrian-only Grand Rue is a lively shopping street leading to the river gorge and the Roman bridge.

Roman Bridge—Two thousand years ago, the Romans cut this sturdy, no-nonsense vault into the canyon rock, and it has survived ever since. Until the 20th century, this was the only way to cross the Ouvèze River. The metal plaque on the wall (Crue du 22-09-92) shows the high-water mark of the record flood that killed 30 people and washed away the valley's other bridges. The flood swept away the modern top of this bridge...but couldn't budge the 55-foot Roman arch.

Upper Town (Ville-Haute)—While there's nothing of particular importance to see in the fortified medieval old town atop the hill, the cobbled lanes and charming fountains make you want to break out a sketchpad. Vaison la Romaine had a prince/bishop starting in the 4th century. He came under attack by the Count of Toulouse in the 12th century. Anticipating a struggle, the bishop abandoned the lower town and built a château on this rocky outcrop (around 1195). Over time, the rest of the townspeople followed, vacating the lower town and building their homes at the base of the château behind the upper town's fortified wall.

To reach the upper town, hike up from the Roman Bridge (passing memorials for both World Wars) through the medieval gate, under the lone tower crowned by an 18th-century wrought-iron bell cage. The château is closed, but a trail to it rewards you with a fine view.

▲**Market Day**—In the 16th century, the pope gave Vaison la Romaine market-town status. Each Tuesday since then, the town has hosted a farmers market. Today, merchants gather with gusto, turning the entire place into a festival of produce. This amazing Tuesday-morning market is worth noting as you plan your itinerary (see "Helpful Hints," above).

Hiking—The TI has good information on relatively easy hikes into the hills above Vaison la Romaine. It's about 90 minutes to the tiny hill town of Le Crestet, though great views begin immediately. To find this trail, drive or walk up past the upper town with the castle on your left, find the chemin des Fontaines, and stay the course as far as you like. Cars are not allowed on the road after about a mile.

Biking—This area is not particularly flat, and it's often hot and windy, making bike-riding a dicey option. But if it's calm out and you lack a car, the five-mile ride to cute little Villedieu is doable (small roads, lovely views). With a little more energy, you can pedal beyond Villedieu on the beautiful road to Mirabel (ask in Villedieu for directions). You can also connect the following villages for a good 11-mile loop ride: Vaison la Romaine, St. Romain-en-Viennois, Puyméras, Faucon, and St. Marcellin-lès-Vaison (TI has details).

Wine-Tasting—Cave la Romaine, a five-minute walk up avenue Général de Gaulle from the TI, offers a variety of great-value wines from nearby villages in a pleasant, well-organized tasting room (daily 8:30–13:00 & 14:00–19:00, avenue St. Quenin, tel. 04 90 36 55 90).

Near Vaison la Romaine

▲**Mont Ventoux and Lavender**—The drive to Mont Ventoux is worth ▲▲▲ if skies are crystal-clear, or in any weather from late June to early August, when the lavender blooms. It also provides a scenic connection between the Côtes du Rhône villages and the Luberon. Allow an hour to drive to the top of this 6,000-foot mountain, where you'll be greeted by cool temperatures, plenty of people, and more white stones than you can imagine.

Mont Ventoux is Provence's rooftop, with astonishing Pyrénées-to-Alps views—but only if it's clear (which it often isn't). Even under hazy skies, it's an impressive place. The top has a barren, surreal lunar-landscape quality, but it's packed with souvenirs, bikers, and hikers. Miles of poles stuck in the rock identify the route (the top is usually snowbound Dec–April). **Le Vendran** restaurant (near the old observatory and Air Force control tower) offers snacks and meals with commanding views. An orientation board is available on the opposite side of the mountaintop.

Between Mont Ventoux and the Luberon, you'll pass through several climate zones and astonishingly diverse landscapes. The scene alternates between rocky canyons, lush meadows, and wildflowers. Thirty minutes east of Mont Ventoux, lavender fields forever surround the rock-top village of Sault (soh), which produces 40 percent of France's lavender essence and has good view cafés.

Getting to Mont Ventoux: To reach Mont Ventoux from Vaison la Romaine, go to Malaucène, then wind up D-974 for 40 minutes to the top (or take D-19 to pleasant little Bedoin, with a fun Monday market; from there, D-974 offers a longer, prettier route to the top). If continuing to Sault (worthwhile only when the lavender blooms), follow signs to Sault. The "Les Routes de la Lavande" brochure suggests driving and walking routes in the area (available online at www.routes-lavande.com or at Sault TI, tel. 04 90 64 01 21).

▲**Ardèche Gorges (Gorges de l'Ardèche)**—These gorges, which wow visitors with abrupt, chalky-white cliffs, follow the Ardèche River through immense canyons and thick forests. To reach the gorges from Vaison la Romaine, drive west 45 minutes, passing through Bollène and Pont Saint-Esprit to Vallon Pont d'Arc (which offers all-day canoe-kayak floats through the gorges). If continuing north, connect Privas and Aubenas, then head back via the autoroute. Endearing little Balazuc—a village north of the gorges, with narrow lanes, flowers, views, and a smattering of cafés and shops—makes a fine stop.

SLEEPING

Hotels here are a good value. Those in the medieval upper town (Ville-Haute) are quieter, cozier, cooler, and a 15-minute walk uphill from the parking lot next to the TI. If you have a car, consider staying in one of the charming Côtes du Rhône villages near Vaison la Romaine (see page 435).

\$\$\$ Hôtel Le Beffroi***, in the upper town, is red-tile-and-wood-beamed classy, with mostly spacious rooms (some with views), a good restaurant, pleasing public spaces, a garden with view tables, and a small pool with more views. The rooms are split between two buildings a few doors apart; the main building is more characteristic (standard Db-€85–100, superior Db-€125, *menus* from €27, driving here is a challenge—tiny lanes—and parking is tight, rue de l'Evêché, tel. 04 90 36 04 71, fax 04 90 36 24 78, www.le-beffroi .com, lebeffroi@wanadoo.fr, Nathalie SE).

\$\$ L'Evêché Chambres, almost next door to Le Beffroi in the upper town, is a cozy, five-room, melt-in-your-chair bed-and-breakfast. The owners (the Verdiers) have an exquisite sense of interior design and are into art—making this place feel like a wood-beamed, leather-couch art gallery (Sb-€65–70, standard Db-€70–80, Db suite-€95–120, the *solanum* suite is worth every euro, Tb-€105–140, rue de l'Evêché, tel. 04 90 36 13 46, fax 04 90 36 32 43, eveche@aol.com).

\$ Hôtel Burrhus**—part art gallery, part hotel—is easily the best value in the lower town. It's central and laid back, with a large, shady terrace over the raucous place Montfort and a floor plan that will confound even the ablest navigator. Ask for one of their new rooms, which are bigger, with cool colors and contemporary decor...worth paying extra for (Db-€45–52, new Db-€54–70, extra bed-€15, air-con in most rooms, for maximum quiet request a back room, 1 place Montfort, tel. 04 90 36 00 11, fax 04 90 36 39 05, www.burrhus.com, info@burrhus.com).

EATING

Vaison la Romaine is a small town with a handful of good, popular eateries—arrive by 19:30 or reserve a day ahead, particularly on weekends. You can eat very well on a moderate budget in the lower town (where you'll find all of my listings), or go for medieval ambience rather than memorable food in the atmospheric upper town (has a view *crêperie* and an air-conditioned pizzeria, open daily, with fair prices). With a car, it's worth venturing to nearby Côtes du Rhône villages to eat (see page 436).

La Bartavelle is *the* place to savor traditional French cuisine in the lower town. Serious yet helpful owner Richard Cayrot has put together a tourist-friendly mix-and-match menu of local options. You get access to the top-end selections even on the €20 bottom-end *menu*—just fewer courses (closed Mon, 12 place Sus-Auze, air-con, reserve ahead, tel. 04 90 36 02 16).

Le Bateleur, almost on the river, is a shy little place with 10 tables and a cuisine that's more Provençal than traditional. It's colorful, formal, and good enough to be popular with the locals—reserve ahead (€25 and €35 *menus*, closed Mon, near Roman bridge at 1 place Théodore Aubanel, air-con, tel. 04 90 36 28 04).

Le Tournesol offers the best €17 dinner value in town—with mostly Provençal dishes and friendly service (June–Oct daily, Nov–May closed Tue–Wed, 30 cours Taulignan, tel. 04 90 36 09 18, owner Patrick S a little E).

Pascal Boulangerie/Café is the best value among the many cafés on place Montfort (at the far end, breakfast and lunch only, closed Thu).

TRANSPORTATION CONNECTIONS

The most central bus stop is at Cave Vinicole.

From Vaison la Romaine by bus to: Avignon (2–3/day, 90 min), **Orange** (2–3/day, 45 min). Bus info: tel. 04 90 36 09 90.

Côtes du Rhône Villages:
Self-Guided Driving Tour

This driving tour introduces you to the characteristic best of the Côtes du Rhône wine road. While circling the region's rugged Dentelles de Montmirail mountain peaks, you'll experience all that's unique about this region—its natural beauty, glowing limestone villages, inviting wineries, and rolling hills of vineyards. As you drive, notice how some vineyards grow at angles, planted this way to compensate for the strong effect of the *mistral* wind.

This trip provides a crash course in Rhône Valley wine, an excuse to meet the locals who make the stuff, and breathtaking scenery—especially late in the day, when the famous Provençal sunlight causes colors to absolutely pop.

ORIENTATION

Officially, the Côtes du Rhône vineyards follow the Rhône River from just south of Lyon to Avignon. Our focus is the southern Provençal section of the Côtes du Rhône, centering on the small area between Châteauneuf-du-Pape and Vaison la Romaine. This eight-stop tour starts just outside wine-happy Rasteau, then returns to Vaison and winds clockwise around the Dentelles de Montmirail, visiting the mountaintop village of Le Crestet, adorable little Suzette, and the famous wine villages of Beaumes-de-Venise, Gigondas, and Séguret. I've listed several wineries *(domaines)* along the way. Before you go, study up with "French Wine-Tasting 101," page 46. But this easy loop is a shame to miss, even if wine isn't your thing.

Without a car, it's tougher, but a representative sampling is doable by bike or bus (2–3 buses/day from Avignon and Orange stop at some Côtes du Rhône villages; consider bus one-way and taxi back). While it's possible as a day trip by car from Arles or Avignon (allow an entire day for the 80-mile round-trip from Avignon), you'll have a more relaxing and intimate experience if you sleep in one of the villages (see page 435).

The best one-day plan: Try to get the first two stops done before lunch (most wineries are closed 12:00–14:00), then complete the loop in the afternoon. This route is picnic-friendly, but there are few shops along the way—stock up before you leave. In addition to being closed at lunchtime, most wineries are also closed on Sundays, holidays, and during the harvest (mid-Sept).

THE TOUR BEGINS

Our tour starts just south of Vaison la Romaine, near Rasteau. From Vaison, follow signs to Avignon or Orange, then follow signs to Roaix and stay on D-975. A well-marked turnoff between Roaix and Rasteau leads uphill to...

❶ **Domaine des Girasols:** Friendly Françoise, her American husband John (both SE), or Mama (Marie-Elizabeth, SE "a leetle") will take your palate on a tour of some of my favorite wines. This is the ideal place to get oriented, because the helpful owners produce a wide variety of wines and understand Americans. Papa Joyet bought this winery about 10 years ago, trading a vegetable business in the big city of Lyon for vineyards in little Rasteau. The setting is postcard-perfect, their wines are now available in the U.S., and son-in-law John (a big Oakland Raiders fan) studied winemaking in the Napa Valley. Mama made those beautiful quilts you see in the tasting room (Mon–Sat 9:00–12:00 & 14:00–18:00, Sun by appointment only, tel. 04 90 46 11 70).

Next, return to Vaison la Romaine and follow signs towards Carpentras, taking the uphill detour five minutes to the ridge-top village of...

❷ **Le Crestet:** This village—founded after the fall of the Roman Empire, when laws were lost and people gathered in high places like this for protection from marauding barbarians—followed the usual hill town evolution. The outer walls of the village did double duty as ramparts and house walls. The castle above (from about 850 A.D.) provided a final safe haven if attacked. The Bishop of Vaison la Romaine was the first occupant, lending little Crestet a certain prestige. With about 500 residents in 1200, Crestet was a very important town in this region. The village reached its zenith in the mid-1500s, when 660 people called Le Crestet home. Le Crestet began its gradual decline when the bishop moved to Vaison la

Côtes du Rhône Driving Route

5 MILES
10 KM

TO ARDECHE GORGES D-94

MIRABEL

VILLEDIEU

D-938

BIKE LOOP

VAISON LA ROMAINE

D-8

RASTEAU

D-5

LE CRESTET

CAIRANNE

SEGURET

❶

❽

❷

D-975

SABLET

DENTELLES DE MONTMIRAIL

MALAUCENE

D-974

❸

TO ORANGE & AVIGNON

GIGONDAS

❼

❹

SUZETTE

❺

LAFARE

D-19

VACQUERAS

❻

D-938

BEDOIN

D-974

TO ORANGE & A-7

BEAUMES-DE-VENISE

D-950

D-974

TO MONT VENTOUX

D-974

CARPENTRAS→

D-942

←D-49

D-942

DCH

TO AVIGNON

TO ISLE-SUR-LA-SORGUE & LUBERON

❶ Domaine des Girasols Winery
❷ Le Crestet
❸ La Col de la Chaine
❹ Suzette
❺ Domaine de Coyeux Winery
❻ Domaine de Durban Winery
❼ Gigondas
❽ Séguret

Romaine in the 1600s, though the population remained fairly stable until World War II. Today about 35 people live within the walls year-round (about 55 during the summer).

As you drive up to Le Crestet, stop by Charley Schmitt's house to pick up his well-done self-guided tour in English (on the road up to the village, it's the first house on the right after passing the "no bus allowed" sign; look for the small solar panel over his door). Charley has spent the last 40 years of his life studying and sketching this village, and he knows every stone. He's 85, speaks no English (his daughter translated the walking tour), and would be honored to sell you his brochure for €3.

Walking-tour brochure in hand, park at the entry of the village and wander the peaceful lanes. Appreciate the amount of work it took to put these locally found stones in place. Notice the elaborate water channels. Le Crestet was served by 18 cisterns in the Middle Ages, and disputes over water were a common problem. Don't miss the peaceful church (€0.50 turns the lights on) and its beautiful stained-glass window behind the altar. Light a candle. The village's only business, café-restaurant **Le Panoramic,** has an upstairs terrace with a view that justifies the name...even if the food is overpriced (see page 436).

Carry on and reconnect with the road below, following signs to Malaucène. As you enter Malaucène, turn right on D-90 (direction: Suzette) just before the Total station. The scenery gets better fast. You'll pass almond and cherry orchards in less than a mile (to the right and left, respectively) as you climb to the mountain pass...

❸ **La Col de la Chaîne (Chain Pass) and the Dentelles de Montmirail:** Get out of your car at the pass (about 1,000 feet) and enjoy the breezy views. Wander around. The peaks in the distance—thrusting up like the back of a stegosaurus—are the Dentelles de Montmirail, a small range running just nine miles basically north to south and reaching 2,400 feet in elevation. Those rocky tops were blown bare by the viscous mistral wind. Below, pine and oak trees mix with scotch broom, which blooms brilliant yellow from April to June. The village below is Suzette (you'll be there soon). The crops growing in front of you contain the classic Mediterranean mix—olives, vines, citrus fruit, and figs. The yellow-signed hiking trail leads to the castle-topped village of Le Barroux (3.5 miles, mostly downhill).

You'll pass countless yellow trail signs along this drive, as the Dentelles provide fertile ground for walking trails. Barely up the road is a small lavender field that is a sight to behold in July. To sleep nearby, try **La Ferme Dégoutaud,** just ahead (see page 436).

With the medieval castle of Le Barroux topping the horizon in the distance (off to the left), drive on to little...

❹ **Suzette:** Tiny Suzette floats on its hilltop, with a small 12th-century chapel, one café, a handful of residents, and the gaggle of houses where they live. Park in Suzette's lot, below and to the left as you enter. Find the big orientation board above the lot (Rome is to your right, 620 kilometers, or 385 miles, away). Look out to the broad shoulders of Mont Ventoux. At 6,000 feet, it always seems to have some clouds hanging around. The top looks like it's snow-covered; if you drive up there, you'll see it's actually white stone.

Look to the village. Suzette's homes once huddled in the shadow of an imposing castle, destroyed during the religious wars of the mid-1500s. **Les Coquelicots** café makes a perfect lunch or drink stop (light meals and snacks; see page 437); if it's warm, consider returning for dinner. Back across the road from the orientation table is a tasting room for **Chateau Redortier** wines (English brochure and well-explained list of wines provided; skip their white, but try the good rosé and two reds). **La Treille's** lovely rooms are on the road just behind you (see page 436).

Continuing in the direction of Beaumes-de-Venise (not Le Barroux), you'll drop down into the lush little village of La Fare. Just after La Fare lies a worthwhile detour and great wine-tasting opportunity...

❺ **Domaine de Coyeux:** The private road winds up and up to this impossibly beautiful setting, with the best views of the Dentelles I found. Olive trees line the final approach, and *Le Caveau* signs lead to a polished tasting room. These wines have an excellent reputation in the area, yet are served in a very relaxed manner. Start with the dry Muscat, then try their delectable Côtes du Rhône Villages red, and finish with their trademark sweet Muscat (wines range €6.50–10/bottle, Mon–Sat 10:00–12:00 & 14:00–18:00, closed Sun, tel. 04 90 12 42 42, some English spoken). After tasting, take time to wander about the vineyards.

Drive on toward Beaumes-de-Venise. On the way, **Restaurant le Redortier** is worth considering for a bite (see page 437). You'll drop out of the hills as you approach Beaumes-de-Venise. To find my next winery, stay straight at the first *Centre-Ville* sign as the road bends left, then carefully track *Domaine de Durban* signs for three incredibly scenic miles to...

❻ **Domaine de Durban:** In this stunning setting, mellow Natasha Leydier will welcome you to her wines. This *domaine* produces appealing whites, reds, and Muscats. Start with the 100 percent Viognier, then try their Viognier-Chardonnay blend. Next, their two reds are very different from each other: one is fruity, and the other—aged in oak—is tannic (both could use another year before drinking, but seemed fine to me). Finish with their well-respected Muscat de Venise (wines cost €4.50–10/bottle, Mon–Sat 9:00–12:00 & 14:00–18:30, closed Sun, tel. 04 90 62 94 26). Picnics are not allowed, though strolling amid the gorgeous vineyards is.

Returning to Beaumes-de-Venise, follow signs for *Centre-Ville*, then Vacqueyras. You'll pass Beaumes-de-Venise's massive cooperative, which represents many growers in this area (big selection, but too slick for my taste; daily 8:30–12:30 & 14:00–19:00). Continue following signs for Vacqueyras (a famous wine village with another cooperative), and then signs for Gigondas and *Vaison par la route Touristique*. Park in the little square of prosperous...

❼ **Gigondas:** This town produces some of the region's best red wines and is ideally situated for hiking, mountain biking, and driving into the mountains. Take a walk above the town—the church is an easy destination, with good views over the heart of the Côtes du

Rhône vineyards. Several good tasting opportunities await you on the main square. **Le Caveau de Gigondas** is best, with a vast selection of tiny bottles for sampling filled directly from the barrel, and a dona-tion-if-you-don't-buy system (daily 10:00–12:00 & 14:00–18:30, 2 doors down from TI). Here you can compare wines from a variety of private producers in an intimate, low-key surrounding. A good list of wines is provided, and the staff is generally helpful. Because of a self-imposed gag rule (so they don't favor the production of a single winery in this co-op showcase), you need to know what you want (see "French Wine Lingo," page 47). To dine very well or to sleep nearby, consider **Hôtel les Florets**, a half mile above town (closed Wed, see page 437).

Gigondas' info-packed **TI** has a list of welcoming wineries, *chambres d'hôte,* and good hikes or drives into the mountains (open daily, closed 12:00–14:00, place du Portail, tel. 04 90 65 85 46). The €2.50 *Chemins et Sentiers du Massif des Dentelles* hiking map is helpful, though not critical, since routes are well-signed. Route #1 is an ideal one-hour walk above Gigondas to superb views from the Belvedere du Rocher du Midi (route #2 extends this hike into a 3-hr loop).

From Gigondas, follow signs to the circular wine village of Sablet—with generally inexpensive yet tasty wines (the TI and wine cooperative share a space in the town center). Next is our finale, the white village of...

❽ Séguret: Blending into the hillside with a smattering of shops, two cafés, made-to-stroll lanes, and a natural spring, this place is popular. Follow signs and park in the lot. The bulky entry arch just above the lot came with a massive gate, which kept bad guys out for centuries. Walk to its right to appreciate how the homes' outer walls provided security in the Middle Ages.

Enter the village through the first passageway *(poterne)* you pass in the arch and get lost. Find Séguret's open washbasin, a hotbed of social activity and gossip over the ages. Public washbasins like this were used right up until World War II. Find the community bread oven *(four banal),* used for festivals and celebrations. Consider climb-ing to the unusual 12th-century church for views. A twisting fig tree growing out of a stone arch greets you en route. The church is usu-ally closed, but worth a look from the outside, as it's built into the rocky hill. High above, on the top of the hill, a castle once protected Séguret. All that's left is a tower that you can only make out from a distance. A four-star hotel/restaurant lies behind the church, with more views. At Christmas, this entire village transforms itself into one big crèche scene (a Provençal tradition that has long since died out in other villages). To dine, consider **La Bastide Bleue**, just below Séguret (see page 437).

From Séguret, Vaison la Romaine is only minutes away, and your driving tour is finished.

SLEEPING

(€1 = about $1.20, country code: 33)
There are great opportunities along the the Côtes du Rhône for drivers who want to experience rural France and get better values, particularly near Vaison la Romaine.

Near Vaison la Romaine

These five accommodations are within a 10-minute drive of Vaison la Romaine.

$$$ At **Château de la Baude******, young Londoner James Ludlam has taken a low-slung Provençal château and transformed it top to bottom. Goldfish greet guests in the courtyard fountain, and six large rooms pamper guests in tastefully decorated and muted tones (unusual in this colorful region). Enjoy the gym, huge pool, and a tennis court that comes with rackets and a ball machine (Db-€150–200, no CC, accepts checks in U.S. dollars, 500 yards from Villedieu, look for signs, tel. 04 90 28 91 53, www.chateaudelabaude.com, reservations@chateaudelabaude.com, SE).

$$$ **Hôtel les Florets****, a half mile above Gigondas, is surrounded by pine trees at the foothills of the Dentelles de Montmirail. It comes with a huge terrace van Gogh would have loved, thoughtfully designed rooms, and an exceptional restaurant (Db-€90, Tb-€110, annex rooms are best, restaurant closed Wed, Gigondas, tel. 04 90 65 85 01, fax 04 90 65 83 80). See page 437 for information about the restaurant.

$$$ **Château de Taulignan*****, on the outskirts of Vaison la Romaine, is a romantic country château guarded by vineyards and pine trees, and offering 12 large rooms (with big beds). It's kid-friendly and comes with a big pool, table tennis, a lush lawn, and dreamy strolling. Owners Michel and Helen are lovingly restoring the castle, stone by stone (Db-€85–100, buffet breakfast-€10, cancellation fees apply to any room—no matter how far ahead you cancel, tel. 04 90 28 71 16, fax 04 90 28 75 04, www.taulignan.com, reservation@taulignan.com). It's five minutes from Vaison la Romaine's TI; follow *Carpentras* signs and look for *Château de Taulignan* signs to the left just as you leave Vaison.

$$ **L'Ermitage** *chambre d'hôte*—five minutes outside Vaison, under the hill town of Le Crestet—is well-run by British expat Nick and native Nicole, who were born for this business. Their rustic farmhouse comes with three big, simple rooms and a pool with magnificent views. They also rent apartments on a weekly basis (Db-€70, Tb-€85, includes breakfast, apartment-€650/week, no CC, turn right off D-938 at Loupiotte restaurant, from Vaison la Romaine follow *Carpentras* signs, tel. 04 90 28 88 29, fax 04 90 28 72 97, www.lermitage.net, nick.jones@wanadoo.fr, SE).

$$ **L'Ecole Buissonnière** *chambres* are run by another charming Anglo-French team, Monique and John, who share their peace and quiet 10 minutes from Vaison la Romaine in a creatively restored farmhouse with three cozy, half-timbered rooms and convivial public spaces. John, who was a guardian in the Camargue, is generous with his in-depth knowledge of the area. The outdoor kitchen allows guests to picnic in high fashion in the well-tended garden (Db-€51–59, Tb-€66–74, Qb-€82–88, includes breakfast, no CC, between Villedieu and Buisson on D-75, tel. 04 90 28 95 19, ecole .buissonniere@wanadoo.fr).

In or near Suzette

These two places are a 20-minute drive from Vaison la Romaine.

$$ **La Treille** *chambres* lie on D-90 between Malaucène and Beaumes-de-Venise in the tiny hamlet of Suzette. Welcoming Madame Garrigou runs this flowery stone home with spacious rooms, some with commanding views and small kitchens. Most rooms are cool, with earth tones, private terraces, and big bathrooms. The pool comes with territorial views, and home-cooked meals may be available—ask (Db-€65–85, Tb/Qb-€89–99, includes breakfast, room size determines price, tel. 04 90 65 03 77, mobile 06 71 73 56 23, fax 04 90 62 93 39).

$$ **La Ferme Dégoutaud** is a splendidly situated and utterly isolated *chambre d'hôte* about halfway between Malaucène and Suzette (well-signed, a mile down a dirt road). Friendly Véronique rents three farm-rustic rooms with many thoughtful touches, a view pool, and table tennis. Ask, and she'll cook you dinner—€20 for the homemade works, including drinks (Db-€58–64, includes breakfast, tel. & fax 04 90 62 99 29, www.degoutaud.fr.st, le.degoutaud@wanadoo.fr). If you plan to spend a week, inquire about her apartments.

EATING

Along the Côtes du Rhône

Drivers enjoy a wealth of country-Provençal dining opportunities in rustic settings, handy to many of the rural accommodations. I've listed these places by distance from Vaison la Romaine (nearest to farthest).

Le Panoramic, in hill-capping Le Crestet, serves average salads, pizzas, and *plats* for more than you should spend at what must be Provence's greatest view tables (open daily for lunch and dinner, tel. 04 90 28 76 42). Come for a drink and view, but if you're really hungry, eat elsewhere. Drivers should pass on the first parking lot and keep climbing to park at la place du Château. The restaurant is to your right as you face the view.

Loupiotte is a simple café-restaurant on the road between Vaison la Romaine and Malaucène, below Le Crestet. They offer pizza (try *la vegeterienne*), pasta, salads, *plats* (consider the grilled lamb with vegetables and fries for €11), and *menus* (from €16). It's nothing fancy, but a good value (closed Mon, tel. 04 90 36 29 50).

Les Coquelicots, a small café surrounded by vines and views in miniscule Suzette, is idyllic. The food is simple, but the setting is memorable (pizza, grilled meats, omelets, May–Sept closed Tue–Wed, Oct–April weekends only, tel. 04 90 62 38 99). At least stop for a drink.

Hôtel les Florets, in nearby Gigondas, is a traditional, family-run place that justifies the drive. Dinners are a sumptuous blend of classic French cuisine and Provençal accents, served with class by English-speaking Thierry (*menus* from €23; see page 435).

La Bastide Bleue sits right on the road just below Séguret. It's blue-shutter Provençal, with outdoor tables in an enclosed courtyard and a warm interior (2-course *menu*-€19, 3-course *menu*-€23, open Thu–Tue for dinner only, closed Wed, just below Séguret, route de Sablet, tel. & fax 04 90 46 83 43).

La Maison Bleue on Villedieu's adorable little square is a pizza-and-salad place with great outdoor ambience; skip it if the weather forces you inside (open for lunch and dinner, closed Wed, tel. 04 90 28 97 02).

Auberge d'Anaïs—at the end of a dirt road 10 minutes from Vaison—is where I go for a true Provençal experience. It has outdoor tables with lights strung overheard, grand views, reliable local cuisine, and Madame Anaïs at the helm. Ask for a table *sur la terrasse* (good *menus* from €15, closed Mon, tel. 04 90 36 20 06). From Vaison, follow signs to Carpentras, then St. Marcellin; signs will guide you from there.

Restaurant le Redortier, in tiny La Fare between Suzette and Beaumes-de-Venise, offers reasonably-priced lunch and dinner options on an outdoor terrace flanked by interior seating. The cuisine is a blend of traditional and Provençal. Madame will take good care of you. Her specialties are lamb with eggplant and duck with fresh pasta (*menus* from €17, good lunch salads and *plats*, closed Tue–Wed, tel. 04 90 65 07 16).

Top Hill Towns of Luberon:
Isle-sur-la-Sorgue and Roussillon

The Luberon region, stretching 30 miles along a ridge of rugged hills east of Avignon, hides some of France's most appealing hill towns and landscapes. Those intrigued by Peter Mayle's books love joyriding through the region, connecting I-could-live-here villages, crumbled castles, and meditative abbeys. Mayle's best-selling *A Year in Provence* describes the ruddy local culture from an Englishman's perspective, as he buys a stone farmhouse, fixes it up, and adopts the region as his new home. This is a great read while you're here.

The Luberon terrain in general (much of which is a French regional natural park) is as appealing as its villages. Gnarled vineyards and wind-sculpted trees separate tidy stone structures from abandoned buildings—little more than rock piles—that seem to challenge city slickers to fix them up. White rock slabs bend along high ridges, while colorful hot-air balloons survey the sun-drenched scene from above.

Getting Around the Luberon

The region's top two towns are Isle-sur-la-Sorgue (with good train connections) and Roussillon (pathetic connections).

By Public Transportation: You have to be determined to reach Roussillon without a car: From Avignon, take a bus to Cavaillon (3/day Mon–Sat, none Sun), where you'll transfer to another bus to Gordes (1–2/day Mon–Sat, none Sun, bus info tel. 04 90 71 03 00). From Gordes, you'll have to taxi to Roussillon (about €15).

Convenient trains get you to Isle-sur-la-Sorgue (station called "L'Isle-Fontaine de Vaucluse") from Avignon (6/day, 30 min) or from Marseille (4/day, 4 hrs).

By Car: Luberon is ideal by car. Roads are scenic and narrow. Pick up the Michelin Local map #332 to navigate. If you're connecting this region with the Côtes du Rhône, consider doing so via Mont Ventoux—one of Provence's most spectacular routes (see page 427).

Isle-sur-la-Sorgue

This sturdy market town—literally, "Island on the Sorgue River"—sits within a split in its crisp, happy little river. (Do not confuse Isle-sur-la-Sorgue with the nearby and plain town of Sorgue.)

Isle-sur-la-Sorgue makes a good base for exploring the Luberon and Avignon (30 min to each by car). After the arid cities and villages elsewhere in Provence, the presence of water at every turn is a welcome change. Called the "Venice of Provence," the Sorgue's extraordinarily clear and shallow flow divides like cells in Isle-sur-la-Sorgue, producing water, water everywhere. The river is incredibly important to the region's economy. The fresh spring water of the many branches of the Sorgue (that divide

in Isle-sur-la-Sorgue) has provided nourishment for crops and power for key industries for centuries.

While Isle-sur-la-Sorgue is renowned for its market days, it is otherwise a pleasantly average town with no important sights and a steady trickle of tourism. It's calm at night and downright dead on Mondays.

Tourist Information: The TI has a line on rooms in private homes, all of which are outside the town (Tue–Sat 9:00–12:30 & 14:00–18:00, Sun 9:00–12:30, closed Mon, in town center, next to church, place de l'Eglise, tel. 04 90 38 04 78).

Helpful Hints

Market Days: The town erupts into a frenzy each Sunday and Thursday, with hardy crafts and local produce. The Sunday market is astounding and famous for its antiques; the Thursday market is more intimate.

Supermarket: A big **Spar** market is on the main ring road, near the Peugeot Car shop and the train station (Mon–Sat 9:00–12:00, Sun 15:00–19:00).

Internet Access: Try **Ty Webanna** (daily 9:00–19:00, closed Sun and Mon morning, 10 rue Autheman, tel. 04 90 38 15 87).

Launderette: It's just off the pedestrian street, rue de la République, at 23 impasse de la République (daily 8:00–20:30).

Bike Rental: The TI has addresses for local bike-rental shops. These towns make good biking destinations from Isle-sur-la-Sorgue: Velleron (5 miles north, flat, a tiny version of Isle-sur-la-Sorgue with waterwheels, fountains, and an evening farmers market Mon–Sat 18:00–20:00); Lagnes (3 miles east, mostly flat, a pretty and well-restored hill town with views from its ruined château); and Fontaine-de-Vaucluse (7 miles northeast, uphill).

Car Rental: Budget France is on rue André Autheman (tel. 04 90 20 64 13).

Parking: Market days are a challenge. If you don't arrive early, traffic is a mess and parking is a headache. You can circle the ring road and look for parking signs. There's a pay lot behind the post office and several lots just west of the roundabout with roads to Carpentras and Fontaine-de-Vaucluse. There's lots of freestyle parking on roads leaving the city. Don't leave anything visible in your car.

Taxi: Call tel. 06 09 06 92 06 or 06 08 68 12 33.

SIGHTS AND ACTIVITIES

In Isle-sur-la-Sorgue

▲**Wander and Explore**—The town has crystal-clear water babbling under pedestrian bridges stuffed with flower boxes, and its old-time carousel is always spinning. Navigate by the town's splintered streams and nine mossy waterwheels, which, while still turning, power only memories of the town's wool and silk industries.

Start your tour at the church next to the TI—where all streets seem to converge—and make forays into the town from there. The 12th-century **church** (Notre-Dame des Anges) has a festive Baroque interior and seems overgrown for today's town. Walk in. The curls and swirls and gilded statues date from an era that was all about Louis XIV, the Sun King. This is propagandist architecture, designed to wow the faithful into compliance. (It was made possible thanks to profits generated from its river-powered industries.) When entering a church like this, the heavens should open up and convince you that whoever built this had unearthly connections.

Wander down rue Danton, in front of the church, to lose the crowds and find three big, forgotten **waterwheels**. These helped put Isle-sur-la-Sorgue on the map in the 1800s. Along with Avignon, this was Provence's cloth-dyeing and textile center. Those stylish Provençal fabrics and patterns you see for sale everywhere were made possible by this river.

Double back to the church, turn left, and find the small stream. Breakaway streams like this run under the town like subways run under Paris. Take a right on the first street after the stream; it leads under a long arch (along rue J.J. Rousseau). Follow this, and keep (mostly) straight all the way to the main river, and then follow it left. You'll come to **Le Bassin** (a pond), where the river enters the town and divides into many branches (across from the recommended Café de Bellevue restaurant). Track as many branches as you can see, then find the round lookout point and take in the pretty scene.

Fishing was Isle-sur-la-Sorgue's first important economic activity—until the waterwheels took over. The sound of the rushing water makes it clear that even small rivers like this are capable of generating power. The river's defensive benefits are also obvious from here. Isle-sur-la-Sorgue was able to prosper in the Middle Ages in spite of its location (situated in a flat valley), thanks to the natural protection this river provided. Walls with big moats ran along the river, but they were destroyed during the French Revolution.

Take a refreshing **riverfront stroll** (or drive) from here. Cross back over the busy roundabout, and head to the left of the orange Delices de Luberon store (or stop to sample its great tapenade selection). You can follow the main river upstream, along the bike lane, as far as you like. The little road meanders about a mile, following the serene course of the clear-as-a-bell river, past waterfront homes, and beneath swaying trees, all the way to Hôtel le Pescador and a riverside café. The wide and shallow Partage des Eaux, where the water divides before entering Isle-sur-la-Sorgue, is perfect for a refreshing swim on a hot day.

Near Isle-sur-la-Sorgue

Fontaine-de-Vaucluse—You'll read and hear a lot about this village, impressively located at the source of the Sorgue River, where the medieval Italian poet Petrarch mourned for his love, Laura. The river seems to magically appear from nowhere (the actual source is a murky, green water hole) and flows through the town past a lineup of cafés, souvenir shops, and enough tourists to make Disney envious. While the setting is beautiful, the trip is worth it only if the spring is flowing—ask your hotelier, and arrive by 9:00 or after 19:00 to avoid crowds.

Canoe Trips on the Sorgue—Another reason to travel to Fontaine-de-Vaucluse is to canoe down the river. If you're really on vacation and committed to going French, consider this five-mile, two-hour trip. A guide escorts small groups in canoes starting in Fontaine-de-Vaucluse and ending in Isle-sur-la-Sorgue; you'll return to Fontaine-de-Vaucluse via shuttle bus (call for departure times: Canoe Evasion, €18, tel. 04 90 38 26 22, and Kayaks Verts, €18, tel. 04 90 20 35 44).

SLEEPING

(€1 = about $1.20, country code: 33)

Pickings are slim for good sleeps in Isle-sur-la-Sorgue, though the few I've listed provide solid values.

$$$ **La Prévoté***** offers the town's most luxurious digs. Its five meticulously decorated rooms—located above their fine restaurant—are each different, but all are done in earth tones. The rooms here have high ceilings, a few exposed beams, beautiful furnishings, and most overlook a branch of the river (standard Db-€130, larger Db-€150, suite Db-€170, no elevator, one block from the church on 4 bis J.J. Rousseau, tel. & fax 04 90 38 57 29, http://laprevote .site.voila.fr, la.prevote@wanadoo.fr).

$$ **Hôtel les Névons****, two blocks from the center (behind the PTT or post office), is concrete-motel-modern outside. Inside, however, it does everything right, with comfortable, air-conditioned rooms, a few family suites, puce-colored halls, a small rooftop pool, and eager-to-please owners, Mireille and Jean-Philippe (Db-€55–60, big Db-€69, Tb-€65–70, Qb-€75–85, Internet access, easy and secure parking, 205 chemin des Névons, tel. 04 90 20 72 00, fax 04 90 20 56 20, www.hotel-les-nevons.com, info@hotel-les-nevons.com).

$$ **Le Pont des Aubes Chambres,** run by sweet Martine (SE), has two huggable rooms in an old, green-shuttered farmhouse right

on the river. From here, you can cross the bridge and walk 15 minutes along the river into Isle-sur-la-Sorgue, or stroll to the recommended Le Mas Blanc restaurant (Db-€65, Tb-€80, no CC, a mile from town at 189 route d'Apt, tel. & fax 04 90 38 13 75, patriceaubert@wanadoo.fr). Martine also rents one-room apartments by the week for €310–350.

$ **Hôtel le Cours de l'Eau** is a gruff place with bargain beds above a café. It's sufficiently clean and nearly quiet (D-€26, Db-€37, on ring road opposite Café de la Sorgue at place Gambetta, tel. & fax 04 90 38 01 18, NSE).

EATING

Restaurant choices (like hotels) are limited in town. Choose between waterfront ambience and quality cuisine. These places are worthwhile, though having a car opens up a world of opportunity.

Begin your dinner with a glass of wine at the cozy **Le Caveau de la Tour de l'Isle** (part wine bar, part wine shop, open Tue–Sat until about 20:00, closed Sun–Mon, 12 rue de la République).

L'Oustau de l'Isle, which serves the town's most reliable and affordable fine cuisine, is well-suited for special dinners (*menus* from €23, open daily, closed Wed–Thu off-season, has backyard terrace, near post office at 21 avenue des Quatre Otages, tel. 04 90 38 54 83).

La Prévoté is the place to really do it up. Its dining room is covered in wood beams, and the place feels country-classy, but not stuffy. It has a branch of the Sorgue running through it, visible through glass windows (*menus* from €42, closed Tue–Wed, 4 rue J.J. Rousseau, on narrow street that runs along left side of church as you face it, tel. 04 90 38 57 29).

Café de Bellevue is my favorite riverfront café, with van Gogh colors, a great setting on Le Bassin (get a waterfront table), and yellow bulbs that create a warm ambience after dark. The owners—friendly American expat Richard, from North Carolina, and Serge (see if you can find the American)—run this place with panache, celebrating American events like the Fourth of July. Show this book, and they'll offer you a free apéritif (€15 *menu*, reasonably-priced *plats* and salads, closed Mon, located at the top of town, tel. 04 90 38 03 63).

The **Fromenterie** bakery next to the PTT (post office) sells really rich quiches.

Experience a decent riverside meal or snack in a dreamy Partage des Eaux setting at café-restaurant **Le Guinguette** (€16 *menu*, salads and *plats*, closed Mon, follow directions for river walk above, tel. 04 90 38 10 61).

Roussillon

With all the trendy charm of Santa Fe on a hilltop, Roussillon will cost you at least a roll of film (and €2 for parking). Roussillon has been a protected village since 1943, and has benefited from a complete absence of modern development. An enormous deposit of ochre gives the earth and buildings here that distinctive red color, and provides this village with its economic base. This place is popular; it's best to visit early or late in the day.

ORIENTATION

Roussillon sits atop Mont Rouge (Red Mountain) at about 1,000 feet above sea level. The village curls around this hospitable mountain, and the exposed ochre cliffs are a short walk south.

Two parking lots are available: one on the northern edge (by the recommended Hôtel Reve d'Ocre), and another on its southern flank, closer to the ochre cliffs. If you approach from Gordes or Joucas, you'll end up at the northern lot. If you're coming from the N-100 and the south, you'll park at the southern lot.

Thursday is Roussillon's market day, and every day is Christmas for thieves—take everything out of your car.

Tourist Information: The little TI is in the center, between the two lots and across from the David restaurant. It posts a list of hotels, *chambres d'hôte*, and late-night doctors. Walkers should get info on trails from Roussillon to nearby villages (April–Oct Mon–Sat 9:00–12:00 & 13:30–18:30, Sun 14:00–18:30; Nov–March Mon–Sat 13:30–17:30, closed Sun, tel. 04 90 05 60 25).

SIGHTS

▲**The Village**—Start at one of Roussillon's two parking lots. For centuries, animals grazed at the lot closer to the ochre cliffs. It then became a school playground, and when there weren't enough kids to support a school, it became a parking lot. Climb a few minutes from either parking lot (follow signs to Castum, pass the Hollywood-set square and go above the church) to the summit of the town. During the Middle Ages, the church tower marked the entrance to the fortified town. Duck into the pretty 11th-century church of St. Michel, and notice the well-worn center aisle and the propane heaters— winters can be frigid in this area. The castle stood just above the church on the top of Mont Rouge. Find the orientation plaque and the dramatic viewpoint, often complete with a howling mistral. While nothing remains of the castle today, the strategic advantage of this site is clear: You can see forever. As you head back down to the village, notice the clamped-iron beams that shore up ancient walls. Examine the different hues of yellow and orange. These lime-finished exteriors, called *chaux* (literally, "limes"), need to be redone about every 10 years. Locals choose their exact color...but in this town of ochre, it's never white.

See how local (or artsy) you can look in what must be the most scenic village square in Provence (place du Pignotte), and watch the river of shoppers. Is anyone playing *boules* at the opposite end? You could paint the entire town without ever leaving the red-and-orange corner of your palette. Many do. While Roussillon receives its share of day-trippers, evenings are romantically peaceful.

▲▲**Ochre Cliffs**—Roussillon was Europe's capital for ochre production until World War II. A stroll to the south end of town, beyond the upper parking lot, will show you why. A brilliant orange path leads through the richly-colored ochre canyon (formerly a quarry), explaining the hue of this village (€2, daily 10:00–17:30; beware: Light-colored clothing and orange powder don't mix).

The value of Roussillon's ochre cliffs was known in Roman times. Once excavated, the clay ochre was rinsed with water to separate it from sand, and bricks of the stuff were dried and baked for deeper hues. The procedure for extracting the ochre did not change much over 2,000 years. Ochre mining became industrialized in late 1700s. Used primarily for wallpaper, linoleum, and wallpaper, ochre reached its zenith just before World War II (after that, cheaper substitutes took over).

SLEEPING

(€1 = about $1.20, country code: 33)

In Roussillon

The TI posts a list of hotels and *chambres d'hôte*.

$$ Hôtel Rêves d'Ocres**, the only hotel in the town center, is run by helpful Sandrine and laid-back Ouaheb (pronounced web). They have been trying to sell the hotel—be ready for changes from this description. It's warm and comfortable, with spacious rooms. Eight of these have view terraces, most with views to Gordes (Db without balcony-€72, Db with balcony-€80, Tb-€95, air-con, route de Gordes, tel. 04 90 05 60 50, fax 04 90 05 79 74, www.hotelrevesdocres.com, contact@hotelrevesdocres.com).

$ Madame Cherel rents very simple rooms with firm mattresses that seem just this side of a youth hostel. There's a common view terrace, and good reading materials are available (D-€32–35, no CC, 3 blocks from upper parking lot, between gas station and school, La Burlière, tel. 04 90 05 68 47). Chatty and sincere Cherel speaks English, is a wealth of regional travel tips, and rents mountain bikes to guests only (€15/day).

In Joucas, near Roussillon

$$ La Maison de Mistral *chambre d'hôte* offers creatively designed and comfortable rooms, all with valley views and a breakfast terrace for lingering. But the best reason to sleep here is to relax over a chilled rosé with the owners, Pierre and Marie-Lucie Mistral, who want to get to know you. Their lack of English doesn't seem to matter (Db-€60, extra person-€15, includes breakfast, no CC, ask nicely and they might cook you a dinner well worth the cost; dead-center in the village by the church, look for the sign on the walking street, rue de l'Eglise; tel. 04 90 05 74 01, mobile 06 23 87 69 02, pmistral@free.fr). Since the Mistrals' daughter runs the town's only hotel, you get access to its pool (see below).

$$ Hostellerie des Commandeurs**, run by sweet Sophie, lacks the panache of their parent's place, but the modern rooms are comfortable and clean (with wall-to-wall carpeting), the location is great, the pool is big, and their restaurant serves fine-value dinners (*menu* from €17). This place, next to a play field, is good for kids. Ask for a south-facing room for the best views (Db-€55–58, extra bed-€16, above park at village entrance on rue Pietonne, tel. 04 90 05 78 01, fax 04 90 05 74 47, www.lescommandeurs.com, hostellerie @lescommandeurs.com, S enough E).

EATING

If dining in Roussillon, choose ambience over cuisine, and enjoy any of the places on the main square. It's a festive place, where children dance while parents dine, and dogs and cats look longingly for leftovers. Restaurants change with the mistral here—what's good one year disappoints the next. Consider my suggestions, and go with what looks best (or look over my suggestions in other Luberon villages).

On the square, **Le Bistrot de Roussillon** (closed Tue, tel. 04 90 05 74 45) and **Minka's Café** (closed Wed, tel. 04 90 05 62 11) go *mano a mano* at dinner, each vying for customers' loyalty. Both are good values, with similar prices, tables on the square, and red-hill-view terraces in the back, though le Bistrot seems more reliable (good *plats* from €14, *menus* from €20). The little **Crêperie-Saladerie** below serves scrumptious and beefy omelets and good salads. **Le Castrum,** on the square, serves good *tartes* with salad (open lunch only). **Chez David**, across from the TI, has views from interior tables; it's elegant, with a good reputation—for a price (*menus* from €30, closed Wed, tel. 04 90 05 60 13).

The
FRENCH RIVIERA

A hundred years ago, celebrities from London to Moscow flocked here to socialize, gamble, and escape the dreary weather at home. The belle époque is today's tourist craze, as this most sought-after, fun-in-the-sun destination now caters to budget travelers as well. Some of the Continent's most stunning scenery and intriguing museums lie along this strip of land—as do millions of heat-seeking tourists. Nice has world-class museums, a grand beachfront promenade, a seductive old town, and all the drawbacks of a major city (traffic, crime, pollution, etc.). But the day trips possible from Nice are easy and varied: Monte Carlo welcomes everyone, with cash registers open; Antibes has a romantic port and silky-sandy beaches; and the hill towns present a breezy and photogenic alternative to the beach scene. Evenings on the Riviera, a.k.a. the Côte d'Azur, were made for a promenade and outdoor dining.

Choosing a Home Base

My favorite home bases are Nice, Antibes, and Villefranche-sur-Mer.

Nice is the region's capital and France's fifth-largest city. With convenient train and bus connections to most regional sights, this is the most practical base for train travelers. Urban Nice also has a full palette of museums, a beach scene that rocks, the best selection of hotels in all price ranges, and good nightlife options. A car is a headache in Nice, though it's easily stored at one of the many parking garages.

Nearby **Antibes** is smaller, with a bustling center, the best sandy beaches I found, good walking trails, and the Picasso Museum. It has frequent train service to Nice and Monaco, and it's easy for drivers.

Villefranche-sur-Mer is the romantic's choice, with a serene setting and small-town warmth. It has finely-ground pebble beaches, good public transportation to Nice and Monaco, easy parking, and hotels in most price ranges.

Planning Your Time

Most should plan a full day for Nice and at least a half day each for Monaco and Antibes. Monaco has a unique energy at night (sights are closed, but crowds are few; consider dinner here), and Antibes is best during the day (good beaches, hiking, and Picasso Museum). The inland hill towns are a lower priority, particularly if you don't have a car.

Hill-town- and nature-lovers should add a night or two inland to explore the charming, hill-capping hamlets near Vence. (But if you're short on time, you may do better exploring the hill towns of Provence.)

Helpful Hints

Museum Pass: The **Riviera Carte Musées** pass, a good value only for serious museumgoers, includes admission to many major Riviera museums, such as Nice's Chagall and Matisse museums, Antibes' Picasso Museum and Fort Carré, La Trophée des Alpes, the International Museum of Perfume in Grasse, and the Exotic Gardens in Eze-le-Village. (It does not include Fondation Maeght in St-Paul-de-Vence, the villas between Nice and Monaco, or Monaco sights.) This will save you money if you're planning to visit more than two museums in a day, or several museums over a few days (€10/1 day, €17/3 days, €27/7 days, buy at any participating sight).

Events: The Riviera is famous for staging major events. Unless you're actually taking part in the festivities, these events give you only room shortages and traffic jams. Here are the three biggies in 2005: Nice Carnival (Feb 11–27), the Grand Prix of Monaco (May 19–22), and the Cannes Film Festival (May 11–22).

Getting Around the Riviera

Nice is perfectly located for exploring the Riviera by public transport. Eze-le-Village, Villefranche-sur-Mer, Antibes, St-Paul-de-Vence, and Cannes are all within a 60-minute bus or train ride of each other.

Minivan Excursions: The TI and most hotels have information on minivan excursions from Nice (€50–60/half day, €80–110/day). **Med-Tour** is one of many (tel. 04 93 82 92 58 or 06 73 82 04 10, www.med-tour.com); **Tour Azur** is a bit pricier (tel. 04 93 44 88 77 or 06 71 90 76 70, www.tourazur.com); and

The French Riviera

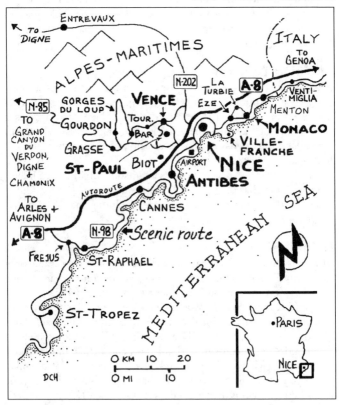

Revelation Tours specializes in English tours (tel. 04 93 53 69 85 or 06 60 02 98 42, www.revelation-tours.com). All companies also offer private tours by the day or half day (check with them for their outrageous prices, about €90/hr).

Bus Station: At Nice's efficient bus station on boulevard Jean Jaurès, you'll find a baggage check (called *messagerie,* €2.50/bag, Mon–Sat 8:00–18:00, closed Sun), a snack bar with sandwiches and drinks, clean WCs (€0.50), and several bus companies. Get schedules and prices from the helpful English-speaking clerk at the information desk in the bus station (tel. 04 93 85 61 81). Buy tickets from the driver on the bus.

Schedules: Here's an overview of public transport options to key Riviera destinations with direct service from Nice. Two bus companies, RCA and Cars Broch, provide service on the same route between Nice, Villefranche-sur-Mer, Eze-le-Village, and Monaco (RCA buses run more frequently). For any bus destination between Nice and Monaco (marked here with a *), you'll pay the same one-way or round-trip (free return only with same company, remember to keep your ticket). For other destinations, the one-way price is listed. Self-serve ticket machines in train stations make ticket purchases easy and fast.

Destination	Bus from Nice	Train from Nice
Villefranche	4/hr, 20 min, €1.80*	2/hr, 10 min, €1.60
Antibes	3/hr, 60 min, €4.30	2/hr, 25 min, €3.70
Monaco	4/hr, 45 min, €3.90*	2/hr, 20 min, €3.20
Cannes	take the train	2/hr, 30 min, €5.20
St-Paul	every 40 min, 45 min, €4.30	none
Vence	every 40 min, 50 min, €4.80	none
Grasse	every 40 min, 75 min, €6.40	none
Eze-le-Village	every 2 hrs, 25 min, €2.60	none
La Turbie	4/day, 45 min, €3	none

Cuisine Scene in the Riviera

The Riviera adds a Mediterranean flair to the food of Provence. While many of the same dishes served in Provence are available throughout the Riviera (see "Cuisine Scene in Provence," 372), you can celebrate the differences and look for anything Italian or from the sea.

Local specialties are bouillabaisse (the spicy seafood stew-soup that seems worth the cost only for those with a seafood fetish), *bourride* (a creamy fish soup thickened with *aioli*, a garlic sauce), and *salade niçoise* (nee-swaz; a tomato, potato, olive, anchovy, and tuna salad). You'll also find these tasty bread treats: *pissaladière* (bread dough topped with onions, olives, and anchovies), *fougasse* (a spindly, lacelike bread), *socca* (a thin chickpea crêpe), and *pan bagnat* (like a *salade niçoise* stuffed into a huge hamburger bun). Italian cuisine is native (ravioli was first made in Nice), easy to find, and generally a good value (*pâtes fraîches* means "fresh pasta"). White and rosé Bellet and the rich reds and rosés of Bandol are the local wines.

Remember, restaurants serve only during lunch (11:30–14:00) and dinner (19:00–21:00, later in bigger cities); cafés serve food throughout the day.

Art Scene in the Riviera

The list of artists who have painted the Riviera reads like a Who's Who of 20th-century art. Pierre-Auguste Renoir, Henri Matisse, Marc Chagall, Georges Braque, Raoul Dufy, Fernand Léger, and Pablo Picasso all lived and worked here—and raved about the region's wonderful light. Their simple, semi-abstract, and—most importantly—colorful works reflect the Riviera. You'll experience the same landscapes they painted in this bright, sun-drenched region, punctuated with views of the "azure sea." Try to imagine the Riviera with a fraction of the people and development you see today.

But the artists were mostly drawn to the uncomplicated lifestyle of fishermen and farmers that has reigned here since time began. As the artists grew older, they retired in the sun, turned their backs on modern art's "isms," and painted with the wide-eyed wonder of children, using bright primary colors, basic outlines, and simple subjects.

Well-organized modern art museums (such as the Picasso Museum in Antibes, and the Chagall and Matisse museums in Nice, described in this chapter) litter the Riviera, allowing art-lovers to appreciate these artists' works while immersed in the same sun and culture that inspired them. Many of the museums were designed to blend the art with the surrounding views, gardens, and fountains, thus highlighting that modern art is not only stimulating, but sometimes simply beautiful.

Nice

Nice (sounds like niece), with its spectacular Alps-to-Mediterranean surroundings, eternally entertaining seafront promenade, and fine museums, is an enjoyable big-city highlight of the Riviera. In its traffic-free old city, Italian and French flavors mix to create a spicy Mediterranean dressing. Nice may be nice, but it's hot and jammed in July and August (reserve ahead). Get a room with air-conditioning *(une chambre avec climatisation)*. Everything you'll want to see in Nice is walkable or a short bus ride away.

ORIENTATION

Most sights and hotels recommended in this book are near avenue Jean Médecin, between the train station and the beach. It's a 20-minute walk from the train station to the beach (or a €10 taxi ride), and a 20-minute walk along the promenade from the fancy Hôtel Negresco to the heart of Old Nice.

You'll no doubt experience the inconvenience of construction in Nice. Three sleek tramway lines are being built (including one that will run along the promenade des Anglais). It's a huge project, and the first line won't open until 2006 at the earliest. Be ready for traffic reroutes and detours in many places.

Tourist Information

Nice's helpful TI has three locations: at the **airport** (mid-June–mid-Sept daily 8:00–21:00, mid-Sept–mid-June closed Sun); next to the **train station** (mid-June–mid-Sept Mon–Sat 8:00–20:00, Sun 9:00–19:00; mid-Sept–mid-June Mon–Sat 8:00–19:00, Sun 9:00–18:00); and facing the **beach** at 5 promenade des Anglais (mid-Sept–mid-June Mon–Sat 9:00–18:00, closed Sun; mid-June–mid-Sept Mon–Sat

8:00–20:00, Sun 9:00–19:00; tel. 08 92 70 74 07 costs €0.34/min, www.nicetourisme.com). Pick up the free Nice map (which lists all the sights, with hours and bus lines), the extensive *Practical Guide to Nice*, and information on regional day trips (such as city maps).

Art-lovers should consider buying a **museum pass** for sights in Nice or throughout the Riviera (sold at any participating sight). The Riviera Carte Musées pass covers many regional sights, including four museums in Nice (Chagall, Matisse, Fine Arts, and Modern and Contemporary Art; €10/1 day, €17/3 days, €27/7 days; for more information, see page 447). A Nice-only museum pass, Carte Passe-Musées 7 Jours, is also available (€6/7 days, does not include Chagall Museum).

Arrival in Nice

By Train: All trains stop at Nice's one main station (Nice-Ville, baggage check available, but closes at 17:45 and all day Sun and holidays). Avoid the suburban stations, and never leave your bags unattended. The TI is next door (to the left as you exit the station), car rental is to the right, and taxis are in front. To reach most of my recommended hotels, turn left out of the station, then right on avenue Jean Médecin. To get near the beach and the promenade des Anglais from the station, continue on foot for 20 minutes down avenue Jean Médecin, or take bus #15 or #17, which both run frequently to place Massena (bus #17 continues to the bus station, *gare routière*). Get off at place Massena and walk five minutes through Old Nice to the beach.

By Car: Driving into Nice from the west (such as from Provence), take the first Nice exit (for the airport—called *Côte d'Azur, Central*) and follow signs for *Nice Centre* and *Promenade des Anglais*. Try to avoid arriving at rush hour, when the promenade des Anglais grinds to a halt (Mon–Fri 17:00–19:30). Hoteliers know where to park (allow €10–18/day). The parking garage at the Nice Etoile shopping center on avenue Jean Médecin is handy to many of my hotel listings (ticket booth on 3rd floor, about €18/day, €10 from 20:00–8:00). All on-street parking is metered.

By Plane: For information on Nice's airport, see "Transportation Connections," page 473.

Helpful Hints

Theft Alert: Nice is notorious for pickpockets. Have nothing important on or around your waist, unless it's in a money belt tucked out of sight (thieves target fanny packs); don't leave anything visible in your car; be wary of scooters when standing at intersections; don't leave things unattended on the beach while swimming; and stick to main streets in Old Nice after dark.

U.S. Consulate: You'll find it at 7 avenue Gustave V (tel. 04 93 88 89 55, fax 04 93 87 07 38).

Canadian Consulate: It's at 10 rue Lamartine (tel. 04 93 92 93 22).

Nice

1 To High Corniche (sky-high route to Monaco)
2 To Middle Corniche (middle route, best for Monaco & Eze-le-Village)
3 To Low Corniche (low route to Villefranche-sur-Mer)
4 Start of Old Nice Walk

Medical Help: Riviera Medical Services has a list of English-speaking physicians. They can help you make an appointment or call an ambulance (tel. 04 93 26 12 70).

Museums: Most Nice museums are closed Tuesdays (except the Modern and Contemporary Art Museum) and free the first Sunday of the month. For information on Nice's museum passes, see "Tourist Information," above.

Supermarket: The big **Monoprix** on avenue Jean Médecin and rue Biscarra has a wide selection of food and cold drinks (closed Sun).

Internet Access: Consider **Web Nice** (daily 9:00–23:00, 25 bis promenade des Anglais, tel. 04 93 88 72 75), **Cyber Café Bio** (cheaper if you buy food or drink, daily 9:00–22:00, near the station at 16 rue Paganini, tel. 04 9 16 89 81), or **Maxi Web** (Mon–Sat 8:00–20:00, closed Sun, 6 bis avenue Durante, tel. 04 93 16 95 56). All three places have familiar American keyboards.

English Bookstore: The Cat's Whiskers has a great selection (closed Sun, 26 rue Lamartine, near recommended Hôtel du Petit Louvre, tel. 04 93 80 02 66).

English Radio: Tune into Riviera-Radio at FM 106.5.

American Express: AmEx faces the beach at 11 promenade des Anglais (where the promenade intersects with Rue du Congrès, tel. 04 93 16 53 53).

Laundry: The self-service **Point Laverie** is at the corner of Rue Alberti and Rue Pastorelli, next to Hôtel Vendôme (open daily).

Renting a Bike (and Other Wheels): Roller Station rents bikes (*vélos*, €5/hr, €10/half-day, €15/day), in-line skates (*rollers*, €5/day), and mini-scooters (*trotinettes*, €5/hr, €6/half day, €9/day). You'll need to leave an ID as deposit (daily 10:00–19:00, across from seaside promenade at 49 quai des Etats-Unis, another location at 10 rue Cassini near place Garibaldi, tel. 04 93 62 99 05).

Rocky Beaches: To make life tolerable on the rocks, swimmers should buy a pair of the cheap plastic beach shoes sold at many shops (flip-flops fall off in the water).

Views: For panoramic views, climb Castle Hill (see page 460).

Getting Around Nice

While walking gets you to most places, you'll want to ride the bus to the Chagall and Matisse museums. Bus fare is €1.40, and an all-day pass is €4.

Taxis are expensive but handy for the Chagall and Matisse museums and the Russian Church (figure €10–14 from promenade des Anglais). They normally only pick up at taxi stands (*tête de station)* or if you call (tel. 04 93 13 78 78).

The hokey tourist train is handy for getting to the castle (see "Tours," next page).

TOURS

Bus Tour—Le Grand Tour Bus provides an expensive hop-on, hop-off option on an open-deck bus with headphone commentary. The full route (about 90 min) includes the promenade des Anglais, old port, Cap de Nice, and the Chagall and Matisse museums on Cimiez Hill (€17/1-day pass, €19/2-day pass, cheaper for seniors and students, €10 for last tour of the day at about 18:45, hourly departures, buy tickets on bus, main stop is on promenade des Anglais, across from plage Beau Rivage, look for signs, tel. 04 92 29 17 00).

Tourist Train—For €6, you can spend 40 embarrassing minutes on the tourist train tooting along the promenade, through the old town, and up to the castle, with a taped English narration. This is a sweat-free way to get to the castle (every 30 min, meet train opposite Albert I park on promenade des Anglais, tel. 04 93 62 85 48).

Segway Tours—The latest technology to reach the Riviera is now available for three-hour English rolls through Nice. These stand-up scooter tours are relaxing, fun, and surprisingly informative (€45, March–Nov daily at 10:30, night tour at 18:30, cash only, reservations required, ages 12 and up, meet at 15 promenade des Anglais in front of Lido Plage, tel. 01 56 58 10 54, www.citysegwaytours.com).

Walking Tour—The TI on the promenade des Anglais organizes guided walking tours of Old Nice from May through October (€12, 1/week, usually Sat mornings, reservations necessary, tel. 08 92 70 74 07).

Local Guide—Pascale Rucker tailors excellent tours in and around Nice to your interests. You can book in advance or on short notice (€80/half-day, €140/day, tel. 04 93 87 77 89, mobile 06 16 24 29 52).

Nice in the Buff:
A Walk Through Old Nice

This fun and informative self-guided walking tour gives a helpful introduction to Nice's bicultural heritage and most interesting neighborhoods. It's best done early in the morning (while the outdoor market still thrives). Allow about two hours at a leisurely pace, with a stop for coffee and a *socca* (chickpea crêpe).

Our tour begins on promenade des Anglais (near the landmark Hôtel Negresco) and ends in the heart of Old Nice (Vieux Nice).

Promenade des Anglais: Welcome to the Riviera. There's something for everyone along this four-mile-long seafront circus. Watch the Europeans at play, admire the azure Mediterranean, anchor yourself to a blue bench, and prop your feet up on the made-to-order guardrail. Later in the day, come back to join the evening parade of tans along the promenade.

For now, stroll like the belle époque English aristocrats for whom the promenade was built. The broad sidewalks of the promenade des

Anglais (literally, "Walkway of the English") were financed by wealthy English tourists who wanted a safe place to stroll and admire the view. The walk was paved in marble in 1822 for aristocrats who didn't want to dirty their shoes or smell the fishy gravel. This grand promenade leads to the old town and Castle Hill.

Start at the pink-domed...

Hôtel Negresco: Nice's finest hotel (also a historic monument) offers the city's most expensive beds and a free "museum" interior (always open—provided you're dressed decently, absolutely no beach attire). March straight through the lobby (as if you're staying there) into the exquisite Salon Royal. The chandelier hanging from the Eiffel-built dome is made of 16,000 pieces of crystal. It was built in France for the Russian czar's Moscow palace...but because of the Bolshevik Revolution in 1918, he couldn't take delivery. Read the explanation of the dome and saunter around counterclockwise: The bucolic scene, painted in 1913 for the hotel, sets the tone. Nip into the toilets for either a turn-of-the-century powder room or a Battle of Waterloo experience. The chairs nearby were typical of the age (cones of silence for an afternoon nap sitting up).

On your way out, pop into the Salon Louis XIV (right of entry lobby as you leave), where the embarrassingly short Sun King models his red platform boots (English descriptions explain the room).

Walk around the back to see the hotel's original entrance (grander than today's)—in the 19th century, classy people stayed out of the sun, and any posh hotel that cared about its clientele would design its entry on the shady north side.

Cross promenade des Anglais, turn left, and—before you begin your seaside promenade—grab a bench at the...

Bay of Angels (Baie des Anges): The body of Nice's patron saint, Réparate, was supposedly escorted into this bay by angels in the 4th century. Face the water. To your right is the airport, built on a landfill. On that tip of land way beyond the runway is Cap d'Antibes. Until 1860, Antibes and Nice were in different countries—Antibes was French, but Nice was a protectorate of the Italian kingdom of Savoy-Piedmont, a.k.a. the Kingdom of Sardinia. (During that period, the Var River—just west of Nice—was the geographic border between these two peoples.) In 1850, the people here spoke Italian and ate pasta. As Italy was uniting, the region was given a choice: Join the new country of Italy or join France (which was enjoying good times under the rule of Napoleon III). The vast majority voted in 1860 to go French...and *voilà!*

To the far left lies Villefranche-sur-Mer (marked by the tower at land's end—and home to lots of millionaires), then Monaco, then Italy. Behind you are the foothills of the Alps (les Alpes Maritimes), which gather threatening clouds that leave the Côte d'Azur alone to enjoy the sunshine more than 300 days each year.

A Walk Through Old Nice

1. Place Masséna
2. Rue St. François de Paule
3. Cours Saleya
4. Rue de la Poissonnerie
5. Rue Droite
6. Place Rosetti
7. Castle Hill

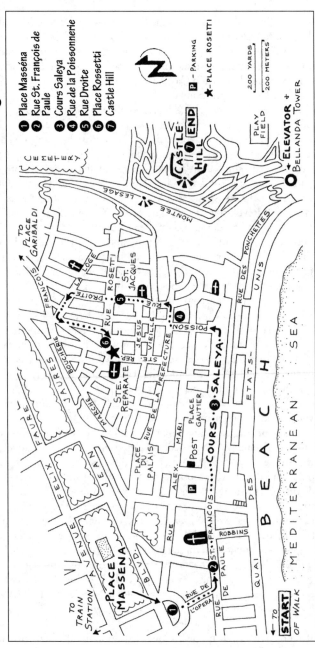

While half a million people live here, pollution is carefully treated—the water is routinely tested and very clean.

Now head to the left and begin...

Strolling the Promenade: The block next to Hôtel Negresco has a lush park and the Masséna Museum (city history, closed for renovation). Nearby sit two other belle époque establishments: the West End and Westminster hotels—English names to help those original guests feel at home. These hotels represent Nice's arrival as a tourist mecca a century ago, when the combination of leisure time and a stable economy allowed tourists to find the sun even in winter.

Even a hundred years ago, there was already sufficient tourism in Nice to justify building its first casino (a leisure activity imported from Venice). An elegant casino stood on pilings in the sea until the Germans destroyed it during World War II. While that's gone, you can see the striking 1920s Art Nouveau facade of the Palais de la Mediterranean, a grand casino and theater. Only the facade survives, and today it fronts a luxury condominium. The less charming Casino Ruhl is farther along (just before the park). Anyone can drop in for some one-armed-bandit fun, but for the tables at night, you'll need to dress up and bring your passport.

Albert I Park is named for the Belgian king who enjoyed wintering here. While the English came first, the Belgians and Russians were also huge fans of 19th-century Nice. The 1960 statue in the park commemorates Nice's being part of France for 100 years.

Walk into the park and continue down the center of the grassy strip between the two boulevards, all the way to place Masséna. The modern sculpture you pass—representing the curve of the French Riviera—is an answer to a prayer for local skateboarders. Walk to the fountains and face them. (To save water, they get high pressure only after 17:00.)

Place Masséna: You're standing on Nice's river, the Paillon (covered since the 1800s). Turn around. You can track the river's route under the green parkway you just walked; it meets the sea at the Casino Ruhl. For centuries, this river was Nice's natural defense. A fortified wall ran along its length to the sea. With the arrival of tourism in the 1800s, Nice expanded over and beyond the river. The rich red coloring of the buildings around you was the preference of Nice's Italian rulers.

Cross the square to the right, towards the Caisse d'Epargne bank and the curved buildings. Follow the steps that lead down past the three palm trees and to rue de l'Opéra (between the curved buildings). Walk down rue de l'Opéra, turning left on...

Rue St. François de Paule: You've entered Old Nice. Peer into the Alziari olive oil shop at #14 (opposite the city hall). Dating from 1868, the shop produces top-quality, stone-ground olive oil. The proud owner, Gilles Piot, claims that stone wheels create less acidity (since metal grinding builds up heat). Locals fill their own containers from the huge vats (the cheapest one is peanut oil, not olive oil). Consider a gift for the olive-oil-lover on your list. A block down on the left (#7), Pâtisserie Auer's grand old storefront has changed little since the pastry shop opened in 1820. The writing on the window says, "Since 1820 from father to son." The royal medallions on the back wall remind shoppers that Queen Victoria fed her sweet tooth here. Across the street is Nice's grand opera house, from the same era. Imagine this opulent jewel buried deep in the old town of Nice back in the 19th century. With all the fancy big-city folks wintering here, the rough-edged town needed some high-class entertainment. The four statues on top represent theater, dance, music, and singing.

Continue on, sifting your way through tacky souvenirs to the cours Saleya (koor sah-lay-yuh).

Cours Saleya: Named for its broad exposure to the sun *(soleil)*, this commotion of color, sights, smells, and people has been Nice's main market square since the Middle Ages (produce market held daily until 13:00—except on Monday, when an antique market takes over the square). Amazingly, part of this square was a parking lot until 1980, when the mayor of Nice had an underground parking garage built.

The first section is devoted to freshly cut flowers that seem to grow effortlessly and everywhere in this ideal climate. Carnations, roses, and jasmine are local favorites in what has been the Riviera's biggest flower market since the 19th century. Fresh flowers are perhaps the best value in this otherwise pricey city.

The boisterous produce section trumpets the season with mushrooms, strawberries, white asparagus, zucchini flowers—whatever's fresh gets top billing.

Place Pierre Gautier (also called Plassa dou Gouvernou—bilingual street signs include the old Niçoise language, an Italian dialect) is where the actual farmers set up stalls to sell their produce and herbs directly. For a good overall view, climb the steps closest to the water (stepping over the trash sacks) above the Grand Bleu restaurant.

From your perch, look up to the hill that dominates to the east. The city of Nice was first settled there by Greeks circa 400 B.C. In the Middle Ages, a massive castle stood there, with turrets, high walls, and soldiers at the ready. With the river guarding one side and the sea the other, this mountain fortress seemed strong—until Louis XIV leveled it in 1706. Nice's medieval seawall ran along the lineup of two-story buildings where you're standing. Now look across place Pierre Gautier to the large "palace." This Ducal Palace was where the kings of Sardinia (the city's Italian rulers until about 1860) would reside when in Nice. Today, it's police headquarters.

Resume your stroll down the center of cours Saleya, stopping when you see La Cambuse restaurant on your left. In front, hovering over the black barrel fire with the paella-like pan on top, is the self-proclaimed Queen of the Market, Thérèse (tehr-ehz). When she's not looking for a husband, Thérèse is cooking *socca*, Nice's chickpea crêpe specialty. Spend €2 for a wad of *socca* (careful—it's hot, but good). If she doesn't have a pan out, that means it's on its way (watch for the frequent scooter deliveries). Wait in line...or else it'll all be gone when you return.

Continue down cours Saleya. The fine golden building at the end is where Henri Matisse lived for 17 years. Turn left at the Civette du Cours café, and head down...

Rue de la Poissonnerie: Look up at #4. Adam and Eve are squaring off, each holding a zucchini-like gourd. This scene (post-apple) represents the annual rapprochement in Nice to make up for the sins of a too-much-fun Carnival (Mardi Gras). Nice residents have partied hard during Carnival for more than 700 years. The iron grill above the door allows air to enter the building, but keeps out uninvited guests. You'll see lots of these open grills in Old Nice. They were part of an ingenious system of sucking in cool air from the sea, through the homes, and out through vents in the roof. Across the street, check out the small Baroque church dedicated to St. Rita, the patron saint of desperate causes. She holds a special place in locals' hearts, and this church is the most popular in Nice.

Turn right on the next street, then left on "Right" Street (rue Droite), into a world that feels like Naples.

Rue Droite: In the Middle Ages, this straight, skinny street provided the most direct route from wall to wall, or river to sea. Stop at Esipuno's bakery (at place du Jésus). Thirty years ago, this baker was voted the best in France, and his son now runs the place. Notice the firewood stacked by the oven. Farther along, at #28, Thérèse (whom you met earlier) cooks her *socca* in the wood-fired oven before she carts it to her barrel on cours Saleya. The balconies of the mansion in the next block mark the Palais Lascaris (1647), a rare souvenir from one of Nice's most prestigious families (free, Wed–Mon 10:00–18:00, closed Tue, worth touring for a peek at 1700s Baroque Italy high life, look up and make faces back at the guys under the balconies).

Turn left on the rue de la Loge, then left again on rue Mascoïnat, to reach...

Place Rossetti: The most Italian of Nice's piazzas, place Rossetti feels more like Rome than Nice. This square comes alive after dark. Fenocchio is popular for its many gelato flavors. Walk to the fountain and stare back at the church. This is the Cathedral of St. Réparate—an unassuming building for a major city's cathedral. The cathedral was relocated here in the 1500s, when Castle Hill was temporarily converted to military-only. The name comes from Nice's patron saint, a teenage virgin named Réparate, whose martyred body floated to Nice in the 4th century, accompanied by angels (remember the Bay of Angels?). The interior is overwhelmingly Baroque. Remember that Baroque was a response to the Protestant Reformation. With the Catholic Church's "Counter-Reformation," the theatrical energy of churches was cranked up—with reenergized, high-powered saints and eye-popping decor.

Back outside the cathedral, the steps leading up rue Rossetti are the most direct path from here to Castle Hill (15 min straight up). If you're pooped, wander back down to quai des Etats-Unis near the beach and ride the elevator (next to Hôtel Suisse, where bayfront road curves right, open daily 10:00–18:00, until 20:00 in summer, one-way-€0.70, round-trip-€1).

Castle Hill (Colline du Château): This hill—in an otherwise flat city center—offers good views over Nice, the port (to the east), the foothills of the Alps, and the Mediterranean. The views are best at sunset or whenever the weather's really clear (park closes at 20:00 in summer, earlier off-season). Until the 1100s, the city of Nice was crammed onto this hilltop, as it was too risky to live in the flatlands below, where marauders were on the rampage. Today, you'll find a waterfall, a playground, two cafés (fair prices), and a cemetery—but no castle—on Castle Hill.

To walk back downtown, follow signs from just below the upper café to Vieille Ville (not Le Port), and turn right at the cemetery, then look for the walkway down on your left.

ACTIVITIES

▲▲**Strolling the Promenade des Anglais**—Sauntering along Nice's four-mile seafront promenade is a must. From the days when wealthy English tourists lined the seaside with grand hotels, to today as a favorite spot for Europeans to enjoy some fun in the sun—this stretch is *the* place to be in Nice.

▲**Wheeling the Promenade**—Get a bike and ride along the coast in both directions (about 30 min each way). Roller Station rents bikes, in-line skates, and mini-scooters (see "Helpful Hints," above). Both of the following paths start along the promenade des Anglais.

The path to the west stops just before the airport at perhaps the most scenic *boules* courts in France. Stop and watch the old-timers while away their afternoon tossing those shiny metal balls (see sidebar on page 125).

In the other direction, you'll round the hill—passing a scenic cape and the town's memorial to both World Wars—to the harbor of Nice, with a chance to survey some fancy yachts. Pedal around the harbor and follow the coast past the Corsica ferry terminal (you'll need to carry your bike up a flight of steps). From there, the path leads to a delightful, tree-lined residential district.

Relaxing at the Beaches—Nice is where the masses relax on the rocks. After settling into the smooth pebbles, you can play beach volleyball, table tennis, or *boules* (see page 125); rent paddleboats, personal watercraft, or windsurfing equipment; explore ways to use your zoom lens as a telescope; or snooze on comfy beach beds with

end tables. You can rent a spot on the beach (mattress and chaise lounge-€12, umbrella-€4, towel-€3). Many hotels have special deals with certain beaches for discounted rental (check with your hotel for details). Consider lunch in your bathing suit (€10 salads and pizzas in bars and restaurants all along the beach). For a peaceful cup of coffee on the beach, stop here first thing in the morning before the crowds hit. *Plage Publique* signs explain the 15 beach no-nos (translated in English).

SIGHTS

Museums

You can get a free pass for bus #15 when traveling between the Chagall and Matisse museums. Ask at either of these museums for this free ticket, which saves you a 20- to 30-minute walk (it's uphill from Chagall to Matisse).

▲▲▲**Chagall Museum (Musée National Marc Chagall)**—Even if you're suspicious of modern art, this museum—with the largest collection of Chagall's work in captivity anywhere—is a delight. After World War II, Chagall returned from the United States to settle in nearby Vence. Between 1954 and 1967, he painted a cycle of 17 large murals designed for, and donated to, this museum. These paintings, inspired by the biblical books of Genesis, Exodus, and the Song of Songs, make up the "nave," or core, of what Chagall called the "House of Brotherhood."

Each painting is a lighter-than-air collage of images that draw from Chagall's Russian-folk-village youth, his Jewish heritage, biblical themes, and his feeling that he existed somewhere between heaven and earth. He believed that the Bible was a synonym for nature, and that color and biblical themes were key ingredients for understanding God's love for his creation. Chagall's brilliant blues and reds celebrate nature, as do his spiritual and folk themes (see sidebar on page 463).

Notice the focus on couples. To Chagall, humans loving each other mirrored God's love of creation. Chagall enjoyed the love of two women in his long life—his first wife, Bella, then Valentina, who gave him a second wind as he was painting these late works. Chagall was one of the few "serious" 20th-century artists to portray unabashed love. Where the Bible uses the metaphor of earthly, physical, and sexual love to describe God's love for humans, Chagall uses unearthly colors and a mystical ambience to celebrate human love. Chagall's canvases are hard to interpret on a literal level, but they capture the rosy spirit of a man in love with life.

On your way out, be sure to visit the three Chagall stained-glass windows in the auditorium (depicting God's creation of the universe).

Cost and Hours: €5.50, covered by Riviera Carte Musées pass, Oct–June Wed–Mon 10:00–17:00, July–Sept Wed–Mon 10:00–18:00, closed Tue, tel. 04 93 53 87 31, www.musee-chagall.fr. For information on getting to the museum, see page 453.

▲▲**Matisse Museum (Musée Matisse)**—This museum, worth ▲▲▲ for his fans, contains the world's largest collection of Matisse paintings. It offers a painless introduction to the artist, whose style was shaped by Mediterranean light and by fellow Côte d'Azur artists Pablo Picasso and Pierre-Auguste Renoir.

Henri Matisse, the master of leaving things out, could suggest a woman's body with a single curvy line—leaving it to the viewer's mind to fill in the rest. Ignoring traditional 3-D perspective, he used simple dark outlines saturated with bright blocks of color to create recognizable but simplified scenes composed into a decorative pattern to express nature's serene beauty. You don't look "through" a Matisse canvas, like a window; you look "at" it, like wallpaper.

Matisse understood how colors and shapes affect us emotionally. He could create either shocking, clashing works (Fauvism) or geometrical, balanced, harmonious ones (later works). While other modern artists reveled in purely abstract design, Matisse (almost) always kept the subject matter at least vaguely recognizable. He used unreal colors and distorted lines not just to portray what an object looks like, but also to express the object's inner nature (even inanimate objects). Meditating on his paintings helps you connect with nature—or so Matisse hoped.

As you wander the museum, look for motifs, including fruit, flowers, wallpaper, and interiors of sunny rooms—often with a window opening onto a sunny landscape. Another favorite subject is the odalisque (harem concubine)—usually shown sprawled in seductive poses and with a simplified, masklike face.

Notice works from his different periods. Room 9 houses paintings from his formative years as a student. In Room 10, his work evolves through many stages, becoming simpler with time. Upstairs, in and around Room 17, you'll find sketches and models of his famous Chapel of the Rosary in nearby Vence (see page 502) and related religious work. On the same floor, there are rooms dedicated

Chagall's Style

Chagall uses a deceptively simple, almost childlike style to paint a world that's hidden to the eye—the magical, mystical world below the surface. Here are some of his techniques:

- **Deep, radiant colors,** inspired by Fauvism and Expressionism.
- **Personal imagery,** particularly from his childhood in Russia—smiling barnyard animals, fiddlers on the roof, flower bouquets, huts, and blissful sweethearts.
- **A Hasidic Jewish perspective,** the idea that God is everywhere, appearing in everyday things like nature, animals, and humdrum activities.
- **A fragmented Cubist style,** a multifaceted, multidimensional style perfect for capturing the multifaceted, multidimensional, colorful complexity of God's creation.
- **Overlapping images,** like double-exposure photography, with faint images that bleed through—suggesting there's more to life under the surface.
- **Stained-glass-esque,** dark, deep, earthy, "potent" colors, and simplified, iconic, symbolic figures.
- **Gravity-defying compositions,** with lovers, animals, and angels twirling blissfully in midair.
- **Happy,** not tragic; despite the violence and turmoil of World Wars and Revolution, he painted a world of personal joy.
- **Childlike simplicity,** with heavy outlines, filled in with Crayola colors that often spill over the lines. Major characters in a scene are bigger than the lesser characters. The smiling barnyard animals, the bright colors, the magical events presented as literal truth.... Was Chagall a lightweight? Or a lighter-than-air-weight?

to his paper cutouts and his *Jazz* series. Throughout the building are souvenirs from his travels, which inspired much of his work.

The museum is in a 17th-century Genoese villa, set in an olive grove amid the ruins of the Roman city of Cemenelum. Part of the ancient Roman city of Nice, Cemenelum was a military camp that housed as many as 20,000 people.

Cost and Hours: €4, covered by Riviera Carte Musées pass, Wed–Mon 10:00–18:00, closed Tue, tel. 04 93 81 08 08, www.musee-matisse-nice.org.

Getting to the Matisse Museum: It's a confusing but manageable 45-minute walk from the top of avenue Jean Médecin (and the train station). And it's a 20- to 30-minute walk from the Chagall Museum.

Buses #15 and #17 serve the Matisse and Chagall Museums

from the eastern side of avenue Jean Médecin (#15 runs more frequently-6/hr, #17-3/hr, €1.40). The bus stop for Matisse (called Arènes) is on avenue de Cimiez, two blocks up from Chagall. If connecting the museums by bus, ask for a free bus pass with your museum ticket.

To **walk** to the Matisse Museum, go to the train-station end of avenue Jean Médecin and turn right onto boulevard Raimbaldi along the overpasses, then turn left under the overpasses onto avenue Raymond Comboul. Once under the overpass, angle to the right up avenue de l'Olivetto to the alley (with the big wall on your right). A pedestrian path soon emerges, and it leads up and up to signs for both Chagall and Matisse.

Modern and Contemporary Art Museum (Musée d'Art Moderne et d'Art Contemporain)—This ultramodern museum features an enjoyable collection of art from the 1960s and 1970s, including works by Andy Warhol and Roy Lichtenstein, and offers frequent special exhibits.

Cost, Hours, Location: €4, covered by Riviera Carte Musées pass, Tue–Sun 10:00–18:00, closed Mon, on promenade des Arts near bus station, tel. 04 93 62 61 62, www.mamac-nice.org.

Molinard Perfume Museum—The Molinard family has been making perfume in Grasse (about an hour's drive from Nice) since 1849. Their Nice store has a small museum in the back illustrating the story of their industry. Back when people believed water spread the plague (Louis XIV supposedly bathed less than once a year), doctors advised people to rub fragrances into their skin and then powder their bodies. Back then, perfume was a necessity of everyday life.

Room 1 shows photos of the local flowers used in perfume production. Room 2 shows the earliest (18th-century) production method. Petals would be laid on a bed of animal fat. After baking in the sun, the fat would absorb the essence of the flowers. Petals would be replaced daily for two months until the fat was saturated. Models and old photos show the later distillation process (660 pounds of lavender would produce only a quarter-gallon of essence). Perfume is "distilled like cognac and then aged like wine." Room 3 shows the desk of a "nose." Of the 150 real "noses" (top perfume creators) in the world, more than 100 are French. You are welcome to enjoy the testing bottles before heading into the shop.

Cost, Hours, Location: Free, daily 10:00–19:00, sometimes closed Mon off-season, just between beach and place Masséna at 20 rue St. François de Paule, tel. 04 93 62 90 50, www.molinard.com.

Other Nice Museums—These museums are decent rainy-day options. The **Fine Arts Museum** (Musée des Beaux-Arts), with 6,000 works from the 17th to 20th centuries, will satisfy your need for a fine-arts fix (€4, covered by Riviera Carte Musées pass,

Tue–Sun 10:00–18:00, closed Mon, 3 avenue des Baumettes, western end of Nice, tel. 04 92 15 28 28). The **Archaeological Museum** (Musée Archeologique) displays Roman ruins and various objects from the Romans' occupation of this region (€4, Wed–Mon 10:00–18:00, closed Tue, near Matisse Museum at 160 avenue des Arènes, tel. 04 93 81 59 57). Nice's city museum, **Museum Masséna** (Musée Masséna), is closed until at least 2006.

More Sights

Russian Cathedral (Cathédrale Russe)—Nice's Russian Orthodox church—claimed to be the finest outside Russia—is worth a visit. Five hundred rich Russian families wintered in Nice in the late 19th century. Since they couldn't pray in a Catholic church, the community needed a worthy Orthodox house of worship. Czar Nicholas I's widow saw the need and provided the land (which required tearing down her house). Czar Nicholas II gave this church to the Russian community in 1912. (A few years later, Russian comrades—who didn't winter on the Riviera—assassinated him.) Here in the land of

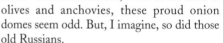

olives and anchovies, these proud onion domes seem odd. But, I imagine, so did those old Russians.

Step inside (pick up English info sheet). The one-room interior is filled with icons and candles, and the old Russian music adds to the ambience. The icon wall divides things between the spiritual world and the temporal world of the worshippers. Only the priest can walk between the two worlds, by using the "Royal Door." Take a close look at items lining the front (starting in the left corner). The angel with red boots and wings—the protector of the Romanov family—stands over a symbolic tomb of Christ. The tall, black, hammered-copper cross commemorates the massacre of Nicholas II and his family in 1918. Notice the Jesus icon near the Royal Door. According to a priest here, as the worshipper meditates, staring deep into the eyes of Jesus, he enters a lake where he finds his soul. Surrounded by incense, chanting, and your entire community...it could happen. Farther to the right, the icon of the Virgin and Child is decorated with semi-precious stones from the Ural Mountains. Artists worked a triangle into each iconic face—symbolic of the Trinity.

Cost, Hours, Location: €2.50, daily 9:00–12:00 & 14:30–18:00, closes 17:00 off-season, chanted services Sat at 17:30 or 18:00, Sun at 10:00, no tourist visits during services, no shorts, 10-min walk behind station at 17 boulevard du Tzarewitch, tel. 04 93 96 88 02.

SLEEPING

Don't look for charm in Nice. Go for modern and clean, with a central location and, in summer, air-conditioning. I've divided my sleeping recommendations into three areas: between the train station and Nice Etoile shopping center, near Old Nice and the beaches, and in a more stately area between the station and promenade des Anglais (by boulevard Victor Hugo).

Reserve early for summer visits. The rates listed here are for April through October. Prices generally drop €10–20 from November through March, and can increase dramatically during the Nice Carnival (Feb 11–27 in 2005), Monaco's Grand Prix (May 19–22 in 2005), and the Cannes film festival (May 11–22 in 2005). June is convention month, and Nice is one of Europe's top convention cities—so book ahead.

Near the Train Station

Most hotels near the station are overrun, overpriced, and loud. Here are the pleasant exceptions (most are between Old Nice and the train station, near avenue Jean Médecin and boulevard Victor Hugo). For parking, ask your hotelier, or see "Arrival in Nice—By Car," page 451.

$$$ Hôtel Vendôme*, a mansion set off the street, gives you a whiff of the belle époque, with pink pastels, high ceilings, and grand staircases. Rooms are modern and come in all sizes. The best have balconies—request *"une chambre avec balcon"* (Sb-€88–95, Db-€105–125, Tb-€120–140, buffet breakfast-€10, air-con, parking-€10/day, 26 rue Pastorelli, tel. 04 93 62 00 77, fax 04 93 13 40 78, www.vendome-hotel-nice.com, contact@vendome-hotel-nice.com).

$$ Hôtel Excelsior*, one block below the station, is a diamond in the rough. You'll find turn-of-the-century decor, a small but lush garden courtyard, and pleasant rooms with real wood furnishings. Rooms on the garden are best in the summer; streetside rooms have balconies and get winter sun (standard Db-€90, *prestige* Db-€120, air-con, 19 avenue Durante, tel. 04 93 88 18 05, fax 04 93 88 38 69, www.excelsiornice.com, excelsior.hotel@wanadoo.fr).

$$ Hôtel St. Georges, a block away, is big and bright, with a backyard garden, reasonably clean and comfortable rooms, and happy Jacques at the reception (Sb-€59, Db-€69, Tb with 3 separate beds-€87, extra bed-€16, air-con, 7 avenue Georges Clémenceau, tel. 04 93 88 79 21, fax 04 93 16 22 85, www.hotelsaintgeorges.fr, nicefrance.hotelstgeorges@wanadoo.fr).

$ Hôtel Clémenceau, run by the charming La Serres, is an exceptional value with a basic, homey feel. Rooms—some with balconies, some without closets, all air-conditioned—are mostly spacious and traditional (S-€31, Sb-€43, D-€43, Db-€58, Tb-€69, Qb-€84, kitchenette-€8 extra and only for stays of at least 3 nights,

Sleep Code

(€1 = about $1.20, country code: 33)
S = Single, D = Double/Twin, T = Triple, Q = Quad,
b = bathroom, s = shower only, no CC = Credit Cards not
accepted, * = French hotel rating (0–4 stars). Hotels speak
English, have elevators, and accept credit cards unless otherwise
noted.

To help you sort easily through these listings, I've divided
the rooms into three categories based on the price for a standard
double room with bath:

$$$ **Higher Priced**—Most rooms €95 or more.
$$ **Moderately Priced**—Most rooms between €65–95.
$ **Lower Priced**—Most rooms €65 or less.

no elevator, 3 avenue Georges Clémenceau, 1 block west of avenue
Jean Médecin, tel. 04 93 88 61 19, fax 04 93 16 88 96, hotel
-clemenceau@wanadoo.fr, Marianne).

$ **Hôtel du Petit Louvre*** is basic, but a good hostel-like budget
bet, with playful owners (the Vilas), art-festooned walls, and adequate rooms (S-€38, Ds-€44, Db-€49, Tb-€57, pay on arrival, 10
rue Emma Tiranty, tel. 04 93 80 15 54, fax 04 93 62 45 08,
petilouvr@wanadoo.com).

Near Old Nice

$$$ **Hôtel Masséna******, in an elegant building a few blocks from
place Masséna, is a consummate business hotel that offers 100 four-
star rooms with all the comforts at reasonable rates (small Db-€120,
larger Db-€150, still larger Db-€215, extra bed-€30, some non-
smoking rooms, Internet access, reserve parking ahead-€18/day, 58
rue Gioffredo, tel. 04 92 47 88 88, fax 04 92 47 88 89, www.hotel
-massena-nice.com, info@hotel-massena-nice.com).

$$$ **Hôtel Suisse***** has Nice's best ocean views for the money,
and is surprisingly quiet given the busy street below. Rooms are
comfortable, with air-conditioning and modern conveniences.
There's no reason to sleep here if you don't land a view, so I've listed
prices only for view rooms—many of which have balconies (Db-
€120–155, breakfast-€14, 15 quai Rauba Capeu, tel. 04 92 17 39 00,
fax 04 93 85 30 70, hotelsuisse.nice@wanadoo.fr).

$$$ **Hôtel Mercure*****, wonderfully situated on the water
behind cours Saleya, offers tastefully designed rooms (some with
beds in a loft) at good rates for the location (Sb-€94, Db-€108–120,
buffet breakfast-€12, air-con, 91 quai des Etats-Unis, tel. 04 93 85
74 19, fax 04 93 13 90 94, h0962@accor-hotels.com).

Nice Hotels

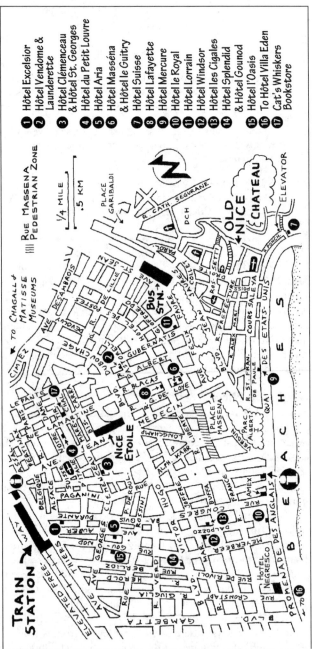

1. Hôtel Excelsior
2. Hôtel Vendome & Launderette
3. Hôtel Clemenceau & Hôtel St. Georges
4. Hôtel du Petit Louvre
5. Hôtel Aria
6. Hôtel Masséna & Hôtel le Guitry
7. Hôtel Suisse
8. Hôtel Lafayette
9. Hôtel Mercure
10. Hôtel le Royal
11. Hôtel Lorrain
12. Hôtel Windsor
13. Hôtel les Cigales
14. Hôtel Splendid & Hôtel Gounod
15. Hôtel l'Oasis
16. To Hôtel Villa Eden
17. Cat's Whiskers Bookstore

$$ Hôtel Lafayette*** looks big and average from the outside, but inside, it's a cozy, good value that offers 18 sharp, spacious, three-star rooms at two-star rates, all one floor up from the street. Sweet Sandrine will take good care of you (standard Db-€77–93, spacious Db-€87–105, extra bed-€18, central air-con, no elevator, 32 rue de l'Hôtel des Postes, tel. 04 93 85 17 84, fax 04 93 80 47 56, lafayette@nouvel-hotel.com).

$$ Hôtel le Guitry*** is a small place with 16 rooms. Half are traditional, half are just renovated and *très* plush, and a few have little natural light (Db-€70–90, big family room-€125, central air-con, 6 rue Sacha Guitry, tel. 04 93 80 83 83, fax 04 93 13 02 91, dynamo Geraldine S enough E).

$ Hôtel Lorrain** is very basic, with kitchenettes in all of its large, linoleum-floored rooms. It's a classic budget place, with no frills, conveniently located one block from the bus station and Old Nice (Db-€48, extra bed-€25, 6 rue Gubernatis, push top buzzer to release door, tel. 04 93 85 42 90, fax 04 93 85 55 54, hotellorrain@aol.com).

Uptown, Between the Station and Promenade des Anglais

$$$ Hôtel Windsor*** is a snazzy, well-run garden retreat with contemporary rooms, including some—designed by modern artists—that defy explanation (pass on the *artiste* rooms and ask for a traditional room). It has a swimming pool and gym (both free for guests), and a €10 sauna (Db-€105–155, extra bed-€20, breakfast-€10, rooms over garden worth the higher price, Internet access, 11 rue Dalpozzo, tel. 04 93 88 59 35, fax 04 93 88 94 57, www.hotelwindsornice.com, contact@hotelwindsornice.com).

$$$ Hôtel Les Cigales*** is a smart little pastel place with tasteful decor, 19 newly renovated rooms, air-conditioning, and a slick upstairs terrace, all well-managed by friendly Mr. Valentino (standard Db-€115, big Db-€160, breakfast-€10, 16 rue Dalpozzo, tel. 04 97 03 10 70, fax 04 97 03 10 71, www.hotel-lescigales.com, infos@hotel-lescigales.com).

$$$ Hôtel Splendid*** is a worthwhile splurge if you miss your Hilton. The rooftop pool, whirlpool tub, and panoramic breakfast room alone almost justify the cost...but throw in good rooms (some non-smoking), a free gym, Internet access, and air-conditioning, and you're as good as home (Db-€225, deluxe Db with terrace-€250, suites-€335, breakfast-€16, free breakfast with minimum 3-night stay, parking-€19/day, 50 boulevard Victor Hugo, tel. 04 93 16 41 00, fax 04 93 16 42 70, www.splendid-nice.com, info@splendid-nice.com).

$$$ Hôtel Gounod*** is behind Hôtel Splendid and shares the same owners, who allow its clients free access to Hôtel Splendid's pool, whirlpool tub, and other amenities. Don't let the lackluster lobby fool you. Its fine rooms are big, air-conditioned, and richly decorated, with high ceilings—though they can be musty (Db-€125–140, palatial 4-person suites-€215, breakfast-€10, parking-€12/day, 3 rue Gounod, tel. 04 93 16 42 00, fax 04 93 88 23 84, www.gounod-nice.com, info@gounod-nice.com).

$$$ **Hôtel Aria***** is a soft-yellow, very sharp, big-city refuge with 30 comfortable rooms, half of which overlook a small park. This place is well run and a good value (Db-€95–110, junior suite-€150, extra bed-€20, buffet breakfast-€9, air-con, 15 avenue Auber, tel. 04 93 88 30 69, fax 04 93 88 11 35, www.aria-nice.com, reservation@aria-nice.com).

$$$ **Hôtel le Royal***** stands shoulder-to-shoulder on the promenade des Anglais with the big boys (hôtels Negresco and Westminster). It feels like a retirement-home-turned-hotel (don't expect an enthusiastic reception), but offers solid comfort with air-conditioning at €100–200 less than its more famous neighbors. The mini-suites are well worth the extra euros (seaview rooms: Sb-€100, Db-€130, Db mini-suite €150; city-facing rooms: Sb-€80, Db-€100; 23 promenade des Anglais, tel. 04 93 16 43 00, fax 04 93 16 43 02, royal@vacancesbleues.com).

$$$ **Hôtel l'Oasis***** is just that. This orange-pastel hotel sits away from the street, surrounding a large, flowery courtyard. Its 40 non-smoking rooms are also calming, with air-conditioning, earth tones, pleasing fabrics, sharp bathrooms, and reasonable rates. This hotel works with an English travel agency, so many guests are British, and the place is often booked long in advance (Sb-€75, Db-€90–120, Tb-€120, prices include breakfast, 23 rue Gounod, tel. 04 93 88 12 29, fax 04 93 16 14 40).

$$ **Hôtel Villa Eden**** is the one little belle époque time-warp place among the sprawling waterfront hotels lining the promenade des Anglais. This former mansion of a Russian aristocrat now rents 13 rooms with a faded and charming, family-run ambience. It's set back enough to lose the street noise and much of the sea view, but if you want to be close to the beach, this is a good budget option (Db-€63–69, extra bed-€15, 10-minute walk beyond Hôtel Negresco, bus #12 or #23 from station, 99 Promenade des Anglais, tel. 04 93 86 53 70, fax 04 93 97 67 97, hotelvillaeden@caramail.com).

EATING

My recommended restaurants are concentrated in the same neighborhoods as my favorite hotels. The promenade des Anglais is ideal for picnic dinners on warm, languid evenings, and the old town is perfect for restaurant-shopping. Gelato-lovers should save room for **Fenocchio** (on place Rossetti in Old Nice, 86 flavors from tomato to lavender, daily until 23:30). Ice cream cone in hand, you can join the evening parade along the Mediterranean (best view at night is from east end of quai des Etats-Unis, on tip below Castle Hill).

Old Nice, on or near Cours Saleya

Nice's dinner scene converges on cours Saleya (koor sah-lay-yuh)—entertaining enough in itself to make the generally mediocre food of its restaurants a good value. It's a fun, festive place to compare tans and mussels. Even if you're eating elsewhere, wander through here in the evening.

La Cambuse offers a refined setting and fine cuisine for those who want to eat on cours Saleya without sacrificing quality (allow €30–40 per person, open daily, at #5, tel. 04 93 80 82 40).

Le Safari has the best "eating energy" on the cours Saleya and serves all afternoon (open daily, at Castle Hill end at #1, tel. 04 93 80 18 44).

Nissa Socca offers good, cheap Italian cuisine and a lively atmosphere a few blocks from cours Saleya (Mon–Sat from 19:00, closed Sun, arrive early, a block off place Rossetti on rue Ste. Réparate, tel. 04 93 80 18 35).

L'Acchiardo, deeper in the old city, is a budget traveler's friend, with simple, hearty, traditional cuisine at bargain prices in a homey setting (€13 dinner *plats*, closed Sat–Sun, 38 rue Droite, tel. 04 93 85 51 16).

Lou Pilha Leva offers a fun, *très* cheap dinner option with *niçoise* specialties and outdoor-only benches. Order your food from one side and drinks from the other (open daily, located where rue de la Loge and Centrale meet in Old Nice).

L'Univers, a block off place Masséna, has earned a Michelin star while maintaining a warm ambience. This elegant place is as relaxed as a "top" restaurant can be, from its casual decor to the tasteful dinnerware. But when the artfully presented food arrives, you know this is high cuisine (*menus* from €40, closed Sun, 53 boulevard Jean Jaurès, tel. 04 93 62 32 22, plumailunivers@aol.com).

Restaurant Castel is your best beach option. Eating here, you almost expect Don Ho to grab a mike. You're right on the beach below Castle Hill, perfectly positioned to watch evening swimmers get in their last laps as the sky turns pink and city lights flicker on. Lunch views are unforgettable—you can even have lunch at your beach chair if you've rented one. Arrive before sunset and linger long enough to merit the few extra euros the place charges (open daily, salads and pastas-€13–15, main courses-€24, Panaché de la Mer is a good sampling of seafood and vegetables, 8 quai des Etats-Unis, tel. 04 93 85 22 66).

Close to Recommended Hotels near the Station

These restaurants lie closer to most recommended hotels, within a few blocks of avenue Jean Médecin, near the Nice Etoile shopping center.

Old Nice Hotels and Restaurants

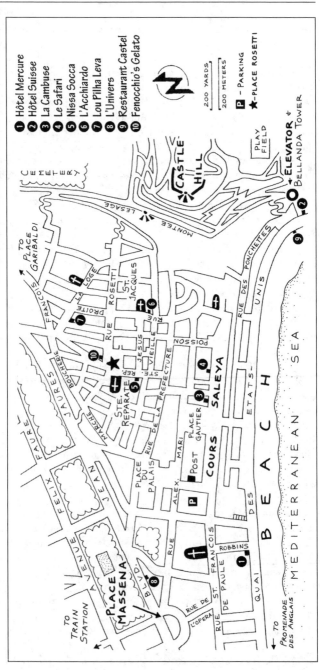

1. Hôtel Mercure
2. Hôtel Suisse
3. La Cambuse
4. Le Safari
5. Nissa Socca
6. L'Acchiardo
7. Lou Pilha Leva
8. L'Univers
9. Restaurant Castel
10. Fenocchio's Gelato

Reserve ahead at enchanting little **Bistrot Les Viviers** for the most authentic *niçoise* cuisine in this book. Fish is their forte (allow €35 per person for dinner, lunch *menus* from €16, closed Sun, 22 rue Alphonse Karr, 5-min walk west of avenue Jean Médecin, tel. 04 93 16 00 48). Make sure to reserve for the *bistrot*, not their stuffier restaurant next door (prices are the same, ambience is different).

Charming **La Cantine de Lulu** is a fine value, wonderfully small, and Czech-owned, with homemade recipes from Nice to Prague (closed Sat–Mon, 26 rue Alberti, tel. 04 93 62 15 33).

La Part des Anges, an atmospheric wine shop with a few tables in the rear, serves a limited, mouthwatering menu with a large selection of wines (open daily for lunch, Fri–Sat only for dinner, reserve ahead, 17 rue Gubernatis, tel. 04 93 62 69 80).

Laid-back cafés line up along the broad sidewalk on rue Biscarra (just east of avenue Jean Médecin behind Nice Etoile, all closed Sun). **L'Authentic**, **Le Vin sur Vin**, and **Le Cenac** are all reasonable (L'Authentic is best, Le Cenac is cheapest).

Lou Mourleco is *niçoise traditionnel*. Because it serves only what's fresh, the menu changes constantly (*menus* from €20, air-con, closed Sun–Mon, 15 rue Biscarra, tel. 04 93 80 80 11).

Le Côte Grill, a block from Nice Etoile, is bright, cool, and easy, with a salad bar, air-conditioned rooms, and a large selection at reasonable prices (open daily, 1 avenue Georges Clémenceau, tel. 04 93 82 45 53).

NIGHTLIFE

Nice's bars play host to the Riviera's most happening late-night scene, full of jazz and rock 'n' roll. Most activity focuses on Old Nice, near place Rossetti. Plan on a cover charge or expensive drinks. If you're out very late, avoid walking alone. The plush and smoky bar at Hôtel Negresco is fancy-cigar old English.

TRANSPORTATION CONNECTIONS

For train and bus schedules from Nice to nearby towns, see "Getting Around the Riviera," page 447. Note that most long-distance train connections to other French cities require a change in Marseille.

From Nice by train to: Marseille (19/day, 2.75 hrs), **Cassis** (7/day, 3 hrs, transfer in Toulon or Marseille), **Arles** (11/day, 3.5 hrs, 10 with change in Marseille), **Avignon** (10/day, 4 hrs, a few direct, most require transfer in Marseille), **Paris'** Gare de Lyon (14/day, 5.5–7 hrs, 6 with change in Marseille), **Aix-en-Provence** TGV station (10/day, 3.5 hrs, transfer in Marseille probable), **Chamonix** (4/day, 11 hrs, 2–3 transfers), **Beaune** (7/day, 7 hrs, transfer in Lyon), **Munich** (2/day, 12 hrs with 2 transfers, one night

Nice Restaurants

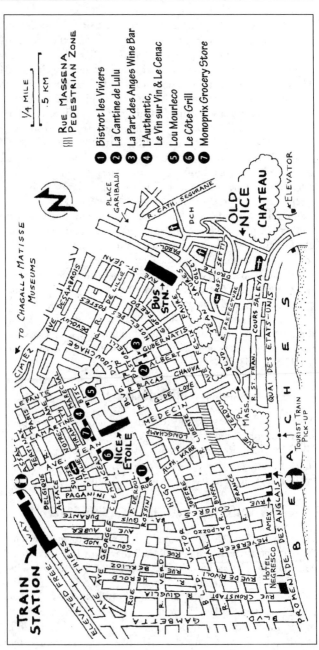

||| RUE MASSENA PEDESTRIAN ZONE

1 Bistrot les Viviers
2 La Cantine de Lulu
3 La Part des Anges Wine Bar
4 L'Authentic, Le Vin sur Vin & Le Cenac
5 Lou Mourleco
6 Le Côte Grill
7 Monoprix Grocery Store

train with a transfer in Verona), **Interlaken** (1/day, 12 hrs), **Florence** (4/day, 7 hrs, transfers in Pisa and/or Genoa, night train), **Milan** (4/day, 5–6 hrs, 3 with transfers), **Venice** (3/day, 3/night, 11–15 hrs, 5 require transfers), **Barcelona** (3/day, 11 hrs, long transfer in Montpellier, or a direct night train).

Nice's Airport (Aéroport de Nice Côte d'Azur)

Nice's easy-to-navigate airport is on the Mediterranean, about 20 minutes west of the city center. Planes go about hourly to Paris (1-hr flight, about the same price as a train ticket). There are two terminals (1 and 2) used by domestic and international flights. Both terminals have TIs, banks, taxis, and buses to Nice (www.nice.aeroport.fr, tel. 08 20 42 33 33 or 04 89 88 98 28).

Taxis into the center are expensive, charging €30 to Nice hotels and €50 to Villefranche-sur-Mer. Taxis stop outside door *(Porte)* A-1 at Terminal 1 and outside Porte A-3 at Terminal 2.

Three **bus** lines run from both terminals into Nice. Bus #99 runs nonstop to the main train station (€3.50, 2/hr, 8:00–21:00, 30 min, drops you within a 10-min walk of many recommended hotels); the yellow "NICE" bus #98 goes to the bus station *(gare routière,* €3.50, 3/hr, 30 min) and will also take you to the train station upon request 6:00–8:00 and after 21:00 (ask driver for *"la gare SNCF"*). The slower, cheaper local bus #23 serves stops between the airport and train station (€1.40, 4/hr, 50 min, direction: St. Maurice).

Buy tickets in the **bus information office** (Terminal 1 only) or from the driver. To reach the bus information office and bus stops at Terminal 1, turn left after passing customs and exit the doors at the far end (buses #98 and #99 use platform 1, bus #23 uses platform 6). Buses serving Terminal 2 are well-signed to the right as you exit (bus #98 stops at platform 5, bus #99 uses platform 4, and bus #23 uses platform 6).

To get to **Villefranche-sur-Mer** from the airport, take the yellow "NICE" bus #98 to the bus station *(gare routière),* and transfer to the Villefranche-sur-Mer bus (bus #100, €1.70, 4/hr).

Buses also run hourly directly from the airport to **Antibes** (line #200, €8, 20 min) and to **Monaco** (line #110 express on the freeway, €14, 50 min).

Villefranche-sur-Mer

Villefranche offers travelers an easygoing slice of small-town Mediterranean life just 15 minutes from more high-powered Nice and Monaco. This town feels Italian—with soft orange buildings, steep, narrow streets spilling into the sea, and pasta with pesto. Luxury yachts glisten in the bay, a reminder to those lazing along the harborfront that Monaco is just down the coast. Sand-pebble beaches, a handful of interesting sights, and quick access to Cap Ferrat keep visitors just busy enough.

Originally a Roman port, Villefranche was overtaken by 5th-century barbarians. Villagers fled into the hills, where they stayed and farmed their olives. In 1295, the Duke of Provence—like much of Europe—was threatened by the Saracen Turks. He asked the hillside olive farmers to move down to the water and establish a front line against the invaders—denying them a base from which to attack Nice. In return for tax-free status, they stopped farming, took

up fishing, and established *Ville-* (town) *franche* (without taxes). Since there were many such towns, this one was specifically "Tax-free town on the sea" *(sur Mer)*. Around 1560, the Duke of Savoy built the town an immense citadel (which you can still tour). Today—because two-thirds of its 8,000 people call this their primary residence—Villefranche feels more like a real community than neighboring Riviera towns.

ORIENTATION

Tourist Information

The TI is in Jardin François Binon, below the main bus stop (July–Aug daily 9:00–19:00, Sept–June Mon–Sat 9:00–12:00 & 14:00–18:30, closed Sun, a 20-min walk or €10 taxi from train station, tel. 04 93 01 73 68, www.villefranche-sur-mer.com). Pick up the brochure detailing a self-guided walking tour of Villefranche and information on boat rides. If you plan to visit Cap Ferrat, ask for the simple brochure-map showing the walks around this peninsula and information on the Villa Ephrussi de Rothschild's gardens (see "The Three Corniches: Villefranche to Monaco," page 481).

Arrival in Villefranche

By Train: Villefranche's train station is a level 15-minute walk along the water from the old town (taxi-€10).

By Bus: Buses from Nice and Monaco drop you just above the TI. The old town and most hotels are downhill. The stop for buses going back to Nice is across the street from where you were left (buses run every 10–15 min). Bus #111 to Cap Ferrat uses the same Villefranche stops.

By Car: From Nice's port, follow signs for Menton, Monaco, and Basse Corniche. In Villefranche, take the road next to the TI into the city. For a quick visit to the TI, park at the nearby pay lot.

You'll find the free Parking Fossés a bit farther down—better for longer visits (well-signed from main road). Some hotels have parking.

Helpful Hints

Market Day: An antiques market enlivens Villefranche on Sundays (on place Amélie Pollonnais by Hôtel le Welcome and in Jardin Binon by the TI). On Saturday mornings, a small food market sets up by the TI (only in Jardin François Binon).

Internet Access: Chez Net, an "Australian International Sports Bar Internet Café," is a fun place to get a late-night drink or check your e-mail (€2.50/15 min, open daily, place du Marché).

Laundry: The self-service launderette is just below the main road, opposite 6 avenue Sadi Carnot (daily 8:00–20:00).

Taxi: Beware of taxi drivers who overcharge—the normal weekday, daytime rate to central Nice is about €30; to the airport, figure about €50; and the trip to the main street level from the waterfront should be around €10 (tel. 04 93 6 70 19).

Sports Fans: Lively *boules* action takes place each evening just below the TI and the huge soccer field.

SIGHTS

The Harbor—Browse Villefranche's miniscule harbor. Only eight families still fish to make money. Gaze out to sea and marvel at the huge yachts that call this bay home. (You might see well-coiffed captains being ferried in by dutiful mates to pick up their statuesque call girls.) Local guides keep a list of the world's 100 biggest yachts and talk about some of them like they're part of the neighborhood.

Parallel to the beach and about a block inland, you can walk the mysterious rue Obscura—a covered lane running 400 feet along the medieval rampart.

Chapel of St. Pierre (Chapelle Cocteau)—This chapel, decorated by artist, poet, and filmmaker Jean Cocteau, is the town's cultural highlight. A mean fisherwoman collects a €2 donation for the fishermen's charity, then sets you free to enjoy the chapel's small but delightful interior. In 1955, Jean Cocteau covered the barrel-vaulted chapel with heavy black lines and pastels. Each of the Cocteau scenes—the Gypsies of Stes-Maries-de-la-Mer who dance and sing to honor the Virgin; girls wearing traditional outfits; and three scenes from the life of St. Peter—are explained in English (€2, Tue–Sun 9:30–12:00 & 15:00–19:00, closed Mon, below Hôtel Welcome).

Citadel—The town's immense castle was built by the Duke of Savoy to defend against the French in the 1500s. When the region joined

France in 1860, it became just a barracks. In the 20th century, with no military use, the city started using the citadel to house its police station, City Hall, and two art galleries.

Church—The town church features a fine crucifix—carved, they say, from a fig tree by a galley slave in the 1600s.

Boat Rides (Promenades en Mer)—These little cruises, with English handouts, are offered one or two days a week (June–Sept only, €11/1 hr, €16/2 hrs, across from Hôtel Welcome, tel. 04 93 76 65 65).

Beach Walk—A pleasant walk under the citadel, along a nearly beach-level rampart, connects the yacht harbor with the old town and beach. Stroll Villefranche's waterfront beyond the train station away from the town for postcard views back to Villefranche and a quieter beach (ideal picnic benches); consider extending your walk to Cap Ferrat (see page 482). Even if you're sleeping elsewhere, consider an ice-cream-licking village stroll here.

SLEEPING

(€1 = about $1.20, country code: 33)

There's a handful of hotels to choose from in Villefranche. The ones I list have at least half of their rooms with sea views—well worth paying extra for. The rooms at both of my first two listings, while different in cost, are about the same in comfort. Hôtel Welcome sits on the harbor in the center; Hôtel la Flore is a 10-minute walk from the old town, but has a pool and free parking.

$$$ **Hôtel Welcome***** is right on the water in the old town—all 36 balconied rooms overlook the harbor. You'll pay top price for all the comforts in a very smart, professional hotel that seems to do everything right, and couldn't be better located ("comfort" Db-€164, bigger "superior" Db-€189, suites-€299–340, extra bed-€35, buffet breakfast-€12, air-con, parking garage-€16/day, 1 quai Amiral Courbet, tel. 04 93 76 27 62, fax 04 93 76 27 66, www.welcomehotel.com, resa@welcomehotel.com.).

$$$ **Hôtel la Flore***** is for you if your idea of sightseeing is to enjoy the view from your bedroom deck, the dining room, or the pool (Db with no view-€90–125, Db with view and deck-€135, Db mini-suite-€195, extra bed-€34, Qb loft with huge terrace-€220, prices 10–15 percent cheaper Oct–March, air-con, elevator, pool, free parking, fine restaurant, just off main road high above harbor, 5 boulevard Princesse Grace de Monaco, 2 blocks from TI towards Nice, tel. 04 93 76 30 30, fax 04 93 76 99 99, www.hotel-la-flore.fr, hotel-la-flore@wanadoo.fr, SE).

$$$ **Hôtel la Fiancée du Pirate** is best for drivers, as it's above Villefranche on the Middle Corniche. Friendly Nadine (SE) offers 15 clean and comfortable rooms. Choose between larger rooms

Villefranche-sur-Mer

1. Hôtel Welcome
2. Hôtel la Flore
3. Hôtel Provençal
4. Hôtel de la Darse
5. Hôtel Vauban
6. Restaurants les Palmiers, Michel's & le Cosmo
7. Restaurant la Mère Germaine
8. Restaurant la Grignotière
9. Lounge Beach Café
10. Chez Net Bar & Internet
11. Boat Tours
12. Launderette
13. Bus Stop (from Nice; to Monaco & Cap Ferrat)
14. Bus Stop (to Nice; from Monaco & Cap Ferrat)

P – Parking
T – Taxi Stand

TO EZE + MONACO VIA LOW CORNICHE ROAD

TRAIN STATION

BEACH

TO CAP FERRAT ON FOOT

BLVD. NAPOLEON

AVE. GEORGES CLEMENCEAU

QUAI PONCHARD

QUAI AM. COURBET

ALBERT 1

AVE. GALLIENI

OLD TOWN

R. DU BARON

RUE OBSCURE

Post

AVE. CH. JEUN.

AVE. SADI

AVE. JOFFRE

AVE. CARNOT

CHAPEL OF ST. PIERRE

AVE. VERDUN

AVE. DUVAL

ALLÉE

PLAY AREA

CITADEL

SCENIC WALKWAY

AVE. FOCH

TO NICE

DE GAULLE

PLAY AREA

AVENUE

200 YARDS
200 METERS

PORT DE LA DARSE

QUAI CORDERIE

MEDITERRANEAN SEA

DCH

inside the building with air-conditioning (Db-€95–120), or view rooms on the garden patio (Db-€115–135, no air-con). There's a pool, garden, spacious *salon de thé*, breakfast terrace with partial views of Cap Ferrat and the sea, and even a small children's play area (8 boulevard de la Corne d'Or, Moyenne Corniche N7, tel. 04 93 76 67 40, fax 04 93 76 91 04, www.fianceedupirate.com, info @fianceedupirate.com).

$$ **Hôtel le Provençal**** is a big place crying out for an interior designer. The uninspired yet comfortable-enough rooms are a fair value, with some fine views and balconies (Db-€63–110, most around €80, Tb-€80–120, extra bed-€10, skip cheaper non-view rooms, 10 percent off with this book and a 2-night stay in 2005, air-con, right below the main road, a block from TI at 4 avenue Maréchal Joffre, tel. 04 93 76 53 53, fax 04 93 76 96 00, www .hotelprovencal.com, provencal@riviera.fr).

$ **Hôtel la Darse**** , a shy and unassuming little hotel sitting in the shadow of its highbrow brothers, offers a simple, low-key alternative right on the water at Villefranche's old port. The dull hallways disguise rooms that are quiet and reasonably comfortable; those facing the sea have million-dollar-view balconies (non-view Db-€52–62, view Db-€64–76, extra bed-€10, from TI walk or drive down avenue Général de Gaulle to the old Port de la Darse, tel. 04 93 01 72 54, fax 04 93 01 84 37, hoteldeladarse@wanadoo.fr, SE). Major renovations are planned in 2005—the hotel might be closed until spring, and prices could increase.

$ **Hôtel Vauban*** , two blocks down from the TI, is a curious place that makes me feel like I'm in a brothel, with 15 basic rooms and decor as Old World as the owner (non-view Db-€45, view Db-€70, no CC, 11 avenue Général de Gaulle, tel. 04 93 76 62 18, e-what?, NSE).

EATING

Comparison-shopping is half the fun of dining in Villefranche. Make an event out of a pre-dinner stroll through the old city. Check what looks good on the lively place Amélie Pollonnais above the Hôtel Welcome, saunter the string of candlelit places lining the waterfront, and consider the smaller, cheaper eateries embedded in the old city's walking streets.

Les Palmiers is a beachy place buzzing with cheery diners (hearty salads and pizza-€9, open daily, on place Amélie Pollonnais, tel. 04 93 01 71 63).

Michel's, on the other side of the fountain, is more romantic and stylish (allow €35–40 per person, closed Tue, tel. 04 93 76 73 24).

Le Cosmo Restaurant is next door, with great tables overlooking the harbor and the Cocteau chapel's facade (floodlit after some wine, Cocteau pops). It serves nicely presented gourmet dishes with less fun but better quality than Les Palmiers (fine salads and pastas- €10, great Bandol red wine, open daily, place Amélie Pollonnais, tel. 04 93 01 84 05).

La Mère Germaine, right on the harborfront, is the only place in town classy enough to lure a yachter ashore. It's dressy, with fine service and a harborside setting. The name comes from when the current own- er's grandmother fed hungry GIs in World War II. Try the bouill- abaisse, served with panache (€57 per person, or a mini-version for €39, €34 *menu*, open daily, reserve harborfront table, tel. 04 93 01 71 39).

Disappear into Villefranche's walking streets and find cute little **La Grignotière,** serving a €29 *gourmet menu* (open daily, 3 rue Poilu, tel. 04 93 76 79 83).

Lounge Beach Café, on the beach below the train station, is worth considering for the best view of Villefranche and decent food at reasonable prices. This place also works well for lunch or a drink with a view (salads, pastas, and à la carte, open daily, tel. 04 93 01 72 57).

Souris Gourmande ("Gourmet Mouse") is handy for a sand- wich, to take away or eat there (daily 11:30–19:30, closed Fri in winter, behind Hôtel Welcome, €4 made-to-order sandwiches...be patient and get to know your chef, Albert). Sandwich in hand, there are plenty of great places to enjoy a harborside sit.

TRANSPORTATION CONNECTIONS

The last bus leaves Nice for Villefranche at about 19:45; the last bus from Villefranche to Nice leaves at about 21:00; and one train runs later (24:00).

From Villefranche by train to: Monaco (2/hr, 10 min), **Nice** (2/hr, 10 min), **Antibes** (2/hr, 40 min).

By bus to: Cap Ferrat (6/day, 10 min), **Monaco** (4/hr, 25 min), **Nice** (4/hr, 15 min).

The Three Corniches:
Villefranche to Monaco

Nice, Villefranche-sur-Mer, and Monaco are linked with three coastal routes: the Low, Middle, and High Corniches. The roads are nicknamed for the decorative frieze that runs along the top of a building (cornice). Each Corniche offers sensational views and a dif- ferent perspective on this exotic slice of real estate.

Low Corniche: The *Basse Corniche* (often called *Corniche Inférieure*) strings ports, beaches, and villages together for a traffic- filled ground-floor view. It was built in the 1860s (along with the new train line) to bring people to the casino in Monte Carlo. When this Low Corniche was finished, many hill-town villagers came down and started the communities that line the sea today. Before 1860, the population of the coast between Villefranche-sur-Mer and Monte Carlo was zero.

Middle Corniche: The *Moyenne Corniche* is higher, quieter, and far more impressive. It runs through Eze (described below) and provides breathtaking views over the Mediterranean, with several scenic pullouts (the pullout above Villefranche-sur-Mer is particularly stunning).

High Corniche: Napoleon's crowning road-construction achievement, the *Grande Corniche,* caps the cliffs with staggering views from almost 1,600 feet above the sea. It is actually the Via Aurelia, used by Romans to conquer the West.

Villas: Driving from Villefranche-sur-Mer to Monaco, you'll come upon impressive villas. A particularly grand entry leads to the sprawling estate built by King Leopold II of Belgium in the 1920s. Those driving up to the Middle Corniche will look down on this yellow mansion that fills an entire hilltop with a lush garden. This estate was later owned by the Agnelli family (of Fiat fame and fortune), and then by the Safra family (American bankers).

The Best Route: For a ▲▲▲ route, **drivers** should take the Middle Corniche from Nice to Eze, follow signs to the High Corniche *(Grande Corniche/La Turbie)* from there, and after La Turbie, drop down into Monaco. **Buses** travel each route; the higher the Corniche, the less frequent the buses (roughly 5/day on Middle and High, 2/hr on Low; get details at Nice's bus station).

The following villages and sights are listed from west to east, as you'll reach them, from Villefranche-sur-Mer to Monaco.

▲Cap Ferrat—This peninsula decorates Villefranche-sur-Mer's sea views. An exclusive, largely residential community, it's a peaceful eddy off the busy Nice–Monaco route (Low Corniche). You could spend a day on this peninsula, wandering the port village of St. Jean-Cap-Ferrat, touring the Villa Ephrussi de Rothschild mansion and gardens (described below), and walking on sections of the beautiful trails that follow the coast. The **TI** is between the port and Villa Ephrussi (at 59 avenue Denis Séméria, tel. 04 93 76 08 90).

Getting to Cap Ferrat from Villefranche: You can go by **car** (Low Corniche) or **taxi** (allow €15 one-way); ride the **bus** (#111 from main stop in Villefranche, 6/day, 10 min; bus from Nice to Monaco also drops you at edge of the Cap—4/hr, 5 min, a 15-min walk to Villa Ephrussi); or **walk** (50 min from Villefranche). Walkers from Villefranche-sur-Mer go past the train station along the beach and climb the steps at the far end. Continue straight past the mansions (with gates more expensive than my entire house) and make the first right. You'll see signs to the Villa Ephrussi de Rothschild, then to Cap Ferrat's port.

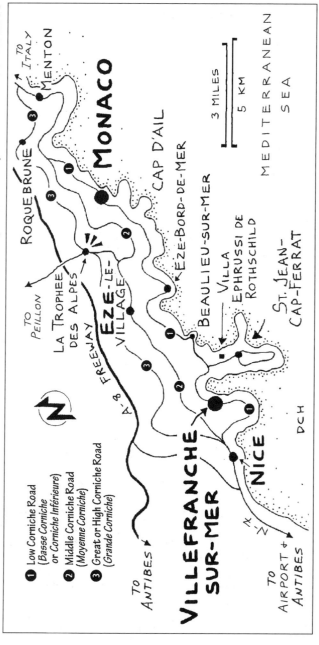

Villefranche, Monaco, and the Corniches

1 Low Corniche Road
   (Basse Corniche
   or Corniche Inférieure)

2 Middle Corniche Road
   (Moyenne Corniche)

3 Great or High Corniche Road
   (Grande Corniche)

Villa Ephrussi de Rothschild—In what seems like the ultimate in Riviera extravagance, Venice, Versailles, and the Côte d'Azur come together in the pastel-pink Villa Ephrussi. Rising above Cap Ferrat, this 1905 mansion comes with territorial views east to Villefranche-sur-Mer and west to Beaulieu.

Start with the well-furnished belle époque **interior** (helpful English handout provided). An 18-minute film (English subtitles) gives background on the life of rich and eccentric Beatrice, Baroness de Rothschild, who built and furnished the place. As you stroll the halls, you'll pass rooms of royal furnishings and personal possessions, including her bathroom case for cruises. A fancy tearoom serves drinks and lunch with a view.

But the gorgeous **gardens** are why most come here. Behind the mansion, stroll through the seven lush gardens, re-created from different parts of the world. The sea views from here are lovely. Don't miss the Alhambra-like Spanish gardens, the rose garden at the far end, and the view back to the house from the "Temple of Love" gazebo.

Cost and Hours: Palace and gardens-€8.50, skippable tour of upstairs-€2 extra, combo-ticket with Villa Grecque Kerylos-€14.50; Feb–Oct daily 10:00–18:00, July–Aug until 19:00; Nov–Jan Mon–Fri 14:00–18:00, Sat–Sun 10:00–18:00; tel. 04 93 01 45 90, www.villa-ephrussi.com. Parking is tricky; a small turnaround is provided at the top.

▲**Eze-le-Village**—Floating high above the sea, flowery Eze-le-Village (don't confuse it with the seafront town of Eze-Bord-de-Mer) is entirely consumed by tourism. This *village d'art et de gastronomie* (as it calls itself) mixes perfume outlets, upscale boutiques, steep cobbled lanes, and magnificent views. Touristy as the place certainly Eze, its stony state of preservation and magnificent hilltop setting make a visit here worthwhile.

Bus stops and parking lots weld the town to the highway (Middle Corniche) that passes under its lowest wall. The **TI** is in the car park below the town (place de Gaulle, tel. 04 93 41 26 00, www.eze-riviera.com).

Come for sunset and stay for dinner to enjoy a more peaceful Eze. You'll dine well at the stone-cozy **Le Troubador** (€30 *menu*, closed Sun–Mon, 4 rue du Brec, tel. 04 93 41 19 03), or for less, with better views, at the basic **Nid de L'Aigle** ("Eagle's Nest," closed Wed except in summer, tel. 04 93 41 19 08).

Getting to Eze-le-Village: There are two Ezes: Eze-le-Village (the spectacular hill town, your destination) and Eze-Bord-de-Mer (a dull beach town far below Eze-le-Village). Eze-le-Village is about

20 minutes east of Villefranche-sur-Mer on the Middle Corniche. There are six buses per day from Nice to Eze-le-Village (3 on Sun), or you can take the train to Eze-Bord-de-Mer and take the shuttle bus up to Eze-le-Village (€4, May–Oct only, daily 9:30–18:30, 8/day; or allow €22 one-way for a taxi between the two Ezes).

▲▲**La Trophée des Alpes**—High above Monaco, on the High Corniche in the village of La Turbie, lies one of this region's most evocative historic sights (with dramatic views over the entire country of Monaco as a bonus). This massive Roman monument commemorates Augustus Caesar's conquest of the Alps and its 44 hostile tribes. It's exciting to think that, in a way, La Trophée des Alpes celebrates a victory that kicked off the Pax Romana—joining Gaul and Germania, freeing up the main artery of the Roman Empire, and lacing together Spain and Italy.

Walk around the monument and notice how the Romans built a fine quarried-stone exterior, filled in with rubble and coarse concrete. Flanked by the vanquished in chains, the towering inscription tells the story: It was erected "by the senate and the people to honor the emperor." The monument was restored in the 1930s and 1940s with money from the Tuck family of New Hampshire.

The one-room museum shows a reconstruction and translation of the dramatic inscription, listing all the feisty alpine tribes that put up such a fight (€5, daily 9:30–11:30 & 13:00–18:30, tel. 04 93 41 20 84). Escorts from the museum take people up the monument, but it's not worth waiting for.

Nearby, the charming village of **La Turbie** is less touristy than others around here, and has plenty of cafés and restaurants.

Getting to La Trophée des Alpes: By **car**, take the High Corniche to La Turbie (10 min east of, and above, Eze-le-Village). At La Regence Café in La Turbie, turn right for the gate to the monument and parking lot. You can also get here by **bus** from Nice or Monaco (from either: €3, 4/day, 45 min; last bus returning to Nice is at about 18:00).

Monaco

Despite overdevelopment, high prices, and wall-to-wall daytime tourists, Monaco (mah-nah-koh) is a Riviera must. Monaco is on the go. Since 1929, cars have raced around the port and in front of the casino in one of the world's most famous auto races, the Grand Prix of Monaco (May 19–22 in 2005). The new breakwater—constructed elsewhere and towed in by sea—enables big cruise ships to actually dock here. The district of Fontvieille, reclaimed from the sea, bristles with luxury high-rise condos. But don't look for anything too deep in this glittering tax haven. Two-thirds of its

30,000 residents live here because there is no income tax—leaving fewer than 10,000 true Monegasques.

This miniscule principality (0.75 square mile) borders only France and the Mediterranean. The country has always been tiny, but it used to be...less tiny. In an 1860 plebiscite, Monaco lost two-thirds of its territory when the region of Menton voted to join France. To compensate, France suggested Monaco build a fancy casino and promised to connect it to the world with a road (the Low Corniche) and a train line. This opened the way for a high-class tourist boom that has yet to let up.

While "independent," Monaco is run as a piece of France. A French civil servant appointed by the French president—with the blessing of Monaco's Prince Rainier—serves as state minister and manages the place. Monaco's phone system, electricity, water, and so on, are all French.

Monaco is a business, and Prince Rainier is its CEO. While its famous casino provides only 5 percent of the state's revenue, its 43 banks—which offer an attractive way to hide your money—are hugely profitable. The prince also makes money with a value-added tax (19.6 percent, the same as in France), plus real estate and corporate taxes.

The glamorous romance and marriage of the American actress Grace Kelly to Prince Rainier added to Monaco's fairy-tale mystique. Grace Kelly first came to Monaco to star in the 1955 Hitchcock film *To Catch a Thief*, in which she was filmed racing along the Corniches. Later, she married her prince and adopted the country. Tragically, Monaco's much-loved Princess Grace died in a car wreck on that same Corniche in 1982.

It's a special place...there are more people in Prince Rainier's philharmonic orchestra (about 100) than in his army (about 80 guards). His princedom is well-guarded, with police and cameras on every corner. (They say you could win a million dollars at the casino and walk through the wee hours to the train station without a worry.) Stamps are so few, they increase in value almost as soon as they're printed. And collectors snapped up the rare Monaco versions of euro coins (with Prince Ranier's portrait) so quickly that many locals have never even seen one.

ORIENTATION

The principality of Monaco consists of three distinct tourist areas: Monaco-Ville, Monte Carlo, and La Condamine. Monaco-Ville fills the rock high above everything else. This is the oldest section, home

Monaco

- **T** – ACCESS TO TRAIN STATION
- **P** – PARKING

300 YARDS
300 METERS

TO MENTON

FRANCE

TO MENTON

MIDDLE CORNICHE

BLVD. PRINCESSE CHARLOTTE

JARDIN EXOTIQUE

TO NICE

BLVD. DU

BLVD. RAINIER III

RUE GRIMALDI

AVE. COSTA

PLACE DU CASINO

AVE. D'OSTENDE

BLVD. MOULINS

AVE. SPEL.

LOEWS CASINO

CASINO

PALAIS DES CONGRES & "LE CASINO"

MONTE-CARLO

JARDIN EXOTIQUE

TO NICE

R. PRIN. CAR.

PLACE D'ARMES

BLVD. ALBERT

PORT LOTSA YACHTS!

MONACO-VILLE

RAMPE MAJOR

AVE. DE LA PORTE NEUVE

POST

MONTE CARLO STORY & **P** "LE PALAIS"

BLVD.

TO NICE

PALACE & NAPOLEON COLLECTION

CATHEDRAL

OLD TOWN

COUSTEAU AQUARIUM

FONT-VIEILLE

BOTANICAL GARDEN

- **1** Hôtel de France
- **2** Pan Bagnat sandwiches at rue Basse #8
- **3** Local bus stops
- **4** Bus stops FROM Nice
- **5** Bus stops TO Nice

to Prince Rainier's palace and all the sights except the casino. Monte Carlo is the area around the casino. And La Condamine is the port (which divides Monaco-Ville and Monte Carlo). You may also pass through a fourth, less-interesting area, Fontvieille.

Buses #1 and #2 link all areas (one ticket-€1.40, four tickets-€3.50, until 21:00, 10/hr, less on Sun). From the port (and train station), it's a 15-minute walk to the Prince's Palace or to the casino (40 min from palace to casino).

Telephone Tip: To call Monaco from France, dial 00, then 377 (Monaco's country code) and the eight-digit number. Within Monaco, simply dial the eight-digit number.

Tourist Information

The main TI is near the casino (2 boulevard des Moulins, Mon–Sat 9:00–19:00, Sun 10:00–12:00), but there's a handier branch in the train station (daily in summer 8:00–19:30, less off-season, tel. 00-377/92 16 61 16 or 00-377/92 16 61 66, www.monaco-tourisme .com). From June to September, you'll find information kiosks in the Monaco-Ville parking garage and on the port.

Arrival in Monaco

By Bus from Nice and Villefranche: There are three stops in Monaco, in order from Nice: in front of a tunnel at the base of Monaco-Ville (place d'Armes), on the port, and below the casino (on avenue d'Ostende). The first stop is the best starting point. From there, you can walk up to Monaco-Ville and the palace (10 min straight up), or catch a local bus (lines #1 or #2). To reach the bus stop and steps up to Monaco-Ville, cross the street right in front of the tunnel and walk with the rock on your right for about 200 feet.

Keep your receipt for the return ride to Nice or Villefranche (RCA buses run twice as often as Cars Broch). The bus stop back to Nice is across the major road from your arrival point, at the light. The last bus leaves Monaco for Nice at about 20:00 (last train leaves about 23:30).

By Train from Nice: The train station is in central Monaco, about a 10-minute walk to the casino in Monte Carlo or the port, and 25 minutes to the palace in Monaco-Ville.

This is a long, underground station with many services. The TI, baggage check, and ticket windows are up the escalator at the Italy end of the station. There are three exits: two from the train platform level (one at each end) and one from above the platforms, up the escalator, past the TI. To walk to the casino, use this upper exit (go past TI, then up the elevator, then exit station and turn left on boulevard Princesse Charlotte and turn right on rue Iris; allow 10 min).

To reach Monaco-Ville and the palace from the station, take one of the two platform-level exits. The exit near the Italy end of the platform leads to the port and the bus stop for city buses #1 and #2, serving Monaco-Ville and the casino (follow *Sortie la Condamine* and go down two escalators, then go left, following Access Port signs). The port is a few blocks downhill from this exit, from which you can walk another 20 minutes to the palace (or casino, though this is the longer way there). The other platform-level exit is at the Nice end of the tracks (signed *Sortie Fontvieille*), which takes you along a long tunnel (TI annex at end) to the foot of Monaco-Ville; from here, it's a 15-minute walk to the palace.

To take the short-but-sweet coastal **walking path** into Monaco's Fontvieille district, get off the train one station before Monaco, in Cap d'Ail. Turn left out of the little station and walk 50 yards up the road, then turn left, going downstairs and under the tracks. Turn left onto the coastal trail, and hike the 20 minutes to Fontvieille. Once you reach Fontvieille, it's a 15-minute uphill hike to Monaco's sights.

By Car: Follow *Centre-Ville* signs into Monaco, then follow the red-letter signs to parking garages at *Le Casino* (for Monte Carlo) or *Le Palais* (for Monaco-Ville). The first hour of parking is free; the next costs €3.50.

Getting Around Monaco

In addition to the city bus system (described under "Orientation," above), here are your other transportation options.

Tourist Train: "Azur Express" tourist trains begin at the aquarium and pass by the port, casino, and palace (€6, 30 min, 2/hr, 10:30–18:00 in summer, 11:00–17:00 in winter depending on weather, taped English commentary, tel. 00-377/92 05 64 38).

Taxis: If you've lost track of time at the casino, you can call the 24-hour taxi service (tel. 00-377/93 15 01 01)...provided you still have enough money to pay for the cab home.

SIGHTS

Monaco-Ville

All of Monaco's sights (except for the casino) are in Monaco-Ville, packed within a few Disney-esque blocks. From anywhere in Monaco, you can get to the palace square, place du Palais (Monaco-Ville's sightseeing ground zero), by taking bus #1 or #2 to place de la Visitation (leave bus to the right and walk straight 5 min, passing a fountain). If you're walking up from the port, the well-marked lane leads directly to the *Palais*.

Palace Square (Place du Palais)—This square is the best place to get oriented to Monaco, as it offers views on both sides of the rock. Facing the palace, go to the right and look out over the city. This little, pastel Hong Kong look-alike was born on this rock in 1215 and has managed to remain an independent country for most of its nearly 800 years. Looking beyond the glitzy port, notice the faded green roof above and to the right: the casino that put Monaco on the map.

Now walk to the statue of the monk grasping a sword near the palace. Meet **François Grimaldi**, a renegade Italian dressed as a monk, who captured Monaco in 1297 and began the dynasty that still rules the principality. Prince Rainier is his great-great-great...grandson, which makes Monaco's royal family Europe's longest-lasting dynasty.

Walk to the opposite side of the square and the Louis XIV **cannonballs**. Down below is Monaco's newest area, Fontvieille, where much of its post-WWII growth has been. Prince Rainier has continued (some say, been obsessed with) Monaco's economic growth, creating landfills (topped with homes, such as Fontvieille), flashy ports, new beaches, and the new rail station. Today, thanks to Prince Rainier's efforts, tiny Monaco is a member of the United Nations. The current buzz is about how soon he'll hand over the reign of the principality to his son, Albert.

You can buy Monaco stamps (popular collectibles, or mail from here) at the post office (PTT) a few blocks down rue Comte Félix Gastaldi.

Prince's Palace (Palais Princier)—A medieval castle sat where Monaco's palace is today. Its strategic setting has had a lot to do with Monaco's ability to resist attackers. Today, Prince Rainier and his son, Albert, live in the palace; princesses Stephanie and Caroline live just down the main street. The palace guards protect the prince 24/7, and still stage a Changing of the Guard ceremony with all the pageantry of an important nation (daily at 11:55, fun to watch, but jam-packed). Automated and uninspired tours (in English) take you through part of the prince's lavish palace in 30 minutes. The rooms are well-furnished and impressive, but interesting only if you haven't seen a château lately (€6, June–Sept daily 9:30–18:00, Oct daily 10:00–17:00, closed Nov–May, tel. 00-377/93 25 18 31).

Napoleon Collection—Napoleon occupied Monaco after the French Revolution. This is the prince's private collection of what Napoleon left behind: military medals, swords, guns, letters, and, most interesting, his hat. I found this collection more appealing than the palace (€4, June–Sept daily 9:30–18:00, Oct daily 10:00–17:00, Dec–May Tue–Sun 10:30–12:30 & 14:00–17:00, closed Mon, next to palace entry).

Cathedral of Monaco (Cathédrale de Monaco)—The somber cathedral, rebuilt in 1878 to show Monaco cared for more than just its new casino, is where centuries of Grimaldis are buried. Circle behind the altar (counterclockwise). The last tomb—Gratia Patricia, MCMLXXXII—is where Princess Grace was buried in 1982 (cathedral open daily 8:30–19:00, until 18:00 in winter).

As you leave the cathedral, step across the street and look down on the newly-reclaimed Fontvieille district and the fancy condos that contribute to the incredible population density of this miniscule country. The adjacent and immaculately maintained Jardin Botanique offer more fine views and a good place to picnic.

Cousteau Aquarium (Musée Océanographique)—Prince Albert I built this impressive, cliff-hanging aquarium in 1910 as a monument to his enthusiasm for things from the sea. One wing features Mediterranean fish; tropical species swim around the other (all well-described in English). Jacques Cousteau directed the aquarium for 17 years. The fancy Albert I Hall upstairs houses the museum (no English), featuring models of Albert and his beachcombers hard at work (aquarium and museum-€12, kids-€6, April–June and Sept daily 9:30–19:00, July–Aug 9:30–19:30, Oct–March 10:00–18:00, at opposite end of Monaco-Ville from palace, down the steps from Monaco-Ville bus stop, tel. 00-377/93 15 36 00, www.oceano.mc).

Monte Carlo Story—The informative 35-minute film gives a helpful account of Monaco's history and offers a comfortable soft-chair break from all that walking (€6.50, usually on the hour, Jan–June and Sept–Oct daily 14:00–17:00, July–Aug 14:00–18:00, closed Nov–Dec, you can join frequent extra showings for groups, English headphones; from aquarium, take escalator into parking garage, then take elevator down and follow signs).

Monte Carlo

▲**Casino**—Monte Carlo, which means "Charles' Hill" in Spanish, is named for the local prince who presided over Monaco's 19th-century makeover. Begin your visit to Europe's most famous casino in the park above the traffic circle. In the mid-1800s, olive groves stood here. Then, with the construction of this casino, spas, and easy road and train access, one of Europe's poorest countries was on the Grand Tour map—*the* place for the vacationing aristocracy to play. Today, Monaco has the world's highest per-capita income.

The casino is designed to make the wealthy feel comfortable while losing money. Charles Garnier designed this casino (with an opera house inside) in 1878, in part to thank the prince for his financial help in completing Paris' Opéra Garnier (which Garnier also designed). The central doors provide access to slot machines, private gaming rooms, and the opera house. The private gaming rooms occupy the left wing of the building.

Count the counts and Rolls-Royces in front of Hôtel de Paris

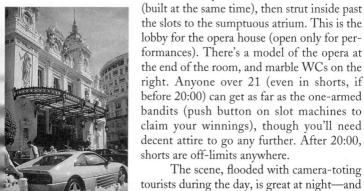

(built at the same time), then strut inside past the slots to the sumptuous atrium. This is the lobby for the opera house (open only for performances). There's a model of the opera at the end of the room, and marble WCs on the right. Anyone over 21 (even in shorts, if before 20:00) can get as far as the one-armed bandits (push button on slot machines to claim your winnings), though you'll need decent attire to go any further. After 20:00, shorts are off-limits anywhere.

The scene, flooded with camera-toting tourists during the day, is great at night—and downright James Bond–like in the private rooms. The park behind the casino offers a peaceful café and a good view of the casino's rear facade and of Monaco-Ville.

If paying an entrance fee to lose money is not your idea of fun, access to all games in the new, plebeian, American-style Loews Casino, adjacent to the old casino, is free.

Cost and Hours: The first rooms, Salons Européens, open at 12:00 and cost €10 to enter. The glamorous private game rooms—where you can rub elbows with high rollers—open at 16:00, others not until 21:00, and cost an additional €10 (and you must show your passport). A tie and jacket (necessary in the evening) can be rented at the bag check for €30 plus a €40 deposit. Dress standards for women are far more relaxed (only tennis shoes are a definite no-no, tel. 00377/92 16 20 00, www.casino-monte-carlo.com).

Take the Money and Run: The return bus stop to Nice is at the top of the park above the casino on avenue de la Costa. To return to the train station from the casino, walk up the parkway in front of the casino, turn left on boulevard des Moulins, turn right on impasse de la Fontaine, climb the steps, and turn left on boulevard Princesse Charlotte (entrance to train station is next to Parking de la Gare; look for *Gare SNCF* sign).

SLEEPING AND EATING

(€1 = about $1.20, country code: 377)
For many, Monaco is best after dark.

The perfectly pleasant **$$ Hôtel de France**** is reasonable (Sb-€72, Db-€94, includes breakfast, 6 rue de la Turbie, near west exit from train station, tel. 00-377/93 30 24 64, fax 00-377/92 16 13 34, hotel-france@monte-carlo.mc).

Several cafés serve basic fare at reasonable prices (day and night) on the port, along the traffic-free rue Princesse Caroline. In Monaco-Ville, you'll find good *pan bagnat* and other sandwiches at 8 rue Basse, just off the palace square.

TRANSPORTATION CONNECTIONS

From Monaco by train to: Nice (2/hr, 20 min), **Villefranche-sur-Mer** (2/hr, 10 min), **Antibes** (2/hr, 45 min).

By bus to: Nice (4/hr, 40 min), **Villefranche-sur-Mer** (4/hr, 25 min).

The last bus leaves Monaco for Villefranche-sur-Mer and Nice at about 20:00; the last train leaves Monaco for Villefranche-sur-Mer and Nice at about 23:30.

Antibes

Antibes has a down-to-earth, easygoing ambience that's rare for this area. Its old town is postcard-perfect: a cluster of red-tiled roofs rising above the blue Mediterranean, watched over by twin medieval lookout towers and wrapped in a rampart. Visitors making the 30-minute trip from Nice browse Europe's biggest yacht harbor, snooze on a sandy beach, loiter through an enjoyable old town, stumble upon characteristic markets, and climb to a castle filled with Picassos.

Though it's much smaller than Nice, Antibes has a history that goes back just as far. Both towns were founded by Greek traders in the 5th century B.C. To the Greeks, Antibes was "Antipolis"—the town *(polis)* opposite *(anti)* Nice. For the next several centuries, Antibes remained in the shadow of its neighbor. By the turn of the 20th century, the town was a military base—so the rich and famous partied elsewhere. But when the army checked out after World War I, Antibes was "discovered" and enjoyed a particularly roaring '20s—with the help of party animals like Rudolph Valentino and the rowdy-yet-very-silent Charlie Chaplin. Fun-seekers even invented water skiing right here in the 1920s.

ORIENTATION

Antibes' old town lies between the port and boulevard Albert 1er and avenue Robert Soleau. Place Nationale is the old town's hub of activity. Lively rue Aubernon connects the port and the old town. Stroll along the sea between the Picasso Museum and place Albert 1er (where boulevard Albert 1er meets the water); the best beaches lie just beyond place Albert 1er, and the path is beautiful. Good play areas for children are on place des Martyrs de la Résistance (close to recommended Hôtel Relais du Postillon).

Tourist Information

There are two TIs. The most convenient is located in the old town, just inside the walls at 21 boulevard d'Aguillon (unpredictable hours, generally June–Aug daily 9:00–21:00, Sept–May Mon–Fri 10:00–12:00 & 14:00–17:00, closed Sat–Sun, tel. 04 93 34 65 65, www.antibes-ville.com). The big Maison de Tourisme is in the newer city, east of the old town where boulevard Albert 1er and rue de la République meet at 11 place Général de Gaulle (July–Aug daily 9:00–19:00, Sept–June Mon–Sat 9:00–12:30 & 13:30–18:00, closed

Sun, tel. 04 92 90 53 00, www.antibes-juanlespins.com). At either TI, pick up the excellent city map and the interesting brochure with a walking tour of old Antibes (in English), and get details on the hikes described below. The Nice TI has Antibes maps; plan ahead.

Arrival in Antibes

By Train: To get to the port (5-min walk), cross the street in front of the station and follow avenue de la Libération downhill. To reach the main TI in the modern city (15-min walk), exit right from the station on avenue Robert Soleau; follow *Maison du Tourisme* signs to place Général de Gaulle. Or hop on the free minibus (see "Getting Around Antibes," below; exit station to the right and cross the street to the park).

By Bus: The bus station is at the edge of the old town on place Guynemer, a block below the TI (info desk open Mon–Sat 8:30–12:00 & 14:30–17:30, closed Sun, public WCs around back).

By Car: Day-trippers should follow *Centre-Ville* and *Vieux Port* signs, and park near the old town walls—as close to the beach as you can (first 30 min free, then about €4/3 hrs, €8/day). Enter the old town through the last arch on the right. If you're sleeping here, hotels are signed; get advice from your hotelier on where to park.

Getting Around Antibes

A free **minibus** *(Minibus Gratuit* or *Navette Gratuite)* circles Antibes (Mon–Sat 7:30–19:30, not on Sun). There are four different circuits, two of which are useful for tourists. Line #1 goes from Fort Carré to the old port, the old town, the ramparts, and back again (every 15 min). Line #2 connects the train station to the main TI at place de Gaulle and to the port every 25 mins. Stops are tricky to find—look for bus stop signs around town (the TI has a small map).

A **tourist train** offers several circuits around old Antibes, the port, and the ramparts (€6.50, departs from place de la Poste, ask about schedule, tel. 06 03 35 61 35). It even has daily departures to Juan-les-Pins (see "Sights," page 496).

To call a **taxi**, dial 04 93 67 67 67.

Helpful Hints

Laundry: A full-service launderette is near the market hall on rue de la Pompe (Mon–Sat 9:00–12:00 & 14:30–19:00, closed Sun).

Bookstore: Heidi's English Bookshop has a great selection of new and used books (daily 10:00–19:00, 24 rue Aubernon).

Introductory Walking Tour of Antibes

This quick walk will help you get your bearings. Begin at the train station (or harborside parking lot), and stroll the **harbor** along

Antibes

To Fort Carre & Nice

TRAIN STN.

PORT VAUBAN

VIEUX PORT

AVE. DU 24 NOV.

AVE. DE LA LIBERATION   AVE. DE VERDUN

BEST PARKING

ARCH

AVE. ROBERT

AVE. THIERS

AVE. MISTRAL

BLVD. D'AIGUILLON

ANDRE

PLAGE DE LA GRAVETTE

PLACE NATIONALE

TOURIST TRAIN PICK-UP

RUE VAUBAN

RUE DE LA REPUBLIQUE

R. SALEURS

AUB.

THURET

PALM.

CLEM.

SADE

RUE CLOSE

RUE DU REVELY

COURS MASSENA

AMIRAL DE GRASSE

CATHEDRAL

PICASSO MUSEUM

CHATEAU GRIMALDI

SOLEAU

PLACE DE GAULLE

BUS STN.

BLVD. WILSON

BLVD. ALBERT 1er

HISTORY & ARCHAEOLOGY MUSEUM

PROM. AMIRAL

BLVD. GEN. MAIZIERES

BLVD. LECLERC

SQUARE ALBERT 1er

TO ❶ ← RUE BOURGEOIS

200 YARDS

200 METERS

Ⓑ – MINIBUS STOP

🅿 – PARKING

TO
PLAGE SALVIS,
CAP D'ANTIBES & ❺

❶ To Hôtel le Mas Djoliba
❷ Auberge Provençale
❸ Modern Hôtel
❹ Hôtel Relais du Postillon
❺ To Hôtel Beau Site
❻ Hôtel le Cameo
❼ Restaurant le Vauban

❽ Restaurant l'Ecureuil
❾ Restaurant Chez Juliette
❿ Restaurant les Vieux Murs
⓫ Le Café Jardin
⓬ Heidi's English Bookshop
⓭ Market Hall
⓮ Launderette

avenue de Verdun. Locals claim that
this is Europe's biggest yacht harbor,
with 1,600 stalls. At the end of the
yachts (quai des Pêcheurs), you'll see
the pathetic remains of a once-hearty
fishing fleet. The Mediterranean is getting fished out. Most of the seafood
you'll eat here comes from fish farms or
the Atlantic.

Cross through the old gate under the ramparts to enter the
old town. Because Antibes was the last fort before the Italian border,
the French king made sure the ramparts were strong and well-
defended. Today, the town is the haunt of a large community of
English, Irish, and Aussie boaters who help crew the giant yachts of
the rich and famous. (That explains the Irish pubs and English
bookstores.) Drop by the cute, shell-shaped **plage de la Gravette**,
an adorable public beach tucked right in the middle of old Antibes.

Continue following the ramparts to the 16th-century, white-
stone **Château Grimaldi**. The castle stands on prime real estate:
This site has been home to the acropolis of the Greek city of
Antipolis, a Roman fort, and a medieval bishop's palace. This
château was the home of the Grimaldi family (who still rule
Monaco), and today it houses the Picasso Museum (listed below).
The neighboring **cathedral** is built over a Greek temple.

Notice the two **towers**. They symbolized society's two dominant land-owning classes: the Church and the nobility. (In 1789, the
Revolution changed all that.) From the bluff below the castle, you
can see **Cap d'Antibes** crowned by its lighthouse and studded with
mansions (see "Cap d'Antibes Hike," below).

The ramparts lead to the **History and Archaeology Museum**
(see below). Just before that (at rue du Haut Castelet), hook inland
and explore the charming, cobbled **pedestrian zone** around rue du
Haut Castelet and rue du Bas Castelet. Poking around Antibes'
peaceful back lanes, gradually work your way back to the entertaining covered **market hall** on cours Masséna.

SIGHTS

▲▲**Picasso Museum (Musée Picasso)**—In the early 20th century,
Antibes' castle (Château Grimaldi) was home to an obscure little
museum that nobody cared about. Then its director had a brain-
storm: Offer the castle to Pablo Picasso as a studio. Picasso lived in
the castle for four months in 1946, where he cranked out an amazing
amount of art—and the resulting collection put Antibes on the
tourist map.

Sitting serenely where the old town meets the sea, this museum

Picasso in Antibes

In the summer of 1946, 65-year-old Pablo Picasso was reborn. World War II was over, and Picasso could finally escape the gray skies and gray uniforms of Nazi-occupied Paris. Enjoying worldwide fame and the love of 23-year-old Françoise Gilot (who would soon have Picasso's babies Claude and Paloma), he moved to Antibes. He spent mornings swimming in the Mediterranean, days painting, evenings partying with friends, and late nights painting again, like a madman. Ever-restless Picasso had finally found his Garden of Eden and rediscovered his *joie de vivre*.

For four months, Picasso worked in a sun-bathed studio in the Château Grimaldi, with a wide-angle view of the Bay of Antibes. Dressed in rolled-up white pants and a striped sailor's shirt, bursting with pent-up creativity, he often cranked out more than a painting a day. Only when the chill and damp of winter set in did he abandon the studio. In a gesture of gratitude uncharacteristic of the stingy Spaniard, he donated all the work he'd done at the Château—nearly 200 paintings and drawings—to create the Picasso Museum we visit today.

These works set the tone for Picasso's postwar art: sunny, light-hearted, childlike, experimenting in new media, and using motifs of Greek mythology, the sea, and animals (such as birds and goats).

offers a remarkable collection of Picasso's work: paintings, sketches, and ceramics. Picasso said that if you want to see work from his Antibes period, you'll have to see it in Antibes. You'll understand why Picasso liked working here. Several photos of the artist and a movie of him hard at work (when making art, he said he was "working" rather than "painting") make this already intimate museum even more so. In his famous *La Joie de Vivre* (the museum's highlight), there's a new love in Picasso's life, and he's feelin' groovy.

The museum also displays works by Nicolas de Stael (1914–1955), who spent his final lonely winter in Antibes near the château, where he committed suicide by jumping out a window. There's also a sculpture terrace overlooking the Bay of Antibes, featuring works by local artists (such as Germaine Richier), as well as by Picasso's friend Joan Miró *(Sea Goddess)*.

Cost and Hours: €5, covered by Riviera Carte Musées pass, June–Sept Tue–Sun 10:00–18:00, July–Aug Wed and Fri until 20:00; Oct–May Tue–Sun 10:00–12:00 & 14:00–18:00, always closed Mon (tel. 04 92 90 54 20).

History and Archaeology Museum (Musée d'Histoire et d'Archéologie)—Displaying Greek, Roman, and Etruscan odds and ends, this is the only place to get a sense of this city's ancient roots. I liked the 2,000-year-old lead anchors (€3, no English explanations, June–Sept Tue–Sun 10:00–18:00, July–Aug Wed and Fri until 20:00; Oct–May Tue–Sun 10:00–12:00 & 14:00–18:00, always closed Mon; on the water between Picasso Museum and place Albert 1er).

▲Market Hall (Marché Provençal)—The daily market bustles under a 19th-century canopy, with flowers, produce, Provençal products, and beach accessories (in old town behind Picasso Museum on cours Masséna). The market wears many appealing hats: produce daily except Monday until 13:00; handicrafts Thursday through Sunday in the afternoon; and romantic outdoor dining in the evenings.

Other Markets—Antibes' lively antique/flea market fills place Nationale and place Audiberti (next to the port) on Saturdays (7:00–18:00). Its clothing market winds through the streets around the post office (rue Lacan) on Thursdays (9:00–18:00).

Fort Carré—This impressively situated citadel, dating from 1487, was the last fort inside France. It protected Antibes from Nice, which until 1860 was part of Italy. You can tour this unusual four-pointed fort—at its height, it held 200 soldiers—but there's precious little to see inside. People visit for the stunning views (€3, covered by Riviera Carte Musées pass, includes tour, June–Sept daily 10:15–17:30, Oct–May daily 10:15–16:00).

Scenic footpaths link the fort to the port along the sea. It's a 30-minute portside walk from the old town to the fort (or taxi there and walk back). By foot or car, follow avenue du 11 Novembre around the port, stay on the main road (walkers can follow path by sports fields), then park on the beach just after the soccer field. A signed dirt path leads to Fort Carré. Keep following green-lettered signs to *Le Fort/Sens de la Visite.*

Beaches (Plages)—The best beaches stretch between Antibes' port and Cap d'Antibes, and the very best (plage de la Salis and plage du Ponteil) are just south of place Albert 1er. All are golden and sandy. Plage de la Salis is busy in summer, but it's manageable, with snack stands every so often and views of the old town. The closest beach to the old town is at the port (plage de la Gravette)  and remains relatively calm in any season.

Juan-les-Pins—This village, across the Cap d'Antibes isthmus from Antibes, is where the action is in the evenings. It's a modern beach resort with good beaches, plenty of lively bars and restaurants, and a popular jazz festival in July. Buses, trains, and even a tourist train (see "Getting Around Antibes," above) make the 10-minute connection to and from Antibes constantly.

HIKES AND DAY TRIPS

From place Albert 1er (where boulevard Albert 1er meets the beach), there's a great view of plage de la Salis and Cap d'Antibes. That tower on the hill is your destination for the first walk described below. The longer "Cap d'Antibes Hike" begins on the next beach, just over that hill.

▲▲**Chapelle et Phare de la Garoupe**—The sensational views (best at sunset) from this chapel and lighthouse more than make up for the 25-minute uphill climb from the far end of plage de la Salis (a block after Maupassant Apartments, follow pedestrian-only chemin du Calvaire up to lighthouse tower). An orientation table explains that you can see from Nice to Cannes and up to the Alps. By car, follow signs for Cap d'Antibes, then look for signs to Chapelle et Phare de la Garoupe.

▲**Cap d'Antibes Hike (Sentier Touristique Piétonnier de Tirepoil)**—At the end of the mattress-ridden plage de la Garoupe (over the hill from lighthouse) is a well-maintained trail around Cap d'Antibes. The beautiful path follows the rocky coast below exclusive mansions for about two miles, then heads inland, ending at the recommended Hôtel Beau-Site (and bus stop). You can walk as far as you'd like and then double back, or do the whole loop (allow 2 hrs, use the TI Antibes map). Locals call this the "Bay of Millionaires."

To get to the trail from Antibes, take **bus** #2A from the bus station to the La Fontaine stop at the Hôtel Beau-Site (every 40 min, return stop is 50 yards down on opposite side, get return times at station, also posted at stop). Walk 10 minutes down to plage de la Garoupe and start from there. By **car**, follow signs to Cap d'Antibes, then plage de la Garoupe, and park there. The trail begins at the far-right end of plage de la Garoupe.

Marineland and Parc de la Mer—A few backstrokes from Antibes, Parc de la Mer is a massive waterworld of waterslides, miniature golf, exhibits, and more. Marineland anchors this sea park extravaganza, with shows featuring dolphins, sea lions, and killer whales (Marineland only—adults-€32, kids-€23, prices €2 more in July–Aug and €6 less in winter; the whole shebang—adults-€39, kids-€30; various combo-tickets available for aquasplash waterslides, miniature golf, and other attractions; daily 10:00–19:00, until 22:00 July–Aug, tel. 04 93 33 49 49, www.marineland.fr). The park is five minutes on foot from the train station in Biot (between Nice and Antibes); exit Biot's station and walk toward Nice, following the signs. By car, the park is signed from RN-7, several miles from Antibes toward Nice.

More Day Trips from Antibes—Antibes is halfway between Nice and Cannes (easy train service to both), and close to the artsy pottery and glassblowing village of Biot, home of the Fernand Léger Museum (frequent buses, get details at TI).

SLEEPING

(€1 = about $1.20, country code: 33)

The best Antibes hotels require a car or taxi—central pickings are slim in this city, where most hoteliers seem more interested in their restaurants.

Outside the City Center

$$$ Hôtel Pension le Mas Djoliba*** is a good splurge, but best for drivers (since it's a 15-min walk from the beach and old Antibes, and a 25-min walk from the train station). Reserve early for this tranquil, bird-chirping, flower-filled manor house where no two rooms are the same. After a busy day of sightseeing, dinner by the pool is a treat (they request that you dine here May–Sept). You'll be in good hands with sweet Stephanie serving and Sylvan cooking with market-fresh products (Db with breakfast and dinner-€80–96 per person, Db room only-€85–125, several good family rooms-€160–170, suite-€210, breakfast-€10, 29 avenue de Provence; from boulevard Albert 1er, look for blue signs and turn right up avenue Gaston Bourgeois; tel. 04 93 34 02 48, fax 04 93 34 05 81, www.hotel-djoliba.com, hotel.djoliba@wanadoo.fr).

$$ Hôtel Beau Site*** is my only listing on Cap d'Antibes, a 10-minute drive from the old town. It's a fine value if you want to get away, but not *too* far away. This place is a sanctuary, with friendly owners (Nathalie SE), a pool, a big patio, and easy parking. The 30 plush and well-cared-for rooms are priced fairly (standard Db-€67–77, bigger Db-€87–92, extra bed-€25, bikes available, 141 boulevard Kennedy, tel. 04 93 61 53 43, fax 04 93 67 78 16, www.hotelbeausite .net, hbeausit@club-internet.fr). From the hotel, it's a 10-minute walk down to the crowded plage de la Garoupe and a nearby hiking trail (see "Hikes and Day Trips from Antibes," above).

In the City Center

$$ Modern Hôtel** this spick-and-span, well-run place is in the pedestrian zone. The 17 standard-size rooms, each with air-conditioning and pleasing decor, are an excellent value (Sb-€55–60, Db-€64–76, €10 more in summer, 1 rue Fourmillière, tel. 04 92 90 59 05, fax 04 92 90 59 06).

$$ Hôtel Relais du Postillon**, on a thriving square, offers 15 small, tastefully designed rooms, all with names instead of numbers, accordion bathrooms in need of TLC, and owners who take more pride in their well-respected restaurant (Db-€46–84, price depends on size and whether you're facing courtyard or park, *menus* from €32, 8 rue Championnet, tel. 04 93 34 20 77, fax 04 93 34 61 24, postillon @atsat.com, SE).

$$ Auberge Provençale*, on charming place Nationale, has a popular restaurant and seven Old World rooms (those on the square get all the noise, day and night), with nonexistent management and a couldn't-care-less-if-you-stayed-here attitude (Db-€63–85, Tb-€72–94, Qb-€110, reception in restaurant, 61 place Nationale, tel. 04 93 34 13 24, fax 04 93 34 89 88). Their huge loft room, named "Céline," faces the back and comes with a royal canopy bed and a dramatic open-timbered ceiling for no extra charge.

$ **Hôtel le Cameo**** is a rambling, refreshingly non-aggressive old place above a bustling bar (where you'll find what reception there is). The public areas are dark, but the nine very simple, linoleum-lined rooms are almost huggable. All open onto the delightful place Nationale, which means you don't sleep until the restaurants close (Ds-€50, Db-€60, Ts-€59, Tb-€69, 5 place Nationale, tel. 04 93 34 24 17, fax 04 93 34 35 80, NSE).

EATING

The old town is crawling with possibilities. Lively place Nationale is filled with tables and tourists (great ambience), while locals seem to prefer the restaurants along the market hall. Take a walk and judge for yourself, considering these suggestions. Romantics and those on a budget should buy a picnic dinner and head for the beach.

Le Vauban is near the port, with an appealing interior and reasonably-priced salads and *plats* (*menus* from €20, open daily, 7 rue Thuret, tel. 04 93 34 33 05).

Le Café Jardin, serves simple food and has a quiet, hidden garden terrace behind the café (look for *Jardin* sign pointing through a door in the back, left of café; open Mon–Sat for lunch only, also open for dinner July–Aug, always closed Sun, 8 rue James Close, tel. 04 93 34 42 66).

L'Ecureuil (or "Casa Amando" in Spanish) is a fun, inexpensive place to try paella in the traffic-free zone. Señor and Madame Carramal are the friendly owners—he's Spanish, which explains why the paella is so *bueno* (closed Sun–Mon, 17 rue Fourmillière, tel. 04 93 34 07 97).

The recommended hotels **Auberge Provençale** (seafood specialties) and **Relais du Postillon** (cozier decor and an interior courtyard) both offer well-respected cuisine with *menus* for €30–35 (both open daily).

Chez Juliette, just off place Nationale, offers budget meals (*menus* from €14, closed for lunch and on Mon, rue Sade, tel. 04 93 34 67 37).

Les Vieux Murs is the place to splurge in Antibes for regional specialties. Its candlelit, red-tone, *très romantique* interior overlooks the sea (€40 *menu*, open daily June–mid-Sept, closed Tue off-season, along ramparts beyond Picasso Museum at 25 promenade Amiral de Grasse, tel. 04 93 34 06 73).

TRANSPORTATION CONNECTIONS

TGV and local trains serve Antibes' little station.

From Antibes by train to: Cannes (2/hr, 15 min), **Nice** (2/hr, 25 min), **Villefranche-sur-Mer** (2/hr, 40 min), **Monaco** (2/hr, 60 min), **Marseille** (16/day, 2.25 hrs).

By bus to: Cannes (3/hr, 25 min), **Nice Airport** (1/hr, 40 min), **Biot** (2/hr, 20 min).

Inland Riviera

For a verdant, rocky, fresh escape from the beaches, head inland and upwards. Some of France's most perfectly-perched hill towns and splendid scenery are overlooked in this region more famous for beaches and bikinis. Driving is the easiest way to get around, though the bus gets you to many of the places described. Vence and St-Paul-de-Vence are well served by bus from Nice every 30 minutes (see "Getting Around the Riviera," page 447). Buses to Tourrettes leave from Vence daily except Sunday (7/day, 15 min, tel. 04 93 42 40 79).

Vence

Vence is a well-discovered yet appealing hill town high above the Riviera. While growth has spread outside its old walls, the mountains are front and center and the breeze is fresh in this engaging town that bubbles with workaday life and ample tourist activity.

Tourist Information: Vence's fully loaded TI is at 8 place du Grand Jardin. It offers bus schedules, English brochures on the cathedral, and a city map with a well-devised, self-guided walking tour (25 stops, incorporates informative English wall plaques). They also publish a list of Vence art galleries with English descriptions of the collections (May–Sept Mon–Sat 9:00–18:00, Sun 9:00–13:00; Oct–April Mon–Sat 9:00–13:00 & 14:00–17:00, closed Sun; tel. 04 93 58 06 38).

Market days in the Cité Historique are on Tuesday and Friday mornings. There's a big, day-long antique market on place du Grand Jardin every Wednesday.

Arrival in Vence
By Bus: The bus stop is on place du Grand Jardin, next to the TI (schedules are posted in the window).

By Car: Follow signs to *Cité Historique,* and park where you can. The most central pay lot is at place du Grand Jardin.

SIGHTS

Stroll the narrow lanes of the old town (Cité Historique), using the TI's self-guided tour map. Enjoy a drink on a quiet square, sample art galleries, and find the small cathedral with its Chagall mosaic.

Château de Villeneuve—This 17th-century mansion bills itself as "one of the Riviera's high temples of modern art," with a rotating collection. Check with the TI to see what's playing (€4, Tue–Sun 10:00–12:30 & 14:00–18:00, closed Mon, tel. 04 93 58 15 78).

Chapel of the Rosary (Chapelle du Rosaire)—The chapel, a 20-minute walk from town, was designed by Henri Matisse as thanks to the Dominican sister who had taken care of him (he was 81 when the chapel was completed). The chapel is a simple collection of white walls, laced with yellow, green, and blue stained-glass windows and charcoal black-on-white tile sketches. The sunlight filtered through glass does a cheery dance across the sketches. The experience may be a bit subtle for all but his fans, for whom this is a rich and rewarding pilgrimage (€2.50, Mon and Wed 14:00–17:30, Tue and Thu 10:00–11:30 & 14:00–17:30, Sun only open for Mass at 10:00 followed by tour of chapel, closed Fri–Sat and Nov, tel. 04 93 58 03 26). To reach the chapel from the Vence TI, turn right out of the TI and walk down avenue Henri Isnard, then right on avenue de Provence, following signs to *St. Jeannet*. Or take the little white train that runs to the chapel from in front of the TI (round-trip-€4, 1/hr).

SLEEPING

$$$ Hôtel la Villa Roseraie* is a Provençal paradise with a pool, lovely garden, and 14 *charmantes* rooms on the fringe of the city (Db-€110–145, most around €125, parking, easy walk to Matisse's chapel and a 15-min walk to TI, along the road to Col de Vence at 128 avenue Henri Giraud, tel. 04 93 58 02 20, fax 04 93 58 99 31).

$$ L'Auberge des Seigneurs, in the old city, has six appealing rooms with wood-accented character, red-tiled floors, and a low-key, friendly feel (spacious Sb-€48, Db-€65–72, no elevator, place du Frêne, tel. 04 93 58 04 24, fax 04 93 24 08 01). It's a short walk from the bus stop and TI: turn right out of the TI, then right again, then left.

EATING

Tempting outdoor places fill the old city; every place looks good to me.

La Pêcheur de Soleil Pizzeria offers inexpensive meals on a quiet square (daily July–Aug, otherwise closed Sun–Mon, 1 place Godeau, tel. 04 93 58 32 56).

For an untouristy, full-blown dinner, try **L'Auberge des Seigneurs,** and dine by the chimney in which your dinner is cooked (*menus* from €29, closed Sun–Mon; see "Sleeping," above).

MORE SIGHTS IN THE INLAND RIVIERA

St-Paul-de-Vence—The most famous of Riviera hill towns, and the most-visited village in France, feels that way—like an overrun and over-restored artist-shopping-mall. Wall-to-wall upscale galleries and ice cream shops compete for the attention of hordes of day-trippers. Avoid visiting

between 11:00 and 18:00 (I avoid it completely). If you must go, meander deep into St-Paul-de-Vence's quieter streets and wander far to enjoy the panoramic views (**TI** in Maison Tour on rue Grande, tel. 04 93 32 86 95).

▲**Fondation Maeght**—This inviting, pricey, and far-out private museum is situated above St-Paul-de-Vence. Fondation Maeght (fohn-dah-shown mahg) offers a fine introduction to modern Mediterranean art by gathering many of the Riviera's most famous artists under one roof. The founder, Aimé Maeght, long envisioned an ideal exhibition space for the artists he supported and befriended as an art dealer. He purchased a dry piece of hilltop land, planted more than 35,000 plants, and hired an architect (José Luis Sert) with the same vision.

A sweeping lawn laced with amusing sculptures and bending pine trees greets visitors. On the right, a chapel designed by Georges Braque—in memory of the Maeghts' young son, who died of leukemia—features a moving purple stained-glass window over the altar. The unusual museum building is purposefully low-profile, to let its world-class modern art collection take center stage. Works by Fernand Léger, Joan Miró, Alexander Calder, Georges Braque, and Marc Chagall are thoughtfully arranged in well-lit rooms. The backyard of the museum has views, a Gaudí-esque sculpture labyrinth by Miró, and a courtyard filled with wispy works of Alberto Giacometti. The only permanent collection in the museum consists of the sculptures, though the museum tries to keep a good selection of paintings by the famous artists here all year.

Cost and Hours: €11.50, €2.50 to take photos, not covered by Riviera Carte Musées pass, July–Sept daily 10:00–19:00, Oct–June 10:00–12:30 & 14:30–18:00, great gift shop and cafeteria, tel. 04 93 32 81 63, www.maeght.com.

Getting There: It's a steep (uphill) 15-minute walk from St-Paul-de-Vence; blue signs indicate the way (use St-Paul-de-Vence bus stop; parking is available at the top, though lot can be full).

Tourrettes-sur-Loup—The town, hemmed in by forests, looks ready to skid down its abrupt hill. Tourrettes-sur-Loup is small, with no sprawl. Wander its steep streets. You'll still find some arts and crafts, though much less than in the "Vence towns." Plunge deep to find good views, as well as Tom's ice cream. Known as the "Cité des Violettes," Tourrettes-sur-Loup produces more violets than anywhere else in France, most of which end up in bottles that make you smell better. Wednesday is market day on place de la Libération. Fabulous views of Tourrettes-sur-Loup await a minute away on the drive to Pont-du-Loup.

Sleeping and Eating: $$ **L'Auberge de Tourettes*****, an exquisite restaurant at the western edge of town, produces new *menus* each day. It's ideal for lunch with a view (good *plats*-€16, dinner *menus* from €45, restaurant closed Tue–Wed). Its six thoughtfully designed rooms—some with sea views and all with access to a view terrace—seem to go unnoticed (mountain-side Db-€90, grand-view-side Db-€110, buffet breakfast-€11, 11 route de Grasse, tel. 04 93 59 30 05, fax 04 93 59 28 66, www.aubergedetourettes.com).

Confiseries Florian—The candied-fruit factory hides between trees down in Pont-du-Loup (though their big, bright sign is hard to miss). Ten-minute tours of their factory leave regularly, covering the candied-fruit process and explaining the use of flower petals (like violets and jasmine) in their products. Everything they make is fruit-filled—even their chocolate (with oranges). The tour ends with a tasting of the *confiture* in the dazzling gift shop.

Cost and Hours: Free, request a tour with English commentary, daily 9:00–12:00 & 14:00–18:30, tel. 04 93 59 32 91.

La Route Napoleon: North to the Alps

After getting bored in his toy Elba empire, Napoleon gathered his entourage, landed on the Riviera, bared his breast, and told his fellow Frenchmen, "Strike me down or follow me." France followed. But just in case, he took the high road, returning to Paris along the route known today as La Route Napoléon. (Waterloo followed shortly afterward.)

By Car: The route between the Riviera and the Alps is beautiful (from south to north, follow Digne, Sisteron, and Grenoble). An assortment of pleasant villages with inexpensive hotels lies along this route, making an overnight easy. Little Entrevaux feels forgotten and still stuck in its medieval shell. Cross the bridge, meet someone friendly, and consider the steep hike up to the citadel (€2). Sisteron's Romanesque church and view from the citadel above make this town worth a quick leg stretch. If a night in this area appeals, stay farther north, surrounded by mountains. Tiny Clelles has a good hotel: $ **Hôtel Ferrat****, a simple, family-run mountain hacienda at the base of Mont Aiguille (after which Gibraltar was modeled) is a good place to break this train trip. Enjoy your own *boules* court, swimming pool, and good restaurant (Db-€45–58, tel. 04 76 34 42 70, fax 04 76 34 47 47, hotelferrat@wanadoo.fr).

By Train: Narrow-Gauge Train into the Alps (Chemins de Fer de Provence)—Leave the tourists behind and take your kids on the scenic train-bus-train combination that runs between Nice and Digne through canyons, along whitewater rivers, between snow-capped peaks, and through many tempting villages (Nice to Digne: 4/day, 3 hrs, €17.50, 25 percent discount with railpass, departs Nice from the South Station—Gare du Sud—about 10 blocks behind the city's main station, 4 rue Alfred Binet, tel. 04 97 03 80 80).

Start with a 9:00 departure and go as far as you want. Little **Entrevaux** is a good destination (about 2 scenic hours from Nice, €9, see description above). Climb high to the citadel for great views. The train ends in **Digne** where you can catch a main-line train (covered by railpass) to other destinations—or better, take the bus (quick transfer, free with railpass) to **Veynes** (6/day, 90 min), where you can then catch the most scenic two-car train to **Grenoble** (5/day, 2 hrs). From Grenoble, connections are available to many destinations.

To do the entire trip from Nice to Grenoble in one day, you must start with the 9:00 departure from Nice (arrives Grenoble about 18:00).

The

FRENCH ALPS
(Alpes-Savoie)

Savoie grows Europe's highest mountains and is the top floor of the French Alps (the lower Alpes-Dauphiné lie to the south). More than just a pretty-peaked face, stubborn Savoie maintained its independence from France until 1860, when mountains became targets, rather than obstacles for travelers. Its borders once extended south to the Riviera and far west across the Rhône Valley. Home to skier Jean-Claude Killy and the first winter Olympics (1924 in Chamonix), today's Savoie is France's mountain-sports capital, with 15,771-foot Mont Blanc as its centerpiece. With wood chalets overflowing with geraniums and cheese fondue in every restaurant, Savoie feels more Swiss than French.

The scenery is drop-dead spectacular. Serenely self-confident Annecy is a postcard-perfect blend of natural and man-made beauty. In Chamonix, it's just you and Madame Nature—there's not a museum or important building in sight. If the weather's right, take Europe's ultimate cable-car ride to the 12,600-foot Aiguille du Midi in Chamonix.

Planning Your Time

Hemmed in by mountains, lakefront Annecy has boats, bikes, and hikes for all tastes and abilities. Its trademark arcaded walking streets and good transportation connections (most trains to Chamonix pass through Annecy) make it a convenient stopover. But if you're pressed for time and antsy for Alps, go straight to Chamonix. There you can skip along alpine ridges, glide over mountain meadows, zip down the

The French Alps

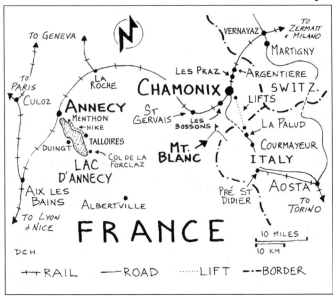

mountain on a wheeled luge, or explore riverside paths on a mountain bike. Plan a minimum of two nights and one day in Chamonix, and try to work in a night in Annecy. Since weather is everything, get the forecast by calling Chamonix's TI, and if it looks good, get thee to Chamonix; if it's gloomy, Annecy offers more to do. Both Chamonix and Annecy are overwhelmed with tourists in summer. (If you're driving or taking the train from here to the Riviera, see "La Route Napoléon" tips at the end of the previous chapter.)

Getting Around the Alps

Annecy and Chamonix are well connected by trains. Buses run from Chamonix to nearby villages, and the Aiguille du Midi lift takes travelers from Chamonix to Italy over Europe's most scenic border crossing.

Cuisine Scene in Savoie

Savoie cuisine is mountain-hearty. Its Swiss-similar specialties include *fondue savoyarde* (melted Beaufort and Comté cheeses and local white wine, sometimes with a dash of Cognac), raclette (chunks of semi-melted cheese served with potatoes, pickles, sausage, and bread), *tartiflettes* (hearty scalloped potatoes with melted cheese), *poulet de Bresse* (the best chicken in France), *Morteau* (smoked pork sausage), *gratin savoyard* (a potato dish with cream, cheese, and garlic), and fresh fish. Local cheeses are Morbier (look for a charcoal streak down the middle), Comté (like Gruyère), Beaufort (aged for two years, hard and strong), Reblochon (mild and creamy), and Tomme de Savoie (mild and semi-hard). Evian water comes from Savoie, as does Chartreuse liqueur. Apremont and Crépy are two of the area's surprisingly good white wines. The local beer, Baton de Feu, is more robust than other French beers.

Remember, restaurants serve only during lunch (11:30–14:00) and dinner (19:00–21:00, later in bigger cities); cafés serve food throughout the day.

Annecy

There's something for everyone in this gorgeous lakefront city that knows how to be popular: mountain views, flowery cobbled lanes that meander along its river and canals, a château that lurks above, and swimming in—or boating on, or biking around—the translucent lake. Sophisticated yet outdoors-oriented Annecy (ahn-nuh-see) is France's answer to Switzerland's Luzerne, and, while you may not have glaciers knocking at your door, as in nearby Chamonix, the distant peaks paint a darn pretty picture with Annecy's lakefront setting. Annecy has a few museums, but don't kid yourself—you're here for its lovely setting and strollable streets.

ORIENTATION

Modern Annecy sprawls for miles, but we're interested only in its compact old town, tucked back in the southwest corner of the lake. The old town is split by the Thiou River and bounded by the château to the south, the TI and rue Royale to the north, rue de la Gare to the west, and, above all, the lake to the east.

Tourist Information

The TI is a few blocks from the old town, across from the big grass field in the brown-and-glass Bonlieu shopping center (mid-May–mid-Sept daily 9:00–18:30, mid-May–mid-Sept daily 9:00–12:30 & 13:45–18:30, closed Sun Nov–March, 1 rue Jean Jaurès, tel. 04 50 45 00 33, www.lac-annecy.com). Get a city map, the *Town Walks* walking-tour brochure (several different, mildly interesting walks described), the map of the lake showing the bike trail, and, if you're spending a few days, the helpful *Annecy Guide*, which has everything a traveler needs to know. Ask about summertime walking tours in English (€6, normally Tue and Fri at 16:00). You'll also find TIs in virtually every village on the lake: Talloires, Menthon-St. Bernard, Veyrier du Lac, Bout du Lac, St. Jorioz, and Sévrier.

Annecy

1. Splendid Hôtel
2. Hôtel du Palais de l'Isle
3. Jardin du Château B&B
4. Hôtel Ibis
5. Hôtel du Château
6. Hôtel de Savoie
7. Hôtel Kyriad
8. Hôtel Central
9. Hôtel des Alpes
10. Rest. le Freti & Café l'Estaminet
11. Rest. le Grenier du Pere de Jules
12. Rest. Auberge du Lyonnais
13. To le Bistro du Port
14. Launderette
15. Internet Café
16. Monoprix Store
17. Bike Rental

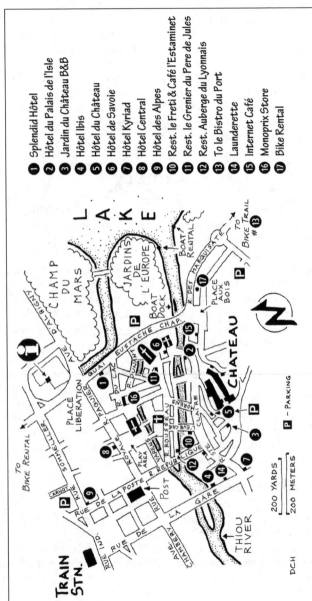

Arrival in Annecy

By Train: To reach the old town and TI, leave the station (baggage check not available), veer left at street level, and cross the big road to the pinkish Hôtel des Alpes. Continue a few blocks down rue de la Poste then turn left on rue Royale for the TI and some hotels, or continue straight to more recommended hotels.

By Car: Annecy is a traffic mess; try to arrive very early, during lunch, or late in the day in high season. Avoid most of the snarls by taking the *Annecy Sud* exit from the autoroute and following Albertville signs. Upon entering Annecy, turn left at the roundabout below the hospital for the city center. (Don't follow signs for *Annecy-le-Vieux;* it's another town entirely). Refer to my map to find these parking lots: You can park free right on the lake with the buses opposite the boat dock (few spaces for cars, but this might be your lucky day), or follow *Château* signs to park free above the old town at Annecy's château (this small lot is also often full). You'll have better luck further away; try Parking Carnot (off rue Carnot near the train station, follow *Gare SNCF* signs) or at place des Romaines (further on rue Carnot). There are several pay lots close by (allow €1.50/hr, the Hôtel de Ville's parking structure is as central as you can get). Those staying at a hotel get free overnight parking at a public lot, but only if they ask at their hotel.

Helpful Hints

Market Days: A thriving outdoor market occupies most of the old-town center on Tuesday, Friday, and Sunday mornings.

Department Store: The **Monoprix** is at the corner of rue du Lac and rue Notre-Dame (8:30–19:30, closed Sun, supermarket on first floor).

Internet Access: L'Emailerie serves drinks and has American keyboards and high-speed connections (daily 10:30–12:30 & 14:30–19:30, across from green Vivaldi restaurant, near lake on Faubourg des Annonciades, tel. 04 50 10 18 91).

Laundry: The launderette is at the western edge of the old town where rue de la Gare meets rue Ste. Claire (daily 7:00–21:00, 4 rue de la Gare).

Bike and Skate Rental: It's best to ask at the TI, as bike shops come and go here. Try **Roule Ma Poule,** near the cruise boats (daily 9:00–12:30 & 14:00–19:00, 4 rue Marquisats, tel. & fax 04 50 27 86 83).

Bad Weather: If it's raining, consider a day trip to Lyon (7 trains/day, 2 hrs, see description in Burgundy chapter). The last train to Annecy usually leaves Lyon at about 20:00, allowing a full day in the big city.

SIGHTS AND ACTIVITIES

Strolling—Most of the old city is wonderfully traffic-free. The river, canals, and arcaded streets are made for ambling. The TI's *Town Walks* brochure describes Annecy with basic historical information. Get lost—the water is your boundary. Surrender to the luscious ice-cream shops and waterfront cafés.

Museum of Annecy (Palais de l'Ile)—This serenely situated, 13th-century building cuts like the prow of a ship through the heart of the Thiou river. Once a prison, now a boring museum, it held French Resistance fighters during World War II (€3.20, June–Sept Wed–Mon 10:30–18:00, Oct–May Wed–Mon 10:00–12:00 & 14:00–18:00, closed Tue year-round).

Château Museum (Musée-Château d'Annecy)—The castle was built in the late 1100s by aristocrats from nearby Geneva. Today, it houses a dull museum that mixes local folklore, anthropology, natural history, and modern and fine art with great views over the lake and city. The only compelling reason to enter the château is for the view (€5, same hours as Museum of Annecy).

▲Boating—Rent a paddleboat equipped with a slide (about €10/30 min, €14/hr) or a motorboat (about €26/30 min, €42/hr) and tool around the lake. It's incredibly clear (this is one of Europe's cleanest lakes) and warmer than you'd think.

Compagnie des Bateaux du Lac d'Annecy offers worthwhile lake cruises. The one-hour cruise makes no stops but has many departures (€10, 12/day April and Sept, 18/day in summer). The two-hour cruises, called *Circuit Omnibus,* make stops at several villages around the lake (€12, 3/day); these are ideal for hikers and bikers (see below). The elaborate dinner and dancing cruises look like fun (€45–67 *menus*). Get schedules and prices for all boat trips at the TI or on the lake behind Hôtel de Ville (tel. 04 50 51 08 40, www.annecy-croisieres.com).

For a decent workout and a rewarding full-day excursion, take the 10:30 boat to **Menthon-St. Bernard** (€4.20), hike 2.5 hours to lovely **Talloires,** then catch the boat back to Annecy (€5.10). From the boat dock in Menthon-St. Bernard, walk to the right along the shore toward the large palace and follow the signposts for Roc de Chère. The path leads up and over the Roc, passing the Golf de Talloires. The last stretch into Talloires drops steeply—wear good shoes. Cross Talloires to the port and beach (swim and lunch there) and catch the 15:00 boat back to Annecy to arrive about 16:15 (the last boat for Annecy from Talloires leaves at 17:30).

▲Biking—Annecy was made for biking; it's an ain't-it-great-to-be-alive way to poke around the lake and test waterfront cafés and parks. A terrific bike trail *(piste cyclable)* runs along the entire west side of the lake (smart to wear sunglasses and bring water; for rental info, see "Helpful Hints," above). The small village of Duingt is seven level miles away and makes a good destination. Steady bikers make it in 45 minutes, but laid-back cyclists need at least an hour. You can ride to Duingt and take the *Omnibus* boat back to Annecy (€7, 3 departures/day from Duingt normally at 11:45, 15:30, and 18:00, verify at boat dock or TI, bikes allowed).

To get to Duingt, leave Annecy on the main road (N-508) with the lake on your left, and join the bike trail. Once the painted bike lane ends in Sévrier, you'll see a sign for the trail *(piste cyclable)* to the left. Follow it to Duingt (exit the trail just before the tunnel for Duingt, ride down to main road and turn right, then find the small green boat dock shelter just after the castle).

This route also works well in reverse: Take the *Omnibus* boat to Duingt and pedal back (turn right when you get off the boat, and join the bike trail behind Duingt's tall church). The trail beyond Duingt is beautiful, as the lake narrows—hardy cyclists can make it all the way around the lake in about three hours (along small roads on opposite side of lake with one good hill).

Driving—For the best car-accessible views overlooking Annecy, drive 12 miles to Col de la Forclaz (3,600 feet, restaurants with view terraces). Take D-508 south along the lake past Duingt and turn left on D-42 a few minutes after leaving the lake (allow 45 min one-way with traffic). This also ties in easily with the scenic route to Chamonix via N-508.

SLEEPING

Annecy is popular—book your hotel ahead if you can, particularly on weekends and during the summer. Hotel rates drop from about mid-October through late April, and generally increase in summer. Most hotels can help you find free overnight parking (in lots, after 18:00 until 9:00).

Hôtel du Château and Jardin du Château Bed & Breakfast are at the foot of the château (limited but free parking at château), up rampe du Château from the old town. The rest of my listings are in the pedestrian-friendly town center and tend to be noisier (ask about parking deals). If a hotel does not have a Web site listed below, try Annecy's, www.lac-annecy.com.

$$$ **Splendid Hôtel** *** makes a striking impression, with its grand facade, neon sign, and flags. This business hotel, with every comfort, sits on Annecy's busiest street, across from the park and the TI (Sb-€95–105, Db-€105–115, breakfast buffet-€13, air-con, big beds, some non-smoking rooms, 4 quai Eustache Chappuis, tel. 04 50 45 20 00, fax 04 50 45 52 23, www.splendidhotel.fr).

$$$ **Hôtel du Palais de l'Isle*** has a romantic canalside location in the thick of the old town, and 33 stylish, contemporary

---

Sleep Code

(€1 = about $1.20, country code: 33)
S = Single, **D** = Double/Twin, **T** = Triple, **Q** = Quad,
b = bathroom, **s** = shower only, **no CC** = Credit Cards not
accepted, **SE** = Speaks English, **NSE** = No English, * = French
hotel rating system (0–4 stars). You can assume a hotel takes
credit cards unless you see "no CC" in the listing.

To help you sort easily through these listings, I've divided
the rooms into three categories based on the price for a standard
double room with bath:

$$$ **Higher Priced**—Most rooms €90 or more.
 $$ **Moderately Priced**—Most rooms between €60–90.
  $ **Lower Priced**—Most rooms €60 or less.

---

rooms, several with canal or rooftop views (Sb-77–95, Db-€85–105, deluxe Db-€125, grand suites-€235, buffet breakfast-€10.50, air-con, Internet access, elevator, 13 rue Perrière, tel. 04 50 45 86 87, fax 04 50 51 87 15, www.hoteldupalaisdelisle.com).

$$ At **Jardin du Château Bed & Breakfast**, friendly Anne-Marie and Jean-Paul have created Annecy's highest urban refuge (near the Château entry). Their chalet *chambre d'hôte* comes with a small garden and eight modern yet comfy rooms, all with kitch-enettes, and some with views and balconies. Jean-Paul doubles as a mountain guide and has a wealth of information (Db-€64–94, good family rooms-€80–115, no CC, no elevator, bike rental, closed Nov-April, 1 place du Château, tel. & fax 04 50 45 72 28, jardinduchateau@wanadoo.fr, SE).

$$ **Hôtel Ibis**** is a decent chain hotel option, with narrow rooms, a canalside breakfast room, and easy underground parking. It's well-situated on a modern courtyard on the edge of the old town, a few blocks from the train station (Db-€80, buffet breakfast-€6, air-con in summer, elevator, 12 rue de la Gare, tel. 04 50 45 43 21, fax 04 50 52 81 08, www.ibishotel.com, H0538@accor-hotels.com).

$$ **Hôtel du Château**** family-run by the Zulianis, is just below the château and comes with a great view terrace. Its 15 rooms are bright, spotless, and basic, with linoleum wallpaper; about half have views, and all have updated bathrooms with showers. It's first come, first get for the precious few free parking spots (Db-€58–64, Tb-€70, Qb-€80, Internet access, no elevator, 16 rampe du Château, tel. 04 50 45 27 66, fax 04 50 52 75 26, www.annecy-hotel.com, hotelduchateau@noos.fr, SE).

$$ **Hôtel de Savoie**** run by engaging Monsieur and Madame Lavorel, is the antithesis of a modern chain hotel. Don't let the car-peted doors fool you—rooms are well-tended, cheery, and

comfortable. Every room is different, several have great views (worth the extra euros), and there are three cheap singles (S-€52, Db without view-€62–72, Db with canal view-€82, no elevator, near the canal a block from the lake, 1 place St. François, tel. 04 50 45 15 45, fax 04 50 45 11 99, www.hoteldesavoie.fr).

$$ Hôtel Kyriad**, a block down from Hôtel Ibis, is a better hotel-chain option. It's well-run, with 24 surprisingly charming and well-designed rooms (Db-€65–76, Tb-€74–88, Qb-€86–99, air-con, no elevator, 1 faubourg des Balmettes, tel. 04 50 45 04 12, fax 04 50 45 90 92, annecy.hotel.kyriad@wanadoo.fr).

$ Hôtel Central* is just that. This simple and homey place sits behind an ivy-covered courtyard off a big pedestrian street (Ds-€37, Db-€42, extra person-€7, no elevator, 6 bis rue Royale, tel. 04 50 45 05 37, fax 04 50 51 80 19, stefanpicollet@hotmail.com, informal owner Stefan SE).

$ Hôtel des Alpes** offers immaculate, comfortable, and bright rooms, just across from the train station at a busy intersection (Sb-€43, Db-€52–62, Tb-€64, Qb-€75, no elevator, 12 rue de la Poste, tel. 04 50 45 04 56, fax 04 50 45 12 38, www.hotelcentralannecy.com—in French only).

EATING

Don't come to Annecy in search of a fine dining experience. Pizzerias, *crêperies*, and cafés are plentiful, and a good solution for most. The touristy old city is well stocked with forgettable restaurants, and while you'll pay more to eat with views of the river or canal, the experience is uniquely Annecy. The ubiquitous and sumptuous *gelati* shops remind us that we're not far from Italy. If it's sunny, assemble a gourmet picnic at the arcaded stores, and dine lakeside. Wherever you eat, don't miss an ice-cream-licking stroll along the lake after dark.

Le Freti, with a friendly waitstaff, is the most reliable restaurant I have found in Annecy. It's where locals go for mouthwatering fondue, raclette, or anything else with cheese. Each booth comes with its own outlet for melting raclette (fondue-€11, good salads and onion soup, open daily, walk through door at 12 rue Ste. Claire, it's on first floor, tel. 04 50 51 29 52).

If Le Freti sounds cheesy, go next door to **Café l'Estaminet** for a Belgian welcome, where you'll get salads, omelettes, pasta, mussels, fries, and more for fair prices. There's a silver backyard deck hanging over the river (closed Mon, 8 rue Ste. Claire, tel. 04 50 45 88 83).

Le Grenier du Pere de Jules is like eating in an alpine folk museum with stuffed mountain animals, rusted tools, and all sorts of knickknacks. The cuisine is as alpine as the decor, with fondue, raclette, and other cheese dishes. Portions are generous and hearty (daily, 11 rue Grenette, tel. 04 50 45 41 18).

Auberge du Lyonnais is a well-respected and classy place that specializes in seafood, with a brilliant setting on the river (indoor and outdoor seating). The outgoing owners love Americans; ask him about his many trips to the States and about his Ford pickup (*menus* from €28, daily, 9 rue de la République).

Near Annecy

Many cafés and restaurants ring Annecy's postcard-perfect lake. If you have a car and need views, prowl about the many lakefront villages. **Le Bistro du Port**, a nautical place with blue deck chairs, is beautifully situated at the boat dock in Sévrier. It's not cheap, but the setting is sensational (salads-€10, main course-€15–20, €28 *menus*, closed Mon–Tue except summers, Port de Sévrier, tel. 04 50 52 45 00).

TRANSPORTATION CONNECTIONS

From Annecy by train to: Chamonix (8/day, 2.5 hrs, change in St. Gervais), **Beaune** (9/day, 5 hrs, change in Lyon), **Nice** (8/day, 7–9 hrs, transfer in Lyon or Valence), **Paris'** Gare de Lyon (11/day, 4–5 hrs, many with change in Lyon, night train).

Chamonix

Bullied by snow-capped peaks, churning with mountain lifts, and littered with hiking trails, the resort of Chamonix (shah-moh-nee) is France's best base for alpine exploration. Officially called Chamonix-Mt. Blanc, it's the largest of five villages at the base of Mont Blanc. Chamonix's purpose in life has always been to accommodate visitors with some of Europe's top alpine thrills—it's super-busy in the summer and on winter holidays, but peaceful at other times. Chamonix's sister city is Aspen, Colorado.

Planning Your Time

Ride the lifts early (crowds and clouds roll in later in the morning) and save your afternoons for lower altitudes. If you have one sunny day, spend it this way: Start with the Aiguille du Midi lift (go as early as you can, reservations possible and recommended in July–Aug), take it all the way to Helbronner (hang around the rock needle longer if you can't get to Helbronner), double back to Plan de l'Aiguille, hike to Montenvers and the Mer de Glace (only with good shoes, and snow level permitting), and take the train down

Chamonix Quick History

1786 Jacques Balmat and Michel-Gabriel Paccard are the
first to climb Mont Blanc

1818 First ascent of Aiguille du Midi

1860 After a visit by Napoleon III, the trickle of nature-
loving visitors to Chamonix turns to a gush

1924 First winter Olympics held in Chamonix

1955 Aiguille du Midi *téléphérique* (gondola lift) opens to
tourists

2005 Your visit

from there. If the weather disappoints or the snow line's too low,
hike the Petit Balcon Sud or Arve river trails.

ORIENTATION

Eternally white Mont Blanc is Chamonix's southeastern limit; the
Aiguilles Rouges mountains form the northwestern border. The
frothy Arve River splits Chamonix in two. The small pedestrian zone,
just west of the river, and rue du Docteur Paccard and rue Joseph
Vallot make up Chamonix's core. The TI is west of the river, just
above the pedestrian zone, while the train station is east of the river.

Tourist Information

Come to the TI on arrival to best plan your attack. Get the weather
forecast, then pick up maps: the free town and valley map, the
"panorama" map of all the valley lifts, and consider the €4 hiking
map called *Carte des Sentiers* (see "Chamonix Area Hikes," page
525). Ask for hours of lifts (important), about the new lift pass,
Multipass (see under "Getting Around the Valley," below), biking
information, and any help with hotel reservations (July–Aug daily
8:30–19:00, Sept–June daily 9:00–12:30 & 14:00–18:30, may be
closed Sun off-season, on place du Triangle de l'Amitié, next to
Hôtel Mont Blanc, one block above pedestrian zone, tel. 04 50 53
00 24, fax 04 50 53 58 90, www.chamonix.com).

For a good mountain viewpoint, leave the TI and walk between
the church and the Office de la Haute Montagne. Climb the stone
steps that lead over a road, then up more steps to a small parklike
area (good picnic spot). Mont Dru, the dominant peak to the left,
towers above the Mer de Glace glacier. Burly, rounded Mont Blanc
stands high to the right. The menacing glacier seems to threaten
Chamonix—in very sloooow motion.

Chamonix Valley Overview

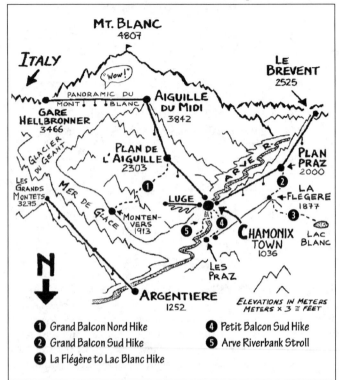

1. Grand Balcon Nord Hike
2. Grand Balcon Sud Hike
3. La Flégère to Lac Blanc Hike
4. Petit Balcon Sud Hike
5. Arve Riverbank Stroll

Arrival in Chamonix

By Train: Walk straight out of the station (no baggage check available) and up avenue Michel Croz. In three blocks, you'll hit the town center; turn left at the big clock, then right for the TI.

By Car: For most of my hotels and the TI, take the *Chamonix Nord* turnoff (second exit coming from Annecy) and park in the lot adjacent to the large traffic circle near Hôtel Alpina or at your hotel. To reach the hotels I list for drivers, take the *Chamonix Sud* exit (first exit). Most parking is metered, though your hotel can direct you to free parking.

The Mont Blanc tunnel allows quick access from Chamonix to Italy (one-way-€30, round-trip-€40, €360 if you're driving a truck, www.tunnelmb.com).

Getting Around the Valley

Note that lifts and cogwheel trains are named for their highest destination (e.g., Aiguille du Midi, Montenvers, and Le Brévent).

By Lifts: Gondolas *(téléphériques)* climb mountains all along the valley, but the best one leaves from Chamonix (see "Sights and Activities," page 520). While sightseeing is optimal from the Aiguille du Midi gondola, hiking is more accessible from the Le Brévent gondola (less snow and many views of Mont Blanc). Kids ages 4–11 *(enfants)* ride for 30 percent less; kids 12–15 *(juniors)* for 15 percent less.

The lift to Aiguille du Midi is open in both summer and winter (closures possible in May and late Oct–early Dec, call TI for exact dates). However, the *télécabines* on the Panoramic Mont Blanc lift to Helbronner (Italy) run only from May or June to early October, and even then only in good weather (call the TI to confirm). Other area lifts are open from January to mid-April and from mid-June to late September.

Ask at the first lift or the TI about the new Multipass, allowing access to every gondola in the Chamonix valley and the train to Montenvers. The pass is valid for 36 hours, with day increments after that, includes the reservation fee for Aiguille du Midi, and allows you to bypass lift ticket lines. While prices were not available at the time of this writing, Multipass appears to pay for itself with the Aiguille du Midi lift trip to Helbronner alone (about €50).

By Foot: See "Chamonix Area Hikes," page 525.

By Bike: The TI has a brochure showing bike-rental shops and the best biking routes. The peaceful river valley trail is ideal for bikes and pedestrians.

By Bus or Train: One road and one scenic rail line lace together the towns and lifts of the valley. Local buses run hourly off-season, and twice an hour in summer to valley villages (main stop is 200 yards to the right when you leave the TI, past Hôtel Mt. Blanc, look for the bus shelters). Direction: *le Tour* takes you toward les Praz and Switzerland, direction: *les Houches* takes you the opposite direction.

Helpful Hints

Beat the Crowds: Take the first lift to beat the crowds and afternoon clouds. Consider breakfast at "le top."

Internet Access: Internet stations are easy to find in Chamonix (there's even one at the McDonald's near the train station); ask your hotel or the TI for the nearest place. **I-Quest** is well-equipped (daily 16:00–20:00, opens at 14:00 if it's raining, enter galerie Blanc Neige at 266 rue Docteur Paccard).

Laundry: Laverie Alpina (look for *Pressing* sign) is in the Galerie Alpina shopping center. Charming Marie-Paule will do your laundry for the cost of the washer and dryer if she has time (allow €9 for a load, leave a small tip, daily 8:00–12:00 & 14:00–17:30, no midday closing, open until 19:00 in summer, closed Sun and midday off-season, tel. 04 50 53 30 67).

Another Laverie is one block up from the Aiguille du Midi lift, down the small lane on via d'Aoste (daily 9:00–20:00, instructions in English).

SIGHTS AND ACTIVITIES

▲▲▲**Aiguille du Midi** (ay-gwee doo mee-dee)—This is easily the valley's (and arguably, Europe's) most spectacular and popular lift. If the weather's clear, the price doesn't matter. Pile into the *téléphérique* (gondola) and soar to the tip of a rock needle 12,600 feet above sea level. Chamonix shrinks as trees fly by, soon replaced by whizzing rocks, ice, and snow until you reach the top. No matter how sunny it is, it's cold. The air is thin. People are giddy. Fun things can happen at Aiguille du Midi if you're not too winded to join the locals in the halfway-to-heaven tango.

From the top of the lift station, cross the bridge and ride the elevator through the rock to the summit of this pinnacle (€3 in high season, free off-season). Missing the elevator is the kind of Alpus Interruptus I'd rather not experience. The Alps spread out before you. In the distance and behind a broader mountain, you can see the bent little Matterhorn; the tall, shady pyramid listed in French on the observation table as "Cervin—4,505 meters" (14,775 feet). And looming just over there is **Mont Blanc**, the Alps' highest point at 4,810 meters (15,771 feet). Use the free telescope to spot mountain climbers; over 2,000 scale this mountain each year. Dial English, and let the info box take you on a visual tour. Check the temperature next to the elevator. Plan on 32 degrees Fahrenheit, even on a sunny day. Sunglasses are essential.

Explore Europe's tallest lift station. More than 150 yards of tunnels lead to a cafeteria, restaurant, gift shop, and the icicle-covered gateway to the glacial world. This "ice tunnel" is where summer skiers and mountain climbers depart. Just observing is exhilarating. Peek down the icy cliff and ponder the value of an ice ax.

Next, for your own private glacial dream world, get into the little red *télécabine* (called Panoramic Mont Blanc) and head south to **Helbronner Point**, the Italian border station. This line stretches three miles with no solid pylon. (It's propped by a "suspended pylon," a line stretched between two peaks 1,300 feet from the Italian end.) In a gondola for four, you'll dangle silently for 40 minutes as you glide over the glacier to Italy. Hang your head out the window; explore every corner of your view. From Helbronner Point, you can continue down into Italy (see "Transportation Connections," page 533), but there's really no point unless you're traveling that way.

From Aiguille du Midi, you can ride all the way back to Chamonix, or better (if you like to hike and are wearing good shoes), get off halfway down at **Plan de l'Aiguille** and take a hike plus a

Over the Alps: France to Italy

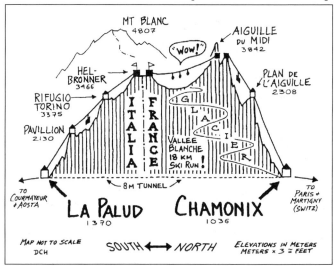

train ride down to Chamonix. From Plan de l'Aiguille, hike 15 minutes down to the refuge, which has great views and reasonable lunches (wooden building, closed and unmarked off-season). From the refuge, go right and hike the spectacularly scenic, undulating, and at times quite strenuous two- to three-hour trail to Montenvers (overlooking the Mer de Glace glacier; see "Mer de Glace" and "Chamonix Area Hikes—Hike #1," below). From Montenvers, ride the train (€11) into Chamonix. Don't hike all the way down to Chamonix from Plan de l'Aiguille or Montenvers-Mer de Glace; it's a long, steep walk through thick forests with few views.

To beat the hordes and clouds, ride the Aiguille du Midi lift (up and down) as early as you can. To beat major delays in August, leave no later than 7:00 (first lift departs at about 6:00). If the weather has been bad and turns good, expect crowds in any season (worse on weekends). If it's clear, don't dillydally. Lift hours are weather- and crowd-dependent, but generally run daily from 7:00 to 17:00 in summer; 8:00 to 16:45 in May, June, and September; and 8:00 to 15:45 in winter. The last *télécabine* (called Panoramic Mont Blanc) departure to Helbronner is about 14:00, and the last train down from Montenvers is about 16:00.

Hours: In peak season, smart travelers reserve the Aiguille du Midi lift in advance, either at the information booth next to the lift (open mid-June–mid-Sept) or by telephone (year-round, tel. 08 92 68 00 67, €0.34/min, automated reservations in English). For €2, you can reserve up to 10 days in advance, and you must pick up your reservation at the lift station at least 30 minutes before your departure. Note that you can't reserve the *télécabines* to Helbronner.

Costs: The following prices are approximate ticket costs for summer (slightly less off-season, ask about the special family rates). From Chamonix to: Plan de l'Aiguille—round-trip-€16 (one-way-€14); Aiguille du Midi—round-trip-€35 (one-way-€30, not including parachute); the Panoramic Mont Blanc *télécabine* to Helbronner—round-trip-€52 (one-way-€40). If you are planning to stop at Plan de l'Aiguille on the way back down and hike to Montenvers (see "Mer de Glace" and "Chamonix Area Hikes—Hike #1," below), ask about a *spécial randonée* ticket for about €32.

Tickets from Aiguille du Midi to Helbronner are sold at both base and summit lift stations with no difference in price (round-trip-€19, one-way-€12). It's €24 to drop into Italy (sold at Helbronner, other currencies also accepted). *Si,* you can bring your luggage.

The new Multipass might save you money—ask at the TI (see page 519).

Time to Allow: Chamonix to Aiguille du Midi—20 minutes one-way, two hours round-trip, three to four hours in peak season; Chamonix to Helbronner—90 minutes one-way, three to four hours round-trip, longer in peak season. On busy days, minimize delays by making a reservation for your return lift time upon arrival at the top. (For information on Aiguille du Midi, call 04 50 53 30 80.)

▲**Mer de Glace (Montenvers)**—From Gare de Montenvers (the little station over the tracks from Chamonix's main train station), the cogwheel Train du Montenvers toots you up to tiny Montenvers (mohn-ton-vare). There you'll see a rapidly moving and dirty glacier called the Mer de Glace (mayr duh glahs), or Sea of Ice, and a fantastic view up the white valley (Vallée Blanche) of splintered, snow-capped peaks (round-trip-€15, one-way-€11, 8:30–17:00, last train down at 16:00–17:30 off-season, 18:30 in summer, confirm times).

France's largest **glacier**, at six miles long, is impressive from above and below. Exit the station and walk to the view deck. The glacier extends under the dirt about a half mile downhill to the left. Imagine that it recently rose as high as the vegetation below (easy to see the dirt banks left in its wake). In 1860, this glacier stretched all the way down to Chamonix. They say this fast-moving glacier is just doing its cycle thing, growing and shrinking—a thousand years ago, cows grazed on grassy fields here. The funky **ice caves** embedded in the glacier are filled with ice sculptures (take the small gondola down from the train station, €7 round-trip to the caves, includes entry, or hike down 20 min and pay €3 to enter). If you've already seen a glacier up close, you might skip this one.

Now look up to the peaks (find the orientation charts). Monsieur Dru's powerful spire dominates your view (at about 11,700 feet). It was first scaled in 1860, and was recently free-climbed (no ropes, belays, etc.; just firm fingers and sticky feet). The smooth snow field to its left (Les Grands Montets) is the top of the ski run for the opposite side. From here, you can wander right, down toward the glacier, passing a viewpoint snack stand/café and a small exhibit on crystals (with English information). Or wander left to **Refuge-Hôtel le Montenvers,** where you'll find a full-service restaurant, view tables, and a cozy interior—consider a night here. The three-hour trail to Plan de l'Aiguille begins here (see page 525). Consider hiking toward Plan de l'Aiguille as far as you feel like—the views get better the higher you climb (follow signs on the stone building opposite the hotel; you want *sentier gauche*).

▲**Luge (Luge d'été)**—Here's something for thrill-seekers: Ride a chairlift up the mountain and scream as you shoot down a twisty, banked, concrete slalom course on a wheeled sled. Chamonix has two roughly parallel luge courses. While each course is just over a half mile and about the same speed, one is marked for slower bob-sledders and the other for speed demons. Young or old, hare or tor-toise, any fit person can manage a luge. Don't take your hands off your stick; the course is fast and slippery. *Freinez* signs tell you when to brake. The luge courses are set in a grassy park with kids' play areas (one ride-€5, six rides-€25, 12 rides-€42, rides can be split with companions and tickets are good for a month, July–Aug daily 10:00–19:30, June 15–30 & Sept 1–15 daily 13:30–18:00, otherwise weekend and holiday afternoons only, call for spring and fall hours, closed in winter, 15-min walk from town center, over the tracks from train station, follow signs to *Planards*, tel. 04 50 53 08 97).

▲▲▲**Paragliding (Parapente)**—When it's sunny and clear, the skies above Chamonix are filled with colorful, parachute-like sails that circle the valley like birds of prey. For €90, you can join the fes-tival of color and launch yourself off a mountain in a tandem parasail with a trained, experienced pilot. Consider **Summits Parapente** (smart to reserve a day ahead, open year-round, tel. 04 50 53 50 14, fax 04 50 55 94 16, across from Galerie Alpina at 27 allée du Savoy, www.summits.fr/parapente_chamonix).

To get a sneak preview, walk to the main landing area and observe these courageous "sailors" perfect their landing (see "Chamonix Area Hikes—Hike #5: Arve Riverbank Stroll and Paragliding Landing Field," below). Even if you have no intention of jumping off a cliff, wander over to this grassy field and enjoy the spectacle.

▲▲▲**Gondola Lifts** *(Téléphériques)* **to Le Brévent and La Flégère**—While Aiguille du Midi gives a more spectacular ride, the Le Brévent and La Flégère lifts offer distinctly different hiking and viewing options, as you get unobstructed panoramas across to the Mont Blanc range from this opposite side of the valley. The Le Brévent (luh bray-vahn) lift is in Chamonix; the La Flégère (lah flay-zhair) lift is in nearby Les Praz (lay prah). The lifts are

Chamonix Valley Hikes and Lifts

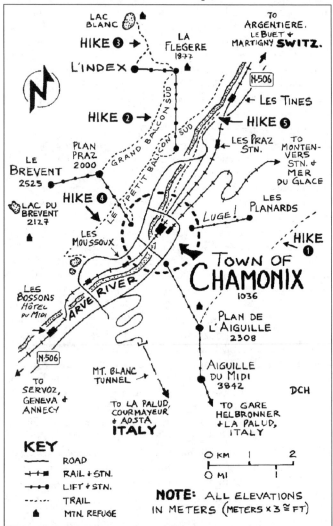

connected by a scenic hike or by bus along the valley floor (see "Chamonix Area Hikes—Hike #2," below); both have sensational view cafés for non-hikers.

Le Brévent lift is a steep, 10-minute walk up the road above Chamonix's TI. This *téléphérique* stops halfway up at Planpraz station (round-trip costs about €11, one-way-€9, nice restaurant, great views and hiking) and continues to Le Brévent station at the top with more views and hikes, though Planpraz offers plenty for me (round-trip-€16, one-way from Chamonix-€13, daily 9:00–16:00, July–Aug daily 8:00–17:00, closed end of April–mid-June plus Oct, tel. 04 50 53 13 18).

La Flégère lift runs from the neighboring village of Les Praz with just one stop at La Flégère station (round-trip-€11, one-way-€9, daily 8:40–16:00, summer 7:40–17:00, closed end of April–mid-June plus Oct, tel. 04 50 53 18 58). Hikes to Planpraz and Lac Blanc leave from the top of this station.

Chamonix Area Hikes

Your first stop should be at the full-service **Maison de la Montagne**, across from the TI. On the third floor, the **Office of the High Mountain** (Office de Haute-Montagne) can help you plan your hikes and tell you about trail and snow conditions (9:00–12:00 & 15:00–18:00, closed Sun except in summer, tel. 04 50 53 22 08, www.ohm-chamonix.com—in French only). The staff speaks enough English, has maps everywhere and some English hiking guidebooks (you can photocopy key pages), and, most importantly, offers vital weather reports. The region's hiking map, *Carte des Sentiers*, is extremely helpful; you can pick it up at the TI (€4). Ask to look at the trail guidebook (sold in many stores, includes the *Carte des Sentiers* trail map).

At **Compagnie des Guides de Chamonix** on the ground floor, you can hire a guide to take you hiking for the day (€250), help you scale Mont Blanc, or hike to the Matterhorn and Zermatt (€670 for the two-day climb up Mont Blanc, Tue–Sat 9:00–12:00 & 15:30–19:00, closed Sun–Mon off-season, tel. 04 50 53 00 88, fax 04 50 53 48 04, www.chamonix-guides.com).

I've described three challenging hikes (#1–3), one moderately difficult hike (#4), and an easy walk (#5; see map on page 524). These hikes give nature-lovers of almost any ability a good opportunity to enjoy the valley in just about any weather. Start early, when the weather's generally best. This is critical in summer; if you don't get in the lifts by 8:30, you'll join a conveyor belt of hikers. If starting later or walking longer, confirm lift closing hours, or you'll end up with a long, steep hike down.

For your hike, pack sunglasses, sunscreen, rain gear, water, and snacks. Wear warm clothes and good shoes. Trails are rocky and uneven. Take your time, watch your footing, don't take shortcuts, and make sure to say "*Bonjour!*" to your fellow hikers.

▲▲▲**Hike #1: Plan de l'Aiguille to Montenvers-Mer de Glace (Grand Balcon Nord)**—This is the most efficient way to incorporate a two- to three-hour high-country hike into your ride down from the valley's greatest lift, and check out a glacier to boot. The well-used trail rises, but mostly falls (dropping 1,500 feet), and is moderately difficult, provided the snow is melted (get trail details at the Office of the High Mountain, above). Some stretches are steep and strenuous, with uneven footing and slippery rock. From the Aiguille du Midi lift, get off halfway down at Plan de l'Aiguille and follow signs to the unmarked wooden Refuge-Hôtel Montenvers (reasonable food and drinks, closed off-season, see page 532). From there, take a right and follow *Montenvers* signs for about an hour. If you don't see signs, ask for the way to Montenvers: *"Quelle direction à Montenvers?"* (kell dee-reck-shown ah mohn-ton-vare). When the trail splits, follow signs up the steep trail to Signal Montenvers (more scenic and easier), rather than to the left towards Montenvers (it may look easier at first, but it becomes extremely narrow). At this point, you'll grind it out up and up to the best views of the trail. It's a long, steep, and incredibly scenic drop to Montenvers and the Mer de Glace (€11 train back to Chamonix at the small gondolas; don't walk the rest of the trail down). Snow covers this trail generally until June.

▲▲**Hike #2: La Flégère to Planpraz (Grand Balcon Sud)**—This glorious hike undulates above Chamonix valley and offers staggering views of Mont Blanc and countless other peaks, glaciers, and wildflowers. With just 370 feet of difference in elevation between La Flégère and Planpraz lift stations, this hike, while it has its ups and downs, is relatively easy, but still requires serious stamina. You can do it in either direction, but I prefer starting at La Flégère, which is how I've described the hike.

From Chamonix, drive five minutes, then walk 40 minutes along the Arve River (see "Hike #5: Arve Riverbank Stroll," below); or take the Chamonix bus (every 30–60 min, 10-min ride) to the tiny village of Les Praz and La Flégère lift station. Ride the lift up to La Flégère (€9) and walk down to the Refuge-Hôtel La Flégère. Find the signs to Planpraz (you don't want Les Praz-Chamonix—that's straight down), then hike the rolling Grand Balcon Sud to Planpraz station, the midway stop on the Le Brévent lift line (allow 2.5 hrs). Take the Planpraz lift down to Chamonix (€9) and skip the steep hike down (as I've mentioned, you can do this route in reverse, but you'd have to walk backwards). Ask for the round-trip rate allowed with La Flégère and Planpraz (Le Brévent) lifts, available at either lift (saves €6).

▲▲**Hike #3: La Flégère to Lac Blanc** (lock blah)—This is the most demanding hiking trail of those I list; it climbs steeply and steadily over a rough, boulder-strewn trail for 90 minutes to snowy Lac Blanc (some footing is tricky, and good shoes or boots are essential). I like this trail, as it gets you away from the valley edge and opens views to peaks you don't see from other hikes. The destination is a frigid, snow-white lake surrounded by peaks, and a nifty chalet-refuge offering good lunches (and dinners with accommodations). The views on the return trip are breathtaking. Check for snow conditions on the trail, and go early (particularly in summer), as there is no shade and this trail is popular. Follow directions from Hike #2 to La Flégère station (above), then walk out the station's rear door past the orientation table and view area, and follow signs to Lac Blanc. The trail is well-signed and improves in surface quality as you climb. While you can eliminate a good portion of the uphill hiking by riding the lift up to L'Index from La Flégère, use caution before continuing your hike. The trail from L'Index to Lac Blanc generally requires serious skill and equipment because of snow; ask before you go out.

▲**Hike #4: Petit Balcon Sud**—This trail runs above the valley on the Brévent side from the village of Servoz to Argentiere, passing Chamonix about halfway, and is ideal when snow or poor weather make other hikes problematic. No lifts are required—just firm thighs to climb up to and down from the trail. Access paths link villages below. Once you're up, the trail rises and falls with some steep segments and uneven footing, but is generally very manageable. To reach the trail from Chamonix, walk up to Le Brévent lift station, then follow the asphalt road to the left of the lift leading uphill; it turns into a dirt road that signs mark as the Petit Balcon Sud trail. After about 20 minutes on the dirt road, a sign for the Petit Balcon Sud points left and up a smaller trail. This segment of the hike doubles back above Chamonix, taking you toward Servoz (keep following Petit Balcon Sud). Go as far as you like, taking any trail down (signed to the village below). For an easier hike to **Les Praz** (where you can take the Arve River trail back to Chamonix), bypass this Petit Balcon turnoff and stay on the dirt road. After about 30 minutes, follow La Floria signs right and join the Petit Balcon Sud trail, then find Les Praz signs to get down the hill (a worthwhile 20-min round-trip detour leads to **la Floria chalet,** with drinks, snacks, tables, and views, open mid-June–late Sept; at about the same junction, you'll see a shortcut back to Chamonix through the woods). Continuing to Les Praz, when you reach the asphalt road below, turn left to explore the village and connect with the river trail back to Chamonix (right immediately after bridge), or turn right for the bus stop back to Chamonix (figure it takes the bus 20 min to reach Les Praz from the time posted in Le Tour).

Hike #5: Arve Riverbank Stroll and Paragliding Landing Field—For a level, forested-valley stroll, follow the Arve River toward Les Praz. Cross the river from Chamonix's Hôtel Alpina, turn left, and walk until you pass the last red clay tennis court. Cross two bridges to the left and turn right along the rushing Arve River (river to your right). Several trails loop through these woods; if you continue walking straight, you'll reach Les Praz—a pleasant destination with several cafés and a charming village green. If you stay right after the tennis courts (passing the piles of river dirt excavated to keep the river from flooding) you'll come to a grassy landing field, Parapente, where paragliders hope to touch down. Walk to the top of the little grassy hill for fine Mont Blanc views and a great picnic spot. The recommended Micro Brasserie de Chamonix is nearby (see "Eating," page 533).

DAY TRIPS

A Day in French-Speaking Switzerland—There are plenty of tempting alpine and cultural thrills just an hour or two away in Switzerland. A road-and-train line sneaks you scenically from Chamonix to the Swiss town of Martigny. While train travelers cross without formalities, drivers are charged a one-time fee of 40 Swiss francs (€30) for a permit to use Swiss autobahns.

A Little Italy—The remote Valle d'Aosta and its historic capital city of Aosta are a spectacular gondola ride over the Mont Blanc range. The side-trip is worthwhile if you'd like to taste Italy (spaghetti, gelato, and cappuccino), enjoy the town's great evening ambience, or look at the ancient ruins in Aosta (often called the "Rome of the North").

Take the spectacular lift (Aiguille du Midi-Helbronner) to Italy, described on page 520. From Helbronner, catch the €24 lift down to La Palud and take the bus to Aosta (hrly, change in Courmayeur). Aosta's train station has connections to anywhere in Italy.

For a more down-to-earth experience, you can take the bus from Chamonix to Aosta (90 min). Get schedules at the TI or the bus station (located at train station). Drivers can simply drive through the Mont Blanc tunnel (round-trip-€40, one-way-€30, www.tunnelmb.com).

SLEEPING

(€1 = about $1.20, country code: 33)
Reasonable hotels and dorm-like chalets abound in Chamonix, with easy parking and easy access from the train station. With the helpful TI, you can find budget accommodations anytime. The period from mid-July to mid-August is most difficult, when some hotels have five-day minimum-stay requirements. Prices tumble off-season (outside July–Aug and Dec–Jan). Many hotels and restaurants are closed in April, June, and November, but you'll still find a room and a meal. If you want a view of Mont Blanc, ask for *côté Mont Blanc* (coat-ay mohn blah). Summertime travelers should seriously consider a night high above in a refuge-hotel.

All hoteliers speak English. Many hotels have elevators. Big buffet breakfasts may be available for an extra charge, unless otherwise noted (a few include breakfast in their price, read carefully). Price ranges usually reflect low-to-high season rates.

In the City Center

$$$ Hôtel Gourmets et Italy*** is a sharp, 40-room, well-run place with cozy public spaces, a cool riverfront terrace, and balcony views from many of its appealing rooms (closed late April–early June, standard Db–€70, larger Db with Mont Blanc view–€110, extra person-about €16, 2 blocks from casino on Mont Blanc side of river, 96 rue du Lyret, tel. 04 50 53 01 38, fax 04 50 53 46 74, www.hotelgourmets -chamonix.com, hgicham@aol.com, helpful Erique speaks perfect English).

$$ Hôtel de l'Arve** has a contemporary alpine feel, with comfortable view rooms right on the Arve River looking up at Mont Blanc, or cheaper rooms without the view. The wood accents, fireplace lounge, pleasant garden, sauna, climbing wall, and easy parking add to the appeal. The half-pension option is a good value at €20 extra per person for a buffet breakfast and simple four-course dinner; let them know ahead if you want it (open year-round, standard Db-€56–80, larger or view Db-€64–94, big view room-€74–108, Tb-€90–120, extra person-€12.50, behind huge Hôtel Alpina, 60 impasse des Anémones, tel. 04 50 53 02 31, fax 04 50 53 56 92, www.hotelarve-chamonix.com, contact@hotelarve-chamonix.com, Isabelle and Beatrice SE).

$$ Hôtel Richemond**, with an almost retirement-home feel in its faded-alpine-elegant public spaces, is dead center and my closest listing to the Aiguille du Midi lift. The same family has run this hotel since it was built in 1914. Rooms are traditional, comfortable, and generally spacious, with period furniture. There's also an outdoor terrace and a game room with a pool table, "flipper" (pinball), and table tennis (Sb-€55–63, Db-€86–99, Tb-€106–127, includes buffet breakfast, 228 rue du Docteur Paccard, tel. 04 50 53 08 85, fax 04 50 55 91 69, www.richemond.fr, richemond@wanadoo.fr, Claire SE and brother Bruno loves Americans).

$$ Chalet Beauregard, Chamonix's most welcoming *chambre d'hôte*, is a short but steep walk above the TI. It's relaxed and peaceful, with a private garden, table tennis, and swings. Five of its seven cushy rooms have balconies with grand views (Sb-€49–89, Db-€69–99, Tb-€89–129, ask about the amazing top floor suite-€135–195, no CC, but personal checks in U.S. dollars accepted, includes breakfast, free parking, may require 5-day minimum in summer, often closed in May, on road to Le Brévent lift, 182 rue de La Mollard, tel. & fax 04 50 55 86 30, cell 06 30 52 63 97, www.chalet-beauregard.com, info@chalet-beauregard.com, friendly Manuel and Laurence SE).

$ Hôtel au Bon Coin**, a few blocks toward the town center from the Aiguille du Midi lift, is a modest, wood-paneled place with great views, private balconies, and thinnish walls in most of its spotless, well-maintained rooms. The cheaper rooms lack views and

Chamonix Town

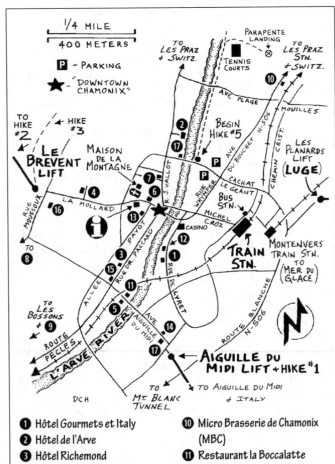

1. Hôtel Gourmets et Italy
2. Hôtel de l'Arve
3. Hôtel Richemond
4. Chalet Beauregard B&B
5. Hôtel au Bon Coin
6. Hôtel le Chamonix
7. Hôtel Touring & Super U Grocery
8. To Auberge du Bois Prin & B&B la Girandole
9. To Hôtel l'Aiguille du Midi
10. Micro Brasserie de Chamonix (MBC)
11. Restaurant la Boccalatte
12. Restaurant Chez Nous
13. Restaurant la Calèche & Midnight Express
14. Crêperie Bretonne
15. Restaurant le Panier & Internet Café
16. Café la Cabolée
17. Launderettes (2 locations)

private bathrooms (closed late April–mid-June, D-€40, Ds-€46, Db with view and balcony-€62, Tb-€65, Qb-€82, 80 avenue de L'Aiguille du Midi, tel. 04 50 53 15 67, fax 04 50 53 51 51, hotel.auboncoin@wanadoo.fr, Dermot and Julie SE).

$ Le Chamonix **, across from the TI and above a café, offers red carpets and wood paneling with good-value rooms, but no elevator. Many rooms facing Mont Blanc have great views, little balconies, and some noise from *le café* below (standard Db-€46–68, standard Db with Mont Blanc view-€52–72, Tb-€63–90, Qb-€72–100, no elevator, rue de l'Hôtel de Ville, tel. 04 50 53 11 07, fax 04 50 53 64 78, www.hotel-le-chamonix.com, hotel-le-chamonix@wanadoo.fr, SE).

$ Hôtel Touring** has basic but cavernous rooms (many with 4 beds), some saggy mattresses, and no elevator, but employs a friendly British staff and is a good option for families (Ds-€44–52, Db-€66, third person-€15, fourth person-€10 more, 95 rue Joseph Vallot, tel. 04 50 53 59 18, fax 04 50 53 97 71, www.hoteltouring-chamonix.com, hoteltouring@aol.com).

Outside Chamonix

A few minutes above Chamonix, these places are practical only by car.

$$$ Auberge du Bois Prin****, my only four-star listing, has the best views I found, cozy ambience, and a melt-in-your-chair restaurant. Rooms are closer to three- than four-star in comfort, but it's the view that makes this place worthwhile. Five of the 11 rooms in this flowery chalet come with a balcony facing Mont Blanc (Db-€181–219, Tb-€238–265, includes breakfast, sauna, Jacuzzi, elevator, *menus* from €27.50 for guests, follow Les Moussoux from Chamonix Sud exit, tel. 04 50 53 33 51, fax 04 50 53 48 75, www.boisprin.com).

$$ Chambre d'Hôte la Girandole, above Auberge du Bois Prin, may be the highest home in Chamonix, with three ground-floor rooms, three good bathrooms in the hall, and immense views from the flowery garden (Sb-€53, Db-€64, includes breakfast, no CC, 46 chemin de la Perseverance, tel. 04 50 53 37 58, fax 04 50 55 81 77, la-girandole@wanadoo.fr).

Near Chamonix

If Chamonix overwhelms you, spend the night in one of the valley's overlooked, lower-profile villages.

$$ Hôtel l'Aiguille du Midi** lies in the village of Les Bossons, about two miles from Chamonix toward Annecy. Self-assured, English-speaking Martine Farini runs this mountain retreat in a parklike setting, with a swimming pool, tennis court, whirlpool tub, table tennis, and a laundry room to boot. The alpine-comfortable rooms aren't big, and you won't care. The pricey, classy restaurant offers good à la carte options and a required half pension in summer

(Db-€69–80, Tb-€99, Qb-€118, elevator, €20–43 *menu* or à la carte for the public, easy by train, get off at Les Bossons, tel. 04 50 53 00 65, fax 04 50 55 93 69, www.hotel-aiguilledumidi.com, hotel-aiguille -du-midi@wanadoo.fr).

Refuges and Refuge-Hôtels near Chamonix

Chamonix has the answer for hikers who want to sleep high up, but don't want to pack tents, sleeping bags, stoves, or food: refuge-hôtels (generally open mid-June–mid- or late Sept, depending on snow levels). Refuge-hôtels usually have some private rooms (and dorm rooms), hot showers down the hall, and restaurants. Reserve in advance (a few days are generally enough), then pack your small bag for a memorable night among new international friends. The **Office of the High Mountain** in Chamonix can explain your options (see "Chamonix Area Hikes," above).

Refuge-Hôtels: $$ Refuge-Hôtel Montenvers is a great experience at the Montenvers train stop and Chamonix's oldest refuge. It was built in 1890 as a climbing base for mountain guides before the train, so materials had to be gathered from nearby. The five simple, wood-cozy rooms and dining room feel as though they haven't been modified since they were built (half pension in a double room-about €50/person, €35/person in dorm room, good showers down the hall, tel. 04 50 53 87 70, fax 04 50 55 38 55, restauration.montenvers @compagniedumontblanc.fr). For directions, see "Hike #1," page 525). **$ Refuge-Hôtel La Flégère** hangs on the edge and is also at a lift station. It's simpler, but ideally located for hiking to Lac Blanc or Planpraz (3 private rooms with 5 beds, many dorm beds, half pension-€37/person, fireplace, cozy bar-café, right at La Flégère lift, tel. 06 03 58 28 14). For directions, see "Hike #2," page 526.

EATING

You have two basic dining options in Chamonix—cozy, traditional *Savoyarde* restaurants serving fondue, raclette, and the like; or big cafés in central locations serving a wide variety of dishes (including regional specialties), and allowing you to watch rivers of hikers return from a full day in the mountains. Prices are roughly the same; you choose. If it's a beautiful day, take an outdoor table at a central café; if you're dining inside, go local and consider these places:

Chez Nous has *Savoyarde* specialties with down-to-earth, wooden-bench ambience and fair prices (€15 *menu*, great fondue comes with a green salad and potatoes, open daily, turn right at casino, 78 rue du Lyret, tel. 04 50 53 91 29).

La Calèche presents delectable regional dishes in a warm, hyper-decorated, alpine setting. The owner must be a collector, as you'll dine amid antique dolls, cuckoo clocks, copper pots, animal trophies, and more. Servers sport traditional outfits to complete the picture. It's centrally located, just off place Balmat (€20 *menu*, €24 *menu* is much better, daily, 18 rue du Docteur Paccard, tel. 04 50 55 94 68).

At **Crêperie Bretonne**, friendly, English-speaking owners Anne and Didier serve delicious, inexpensive crêpes. It's near the Aiguille du Midi lift and works for lunch or dinner (daily, 199 avenue de l'Aiguille du Midi, tel. 04 50 53 16 04).

La Boccalatte serves a good, simple lunch or dinner, with a lively atmosphere, near the Aiguille du Midi. Choose from a large selection of local specialities and 20 kinds of beer. It's run by friendly Alsatian, English-speaking Thierry (daily 12:00–22:00, happy hour 17:00–19:00, across from Hôtel au Bon Coin, 59 avenue de l'Aiguille du Midi, tel. 04 50 53 52 14).

La Cabolée, next to La Brévent station, is a hip eatery with great omelettes and a wonderful view from its outdoor tables (closed mid May–mid-June).

Le Panier is where locals go for traditional French (not local) cuisine like grandma made. The place is charmingly elegant in spite of its mini-mall location, and deserving of its solid reputation (*menus* from €30, closed Wed, in Galerie Blanc Neige above I-Quest Internet service at 266 rue Docteur Paccard, tel. & fax 04 50 53 98 77).

Micro Brasserie de Chamonix (with MBC sign) is a knockoff of microbrew pubs we have at home, and *the* place to hang out after a day of parasailing or rappelling. It's not central, across from the *parapente* landing strip (see "Hike #5," page 527), but it's reasonable and lively. Come here for a homemade brew, a glass of wine, or a pub dinner, and expect crowds of twenty- and thirtysomethings (daily 16:00–02:00, 350 route du Bouchet, tel. 04 50 53 61 59).

Midnight Express serves tasty sandwiches until late, from the little stand across from the recommended La Caleche restaurant. Try a Pain Rond-Rustique (round bread rustic sandwich).

TRANSPORTATION CONNECTIONS

Bus and train service to Chamonix is surprisingly good. You'll find helpful bus and train information desks at the train station. Remember, if you have a France-only railpass, your train might take you via Switzerland (e.g., some Paris and Colmar trains).

From Chamonix by train to: Annecy (5/day, 2.5 hrs, change in St. Gervais), **Beaune** and **Dijon** (5/day, 7 hrs, changes in St. Gervais and Lyon), **Nice** (5/day, 10 hrs, change in St. Gervais and Lyon), **Arles** (5/day, 8.5 hrs, change in St. Gervais and Lyon), **Paris'** Gare de Lyon (8/day, 7 hrs, change in Switzerland in Martigny and Geneva or Lausanne, handy night train with one change in nearby

St. Gervais), **Martigny, Switzerland** (10/day, 1.5 hrs, scenic trip), **Geneva, Switzerland** (3/day, 3.5 hrs, changes in St. Gervais, La Roche-sur-Foron, and Annemasse).

By bus: Buses provide service to destinations not served by train, and also to some cities that *are* served by train—but at a lower cost and higher speed. Get information at the TI or bus station *(gare routière)*; the information office is outside Chamonix's SNCF train station (tel. 04 50 53 01 15). Long-distance buses depart from the train station, not from local bus stops.

To Italy: See "Day Trips," page 528.

BURGUNDY and LYON

The rolling hills of Burgundy gave birth to superior wine, fine cuisine, and a sublime countryside. This deceptively peaceful region witnessed Julius Caesar's defeat of the Gauls, then saw the Abbey of Cluny rise from the ashes of the Roman Empire to vie with Rome for religious influence in the 12th century. Burgundy's last hurrah came in the 15th century, when its powerful dukes controlled an immense area stretching north to Holland. Today, bucolic Burgundy runs from about Auxerre in the north to near Lyon in the south, and it's crisscrossed with canals and dotted with quiet farming villages. It's also the transportation funnel for eastern France and makes a convenient stopover for travelers (car or train), with quick access north to Paris or the Alsace, east to the Alps, and south to Provence.

Only a small part of Burgundy is covered by vineyards, but grapes are what they do best. The white cows you see everywhere are Charolais. France's best beef ends up in *bœuf bourguignon*.

Lyon—the gateway to Burgundy, Provence, and the Alps—is easily accessible by train or car. This captivating place is France's most interesting major city after Paris. If you need a city fix, linger in Lyon.

Planning Your Time

With limited time, stay in or near Beaune. It's conveniently located for touring; plan on a half day in Beaune and a half day for the vineyards and countryside.

Burgundy

Lyon, 70 minutes south of Beaune, is France's best-kept urban secret and merits at least one night and a full day. It's also easy enough by train from Beaune for a day trip. If you're driving between Beaune and Lyon, take the detour to adorable Brancion and once powerful Cluny.

If you're in search of off-the-beaten-path Burgundy, visit unspoiled Semur-en-Auxois and France's best-preserved medieval abbey complex at Fontenay (they're both closer to Paris, but doable as a day trip from Beaune). The magnificent church at Vézelay is harder to reach, and is best done as a day trip from Semur-en-Auxois, or on your way to or from Paris.

Getting Around Burgundy

Trains link Beaune with Dijon to the north and Lyon to the south. Less frequent buses cruise the wine route between Dijon, Beaune, and Chalon-sur-Saône. Bikes and minivan tours get nondrivers from Beaune into the countryside. Buses connect Semur-en-Auxois with Dijon and Montbard train stations.

Cuisine Scene in Burgundy and Lyon

Arrive hungry. Considered by many to be France's best, Burgundian cuisine is peasant cooking elevated to an art, and entire lives are spent debating the best restaurants and bistros in Lyon.

Several classic dishes were born in Burgundy: *escargots bourguignon* (snails served sizzling hot in garlic butter), *bœuf bourguignon* (beef simmered for hours in red wine with onions and mushrooms), *coq au vin* (chicken stewed in red wine), and *œufs en meurette* (poached eggs on a large crouton in red wine), as well as the famous Dijon mustards. Look also for *jambon persillé* (cold ham layered in a garlic-parsley gelatin), *pain d'épices* (spice bread), and *gougère* (light, puffy cheese pastries). Native cheeses are Époisses and Langres (both mushy and great) and my favorite, Montrachet (a tasty goat cheese). *Crème de cassis* (black currant liqueur) is another Burgundian specialty; look for it in desserts and snazzy drinks (try a *kir*).

Lyon offers *le top* in French cuisine. Surprisingly affordable, this is an intense gastronomic experience—try the *salade lyonnaise* (croutons, ham, and a poached egg on a bed of lettuce), *andouillettes* (pork sausages), and *quenelles* (large dumplings, best when flavored with fish).

Remember, restaurants serve only during lunch (11:30–14:00) and dinner (19:00–21:00, later in bigger cities); cafés serve food throughout the day.

Wine: Along with Bordeaux, Burgundy is why France is famous for wine. From Chablis to Beaujolais, you'll find it all here: great fruity reds, dry whites, and crisp rosés. The three key grapes are Chardonnay (dry white wines), Pinot Noir (medium-bodied red wines), and Gamay (light, fruity wines, such as Beaujolais). Every village produces its own distinctive wine, from Chablis to Meursault to Chassagne-Montrachet. Road maps read like fine-wine lists. If the wine village has a hyphenated name, the latter half of its name often comes from the town's most important vineyard (e.g., Gevrey-Chambertin, Ladoix-Serrigny). Look for *Dégustation Gratuite* (free tasting) signs, and prepare for serious wine tasting—and steep prices, if you're not careful. For a more relaxed tasting, head for the hills: The less prestigious Hautes-Côtes (upper slopes) produce some terrific and overlooked wines. Look for village cooperatives (usually called *Caveau des Vignerons*), or try our suggestions for Beaune tastings. The least expensive (but still tasty) wines are Bourgogne Ordinaire and Passetoutgrain (both red), and whites from the Mâcon and Chalon areas. If you like rosé, try Marsannay, considered one of France's best. For tips on tasting, see "French Wine-Tasting 101" on page 46.

Beaune

You'll feel comfortable right away in this prosperous and popular little wine capital, where life centers on the production and consumption of the prestigious, expensive Côte d'Or wines. *Côte d'Or* means "golden hillside," and such hillsides are a spectacle to enjoy in late October as the leaves turn.

Medieval monks and powerful dukes of Burgundy laid the groundwork that established this town's prosperity. The monks cultivated wine and the dukes cultivated wealth. Today, one of the world's most important wine auctions takes place here during the third week of November.

ORIENTATION

Beaune is a compact place (pop. 25,000) with a handful of interesting monuments and vineyards on its doorstep. Limit your Beaune ramblings to the town center, lassoed within its medieval walls and circled by a one-way ring road, and find a quiet moment to stroll into the vineyards. All roads and activities converge on the perfectly French square, place Carnot (as do Wednesday and Saturday markets). Beaune is quiet on Sundays and Monday mornings.

Tourist Information

There are two TIs: The main office is in the city center, and an outpost lies on the ring road. The **main TI** is across the street from Hôtel Dieu on place de la Halle (April–Nov Mon–Sat 9:30–19:00, summers until 20:00, Sun 10:00–12:30 & 14:00–18:00; Dec–March Mon–Sat 10:00–18:00, Sun 10:00–13:00 & 14:00–17:00; tel. 03 80 26 21 30). The other **TI** is handy for drivers, across from the post office on the ring road's southeastern corner (Mon–Fri 9:00–12:00 & 14:00–18:00, closed Sat–Sun, look for Porte Marie de Bourgogne on the red banner).

Both TIs have extensive information on wine-tasting inside and outside Beaune, and sell brochures you don't need. They also have a room-finding service, a list of *chambres d'hôte*, and bus schedules. Ask about guided English walking tours (€7, usually at about 12:00, daily July–mid-Sept, call to verify), and pass on their museum pass.

Arrival in Beaune

By Train: To reach the city center from the train station (lockers not available), walk straight out of the station up avenue du 8 Septembre, cross the busy ring road, and continue up rue du Château. Follow it as it angles left and pass the mural on your right (rue des Tonneliers). A left on rue de l'Enfants leads to Beaune's pedestrian zone and place Carnot.

By Bus: Beaune has no bus station—only several stops in the town center. Ask the driver for *le Centre-Ville.* The Jules Ferry (zhul fair-ee) stop is central and closest to the train station; the Clémenceau stop is best for visiting Château de la Rochepot (see page 556). Bus info: tel. 03 80 42 11 00.

By Car: Follow *Centre-Ville* signs to the ring road. Once on the ring road, turn right at the first signal after the modern post office (rue d'Alsace), and park for free a block away in place Madeleine. If the lot is full, look for spaces on surrounding streets.

Helpful Hints

Market Days: Wednesday and Saturday are Beaune's market days, held on place Carnot (until 12:30).

Supermarket: Supermarché Casino has a great selection, a deli, and fair prices (Mon–Sat 8:30–20:00, closed Sun, through the arch off place Madeleine).

Best Wine and Food Stores: Beaune overflows with wine boutiques eager to convince you that their wines are best. The wine shop **Denis Perret** has a good, varied selection in all price ranges and a helpful, English-speaking staff (they can chill a white for your picnic). If you've tasted a wine you like elsewhere, they can usually find a less costly bottle with similar qualities (June–Nov Mon–Sat 9:00–19:00, closed Sun; Dec–May closed 12:00–14:00, 40 place Carnot, tel. 03 80 22 35 47, www.denisperret.fr—in French only). The wine hardware store, **Comptoir du Vin**, is good for wine paraphernalia (Mon–Sat 8:00–12:45 & 13:45–19:00, closed Sun, where rue d'Alsace runs into place Carnot). **Amuse Bouche** displays fine food products beautifully and has many ideas for gifts (7 place Carnot). A few doors down, welcoming **Pain d'Épices** shows off beautiful packages of this tasty and local spice bread, also handy as gifts (1 place Carnot).

Best Souvenir Shopping: The **Athenaeum** has a great variety of souvenirs, including wine and cooking books in English, with a great children's section upstairs (daily 10:00–19:00, across from Hôtel Dieu at 7 rue de l'Hôtel Dieu). And you won't find a bookstore with a better wine bar.

Laundry: Beaune's only launderette is between the train station and place Madeleine (daily 6:30–21:00, 17-19 rue du Faubourg St. Jean).

Bike Rental: See "Getting Around the Beaune Region," page 553.

Car Rental: ADA is cheap and closest to the train station (26 avenue 8 Septembre, tel. 03 80 22 72 90). **Avis** is five blocks

Beaune

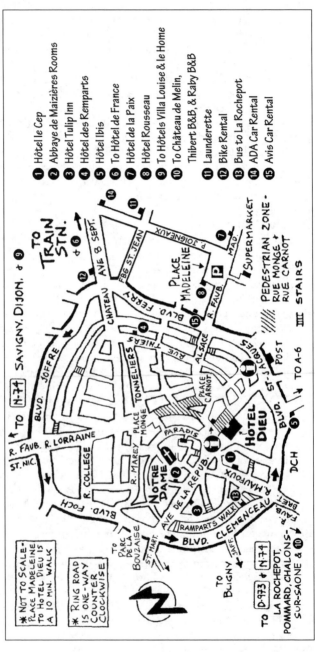

1. Hôtel le Cep
2. Abbaye de Maizières Rooms
3. Hôtel Tulip Inn
4. Hôtel des Remparts
5. Hôtel Ibis
6. To Hôtel de France
7. Hôtel de la Paix
8. Hôtel Rousseau
9. To Hôtels Villa Louise & le Home
10. To Château de Melin, Thibert B&B, & Raby B&B
11. Launderette
12. Bike Rental
13. Bus to La Rochepot
14. ADA Car Rental
15. Avis Car Rental

away on the ring road, near place Madeleine (48 bis Jules Ferry, tel. 03 80 24 96 46).

Taxi: Call 06 09 42 36 80, 06 09 36 06 44, or 06 14 36 43 47.

SIGHTS

Hôtel Dieu

This medieval charity hospital, worth ▲▲▲, is now a museum. The Hundred Years' War and the Black Death plague devastated Beaune, leaving three-quarters of its population destitute. Nicholas Rolin, chancellor of Burgundy (enriched, in part, by his power to collect taxes), had to do something for "his people" (or, more likely, was getting old and wanted to close out his life on a philanthropic, rather than a greedy, note). So, in 1443, Rolin paid to build this hospital. It was completed in just eight years.

Cost and Hours: €5.40, daily April–Nov 9:00–19:30, Dec–March 9:00–11:30 & 14:00–17:30, last ticket sold one hour before closing.

Self-Guided Tour: While the English flier you pick up as you enter is helpful, and you'll find English descriptions throughout, this self-guided tour gives it more meaning. Tour the rooms, which circle the courtyard in a clockwise direction, starting from near the turnstile.

"Courtyard of Honor": Honor meant power, and this was all about showing off. While the exterior of the hospital and the town side of the courtyard are less ostentatious (because there was no point in attracting the pesky 15th-century brigands who looted whatever looked most rewarding), the inner rooftop is dazzling. The colorful glazed tile roof established what became a style recognized as typically "Burgundian." The tiles, which last 300 years, are fired three times: once to harden, then to burn in the color, and finally for the glaze. They were redone in 1902. The building is a lacy Flamboyant Gothic with lots of decor—and more weather vanes than any other building in France.

Paupers' Ward: This grandest room of the hospital was the ward for the poorest patients. The vault, typical of big medieval rooms, was constructed like the hull of a ship. The screen separates the ward from the chapel. Every three hours, the door was opened, and patients could experience Mass from their beds. Study the ceiling. Cross beams are held by the mouths of delightfully carved monsters—each mouth is stretched realistically, and each face has individual characteristics. Between the crossbars are busts of real 15th-century townsfolk—leading citizens, with animals humorously indicating their foibles (e.g., a round-faced glutton next to a pig). This room housed patients until 1949 (see painting, middle left). During epidemics, there were two to a bed.

The carved wooden statue over the door shows a bound

Christ—demonstrating graphically to patients that their savior suffered and was able to empathize with their ordeal. Its realism shows that Gothic art had moved beyond the stiff formality of Romanesque carving. Behind the little window, next to the statue, was the nuns' dorm. The sisters would check on patients from here. Notice the scrawny candle holder; if a patient died in the night, the candle would be extinguished. Study the glass display cases near the beds. Rolin, who believed every patient deserved dignity, provided each patient with a pewter jug, mug, bowl, and plate. But the ward didn't get heat until the 19th century (notice the heating grates on the floor).

Chapel: The hospice was not a place of hope. People came here to die. Care was more for the soul than the body. (Local guides are routinely instructed in writing by American tour companies not to use the word "hospice," because it upsets their clients—but this was a hospice, plain and simple, and back then, death was apparently less disturbing.) The stained glass shows Nicolas Rolin (lower left) and his wife, Guigone (lower right), dressed as a nun to show her devotion. Nicolas' feudal superior, the Duke of Burgundy, is portrayed above him. Notice the action on Golgotha. As Jesus is crucified, the souls of the two criminals crucified with him (portrayed as miniature naked humans) are being snatched up—one by an angel and the other by a red devil. You're standing on tiles with the love symbol (or "gallant device") designed by Nicolas and Guigone (as noble couples often did) to celebrate their love. The letters N and G are entwined in an oak branch, meaning that their love was strong. The word *seule* (only one) and the lone star declare that Guigone is the only star in Nicolas' cosmos.

St. Hugue's Ward: In the 17th century, this smaller ward was established for rich patients. They were more likely to survive, and the decor displays themes of hope, rather than resignation: The series of Baroque paintings lining the walls show the biblical miracles that Jesus performed. As the wealthy would lie in their beds, they'd stare at the ceiling—a painting with the bottom of an angel's foot, surrounded by the sick waiting to be healed by Jesus in his scarlet robe. The syringes in the display case are as delicate as caulking guns.

St. Nicolas Room: Originally part of the kitchen, this room now exhibits more tools of the doctoring trade (amputation saws, pans for blood-letting, and so on). Notice the nearby hatch in the floor, showing the river running below; the hole provided a primitive but convenient disposal system.

Kitchen: The kitchen display here shows a 16th-century rotisserie. When wound up, the cute robot would crank away, and the spit would spin slowly for 45 minutes. The 19th-century stove provided running hot water, which spewed from the beaks of swans.

Pharmacy: The nuns grew herbs out back, and strange and wondrous concoctions were stored in pottery jars. The biggest jar (by the window) was for *theriaca* (literally, "panacea"). The most commonly used medicine back then, it was a syrup of herbs, wine, and opium.

St. Louis Ward: A maternity ward until 1969, this room today displays precious 15th-century prayer books and is lined with fine 16th- and 17th-century tapestries illustrating mostly Old Testament stories. Dukes traveled with tapestries to cozy up the relatively humble places they stayed in while on the road. The 16th-century pieces have better colors, but worse perspective. (The most precious tapestries here are from the 15th century and are displayed in the next room, where everyone is enthralled by the great van der Weyden painting.)

Roger van der Weyden's Last Judgment: This exquisite painting, the treasure of the Hôtel Dieu, was commissioned by Rolin in 1450 for the altar of the Paupers' Ward. He spared no cost, hiring the leading Flemish artist of his day. The entire altarpiece survives. The back side (on right wall) was sliced off so everything could be viewed at the same time. The painting is full of symbolism. Christ presides over Judgment Day. The lily is mercy, the sword is judgment, the rainbow promises salvation, and the jeweled globe at Jesus' feet symbolizes the universality of Christianity's message. As four angels blow their trumpets, St. Michael the archangel—very much in control—determines which souls are heavy with sin. Mary and the apostles pray for the souls of the dead as they emerge from their graves. But notice how both Michael and Jesus are expressionless—at this point, the cries of the damned and their loved ones are useless. In the back row are real people of the day.

The intricate detail, painted with a three-haired brush, is typical of Flemish art. While Renaissance artists employed mathematical tricks of perspective, these artists captured a sense of reality by painting minute detail upon detail. Stare at Michael's robe and wings. Check out John's delicate feet and hands. Study the faces of the damned; you can almost hear the gnashing of teeth. The feet of the damned show the pull of a terrible force. On the far left, notice those happily entering the pearly gates. On the far right—it's the flames of hell (no, this has nothing to do with politics).

Except for Sundays and holidays, the painting was kept closed and people saw only the panels, which now hang on the right wall: Nicolas and Guigone piously at the feet of St. Sebastian—invoked to fight the plague—and St. Anthony, whom patients called upon for help in combating burning skin diseases.

More Sights

Collégiale Notre-Dame—Built in the 12th and 13th centuries, the cathedral was a "daughter of Cluny" (built in the style of the Cluny Abbey; page 568). Except for the 14th-century Gothic front porch addition, it's a fine example of Cluny-style Romanesque architecture. Enter to see the 15th-century tapestries (behind the altar), a variety of stained glass, and what's left of frescoes depicting the life of Lazarus (tapestry open daily 9:30–12:30 & 14:00–19:00).

To get to the Museum of Wine (listed below) from here, walk 30 steps straight out of the cathedral, turn left down a cobbled alley (rue d'Enfer—Hell Street, named for the fires of the Duke's kitchens once located on this street), keep left, and enter the courtyard of Hôtel des Ducs.

Museum of the Wine of Burgundy (Musée du Vin de Bourgogne)—You don't have to like wine to appreciate this folkwine museum, which fills the old residence of the Dukes of Burgundy. The history and culture of Burgundy and wine were fermented in the same bottle. At least wander into the free courtyard for a look at the palace, antique wine presses (in the *cuverie,* or vatting shed), and a concrete model of Beaune's 15th-century street plan (a good chance to understand the town's impressive fortified wall). Inside the museum, you'll see a model of the region, with tools, costumes, and scenes of Burgundian wine history—but no tasting. English explanations are in each room (€5.40, ticket includes Beaune's painting and photography museums each in the City Hall, daily 9:30–18:00, closed Tue in winter).

Ramparts Walk, Parc de la Bouzaise, and Vineyards—Stroll above Beaune along its 13th-century wall to get a sense of its once impressive medieval defenses, then wander into nearby vineyards. From inside the town, most of the rampart is accessible, but has melted into peaceful residential lanes. You can head out rue Maufoux and find the ramp leading to the ramparts (Remparts des Dames) on the right. Wander north along the fortification to the next street (avenue de la République), drop down and turn left, cross the ring road, and leave town, following the same stream that runs under the Hôtel Dieu for three blocks to the park. The vineyards are behind the park, with small roads, paths, and views that are best at sunset (walkers need 15 min from Beaune's center to reach the vineyards; drivers only about 2 min).

WINE-TASTING

In Beaune

Countless opportunities exist for you to learn the fine points of Burgundy's wines (for a price). Shops everywhere offer free tastings that are generally friendly and informative (with the expectation that you'll buy at least one bottle). For tips on wine-tasting, see "French Wine-Tasting 101," page 46.

Several large cellars *(caves)* charge an entry fee, allowing you to taste a variety of wines (with less expectation that you'll buy). Most

Burgundian Wine Quality, 1998–2002

1998   Whites are rich, distinctive, full-bodied, and capable of lasting 10 years. Reds, while less distinctive, are good, with tannic, full-bodied taste.

1999   This is an outstanding vintage, especially for reds, which are supple and easy to drink now, and for the next several years.

2000   This year is a less impressive vintage than the previous two years; reds should be consumed soon, as they lack concentration for aging purposes. Whites are much better.

2001   A difficult growing season, with rain and a late frost, producing reds that are thinner, less consistent, and more tannic than in previous years. Whites fared much better.

2002   Being called by some as the "vintage of the decade," the reds are just now being released. The whites are excellent, with good structure, balance, and pure, clean fruit flavors.

of these *caves* offer some form of introduction or self-guided tour (see also "Minibus Tours of Vineyards near Beaune," page 547). Don't mind the mossy ceilings. Many cellars have spent centuries growing this "angel's hair"—the result of humidity created by the evaporation of the wines stored there.

The following two places (a block apart and close to the TI) charge an entry fee, but then allow you to sample a variety of wines (18 wines for €9, or 7 wines for €6) in atmospheric candlelit cellars.

▲▲▲**Marché aux Vins**—Across the street from the Hôtel Dieu, this is Beaune's wine smorgasbord and the best way to sample its impressive wines. Pay €9 for a wine-tasting cup (yours to keep) and scorecard, then plunge into the labyrinth of candlelit caves dotted with 18 barrels, each offering a new tasting experience (4 Chardonnays, 14 Pinot Noirs). In Burgundy, most whites are Chardonnays, and most reds are Pinot Noirs. You're on your own. Tip: The best reds (bottles you'd pay €100 for in restaurants) are upstairs in the chapel, at the end of the tasting. While you technically have 45 minutes in the cellars, this is rarely enforced—especially if you look like a serious buyer. (Carrying one of their little shopping baskets improves your image.) Discreetly bring some crackers to cleanse your palate and help you really taste the differences (mid-June–mid-Sept daily 9:30–17:30, otherwise daily 9:30–11:30 & 14:00–17:30, tel. 03 80 25 08 20).

▲**Caves des Cordeliers**—Compared to the Marché aux Vins, this cellar is smaller (with 7, rather than 18, wines to taste), but it's just as atmospheric, more historic, and it comes with more personalized help. You enter via a cloister that survives from the original 13th-century Convent des Cordeliers. (The cells upstairs house retired nuns to this day.) After paying and picking up your *tastevin* (tasting cup), tour the historical exhibit upstairs. Then descend into cellars where monks have actually stored their wine for centuries. Surrounded by candlelit barrels sporting opened bottles, you become something like a kid in a candy shop. The "cellar master" (in the coat and tie) speaks English and is happy to teach you about the wine. Your last stop: a classy wine-lovers boutique (€6, 9:30–12:00 & 14:00–18:30, 6 rue de l'Hôtel Dieu, one block toward ring road from Marché aux Vins, tel. 03 80 25 08 85).

Outside of Beaune

The TI has a long list of area vintners for those who want to venture into the countryside. At free tastings, you're expected to buy a bottle or two unless you're with a group tour. The famous *Route des Grands Crus* that connects Burgundy's most prestigious wine villages is disappointing north of Aloxe-Corton, as you're forced onto the unappealing N-74. Consider instead the beautiful routes connecting villages between Beaune and La Rochepot and south to Santenay (e.g., Monthelie, Nantoux, St. Romain, and St. Aubin are all off the famous path and offer ample tastings).

I've listed a few favorites below. For directions to the first three places, see "Bike (or Drive) the Vineyards," page 553. The fourth (La Cave de Pommard) is two miles from Beaune.

Montrachet's Cave Cooperative (Cave Coopérative de Montrachet)—Ten minutes south of Beaune in Puligny Montrachet (pool-ee-knee moan-rah-shay) on the scenic route to Château de la Rochepot, this cellar is king of white wines and represents many local vineyards (€5 for 3 wines, free if you buy, daily 9:30–12:30 & 14:30–19:00, tel. 03 80 21 96 78).

Henri de Villamont—In Savigny-lès-Beaune, find Villamonts' red-brick winery and say hello to English-speaking Annie, who can introduce you to her fine wines (Wed–Mon 10:00–18:00, closed Tue, reasonable prices and good selection, tel. 03 80 21 52 13).

Caveau des Vignerons in Aloxe-Corton—Here you can sample from nine of the 11 makers of this famous wine; prices are very affordable, and easygoing Philippe speaks just enough English (€1–6 per wine, free if you buy, Thu–Mon 10:00–13:00 & 14:00–19:00, closed Tue–Wed, tel. 03 80 26 49 85).

La Cave de Pommard—A short drive or two-mile walk from Beaune leads to this good cellar in Pommard (on the way to or from Château de la Rochepot). From Beaune's ring road, follow Chalon-sur-Saône, then Autun, to reach Pommard. The cellars are just after the Château de Pommard on the right. Visit on your own, and ask to taste from what's available (free, daily 10:00–19:00, several wineries represented, though most come from two *domaines*, tel. 03 80 24 99 00).

Minibus Tours of Vineyards near Beaune—Wine Safari offers minibus wine-tasting tours in three two-hour itineraries (€34, tour #2 is best for beginners, tours depart from TI generally at 12:00, 14:30 & 17:00, tel. 03 80 24 79 12, www.burgundy-tourism -safaritours.com, or call TI to reserve). These English-speaking tours are relaxed, friendly, and get you into the countryside and smaller wineries. **Transco** buses also run from Beaune through all the great wine villages (see "Getting Around the Beaune Region," page 553).

SLEEPING

In the Center

$$$ **Hôtel le Cep****** is the place to stay in Beaune if you have the funds. Buried in the town center, this historic building comes with exquisite public spaces, gorgeous wood-beamed and traditionally decorated rooms, and a restaurant that has long been the talk of the town (standard Sb-€130, standard Db-€165, deluxe Db-€195, suites-€250–350, family duplexes-€500, continental breakfast-€16, air-con, king-size beds, parking-€10/day, 27 rue Maufoux, tel. 03 80 22 35 48, fax 03 80 22 76 80, www.hotel-cep-beaune.com, resa@hotel-cep-beaune.com).

$$$ **Hôtel Tulip Inn***** charges top euro for its central location a block from the basilica, and mixes modern comfort in smaller rooms with a touch of old Beaune. Skip the overpriced breakfast (standard Db €75–88, *superieure* Db-€90–120, extra bed-€15, elevator, cozy public spaces, parking garage-€9/day but a long walk away, 9 avenue de la République, tel. 03 80 24 09 20, fax 03 80 24 09 15, hotel.athanor@wanadoo.fr, SE).

$$ **Abbaye de Maizières***** slumbers near the basilica, deep in Beaune's center, with 12 big, colorful, and basic rooms over a good restaurant in a 12th-century building (Db-€66–110, most about €70, Tb-€88–125, extra bed-€15, no lobby, reception at restaurant, many stairs, parking garage-€5/day, 19 rue des Maizières, tel. 03 80 24 74 64, fax 03 80 22 49 49, French only, contact@abbayedemaizieres .com; if no response, contact Hôtel Tulip Inn, below).

$$ **Hôtel des Remparts***** is a peaceful oasis in a manor house run by the formal Epaillys. They offer rustic-classy and affordable rooms with beamed ceilings, period furniture, a quiet courtyard, and a few great family rooms. Added to the hotel's appeal is free Internet access, laundry service, and bike rental (Db-€76–90, most at €76, bigger rooms are pricier, with elaborate bathrooms, Db suite-€110, Tb-€86–110, Qb-€120, cozy attic rooms, garage-€8/day, 48 rue

Sleep Code

(€1 = about $1.20, country code: 33)
S = Single, **D** = Double/Twin, **T** = Triple, **Q** = Quad,
b = bathroom, **s** = shower only, **no CC** = Credit Cards not
accepted, **SE** = Speaks English, **NSE** = No English, ***** = French
hotel rating system (0–4 stars). You can assume a hotel takes
credit cards unless you see "no CC" in the listing.

To help you sort easily through these listings, I've divided
the rooms into three categories based on the price for a standard
double room with bath:

$$$ Higher Priced—Most rooms €90 or more.
$$ Moderately Priced—Most rooms between €60–90.
$ Lower Priced—Most rooms €60 or less.

Thiers, between train station and main square, just inside ring road,
tel. 03 80 24 94 94, fax 03 80 24 97 08, hotel.des.remparts
@wanadoo.fr, SE).

$$ Hôtel Ibis**, modern with 73 efficient rooms, is an accept-
able last resort for most, but a good first resort if you have kids and
want a pool. The bigger "Club" rooms are worth the extra euros
(standard Db-€67, Club Db-€74, extra person-€10, free parking,
smoke-free floor, air-con, you'll pass it as you enter Beaune from
the autoroute, tel. 03 80 22 75 67, fax 03 80 22 77 17, www
.hotelibis.com, h1363@accorhotels.com). There's another Ibis
Hôtel—along with a gaggle of Motel 6–type places (Db-€40)—
closer to the autoroute.

$ Hôtel de France** lacks character, but is easy for train travelers
and drivers (parking across from the train station). It comes with clean
rooms and Diana the sheepdog. Half pension is required on Friday
and Saturday (Sb-€40–62, Db-€51–75, most at about €60, Tb-
€62–76, air-con, garage-€9/day, 35 avenue du 8 Septembre, tel. 03 80
24 10 34, fax 03 80 24 96 78, hotfrance.beaune@wanadoo.fr, SE).

Place Madeleine

These hotels are a few blocks from the city center and train station,
with easy parking.

$$ Hôtel de la Paix***, a few steps off place Madeleine, is intimate and welcoming, with 14 plush and well-appointed rooms, sev-
eral good family rooms, and a snazzy bar with a pool table (Sb-€55,
Db-€72–75, loft Tb-€95, Qb-€115–130, air-con, 45 rue du
Faubourg Madeleine, tel. 03 80 24 78 08, fax 03 80 24 10 18,
www.hotelpaix .com, contact@hotelpaix.com SE).

$ Hôtel Rousseau is a great-value, no-frills manor house that
turns its back on Beaune's sophistication. Cheerful, quirky, and

hard-to-find owner Madame Rousseau, her pet birds, and charming garden will make you smile, and the tranquility will help you sleep. The cheapest rooms are simple, clean, and just fine. The rooms with showers are like grandma's, with enough comfort (S-€28, D-€33, D with toilet-€43, Db-€54, T with toilet-€53, Tb-€60, Q-€53, Qb-€75, showers down the hall-€3, includes breakfast, no CC, free parking, 11 place Madeleine, tel. 03 80 22 13 59).

Near Beaune

You'll find some exceptional and family-friendly values within a short drive of Beaune. Hotels in famous wine villages are generally pricey and overrated.

Hotels

$$$ Hôtel Villa Louise*** is a small, dreamy place burrowed in the prestigious wine hamlet of Aloxe-Corton, five minutes north of Beaune. Many of its 11 *très* cozy and tastefully decorated rooms overlook vineyards, a small covered pool, and a rear garden made for sipping wine. The English-speaking, winemaking owners—the Perrins—are happy to show you their vaulted cellars (Db-€98–150, Db suite-€200, most about €120, whirlpool tub, sauna, 10 percent off if you mention this book when booking and pay in cash, 21420 Aloxe-Corton, tel. 03 80 26 46 70, fax 03 80 26 47 16, www.hotel-villa-louise.fr, hotel-villa-louise@wanadoo.fr).

$$ Hôtel le Home** sits just off busy N-74, a half mile north of Beaune, with cushy rooms in an old mansion. The rooms in the main building are Laura Ashley–soft (Db-€55–73, Tb-€70–78, top-floor rooms are the most romantic). Rooms on the parking courtyard (only Db-€66) come with stone floors, small terraces, and bright colors (free parking, 138 route de Dijon, tel. 03 80 22 16 43, fax 03 80 24 90 74, www.lehome.fr.)

Chambres d'Hôte

The Côte d'Or has scads of *chambres d'hôte;* get a list at the TI and reserve ahead in the summer. The cliff-dwelling villages of Baubigny, Orches, and Evelles, just under La Rochepot, are my favorite non-Beaune bases with several *chambres d'hôte* (well-signed in the villages).

$$$ Château de Melin, is a little paradise between the villages of Auxey-Duresses and La Rochepot (10 min from Beaune toward La Rochepot). You'll wish you had reserved extra days when you enter the grounds. The well-restored château offers good comfort and big rooms, complete with a small pond, vineyards (tastings available), and gardens to stretch out in (Db-€86–105, Tb-€120, Qb-€135, includes good breakfast, no CC, tel. 03 80 21 21 19, fax 03 80 21 21 72, www.chateaudemelin.com—in French only, friendly Helene SE).

$ **Madame Thibert**, on the lower road between Baubigny and Evelle (signed to Madame Fussi, previous owner), has two comfortable rooms in a modern home over a sweeping lawn (Db-€46, no CC, tel. 03 80 21 84 66, fabienne.thibert@xthibom).

$ **Isabelle Raby** rents three good rooms a half-mile above Baubigny in rocky Orches with the best set-up for families, including a pretty pool, ping pong, swings, and a big grassy area. Ask to see her cellar (Db-€53, Tb-€65, Qb-€75, Quint-€89, includes big breakfast, no CC, tel. & fax 03 80 21 78 45).

EATING

For a small town, Beaune offers a wide range of reasonably priced restaurants. Review our suggestions below carefully before setting out, and reserve ahead to avoid frustrations (especially on weekends).

Eating in the Center

Abbaye de Maizières, in a 12th-century wine warehouse where monks once stored and sold wine, specializes in traditional Burgundian cuisine (with smoked salmon tossed in). The €23 *menu* and setting, complete with centuries-old "angel's hair," make for an ideal introduction to Burgundian cooking (closed Tue, inexpensive wines by the glass, service can be slow, 19 rue des Maizières, tel. 03 80 24 74 64, Alan Siruque SE).

Bistrot Bourguignon is a relaxed, wine bar-bistro with a lengthy wine list and 15 wines available by the glass (order by number from display behind bar). The affordable prices are the same at either bar or table. Come for a glass of wine or to enjoy a light dinner. Dine at the counter, the tables, or in the living room out back. The *bon-vivant* owner, Jean-Jacques, speaks English (daily, on a pedestrian-only street at 8 rue Monge, tel. 03 80 22 23 24).

Le P'tit Paradis is a tiny, yellow, welcoming place on a quiet street across from the wine museum. The cuisine has some Burgundian dishes, but is mostly the product of the Madame Daloz's creative mind; a vegetarian option is always available—just ask. Call ahead to reserve (*menus* from €17, closed Mon–Tue, 25 rue du Paradis, tel. 03 80 24 91 00).

La Ciboulette, friendly and family-run, offers fine cuisine, mixing traditional Burgundian flavors with creative dishes; it's worth the longer walk (*menus* from €19, closed Mon–Tue, from place Carnot, walk out rue Carnot and keep going to 69 rue Lorraine, tel. 03 80 24 70 72).

Le Jardin des Remparts provides the perfect Burgundian splurge. This dressy stone manor house, hiding behind trees, is elegant inside and out (leafy terrace dining in summer), yet the service is relaxed and helpful. The excellent "new cuisine" proudly works with regional products (€30–55 *menus*, 7-course "discovery *menu*" €75,

Beaune Restaurants and Wine Caves

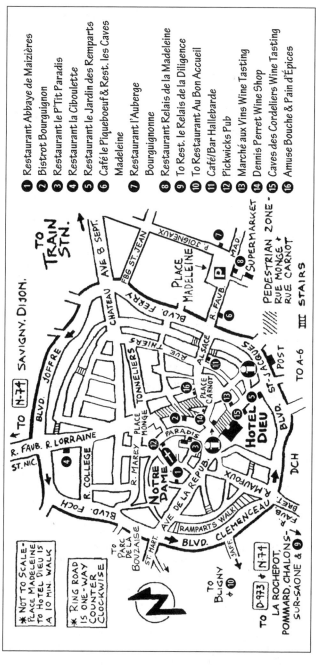

1. Restaurant Abbaye de Maizières
2. Bistrot Bourguignon
3. Restaurant le P'Tit Paradis
4. Restaurant la Ciboulette
5. Restaurant le Jardin des Remparts
6. Café le Piqueboeuf & Rest. les Caves Madeleine
7. Restaurant l'Auberge Bourguignonne
8. Restaurant Relais de la Madeleine
9. To Rest. le Relais de la Diligence
10. To Restaurant Au Bon Accueil
11. Café/Bar Hallebarde
12. Pickwicks Pub
13. Marché aux Vins Wine Tasting
14. Dennis Perret Wine Shop
15. Caves des Cordeliers Wine Tasting
16. Amuse Bouche & Pain d'Épices

closed Sun–Mon, always reserve ahead, just past Hôtel Dieu on ring road at 10 rue de l'Hôtel Dieu, tel. 03 80 24 79 41, lejardin @club-internet.fr).

Place Madeleine

Le Piquebœuf, on the busy ring road, feels like an upscale café, with fair-priced dishes served in a pleasant setting (salads and pizza-€10, *plats du jour*-€10–14, closed Tue, air-con, family-friendly seating upstairs, 2 rue de la Madeleine, tel. 03 80 24 07 52).

Les Caves Madeleine is a wine shop that keeps its cozy little dining room busy. Diners are surrounded by shelves of this week's wines with prices chalked onto bottles. Choose a private table, or join the big convivial communal table, where good food and wine kindle conversation, then lubricate new friendships. The owners are wine merchants who pass their savings on to you. (As you choose a bottle at store prices and add €5 to drink here, top-end wines become affordable). This small place is family-run by the Brelin's son, English-speaking "Lo-lo," who enjoys sharing his love of wine (good wines by the glass, €12 and €22 *menus*, closed Thu and Sun, 8 rue du Faubourg Madeleine, tel. 03 80 22 93 30).

L'Auberge Bourguignonne is solidly Burgundian, with serious service, that proudly displays its awards. Choose from the dressy dining room; the folksy, more traditional dining room; or tables outside on the square (*menus* from €16, some seafood, daily, air-con, reservations smart, 4 place Madeleine, tel. 03 80 22 23 53).

Relais de la Madeleine is Beaune's basic budget diner—with little emphasis on ambience or presentation. It's run by the entertaining "Monsieur Neaux-Problem" (€12.50 *menu*, closed Wed, 44 place Madeleine, tel. 03 80 22 07 47).

Bars

Drop by **Café Hallebarde** for a grand selection of draft beer (24 rue d'Alsace), and, if you're tired of speaking French, pop into the late-night-lively **Pickwicks Pub** (behind church at 2 rue Notre-Dame).

Eating near Beaune

If you have a car, you'll find better values and more character in these rural places (each less then a 10-min drive from town).

Le Relais de la Diligence, a five-minute drive from Beaune, serves the area's best budget Burgundian cuisine, with many *menu* options. The dressy (smoke-free) dining room with sliding-glass walls has you feeling like you're sitting in the vineyard. Or, on a balmy evening, you can eat on the terrace. Either way, as the sun sets, you're enjoying the tasty best of rural Burgundy (*menus* from €17, the *Menu Tutu* for dogs—I'm serious—at €2.50 includes ground hamburger and *pâté*, daily, closed Tue–Wed Oct–May, take

N-74 toward Chagny/Chalon and turn left at L'Hôpital Meursault on D-23, tel. 03 80 21 21 32).

Au Bon Accueil is relaxed and country-cozy, on a hill above Beaune, with great outdoor tables. It's ideal for a relaxed Burgundian lunch or dinner. This place is popular, so call ahead if possible, particularly for weekends and in summer (lunch *menu*-€12, 5-course dinner *menu*-€20, smaller dinner *menu*-€14, closed for dinner Mon–Wed, but open for lunch except Mon, leave Beaune's ring road and take Bligny-sur-Ouche turnoff, you'll see signs a few minutes outside Beaune, tel. 03 80 22 08 80).

TRANSPORTATION CONNECTIONS

From Beaune by train to: Dijon (14/day, 25 min), **Paris'** Gare de Lyon (12/day, 2.5 hrs, 10 require change in Dijon), **Colmar** (5/day, 4–5 hrs, changes in Dijon and in Besançon, Mulhouse, or Beflort), **Arles** (8/day, 4.5 hrs, 9 with change in Lyon and Nîmes or Avignon), **Chamonix** (5/day, 7 hrs, changes in Lyon and St. Gervais, some require additional changes), **Annecy** (5/day, 5 hrs, change in Lyon), **Amboise** (8/day, 6 hrs, most with changes in Dijon and in Paris, arrive at Paris' Gare de Lyon, then Métro to Austerlitz or Montparnasse stations).

The Beaune Region

Getting Around the Beaune Region

By Bus: Transco **bus #44** runs from Beaune through the vineyards and villages south to Chalon-sur-Saône, west to La Rochepot, and north to Dijon. About 10 buses per day link Beaune and Dijon via the famous wine villages; ask at the TI for schedules and stops, or call for information (tel. 03 80 42 11 00).

By Bike: Well-organized, English-speaking Florent at Bourgogne Randonnées has good bikes, bike racks, maps, and thorough countryside itineraries (get his advice on your plan). He can deliver your bike to your hotel anywhere in France (bikes-€3/hr, €15/day, Mon–Sat 9:00–12:00 & 13:30–19:00, Sun 10:00–12:00 & 14:00–17:00, near train station at 7 avenue du 8 Septembre, tel. 03 80 22 06 03, fax 03 80 22 15 58, www.bourgogne-randonnees.com).

SIGHTS

▲▲**Bike (or Drive) the Vineyards**—Hop on a bike in Beaune, and in minutes, you can be immersed in the lush countryside and immaculate vineyards of the Côtes d'Or. The many little-traveled

The Beaune Region

3 MILES
3 KM

TO VEZELAY + PARIS
TO HAUTES COTES DE BEAUNE
TO DIJON

PERNAND-VERG.
SAVIGNY
ALOXE CORTON
N-74
CHOREY
A-31

A-6

TO BLIGNY SUR-OUCHE + CHATEAUNEUF EN-AUXOIS

D-18

D-970

AU BON ACCUEIL REST.

TO IVRY

D-17

ST. ROMAIN

POMMARD

BEAUNE

View

D-973

N-74

ORCHES

MELIN B+B

AUXEY-DURESSES

MEURSAULT

L'HÔPITAL

EVELLE

BAU-BIGNY

LA ROCHEPOT

LE RELAIS DE LA DILIGENCE REST.

View

N-74

D-33

ST. AUBIN

PULIGNY MONTRACHET

A-6

N

CHAGNY

SCENIC ROUTE
GOOD BIKE ROUTE

TO BRANÇION, BEAUJOLAIS + LYON

DCH

roads (and friendly bike-rental place in Beaune—see previous page) make this area perfect for biking. For an easy and very rewarding roll through wine paradise, follow this 10-mile half-day loop from Beaune. It laces together three renowned wine villages—Savigny-les-Beaune, Aloxe-Corton, and Pernand Vergelesses—connecting you with the best of Burgundian nature and village wine culture. (Remember, wine-tasting does not necessarily mean wine-drinking. Bikers needn't be shy about tasting like a professional—spitting, rather than swallowing.) Bring water and snacks, as there is precious little available along this route.

From Beaune's ring road, take N-74 north, following signs to Dijon and then Savigny-lès-Beaune. Entering Savigny, follow the Camping sign to the next intersection. Here, you'll turn right—after a wine-tasting detour 200 yards to the left (direction: Bouilland).

In Savigny-les-Beaune, consider detouring to the winery of **Henri de Villamont** for a tasting (see page 546). Note that this can also be done as you return to Beaune.

Return to the intersection, and follow signs toward Pernand Vergelesses. Turn left at the unsigned T-intersection to join the "main" road, then, after about 30 yards (if you're under 5 tons), take a right and coast down a delightful lane to Aloxe-Corton (you'll see its pointy church spire in the distance). This tiny town, with a world-class reputation among wine enthusiasts, has many tasting opportunities (but no cafés). Within a few steps of the church is the main square (like a small parking lot). The easygoing **Caveau des Vignerons** offers tastings (see page 546).

Back on your bike, leave Aloxe's little square and head up the hill to Pernand Vergelesses, where you can enjoy a well-deserved drink or light meal at the cozy **Happy Bar Luxembourg**. From there, signs lead you back to Beaune. Feel free to dally among the tiny wine lanes off to the right on your return. If you get lost, just keep on pedaling. It's all gorgeous.

For a more rigorous, all-day ride, consider biking (rather than driving) the...

▲**Scenic Vineyard Drive to/from La Rochepot**—Take this lovely, peaceful detour for the best approach to La Rochepot's romantic castle, and to glide through several of Burgundy's most reputed vineyards. Leave Beaune south on N-74 (follow signs for Chalon-sur-Saône) and stay on this major road, passing the famous wine villages of Pommard, Volnay, and Meursault. Turn right onto a tiny road at Puligny-Montrachet (after about 6 miles, you'll see a big sign for Puligny-Montrachet; turn right at the next road, just past the 70 speed limit sign). Take a left at the end of this road, go about two blocks, and turn right at the stop sign.

This will take you to a roundabout with an interesting bronze statue of vineyard workers, and on to **Montrachet's Cave Co-operative** for a wine-tasting (see page 546). From here, follow signs through low-slung vineyards to St. Aubin. A hard right takes you on the N-6 for a short distance; find La Rochepot signs as you bypass St. Aubin. Follow signs for La Rochepot (D-33) over the hills and through the vineyards of the Hautes-Côtes (upper slopes), and you'll come to a dramatic view of the castle (stop mandatory). Turn right when you reach La Rochepot, and follow Le Château signs to the castle (described below).

After visiting the castle, turn right out of its parking lot and drive through Baubigny, Evelles, and rocky Orches. After Orches, climb to the top of Burgundy's world—keeping straight, you'll pass several exceptional lookouts (the village of St. Romain swirls below, and if it's really clear, look for Mont Blanc), then follow signs down to Pommard and Beaune (you'll pass Burgundy's most important wine-barrel-maker, François Frères, in St. Romain; notice the wood slats used for barrel-making).

▲**Château de la Rochepot**—This very Burgundian castle rises above the trees and its village, eight miles from Beaune. It's accessible by car, bike (hilly), or infrequent bus. Cross the drawbridge and knock three times with the ancient knocker to enter. If no one comes, knock harder, or find a log and ram the gate. This pint-size castle is splendid inside and out. Tour half on your own and the other half with a French guide (get the English handout, some tours in English, call ahead, most guides speak some English and can answer questions). Because this castle dates mostly from the 1400s, when gunpowder found its way to Europe, (destroying many medieval castles), it's neither a purely defensive structure (as in the Dordogne) nor a luxury palace (as in the Loire)—it's a little of both.

The furnishings are surprisingly elaborate (some date from the 1700s), given the military look of the exterior. I could sleep well in the Captain's Room, surrounded by nine-foot-thick walls. Don't miss the 15th-century alarmed safe. Notice the colorful doorjamb. These same colors were used to paint many buildings (including castles and churches) and remind us that medieval life didn't consist only of monotonous beige stone. The kitchen will bowl you over; look for the 15th-century walnut high-chair. Climb the tower and see the Chinese room, sing chants in the resonant chapel, and make ripples in the well. (Can you spit a bull's-eye? It's 240 feet down!). Paths outside lead around the castle. Don't leave without driving, walking, or pedaling up D-33 a few hundred yards toward St. Aubin (behind Hôtel Relais du Château) for a romantic view.

To reach the château from Beaune, follow signs for Chalon-sur-Saône from Beaune's ring road, then follow signs to Autun along a lovely 15-minute drive to la Rochepot. Once in the town, turn right a block before the Relais du Château Hôtel to reach the castle (€6, €8.50 if you add tour of exterior offered Sundays at 11:30, private tours in English-€55, call to confirm times, April–June and Sept Wed–Mon 10:00–11:30 & 14:00–17:30, July–Aug Wed–Mon 10:00–18:00, Oct Wed–Mon 10:00–11:30 & 14:00–16:30, closed Tue and Nov–March, tel. 03 80 21 71 37, www.larochepot.com).

Between Beaune and Paris

A Self-Guided Driving Tour

This all-day loop links Châteauneuf-en-Auxois, Semur-en-Auxois, Fontenay, Flavigny, Alise Ste. Reine, and Vézelay. The trip includes vineyards, pastoral landscapes, the Burgundy canal, a Cistercian abbey, Gallic-Roman history, and two medieval villages. (If you're heading to/from Paris, this scenic tour can be done en route or as an overnight stop; accommodations are listed.) It requires a car, Michelin Local map #243, and navigational patience.

Here's your itinerary for a full day in off-the-beaten-path Burgundy. Leave Beaune, following signs for Auxerre and Bligny-sur-Ouche; from Bligny, follow D-33 to Pont d'Ouche (follow signs to Pont du Pany and Dijon), where you'll turn left along the canal, following signs to Château de Châteauneuf. In five minutes, you'll see Châteauneuf-en-Auxois castle looming above (described below). From Châteauneuf, retrace your route to the canal, turn right, and follow Vandenesse (nice picnic spot on its "port," with good views of Châteauneuf), then follow Pouilly-en-Auxois, then Semur-en-Auxois (described below) on D-970. From Semur, follow Montbard, then Fontenay signs to reach the abbey. The abbey is your goal today; allow at least an hour here. With no stops, this one-way drive from Beaune to Fontenay should take about 75 minutes. Return to Beaune along D-905, following signs for Venary les Laumes, and contemplate short detours to Alise Ste. Reine (the "Alésia" battlefield where Caesar defeated the Gauls) and lovely little Flavigny (of *Chocolat* film fame). If you're doing this trip on your way to or from Paris, visit Flavigny and Alise Ste. Reine between Semur-en-Auxois and Fontenay, or skip them. Better yet, sleep in Semur-en-Auxois or Châteauneuf-en-Auxois, and do it all at a sane pace (see below).

Non-drivers can get as far as Semur-en-Auxois by bus (3/day from Montbard or Dijon—early morning, noon, and evening, railpass gets you a free ticket, get ticket at station or at TI in Semur). There are no trains to Semur.

Châteauneuf-en-Auxois

This purely medieval castle, rated ▲, monitored passage between Burgundy and Paris, with hawk's-eye views from its 2,000-foot setting. *Châteauneuf* means "new castle," so you'll see many in France. This one is in the Auxois area, so it's Châteauneuf-en-Auxois (not to be confused with the famous Châteauneuf-du-Pape in Provence). The living hill town, huddling in the shadow of its pit-bull château, merits exploring. Park at the lot in the upper end of the village; don't miss the panoramic viewpoint nearby. The military value of this site is clear from here. Saunter into the village, walk into the courtyard, but skip the château interior (€5, Tue–Sun 10:00–12:00 & 14:00–19:00, closed Mon, get English handout). You'll get better moat views by walking below the castle, passing Hostellerie du Château, and then turning right. You'll find several reasonably priced cafés and restaurants scattered about Châteauneuf.

SLEEPING

For an excellent night's sleep and a great meal, consider **Hostellerie du Château**. This cozy place offers an enticing vacation ensemble: nine comfy, inexpensive rooms with a kid-friendly garden overlooking a brooding castle and a fine restaurant (Db-€47–72 depending on size, plumbing, and view—showers cheaper than baths, extra bed-€10, fine *menus* from €24, tel. 03 80 49 22 00, fax 03 80 49 21 27, www.hostellerie-chateauneuf.com, hdc@hostellerie-chateauneuf.com, family-run by Andre and Florence). Their "Residence" nearby has bigger rooms, but with less character. The **Lady A Barge,** in the canalside village of Vandenesse-en-Auxois, offers tight, cozy rooms on a luxury hotel barge at two-star prices, with views of Châteauneuf's castle. Friendly Lisa cooks an elaborate dinner upon request for €24, including wine (Sb-€45, Db-€55, comes with breakfast, book way ahead in summer, no CC, address: Lady A, Bord du Canal, 21320, Vandenesse-en-Auxois, tel. 03 80 49 26 96, fax 03 80 49 27 00, ladyabarge@yahoo.fr, SE). From the freeway exit in Pouilly-en-Auxois, take D-18 to Vandenesse-en-Auxois to find the canal.

Semur-en-Auxois

If you have time for one more night in Burgundy, spend it here. This happy little town feels real. There are no important sights to digest—just a seductive jumble of Burgundian alleys perched above the meandering Armançon River and behind the town's four massive towers—all beautifully illuminated after dark.

Semur-en-Auxois (suh-moor-ahn-ohx-wah) works well as a base to visit the sights described in this day trip, or as a handy lunch or dinner stop. Semur is also about 45 minutes from the famous church in Vézelay (see page 565) and two hours from Paris, making it an easy first- or last-night stop on your trip. Don't miss the smashing panorama of Semur (best at night) from the viewpoint by the Citroën shop where D-980 and D-954 inter-  sect (see "View over Semur-en-Auxois," page 560).

The helpful **TI** is across from Hôtel Côte d'Or, at Semur's medieval entry (mid-June–Sept Mon–Sat 9:00–19:00, Sun 10:00–12:00 & 15:00–18:00; Oct–mid-June Mon 14:00–17:00, Tue–Sat 9:00–12:00 & 14:00–17:00, closed Sun; 2 place Gaveau, tel. 03 80 97 05 96, www.ville-semur-en-auxois.fr—in French only).

Pick up their city-walking brochure, information on the regional sights, and bike-rental information and suggested routes (hilly terrain). There's an SNCF rail office in the TI where railpass users can get free tickets for the bus to Montbard.

SIGHTS

You can connect the following sights with a short stroll. Begin at the TI, then stop under the Sauvigny gate.

Sauvigny and Guiller Gates—These two impressive gates provided safe entry to Semur in the Middle Ages. If you look up at the 15th-century Sauvigny gate, you can imagine it sliding down to meet a drawbridge that crossed a moat below. The Guiller gate, 100 years older, marked the town's limit in the 1300s.

From here, you enter charming rue Buffon, Semur's oldest commercial street. At the end of this street is the...

Church of Notre-Dame—The town's main sight, the 13th-century Church of Notre-Dame, dominates its small square and is worth a quick look. The same busy man who restored Notre-Dame Cathedral in Paris (and Carcassonne) helped restore this impressive church as well. Wander up the central aisle and notice how perfectly the stained-glass window above Mary's statue is framed by the Gothic arch. Halfway up, you'll notice two contrasting chapels, a Renaissance chapel to your right and a Gothic chapel to your left. Now walk counterclockwise around the ambulatory behind the altar. The first chapel on the right is dedicated to St. Eloi and has unusual stained-glass windows honoring Semur's WWI soldiers. Keep walking, and observe how most capitals are painted, then be dazzled by the colors in the chapel, with Mary draped in rich red. Gothic churches were usually brightly painted, not as you see them today—somber and gray—with the only color provided by stained-glass windows. The beautiful pieces of stained glass around Mary's statue date from the 13th century and are the only originals left. Continue walking around; before leaving the church, take a look at the last chapel on your right. It has a large plaque honoring American soldiers who lost their lives in World War I, and an interesting stained-glass window (Mon–Sat 9:00–12:00 & 14:00–18:30, Sun 14:00–18:30, decent English handout).

Leave with the church to your back and walk down the square, turn left at the bottom on rue du Rempart and see...

Semur's Towers—You'll stand face-to-face with two of Semur's four ominous towers, which were connected by defensive ramparts, encircling the center city in medieval times. Caught in a crossfire between the powerful Dukes of Burgundy and the king of France, Semur's defenses were first destroyed by Louis XI in 1478, then finished off during the wars of religion in 1602. The hilltop setting and river below helped provide a natural defense.

Keep straight for several blocks, and you'll enter a park where Semur's outer defenses once stood. Walk down the road that drops below the walls, turn left at the bottom, and follow the river to lovely views up to Semur. Just after the medieval bridge, look for steps up to your left (rue du Fourneau) to return to the town center.

▲▲**View over Semur-en-Auxois**—Drive or hike downhill from the TI, cross the river, then head uphill and turn left at the top roundabout. Just after the Citroën dealership, you'll find a lookout with an orientation table and a brilliant view of the red roofs, spires, and towers of this medieval city—especially lovely at night. Walkers don't need to go the distance; views are great long before this viewpoint.

SLEEPING

If Semur seduces you into spending a night, do so at **Hôtel les Cymaises**** where you get three-star comfort for the price of two, with comfortable rooms and big beds in a manor house with a quiet courtyard (Db-€59, Tb-€70, two-room Qb-€89–100, 7 rue du Renaudot, private parking, tel. 03 80 97 21 44, fax 03 80 97 18 23, www.hotelcymaises.com, hotel.cymaises@libertysurf.fr).

$ Hôtel des Gourmets*, a simple little place tucked below the main pedestrian street, is good for those on a tight budget (D-€26, Db-€41, T/Q-€32, 5- to 6-person room-€58, extra bed-€5, traditional menus from €14, 4 rue Varenne, tel. 03 80 97 09 41, fax 03 80 97 17 95).

EATING

Enjoy a fun lunch or dinner at **Le Calibressan**, a cozy Franco-American-owned restaurant serving zesty French cuisine with a dash of California. Say hello to friendly Jill (*menus* from €19, cool salad bar, closed Sun–Mon, 16 rue Fevret, tel. 03 80 97 32 40). **L'Entracte** is where everybody goes for pizza, pasta, salads, and more in a relaxed atmosphere (daily, below the church on 4 rue Fevret). The historic *charcuterie* (delicatessen) across from the church can supply your picnic needs.

Abbey of Fontenay

The entire ensemble of buildings making up this isolated Cistercian abbey, rated ▲▲, has survived, giving visitors perhaps the best picture of medieval abbey life in France. In the Middle Ages, it was written, "To fully grasp the meaning of Fontenay and the power of its beauty, you must approach it trudging through the forest footpaths...through the brambles and bogs...in an October rain." But even if you use the parking lot, Fontenay's secluded setting, blanketed in bird song with a garden lovingly used "as a stage set," is truly magical.

This abbey—one of the oldest Cistercian abbeys in France—was founded in 1118 by St. Bernard as a back-to-basics reaction to the excesses of Benedictine abbeys, such as Cluny. The Cistercians worked to recapture the simplicity, solitude, and poverty of the early Church.

Bernard created "a horrible vast solitude" in the forest, where his monks could live like the desert fathers of the Old Testament. They chose marshland ("Cistercian" is derived from "marshy bogs") and strove to be separate from the world (which required the industrious self-sufficiency these abbeys were so adept at). The movement spread, essentially colonizing Europe religiously. In 1200, there were over 500 such monasteries and abbeys in Europe.

Like the Cistercian movement in general, Fontenay flourished through the 13th to 15th centuries. A 14th-century proverb said, "Wherever the wind blows, to Fontenay money flows." Fontenay thrived as a prosperous "mini-city" for nearly 700 years, until the French Revolution, when it became property of the nation and was eventually sold.

Like visitors centuries ago, you'll enter through the abbey's **gatehouse**. The main difference: Anyone with a ticket gets in, and there's no watchdog barking angrily at you (through the small hole on the right). Pick up the English self-guided tour flier with your ticket. Your visit follows the route below (generally clockwise). Arrows keep you on course, and signs tell you which sections of the abbey are private (as its owners still live here).

The **abbey church** is pure Romanesque and built to St. Bernard's specs: Latin cross plan, no fancy stained glass, unadorned columns, nothing to distract from prayer. The lone statue is the 13th-century *Virgin of Fontenay*, a reminder that the church was dedicated to St. Mary. Enjoy the ethereal light. You can almost hear the brothers chanting.

Stairs lead from the front of the church to a vast (16th century) oak-beamed **dormitory** where the monks slept—together, fully dressed, on thin mats. Monastic life was extremely simple: prayer, reading, work, seven services a day, one meal in the winter, two in the summer. Daily rations: a loaf of bread and a quarter liter of wine.

Back down the stairs, you enter the **cloister,** beautiful in its starkness. This was the heart of the community, where monks read, exercised, washed, did small projects—and, I imagine, gave each other those unique haircuts. The shallow alcove (next to church door) once stored prayer books; notice the slots for shelves. Next to that, the chapter room was where the abbot led discussions and community business was discussed. The adjacent monks' hall was a general purpose room, likely busy with monks hunched over tables copying sacred texts (a major work of abbeys). The dining hall, or refectory, also faced the cloister (closed to the public).

Across the peaceful garden stands the huge abbey **forge**. In the 13th century, the monks at Fontenay ran what many consider Europe's first metalworking plant. Iron ore was melted down in ovens with big bellows. Tools were made and sold for a profit. The hydraulic hammer—which became the basis of industrial manufacturing of iron throughout Europe—was first used here. Leaving the building, walk left around the back to see the stream, which was diverted to power the wheels that operated the forge.

Water was vital to abbey life. The pond—originally practical, rather than decorative—was a fish farm (some whoppers survive to this day).

Leave through the gift shop, which was the public chapel in the days when visitors were not allowed inside the abbey grounds (€8.50, daily 10:00–18:00, 20-min drive from Semur via Montbard, no bus, taxi from Montbard-€12, tel. 03 80 92 15 00).

Flavigny-sur-Ozerain

Ten minutes from Semur and five minutes from Alise Ste. Reine, little Flavigny has taken the excitement of its *Chocolat*-covered Hollywood image in stride. This unassuming and serenely situated village feels permanently stuck in the past, with one café, one *crêperie*, and two boutiques. There's little to do here other than appreciate the setting (best from the grassy ramparts). Pick up a map at the **TI** and try the little *anis* (anise) candies (April–Sept 10:00–12:30 & 13:00–19:30, Oct and March daily 10:00–12:30 & 13:00–18:00, closed Nov–Feb, down rue de l'Église in front of church).

Chocolat-lovers will have to be satisfied with a few of the building facades featured in the film; there are no souvenirs or posters to be found, and nary a chocolate shop (locals weren't thrilled with the movie). There are four buildings most should recognize—the most important is the *chocolaterie* (chocolate shop); it's across the square from the church entry, just past La Grange on rue du Four (look for the arched window). The Count's home is today's *Mairie* (City Hall), also opposite the church entry, but to the left as you leave the church. The *coiffure* (hair dresser) is one door down from the TI; look for the white shutters. And what was the Café de la République is three doors up from the TI with an austere facade. Johnny Depp never visited Flavigny, and there is no river here (the river scene was filmed in the Dordogne, near Beynac).

Elsewhere in Flavigny, you can buy the locally produced *anis* candies in pretty tins (great for souvenirs, see them being made 8:30–11:00 Mon–Fri in the Abbey of St. Pierre). You can also visit the ancient Church of St. Genest (14:00–17:45; if closed, ask the town hall next door to open it). The grassy ramparts are worth a stroll for the view (behind the church down rue de la Poterne and out the gate).

SLEEPING AND EATING

L'Ange Souriant Chambre d'Hôte is comfortable and intimate (Sb-€50, Db-€55, Tb-€90, tel. & fax 03 80 96 24 93, www.ange-souriant.com, SE). **Le Relais de Flavigny**, next door, is an appealing little restaurant with seven basic, bargain rental rooms above (S/D-€28, Ss/Ds-€33, *menus* from €13, €10 hearty summertime lunch salads, daily, at bottom of rue de l'Église from church, tel. 03 80 96 27 77, www.le-relais.fr). **La Grange** (the barn) serves farm-fresh fare, including luscious quiche, salad, fresh cheeses, *pâtés*, and fruit pies (July–mid-Sept daily 12:30–16:00, rest of year Sun only, across from church, look for brown doors and listen for lunchtime dining, tel. 03 80 35 81 78).

TRANSPORTATION CONNECTIONS

To reach Flavigny, leave Semur following Venary les Laumes, and look for the turnoff to Flavigny (at the village of Pouillenay). The approach to Flavigny from Pouillenay via D-9 is picture-perfect. Park at the gate or in the lot just below. From this lot, signs lead to Alise Ste. Reine, described below (great views back to Flavigny as you leave).

Alise Ste. Reine

> *"A united Gaul forming a single nation animated by the same spirit could defy the universe."*
>
> —Julius Caesar, *The Gallic Wars*

A five-minute drive from Venary les Laumes, above the vertical little village of Alise Ste. Reine, is where historians think Julius Caesar defeated the Gallic leader Vercingétorix in 52 B.C., thus winning Gaul for the Roman Empire and forever changing France's destiny.

Follow signs to Statue de Vercingétorix, up through the village to the very top, to the park with the huge statue of the Gallic warrior overlooking his Waterloo. Stand as he did, and imagine yourself trapped on this hilltop (see "The Dying Gauls" sidebar, next page).

The Dying Gauls

In 52 B.C., General Julius Caesar and his 60,000 soldiers surrounded Alésia (today's Alise Ste. Reine), hoping to finally end the uprising of free Gaul and establish Roman civilization in France. Holed up inside the hilltop fortress were 80,000 die-hard (long-haired, tattooed) Gauls under their rebel chief, Vercingétorix (pronounced something like "verse in Genesis"). Having harassed Caesar for months with guerrilla-war attacks, they now called on their fellow Gauls to converge on Alésia to wipe out the Romans.

Rather than attack the fierce-fighting Gauls, Caesar's soldiers patiently camped at the base of the hill and began building a wall. In six weeks, they completed a 12-foot-tall stone wall all the way around Alésia (11 miles around), and then a second larger one (13 miles around), trapping the rebel leaders and hoping to starve them out. If the Gauls tried to escape, not only would they have to breach the two walls, they'd first have to cross a steep no-man's-land dotted with a ditch, a moat, and booby traps (like sharp stakes in pits and buried iron spikes).

The starving Gauls inside Alésia sent their women and children out to beg mercy from the Romans. The Romans (with little food themselves) refused. For days, the women and children wandered the unoccupied land, in full view of both armies, until they starved to death.

After months of siege, Vercingétorix's reinforcements finally came riding to save him. With 90,000 screaming Gallic warriors (Caesar says 250,000) converging on Alésia, and 80,000 more atop the hill, Caesar ordered his men to move between the two walls to fight a two-front battle. The Battle of Alésia raged for five days—a classic struggle between the methodical Romans and the impetuous "barbarians." When it became clear the Romans would not budge, the Gauls retreated.

Vercingétorix surrendered, and Gallic culture was finished in France. During the three-year rebellion, one in five Gauls had been killed, enslaved, or driven out. Roman rule was established for the next 500 years, strangling the Gallic/Celtic heritage. Vercingétorix spent his last years as a prisoner, paraded around as a war trophy. In 46 B.C., he was brought to Rome for Caesar's triumphal ascension to power, where he was strangled to death in a public ritual.

Vézelay

For over seven centuries, pilgrims have overrun this hill town to get to its famous church, the Basilica of Ste. Madeleine (rated ▲ for travelers). One of Europe's largest and best-preserved Romanesque churches, it was built to honor its famous relics—the bones of Mary Magdalene, who had been possessed by the devil and then saved.

The basilica's appeal lies in its simplicity, and in the play of light on the pleasing patterns of stones. Notice the absence of distracting decoration and bright colors. To appreciate this austerity, compare this church to another of the same era, Paris' Notre-Dame Cathedral. The effect when you enter the basilica's interior is mesmerizing. The tympanum (semicircular area over the door) and capitals provide what decoration there is through astonishing sculptures. These tell Bible stories in much the same way stained-glass windows do in Gothic churches. Notice how unappealing the newer Gothic apse feels in comparison to the older Romanesque nave. Buy the well-done €5 booklet inside the church (free entry, daily 8:00–19:30). Occasional one-hour English guided **tours** depart from inside the basilica (€3 donation requested, call to get times or to arrange a private tour, tel. 03 86 33 39 50). The view from the park behind the church is sublime.

Vézelay's **TI** is near the church (rue St. Pierre, tel. 03 86 33 23 69). The **Auberge de la Coquille** is a cozy place to eat, with reasonably priced salads, crêpes, and full-course *menus* (daily, halfway up to the church at 81 rue St. Pierre, tel. 03 86 33 35 57).

TRANSPORTATION CONNECTIONS

Vézelay is about 45 minutes northwest of Semur (20 min off the autoroute to Paris). Train travelers go to Avallon and catch the lone bus per day (20 min) that leaves you all day in Vézelay (free with railpass); consider a taxi back (allow €20 one-way, tel. 03 86 32 31 88). More buses run from Montbard's train station, but it's an hour-long trip. Call the Vézelay TI to confirm.

Between Burgundy and Lyon

To connect these towns scenically from Beaune, follow N-74 south to Chagny (Burgundy's ugliest town), find Remigny and follow D-109 to Aluze, then follow D-978 east and D-981 south through Givry, Buxy, and on to Chapaize.

Brancion and Chapaize

An hour south of Beaune by car (12 miles west of Tournus on D-14) are two tiny villages, each with "daughters of Cluny"—churches that owe their existence and architectural design to the nearby and once powerful Cluny Abbey.

Brancion

This is a classic feudal village. Back when there were no nations in Europe, control of land was delegated from lord to vassal. The Duke of Burgundy ruled here through his vassal, the Lord of Brancion. His vast domain—much of south Burgundy—was administered from this tiny fortified town.

Within its walls, the feudal lord had a castle, church, and all the necessary administrative buildings to provide justice, collect taxes, and so on. Perched strategically on a hill between two river valleys, he enjoyed a commanding view of his domain. Brancion's population peaked centuries ago at 60. Today, it's home to only four people...and on its way to becoming a museum town.

The castle, part of a network of 17 castles in the region, was destroyed in 1576 by Protestant Huguenots. After the French Revolution, it was sold to be used as a quarry and spent most of the 19th century being picked apart. While the flier gives a brief tour, the castle is most enjoyable for its evocative angles and the lush views from the top of its keep (€3.50, daily 9:00–18:00).

Wandering from the castle to the church, you'll pass the 15th-century market hall (used by farmers from the surrounding country-side until 1900) and a few other buildings from that period.

The 12th-century church (with faint paintings surviving from 1330) is Romanesque at its pure, unadulterated, fortress-of-God best (thick walls, small windows, once colorfully painted interior, no-frills exterior). From its front door, enjoy a lord's view over one glorious Burgundian estate.

Brancion has one place to eat and sleep: **Auberge du Vieux Brancion** offers traditional Burgundian cooking (lunch *menu*-€12, dinner *menu*-€19) and a perfectly tranquil place to spend the night (simple, frumpy, but cozy rooms, Ds-€37, Db-€56, family rooms-€55–72, tel. & fax 03 85 51 03 83, www.brancion.fr—in French only, friendly owner François SE).

Chapaize

This hamlet, a few miles closer to Beaune, grew up around its Benedictine monastery—only its 11th-century church survives. It's a pristine place (cars park at the edge of town) with a ghost-town café and rustic decay, surrounded by grassy fields. (Nearby Stonehenge-age *menhirs* are evidence that this was sacred ground long before Christianity.) In its classic Romanesque church, study the fine stonework by Lombard masons. (Its lean seems designed to challenge the faith of parishioners.) The WWI monument near the entry—with so many names from such a tiny hamlet—is a reminder that half of all young French men were casualties in the war that *didn't* end all wars. Wander around the back for a view of the belfry and then ponder Chapaize across the street over a *café au lait*.

Cluny

The delightful little town that grew up around the abbey maintains its street plan, with plenty of its original buildings, and even the same population it had in its 12th-century heyday (4,500). Wandering the town, which claims to be the finest surviving Romanesque town in France, enjoy the architectural details on everyday buildings. Much of the town's fortified walls, gates, and towers survive.

Everything of interest is within a few minutes walk of the **TI**. Drivers can follow signs to the TI and park there (pick up the fine "practical guide," daily 10:00–12:30 & 14:00–18:45, 6 rue Mercière, tel. 03 85 59 05 34). The TI is at the base of the "Cheese Tower," so named because it was used to age cheese (or perhaps for the way tourists smell after climbing to the top). The tower offers a fine city view (€1.25, same hours as TI).

A **farmers market** enlivens the old town each Saturday.

Bus connections are meager (3/day, from Chalons-sur-Saône in 75 min, 3/day from Macon in 50 min). There's no train station.

SIGHTS

Museum of Art and Archaeology (Musée Ochier)—The abbey museum fills the palace of the abbot with bits from medieval Cluny and models of the abbey (same cost and hours as abbey). As the abbey is so ruined, a visit here is essential in understanding the site and its former magnificence. Visit this before you explore the ruins.
Site of Cluny Abbey—Much of today's old town stands on the site of what was the largest church in Christendom. It was 555 feet long, with five naves. The whole complex (church plus monastery) covered 25 acres. Revolutionaries destroyed it in 1790. It was later sold and used as a quarry through the 19th century. Today, only the tower and part of the transept still stand. The visitor's challenge: Visualize it. Get a sense of its grandeur. From Hôtel Bourgogne (abbey models in hotel lobby), the scant remains of a transept stretch toward the city museum. The National Stud Farm and a big school

History of Cluny and its (Scant) Abbey

In 1964, St. Benedict (480–547), founder of the first monastery (Montecassino, south of Rome) from which a great monastic movement sprang, was named the patron saint of Europe. Christians and non-Christians alike recognize the impact that monasteries had in establishing a European civilization out of the dark chaos that followed the fall of Rome.

The Abbey of Cluny was the ruling center of the first great international franchise, or chain, of monasteries in Europe. It was the heart of an upsurge in monasticism, of church reform, and an evangelical revival that spread throughout Europe—a phenomenon historians call the Age of Faith (11th and 12th centuries). From this springboard came a vast network of abbeys, priories, and other monastic orders that kindled the establishment of modern Europe.

In 910, 12 monks founded a house of prayer at Cluny, vowing to follow the rules of St. Benedict. The cult of saints and relics was enthusiastically promoted. The order was independent and powerful. From the start, the Abbot of Cluny answered only to the pope (not to the local bishop or secular leader). The abbots of the other Cluniac monasteries were answerable only to the Abbot of Cluny (not to their local bishop or prince). This made the Abbot of Cluny arguably the most powerful person in Europe.

Guides at Cluny attribute the abbey's success to several factors. Most importantly, Cluny was blessed by a series of wise and long-lived abbots who managed to keep out of the costly Crusades that seduced so much of Europe into exciting but futile adventures in the Holy Land. (They believed that, by praising God in a glorious monastic setting, they could reach a "celestial Jerusalem" without even leaving home.) These Benedictines managed to get Europe's warrior class to respect the life and property of noncombatants (monks and clergy). They convinced Europe's noble class—its great landowners—to will their estates to the order in return for perpetual prayers for the benefit of their needy and frightened souls.

From all this grew the greatest monastic movement of the High Middle Ages. A huge church was built at Cluny, where in 1100, it was the headquarters of 10,000 monks who ran nearly a thousand monasteries and priories across Europe. Cluny peaked in the 12th century, then faded in influence (though monasteries continued to increase in numbers and remain a force until 1789).

obliterate much of the floor plan of the abbey. You can tour what little still stands (€6.10, May–Aug daily 9:30–18:30, Sept–April daily 9:30–12:00 & 13:30–17:00, tel. 03 85 59 12 79).

National Stud Farm (Les Haras Nationaux)—Napoleon (who needed *beaucoup de* horses for his army of 600,000) established this horse farm in 1806. You're free to wander among the 19th-century stables—home to 50 thoroughbred stallions. Horses kill time in their stables. If the stalls are empty, they're out doing their current studly duty...creating fine race horses. The gate is next to Hôtel Bourgogne, two blocks from the TI (free, daily 9:00–19:00, pick up free English flier at gate).

SLEEPING

If you're spending the night, consider the comfortable **Hôtel Bourgogne***, which is built into the wall of the abbey's right transept and as central as can be for enjoying the town (Db-87–118, place de l'Abbaye, tel. 03 85 59 00 58, fax 03 85 59 03 73, contact@hotel -cluny.com). It also has a fine restaurant (*menus* from €22).

Taizé

To experience the latest in European monasticism, consider visiting the booming Christian community of Taizé (teh-zay), a few miles north of Cluny. The normal, un-cultlike ambience of this place— with thousands of mostly young, European pilgrims asking each other, "How's your soul today?"—is remarkable.

Brother Roger and his community welcome visitors who'd like to spend a few days getting close to God through meditation, singing, and simple living. While designed primarily for youthful pilgrims in meditative retreat (there are around 5,000 here in a typical week), people of any age are welcome to pop in for a meal or church service.

Taizé is an ecumenical movement—prayer, silence, simplicity— welcoming Protestant as well as Catholic Christians. While it feels Catholic, it isn't. (But, as some of the brothers are actually Catholic priests, Catholics may take the Eucharist.) The Taizé style of worship is well-known among American Christians for its hauntingly beautiful chants. (Songbooks and CDs are the most popular souvenirs.)

Three times a day, the bells ring and worshipers file into the long, low, simple, and modern Church of Reconciliation. It's dim— candlelit with glowing icons—as the white-robed brothers enter. The service features responsive singing of chants (from well-worn songbooks listing lyrics in 19 languages), reading of Bible passages, and silence, as worshipers on crude kneelers stare into icons. The aim: "Entering together into the mystery of God's presence." (Secondary aim: Helping Lutherans get over their fear of icons.)

Drivers follow signs to *La Communauté* and park in a huge lot. Buses serve Taizé from Chalons-sur-Saône to the north and from Macon to the south (3/day, 60 min from each).

The welcome office provides an orientation and daily schedule. Time your visit for a church service (Mon–Sat 8:30, 12:20, and 20:30; Sun 10:00 and 20:30). The Exposition (next to the church) is the thriving community shop, with books, CDs, music, handicrafts, and other souvenirs. The Oyak (near the parking lot) is where those in a less monastic mood can get a beer or burger.

Those on retreat fill their days with worship services, work-shops, simple, relaxed meals, and hanging out in an international festival of people searching for meaning in their lives. Visitors are welcomed free. The cost for a real stay is €10 to €20 per day (based on a sliding scale) for monastic-style room and board. Adults (those over 30) are accommodated in a more comfortable zone, but count on simple dorms. Call or e-mail first if you plan to stay overnight. The Web site explains everything—in 26 languages (Taizé Community, tel. 03 85 50 14 14, www.taize.fr).

Beaujolais Wine Country

Just south of Cluny and north of Lyon, the beautiful vineyards and villages of the Beaujolais (relaxed wine-tastings) make a pleasant detour for drivers. The most scenic and interesting section lies between Mâcon and Villefranche-sur-Saône, a few minutes west of A-6 on D-68. The route runs from the Mâconnais wine region and the famous village of Pouilly-Fuissé, south through Beaujolais' most important villages: Chiroubles, Fleurie, and Juliénas. Look for *Route de Beaujolais* signs, and expect to get lost a few times.

For a pricey but thorough introduction to this region's wines, visit **Hameau du Vin** in Romanèche-Thorins. The king of Beaujolais, Georges DuBœuf, has constructed the perfect introduc-tion to wine at his wine museum, which immerses you into the life of a winemaker and features impressive models, exhibits, films, and videos. You'll be escorted from the beginning of the vine to present-day winemaking, with a focus on Beaujolais wines (€13, includes small tasting and free English headphones, June–Sept daily 9:00–18:00, Oct–May daily 10:00–17:00; in Romanèche-Thorins, look for signs to Hameau du Vin, then *La Gare*, and look for the old train-station-turned-winery; tel. 03 85 35 22 22).

Lyon's TI has information on **afternoon bus excursions** to the Beaujolais (about €35, includes tastings).

Lyon

Straddling the Rhône and Saône Rivers between Burgundy and Provence, Lyon has been among France's leading cities since Roman times. Today, overlooked Lyon is one of France's big-city surprises. In spite of its work-a-day, business-first facade, Lyon is the most historic and culturally important city in France after Paris. Visitors experience two distinctly different-feeling cities: the Old World cobbled alleys, Renaissance mansions, and colorful facades of Vieux Lyon; and the more staid but classy, Parisian-feeling shopping streets of Presqu'île. Once you're settled, this big city feels small, welcoming, and surprisingly untouristy. It seems everyone's enjoying the place—and they're all French.

ORIENTATION

Although it's France's second-largest metropolitan area, Lyon feels peaceful and manageable. Traffic noise is replaced by pedestrian friendliness in the old center. Sightseeing can be done on foot from any of the hotels I list. Nearly all the recommended sights are described in an easy walking tour route. Lyon provides the organized sightseer with a fine, full day of activities.

Lyon's sights are concentrated in three areas: Fourvière Hill, with its white Basilique Notre-Dame glimmering over the city; historic Vieux Lyon, below on the bank of the Saône River; and the Presqu'île (home to recommended hotels), across the Saône. Huge place Bellecour lies in the middle of the Presqu'île.

Planning Your Time

Lyon makes a handy day visit for train travelers, as many trains pass through Lyon, and both stations have baggage check and easy connections to the city center. But those who spend the night can experience the most renowned cuisine in France at pleasing prices.

For a full day of sightseeing: Start on Fourvière Hill (to get here, take the funicular near St. Jean Cathedral in Vieux Lyon), visit the Notre-Dame Basilica, tour the Gallo-Roman Museum, Roman Theaters, and catch the funicular back down to Vieux Lyon. Have lunch in Vieux Lyon and explore the old town and its hidden passageways. Finish your day touring the Museum of Fine Arts, Resistance Center, and early film museum. Many of Lyon's important sights are closed on Mondays or Tuesdays, or both. Dine well in the evening, and cap your day enjoying a stroll through the best-lit city in France.

Drivers connecting Lyon with southern destinations should consider the scenic detour via the Ardèche Gorges (see Lyon's "Transportation Connections," page 585), and those connecting to Burgundy should consider the Beaujolais wine route, then visiting Brancion and Cluny (see page 565).

Tourist Information

The well-equipped TI is generous with helpful, free information (Mon–Sat 9:00–18:00, until 19:00 mid-April–mid-Oct, Sun 10:00–18:00, tel. 04 72 77 69 69, www.lyon-france.com, corner of place Bellecour). Pick up the English version of the city map (with museum information, a good enlargement of central Lyon, and all public parking lots); the map of Vieux Lyon; an event schedule (ask about concerts in the Roman Theater and events at the Opera House); and the *Enjoy Lyon City Guide* (with a directory of shopping and eateries, as well as articles on special aspects of the city).

The TI sells a useful **Lyon City Card** for serious sightseers (1 day-€18, 2 days-€28, 3 days-€38, under 18-half price). This pass includes all Lyon museums, a day pass for the Métro/bus system, a walking tour of Lyon with a live guide or audioguide, and a river cruise. If you plan to visit the Gallo-Roman Museum and the Resistance and Deportation History Center, plus take a guided walking tour, the one-day pass will pay for itself.

The TI's handy **audioguide** (€8/half day) offers good, self-guided walking tours of Vieux Lyon. Live **guided walks** are offered most days at 14:30 (€9, 2 hrs, English/French language, depart from next to St. Jean Métro/funicular station, no need to reserve—just show up, generally 5 days a week, verify times with TI). The well-done *World Heritage Excursions* **guidebook**, sold for €6 at the TI, describes interesting self-guided walking tours (Vieux Lyon and Presqu'île North walks are best).

Arrival in Lyon

By Train: Two train stations serve Lyon—Perrache and Part-Dieu. Many trains stop at both, and through trains connect the two stations every 10 minutes. Both have baggage-check services and are well-served by Métro, bus, and taxi.

The **Perrache station** is more central and within a 20-minute walk of place Bellecour (follow signs to Porte/Place Carnot, then cross place Carnot and walk straight up pedestrian rue Victor Hugo). Or take the Métro (direction: Laurent Bonnevay) two stops to Bellecour and follow *Sortie rue République* signs. The Resistance Center is one stop away from the Perrache station on the T-2 tramway; the stop is below the train station (see "Getting Around Lyon," below, for Métro and tramway tips).

To get to the city center from the **Part-Dieu station,** follow

Sortie Vivier Merle signs outside the station to the Métro. Take it toward Stade de Gerland, transfer at Saxe-Gambetta to the Gare de Vaise route, get off at Bellecour, and follow signs for Sortie rue *République* (see "Getting Around Lyon," below, for Métro help).

Figure about €12 for a **taxi** from either train station to the hotels listed near place Bellecour.

By Car: The city center is fairly easy to navigate, though you'll encounter traffic on the surrounding freeways. To get to the center from the freeways, follow *Centre-Ville* and *Presqu'île* signs, and then follow *place Bellecour* signs. Park in the lots under place Bellecour or place des Celestins (yellow P means "parking lot") or get advice from your hotel. The TI's map identifies all public car parks. Overnight parking (generally 19:00–8:00) is only €3, but day rates are €1.50 per hour. Take everything out of your car.

By Plane: Lyon's sleek little airport, Saint-Exupéry, is a breeze (tel. 08 26 80 08 26, www.lyon.aeroport.fr). It's served by most major European cities, has two flights per hour to Paris' Charles de Gaulle airport, and has a TGV station (12 trains/day from downtown Paris, 2 hrs). Three shuttles *(navettes)* per hour run make the 40-minute trip from the airport to both Lyon train stations for €9 (tel. 04 72 68 72 17). Allow €45 for a taxi.

Helpful Hints

Consulates: The **U.S. Consulate** is at 16 rue de la République (World Trade Center, tel. 04 78 38 33 03), and the **Canadian Consulate** is at 21 rue Bourgelat (tel. 04 72 77 64 07).

Market Days: A colorful produce market stretches along the Saône River between pont Bonaparte and passerelle du Palais de Justice (Tue–Sat until 12:30).

Internet Access: Connectik offers access with a café-lounge atmosphere near place des Celestins. Friendly owners Patrick and Françoise are tuned into numeric art (Mon–Sat 10:00–19:00, closed Sun, 19 quai St. Antoine, tel. 04 72 77 98 85).

Laundry: A launderette is at 7 rue Mercière on the Presqu'île near the Alphonse Juin bridge (daily 6:00–21:00); another is a few steps off the pedestrian street, rue Victor Hugo (daily 7:30–20:30, 19 rue Ste. Helene, between place Bellecour and the Perrache station).

SNCF Train Office: The **SNCF Boutique,** at 2 place Bellecour, is handy for train info, reservations, and tickets (9:00–18:00, closed Sun).

Children's Activities: The Park de la Tete d'Or is vast, with rental rowboats, a miniature golf course, and ponies to ride (across Rhône River from Croix Rousse neighborhood, Métro Massena, tel. 04 72 69 47 60).

Getting Around Lyon

Lyon has a user-friendly public transit system, with two flashy street-car lines (tramways T-1 and T-2), four underground Métro lines (A, B, C, and D), an extensive bus system, and two funiculars. The subway is similar to Paris' Métro in many ways (e.g., routes are signed by *direction* for the last stop on the line), but highly automated, cleaner, and less crowded. There are no turnstiles, no obvious ticket windows, and plenty of coin-op ticket machines (€1.40, 10 rides-€11.20, one day-€4.00, funicular round-trip-€2.80). Buy your ticket (use the black roller to *selectionnez* your ticket, firmly push top button twice to *confirmez* your request, and then insert coins or Visa card). If using the Métro, validate your ticket by punching it in a nearby chrome machine (tramway users validate on the trams). Study the wall maps to be sure of your *direction*; ask a local if you're not certain. Yellow signs are directional, green signs lead to exits. Your ticket is good for one hour of travel, including transfers between Métro, tramways, buses, and funiculars.

SIGHTS

Orientation from Bonaparte Bridge—From this central bridge, spin clockwise, starting by facing the golden statue of the Virgin Mary marking the Notre-Dame Basilica of Fourvière on Fourvière Hill. (It's actually capping the smaller chapel, which predates the church by 500 years.) The basilica is named for the Roman Forum (Fourvière) upon which it sits.

The Metallic Tower (called La Tour Metallique—not La Tour Eiffel), like the basilica, was finished just before World War I. It was originally an observation tower, but today functions only as a TV tower. The church on the riverbank below (St. Jean Cathedral) marks the center of the old town, Vieux Lyon. Upstream, the neoclassical columns mark the Court of Justice (where Klaus Barbie, head of the local Gestapo—a.k.a. "the Butcher of Lyon"—was sentenced to life in prison in the 1980s). Beyond the courthouse, the hill covered with tall, pastel-colored houses is the Croix-Rousse district. The city's silk industry was huge. With the invention of the "Jacquard looms," which required 12-foot-tall ceilings, new factory buildings were needed. The new weaving center grew up on this hill. In 1850, it was thriving, with 30,000 looms. The other side of the river is the district of Presqu'île (literally, "Almost Island"). The peninsula created by the Saône and Rhône rivers coming together is home to Lyon's opera house, city hall, theater, top-end shopping, banks, and all of our recommended hotels. A morning produce market sets up under the trees along the river (just beyond the red bridge, Tue–Sun). Lyon's bridges—including the one you're standing on—were destroyed by the Nazis as they checked out in 1944. Looking

Lyon

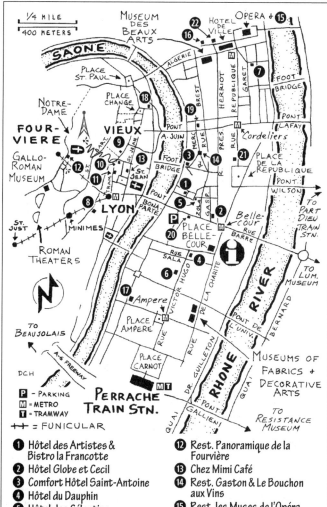

1. Hôtel des Artistes & Bistro la Francotte
2. Hôtel Globe et Cecil
3. Comfort Hôtel Saint-Antoine
4. Hôtel du Dauphin
5. Hôtel des Célestins
6. Hôtel la Residence
7. Hôtel Iris
8. Youth Hostel
9. Rest. les Adrets & les Retrouvailles
10. Restaurant les Lyonnais
11. Restaurant la Machonnerie
12. Rest. Panoramique de la Fourvière
13. Chez Mimi Café
14. Rest. Gaston & Le Bouchon aux Vins
15. Rest. les Muses de l'Opéra
16. Rest. l'Etage
17. Rest. Chez Abel
18. Nardone René Glacier
19. Launderette
20. SNCF Ticket Boutique
21. U.S. Consulate
22. Silk Workshop

downstream, see the stately mansions of Lyon's well-established families. Across the river again, the neo-Gothic St. Georges Church marks the neighborhood of the first silk weavers. The ridge—dominated by a big building—once a seminary for priests, now a state high school—leads back to Mary (see next two listings, below).

If you walk across the bridge and over two blocks, you'll reach the funicular station, where you can ride up to Fourvière Hill to the basilica (catch the train marked Fourvière, not St. Just). From there, you can tour the basilica, enjoy the city view, visit the Roman Theaters and Gallo-Roman Museum, catch another funicular back down, and explore the old town (Vieux Lyon) between the cathedral and the place du Change. From the square it's a short walk back over the river to place des Terreaux (City Hall and Museum of Fine Arts). Note: Lyon's walking tours leave from in front of this funicular station (most days at 14:30, see "Tourist Information," above).

Illuminated Lyon—The statue of Mary was placed atop the Notre-Dame Basilica on December 8, 1852. Spontaneously, the entire city welcomed her with candles in their windows. Each December 8 since, the city glows softly with countless candles. This tradition has spawned an actual industry. Lyon is famous as a model of state-of-the-art floodlighting, and the city hosts conventions on the topic. Each night, over 200 buildings, sites, and public spaces are gloriously floodlit. Paris calls itself the City of Light—but actually, it's Lyon.

Fourvière Hill

Notre-Dame Basilica (Basilique Notre-Dame de Fourvière)—In about 1870, the bishop of Lyon vowed to build a magnificent tribute to the Virgin Mary if the Prussians spared his city (similar deal-making led to the construction of the basilica of Sacré-Cœur in Paris). Building began in 1872, and the church was ready for worship by World War I (daily 6:00–19:00).

Before entering, step back to view the fancy facade, the older chapel on the right (supporting the statue of Mary), and the Eiffel-like TV tower on the left.

You won't find a more Mary-centered church. Inside, everything—floor, walls, ceiling—is covered with fine mosaics. Scenes glittering on the walls tell stories of the Virgin (in Church history on the left, in French history on the right):

First scene on the left: In 431, the Council of Ephesus declared Mary to be the "Mother of God."

Across the nave, first on the right: The artist imagines Lugdunum (Lyon)—the biggest city in Roman Gaul, with 50,000 inhabitants—as the first Christian missionaries arrive. The first Christian martyrs in France (killed in A.D. 177) dance across heaven with the their traditional palm branches.

Next left: In 1571, at the pivotal sea battle of Lepanto, Mary provides the necessary miracle as the outnumbered Christian forces beat those nasty Turks.

Opposite: Joan of Arc hears messages from Mary, rallies the French against the English, and is ultimately burned at the stake.

On the left: Pope Pius I proclaims the dogma of the Immaculate Conception in 1854 (establishing the belief among Catholics that Mary was born without the "Original Sin" of apple-eating Adam and Eve).

Finally, on the right: Louis XIII offers the crown of France to the Virgin Mary (the empty cradle hints that while he had her on the line, he asked, "Could I please have a son?"—and Louis the XIV was born shortly after that). Above marches a parade of pious French kings, from Clovis and Charlemagne to Napoleon (on the far right—with the white cross and red coat). Below are the great Marian churches of France (left to right)—Chartres, Paris' Sacré-Cœur and Notre-Dame, Reims (where most royalty was crowned), and this church. These six scenes all lead to the altar, where Mary reigns as Queen of Heaven.

Exit under the statue of Joan of Arc and descend to the lower church, dedicated to Mary's earthly husband, Joseph. Priorities here are painfully clear,as money ran out on Joseph's church. Today, it's used as a concert venue (notice the spongy-yellow acoustic material covering the vaulting). Leaving on this side of the basilica, and find the humble 16th-century chapel to the Virgin; look up to see the glorious statue of Mary that overlooks Lyon.

Just around this chapel (past the church museum and the recommended Panoramique Restaurant, see "Eating," below) is a terrace with the best view of Lyon. You can see from the Croix-Rousse district to the Bonaparte Bridge, with greater Lyon (1.3 million people) sprawling in the distance. On a clear afternoon, you'll get a glimpse of Mont Blanc (the highest point in Europe, just left of the pencil-shaped skyscraper), looking Blanc as can be.

You can climb the basilica's 278 steps to the observatory tower (€2, April–Sept Wed–Sun 10:00–12:00 & 14:00–18:30, closed Mon–Tue and off-season) for the exercise and about the same view you enjoy from street level.

To get to the Roman Theaters and Gallo-Roman Museum, turn left, walking down rue Roger Radisson. Before entering the museum, get the best overview of the ancient site by taking a left on rue Cleberg, walking half a block, and taking the ramp that leads to the museum's rooftop (leave street just below #15; notice artist's reconstruction of theaters).

▲▲**Roman Theaters and Gallo-Roman Museum (Musée de la Civilisation Gallo-Romaine)**—Constructed in the hillside with views of two Roman Theaters, this museum makes Lyon's importance in Roman times clear. Lyon (founded in A.D. 43) was an important transportation hub for the administration of Roman Gaul (and much of modern-day France). Emperor Caracalla was born in Lugdunum (Roman Lyon).

The big theater (which originally held 10,000) seats 3,000 for concerts today. The smaller theater, an "odeon" (from the Greek "ode," or song), was acoustically designed for speeches and songs. The ground is littered with gravestones and sarcophagi. Between the theaters, original Roman paving stones lead downhill to the funicular station (taking you back into the old town). The site is free and open daily until 19:00.

The fine **Gallo-Roman Museum**, wonderfully explained in English, takes you on a chronological stroll through ancient Lyon. All the artifacts are local ("Gallo-Roman"). The fine bronze chariot dates from the 7th century B.C. The model of Roman Lyon shows a town of 50,000 in its 2nd-century A.D. glory days. (The forum stands where the basilica does today.) Curved stones in an arena were actual seats—inscribed with the names of tribes who sat there. A speech by Emperor Claudius carved into a big black bronze tablet recalls how, in A.D. 48, he worked to integrate Gauls into the empire by declaring that they were eligible to sit in the Roman Senate (English translation on the wall). A mosaic shows a *Ben Hur*–type chariot race and, with the push of a button, you can see the mechanics of a theater stage curtain in action (€4, free on Thu, open Tue–Sun 10:00–18:00, until 17:00 Nov–Feb, closed Mon, tel. 04 72 38 49 30).

The ancient road between the Roman Theaters leads down and out, where you'll find the funicular station. You can take the funicular to Vieux Lyon (look for a car labeled Vieux Lyon, not St. Just), where it will deposit you only a few steps from St. Jean Cathedral.

Vieux Lyon (Old Lyon)

St. Jean Cathedral—Stand back in the square for the best view. This mostly Gothic cathedral took 200 years to build. It doesn't soar as high as its northern French counterparts. Influenced by their Italian neighbors, churches in southern France are typically less vertical than those in the north. This cathedral, while underwhelming inside, is the "primate cathedral of Gaul," serving what's considered the oldest Christian city in France (Mon–Fri 8:00–12:00 & 14:00–19:30, Sat–Sun 14:00–17:00). Outside (turn right as you leave) are the ruins of a mostly 11th-century church, which was destroyed during the French Revolution (the cathedral was turned into a "temple of reason"). What's left of a baptistery from an early Christian church (c. A.D. 400) is under glass.

▲**Old Lyon and Covered Passageways *(Traboules)*—**Lyon offers the best concentration of well-preserved Renaissance buildings in the country. The city grew rich from its trade fairs and banking. From the 16th to 19th centuries, Lyon was the king of

Europe's silk industry, humming with more than 18,000 looms. The fine buildings of the old center were inspired by Italy and financed by the silk industry.

The **Gadagne Museum** tells Lyon's history and comes with a lively puppet museum showcasing the famous Guignol puppets (€4, Wed–Mon 10:45–18:00, closed Tue, between cathedral and place du Change off rue St. Jean at place du Petit Collège).

Rue St. Jean, leading from the cathedral to place du Change, is the main drag, flanked by a parallel road on either side. The city's trademark serpentine passageways *(traboules)* were essentially shortcuts linking the old town's three main streets. These hidden paths give visitors a hide-and-seek opportunity to discover pastel courtyards, lovely loggias, and delicate arches. Spiral staircases were often shared by houses with arches giving several addresses access. The *traboules* provided shelter when silk was being moved from one stage to the next.

Walking along rue St. Jean, you can poke through several passageways (try #52, #28, #27, #26, and #18). Many of Lyon's 315 *traboules* are open to the public (press top button next to streetfront door to release door when entering, push lit buttons to illuminate dark walkways, and slide door-handle levers when leaving). You're welcome to explore from 8:00 until 20:00 if you are quiet and respectful of the residents, and don't go up any stairs. The TI's Vieux Lyon leaflet locates the *traboules* and courtyards. As you wander Vieux Lyon, look for door plaques giving a history of the building and *traboule*. Walking through Lyon's longest *traboule*, at #27 rue de Bœuf (push buttons as you go for mood lighting), you'll understand why Lyon's old town made an ideal center for the Resistance fighters to slip in and out of as they confounded the Nazis.

Place du Change was the banking center of medieval Lyon. This money scene developed after the city was allowed to host trade fairs in 1420. Its centerpiece is France's first stock exchange. From here, it's a short walk across the river to place des Terreaux and the Museum of Fine Arts.

Place des Terreaux—This grand square hosts the Hôtel de Ville (City Hall), the Museum of Fine Arts, and a grand fountain by Bertholdi (the French sculptor who designed America's Statue of Liberty). The fountain features Marianne (the Lady of the Republic) riding a four-horse-powered chariot. The square itself is pretty wet as 69 fountains spurt playfully in a vast grid. (The number 69 represents the fact that the Rhône department is #69 of the 150 or so in France. Check the license plates, and you'll see most have a 69—indicating they're registered in this department.)

Atelier de la Soierie (silk workshop) is just off place des Terreaux (behind Café Le Moulin Joli) and welcomes the public to drop in to see silk printing and screen-painting by hand (free, Mon–Sat 9:00–12:00 & 14:00–19:00, closed Sun).

For a bite to eat, choose from the many cafés on the square: Café Le Moulin Joli (a Resistance hangout during World War II with light bar meals), the recommended restaurant L'Etage (see under "Eating," below), or the very cheap Turkish eateries (with Turkish MTV playing) on rue Puits-Gaillot. Or grab a picnic (or Turkish to go) to enjoy in the fine and shady courtyard inside the Museum of Fine Arts.

▲**Museum of Fine Arts (Musée des Beaux-Arts)**—Located in a former abbey, which was secularized by Napoleon in 1803 and made into a public museum, this fine-arts museum has an impressive collection, ranging from Egyptian antiquities to Impressionist paintings (€6, Wed–Mon 10:00–18:00, opens at 10:30 on Friday, closed Tue, first floor closes 12:00–13:05, second floor closes 13:05–14:15, pick up museum map on entering, picnic-perfect courtyard, 20 place des Terreaux, Métro: Hôtel de Ville).

The first floor offers a stroll through a fine collection of ancient (especially Egyptian) art, medieval art, and Art Nouveau (furniture). The adjacent chapel is a dreamy, Orsay-like display of 19th- and 20th-century statues (including work by Rodin and Bartholdi).

The second floor displays a pretty selection of paintings from many ages and countries (with no famous works, but a fine Impressionist collection). The highlight is a series of pre-Raphaelite-type works called *Le Poeme de l'Ame* ("The Poem of the Soul") by Louis Janmot. This cycle of 18 paintings and 16 charcoal drawings traces the story of the souls of a boy and a girl as they journey through childhood, adolescence, and into adulthood. They struggle with fears and secular temptations before gaining spiritual enlightenment on the way to heaven. The boy loses his faith and enjoys a short but delicious hedonistic fling, which leads to misery in hell. But a mother's prayers intercede, and he reunites with the girl to enjoy heavenly redemption.

More Sights

Lyon's Presqu'île—This bit of land (French for peninsula, and literally meaning "Almost Island") between the two rivers is Lyon's shopping spine, with thriving pedestrian streets. Join the parade of shoppers on sprawling rue de la République (north of place Bellecour) and the teeming rue Victor Hugo pedestrian mall (south of place Bellecour). Peruse the *bouchons* (characteristic bistros—especially characteristic in the evening) of rue Mercière, and relax at a café on place des Terreaux (described above).

Grand Café des Negociants is an ideal stop for a break. This *très élégant* café has been in business since 1864, and feels like it hasn't changed, with its soft leather chairs, painted ceilings, and glass chandeliers (daily, along rue de la République at 2 place Francis-Régaud, tel. 04 78 42 50 05).

Museums of Fabrics and Decorative Arts (Musées des Tissus et des Arts Décoratifs)—These museums fill two buildings (sharing a courtyard and connected with an interior hallway). While filled with exquisite exhibits, they provide little information in English (descriptive sheets upstairs in the Museum of Fabrics, nothing in Museum of Decorative Arts). The Museum of Fabrics traces the development of textile weaving over 2,000 years and shows off some breathtaking silk work. The Museum of Decorative Arts, billed as "an ambience museum," is a luxurious mansion decorated to the hilt with 18th-century furniture, textiles, and tapestries in a plush domestic setting (€5 covers both museums, Tue–Sun 10:00–17:30, closed Mon, Decorative Arts Museum closes 12:00–14:00, 34 rue de la Charité, Métro: Bellecour).

▲▲Resistance and Deportation History Center (Centre d'Histoire de la Résistance et de la Déportation)—Located near Vichy, capital of the French puppet state, and near neutral Switzerland, Lyon was the center of the French Resistance from 1942 to 1945. This excellent museum, once used as a Nazi torture chamber, uses headsets, videos, and excellent English descriptions to tell the inspirational story of the French Resistance. The included headsets are worth the trouble (move slowly and stand near the remote signal boxes). Don't miss the film describing the deportation, shown in a recreated train boxcar (€4, Wed–Sun 9:00–17:30, closed Mon–Tue, 15-min walk from Perrache station across pont Gallieni, then 3 blocks to 14 avenue Berthelot; or, easier, take T-2 tramway from below Perrache station to Centre Berthelot, or ride the Métro to Jean Mace and walk back 3 blocks toward the river).

▲Lumière Museum (Musée Lumière)—Antoine Lumière and his two sons, Louis and Auguste—the Eastman-Kodaks of France—ran a huge factory with 200 workers in the 1880s, producing four million glass photographic plates a day. Then, in 1895, they made the first *cinématograph*, or movie. In 1903, they pioneered the "autochrome" process of painting frames to make "color photos." This museum tells their story.

The highlights are the many screens playing the earliest "movies." The first film reels held about 950 frames, which played at 19 per second, so these first movies were only 50 seconds long. About 1,500 Lumière films are catalogued from between 1895 and 1907. (Notice that each movie is tagged with its "Catalog Lumière" number.) The very first movie ever made features 200 workers piling out of the Lumière factory at the end of a workday.

The museum fills the Villa Lumière, the family's belle époque mansion built in 1902. The ground floor shows movies and the earliest cameras and projectors. Upstairs are exhibits on still photography and the Lumière living quarters (furnished c. 1900). Across the park from the mansion is a shrine at what's left of the warehouse where the first movie was actually shot. In a wonderful coincidence, *lumière* is the French word for "light" (€6, Tue–Sun 10:00–18:30, closed Mon, rue du Premier-Film, Métro: D to Monplaisir-Lumière, tel. 04 78 78 1895, www.institut-lumiere.org). Enjoy your ride on the futuristic (and driverless) Métro D. Sit in the front and command your own underground starship. The museum is half a block from the Monplaisir-Lumière stop.

Nightlife—As Lyon has France's second-largest cultural budget after Paris, there are always plenty of theater and concerts to attend. The TI has all the latest information and schedules. After dinner, a stroll through Lyon's old town and a walk along the river affords a chance to savor the city's famous illuminations. State-of-the-art floodlighting throughout town gives visitors and locals alike a chance to enjoy the grand buildings and public spaces of Lyon after dark. For a lively bar and people-watching scene, prowl rue de la Monnaie (angles off "restaurant row," rue Mercière to the south) and the streets between place des Terreaux and the Opera House.

SLEEPING

(€1 = about $1.20, country code: 33)
Hotels in Lyon are a steal compared to those in Paris. Weekends are generally discounted (about 10 percent) in this city, which thrives on weekday business travel. All hotels listed below are on the Presqu'île near place Bellecour. Hotels have elevators unless otherwise noted, and air-conditioning is a godsend when it's hot.

On or near Place des Celestins (Métro: Bellecour)
$$$ **Hôtel des Artistes*****, ideally located right on place des Celestins, is red-velvet plush, comfortable, professional, and the best value in its price range (standard Sb-€70–82, larger Sb-€89–102, standard Db-€78–88, larger Db-€98–104, standard rooms are plenty comfortable, breakfast-€9, air-con, 8 rue Gaspard-André, tel. 04 78 42 04 88, fax 04 78 42 93 76, hartiste@club-internet.fr, SE).

$$$ **Hôtel Globe et Cecil*****, the most elegant of my listings, offers refined comfort on a refined street, with beautifully decorated, generously sized rooms and sumptuous lounge areas (Sb-€120, Db-€145, includes breakfast, air-con, 21 rue Gasparin, tel. 04 78 42 58 95, fax 04 72 41 99 06, www.globeetcecilhotel.com).

$$ **Comfort Hôtel Saint-Antoine**** is near Saône River on a dingy street with modern, well-appointed rooms and fair rates (Sb-€65–82, Db-€68–84, lower rates listed are for smaller rooms, breakfast-€7.50, Internet access, air-con, 1 rue du Port du Temple, tel. 04 78 92 91 91, fax 04 78 92 47 37, www.hotel-saintantoine.fr).

$$ **Hôtel des Célestins****, just off place des Célestins, is warmly run by Stephanie and Laurent (both SE). In fact, Laurent graduated

from Cornell. Bright, cheery, immaculate rooms come with thoughtful touches. Those on the street side are larger and lighter, while the others are quieter (Sb-€57–61, Db-€61–67, 5 large view rooms for up to 3 people-€70-77, good breakfast-€7.60, 4 rue des Archers, tel. 04 72 56 08 98, fax 04 72 56 08 65, www.hotelcelestins.com, info @hotelcelestins.com).

South of Place Bellecour (Toward Perrache Station)

These two hotels are my closest listings to Perrache train station. They're located on the main pedestrian drag just south of place Bellecour (Métro: Bellecour).

$$ **Hôtel La Residence***** feels big and institutional, but its 68 rooms are air-conditioned, spacious, and well-cared for (Db-€70, Tb-€77, 19 Victor Hugo, tel. 04 78 42 63 28, fax 04 78 42 85 76, www.hotel-la-residence.com).

$ **Hôtel du Dauphin****, run by gentle owner M. LeClerc, is an intimate place, more like a private home than a hotel. It offers 12 quiet and simple rooms with tiny, step-up showers (Sb-€43–49, Db-€54–60, 9 rue Victor Hugo, tel. 04 78 37 18 34, fax 04 72 40 20 84, www.hoteldudauphin-lyon.com).

Near the Opera House

$ **Hôtel Iris**** is the best budget deal I found in Lyon, run by hardworking Cedric, a former bread-baker. He is creatively transforming this historic building (with a brilliant 16th-century stairway) into a sharp little 12-room hotel. Rooms are basic but comfortable, with brown tones and an African motif (D-€32, Db-€40–45, 36 rue de l'Abre Sec, Métro: Hôtel de Ville, tel. 04 78 39 93 80, fax 04 72 00 89 91, www.hoteliris.freesurf.fr). Make your reservation only by phone; Cedric wants to hear your voice.

Lyon's view $ **Youth Hostel** is impressively situated a 10-minute walk above Vieux Lyon (€14-bed in 4–6 bed room, sheet rental-€3, open 24 hrs, kitchen available, no lockers, 45 Montée du Chemin, Métro: Hôtel de Ville, tel. 04 78 15 05 50, www.hihostels .com). Reserve online.

EATING

For the people of Lyon, eating out is a passion. It's what everyone talks about all the time. Here, great chefs are more famous than professional soccer players. Restaurants seem to outnumber cars, yet all seem busy. With an abundance of cozy, excellent restaurants in every price range, it's hard to go wrong—unless you order *tripes* (cow intestines, also known as *tablier de sapeur*), *fois de veau* (calf's liver), *tête de veau* (calf's head)—or decide to dine on Sunday, when almost all restaurants close. Beware, these mouthwatering dishes are very common in small bistros *(bouchons)*, and can be the only choices on cheaper menus. Look instead for these classics: St. Marcellin cheese, *salade lyonnaise* (croutons, ham, lettuce, and poached egg), green lentils *(lentilles)* served on a salad or with sausages, *quenelles de brochet* (fish dumplings in a creamy sauce), and *filet de sandre* (local whitefish).

Lyon's characteristic *bouchons* are small bistros that evolved from the days when Mama would feed the silk workers after a long day. True *bouchons* are simple places with limited selection and seating (just like Mama's), serving only traditional fare. The touristy pedestrian streets of Vieux Lyon and rue Mercière on the Presqu'île are *bouchon* bazaars. While food quality may be better away from these popular restaurant-rows, you can't beat the atmosphere.

Vieux Lyon

Come to Old Lyon for maximum ambience, but for the epicenter of restaurant activity, go to place Neuve St. Jean—survey the scene and menus before sitting down. While quality can vary from year to year, these places have withstood the test of time.

La Machonnerie, a block opposite the cathedral, has almost medieval decor and traditional cuisine. Expect to be greeted by the gregarious owner-chef (*menus* from €19, daily, 36 rue Tramassac, tel. 04 78 42 24 62).

Les Lyonnais, a block north, is more modern, yet appealing, and locally popular, with a photo gallery of loyal customers lining the walls (€19 *menu*, daily, 1 rue Tramassac, tel. 04 78 37 64 82).

Les Retrouvailles, across the road on rue de Bœuf, serves tasty but less traditional Lyonnais cuisine, in a charming setting under wood-beam ceilings. Here your dining experience is carefully managed by friendly owners Pierre *(le chef)* and Odile (€20 and €26 *menus,* closed Sun, 38 rue du Bœuf, tel. 04 78 42 68 84).

Les Adrets has a bigger, rowdier, beer-hall feel and a good, traditional Lyonnais *menu* at €20 (closed Sat–Sun, 30 rue de Bœuf, tel. 04 78 38 24 30).

Chez Mimi, a small, poster-festooned café with a bohemian ambience, is great for an inexpensive salad, omelette, or quiche, and a glass of wine (inside can be smoky, closed Mon–Tue, a block north of the cathedral at 66 rue St. Jean).

Restaurant Panoramique de la Fourvière, atop Fourvière Hill, with a spectacular view overlooking Lyon, serves classic cuisine in a superb setting (*menus* from €20, daily, 9 place de Fourvière, near Notre-Dame Basilica, tel. 04 78 25 21 15).

For Lyon's best ice cream, find **Nardone René Glacier** on the river (daily, 10:00–24:00, 3 place Ennemond Fousseret).

On the Presqu'île

The pedestrian rue Mercière is the epicenter of *bouchons* on the Presqu'île. Along this street, an entertaining cancan of restaurants stretches four blocks from place des Jacobins to rue Grenette. Enjoy surveying the scene and choose whichever eatery appeals.

Gaston, at #41, is hardly traditional, but offers a killer lunch salad bar for €12, fun fondues at dinner, and caged rabbits that make you wonder (tel. 04 72 41 87 86). **Le Bouchon aux Vins,** at #62, has the best atmosphere, plus good lunches at fair prices (daily, tel. 04 78 38 47 40).

La Francotte, an open and appealing zinc-bar bistro on place des Celestins, is good for a relaxing drink or a meal (*menus* from €19, closed Sun, near many recommended hotels at 8 place des Celestins, tel. 04 78 37 38 64).

L'Etage, intimate and wood-paneled, is *the* place to go for up-and-coming Lyon cuisine at its affordable best. Try their *coquilles St. Jacques* and *fondant chocolat*. Reserve ahead (*menus* from €20, closed Sun–Mon, on second floor overlooking place des Terreaux, 4 place des Terreaux, tel. 04 78 28 19 59).

Les Muses de l'Opéra is good for lunch or dinner with a great view (and average quality). Ride the elevator to the seventh floor of the Opera House (dinner *menu*-€29, closed Sun, tel. 04 72 00 45 58).

Chez Abel is the ultimate *bouchon*, far away from restaurant rows and tourists, catering to one kind of client only—local residents. It has a warm, chalet-like interior and a welcoming red-cheeked owner. Servings are generous; the *quenelle de brochet* is downright massive. Consider a *plat du jour* and maybe a salad. Reserve ahead (*menus* from €23, closed Sun–Mon, about 15-min walk south of place Bellecour, a short block from Saône River, at 25 rue Guynemer, tel. 04 78 37 46 18).

TRANSPORTATION CONNECTIONS

After Paris, Lyon is France's most important rail hub. Train travelers find this gateway to the Alps, Provence, the Riviera, and Burgundy is an easy stopover. Two main train stations serve Lyon: Part-Dieu and Perrache. Most trains officially depart from Part-Dieu, though many stop at Perrache, and trains run between the stations every 10 minutes. Double-check which station your train departs from.

From Lyon by train to: Paris (20/day, 2 hrs), **Annecy** (7/day, 2 hrs, most change in Aix-les-Bains), **Chamonix** (10/day, 5 hrs), **Strasbourg** (5/day, 5 hrs), **Dijon** (12/day, 2 hrs), **Beaune** (10/day, 2 hrs, many change in Mâcon), **Avignon** (22/day, 14 to TGV station in 1.5 hrs, 8 to main station in 2.5 hrs), **Arles** (14/day, 2.5 hrs, most change in Avignon, Marseille, or Nîmes), **Nice** (6/day, 5 hrs),

Carcassonne, (6/day, 4 hrs), **Venice** (6/day, 11–13 hrs, most change in Geneva and Milan, night train), **Rome** (4/day, 10–12 hrs, at least one change in Milan, night train), **Florence** (3/day, 10 hrs), **Geneva** (8/day, 2 hrs), **Barcelona** (1 day train, 7 hrs, change in Perpignan; 2 night trains).

Route Tips for Drivers

En route to Provence, consider a three-hour detour through the spectacular Ardèche Gorges: Exit the A-6 autoroute at Privas, and follow the villages of Aubenas, Vallon Pont d'Arc (offers kayak trips), and Pont Saint-Esprit. En route to Burgundy, consider a Beaujolais detour (see page 570).

ALSACE
and NORTHERN FRANCE

The French province of Alsace stands like a flower-child referee between Germany and France. Bounded by the Rhine on the east and the softly rolling Vosges Mountains on the west, this is a lush land of Hansel-and-Gretel villages, sprawling vineyards, and engaging cities. Food and wine are the primary industry, topic of conversation, and perfect excuse for countless festivals.

Alsace has changed hands several times between Germany and France because of its location, natural wealth, naked vulnerability—and the fact that Germany thinks the mountains are the natural border, while France thinks it's the Rhine River.

Having been a political pawn for 1,000 years, Alsace has a hybrid culture: Locals who swear do so bilingually, and the local cuisine features sauerkraut with fine wine. If you're traveling in December, come here for France's most celebrated Christmas markets and festivals.

Colmar is one of Europe's most charming cities—with a small-town warmth and world-class art. Strasbourg is a big-city version of Colmar, worth a stop to see its grand cathedral and feel its relatively high-powered and trendy bustle. The humbling battlefields of Verdun and the bubbly vigor of Reims in northern France are closer to Paris than Alsace, and they follow logically only if your next destination is Paris.

Planning Your Time

Set up in or near Colmar. Allow most of a day for Colmar and a full afternoon for the Route du Vin (Wine Road). If you have one day, wander Colmar's sights until after lunch, and then set out for the Route du Vin. Urban Strasbourg, with its soaring cathedral and thriving center, is an quick 30-minute train ride away. If you can spare an extra half day, spend it there, but with limited time, skip it.

From Alsace to Champagne

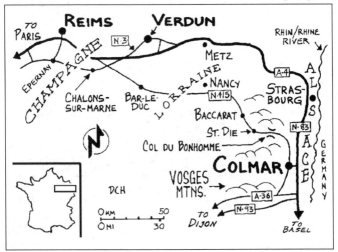

Reims and Verdun are doable by car as stops between Paris and Colmar—if you're speedy. Train travelers with only one day between Colmar and Paris must choose either Reims or Verdun.

Getting Around Alsace

Frequent trains link Colmar and Strasbourg (2/hr, 30 min). Buses and minivan excursions radiate from Colmar to villages along the Route du Vin, and you can rent bikes in Colmar and Turckheim if you prefer to pedal (for details on all of these options, see "Route du Vin," page 602).

Cuisine Scene in Alsace

Alsatian cuisine is a major tourist attraction in itself. The German influence is obvious: sausages, potatoes, onions, and sauerkraut. Look for *choucroute garnie* (sauerkraut and sausage—although it seems a shame to eat it in a fancy restaurant), the more traditionally Alsatian *baeckeoffe* (potato, meat, and onion stew), *rösti* (an oven-baked potato-and-cheese dish), fresh trout, and foie gras. At lunch, or for a lighter dinner, try a *tarte à l'oignon* (like an onion quiche, but better) or *tarte flambée* (like a thin-crust pizza with onion and bacon bits). If you're picnicking, buy some stinky Munster cheese. Dessert specialties are *tarte alsacienne* (fruit tart) and *glace Kugelhopf* (a light cake mixed with raisins, almonds, dried fruit, and cherry liqueur).

Remember, restaurants serve only during lunch (11:30–14:00) and dinner (19:00–21:00, later in bigger cities); cafés serve food throughout the day.

Alsatian Wines

Alsatian wines are named for their grapes, unlike in Burgundy or Provence, where wines are commonly named after villages, or in Bordeaux, where wines are often named after châteaux. White wines dominate in the Alsace. The following wines are made entirely of that grape variety: Sylvaner (fairly light, fruity, and inexpensive), Riesling (more robust than Sylvaner, but drier than the German style you're probably used to), Gewürztraminer (spicy, with a powerful bouquet; good with pâtés and local cheeses), Muscat (very dry, with a distinctive bouquet and taste; best as a before-dinner wine), Tokay Pinot Gris (more full-bodied than Riesling, but fine with many local main courses), Pinot Noir (the local red is overpriced; very light and fruity, generally served chilled), and the tasty Crèmant d'Alsace (the region's good and inexpensive champagne). You'll also see *eaux-de-vie*, powerful fruit-flavored brandies; try the *framboise* (raspberry) flavor.

Colmar

Colmar is a well-pickled old place of 70,000 residents, and it offers a few heavyweight sights in a warm, midsize-town package. Historic beauty was usually a poor excuse for being spared the ravages of World War II, but it worked for Colmar. The American and British military were careful not to bomb the half-timbered old burghers' houses, characteristic red- and green-tiled roofs, and cobbled lanes of Alsace's most beautiful city. The town's distinctly French shutters, combined with the ye olde German half-timbering, gives Colmar a uniquely colorful ambience.

Today, Colmar thrives, with its colorful buildings, impressive art treasures, and German tourists. Schoolgirls park their rickety horse carriages in front of City Hall and are ready to give visitors a clip-clop tour of the old town. Antique shops welcome browsers, and hotel managers hurry down the sleepy streets to pick up fresh croissants in time for breakfast.

ORIENTATION

Assume you will get lost, as there isn't a straight street in Colmar. Thankfully, most streets are pedestrian-only, and it's a lovely town to be lost in. Navigate by the high church steeples and the helpful signs that seem to pop up whenever you need them (directing visitors to the various sights). For tourists, the town center is place Unterlinden (a 15-min walk from the train station), where you'll find the TI, Colmar's most important museum, and a huge and handy Monoprix supermarket/department store. Every city bus starts or finishes on place Unterlinden.

Colmar is most crowded from May through September and during its festive Christmas season. Weekends are busiest (reserve ahead). The impressive music festival fills hotels the first two weeks of July, and the local wine festival rages for 10 days in early August. Open-air markets bustle next to the Dominican Church and St. Martin Cathedral on Thursdays and Saturdays.

Tourist Information

The TI, next to the Unterlinden Museum on place Unterlinden, is generous with printed material. Pick up the excellent city map (describing a good town walk), a Route du Vin (Wine Road) map, information on bike rental, and *Colmar Actualités*, a booklet with bus schedules. Get information about concerts and festivals in Colmar and in nearby villages, and ask about Colmar's Folklore Tuesdays (with folk dancing at 20:30 every Tue mid-May–mid-Sept on place de l'Ancienne Douane). Drivers exploring the Route du Vin can buy the *Blay Foldex Alsace* map (1:175,000, €6). Bikers should get a map of the bike routes (*Le Haut-Rhin à Vélo*, €5.50, suggests routes with estimated timings). The TI also reserves hotel rooms and has *chambres d'hôte* listings for Colmar and the region (April–Oct Mon–Sat 9:00–18:00, until 19:00 July–Aug, Sun 10:00–14:00; Nov–March Mon–Sat 9:00–12:00 & 14:00–18:00, Sun 10:00–14:00, tel. 03 89 20 68 92, www.ville-colmar.fr—in French only). A public WC is 20 yards left of the TI.

Tours: There are no city tours in English, but private English-speaking guides are available through the TI (about €120/3 hrs). Tourist trains depart from the TI (€5.50, 30-min tours, tape-recorded commentary). In the summer, horse-drawn carriages do the same (€6, 30-min tours,). For minivan tours of the Route du Vin, see "Getting Around the Route du Vin," page 603.

Arrival in Colmar

By Train: Before leaving the station, a little history—it was built during Prussian rule with the same plans for the Gdańsk station. Check out the charming 1991 window showing two local maidens about to be run over by a train being rescued by an artist. Opposite, he's shown painting their portraits. To reach the town center from the station (15-min walk, baggage check available at ticket window), walk straight out past Hôtel Bristol, turn left on avenue de la République, and keep walking. Buses #1, #2, and #3 (to the left outside of station) all go from the station to the TI (pay driver).

Buses to the Route du Vin villages stop at the island to the right as you leave the station. Allow €6 for a taxi to a hotel in central Colmar (taxi stand is on left out of the station).

By Car: Follow signs for *Centre-Ville*, then *place Rapp*. There's a 900-spot pay parking garage under place Rapp, and (for now) free lots at Parking du Musée d'Unterlinden (across from Hôtel Primo) and off the ring road near Hôtel St. Martin (follow signs from ring road to Parking de la Vieille Ville). Several hotels have private parking, and those that don't can advise you on where to park. When entering or leaving Colmar on the Strasbourg side, look for the big Statue of Liberty erected on July 4, 2004, to commemorate the 100th anniversary of the death of sculptor Bartholdi.

Helpful Hints

Market Days: Markets take place Thursdays on place de l'Ancienne Douane (mornings only; same square also hosts a flea market first and third Fri), Thursdays on place des Dominicains (all day, no produce), and Saturdays on place St. Joseph (mornings only).

Department Store: The big **Monoprix,** with a supermarket, is across from the TI and Unterlinden Museum (Mon–Sat 8:00–20:00, closed Sun).

Internet Access: Try **Infr@reseau** near the TI at 12 rue du Rempart (Tue–Sat 10:00–20:30, closed Sun–Mon, tel. 03 89 23 98 45) or CyberDidi at 9 rue du Rempart (daily 10:00–23:00, tel. 02 89 29 01 41).

Laundry: You'll find a launderette near the recommended Maison Jund *chambre d'hôte* at 1 rue Ruest, just off the pedestrian street rue Vauban (usually open daily 8:00–21:00).

Bike Rental: Kiosque Colmarvélo is the cheapest around, with the most extensive hours (€3/half day, €5/day; bikes have 5 speeds, medium-width tires, basket, and lock, and a baby seat upon request; daily 9:00–12:00 & 14:00–19:00, tel. 03 89 41 37 90, in kiosk stand at 4 avenue de la République on place Rapp, near the carousel).

Car Rental: The least expensive is **ADA** (22 rue Stanislas, tel. 03 89 23 90 30, www.ada.fr—in French only). **Avis** is at the train station (tel. 03 89 23 16 89). The TI has a long list of others.

Taxis: At the train station, call 03 89 41 40 19; otherwise, call 03 89 80 71 71 or 06 09 42 60 75.

Poodle Care: To give your poodle a shampoo and a haircut (or just to watch the action), drop by **Quatt Pattes** (near Hôtel Rapp at rue Berthe Molly #8).

Introductory Walking Tour of Colmar's Old Town

This walk is good day or night and is a handy way to link the city's three worthwhile sights. Supplement this information by reading the sidewalk information plaques that describe every point of interest in town.

The importance of 15th- to 17th-century Colmar is clear as you wander its pedestrian-friendly old center. It's decorated with 45 buildings classified as historic monuments. In the Middle Ages, most of Europe was fragmented into chaotic little princedoms and dukedoms. Merchant-dominated cities, natural proponents of the formation of large nation-states (a.k.a. globalization), banded together to form "trading leagues" (the World Trade Organizations of their day). The Hanseatic League was the super-league of northern Europe. Prosperous Colmar was the leading member of a smaller league of 10 Alsatian cities, called the Decapolis (founded 1354). The names of the streets you'll walk along bear witness to the merchants' historic importance to Colmar.

Customs House (Koïfhus): Start your tour at the old Customs House. Here, delegates of the Decapolis would meet to sort out trade issues, much like the European Union does in nearby Strasbourg today. Walk under its archway to place de l'Ancienne Douane and face the Frédéric-Auguste Bartholdi statue—arm raised, à la Statue of Liberty—and do a 360-degree spin to appreciate a gaggle of gables. This was the center of business activity in Colmar, with trade routes radiating from here to several major European cities. All goods that entered the city were taxed here. Today, it's the festive site of outdoor wine-tastings on many summer evenings. The soaring, half-timbered commotion of higgledy-piggledy rooftops on the downhill side of the fountain marks the Tanners' Quarters.

Tanners' Quarters: These 17th- and 18th-century rooftops competed for space in the sun to dry their freshly tanned hides, while the nearby river channel flushed the waste products. This neighborhood, restored in about 1970, was a pioneer in the renovation of old quarters funded by the government. Residents had to play along or move out. Follow the statue's left elbow and walk to the end of *Petite* rue des Tanneurs (*not* rue des Tanneurs), turn right (walking along the city's first wall—c. 1230, now built into the row of houses), and take the first left along the stream. On your right is the old market hall (fish, produce, and other products were brought here by flat-bottomed boat). Today, it's Colmar's main market hall, where locals buy produce, meat, and fish. Cross the canal and turn right on quai de la Poissonnerie (wharf of the fishermen), and you'll enter the Petite Venise quarter.

Petite Venise: This neighborhood, a bundle of Colmar's most colorful houses lining the small canal, is extremely popular with tourists, but it's romantic at night, with a fraction of the crowds. It lies between the town's first wall (built to defend against arrows) and its later wall (built in the age of gunpowder). The local river was canalized for medieval industry—to provide water for the tanners,

Colmar

1 Hôtel St. Martin
2 Hôtel Maréchal
3 Hôtel/Restaurant le Rapp
4 Hôtel Turenne
5 Hôtel Ibis
6 Maison Jund Rooms
7 Hôtel Primo 1
8 To Hôtel Bristol
9 La Chaumière Rooms

10 Restaurant la Maison Rouge
11 Winstub Schwendi
12 Restaurant au Fer Rouge
13 Flunch Cafeteria
14 Rest. la Krutenau
   & Wistub la Petite Venise
15 Internet Cafés (2 locations)
16 Launderette
17 Bike Rental
18 Maison Pfister

allow farmers to barge their goods into town, power mills, and so on. Walk several blocks along the flower-box-lined canal to the end of rue de la Poissonnerie. Turn right, walk to the center of the bridge, and enjoy the view. To the right, you'll see examples of the flat-bottom gondolas used to transport goods on the small river. Today, they give tourists sleepy and scenic, 30-minute, €5 canal tours (departure on demand).

Cross the bridge, take the second right on Grande Rue, and stroll several blocks back to the Customs House (green-tiled roof). Turn left, and, with your back to the Customs House, walk uphill along rue des Marchands (Merchants' Street)—one of the most scenic stretches in town. (The ruler of Malaysia recently was so charmed by this street that he had it recreated in Kuala Lumpur.) In two blocks, you come face-to-face with the...

Maison Pfister (Pfister House): This richly decorated merchant's house from 1537, with its external spiral-staircase turret and painted walls, illustrates the city folks' taste for Renaissance humanism (a fine little wine shop fills the ground floor). The man carved into the side of the building the next door up (at #9) was a drapemaker; he's shown holding a bar, Colmar's measure of about one meter. (In the Middle Ages, it was common for cities to have their own units of length; one reason merchants supported the "globalization" of their time was to get rid of different measuring systems.) Look closely at the architecture.

Half-Timbered Houses: House #9 (with the guy holding the bar) shows off the classic half-timbered design—the beams (upright, cross, angular supports) are grouped in what's called (and looks like) "a man." Typical houses are built with a man in the middle, flanked by two "half men." While houses of the rich were made of stone, anyone on a budget built half-timbered. (Although, because of the marshy ground here, all homes sit on a stone lower level.) Originally, proud townsfolk would plaster over their cheap half-timbered walls to create the illusion of a stone house. Then, in the 20th century, half-timbered became charming and they peeled away the plaster, revealing the old beams. You can identify houses that are really made of stone by their windowsills—wood means they're half-timbered; stone indicates the building is stone-built as well. As you explore the town, notice how upper floors are cantilevered out. This was both a structural trick and a tax dodge. A single supporting wall could support more if it rested in from the upper floor's edge. And real-estate taxes were based on the square footage of the ground floor.

If you wander at night, you'll see that Colmar is not only beautifully pedestrianized, but also wonderfully floodlit. Countless small floodlights mixed in with the cobbles illuminate the town at night. They can be changed to give different intensities and colors, keeping Colmar fresh and inviting after dark.

One more block along on the left is the **Bartholdi Museum** (described in "Sights," below). Next door (#28) is Au Dore Carrée, with its charming Art Nouveau facade and interior. Art Nouveau was rare in Colmar—considered an anti-German statement shortly (c. 1900) after the region was taken from France. A passage to the right leads to...

St. Martin Cathedral: The city's golden cathedral, with its lone tower (two were planned) and gleaming tiles, was inspired by Hôtel Dieu in Beaune. Walk left around the cathedral (notice the relief over the main door is not your typical Last Judgment scene, but the three wise men—popular in the Rhineland as the relic heads of the original "We three kings" in Köln's cathedral). Just past the cathedral, head left up the pedestrian-only rue des Serruriers (Locksmiths' Street) to the **Dominican Church** (worth entering, described in "Sights," below). Compare the soaring St. Martin Cathedral with this low-slung, sober structure that perfectly symbolizes Dominican austerity; both the church and cathedral were built at the same time. Continue past the Dominican Church (rue des Serruriers becomes rue des Boulangers—Bakers' Street). Then make a right on rue des Têtes (notice the beautiful stork sign over the *pharmacie* at the corner) Then walk a block to the fancy old house with all the heads (on the right).

Maison des Têtes (House of Heads): Colmar's other famous merchant's house was built in 1609 by a big-shot winemaker and is playfully decorated with 105 faces and masks (the guy in the center has pig's feet). Just to the right, a 1947 bakery sign shows the *boulangerie* basics in Alsace: croissant, *kugelhof*, and baguette). Across the street, study the fine early 20th-century store sign trumpeting the wonders of a butcher (pork, foie gras—with the traditional maiden chasing a goose about to be force-fed), all hung on the beak of a chicken. Angle down the rue de l'Eau (Water Street) opposite Maison des Têtes for a shortcut to the TI and the Unterlinden Museum, with its namesake Linden trees lining the front yard (popular locally for making calming "Lilleul" tea).

SIGHTS

▲▲▲**Unterlinden Museum**—Colmar's touristic claim to fame is one of my favorite museums in Europe. Its extensive yet manageable collection ranges from Roman Colmar to medieval winemaking exhibits, and from traditional wedding dresses to paintings that give vivid insight into the High Middle Ages. Plan on spending extra time in this museum, as its collection is so unusual, exquisite, and varied, and the excellent audioguide (included with your admission) makes the curator your best friend. The museum is one of the most visited in all of France for its devastatingly beautiful *Isenheim Altarpiece*.

Gothic Statues (Room 1): Room one features 14th-century Gothic statues from St. Martin Cathedral, taken in out of the weather after more than 500 years. You can still see the fine attention given to the faces. Take a close look at the 15th-century stained glass; fine details are painted into the glass that no one would see, a jigsaw connected by lead. Around here, glass this old is rare. Most of it was destroyed by rampaging Protestants in the Reformation wars.

Cloister: Step into the delightful cloister (the largest 13th-century cloister in Alsace). This was a Dominican convent founded for noblewomen in 1230. It functioned until the French Revolution, when the building became a garrison. Rooms branch off from here with museum exhibits. Don't miss the wine room, with its classic 17th-century oak presses and finely decorated casks. Wine revenue was used to care for Colmar's poor. The nuns owned many of the best vineyards around, and as this is a sun belt (with less rain than much of southern France), production was excellent. So was consumption. Notice (on the first cask on left) the Bacchus with the distended tummy straddling a keg. The quote from 1781 reads: "My belly's full of juice. It makes me strong. But drink too much, and you lose dignity and health."

Painting Gallery: Left of the wine-press room, enter the painting gallery. Stop first by the spinning case of engravings by Schongauer. He was Albrecht Dürer's master. Throughout the museum, you'll see small photos of engravings illustrating how painters were influenced by other artists' engravings. Most German painters were also engravers (that's how they made money—making lots of copies for sale). The following rooms are filled with wonderfully described (on the audioguide) paintings. As you enjoy the art, remember that Alsace historically is German and part of the upper Rhine Valley. The three kings of Bethlehem fame are prominently featured because their heads ended up as relics in Köln's cathedral (on the Rhine).

Isenheim Altarpiece: The high-light of the museum (and, for me, the city) is Matthias Grünewald's gripping *Isenheim Altarpiece* (c. 1515), actually a series of three different paintings on hinges that pivot like shutters (study the little model on the wall, explained in English). Designed to help people in a medieval hospital  endure horrible skin diseases (such as St. Anthony's Fire, later called rye ergotism)—long before the age of painkillers—it's one of the most powerful paintings ever produced. Germans know this painting like Americans know the *Mona Lisa*.

Stand as if you were a medieval peasant, in front of the center-piece, and let the agony and suffering of the Crucifixion drag its fingers down your face. It's an intimate drama. The point—Jesus' suffering—is drilled home: the weight of his body bending the crossbar (unrealistic—creating to some eyes an almost crossbow effect). His elbows are pulled from their sockets by the weight of his dead body. Those crucified die of asphyxiation, as Jesus' chest implies. His mangled feet are swollen with blood. The grief on Mary's face speaks volumes. In hopes that the intended viewers (the hospital's patients) would know that Jesus understood their suffering, Jesus himself was even painted to appear as if he had a skin disease. Study the faces and the Christian symbolism. Mary is wrapped in the shroud that will cover Jesus. The composition of the sorrow on the left is powerful. On the far left stands St. Sebastian (called upon by those with the plague), and on the right is St. Anthony (the Red Adair of rotten rye).

The Resurrection scene is unique in art history (Grünewald had no master and no students). Jesus rockets out of the tomb as man is transformed into God. As if proclaiming once again, "I am the Light," he is radiant. His shroud is the color of light: Roy G. Biv. Around the rainbow is the "resurrection of the flesh." Jesus' pink and perfect flesh would appeal to the patients who meditated on the scene.

In the nativity scene—set in the Rhineland—much-adored Mary is tender and loving, true to the Dominican belief that she was the intercessor for all in heaven. The three scenes of the painting changed with the church calendar. The happy ending—a psychedelic explosion of Resurrection joy—is the spiritual equivalent of jumping from the dentist's chair directly into a Jacuzzi. The last two panels show the meeting of St. Paul the hermit and St. Anthony.

Rest of the Museum: Downstairs, you'll find a modern art section and Roman and prehistoric artifacts. The upstairs rooms contain local and folk history, with everything from medieval armor to old-time toys.

Cost and Hours: €7, price includes helpful audioguide, May–Oct daily 9:00–18:00, Nov–April Wed–Mon 9:00–12:00 & 14:00–17:00, closed Tue (tel. 03 89 20 15 50).

▲▲**Dominican Church (Eglise des Dominicains)**—Here's another medieval mindblower. In this church, you'll find Martin Schongauer's angelically beautiful *Virgin in the Rosebush* center stage, dating from 1473 but looking as if it were painted yesterday. Here, graceful Mary is shown as a welcoming mother. Jesus clings to her, reminding the viewer of the possibility of an intimate relationship with Mary. The Latin on her halo reads: "Pick me also for your child, O very Holy Virgin." Rather than telling a particular Bible story, this is a general scene...designed to meet the personal devotional needs of any worshipper. Here, nature is not a backdrop; Mary and Jesus are encircled by it. Schongauer's robins, sparrows, and goldfinches bring extra life to an already impressively natural rosebush. The white rose anticipates Jesus' crucifixion. The frame, with its angelic orchestra, dates only from 1900. The contrast provided by the simple Dominican setting heightens the flamboyance of this Gothic masterpiece. Dominican churches were intentionally austere, symbolic of their zeal to purify their faith and compete with the growing popularity of 13th-century heretical movements, such as Catharism, whose message was a simpler faith (€1.30, April–Dec daily 10:00–13:00 & 15:00–18:00, closed Jan–March).

▲**Bartholdi Museum**—This little museum recalls the life and work of the local boy who gained fame by sculpting America's much-loved Statue of Liberty. Frédéric Bartholdi (1834–1904) was a dynamic painter/photographer/sculptor with a passion for the defense of liberty and freedom. Because Prussia took Alsace in 1871, he spent most of his career in Paris, unable to move back to his home of Colmar without becoming a German. He personally devoted years of his life to realizing the vision of a statue of liberty for America standing in New York's harbor. At the ticket desk, study Bartholdi's photo (actually 6 photos in a line) of New York City's harbor in 1876. The first piling of the Brooklyn Bridge is up. Bartholdi added the tiny Statue of Liberty on the far left (along with the boats).

The first floor recreates his high society flat in Paris. The dining room is lined with portraits of his aristocratic family. In the next room hangs a fine portrait of Bartholdi, facing his mother (on a red chair). He was very close to his mom, writing her a letter a day. Many see her features on the Statue of Liberty.

While France would pay for the statue, the United States needed to come up with money for the stand...and this was a very tough sell. Notice the gloomy painting of the Statue of Liberty at the top of the stairs. Bartholdi personally lobbied America to construct the statue, making four trips over 10 years. He traveled with this painting and a full-size model of the torch the statue would ultimately hold to raise money for the pedestal. He took full advantage of the fact that his cousin was the French ambassador to the United States. Finally, the project came together.

The first floor shows off Bartholdi's French work. Notice how his patriotic works tend to have one arm raised—*Vive la France*, God bless America, *Deutschland über alles*...you can fill in the flag-waving blank.

Bartholdi's most famous French work, the *Lion of Belfort*, celebrates the town in Alsace that fought so fiercely in 1871 that it was never annexed into Germany. Photos show the red sandstone lion sitting regally below the mighty Vauban fortress of Belfort—a symbol of French spirit standing strong against Germany.

The second floor is dedicated to his American works—the paintings, photos, and statues Bartholdi made in his many travels to the States. You'll see statues of Columbus and Lafayette (only 19 years old when he came to America's aid) with George Washington. Then the exhibit traces the evolution and completion of the dream of a Statue of Liberty. Fascinating photos show the Eiffel-designed core, the frame being covered with plaster, and then the hand-hammered copper plating, which was ultimately riveted to the frame. The statue was assembled in Paris, unriveted, and shipped to New York, 10 years late...in 1886. The big ear is half size. Curiously, there is absolutely no English posted in this museum (€4, March–Dec Wed–Mon 10:00–12:00 & 14:00–18:00, closed Tue and Jan–Feb, pick up English flier, in heart of old town at 30 rue des Marchands). Several Bartholdi statues grace Colmar's squares.

SLEEPING

Hotels are busy on weekends in May, June, September, and October. Plan ahead. July and August are busy, but there are always rooms—somewhere. Should you have trouble finding a room in Colmar (the TI can help), look in a nearby village, where small hotels and bed-and-breakfasts are plentiful; see my recommendations under "Eguisheim," page 607.

$$$ **Hôtel St. Martin***, near the old Customs House, is a family-run place that began as a coaching inn (in 1361). Its 40 traditional yet well-equipped rooms, with air-conditioning and big beds, are woven into its antique frame. The hotel has three sections (young, middle-aged, and elderly), joined by a peaceful courtyard. All rooms offer solid comfort and character, though the best rooms are in the new (young) wing, with traditional furnishings, stone walls, and plush comfort (Db-€90–105). You'll also find good rooms in the middle-aged wing; the cheapest rooms are the oldest, with showers instead of tubs, and no elevator (Sb-€65–105, Db-€75–125, most about €100, Tb-€116–140, free public parking nearby at Parking de la Vieille Ville, 38 Grand Rue, tel. 03 89 24 11 51, fax 03 89 23 47 78, www.hotel-saint-martin.com, Winterstein family SE).

$$$ **Hôtel Maréchal**** provides Colmar's most famous and characteristic digs in the heart of La Petite Venise, with luxurious rooms and professional service (standard Db-€100–135, Db with whirlpool tub-€135–225, suite Db-€255, parking-€7, 4 place des Six Montagnes Noires, tel. 03 89 41 60 32, fax 03 89 24 59 40, www.hotel-le-marechal.com). Their well-respected restaurant will melt a romantic's heart; you will be encouraged to dine here (*menus* from €35, reserve ahead).

$$$ **Hôtel le Rapp*** is ideally located off place Rapp and offers a variety of rooms for many budgets. Cheapest rooms are small but adequate; the larger rooms are tastefully designed, with queen-size beds. There's also a small basement pool, sauna, Turkish bath, and an indoor/outdoor bar-café. It's well-run and family-friendly, with a big park one block away, and lazy Pastaga, the hotel hound (Sb-€70, Db standard-€80, bigger Db-€90, Db-deluxe Db-€125,

---

Sleep Code

(€1 = about $1.20, country code: 33)
S = Single, **D** = Double/Twin, **T** = Triple, **Q** = Quad,
b = bathroom, **s** = shower only, **CC** = Credit Cards accepted,
no CC = Credit Cards not accepted, **SE** = Speaks English, **NSE** =
No English, * = French hotel rating system (0–4 stars). You can
assume a hotel takes credit cards unless you see "no CC" in the listing.

To help you sort easily through these listings, I've divided
the rooms into three categories based on the price for a standard
double room with bath:

$$$ **Higher Priced**—Most rooms €90 or more.
  $$ **Moderately Priced**—Most rooms between €60–90.
    $ **Lower Priced**—Most rooms €60 or less.

Tb-€130, good buffet breakfast-€9, Internet access, air-con, elevator,
1 rue Berthe Molly, tel. 03 89 41 62 10, fax 03 89 24 13 58,
www.rapp-hotel.com, resa@rapp-hotel.com, SE). Its restaurant
serves a classy Alsatian *menu* with impeccable service (closed Fri).

$$ Hôtel Turenne**** is a good value, with 83 smart rooms in
an historic building. It's a 10-minute walk from the city center, a
15-minute walk from the train station, and is located on a busy street
with easy parking underneath. Rooms are well-appointed, some with
tight bathrooms. A third of the rooms are non-smoking (Sb-€50,
Db-€62–70, Tb-€70, family-friendly studios-€114, parking-€6, air-
con, elevator for most rooms, cozy bar and breakfast room, from
train station walk straight out to avenue Raymond Poincaré, turn
left on rue des Americains, 10 rue de Bâle, tel. 03 89 21 58 58, fax 03
89 41 27 64, www.turenne.com, SE).

$$ Hôtel Ibis****, on the ring road, sells hospital-white, efficient
comfort with tiny bathrooms (Sb-€58–65, Db-€60–72, air-con,
inside parking-€6, outside parking-€3, 11 rue St. Eloi, tel. 03 89 41
30 14, fax 03 89 24 51 49).

$ Maison Jund offers my favorite budget beds in Colmar. This
ramshackle yet magnificent half-timbered house, the home of an
easygoing winemaker (André), feels like a medieval tree house
soaked in wine and filled with flowers. The rooms are simple but
adequately comfortable, spacious, and equipped with kitchenettes.
Most rooms are generally available only April to mid-September,
though five rooms are rented year-round (D-€27, Db/Tb-€35–40,
no breakfast served, free Internet access, 12 rue de l'Ange, tel. 03
89 41 58 72, fax 03 89 23 15 83, www.martinjund.com, martinjund
@hotmail.com). Leave your car at the lot across from the Hôtel
Primo, walk from Unterlinden Museum past Monoprix, and veer

left on rue des Clefs, left on rue Etroite, and right on rue de l'Ange. This is not a hotel, so there is no real reception, though good-natured Myriam (SE) seems to be around, somewhere, most of the time.

$ Hôtel Primo**, near the Unterlinden Museum, is an efficient, bright, nothing-but-the-plastic-and-concrete-basics place to sleep for those who consider ambience a four-letter word. Rooms facing the big square *(grand place)* are far quieter (S/D/T-€29, Sb-€39–49, Db-€49–59, Tb/Qb-€69, small discount for my readers, foam mattresses, Internet access, free parking in big square in front, rooms held until 18:00 if you call, friendly staff, 5 rue des Ancêtres, tel. 03 89 24 22 24, fax 03 89 24 55 96, www.hotel-primo.com, SE). Half the beds have footboards—a problem if you're over six feet tall.

Near the Train Station

$$$ Hôtel Bristol*** couldn't be closer to the station, and, in spite of its Best Western plaque, it has some character, with pleasant public spaces and good, if pricey, rooms (Sb-€78–90, standard Db-€99, big Db-€130, 7 place de la Gare, tel. 03 89 23 59 59, fax 03 89 23 92 26, www.grand-hotel-bristol.fr).

$ La Chaumière*, on a big street two blocks from the station, is above and behind a truly French café and has been run by gentle Madame Servor and her sister, Madame Chouvet, for 40 years. Most of its modest, good-value rooms surround a courtyard off the street (S/D-€30, Sb/Db-€40–43, parking-€4, walk straight out of station and turn left on avenue de la République to #74, tel. 03 89 41 08 99, SE a smidgen).

EATING

Colmar is full of good restaurants offering traditional Alsatian cuisine for €17–25. (Also see "Eating" in nearby Eguisheim, page 610.)

For dining with a canalside view, head into Petite Venise and make your way to the photo-perfect bridge on rue Turenne, where you'll find several picturesque places.

In Petite Venise

La Krutenau's wood tables sprawl along the canal, offering thin pizza-like *tartes flambées* and many desserts. Come for a light meal with ambience (inside or out), a dessert, or a drink on a warm evening (closed Sun–Mon, 1 rue de la Poissonnerie, tel. 03 89 41 18 80).

Wistub "La Petite Venise," buried in the middle of all the canal cuteness, serves well-presented creative dishes with a dash of Vosges mountain inspiration in what feels like a well-polished mountain chalet. Walter and Christel (SE) work hard in their small, eight-table place (among old-time family photos), and are accommodating—they explain their fun chalkboard menus and split desserts with a smile (closed Wed and Sun, 4 rue de la Poissonnerie, tel. 03 89 41 72 59).

In the Old City Center

Winstub Schwendi overflows with outdoor tables and has the lively feel of a German pub (with 10 beers on tap). Choose from a dozen different robust Swiss *rösti* plates or the *tarte flambées;* I like the *strasbourgoise* (€8–14 meals, daily, facing old Customs House at 3 Grand Rue).

La Maison Rouge has a folk-museum interior and noisy sidewalk seating with good, reasonably priced, traditional Alsatian cuisine (€16 and €23 *menus*, try the endive salad and *tarte flambée forestière*, closed Sun, 9 rue des Ecoles, tel. 03 89 23 53 22).

Hôtel-Restaurant le Rapp is a traditional place to savor a slow, elegant meal served with grace and fine Alsatian wine. While *menus* start at €18, if you want to order high on the menu, this is a fine place to do it (closed Fri, great *baeckeoffe* for €16 that makes a whole meal, good salads, they take their vegetarian options seriously, aircon, 1 rue Berthe Molly, tel. 03 89 41 62 10, SE).

Au Fer Rouge serves classic gourmet French cuisine with dressy formality in a charming old building with plateware Dale Chihuly would admire. When locals want to splurge, they come here. The five-course €50 *menu* (served only Mon–Thu) is an adventure you'll long remember (€50–100 for dinner, reserve ahead on weekends, closed Sun–Mon, 52 Grand Rue, tel. 30 89 41 37 24, fax 03 89 23 82 24).

Flunch, at the other end of the extreme, is a family-friendly cafeteria that's tastefully decorated. It serves cheap, easy-to-order food and has a good €4 salad bar (daily until 22:00, 10 place Rapp).

TRANSPORTATION CONNECTIONS

From Colmar by train to: Strasbourg (2/hr, 30 min), **Reims** (6/day, 6 hrs, changes in Strasbourg or Mulhouse and Metz or Chalon), **Beaune** (6/day, 4–5 hrs, changes in Besançon, Mulhouse, or Beflort and Dijon), **Paris'** Gare de l'Est (12/day, 5.5 hrs, change in Strasbourg, Dijon, or Mulhouse), **Amboise** (8/day, 9 hrs, via Paris), **Basel**, Switzerland (13/day, 1 hr), **Karlsruhe**, Germany (10/day, 2.5 hrs, best with change in Strasbourg; from Karlsruhe, it's 90 min to Frankfurt, 3 hrs to Munich).

Route du Vin
(The Wine Road)

Alsace's Route du Vin is an asphalt ribbon that ties 90 miles of vineyards, villages, and feudal fortresses into an understandably popular tourist package. This is a sunbelt that gets less rain than much of southern France. The generally dry, sunny climate has made for good wine and happy tourists since Roman days. Colmar and Eguisheim are ideally located for exploring the 30,000 acres of vineyards blanketing the hills from Marlenheim to Thann.

If you have only a day, focus on towns within easy striking range of Colmar. Top stops are Eguisheim, Kaysersberg, Hunawihr, Ribeauvillé, and the too-popular Riquewihr. Be careful not to overdose on all the half-timbered cuteness. Two or three villages are sufficient for most. As you tour this region, you'll see storks' nests on many church spires and city halls, thanks to a campaign to reintroduce the birds to this area. (Nests can weigh as much as 1,000 pounds.)

Get a map of the Route du Vin from any TI. Review "French Wine-Tasting 101" (page 46) and information on half-timbered architecture (page 594).

Most towns have wineries that give tours (some charge a fee), and many small producers open their courtyards and offer free tastings. The modern cooperatives at Eguisheim, Bennwihr, Hunawihr, and Ribeauvillé, created after the destruction of World War II, provide a good look at a more modern and efficient method of production.

Learn to recognize the basic grapes: Reisling is the king of Alsatian grapes. The name comes from the German word that describes its slightly smoky, gasoline smell. Gewürztraminer is "the lady's wine"—its bouquet is like a rosebush, its taste is fruity, and its aftertaste is spicy. In fact, it's named by the German word for "spicy." Crèmant d'Alsace, the Alsatian champagne, is very good—and much cheaper. The French term for headache, if you really get "Alsauced," is *mal de tête*.

Towns have a special vibrancy during their weekly morning farmers' markets (Friday: Turckheim, Monday: Kaysersberg, Saturday: Ribeauvillé and Colmar—behind station near St. Joseph's church). Riquewihr and Eguisheim have no market days.

Getting Around the Route du Vin

If you're driving, buy a good regional map (1:200,000 or better) before heading out.

By Bus: Several private companies run buses connecting Colmar's train station with most villages along the Route du Vin. In general, departures are fairly frequent except on Sundays. Kaysersberg has good service and makes an easy day trip from Colmar; Riquewihr, Hunawihr and Ribeauvillé have decent service, but service to Eguisheim is minimal (Mon–Sat schedules from Colmar to Eguisheim: 3/day, 20 min; to Kaysersberg: almost hrly, 25 min; to Riquewihr, Bennwihr, Hunawihr, Turckheim, and Ribeauvillé: 6/day, 30–45 min). Allow €1.50 to €3 one-way to these villages. Schedules are posted where buses stop, and on the bus island to the left of the station as you face it. You can also pick up your own schedules at the

Alsace's Route du Vin

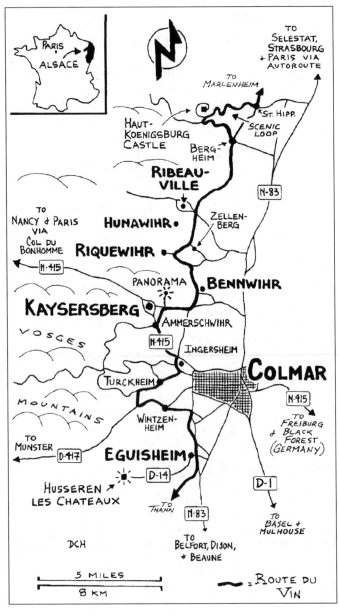

TI. Buy tickets from the driver. Eguisheim buses stop at the lower end of town at the PTT, Kaysersberg buses have blue accents.

By Taxi: Allow €14 from Colmar to Eguisheim, €25–30 from Colmar or Eguisheim to Kaysersberg (call friendly Taxi-William at 06 14 47 21 80, or another taxi at 03 89 80 71 71).

By Minivan Tour: Cheerful Jean-Claude Werner leads **Les Circuits d'Alsace** day trips in a comfortable minivan (small groups: min 2, max 7; in English and/or Japanese, great sound system on comfy, air-con bus). His informative tours include a few delightful, very short vineyard walks. Jean-Claude's enthusiasm and personal touches add to the experience. Wine-tastings can be arranged on request. Half-day tours for €50 visit three towns, generally Kaysersberg, Turckheim, and Eguisheim. Full-day tours for €93 add a couple more towns and the Haut-Koenigsbourg Castle (5 percent discount with a copy of this book, reserve directly with Jean-Claude, pickup at your hotel, tel. 03 89 41 90 88, mobile 06 88 40 21 02, www.alsace-travel.com, werner@alsace-travel.com).

By Bike: The Route du Vin's more or less level terrain and abundant bike trails make cycling a reasonable option, particularly once you get to the villages (see "Helpful Hints," page 591, for bike rental in Colmar). To save yourself the ride out of Colmar, rent a bike in Turckheim (84 Grand Rue, tel. & fax 03 89 27 06 36). Colmar to Eguisheim to Turckheim and back makes an easy 15-mile, half-day circuit; add Kaysersberg for a full-day's outing. Most key roads leaving Colmar have a painted bike lane. With a small bike lane, the route to Eguisheim from Colmar is a level snap, though it's entirely on busy city streets (biking to Eguisheim is a practical means of visiting this village, given the poor bus service and easy bike access). From Eguisheim, you can pedal along small vineyard roads. Figure pedaling steadily for 60 minutes on mostly busy roads to Kaysersberg from Colmar (bike lane on the main road from Colmar, route du Colmar). Get advice and a good map from a bike shop, and avoid major roads—except for those you use to leave Colmar (for directions, see "By Car," below).

By Car: To reach the Route du Vin north of Colmar, leave Colmar from the train station, following signs to Epinal. In Wintzenheim, follow signs to Turckheim, then find D-10 (Route du Vin) to Ingersheim (Kaysersberg is a short detour from here), Riquewihr, Hunawihr, Ribeauvillé, and Château du Haut-Koenigsbourg. Look for Route du Vin signs. For Eguisheim, leave Colmar on N-83 toward Belfort.

By Foot: Well-signed walking trails *(Sentiers Viticoles)* connect Route du Vin villages through the vineyards (get info at local TIs and see our walking trails under "Sights," below); hikers can climb to the higher ruined castles of the Vosges mountains (Eguisheim and Ribeauvillé are good bases). The Sentier Viticole connecting

Kaysersberg and Riquewihr is a good two-hour walk that works well with buses from Colmar (see "Kaysersberg," below).

SIGHTS

Along the Route du Vin, North of Colmar

These sights are listed from south to north.

Eguisheim—This is the most charming village of the region (described on page 607).

Turckheim—The pleasant town, with a fine square and garden-filled moat, is refreshingly untouristy, just enough off the beaten path to be overlooked. WWII buffs will be interested in its "Colmar Pocket" museum chronicling the American push to take Alsace from the Nazis.

Kaysersberg—The town has WWII sights, Dr. Albert Schwietzer's house, and plenty of hiking opportunities (described on page 610).

Riquewihr—This little village is so picturesque today because it was so rich centuries ago; you can tell its old wealth because it has the most stone houses of any place in Alsace. The walled village is crammed with tourist shops, cafés, galleries, cobblestones, and flowers. Sharpen your elbows if you arrive with the many groups in the afternoon. (**TI** tel. 03 89 47 80 80.)

You'll enter at the lower end under the Hôtel de Ville (City Hall). Within a few yards, you'll see the tourist train (€5.50, next departure time posted, 30 min, headset-recorded tour through vineyards). Try the excellent and free wine-tasting at Caves Dopff et Irion (uphill from Hôtel de Ville, daily 10:00–19:00, tel. 03 89 47 92 51). The wonderful "air-conditioning" is completely natural—you're in a cave.

Shop and browse, sampling fresh local baked goods given free to tourists, to the top of town, where you'll find one of best bell towers in the region (1291). The Dolden Museum (at the tower) shows off farm and winemaking tools). Check out the engraving of 13th-century Riquewihr by the fountain. Walks both inside and outside the ramparts begin from here. (The best walk is to the left or south.)

Zellenberg—This town has an impressive setting and is worth a quick stop for the views from either side of its narrow perch.

Hunawihr—This bit of wine-soaked Alsatian cuteness is far less visited than its more famous neighbors, and comes complete with a 16th-century fortified church that today is shared by Catholics and Protestants (the Catholics are buried next to the church; the Protestants are buried outside the church wall). Park below in the village at the sheltered picnic tables and follow the trail up to the church, then loop back through the village. Kids enjoy Hunawihr's small stork park, Parc des Cigognes (April–Nov daily 10:00–12:00

& 14:00–18:00, closed Oct–March, other animals take part in the afternoon shows). Eat well at **Winstub Suzel,** near the church (€16–22 *menus,* closed Tue, 2 rue de l'Eglise, tel. 03 89 73 30 85).

Ribeauvillé—Come here to hike. Two brooding castles hang above this pleasant town seldom visited by Americans. The steep castle trail leaves from the top of the town (at Hôtel Trois Châteaux, park in city lot here). Allow 45 minutes one-way, or just climb 10 minutes for a view over the town.

Château de Haut-Kœnigsbourg—This granddaddy of Alsatian castles, strategically situated on a rocky spur high above the flat Rhine plain, protected the passage between Alsace and Lorraine for centuries. Its pink stones, characteristic of the region, were quarried from Vosges mountains. Rebuilt in the early 20th century, this well-furnished castle illustrates Germanic influence in Alsatian history. Its furnishings attempt to show castle life from 15th through 17th centuries. There's little English, so you need the informative 90-minute audioguide (€7, audioguide-€4, June–Aug daily 9:30–18:00, April–May and Sept 9:30–17:00, March and Oct 9:45–16:30, Nov–Feb closed 12:00–13:00, about 15 min north of Ribeauvillé above St. Hippolyte).

Vieil-Armand WWI Memorial—This powerful memorial evokes the slaughter of the Western Front in World War I, when Germany and France bashed heads for years in a War of Attrition. It's up a windy road above Cernay (20 miles south of Colmar). From the parking lot, walk 10 minutes to the vast cemetery, and walk 30 more minutes through trenches to a hilltop with a grand Alsatian view. Here you'll find a stirring memorial statue of French soldiers storming the trenches in 1915 and 1916, facing near-certain death.

Eguisheim

Just a few miles south of Colmar's suburbs, this circular, flower-festooned little wine town (pop. 1,600) is almost too cute. It's ideal for a relaxing lunch and vineyard walks, and makes a good small-town base for exploring Alsace. It's a cinch by car (easy parking) and by bike, but barely accessible by bus. Consider taking the bus one-way and taxi the other to Colmar or other villages (bus schedules available at TIs).

The **TI** has information on accommodations, festivals, vineyard walks, and Vosges mountain hikes (Mon–Sat 9:30–12:00 & 14:00–18:00, closed Sun, 22 Grand Rue, tel. 03 89 23 40 33, www .ot-eguisheim.fr). They're happy to call a taxi for you. An Internet café is on rue du Rampart Nord.

While Eguisheim's wall is gone, the rue des Ramparts (Nord and Sud) survives, scenically circling the village. The main drag, Grand Rue, bisects the circle leading to a town square that's as darling as a

Grimms' fairy tale. Start your visit at the bottom of town (TI) and circle the ramparts clockwise (walking up rue du Rampart Sud). Cut into the town center to enjoy the main square. Then lose all sense of discipline, sampling the shops, cafes, and fruit of the local vine.

Back on the rue des Ramparts, you'll see that what was the moat is now lined with 13th- to 17th-century houses—a cancan of half-timbered charm. You're actually walking a lane between the back of fine homes (on the left) and their barns (on the right). Look for emblems of daily life, religious and magical symbols, dates on lintel stones, and so on. The most scenic and higgledy-piggledy view in town is right at the start of the loop (at the tight Y in the road, go left and uphill). Rue du Rampart Sud is more picturesque than Rue du Rampart Nord, but I'd walk the entire circle. (The government pays 15 percent of any work locals do on their exteriors.)

Eguisheim's main square, **place du Château,** lined with fine Renaissance houses, marks the heart of the old town. The castle is privately owned (closed to public). Surviving bits of its 13th-century, eight-sided wall circle the chapel, built in neo-Romanesque-style on the site of the castle's keep in 1895. While it is of little historic importance, it's worth a peek to see how a Romanesque chapel may have been painted (drop any coin into the €.50 box for light). The 19th-century fountain sports a statue of Pope St. Leo IX (1048–1054), the only Alsatian pope. Eguisheim's most famous son was a saint to boot.

Exploring the town, you may come upon some of its 20 "tithe courtyards." These once administered nearby farmland, which belonged to the church but was given to locals in return for 10 percent of their production. With so many of these courtyards, it's safe to conclude that the farming around here was excellent.

Don't leave without visiting one of Eguisheim's countless cozy **wineries,** or the big and modern **Wine Cooperative** (Wolfberger, Cave Vinicole d'Eguisheim, daily 8:00–12:00 & 14:00–18:00, 6 Grand Rue, tel. 03 89 22 20 20).

Views over Eguisheim: If you have a car, follow signs up to Lis Husseren and Les Cinq Châteaux, then walk 20 minutes to the ruined castle towers for a good view of the Vosges mountains above and vineyards below. By mountain bike or on foot, find any path through vineyards above Eguisheim for nice views (the TI has a free map, *Canton de Wintzenheim en balade*). For a bracing and scenic 90-minute round-trip hike, walk uphill on Grande Rue, cross the ring road leaving Eguisheim's town center, and turn left at the *Camping* arrow. Pass the campground, then follow Sentier Viticole signs past the little Stork Park and keep straight. The five châteaux of Les Husseren float above on your right. Sentier Viticole signs will lead you on a loop trip through the vineyards to the village of Husseren at the base of those castles, then back to Eguisheim.

SLEEPING

(€1 = about $1.20, country code: 33)

Hotels

$$$ **Hôtel St. Hubert***** offers polished and modern German, hotel-like comfort, an indoor pool and sauna, vineyards out your window, and a warm welcome (15 rooms, Db-€78, bigger Db-€100, Db suite-€120, extra bed-€16, buffet breakfast-€10, 4 rooms have patios, free pickup at Colmar's train station if reserved in advance, 6 rue des Trois Pierres, tel. 03 89 41 40 50, fax 03 89 41 46 88, www.hotel-st-hubert.com, Karen SE).

$$$ **Hostellerie du Château*****, part art gallery, part hotel, provides stylish, contemporary luxury on the main square (Db-€80–94, extra bed-€16, a few rooms overlook the pretty square, 2 place du Château St. Léon IX, tel. 03 89 23 72 00, fax 03 89 41 63 93, www.hostellerieduchateau.com, info@hostellerieduchateau.com).

$$ **Auberge Alsacienne***** is picturesque, with small, tastefully designed rooms and rental bikes for guests (Db-€55–65, Tb-€75, 12 Grand Rue, tel. 03 89 41 50 20, fax 03 89 23 89 32, auberge-alsacienne@wanadoo.fr, Dutroe speaks a little English).

$ **Auberge du Rempart** is atmospheric, with white, bright, and airy rooms deep inside the town (standard Db-€50, bigger Db-€65, great family suite-€90, 3 rue des Remparts Sud, near TI, tel. 03 89 41 16 87, fax 03 89 41 06 50, www.auberge-du-rempart.com, auberge-du-rempart@wanadoo.fr).

Chambres d'Hôte

While none of these owners speak English, they're creative at communicating. Please remember to cancel if you reserve a room and can't use it.

$$ **Madame Hertz-Meyers**, your Alsatian grandmother who wishes you spoke French so she could chat with you, welcomes you with mostly big rooms in a mansion surrounded by vineyards, only 200 feet from the village. Rooms in the main house are great for families and better than her two modern apartments (Sb-€46, Db-€53–60, Tb-€75, includes breakfast, no CC, 3 rue du Riesling; look for sign Albert-Hertz, Dégustation-Vente, walk into courtyard and ring bell; check-in after 18:00 unless otherwise prearranged by fax, tel. & fax 03 89 23 67 74).

$ **Monique Freudenreich** rents spacious, light, and decent rooms at a good price. Charming Mme. Freudenreich, who loves America, is learning English, but still relies on her son Alexandre to translate. They will pick you up in Colmar if you book ahead (Db-€42, includes breakfast, no CC, one block from TI, 4 cour Unterlinden, tel. & fax 03 89 23 16 44, maisonhotes@aol.com).

$ **Madame Dirringer's** is a formal place, with four comfortable rooms facing a traditional courtyard (Db-€32–35, good family room, breakfast-€6, no CC, 11 rue du Riesling, tel. 03 89 41 71 87).

$ **Madame Bombenger's** modern, graceful home has nice views into the vineyards and over Eguisheim (Db-€46, includes breakfast, 3 rue des Trois Pierres, tel. & fax 03 89 23 71 19, mobile 06 61 94 31 09).

EATING

The Charcuterie on place du Château has killer quiche to go and everything you need for a fine picnic (daily until 19:00). You can picnic on the wood benches by the fountain.

For a sit-down meal, **Auberge de Trois Châteaux** is very Alsatian, with cozy ambience and traditional cuisine (€16 and €19 *menus* and reasonable *plats du jour*, closed Tue–Wed, 26 Grand Rue, tel. 03 89 23 70 61).

Auberge Alsacienne offers regional cuisine in a more refined setting (closed Sun–Mon, 2 courses-€16, 3 courses-€25, 12 Grand Rue, tel. 03 89 41 50 20).

Auberge du Rempart is best for outdoor dining in a pleasant courtyard around a fountain. Come here for less expensive and lighter meals and good *tarte flambées* (closed Mon, closed Sun off-season, 3 rue des Remparts Sud, near TI, tel. 03 89 41 16 87).

Kaysersberg

Albert Schweitzer's hometown offers a cute jumble of 15th-century homes under a romantically ruined castle, with easy vineyard trails at its doorstep, and lots of tourists. Frequent buses from Colmar make Kaysersberg an easy day trip. Catch buses back to Colmar across the road from the bus shelter where riders are dropped coming from Colmar (a block from post office).

The **TI** is inside Hôtel de Ville near the town's main entry (closed Sun, tel. 03 89 78 22 78, WCs under arch next door). Walkers can pick up the free *Sentier Viticole* map for hiking between wine villages and bus schedules (from their destination back to Colmar). Serious walkers can buy the trail map (see "Walking Trails from Kaysersberg," below). The TI also has information on bike rental.

Strolling through Kaysersberg is a treat. Walking up the main drag through the town, you'll see **St. Croix Church** (daily 9:00–16:00, unique crucifix in front of a fine 1518 altarpiece—push button for light); colorful shops (pop into the Moulin des Arts—a touristy shopping mall with waterwheels); the humble town museum (€2, daily 14:00–18:00), and its 16th-century bridge. As the Nazis were preparing to evacuate, they planned to destroy the bridge. Locals reasoned with the commander, agreeing to dig an anti-tank ditch just beyond the bridge—and the symbol of the town was saved. Just beyond, you'll come to **Dr. Albert Schweitzer's house**, a small and disappointing museum. It has two rooms of scattered photos and artifacts from his time in Africa, without a word of English (€2, daily 9:00–12:00 & 14:00–18:00, closed Nov–Easter, 126 rue du Général de Gaulle). The square across the street hosts a thriving market each Monday until noon.

Walking Trails from Kaysersberg: Well-marked trails depart from just outside the TI (walk under arch next to TI and find trail signs). Turn left on the trail to hike up to the **castle** (free, fine views and benches, 113 steps up a dark stairway to the tower). Hikers can continue past the castle for more views and walks on vineyard roads. This also leads to the well-signed, longer route to Riquewihr (2.5 hrs).

For an easier hike to Riquewihr, turn right (rather than left) on the same trail back down by the TI. You'll start on a bike path *(piste cyclable)* to Kientzheim, then join the trail (marked Sentier Viticole) to Riquewihr (where buses can take you back to Colmar).

World War II Sights: The hill just north of Kaysersberg is soaked in WWII blood. Towns around it have gray-tiled, rather than red-tiled, roofs (indicating they were entirely destroyed and rebuilt). **Kientzheim** has an American-made tank parked in its front yard and a wine museum in its castle grounds. In 2004, the refreshing system of a tiny stream of water trickling down its streets (standard before WWII) was restored. Both Sigolsheim (scene of fierce fighting—note its sterile, rebuilt Romanesque church) and Bennwihr are modern, as they were taken and lost a dozen times by the Allies and Nazis, and entirely destroyed. Today, the hill is still called "Bloody Hill," as it was nicknamed by German troops. Between its cemeteries, you'll find some of the best vines on the Route du Vin.

A **WWII Monument** stands atop Bloody Hill. The spectacular setting, best at sunset, houses a monument to the American divisions that helped liberate Alsace in World War II (find the American flag). Up the lane, a beautiful cemetery is the final resting place of 1,600 men who fought in the French army (many gravestones are Muslim—for soldiers from France's North African colonies—Morocco, Algeria, and Tunisia. From this brilliant viewpoint, you can survey the entire southern section of the Route du Vin and into Germany. The hard-to-find road to the memorial leaves from the center of Sigolsheim (follow Necropole and Cimitière signs, turning at Pierre Sparr winery, then keep straight and climb into the vineyards).

Sleeping in Kaysersberg: **Hôtel L'Arbre Vert**** gives you three-star comfort at two-star prices (Db-€60–70, across from Albert Schweitzer's house at top end of town, 1 rue Haute du Rempart, tel. 03 89 47 11 51, fax 03 89 78 13 40).

Strasbourg

Strasbourg is urban Alsace at its best, and it feels like a giant Colmar with water and streetcars. It's a progressive, livable city, with generous space devoted to pedestrians, scads of bikes, sleek trams, meandering waterways, and a young, lively mix of university students, Eurocrats, and street people. This place has an Amsterdam-like feel. Situated just west of the Rhine River, Strasbourg provides the ultimate blend of Franco-Germanic culture, architecture, and ambience. A living symbol of the perpetual peace between France and Germany, Strasbourg was selected as home to the European Parliament, the European Council (sharing administrative responsibilities for the European Union with Brussels, Belgium), and the European Court of Human Rights. Strasbourg makes a good day trip from Colmar or a handy stop en route to Paris (baggage check available). None of its museums are compelling—you're here to see the cathedral, wander the waterways, and take a bite out of the big city. Plan on three hours to do my loop walk, starting at Strasbourg's dazzling cathedral (try to be here by 12:15 for the clock's best performance, see "Sights," next page) and ending with La Petite France (ideally for lunch).

Tourist Information

There's a TI at the train station and another next to the cathedral. The **train station TI** is far quieter (outside the station and one floor down, daily, year-round, 9:00–18:00). The **main TI** faces the cathedral at 17 place de la Cathédrale (Mon–Sat 9:00–19:00, Sun 9:00–18:00, tel. 03 88 52 28 28, www.strasbourg.com). Buy the €1 city map (which describes a decent walking tour in English), or pay €6 for a Walkman cassette tour that covers the cathedral and old city in more detail than most need (available only at the main TI and includes a cute little map of the route, allow 90 min). The TI also has bike maps for the city and surrounding areas.

The €11 **Strasbourg Pass** (valid 3 days) is a great value if you plan to see even just a handful of sights; it includes one museum free (half-off coupons for others), the cathedral narthex view and astrological clock entries, the boat cruise, free bike for a day, and half off a Walkman tour.

Arrival in Strasbourg

By Train: After stopping by the station TI (baggage check in station), walk 15 urban minutes to the cathedral. Cross the big square and walk past Hôtel Vendôme and up rue du Maire Kuss, cross the river, and continue up serpentine rue du 22 November all the way to place Kleber. Cross bustling place Kleber, maintaining the same direction, then turn right on the huge pedestrian street (rue des Grandes

Arcades). Turn left on rue des Hallebardes, then follow that spire.

To get from the train station to the city center by public transportation, catch the caterpillar-looking tram that leaves the station one floor below the TI (buy €1.20 tickets from machines on platforms, then validate in skinny machines). Take Tram A (direction: Illkirch) three stops to Grande Rue, two blocks from the cathedral. (You can return to the station, Gare Centrale, from same stop, direction: Hautepierre.)

By Car: Follow *Gare Centrale* signs and park under the train station, or look for *Centre-Ville/Cathédrale* signs to park closer to the center (and encounter more traffic). Parking lots are well-marked— place Gutenberg and place du Château are close to the cathedral, though the larger Austerlitz lot works fine. Pay to park safe here.

By Plane: The user-friendly Strasbourg-Entzheim airport (tel. 03 88 64 67 67), with frequent and often inexpensive flights to Paris, is easily accessible via tram and shuttle bus: From the airport, catch the shuttle bus (*navette*, 3/hr) to the Baggarsee stop, where Tram A runs frequently to the city center, stopping at the train station and cathedral (allow €6 and 30 min total).

Helpful Hints

U.S. Consulate: It's at 15 rue d'Alsace (tel. 03 88 35 31 04, fax 03 88 23 07 17.)

Quiet Transportation: Beware of quiet streetcars and bicycles; look both ways before crossing streets. Bikes are allowed on pedestrian streets.

Bike Rental: You can rent bikes near the station at **Velocation** (4 rue du Maire Kus, half-day-€4, tel. 03 88 23 56 75).

Taxi: Call 03 88 36 13 13.

SIGHTS

▲▲**Strasbourg Cathedral (Cathédrale de Notre-Dame)**—Stand in front of Hôtel de la Cathédrale and crane your neck up. If this church, with its single soaring spire and pink sandstone color, wows you today, imagine its impact on medieval tourists. The delicate Gothic style of the cathedral (begun in 1176, not finished until 1429) is another Franco-German mixture that somehow survived the French Revolution, the Franco-Prussian war, World War I, and World War II. The square in front of the cathedral makes the ideal stage for street performers—it's like a medieval fair from one thousand years ago.

Before entering the cathedral, look around. This square was Roman 2,000 years ago. Then, as well as now, it was the center of activity. The dark, half-timbered building to your left next to the TI was the home of a wealthy merchant in the 16th century, and symbolizes the virtues of capitalism that Strasbourg has long revered. Goods were sold under the ground floor arches; owners lived above.

Strasbourg made its medieval mark as a trading center, taking advantage of its location at the crossroads of Europe and its river-accessible location to charge tolls for the movement of goods. Its strong economy allowed for the construction of this remarkable cathedral. Strasbourg's location also made it susceptible to new ideas. Martin Luther's theses were posted on its main doors, and after the wars of religion, this cathedral was Protestant for over 100 years. It took Louis XIV to return it to Catholicism (in 1621).

As you enter the cathedral, notice the sculpture over the left portal (complacent, spear-toting Virtues getting revenge on those nasty Vices). Enter and walk down the center. The stained glass on the lower left shows various rulers of Strasbourg, while the stained glass on your right depicts Bible stories. An ornate, gold-leafed organ hangs above the second pillars. Walk to the choir and stare at the stained-glass image of Mary; find the European Union flag at the top.

In the right transept is a high-tech, 15th-century **astronomical clock** (restored in 1883) that gives a ho-hum performance every 15 minutes (keep your eye on the little angel about 15 feet up, slightly left of center), better on the half hour (angel on the right), and best at 12:30 (everybody gets in the act, including a rooster and 12 apostles—for the 12 hours). Arrive by 12:00 outside the right transept, buy your €1 ticket, then enter and hear an explanation of the clock's workings—and beware of pickpockets.

For €3, you can climb 330 steps to the top of the narthex for an amazing view (access on right side of cathedral, cathedral open daily 7:00–11:35 & 12:40–19:00; tower open April–Sept daily 9:00–17:00, Oct–March daily 9:00–16:30).

Before leaving this area, investigate the impressive network of smaller pedestrian streets that connect the cathedral with the huge place Kleber (home to various outdoor markets depending on the day of the week). Each street is named for the primary trade that took place there.

Museums near the Cathedral—These museums sit just outside the cathedral's right transept and are interesting only for aficionados with particular interests or a full day in Strasbourg. They're all free the first Sunday of the month.

Palais Rohan: This stately palace houses three museums—the **Museum of Decorative Arts** (big rooms with red velvet chairs), the **Museum of Fine Arts** (a small, well-displayed collection of paintings from Middle Ages to Baroque, some by artists you would recognize), and the **Archaeological Museum**, which is the best of the three, with a stellar presentation of Alsatian civilization through the millennia, with English explanations (€4 each, Wed–Mon 10:00–18:00, closed Tue, 2 place du Château).

Museum of the Cathedral (Musée de l'Oeuvre Notre-Dame): The well-organized museum has plenty of artifacts from the cathedral and includes an English audioguide in the admission (€4, Tue–Sun 10:00–18:00, closed Mon, 3 place du Château).

Alsatian Museum: An extensive collection of Alsatian folk art is presented in one of Strasbourg's oldest and most characteristic homes, along with scenes from daily life, house interiors, tools, as well as the life of a wine-maker, but without English explanations (€4, daily 14:00–18:00, across the river and down one block from the boat dock at 23 quai St Nicholas).

Boat Ride on the Ill River—Popular glass-topped boats do loop trips around Strasbourg in 70 minutes. The boats are air-conditioned and sufficiently comfortable; either side has fine views. It's a nice break from walking and gives a water-oriented perspective on the city. You'll pass through two locks as you circle the old city clockwise. The highlight for me was cruising by the European Parliament buildings and the European Court of Human Rights (adults-€7, under 18-half price, 70 min, good English commentary with live guide or audioguide, 2 boats/hr, April–Oct 9:30–21:00, May–Sept 9:30–22:00, Nov–March 10:30–13:00 & 14:30–16:00, dock is 2 blocks outside cathedral's right transept, where rue Rohan meets the river).

La Petite France—Historic home to Strasbourg's tanners, millers, and fishermen, this almost-too-charming area is laced with canals, crowned with magnificent half-timbered homes, carpeted with cobblestones, and filled with tourists. From the cathedral, retrace your steps down rue des Hallebardes to the merry-go-round, then continue straight, following rue Gutenberg. Cross big rue des Francs Bourgeois and keep straight (now on Grande Rue). Turn left on the fourth little street (rue du Bouclier, street signs are posted behind you), and make your way to the middle of the bridge (pont St. Martin). Gaze at the various locks and the channels that meet here. Walk down to the river, following the walkway past the lock deep into La Petite France. Make friends with a leafy café table on place Benjamin Zix, or find the siesta-perfect parks between the canals across the bridge at rue des Moulins. Climb the once-fortified grassy wall (Barrage Vauban) for an okay view—the glass structure behind you is the new modern art museum (interesting more for its architecture than its collection). La Petite France's coziest cafés line the canal on quai de la Bruche near the barrage. From here, it's a 10-minute walk back to the station (with river on your left walk along quai de Turkheim, cross the third bridge and find rue du Maire Kuss).

SLEEPING

(€1 = about $1.20, country code: 33)
You'll find a handy launderette near both listed hotels on rue des Veaux.

$$$ **Hôtel Cathédrale***, comfortable and contemporary, has a Jack-and-the-beanstalk spiral stairway (elevator also available one floor up) and a hopelessly confusing floor plan. This modern yet

atmospheric place lets you stare at the cathedral point-blank from your room. Skip the cheaper rooms *sans* view, and splurge (Db with view-€150, small Db without view-€85–110, larger Db with no view-€120, prices include good buffet breakfast in a room with a view, air-con, Internet access, free bicycles can be reserved for up to 2 hrs, laundry service, good to reserve a parking space ahead—only 5 available-€16, 12 place de la Cathédrale, tel. 03 88 22 12 12, toll free in France 08 00 00 00 84, fax 03 88 23 28 00, www.hotel-cathedrale.fr, reserv@hotel-cathedrale.fr, SE).

$$ Hôtel Suisse**, across from the cathedral's right transept and off place du Château, is a low profile, dark, central, and solid two-star value (Sb-€52–62, Db-€72–77, extra person-€10, elevator, 2 place de la Râpe, tel. 03 88 35 22 11, fax 03 88 25 74 23, www.hotel-suisse.com, info@hotel-suisse.com, SE).

EATING

Atmospheric *winstubs* serving affordable salads and *tarte flambée* are a snap to find. If the weather is nice, head for **La Petite France** and choose ambience over cuisine—dine outside at any café/*winstub* that appeals to you.

For a real meal, skip the touristy restaurants on the cathedral square and consider these nearby places, both one block behind the TI, and both closed on Sunday (go left out of the TI, then take the first left through the passageway and keep walking): **Chez Yvonne** (marked *S'Burgerstuewel* above windows) has a tradition of good food, pleasant staff, and reasonable prices (allow €20–25, daily, 10 rue du Sanglier, tel. 03 88 32 84 15). Half a block left down rue du Chaudron at #3 lies **Le Clou Winstub,** with €10 salads and €14 *plats du jour* (closed Sun, tel. 03 88 32 11 67).

TRANSPORTATION CONNECTIONS

Strasbourg makes a good side-trip from Colmar or a stop on the way to or from Paris.

From Strasbourg by train to: Colmar (hrly, 50 min), **Paris'** Gare de l'Est (14/day, 4.5 hrs, 6 require changes), **Karlsruhe**, Germany (16/day, 1.5 hrs, 11 with change in Appenweier), **Basel**, Switzerland (hrly, 2 hrs).

Verdun

Few traces of World War I remain in Europe today, but Verdun provides a fine and hard-hitting tribute to the almost one million lives lost in the battles fought here. While the lunar landscape of that war is now forested over, craters and trenches are still visible. Millions of live bombs lie in vast cordoned-off areas, and every year, French farmers and hikers are injured by unexploded mines. Drive or ride through the eerie moguls surrounding Verdun, and stop at melted-sugar-cube forts and plaques marking where towns once existed. With three hours and a car or easy taxi rides, or a full day and a bike (and a strong heart), you can see the most stirring sights and appreciate the tremendous scale of the battles. The town of Verdun is not your destination, but a starting point for your visit into the nearby battlefields.

Tourist Information

The TI is just across the river (cross pont Chausée) east of the city center on place de la Nation (May–Sept daily 8:30–18:30, Oct–April closed 12:00–14:00 and at 18:00, tel. 03 29 86 14 18).

Arrival in Verdun

By Train: Walk straight out of the station and down avenue Garibaldi to the town center.

By Car: Follow signs to the town center *(Centre-Ville)*, place de la Nation, and Porte Chatel; you'll pass the TI just before crossing the river.

Getting Around the Verdun Battlefield

The TI has good maps of the battlefield remains, which are situated on two sides of the Meuse River; the *rive droite* (right bank) has more sights. By following signs to Fort Douaumont and the Ossuaire, you'll pass Mémorial-Musée de Fleury.

With a Car: Start at the TI, pick up the information you need, then head east on avenue du Général Mangin, turn left on D-964, then right on to D-112 and look for signs to Douaumont (follow D-913 to Douaumont). You can **rent a car** at the train station (about €45–60 per day with 120 kilometers/80 miles included, **Hertz:** tel. 03 29 86 58 58).

Without a Car: Four-hour, French-language **minivan tours** of the battle sites are available June through September and leave the TI around 14:00 (€26, guides usually speak some English, English handouts are available). You can rent a bike opposite Verdun's train station at **Cycles Flavenot** (closed Sun–Mon, tel. 03 29 86 12 43). Round-trip, it's about a 20-mile ride along mostly level terrain (follow directions given above, you'll pass the TI on your way).

While **taxis** can take visitors through the battlefields (no English), the best plan is to have them drop you at L'Ossuaire (see "Sights," below) and pick you up a few hours later at Fort Douaumont, a 20-minute walk away (€18 each way, tel. 03 29 86 05 22).

SIGHTS

▲▲**Battlegrounds**—After the annexation of Alsace and Lorraine following the Franco-Prussian war in 1871, Verdun was a short 25 miles from the German border. This was too close for comfort for the French, who invested mightily in the fortification of Verdun, hoping to discourage German thoughts of invasion. The plan failed. At the onset of World War I, the Germans wanted to strike a quick knockout punch at the heart of the French defense to demoralize them and force a quick surrender. They chose Verdun as the ultimate symbol of French pride. The French chose to fight to the bitter end.

Soft, forested lands hide the memories of the vicious battles that took place here during 1916. Thirteen once-thriving villages were caught in the middle and obliterated, never to resurrect. Only small monuments remind us that they ever existed.

There are three compelling sights to visit in this area: Mémorial-Musée de Fleury, L'Ossuaire, and Fort Douaumont.

Start with **Mémorial-Musée de Fleury**. The museum is built on the site of a village (Fleury) lost during the fighting. Its centerpiece is the re-creation of a battlefield, with hard-hitting photos, weaponry displays, and a worthwhile 15-minute movie narrated in English with headphones (€7, May–mid-Sept 9:00–18:00, mid-Sept–April 9:00–12:00 & 14:00–17:00, until 18:00 mid-Sept–Oct, closed Jan).

L'Ossuaire de Douaumont is the tomb of 130,000 French and Germans whose last homes were the muddy trenches of Verdun (May–Aug daily 9:00–18:30, Sept and April daily 9:00–12:00 & 14:00–18:30, Oct & March 9:00–12:00 & 14:00–17:30, closes at 17:00 in Nov, Dec 14:00–17:00 only, closed Jan–mid-Feb). Look through the low windows for a bony memorial to those whose political and military leaders asked them to make the "ultimate sacrifice" for their countries. Enter the monument and experience a humbling and moving tribute. Reflect on a war that left half of all Frenchmen aged 15 to 30 dead or wounded. Climb the tower for a territorial view and don't miss the thought-provoking 20-minute film (€3.50, includes tower; theater in basement, ask for English version). The little coin-op picture boxes in the gift shop are worth a look if you don't visit Mémorial-Musée de Fleury (turn through all of the old photos before time expires, tel. 03 29 84 54 81).

Before leaving, walk to the cemetery and listen for the eerie buzz of silence and peace. Rows of 15,000 Christian crosses and Muslim headstones (oriented toward Mecca) decorate the cemetery. Moroccan soldiers were instrumental in France's ultimate victory at Verdun, a fact often overlooked by right-wing politicians in France. You can visit the nearby **Tranchée des Baïonnettes**, where an entire company of soldiers was buried alive in their trench (the soldiers' bayonets remained above ground until recently).

Verdun

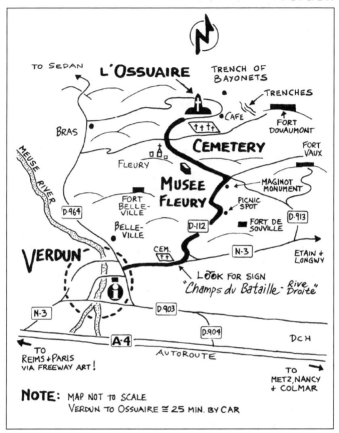

The nearby **Fort Douaumont** (same hours as L'Ossuaire) was a strategic command center for both sides at various times. It's more interesting from the outside than the inside (walk on top and notice the round, iron-gun emplacements that could rise and revolve). A walk inside (€3, daily 10:00–13:00 & 14:00–18:00, no midday break in summer) completes the picture, with long, damp corridors and a German memorial on the spot where 1,600 Germans were killed by a single blast. Halfway between L'Ossuaire and Fort Douaumont (on either side of the road) are clearly visible trenches. Village Détruit signs indicate where villages were entirely destroyed; only monuments remain to mark their existence.

Citadelle Souterraine—This is a disappointing visit through the tunnels of the French Command in downtown Verdun. While it tries to re-create the Verdun scene, it's not worth your time.

TRANSPORTATION CONNECTIONS

From Verdun by train to: Colmar (5/day, 4–6 hrs, best with changes in Metz and Strasbourg), **Reims** (4/day, 3 hrs, most with change in Chalon), **Paris'** Gare de l'Est (5/day, 3 hrs, change in Metz or Chalon).

Reims

Deservedly famous for its cathedral and its champagne, contemporary Reims (rance, rhymes with France) is a prosperous, modern city. Rebuilt after being leveled in World War I, Reims is 90 minutes from Paris by car or train and makes a good day trip or handy stop for travelers en route elsewhere. Most sights of interest (champagne *caves,* or cellars, included) are within a 20-minute walk from the cathedral.

To best experience contemporary Reims, wander the busy shopping streets between the cathedral and the train station; rue de Vesle, rue Condorcet, and place Drouet d'Erlon are best.

Tourist Information: The TI is outside the cathedral's left transept (Easter–mid-Oct Mon–Sat 9:00–19:00, Sun 10:00–18:00; mid-Oct–Easter Mon–Sat 9:00–18:00, Sun 11:00–17:00, free map shows champagne *caves,* Internet access available, public WCs across street, tel. 03 26 77 45 25, www.tourisme.fr/reims). Ask about tours of the cathedral in English (2–3/day Sat–Sun, summer only), and skip the costly audioguide tour (covers the city and cathedral).

Arrival in Reims

By Train: To get to the cathedral by foot (15-min walk), walk straight out of the station (baggage check available) and through the park, cross the huge boulevard Joffre and boulevard Foch, and stroll up the pedestrian place Drouet d'Erlon. Turn left on rue Condorcet, then right on rue de Talleyrand, to reach the cathedral. Most buses leaving from the front of the station (station side of the street) will take you close to the cathedral (verify with driver, get off at stop Grand Théâtre).

By Car: Follow *Centre-Ville* and *Cathédrale* signs and park on the street approaching the cathedral (rue Libergier) or in the well-signed Parking Cathédrale structure.

SIGHTS

▲▲▲**Cathedral**—The cathedral of Reims is a glorious example of Gothic architecture, with the best west portal anywhere (inside and outside). Since medieval churches always face east, you enter the west portal. Clovis, the first king of the Franks, was baptized here in

A.D. 496 (thus determining France's religion). Ever since, Reims' cathedral has served as *the* place for the coronation of French kings and queens. Self-assured Joan of Arc led a timid Charles VII here to be crowned in 1429. This event rallied the French around their king to push the English out of France and end the Hundred Years' War. The cathedral houses many treasures, great medieval stained glass, and a luminous set of Marc Chagall stained-glass windows from 1974 that somehow fit well into this ancient stone structure. Informative English explanations are provided along the right aisle and offer sufficient historical detail (including the Chagall windows) for most travelers (daily 7:30–19:30).

Palais de Tau—This former Archbishop's Palace houses artifacts from the cathedral (mostly tapestries and stone statues) in impressive rooms—these guys lived well. There is sadly little English information, and while I enjoyed seeing eye-to-eye with the original statues from the cathedral's facade—particularly the huge Goliath that hangs above the entry's rose window—this museum isn't worth the time for most (€6.50, May–Aug Tue–Sun 9:30–18:30, Sept–April Tue–Sun 9:30–12:30 & 14:00–17:30, closed Mon).

▲**Champagne Tours**—Reims is the capital of the Champagne region. While the bubbly stuff's birthplace was closer to Epernay, you can tour a champagne cave right in Reims. All charge for tastings and are open daily; the last tours usually depart about an hour before midday and afternoon closings—the hours listed below reflect the hours of the last visit. All but the four listed below must be reserved in advance to visit.

Mumm is closest to the train station and offers three kinds of worthwhile visits. The "traditional" (€7, 1 hr) includes a good 10-minute video explaining the history of Mumm and the champagne-making process, a tour of the cellars, where 25 million bottles are stored, and a small museum of old champagne-making contraptions. The tour ends with a glass of Cordon Rouge. The "enological visit" offers all that, plus a "guided" tasting at the end (€13 for 2 tastes, €18 for 3, 1.5 hrs). You can also add a "vineyard visit" by minivan (€25, 3 hrs), but only by reservation in advance (March–Sept daily 9:00–11:00 & 14:00–17:00, Oct–Feb weekend afternoons, tel. 03 26 49 59 70, www.champagne-mumm.com). Mumm is four blocks left out of the train station, on the other side of place de la République at 34 rue du Champs de Mars. Don't go in #29 on the left-hand side of the street, as shown on the city map; the visits are in the building on the right, #34, at the end of the courtyard. Follow signs for Visites des Caves.

The next three places cluster near each other about 25 minutes by foot southeast of the cathedral (from behind cathedral's right transept, walk down rue de l' Université, then rue du Barbâtre; figure €7 for a one-way taxi from the train station). **Taittinger** does a great job of trying to convince you they're the best. After seeing their

Reims

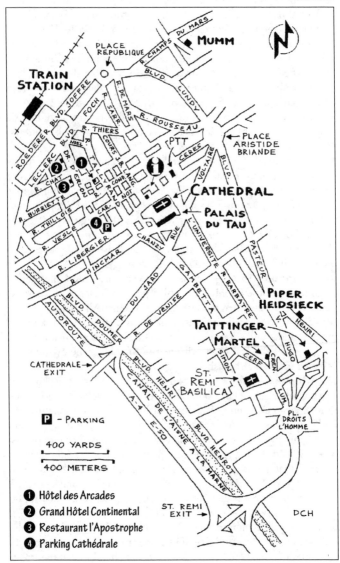

Mumm

PLACE RÉPUBLIQUE

DU MARS

R. CHAMPS

BLVD. LUNDY

TRAIN STATION

R. DE MARS

R. ROUSSEAU

BLVD. JOFFRE

FOCH

R. SARR

ROEDERER

BLVD. LECLERC

DR. CHAT

R. THIERS

NOEL

COURS J.

R. TAL

R. DE PÉRON

PTT

CERES

← PLACE ARISTIDE BRIANDE

VOLTAIRE

BLVD.

❷

❶

❸

R. BURRIETTE

R. THILLOIS

CONT.

R. RAZ

NOT

CAR.

❹ P

CATHEDRAL

PALAIS DU TAU ←

R. VESLE

R. LIBERGIER

R. HINCMAR

CHANZY

RUE

R. UNIVERSITÉ R. BARBATRE

PASTEUR

AUTOROUTE

BLVD. P. DOUMER

P. DU JARD

R. DE VENISE

GAMBETTA

PIPER HEIDSIECK

TAITTINGER

MARTEL

HUGO

HENRI

CATHEDRALE → EXIT

BLVD. HENRI

CANAL DE L'AISNE À LA MARNE

A-4 E-50

SIMON

CERE

CREN

ST. REMI BASILICA

LUM.

PL. DROITS L'HOMME

BLVD. HENROT

P – PARKING

400 YARDS

400 METERS

ST. REMI EXIT →

DCH

❶ Hôtel des Arcades
❷ Grand Hôtel Continental
❸ Restaurant l'Apostrophe
❹ Parking Cathédrale

movie (in comfortable theater seats), follow your guide down into some of the three miles of chilly chalk caves, many dug by ancient Romans. Popping corks signal when the tour's done and the tasting's begun (€7, includes tasting, 1 hr, Mon–Fri 9:30–11:00 & 14:00–16:30, Sat–Sun 9:00–11:00 & 14:00–17:00, Dec–Feb closed weekends, 9 place St. Nicaise, tel. 03 26 85 84 33, www.taittinger .com). **Piper Heidsieck** offers a short, Disneyesque train-ride tour and tasting (€7 for 1 sample, €13 for 3 samples, daily 9:00–11:45 & 14:00–17:00, Jan–Feb closed Tue–Wed, one block beyond Taittinger up boulevard Victor Hugo to 51 boulevard Henri Vasnier, tel. 03 26 84 43 44, www.piper-heidsieck.com). **Martel** is nearby, less famous, and the best deal, with a we-try-harder attitude. Their €5, 50-minute tour includes a film, a tour of their cellars, and a tasting of three different champagnes (open through lunch, daily 10:00–18:00, 17 rue des Créneaux, tel. 03 26 82 70 67).

SIGHTS

Near Reims

Epernay—Champagne purists may want to visit Epernay (16 miles away, well-connected to Paris and Reims), where the granddaddy of champagne houses, **Moët et Chandon**, offers tours with three tasting possibilities (€7 for single tasting, €16 for 2 tastes, €20 for 3, daily 9:30–11:30 & 14:00–16:30, tel. 03 26 51 21 00). According to the story, it was near here in about 1700 that the monk Dom Perignon, after much fiddling with double fermentation, stumbled onto this bubbly treat. On that happy day, he ran through the abbey shouting, "Brothers, come quickly...I'm drinking stars!"

Route de la Champagne—Drivers can joyride through the scenic and prestigious vineyards just south of Reims. Follow D-9 south to Cormontreuil, then Louvois, then Bouzy, to see the chalky soil and vines that produce Champagne's costly wines. Many of the villages have small hotels if you'd like to sleep surrounded by vineyards.

SLEEPING

(€1 = about $1.20, country code: 33)
It's hard to differentiate between the scads of hotels lining the vast pedestrian place Drouet d'Erlon.

$$ **Grand Hôtel Continental***** is a business hotel that offers reasonable three-star comfort, pleasant public spaces, and frequent specials (standard Db-€55–65, Db suites-€105–120, Tb/Qb-€110–220, suites are less in summer, buffet breakfast-€10, elevator, laundry service, parking-€5, 93 place Drouet d'Erlon, tel. 03 26 40 39 35, fax 03 26 47 51 12, www.grandhotelcontinental.com, grand -hotel-continental@wanadoo.fr, friendly owner Philippe SE).

$ **Hôtel des Arcades**** is modern but basic (Sb or Db-€47, Tb-€60, elevator, parking-€6, 16 passage Subé, off rue Condorcet in mall opposite merry-go-round, tel. 03 26 88 63 74, fax 03 26 40 66 56, hotel.des.arcades@wanadoo.fr).

EATING

L'Apostrophe wins the snazziness contest, with a library-like interior and a lively bar scene in the rear (look for their specials, daily, 59 place Drouet d'Erlon, tel. 03 26 79 19 89).

TRANSPORTATION CONNECTIONS

From Reims by train to: Epernay (12/day, 30 min), **Verdun** (4/day, 3 hrs, most with change in Chalon), **Paris'** Gare de l'Est (12/day, 1.5 hrs), **Colmar** (6/day, 6 hrs, several changes).

APPENDIX

French History in an Escargot Shell

Around the time of Christ, Romans "Latinized" the land of the Gauls. With the 5th-century fall of Rome, the barbarian Franks and Burgundians invaded. Today's France evolved from this unique mix of Latin and Celtic cultures.

While France wallowed with the rest of Europe in medieval darkness, it got a head start in its development as a nation-state. In 507, Clovis established Paris as the capital of his Christian Merovingian dynasty. Clovis and the Franks would eventually become Louis and the French. Charles Martel stopped the spread of Islam by beating the Spanish Moors at the Battle of Poitiers. And Charlemagne, the most important of the "Dark Age" Frankish kings, was crowned Holy Roman Emperor by the pope in 800. Charles the Great presided over the "Carolingian Renaissance" and effectively ruled a vast-for-the-time empire.

The Treaty of Verdun (843), which divided Charlemagne's empire among his grandsons, marks what could be considered the birth of Europe. For the first time, a treaty was signed in vernacular languages (French and German), rather than in Latin. This split established a Franco-Germanic divide, and heralded an age of fragmentation. While petty princes took the reigns, the Frankish king ruled only Ile-de-France, a small region around Paris.

Vikings, or Norsemen, settled in what became Normandy. Later, in 1066, these "Normans" invaded England. The Norman king, William the Conqueror, consolidated his English domain, accelerating the formation of modern England. But his rule also muddied the political waters between England and France, kicking off a centuries-long struggle between the two nations.

In the 12th century, Eleanor of Aquitaine (a separate country in southwest France) married Louis VII, king of France, bringing

Aquitaine under French rule. They divorced, and she married Henry of Normandy, soon-to-be Henry II of England. This marital union gave England control of a huge swath of land from the English Channel to the Pyrénées. For 300 years, France and England would struggle over control of Aquitaine. Any enemy of the French king would find a natural ally in the English king.

In 1328, a French king (Charles IV) died without a son. The English king (Edward III) was his nephew and was interested in the throne. The French resisted. This pitted France, the biggest and richest country in Europe, against England, which had the biggest army. They fought from 1337 to 1453 in what was modestly called the Hundred Years' War.

Regional powers from within France sided with England. Burgundy actually took Paris, captured the royal family, and recognized the English king as heir to the French throne. England controlled France from the Loire north, and things looked bleak for the French king.

Enter Joan of Arc, a 16-year-old peasant girl driven by religious voices. France's national heroine left home to support the dauphin Charles VII (boy prince, heir to the throne but too young to rule). Joan rallied the French, ultimately inspiring them to throw out the English. In 1430, Joan was captured by the Burgundians, who sold her to the English, who convicted her of heresy and burned her at the stake in Rouen. But the inspiration of Joan of Arc lived on, and by 1453, English holdings on the Continent had dwindled to the port of Calais.

By 1500, a strong, centralized France had emerged, with borders similar to today's borders. Her kings (from the Renaissance François I through the Henrys and all those Louis) were model divine monarchs, setting the standards for absolute rule in Europe.

Outrage over the power plays and spending sprees of the kings, coupled with the modern thinking of the Enlightenment—whose leaders were the French *philosophes*—led to the French Revolution (1789) and the end of the *ancien régime*, as well as its notion that some are born to rule, while others are born to be ruled.

But the excesses of the Revolution led to the rise of Napoleon, who ruled the French empire as a dictator until his excesses ushered him into a South Atlantic exile. The French settled on a compromise role for their leader. The modern French king was himself ruled by a constitution. Rather than dress in leotards and powdered wigs, he went to work in a suit with a briefcase.

The 20th century spelled the end of France's reign as a military and political superpower. Devastating wars with Germany in 1870, 1914, and 1940, and the loss of her colonial holdings, left France with not quite enough land, people, or production to be a top player on a global scale.

> ### *"La Marseillaise"*
>
> There's a movement in France to soften the lyrics of their national anthem. Sing it now...before it's too late.
>
> *Allons enfants de la Patrie,* (Let's go, children of the fatherland,)
> *Le jour de gloire est arrivé.* (The day of glory has arrived.)
> *Contre nous de la tyrannie* (The blood-covered flag of tyranny)
> *L'étendard sanglant est levé.* (Is raised against us.)
> *L'étendard sanglant est levé.* (Is raised against us.)
> *Entendez-vous dans les campagnes* (Do you hear these ferocious soldiers)
> *Mugir ces féroces soldats?* (Howling in the countryside?)
> *Qui viennent jusque dans nos bras* (They're nearly in our grasp)
> *Egorger vos fils et vos compagnes.* (To slit the throats of your sons and your women.)
> *Aux armes citoyens,* (Grab your weapons, citizens,)
> *Formez vos bataillons,* (Form your battalions,)
> *Marchons, marchons,* (March on, march on,)
> *Qu'un sang impur* (So that their impure blood)
> *Abreuve nos sillons.* (Will fill our trenches.)

France in the 21st century is the cultural capital of Europe and a leader in the push to integrate Europe into one unified economic power. When that happens, Paris will once again emerge as a superpower capital.

Contemporary Politics in France

The key political issues in France today are high unemployment (about 9 percent), high taxes (about 45 percent of Gross Domestic Product), a steadily increasing percentage of ethnic minorities (almost 10 percent of France's population is Muslim), and the need to compete in a global marketplace. The challenge is to address these issues while maintaining the social benefits the French expect from their government. As a result, national policies seem to conflict with each other (e.g., France supports the lean economic policies of the European Union, but recently reduced the French workweek to 35 hours).

The unification of Europe has been powered by France and Germany. The 25-member European Union, well on its way to becoming a "United States of Europe," is dissolving borders and freeing up trade. Many EU members, including France, share one currency—the euro.

French national politics are complex. While only two parties dominate American politics, France has six major parties and several smaller ones. From left to right, the major parties include the reformed Communists (PCF—Parti Communiste Français), the environmental party (Les Verts, "The Greens"), the moderate Socialists (PS—Parti Socialiste), the aristocratically conservative UDF (Union pour la Démocratie Française), the center-right UMP (Union pour la Majorité Présidentielle), and the racist and isolationist Front National. In general, the UDF and UMP split the conservative middle ground, and the Socialists dominate the liberal middle ground. But in France, unlike in the United States, informal coalitions are generally necessary for any party to "rule."

You've likely read about the Front National party, led by Jean-Marie Le Pen. Le Pen's "France for the French" platform calls for the expulsion of ethnic minorities and broader police powers. Although the Front National has a staunch voter base of about 15 percent, the recent rise in unemployment and globalization worries have increased its following, allowing Le Pen to nudge the political agenda to the right. On the far left, the once powerful Communists (PCF) draw only about 5 percent of the popular vote, forcing them to work more flexibly with the less radical Socialists and the Green party. This left end of the political spectrum in France sees its fortunes rise when the economy is strong, and fall when it's weak.

While the French president is elected by popular vote every five years, he is more of a figurehead than his American counterpart. The more powerful prime minister is elected by the parliament (Assemblée Nationale) and confirmed by the new president. With five major parties, a single majority is rare—it takes a coalition to elect a prime minister. While the right had been more successful in marshaling its supporters under Chirac (President Jacques Chirac and Prime Minister Jean-Pierre Raffarin are both conservatives), recent election results have demonstrated a resounding preference for Socialist candidates. The next presidential election, in 2007, should be a fascinating contest.

TRAVELER'S TOOL KIT

Let's Talk Telephones
Dialing Direct
Here's a primer on making direct phone calls. For information specific to France, see "Telephones" in the introduction.

Making Calls Within a European Country: About half of all European countries use area codes (like we do); the other half uses a direct-dial system without area codes.

To make calls within a country that uses a direct-dial system (France, Belgium, the Czech Republic, Denmark, Italy, Portugal, Norway, Spain, and Switzerland), you dial the same number whether you're calling across the country or across the street.

In countries that use area codes (such as Austria, Britain,

Finland, Germany, Ireland, the Netherlands, and Sweden), you dial the local number when calling within a city, and you add the area code if calling long-distance within the country.

Making International Calls: You always start with the international access code (011 if you're calling from America or Canada, or 00 from Europe), then dial the country code of the country you're calling (see chart below).

What you dial next depends on the phone system of the country you're calling. If the country uses area codes, drop the initial zero of the area code, then dial the rest of the number.

Countries that use direct-dial systems (no area codes) vary in how they're accessed internationally by phone. For instance, if you're making an international call to the Czech Republic, Denmark, Italy, Norway, Portugal, or Spain, simply dial the international access code, country code, and phone number. But if you're calling France, Belgium, or Switzerland, drop the initial zero of the phone number.

Country Codes

After you've dialed the international access code (00 if calling from Europe, 011 if calling from the United States or Canada), then dial the code of the country you're calling.

Austria—43	Ireland—353
Belgium—32	Italy—39
Britain—44	Morocco—212
Canada—1	Netherlands—31
Croatia—385	Norway—47
Czech Rep.—420	Poland—48
Denmark—45	Portugal—351
Estonia—372	Slovenia—386
Finland—358	Spain—34
France—33	Sweden—46
Germany—49	Switzerland—41
Gibraltar—350	Turkey—90
Greece—30	U.S.A.—1

Useful French Phone Numbers

Note that calls made to numbers starting with 08 are billed by the minute (about €0.30/min).

Directory Assistance for France (some English spoken): tel. 12
Collect Calls to the U.S.: tel. 00 00 11

Emergency and Medical Needs

Police: tel. 17
Emergency Medical Assistance: tel. 15

European Calling Chart

Just smile and dial, using this key:
AC = Area Code, LN = Local Number.

European Country	Calling long distance within ...	Calling from the U.S.A./ Canada to ...	Calling from a European country to ...
Austria	AC + LN	011 + 43 + AC (without the initial zero) + LN	00 + 43 + AC (without the initial zero) + LN
Belgium	LN	011 + 32 + LN (without initial zero)	00 + 32 + LN (without initial zero)
Britain	AC + LN	011 + 44 + AC (without initial zero) + LN	00 + 44 + AC (without initial zero) + LN
Czech Republic	LN	011 + 420 + LN	00 + 420 + LN
Denmark	LN	011 + 45 + LN	00 + 45 + LN
Estonia	LN	011 + 372 + LN	00 + 372 + LN
Finland	AC + LN	011 + 358 + AC (without initial zero) + LN	00 + 358 + AC (without initial zero) + LN
France	LN	011 + 33 + LN (without initial zero)	00 + 33 + LN (without initial zero)
Germany	AC + LN	011 + 49 + AC (without initial zero) + LN	00 + 49 + AC (without initial zero) + LN
Gibraltar	LN	011 + 350 + LN	00 + 350 + LN From Spain: 9567 + LN
Greece	LN	011 + 30 + LN	00 + 30 + LN

European Country	Calling long distance within …	Calling from the U.S.A./ Canada to …	Calling from a European country to …
Ireland	AC + LN	011 + 353 + AC (without initial zero) + LN	00 + 353 + AC (without initial zero) + LN
Italy	LN	011 + 39 + LN	00 + 39 + LN
Morocco	LN	011 + 212 + LN (without initial zero)	00 + 212 + LN (without initial zero)
Netherlands	AC + LN	011 + 31 + AC (without initial zero) + LN	00 + 31 + AC (without initial zero) + LN
Norway	LN	011 + 47 + LN	00 + 47 + LN
Portugal	LN	011 + 351 + LN	00 + 351 + LN
Spain	LN	011 + 34 + LN	00 + 34 + LN
Sweden	AC + LN	011 + 46 + AC (without initial zero) + LN	00 + 46 + AC (without initial zero) + LN
Switzerland	LN	011 + 41 + LN (without initial zero)	00 + 41 + LN (without initial zero)
Turkey	AC (if no initial zero is included, add one) + LN	011 + 90 + AC (without initial zero) + LN	00 + 90 + AC (without initial zero) + LN

- The instructions above apply whether you're calling a fixed phone or cell phone.

- The international access codes (the first numbers you dial when making an international call) are 011 if you're calling from the U.S.A./Canada, or 00 if you're calling from anywhere in Europe.

- To call the U.S.A. or Canada from Europe, dial 00, then 1 (the country code for the U.S.A. and Canada), then the area code and number. In short, 00 + 1 + AC + LN = Hi, Mom!

Consulates and Embassies

U.S. Consulate in Paris: Open Mon–Fri 9:00–12:30 & 13:00–15:00, 2 rue St. Florentin, Mo: Concorde, tel. 01 43 12 22 22, www.amb-usa.fr/consul/consulat.htm.

U.S. Embassy in Paris: 2 avenue Gabriel (to the left as you face Hôtel Crillon), Mo: Concorde, tel. 01 43 12 22 22.

Canadian Consulate and Embassy in Paris: 35 avenue Montaigne, Mo: Franklin D. Roosevelt, tel. 01 44 43 29 00.

U.S. Consulate in Strasbourg: 15 rue d'Alsace, tel. 03 88 35 31 04, fax 03 88 23 07 17.

U.S. Consulate in Lyon: 16 rue de la République, World Trade Center, tel. 04 78 38 33 03.

Canadian Consulate in Lyon: 21 rue Bourgelat, tel. 04 72 77 64 07.

U.S. Consulate in Nice: 7 avenue Gustave V, tel. 04 93 88 89 55, fax 04 93 87 07 38 (the Consular Agency does *not* provide visa services; Paris is the nearest office for these services).

Canadian Consulate in Nice: 10 rue Lamartine, tel. 04 93 92 93 22.

Paris Information

Tourist Information: tel. 08 92 68 31 12 (recorded info with long menu)

American Church: tel. 01 40 62 05 00

American Hospital: tel. 01 46 41 25 25

Lost or Stolen Credit Cards

Visa: tel. 08 00 90 11 79 or U.S. tel. 410/581-9994

MasterCard: tel. 08 00 90 13 87 or U.S. tel. 636/722-7111

American Express: tel. 01 47 77 72 00 or U.S. tel. 336/393-1111

Diner's Club: Call U.S. collect 00-1-702-797-5532

Travel Advisories

U.S. Department of State: U.S. tel. 202/647-5225, www.travel.state.gov

Centers for Disease Control and Prevention: U.S. tel. 877/FYI-TRIP, www.cdc.gov/travel

Canadian Department of Foreign Affairs: Canadian tel. 800/267-6788, www.dfait-maeci.gc.ca

Travel Companies in Paris

Access Voyages: 6 rue Pierre Lescot, Mo: Châtelet, tel. 01 44 76 84 50

Any Way: 46 rue des Lombards, Mo: Châtelet or Hôtel de Ville, tel. 01 40 28 00 74

Cash & Go: 34 avenue des Champs-Elysées, Mo: Franklin D. Roosevelt, tel. 01 53 93 63 63

Airports in Paris
Aéroport Charles de Gaulle: tel. 01 48 62 22 80, www.adp.fr
Aéroport d'Orly: tel. 01 49 75 15 15, www.adp.fr

Airlines
Aer Lingus: tel. 01 70 20 00 72
Air Canada: tel. 08 25 88 08 81
Air France: tel. 08 20 82 08 20
Alitalia: tel. 08 02 31 53 15
American Airlines: tel. 08 10 87 28 72
British Airways: tel. 08 25 82 54 00
BMI British Midlands: tel. 01 41 91 87 04
Continental: tel. 01 42 99 09 09
Delta: tel. 08 00 35 40 80
Iberia: tel. 08 02 07 50 75
Icelandair: tel. 01 44 51 60 51
KLM: tel. 08 90 71 07 10
Lufthansa: tel. 08 20 02 00 30
Northwest: tel. 08 90 71 07 10
Olympic: tel. 01 44 94 58 58
SAS: tel. 08 25 32 53 35
Swiss: tel. 08 20 04 05 06
United: tel. 08 10 72 72 72
US Airways: tel. 08 10 63 22 22

Train Information
SNCF Reservations and Information: tel. 3635

Car Leasing in France
Auto France: U.S. tel. 800-572-9655, U.S. fax 201/934-7501, www.autofrance.net
Europe by Car: U.S. tel. 800-223-1516, www.europebycar.com

Hotel Chains
Country Home Rental: www.gites-de-france.fr/eng or www.gite.com
Huge Chain of Hotels: www.accorhotels.com (handles Ibis, Mercure, and Novotel hotels)
Ibis Hotels: tel. 08 92 68 66 86; from United States, dial 011 33 8 92 68 66 86, www.ibishotel.com
Kyriad Hotels: tel. 08 25 00 30 03; from United States, dial 011 33 1 64 62 46 46, www.kyriad.com
Mercure Hotels: tel. 08 25 88 33 33, www.mercure.com

Youth Hostels
Hostelling International-U.S.A.: U.S. tel. 202/783-6161, www.hiayh.org

Hostelling International-Canada: Canadian tel. 800-663-5777, www.hostellingintl.ca

Public Holidays and Festivals

Many sights close down on national holidays, and weekends around those holidays are often wildly crowded with vacationers (book your hotel room for the entire holiday weekend well in advance). Note that this isn't a complete list; holidays often strike without warning.

For specifics and a more comprehensive list of festivals, contact the French tourist information office in the United States (see page 5) and visit www.franceguide.com, www.whatsonwhen.com, and www.festivals.com.

Jan 1:	New Year's Day
Jan 6:	Epiphany
Feb 11–27:	Carnival (Mardi Gras, parades, fireworks), Nice
March 27:	Easter Sunday
March 28:	Easter Monday
April 29–May 2:	Labor Day weekend
May:	Versailles Festival (arts), Versailles; Festival Jeanne d'Arc (pageants), Rouen
May 5–8:	Ascension weekend
May 8:	VE Day
May 11–22:	Cannes Film Festival, Cannes
May 15:	Pentecost
May 19–22:	Monaco Grand Prix (auto race), Monaco
June:	Marais Festival (arts), Paris
June 21:	Music Festival (Fête de la Musique), concerts and dancing in the streets throughout France
July:	Nice Jazz Festival (www.nicejazzfest.com); Avignon Festival (theater, dance, music, www.festival-avignon.com); Tour de France (ends in Paris, www.letour.fr); Beaune International Music Festival; Music and Opera Festival (performed in Roman theater, www.choregies.asso.fr), Orange; "Jazz at Juan" International Jazz Festival, Antibes/Juan-les-Pins; International Music Festival (www.festival-colmar.com), Colmar
July 14:	Bastille Day (fireworks, dancing, and revelry all over France)
August:	International Fireworks Festival, Cannes

2005

JANUARY
S	M	T	W	T	F	S
						1
2	3	4	5	6	7	8
9	10	11	12	13	14	15
16	17	18	19	20	21	22
23/30	24/31	25	26	27	28	29

FEBRUARY
S	M	T	W	T	F	S
		1	2	3	4	5
6	7	8	9	10	11	12
13	14	15	16	17	18	19
20	21	22	23	24	25	26
27	28					

MARCH
S	M	T	W	T	F	S
		1	2	3	4	5
6	7	8	9	10	11	12
13	14	15	16	17	18	19
20	21	22	23	24	25	26
27	28	29	30	31		

APRIL
S	M	T	W	T	F	S
					1	2
3	4	5	6	7	8	9
10	11	12	13	14	15	16
17	18	19	20	21	22	23
24	25	26	27	28	29	30

MAY
S	M	T	W	T	F	S
1	2	3	4	5	6	7
8	9	10	11	12	13	14
15	16	17	18	19	20	21
22	23	24	25	26	27	28
29	30	31				

JUNE
S	M	T	W	T	F	S
			1	2	3	4
5	6	7	8	9	10	11
12	13	14	15	16	17	18
19	20	21	22	23	24	25
26	27	28	29	30		

JULY
S	M	T	W	T	F	S
					1	2
3	4	5	6	7	8	9
10	11	12	13	14	15	16
17	18	19	20	21	22	23
24/31	25	26	27	28	29	30

AUGUST
S	M	T	W	T	F	S
	1	2	3	4	5	6
7	8	9	10	11	12	13
14	15	16	17	18	19	20
21	22	23	24	25	26	27
28	29	30	31			

SEPTEMBER
S	M	T	W	T	F	S
				1	2	3
4	5	6	7	8	9	10
11	12	13	14	15	16	17
18	19	20	21	22	23	24
25	26	27	28	29	30	

OCTOBER
S	M	T	W	T	F	S
						1
2	3	4	5	6	7	8
9	10	11	12	13	14	15
16	17	18	19	20	21	22
23/30	24/31	25	26	27	28	29

NOVEMBER
S	M	T	W	T	F	S
		1	2	3	4	5
6	7	8	9	10	11	12
13	14	15	16	17	18	19
20	21	22	23	24	25	26
27	28	29	30			

DECEMBER
S	M	T	W	T	F	S
				1	2	3
4	5	6	7	8	9	10
11	12	13	14	15	16	17
18	19	20	21	22	23	24
25	26	27	28	29	30	31

Aug 15:	Assumption of Mary
Sept:	Fall Arts Festival (Fête d'Automne), Paris; Wine harvest festivals in many towns
Oct 29–Nov 1:	All Saints' Day weekend
Nov 19–20:	Wine Auction and Festival (Les Trois Glorieuses), Beaune
Nov 11–13:	Armistice Day weekend
Dec:	Christmas Market, Strasbourg
Dec 17–Jan 3:	Winter holidays
Dec 25:	Christmas Day

Climate

First line, average daily low temperature; second line, average daily high; third line, days of no rain.

	J	F	M	A	M	J	J	A	S	O	N	D
Paris												
	34°	34°	39°	43°	49°	55°	58°	58°	53°	46°	40°	36°
	43°	45°	54°	60°	68°	73°	76°	75°	70°	60°	50°	44°
	14	14	19	17	19	18	19	18	17	18	15	15
Nice												
	35°	36°	41°	46°	52°	58°	63°	63°	58°	51°	43°	37°
	50°	53°	59°	64°	71°	79°	84°	83°	77°	68°	58°	52°
	23	22	24	23	23	26	29	26	24	23	21	21

Numbers and Stumblers

- Europeans write a few of their numbers differently than we do. 1 = 1, 4 = 4, 7 = 7. Learn the difference or miss your train.
- In Europe, dates appear as day/month/year, so Christmas is 25/12/05.
- Commas are decimal points and decimals commas. A dollar and a half is $1,50 and there are 5.280 feet in a mile.
- When pointing, use your whole hand, palm down.
- When counting with fingers, start with your thumb. If you hold up your first finger to request one item, you'll probably get two.
- What Americans call the second floor of a building is the first floor in Europe.
- Europeans keep the left "lane" open for passing on escalators and moving sidewalks. Keep to the right.

Metric Conversion (approximate)

1 inch = 25 millimeters	32 degrees F = 0 degrees C
1 foot = 0.3 meter	82 degrees F = about 28 degrees C
1 yard = 0.9 meter	1 ounce = 28 grams
1 mile = 1.6 kilometers	1 kilogram = 2.2 pounds
1 centimeter = 0.4 inch	1 quart = 0.95 liter
1 meter = 39.4 inches	1 square yard = 0.8 square meter
1 kilometer = 0.62 mile	1 acre = 0.4 hectare

Converting Temperatures: Fahrenheit and Celsius

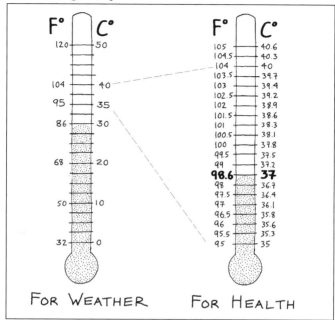

For Weather   For Health

Making Your Hotel Reservation

Most hotel managers know basic "hotel English." Faxing or e-mailing are the preferred methods for reserving a room. They're more accurate than telephoning and much faster than writing a letter. Use this handy form for your fax or find it online at www.ricksteves.com/reservation. Photocopy and fax away.

One-Page Fax

To: _____ @ _____
           hotel   **fax**

From: _____ @ _____
              name   **fax**

Today's date: _____/_____/_____
                day   month   year

Dear Hotel _____ ,
Please make this reservation for me:

Name: _____

Total # of people:_____ # of rooms: _____ # of nights: _____

Arriving: _____/_____/_____   My time of arrival (24-hr clock): _____
         day month year   (I will telephone if I will be late)

Departing: _____/_____/_____
          day month year

Room(s): Single _____ Double _____ Twin _____ Triple _____ Quad _____

With: Toilet _____ Shower _____ Bath _____ Sink only _____

Special needs: View ____ Quiet ____ Cheapest ____ Ground Floor ____

Please fax, mail, or e-mail confirmation of my reservation, along with the type of room reserved and the price. Please also inform me of your cancellation policy. After I hear from you, I will quickly send my credit-card information as a deposit to hold the room. Thank you.

_____
Signature

_____
Name

_____
Address

_____
City   **State**   **Zip Code   Country**

_____
E-mail Address

French Survival Phrases

When using the phonetics, try to nasalize the n̲ sound.

Good day.	**Bonjour.**	bohn̲-zhoor
Mrs. / Mr.	**Madame / Monsieur**	mah-dahm / muhs-yur
Do you speak English?	**Parlez-vous anglais?**	par-lay-voo ahn̲-glay
Yes. / No.	**Oui. / Non.**	wee / nohn̲
I understand.	**Je comprends.**	zhuh kohn̲-prahn̲
I don't understand.	**Je ne comprends pas.**	zhuh nuh kohn̲-prahn̲ pah
Please.	**S'il vous plaît.**	see voo play
Thank you.	**Merci.**	mehr-see
I'm sorry.	**Désolé.**	day-zoh-lay
Excuse me.	**Pardon.**	par-dohn̲
(No) problem.	**(Pas de) problème.**	(pah duh) proh-blehm
It's good.	**C'est bon.**	say bohn̲
Goodbye.	**Au revoir.**	oh vwahr
one / two	**un / deux**	uhn̲ / duh
three / four	**trois / quatre**	twah / kah-truh
five / six	**cinq / six**	san̲k / sees
seven / eight	**sept / huit**	seht / weet
nine / ten	**neuf / dix**	nuhf / dees
How much is it?	**Combien?**	kohn̲-bee-an̲
Write it?	**Ecrivez?**	ay-kree-vay
Is it free?	**C'est gratuit?**	say grah-twee
Included?	**Inclus?**	an̲-klew
Where can I buy / find...?	**Où puis-je acheter / trouver...?**	oo pwee-zhuh ah-shuh-tay / troo-vay
I'd like / We'd like...	**Je voudrais / Nous voudrions...**	zhuh voo-dray / noo voo-dree-ohn̲
...a room.	**...une chambre.**	ewn shahn̲-bruh
...a ticket to ___.	**...un billet pour ___.**	uhn̲ bee-yay poor
Is it possible?	**C'est possible?**	say poh-see-bluh
Where is...?	**Où est...?**	oo ay
...the train station	**...la gare**	lah gar
...the bus station	**...la gare routière**	lah gar root-yehr
...tourist information	**...l'office du tourisme**	loh-fees dew too-reez-muh
Where are the toilets?	**Où sont les toilettes?**	oo sohn̲ lay twah-leht
men	**hommes**	ohm
women	**dames**	dahm
left / right	**à gauche / à droite**	ah gohsh / ah dwaht
straight	**tout droit**	too dwah
When does this open / close?	**Ça ouvre / ferme à quelle heure?**	sah oo-vruh / fehrm ah kehl ur
At what time?	**À quelle heure?**	ah kehl ur
Just a moment.	**Un moment.**	uhn̲ moh-mahn̲
now / soon / later	**maintenant / bientôt / plus tard**	man̲-tuh-nahn̲ / bee-an̲-toh / plew tar
today / tomorrow	**aujourd'hui / demain**	oh-zhoor-dwee / duh-man̲

In the Restaurant

I'd like / We'd like...	Je voudrais / Nous voudrions...	zhuh voo-dray / noo voo-dree-oh<u>n</u>
...to reserve...	...réserver...	ray-zehr-vay
...a table for one / two.	...une table pour un / deux.	ewn tah-bluh poor uh<u>n</u> / duh
Non-smoking.	Non fumeur.	noh<u>n</u> few-mur
Is this seat free?	C'est libre?	say lee-bruh
The menu (in English), please.	La carte (en anglais), s'il vous plaît.	lah kart (ah<u>n</u> ah<u>n</u>-glay) see voo play
service (not) included	service (non) compris	sehr-vees (noh<u>n</u>) koh<u>n</u>-pree
to go	à emporter	ah ah<u>n</u>-por-tay
with / without	avec / sans	ah-vehk / sah<u>n</u>
and / or	et / ou	ay / oo
special of the day	plat du jour	plah dew zhoor
specialty of the house	spécialité de la maison	spay-see-ah-lee-tay duh lah may-zoh<u>n</u>
appetizers	hors-d'oeuvre	or-duh-vruh
first course (soup, salad)	entrée	ah<u>n</u>-tray
main course (meat, fish)	plat principal	plah pra<u>n</u>-see-pahl
bread	pain	pa<u>n</u>
cheese	fromage	froh-mahzh
sandwich	sandwich	sah<u>n</u>d-weech
soup	soupe	soop
salad	salade	sah-lahd
meat	viande	vee-ah<u>n</u>d
chicken	poulet	poo-lay
fish	poisson	pwah-soh<u>n</u>
seafood	fruits de mer	frwee duh mehr
fruit	fruit	frwee
vegetables	légumes	lay-gewm
dessert	dessert	duh-sehr
mineral water	eau minérale	oh mee-nay-rahl
tap water	l'eau du robinet	loh dew roh-bee-nay
milk	lait	lay
(orange) juice	jus (d'orange)	zhew (doh-rah<u>n</u>zh)
coffee	café	kah-fay
tea	thé	tay
wine	vin	va<u>n</u>
red / white	rouge / blanc	roozh / blah<u>n</u>
glass / bottle	verre / bouteille	vehr / boo-teh-ee
beer	bière	bee-ehr
Cheers!	Santé!	sah<u>n</u>-tay
More. / Another.	Plus. / Un autre.	plew / uh<u>n</u> oh-truh
The same.	La même chose.	lah mehm shohz
The bill, please.	L'addition, s'il vous plaît.	lah-dee-see-oh<u>n</u> see voo play
tip	pourboire	poor-bwar
Delicious!	Délicieux!	day-lee-see-uh

For more user-friendly French phrases, check out *Rick Steves' French Phrase Book and Dictionary* or *Rick Steves' French, Italian & German Phrase Book*.

INDEX

RESEARCHER

KRISTEN KUSNIC

Kristen Kusnic, lover of all things French, leads tours and researches guidebooks for Rick Steves. She lived for a year each in the south of France and in Berlin, becoming fluent in French, German, and red wine. When she's not in Europe, Kristen calls Seattle home.

Start your trip at
www.ricksteves.com

Rick Steves' website is packed with over 3,000 pages of timely travel information. It's also your gateway to getting FREE monthly travel news from Rick — and more!

Free Monthly European Travel News

Fresh articles on Europe's most interesting destinations and happenings. Rick will even send you an e-mail every month (often direct from Europe) with his latest discoveries!

Timely Travel Tips

Rick Steves' best money-and-stress-saving tips on trip planning, packing, transportation, hotels, health, safety, finances, hurdling the language barrier...and more.

Travelers' Graffiti Wall

Candid advice and opinions from thousands of travelers on everything listed above, plus whatever topics are hot at the moment (discount flights, packing tips, scams...you name it).

Rick's Annual Guide to European Railpasses

The clearest, most comprehensive guide to the confusing array of railpass options out there, and how to choo-choose the railpass that best fits your itinerary and budget. Then you can order your railpass (and get a bunch of great freebies) online from us!

Great Gear at the Rick Steves Travel Store

Enjoy bargains on Rick's guidebooks, planning maps and TV series DVDs—and on his custom-designed carry-on bags, wheeled bags, day bags and light-packing accessories.

Rick Steves Tours

Every year more than 5,000 lucky travelers explore Europe on a Rick Steves tour. Learn more about our 26 different one-to-three-week itineraries, read uncensored feedback from our tour alums, and sign up for your dream trip online!

Rick on TV

Read the scripts and see video clips from the popular Rick Steves' Europe TV series, and get an inside look at Rick's 13 newest shows.

Respect for Your Privacy

Ordering online from us is secure. When you buy something from us, join a tour, or subscribe to Rick's free monthly travel news e-mails, we promise to never share your name, information, or e-mail address with anyone else. You won't be spammed!

Have fun raising your Travel I.Q. at
www.ricksteves.com

Travel smart…carry on!

The latest generation of Rick Steves' carry-on travel bags is easily the best—benefiting from two decades of on-the-road attention to what really matters: maximum quality and strength; practical, flexible features; and no unnecessary frills. You won't find a better value anywhere!

Convertible, expandable, and carry-on-size:

Rick Steves' Back Door Bag $99

This is the same bag that Rick Steves lives out of for three months every summer. It's made of rugged water-resistant 1000 denier Cordura nylon, and best of all, it converts easily from a smart-looking suitcase to a handy backpack with comfortably-curved shoulder straps and a padded waistbelt.

This roomy, versatile 9" x 21" x 14" bag has a large 2600 cubic-inch main compartment, plus three outside pockets (small, medium and huge) that are perfect for often-used items. And the cinch-tight compression straps will keep your load compact and close to your back—not sagging like a sack of potatoes.

Wishing you had even more room to bring home souvenirs? Pull open the full-perimeter expando-zipper and its capacity jumps from 2600 to 3000 cubic inches. When you want to use it as a suitcase or check it as luggage (required when "expanded"), the straps and belt hide away in a zippered compartment in the back.

Attention travelers under 5'4" tall: This bag also comes in an inch-shorter version, for a compact-friendlier fit between the waistbelt and shoulder straps.

Convenient, durable, and carry-on-size:

Rick Steves' Wheeled Bag $119

At 9" x 21" x 14" our sturdy Rick Steves' Wheeled Bag is rucksack-soft in front, but the rest is lined with a hard ABS-lexan shell to give maximum protection to your belongings. We've spared no expense on moving parts, splurging on an extra-long button-release handle and big, tough inline skate wheels for easy rolling on rough surfaces.

This bag is not convertible! Our research tells us that travelers who've bought convertible wheeled bags never put them on their backs anyway, so we've eliminated the extra weight and expense.

Rick Steves' Wheeled Bag has exactly the same three-outside-pocket configuration as our Back Door Bag, plus a handy "add-a-bag" strap and full lining.

Our Back Door Bags and Wheeled Bags come in black, navy, blue spruce, evergreen and merlot.

For great deals on a wide selection of travel goodies, begin your next trip at the Rick Steves Travel Store!

Visit the Rick Steves Travel Store at
www.ricksteves.com

Rick Steves

COUNTRY GUIDES 2005

France
Germany & Austria
Great Britain
Ireland
Italy
Portugal
Scandinavia
Spain
Switzerland

CITY GUIDES 2005

Amsterdam, Bruges & Brussels
Florence & Tuscany
London
Paris
Prague & The Czech Republic
Provence & The French Riviera
Rome
Venice

BEST OF GUIDES

Best European City Walks & Museums
Best of Eastern Europe
Best of Europe

More *Savvy*. More *Surprising*. More *Fun*.

PHRASE BOOKS & DICTIONARIES

French
French, Italian & German
German
Italian
Portuguese
Spanish

MORE EUROPE FROM RICK STEVES

Easy Access Europe
Europe 101
Europe Through the Back Door
Postcards from Europe

DVD RICK STEVES' EUROPE

Rick Steves' Europe All Thirty
   Shows 2000–2003
Britain & Ireland
Exotic Europe
Germany, The Swiss Alps
   & Travel Skills
Italy

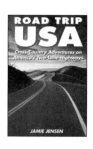

For a complete list of Rick Steves' guidebooks, see page 7.

Thanks to Gene Openshaw for sharing his knowledge of art and history; to Steve's wife, Karen Lewis Smith, for her assistance covering French cuisine; and to Steve's son, Travis, for help with children's activities.

Avalon Travel Publishing
An Imprint of Avalon Publishing Group, Inc.
1400 65th Street, Suite 250
Emeryville, CA 94608

Printed in the U.S.A. by Worzalla. Second printing April 2005.
Distributed to the book trade by Publishers Group West.

For the latest on Rick's lectures, guidebooks, tours, and public television series, contact Europe Through the Back Door, Box 2009, Edmonds, WA 98020, 425/771-8303, fax 425/771-0833, www.ricksteves.com, rick@ricksteves.com.

ISBN 1-56691-620-8
ISSN 1084-4406

Europe Through the Back Door Managing Editor: Risa Laib
Europe Through the Back Door Editors: Jennifer Hauseman, Christine Grabowski, Lauren Mills, Cameron Hewitt
Avalon Travel Publishing Series Manager: Roxanna Font
Avalon Travel Publishing Editor: Patrick Collins
Research Assistance: Kristen Kusnic, Cameron Hewitt (Basque Country)
Copy Editor: Mia Lipman
Indexer: Judy Hunt
Production & Typesetting: Patrick David Barber
Cover Design: Kari Gim, Laura Mazer
Interior Design: Amber Pirker, Jane Musser, Laura Mazer
Maps & Graphics: David C. Hoerlein, Lauren Mills, Zoey Platt, Mike Morgenfeld
Front cover photos: Front image © John Elk III; Back image, Semur, France © Steve Smith
Front matter color photos: p. i, Provence © Paul Orcutt; p. viii, Eiffel Tower, Paris © Veronica Garbutt/Lonely Planet Images
Avalon Travel Publishing Graphics Coordinator: Susan Snyder